D0215057

LEADERSHIP IN HIGHER EDUCATION

LEADERSHIP IN HIGHER EDUCATION

A Handbook for Practicing Administrators

EDITED BY
Bob W. Miller,
Robert W. Hotes,
and
Jack D. Terry, Jr.

GREENWOOD PRESS
Westport, Connecticut • London, England

LIBRARY

FEB 28 1984

UNIVERSITY OF THE PACIFIC
416006

Library of Congress Cataloging in Publication Data

Main entry under title:

Leadership in higher education.

Bibliography: p.
Includes index.
1. Education, Higher—Administration.   2. Leadership.
I. Miller, Bob W.   II. Hotes, Robert W.   III. Terry,
Jack D.
LB2341.L268 1983   378'.1   82-15579
ISBN 0-313-22263-0 (lib. bdg.)

Copyright © 1983 by Bob W. Miller, Robert W. Hotes, and Jack D. Terry, Jr.

All rights reserved. No portion of this book may be
reproduced, by any process or technique, without the
express written consent of the publisher.

Library of Congress Catalog Card Number: 82-15579
ISBN: 0-313-22263-0

First published in 1983

Greenwood Press
A division of Congressional Information Service, Inc.
88 Post Road West
Westport, Connecticut 06881

Printed in the United States of America

10 9 8 7 6 5 4 3 2 1

Contents

Figures

Tables

Preface

This handbook on leadership and general administration in higher education has been written from both the theoretical and practical aspects. It is written for those administrators who are active in the profession today as well as for those who desire to be leaders in the future. Most higher education administrators spend a lifetime trying to attain leadership abilities and attempting to implement and understand general administration practices.

There are many managers and administrators in the field of higher education; however, there is a very small percentage of true leaders. There will always be a position for those administrative leaders who are effective and efficient. One assumption made in the process of writing this book is that any person can be a more effective leader if he or she has the appropriate education. Not everyone can be a great leader or even a good one, but if a person has some natural leadership traits or characteristics, improvement can definitely be made. The better the "raw materials" such as appearance, personality, attitude, and education, the greater the potential success in administrative leadership.

This book is written in the interest of providing the administrator in higher education with assistance in planning, controlling, directing, organizing, and coordinating within his or her organization. The book also covers basic areas such as general administration, motivation, personnel, program development and evaluation, finance, public relations, communications, student development, instructional programs, faculty unionism, women executives, learning resources, and so forth.

The three principal authors have combined a number of years of practical administration experience. Other professionals in the field of higher education administration have joined them in writing portions of the book. The authors all believe that present and future administrative leaders must be able to help people identify emerging problems and issues, and to provide leadership in decision making to bring about proper alternatives in the solution to those problems. In developing this book, an attempt has been made to incorporate integrated concepts from political science, the management sciences, social psychology, psychology, and sociology.

The editors wish to express special thanks to artist Lynn Waibel Hotes for her help in improving some of the graphic materials in this volume.

This book should be of considerable value and benefit to practicing administrators as well as to college and university students of higher education administration. Other students of education can benefit from understanding problems and possibilities in educational organization and administrative leadership.

Notes on the Contributors

GARY R. BEAUCHAMP is Instructor of Communications at Amber University, Dallas. He has been concerned primarily with training leaders in administration techniques in the religious setting. He conducts communication, leadership and administration, and Church Growth Seminars, and is a popular lecturer and feature speaker for colleges, universities, and conventions throughout the country. He has authored *God Loved the Single, Too, The Mixed Marriage, Instilling Spiritual Concepts in Youth,* and *The 20th Century Sermons.* He is chief administrative officer and minister for the Garland Road Church of Christ of Dallas, Texas.

MARLENE H. BREWER is an Assistant Professor of Nursing in the School of Nursing at the University of Texas at Arlington. She previously was Coordinator of the Department of Nursing, Butler County Community College, Pennsylvania. She has been a consultant to numerous community colleges in several states, assisting them in their formulation of career-ladder nursing curricula. She has conducted a study on factors associated with job satisfaction of nursing educators in middle management positions. She is the past President of the Denver Chapter, Association of Seventh-day Adventist Nurses, and President-elect of Delta Theta Chapter, Sigma Theta Tau.

PAULA S. BRIN is an English instructor at Hutchinson Community College in Hutchinson, Kansas. She is also a Ph.D. candidate in Higher Education Administration at North Texas State University.

S. JAMES CORVEY is Associate Dean of Learning Resources at Mountain View College of the Dallas County Community College System. He was formerly Director of Learning Resources, Houston Community College; Director of Central Technical Processing at Miami-Dade Community College; Law Librarian for a law firm in Rochester, New York; and Catalog Librarian at Florida Atlantic University. He has done consultant work throughout the United States and on an international basis.

ROBERT W. HOTES is Manager of Training for a division of Denny's Inc., Fort Worth, Texas. He was formerly Information Services Specialist for the Okaloosa-Walton Junior College district of Florida. His major research interests include the development and evaluation of instructional systems for technical training and the transfer of technology from industrialized nations to developing societies, through training. He coauthored and edited *The Administration of Learning Resources Centers,* and has several journal publications in the field of instructional systems. He is an Accredited Personnel Diplomate (APD) in the Field of Training and Human Resources Development and a member of The Academy of Management.

RON HUGHES is an Assistant Professor of Tele-Communications at Texas Tech University. He teaches Broadcast Communications, Management, and Television Production. He formerly was at Morehead State University in Kentucky where his position was Production Manager for the radio station, Coordinator for Radio and Television and held the rank of Assistant Professor. Hughes has also worked in business and industry in Lubbock, Texas.

JOE IBIOK is an Educational Director for the government of Nigeria. He taught economics at North Texas State University, where he received his Ph.D. in Higher Education Administration. Prior to his United States educational experiences, he was in the banking business in Calabar and Enugu, Nigeria.

HAZEL M. JAY is an Associate Professor and Associate Dean at the University of Texas at Arlington and was previously a member of the faculty at Texas Woman's University. She has contributed authoritatively to the conceptual and theoretical bases of nursing practice.

FLOYD T. KING, JR., is Professor of Chemistry at Northlake Community College. He previously was Division Chair of the Science/Tech Division at Richland Community College and Dallas County Community College District for four years.

ROGER KINSETH is the Associate Dean of Technical Occupational Programs at Cedar Valley Community College of the Dallas County Community College District in Dallas. He has also served as Department Chairperson of Air-Conditioning and Instructor of Air-Conditioning at the South Campus of Tarrant County Junior College in Fort Worth. He has been a commercial construction executive in business and industry.

THEODORE R. LAABS is Director of Graphics and Production in the Learning Resource Center at the Northeast Campus of Tarrant County

Junior College in Fort Worth, Texas. Prior to this he was Dean of Learning Resources at Galveston Community College in Texas. Laabs also served as Library Specialist at Waukesha County Technical Institute in Pewaukee, Wisconsin.

JO LYNN LLOYD is an Instructor in Sociology at Dallas Baptist College. She received her B.A. and M.A. degrees, in Sociology and Community College Administration, from East Texas State University. She is presently completing work on her Ph.D. in Higher Education Administration at North Texas State University.

MICHAEL M. MAYALL is Professor of Behavioral Science and Chairman of the Department of Behavioral Occupations and Psychology at Tarrant County Junior College in Fort Worth, Texas. He has also served in a variety of administrative positions at Dallas County Community College and the University of Oregon. He has authored numerous articles for professional journals.

JAMES S. McELHANEY, JR., is Field Center Coordinator for the Employment Opportunity Pilot Project of the Department of Labor, a program designed to test various alternatives to welfare among the employable poor. He was previously an Associate Professor and Director of Radio/Television/Film at Baylor University, and Coordinator of Communications and Development for the University System of South Texas (formerly the Texas A & I University System). He has contributed to the *Journal of Communication* and has extensive production and directing credits in both film and television.

MARGARET McELROY is an Associate Professor in the College of Nursing graduate program at Texas Woman's University. She is a doctoral candidate in Higher Education Administration at North Texas State University. She is currently President of the Beta Beta chapter of Sigma Theta Tau and has recently completed a three-year term as Secretary of the Texas Nurses' Association.

BOB W. MILLER is a professor and director of Community College Programs at North Texas State University. His duties include directing three doctoral programs, directing Community College Programs, public relations and Liaison with fifty-five community colleges in Texas and Professor of Higher Education Administration, and Public School Administration. Former positions for Bob W. Miller are Tarrant County Junior College in Fort Worth and McClennan Community College in Waco where he was Academic Dean; Director of Personnel and Professional Development at Tarrant County Junior College, Fort Worth; Director of Placement—University level; Director of Student Teachers—University level; Director of Public Relations—University level; Professor of Educational Administration—University level (other universities); Executive Director of The West Texas Innovative Education Center for two colleges and 29 public schools; Public School Administration at all levels; Varsity Coach for basketball, baseball, and track; Teacher in Public Schools and at the Graduate Level in three universities. Has served as a consultant throughout the United States, Canada, Mexico and the Caribbean; He is the author of *Higher Education and The Community College* and a coauthor of *The Administration of Learning Resources* (both by the University Press of America); Has written numerous articles.

ROSE M. NIESWODOMY is Assistant Professor of Nursing at Texas Woman's University. She is a member of the College of Nursing Curriculum Committee and Chairperson of the Academic Committee for the school board. She has been a faculty team leader and surgical nursing supervisor. She recently completed a nationwide research study titled "Research Productivity of Nurse Educators."

RHEY NOLEN is a government and history instructor at Tyler Junior College, Tyler, Texas, in the Division of Social Science. Prior to this he was an administrator in the Denton State School of Denton, Texas.

MARY J. OSENTOWSKI is Division Chairperson, Communications, Richland College, one of the colleges within the Dallas County Community College District. She recently completed a "Career Development Project" internship with the Communications Division Chairperson at Richland College.

MICHAEL ROSS is Assistant Director of Occupational Education for the Dallas County Community College District. He was formerly the Division Chairman for the Science/Math Division at El Central College in Dallas. He has also served as Director of Cooperative Education and an instructor in the Drafting and Design Department of the college. He has also taught at Henderson County Junior College in Athens, Texas.

CAROLYN K. SCHROEDER is a principal in the Dallas Independent School District. Previously she served as a Community Specialist for schools undergoing desegregation and as an assistant principal in impacted K-6 Centers. She has made extensive professional contributions at the local and state levels through various publications, as President of the Dallas Association of Texas Educators, President and Secretary of the North Texas Professional Administrators and Supervisors Council, and as Legislative Chairman of the Association of Texas Educators.

JACK D. TERRY, JR. is Dean of the School of Religious Education at Southwestern Baptist Theological Seminary and is Professor of Foundations of Education. He was previously a member of the faculty at Hardin-Simmons University, Abilene, Texas. He is coauthor of *The Administration of Learning Resources Centers*. He has authored and produced twenty-six videotapes and *Learning Guide* for a teacher-training course for teachers and leaders of learning groups. He is active in teacher-training conferences and as a guest lecturer in the U.S. and abroad.

RUTH J. WATKINS is Associate Dean of Instructional Learning Resources at El Centro College in Dallas. Prior to this she was Associate Dean of Learning Resources at Cedar Valley Community College in Dallas and was an Instructional Development Consultant and Instructor at Tarrant County Junior College in Fort Worth. She has published articles in national journals in the fields of higher education administration and instructional technology.

LEADERSHIP
IN HIGHER
EDUCATION

1

Administrative Organization in Higher Education

ROGER KINSETH AND BOB W. MILLER

The administration of institutions of higher education is a very complex, challenging, and, in many instances, frustrating undertaking. The administrator must deal with many groups, among them students, faculty, other administrators, federal, state, and local governing agencies, accreditation agencies, business and professional organizations, service clubs, and alumni. In order to effectively manage this task, today's administrator must be thoroughly familiar with the various ground rules, regulations, and laws that pertain to higher education. In addition, the administrator must be sensitive to the needs of the populations served by the institutions, the pressures exerted by outside groups, and the internal functioning of the institution.

DEFINITIONS

Accrediting agencies—Regional accrediting bodies which develop a set of standards for the purpose of accrediting the institution as a whole. The regional accrediting agency assures that the total program of a complex institution is coordinated, administered, and held in proper balance.

Chief administrative officer—Directly responsible to the local governing body for insuring that the institution is in compliance with the rules, laws, and various regulations impacted by the various internal and external agencies.

Federal control—Multiple laws enacted by the federal government which assure the high quality of various forms of educational programs and provide funds to assist those programs.

Local governing board—The legislative and policy-making body of an institution of higher education charged with the oversight and control of the institution's activities.

FEDERAL CONTROL AND REGULATION

In the Constitution of the United States, education is not mentioned. However, from the time of the first settlers in America, an educational system evolved. Until the Civil War, educational systems were developed, financed, and controlled by state or local governments or by various religious groups.

The role of the federal government in education increased greatly with the passing of the Morrill Act of 1862. Even though there were state universities in existence, those institutions dealt primarily with the professions (i.e., law, medicine) and the liberal arts. The Morrill Act provided for the creation of land grant colleges primarily to teach agriculture, engineering, and homemaking. Although the federal government provided funds to the states, there was no federal supervision.

FIGURE 1
Selected relationships of U.S. Department of Education

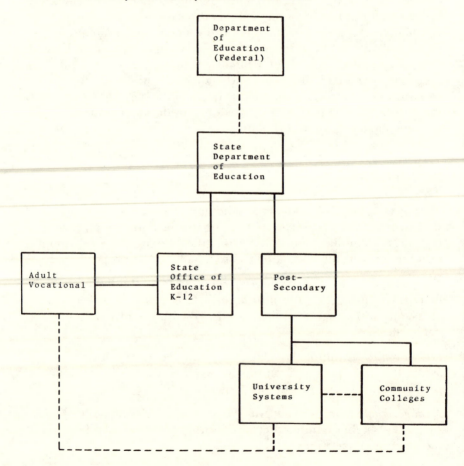

The role of the federal government further expanded in 1917 when Congress enacted the Smith-Hughes Act for the advancement of vocational education. For the first time, there was federal supervision of the expenditure of federal funds for education. This act marked the increasing involvement of the government in education.

In 1867, following the Civil War, the Federal Office of Education was formed to promote education, primarily by collecting and disseminating information. Its name later was changed to Bureau of Education and finally, in 1933, to United States Office of Education.

Since 1958, when the National Defense Education Act was passed shortly after the successful launching of the Soviet Sputnick, many other acts have been enacted that have further increased the federal role in education.[1] (See Figure 1.)

The major functions of the United States Office of Education are as follows:

Promotes education

Aids in the administration of funds for education

Issues publications and periodicals

Maintains a national library of education in Washington

Conducts local, state, and national surveys[2]

ACCREDITING AGENCIES

Institutions of higher education in the United States have no single accrediting agency, but six regional agencies:

Commission on Institutions of Higher Education of the Middle States Association of Colleges and Secondary Schools

Commission on Institutions of Higher Education of the New England Association of Colleges and Secondary Schools, Inc.

Commission on Colleges and Universities of the North Central Association of Colleges and Secondary Schools

Commission on Colleges of the Southern Association of Colleges and Schools

Northwest Association of Schools and Colleges

Accrediting Commission for Senior Colleges and Universities of the Western Association of Schools and Colleges[3]

While all of the above-listed accrediting agencies are independent of one another, they are largely parallel in aims and functions. There exists a great deal of cooperation and exchange of ideas between these regional accrediting agencies.

The *Standards of the College Delegate Assembly* of the Southern Association of Colleges and Schools will be discussed in this chapter as being representative of all the regional accrediting agencies. Reference to other accrediting agencies will be made where necessary to provide a national scope.

The Commission on Colleges sees its task as intimately related to the traditional public philosophy of the United States—that free men can and ought to govern themselves, and that they do so best through a representative, flexible, and responsive system.[4]

It is the feeling of the Commissions that regional accreditation is preferable to national or state accreditation because a large, national agency might become unwieldy and not sensitive to regional needs. On the other hand, provincialism tends to threaten the smaller unit.

The Commission regards as its basic function the accreditation of the institution as a whole. It recognizes that accreditation of professional schools, divisions, or departments within complex colleges and universities is also provided by other recognized accrediting organizations. Although it cooperates with these agencies, the Commission retains the right and responsibility of assuring that the total program of a complex institution is coordinated, administered, and held in proper balance.[5]

A new institution may apply for candidate status with the Commission. After receiving full accreditation, each member institution must conduct a comprehensive self-study every ten years. This self-study is evaluated at the institution by a qualified committee of educators.

The Commission has eleven standards by which each institution is evaluated. However, meeting each standard is not all that is required for accreditation by and membership in the Southern Association. While the Commission is concerned with the many factors referred to in the standards, its final concern is with the totality of the effort and the atmosphere in which it is carried out. This assessment overrides smaller considerations as the decision whether or not to grant or renew membership is approached. Following is a list of the eleven standards of the Southern Association and the major areas contained within each standard:

Southern Association of Colleges and Schools

Standard One—Purpose

Standard Two—Organization and Administration

Descriptive Titles and Terms

Governing Boards

Advisory Committees

Library

Financial Resources

Standard Eleven—Research

Administration

Institutional Control

Primacy of Teaching Obligations

Faculty Morale

Expenditure of Research Funds

Freedom of Investigation[6]

In addition to acquiring regional accreditation, many programs must be accredited by special accrediting agencies. Among these agencies are: American Bar Association, American Chemical Society, American Medical Association, Federal Aviation Agency, Federal Communications Commission, State Nursing Board, and the National Council for Accreditation of Teacher Education

LOCAL GOVERNING BOARDS

The legal authority and responsibility for the operation of public junior community colleges is usually vested in an elected group of residents of the particular district. It may be called the Board of Education, Board of Regents, Board of Governors, or the District Junior Community College Committee. However, the most commonly used term is Board of Trustees.

The board has the responsibility of formulating broad public policy in community college education. It functions as the legislative and policy-making body charged with the oversight and control of college activities. The board will usually delegate to the chief executive officer, commonly called the president or chancellor, the function of implementing the policy as established by the board. Following are the responsibilities of the Board of Trustees of a typical community college:

Adopt and periodically review a statement of philosophy which clarifies basic educational beliefs and educational responsibilities of the district to the community.

Determine the quality of professional leadership needed to carry out the philosophy and objectives of the district; select and appoint the Chancellor of the district.

Approve uniform policies regarding admission, retention, scholastic standards, record keeping, registration practices, and regulations for student conduct.

Review and take appropriate action on matters relating to site selection and physical plant development.

Provide ways and means of financial support; approve the annual budget; review and approve expenditures.

Approve courses and curricula for inclusion in educational programs of the colleges.

Formulate such additional policies as are necessary to promote the educational program of the colleges.

Consider and act upon administrative recommendations concerning appointment, retention or dismissal of district employees.

Review administrative recommendations and take action concerning employee benefit programs.

Consider communications and requests from citizens and organizations on matters of policy, administration and other items of public concern affecting the district.

Serve as a final adjudicating agency for students, employees and citizens of the college district on matters of Board policy.

Bear the legal responsibility for all aspects of the operation of the district.[7]

In most states the members of the governing board are elected. However, in several states they are appointed by the governor, or in the case of a city college system, they may be appointed by the mayor. Board members of private institutions that are church affiliated are often appointed by the governing body of that particular denomination.

Usually Board members are volunteers and receive no compensation for serving. The members have no individual authority. Their only authority is vested in the Board as a whole. They have a "fiduciary duty" to act in the best interest of their institution and not in the interest of any single individual when a conflict of interest arises.

If state law permits, many trustees are granted limited indemnification for any loss they may incur by reason of their service to the institution. Even though trustees may have limited indemnification or be protected somewhat by the Doctrine of Sovereign Immunity, there recently has been much judicature in the area of civil liability. The most common types of civil liability assessed against trustees and administrators are contract liability, tort liability, violation of constitutional rights, and liability for breach of fiduciary trust.

STATE REGULATION AND CONTROL

In the early years of development of the junior college movement, many communities organized junior colleges at a rapid rate. This resulted in a variety of administrative controls. Because of this rapid growth, many states developed standards for the establishment and control of junior colleges. Several states have boards on the state level for the supervision of public junior/community colleges. Among them are Arizona, Illinois, Massachusetts, Minnesota, Virginia, and Washington. In Oregon, Pennsylvania, and Utah, the public junior/community colleges are under the State Board of Education. Other states have a comprehensive administrative structure encompassing universities, colleges, and two-year colleges; California is one of these states. Authority exercised by the various states to administer, control, and regulate two-year colleges is usually based on the power of the state legislatures to appropriate funds for the operation of the colleges.

In Texas five regulatory bodies supervise higher education. They are: Board of Regents—University of Texas System, Board of Regents—Texas A & M University System, Board of Regents—State Senior Colleges and Universities, Coordinating Board—Texas College & University System, and Texas Education Agency.

Public junior/community colleges in Texas deal with two state regulatory bodies: the Coordinating Board and the Texas Education Agency. The Coordinating Board administers the university parallel curriculum offered in the community colleges, while the Texas Education Agency administers post-secondary occupational and technical education, adult and continuing education, and the teacher education and certification programs in the state universities. The organizational structure of the Texas Education Agency is shown in Figure 2.

Relationships between four-year colleges and universities and two-year comprehensive community colleges vary from regional association to regional association and from state to state. In California, for example, a multilevel structure of post-secondary education has been established, with metropolitan universities and campuses enjoying the greatest prestige, while regional state colleges and two-year community colleges form a second grouping. In most states throughout the nation there is a degree of rivalry among universities, colleges, and college systems, with increasing competition for legislative attention and funding.

In all regions throughout the United States, the ideal for state influence on higher education has been coordination rather than control. In recent years, however, California, Texas, Florida, and several other states have taken steps to exercise a kind of "quality control" function in relation to degrees and programs. In the atmosphere of increased competitiveness which prevails in today's market for post-secondary education, greater intervention by state boards of higher education will be likely. The federal government, through its establishment of a separate cabinet-level post for education, has indicated a growing concern for the improvement of the quality of American higher education.

FIGURE 2
Texas Education Agency

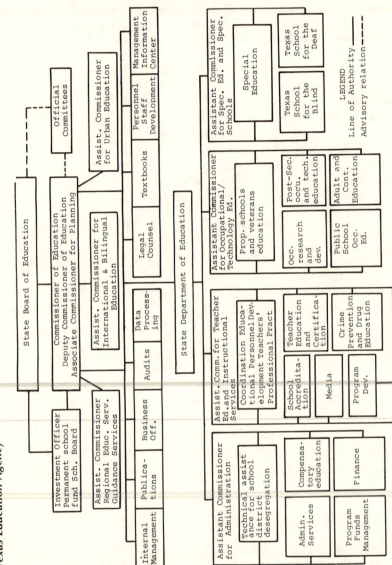

Texas Education Agency, 1973

A major source of apprehension on the part of many administrators in higher education is the possibility that individual initiative in innovation and curriculum will be precluded by increased state and federal intervention in higher education. In the perception of many educators, the reins of effective governance in higher education *must* remain at the individual college and university level. It is doubtful that a single, national controlling board for higher education could effectively deal with the different characteristics which are at present evident among the institutions that form the various regional accrediting agencies. Therefore, it is likely that control of higher education will remain with the states and regions.

CHIEF ADMINISTRATIVE OFFICER

The ultimate responsibility for insuring that the college or university is in compliance with the rules, laws, and regulations of the various agencies under discussion rests with the chief administrative officer of the institution. This person may be called the president, the provost, or often in the case of multi-campus/college districts, the chancellor. Depending on the type and size of the institution, the duties of the chief administrator vary widely. To assist the chief administrative officer in carrying out the duties and responsibilities, several vice-presidents or deans are often employed.

Following is a representative list of the duties charged to the chief administrative officer:

1. Operation and development of the institution as a whole and of each of its parts.
2. Service as the chief administrative officer and the principal educational officer of the institution.
3. Maintaining and promoting a broad view of the objectives and the mission of the institution.
4. Planning, developing, and administering all institutional activity.
5. Developing and maintaining a program of instruction, research, and service suited to the needs of the institution's sponsors and of all the students admitted.
6. Recruiting and maintaining a high-quality instructional, research, and administrative staff.
7. Recruiting, admitting, and supervising a qualified student body.
8. Developing plans to finance the required capital and current budgets of the institution.

TABLE 1

Frequency of the duties performed by presidents by percentages in one hundred forty public junior colleges arranged in categories from less than 500 to more than 2000 students

	Duties	Total
1.	Coordinates the activities of the various divisions of the college	100
2.	Acts as professional advisor to the board	100
3,	Keeps the board advised of the appointment and discharge of staff members	100
4.	Is responsible for the execution of policies and regulations of the governing board	100
5.	Directs the public relations work of the college	93
6.	Presides at faculty meetings	25
7.	Presides at commencement and confers degrees and diplomas	100
8.	Teaches regularly scheduled classes	11
9.	Is responsible for the preparation of the budget	75
10.	Is responsible for the purchase of equipment and supplies	54
11.	Is responsible for maintaining an accurate inventory of college properties and equipment	39
12.	Is responsible for accounting for all monies of the college	50
13.	Maintains supervision and direction of all persons employed in the care, custody, and operation of the plant	50
14.	Is responsible for the operation of the bookstore	32
15.	Is responsible for seeing all faculty members carry a proper teaching load and maintain a satisfactory quality of work	17

9. Developing and maintaining modern procedures in plant maintenance, purchasing, budgeting, accounting, auditing, and financial reporting.

10. Developing a sound, streamlined administrative structure for the institution, to the end that all employees will be properly assigned and supervised.

11. Developing communication channels between and among all staff and student groups in the institution.

12. Regularly disseminating information about the institution to other agencies related to the constituency; to cultural, civic, and business organizations; to the alumni; and to the general public.[8]

A 1968 study by Harold F. Landrith determined that the duties of presidents do not vary greatly except in one area: Presidents of smaller institutions more frequently prepare budgets and purchase equipment than do presidents in larger community colleges.[9]

ADVISORY COMMITTEES

Advisory committees are utilized by the technical/occupational programs in the community college. These committees are made up of members of business and industry, high school instructors, or other persons involved in the technical/occupational area. Advisory committees are utilized to assist, advise, and counsel those who operate new, complicated, and changing technical/occupational programs. The efforts of the committee should be evident in the quality of instruction and program received by the students.

Advisory committee members are called upon for service to (1) help evaluate the program of instruction; (2) help keep the colleges informed of changes in technology and labor requirements; (3) inform the community of occupational programs; (4) assess program needs in terms of the entire community; (5) assist in recruitment and placement of students; (6) serve as a channel of communication between colleges and community; (7) suggest ways for improving public relations; and (8) recommend competent personnel as potential instructors.

The duties and responsibilities of the various components involved in the administration and regulation of institutions of higher education, especially community colleges, are described briefly above. Due to increasing demands by taxpayers, interest groups, and various federal, state, and local governmental agencies, the role of the administrator is becoming increasingly complex. Only by constant study and awareness of all aspects of administration can today's college administrator function effectively and efficiently in dealing with this myriad of problems.

NOTES

1. John H. Ferguson and Dean E. McHenry, *The American System of Government* (New York, McGraw-Hill, 1969), p. 618.

2. Harry G. Good and James D. Teller, *A History of Western Education* (New York: MacMillan, 1969), p. 478.

3. Harold F. Landrith, *Introduction to the Community Junior College*, (Danville, Ill.: Interstate Printers and Publishers, 1971), p. 297.

4. *Standards of the College Delegate Assembly* (Atlanta: Southern Association of Colleges and Schools, 1977), p. 1.

5. Ibid., p. 2.

6. Ibid., pp. 3–34.

7. *Board of Trustees Policies and Administrative Procedures Manual*, (Dallas: Dallas County Community College District, 1977), p. 11B.

8. Landrith, *Introduction to the Community Junior College*, p. 299.

9. Landrith, *Introduction to the Community Junior College*, pp. 137–38.

2

Theories of Administration

MARGARET MC ELROY AND JACK D. TERRY, JR.

American society has become institutionalized in the past seventy-five years. Social tasks previously done by the family unit are now accomplished by organizations or institutions. With the development of institutions or organizations which perform functions in a variety of domains—commerce, industry, health care, education, and government—there has developed a need for management. Peter Drucker describes management as the organ of the institution. " . . . [it] is independent of ownership, rank, power . . . is professional—management is a function, a discipline, a task to be done; and managers are the professionals who practice this discipline. . . ."[1]

A contemporary issue is the concern for the theoretical basis of administration. Questions to be answered are: Should there be a scientific approach to administration? What is the nature of theory? What are the prevailing theories of administration?

DEFINITIONS

Administration—The managing of a business, office, school, etc. The group of persons in charge of the management of affairs.

Authoritarian leadership—Associated with bureaucratic organizational structure. Authority comes downward.

Conflict model—A model in which organization is conceived as a basis of group differences, not individual differences. Conflict acts as a stimulus to proffer competition in an effort to reduce conflict among groups.

Conflict theory—A theory that views organization as the hierarchy of subordinate-superordinate relationships within the social system which allocates, integrates, and facilitates in order to achieve goals of that social system.

Decision-making theory—A theory that may be equated with the problem-solving process which assists an organization to pass judgement on a problem and thereby terminate a controversy.

Democratic leadership—Associated with a participative structure of organization. Authority stems from the group.

Laissez-faire leadership—Associated with individual independent decision making outside any organizational structure.

Life-style cycle theory leadership—Associated with an understanding of the relationship between an effective style of leadership and the level of maturity of the members of the organization.

Management—The controlling, handling, and directing of a business, office, school, etc. The group of persons who skillfully administer the guidance of the affairs.

Motivational theory—A theory that considers organization as a cooperative system which is conscious, deliberate, and purposeful.

Rational model—A model in which organization is conceived as a means for the realization of announced group goals.

Systems theory—A theory of administration which is organized in such a manner as to accomplish objectives and goals.

HISTORY OF THE THEORIES OF ADMINISTRATION

There is a controversy between theorists and scientists on the question of whether or not management is a discipline with its own organized body of knowledge. The debate has advanced beyond this matter of art vs. science, and management is considered generally as something to be learned, and thus a discipline. As a discipline, it is more than an array of traits and talents which ensure success to those so endowed.

In the early years of the twentieth century, the approach to the study of management was functional rather than theoretical. Writers of that time spoke more of principles than of theories. The emphasis in management was first a task-oriented one, progressing to a manager-oriented one, and then to one concerned with the worker. Chester I. Barnard published his still-used organizational theory of cooperative systems in 1938. Barnard combines both of the major influences discussed in his concepts of effectiveness and efficiency.

Effectiveness had to do with achieving goals and getting the job done. Efficiency was person-oriented and had much to do with the satisfaction of the worker within the organization. Elton Mayo and Fritz J. Roethlisberger carried on the Hawthorne studies in the early thirties. The work of these individuals introduced into administrative thinking the importance of observing what managers do and analyzing these actions to determine the underlying theory of the administrative function. These works are viewed as scientific in nature. In addition, they illustrate an introduction of the behavioral approach to the study of management.

The concern over theory, research, and practice in administration gathered momentum in the post-World War II years. Research in the social sciences had increased very rapidly and was reflected in what has been referred to as the "New Movement in educational administration."[2] Individuals such as Jacob W. Getzels, Herbert A. Simon, Daniel Griffiths, and Andrew W. Halpin became prominent as leaders in this movement. Its development began with dissatisfaction on the part of a group of professors of educational administration with the current methods of training administrators. At that time neither theory nor research formed the basis of instruction; personal experiences of the professors in school administration became the content of the courses. Getzels and his associates refer to the "trait" and "technology" points of view about administration as the "uncodified art" and "prescriptive" views. They describe a third view as one in which the focus of administration must be on "conceptualizations and theories—not on simply directions to be followed but on complex relations to be understood."[3] Simon was especially concerned that administrators be able to improve the decision-making process. Griffiths illustrates how social science contributes to the building of administrative sciences.

In 1947 a conference was attended by these "dissatisfied" professors who with the American Association of School Administrators secured funding for a research and development program from the Kellogg Foundation. In 1950 centers for this program opened at eight universities.

In a 1953 conference of professors of educational administration, there was a noticeable shift from concerns related to procedure, to concerns related to theory. Getzels made a strong plea for theory-oriented research at this particular meeting.[4]

In 1954 a group of behavioral scientists met with professors of educational administration. At that time the scientists criticized the quality of research being done in education, indicating that it was "a-theoretical" in nature. This has been described as "the first real" confrontation between behavioral scientists and professors of educational administration.[5]

James Thompson, a professor of sociology and business administration, described several advantages of administration theory: (1) preparing students for change with a view of the administration process as a "complex of simultaneously variable factors"; (2) offering a way of thinking "which would allow the administrator to incorporate knowledge produced by the several disciplines"; (3) alerting students to the results of research; and (4) preparing students for "growth through their own later experience."[6]

As stated by Halpin, the leaders of the New Movement emphasized that (1) the role of theory be recognized and that nakedly empirical research be rejected in favor of hypothetico-deductive research in history; (2) educational administration not be viewed provincially, and especially not as distinct from other kinds of administration—administration as administration, without adjectival qualifiers, is a proper subject for study and research; and (3) because education can be construed best as a social system, educational administration must, in turn, draw heavily from insights furnished by the behavioral sciences.[7]

Five research studies were considered as substantive achievements of the New Movement. One was on leadership behavior of superintendents (Halpin); another on administration as a social process (Getzels); a third on personality characteristics and administrative performance of principals (Hemphill and his associates); a fourth on place-bound and career-bound superintendents in relation to effecting organization change (Carlson); and a fifth study was on the organizational climate in elementary schools.[8] Out of these studies concepts and theories developed, although Halpin reflects pessimism in an article published in 1969 in which he indicates that the movement began to run down because the idea of theory in administration was oversold and because of lack of ability to attract enough quality manuscripts.[9]

Although the movement for development of a theoretical base in educational administration lost its momentum, it left its mark. There is a developing theory, or theories, of administration, which is considered a discipline with a base that is scientific in nature. This statement is based upon the perceptions of most authorities in the area of higher educational administration. Drucker views management as being scientific in nature when he describes it as "a discipline, or at least capable of becoming one."[10] It appears that management has become a field for the scientific study of how organizations and people in organizations do and can behave.

Organizations may consist of leaders who exhibit a variety of behaviors and traits, workers who display complex and constantly varying motivational patterns, and a structure that establishes tasks ranging along a simple-to-complex continuum. Administrative theory is a tool for systematizing the spirit of inquiry about organizations. It allows the administrator to rise above the unexamined assumptions he may have generated from experience alone or learned from fellow administrators.[11]

THE NATURE AND DEVELOPMENT OF THEORY

Understanding of the nature and development of theory must be based upon a common understanding of the involved terminology. Theory has two functions, one concerned with description and the other with explanation. In order to provide for a terminology which will not constantly involve a tangle of confusions, a definition of theory is presented; a "theory" is a set of assumptions from which can be derived, by purely logico-mathematical procedures, a larger set of empirical laws. The theory thereby furnishes an explanation of these empirical laws and unifies the originally heterogeneous areas of subject matter characterized by those empirical laws.[12]

Getzels, James Lipham, and Ronald Campbell list three functions of theory in the study and practice of administration—taxonomic, explanatory, and heuristic.[13] Others define theory as a deductively connected set of laws. In general, a theory might be considered as a principle or assumption which serves to explain, predict, and question phenomena, and from which laws are derived.

Since theory is derived from a framework of concepts, it is appropriate to discuss the meaning of *concept*. According to Griffiths a concept is simply a term to which a particular meaning has been attached. The lack of appropriate concepts has made it very difficult to adequately describe administrative situations or administrative behavior. A concept is now considered to be operational if a link to other operational concepts can be clearly demonstrated.[14] Concept has also been referred to as a "descriptive term, or observable." It is found in everyday experience, "susceptible to direct sensory observation," and defined by popular acceptance.

Griffiths refers to the steps in theory construction as stages in the development of a science. He describes his approach as the "level" approach, with sensitizing concepts at the lowest level, integrating concepts at the middle level, and theory at the top level. Sensitizing concepts are those which draw attention to specific behaviors associated with administrative activity. Integrating concepts order the relationships among a number of sensitizing concepts. This approach is illustrated in Figure 3. According to Griffiths, the theory builder has useful thoughts, opinions, and ideas (presumptions), which he follows up by observation and description of the administrative behavior noted. Explanation of the observation is attempted on one of the three levels, but levels may be skipped or returned to from a higher level.[15]

Figure 4 illustrates the concept that the administrator attempts to insure goal achievement by control. Rather than confronting the person directly, he controls by rules. This keeps the visibility of power relations down and thus lowers the interpersonal tension level. The lowered tension level increases the use of rules.[16]

Figure 5 depicts an example of a more complex integrative administrative act, where a consequence occurred which the administrator did not anticipate. When the general rule can only imply what is minimum acceptable behavior and only minimum behavior occurs, there will be an increased gap between the organizational goals and the attainment of the goals, resulting in closer supervision. Closer supervision leads to increased visibility of power relations, which in turn leads to an elevated

FIGURE 3
Paradigm for theory development

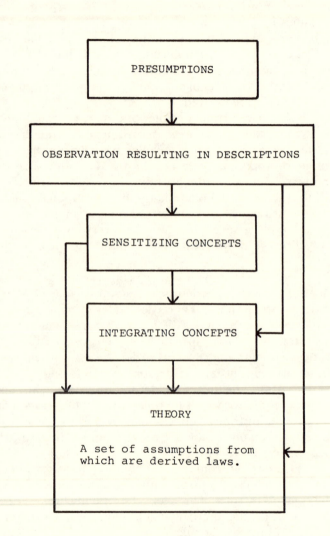

Griffiths, *The Nature and Planning of Theory*, P. 35.

FIGURE 4
Anticipated consequences of demand for control

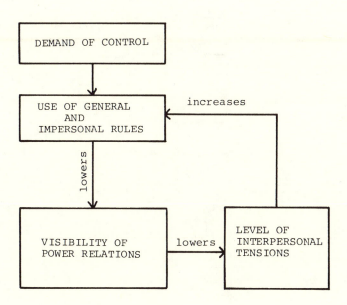

Griffiths, Daniel E., *"The Nature and Planning of Theory"*, p. 42.

level of interpersonal tension. The elevated tension leads to decreased effectiveness in the use of rules as a means of control.[17] The more the organization is in a state of nonsatisfaction, the closer the supervision is likely to be. The more satisfactorily the organization is functioning, the less the need for supervision.

An analysis of the illustrated integrative concepts shows that their value lies in the fact that they order the less complex concepts and maintain an appropriate relationship between them. Thus the goal is still achieved by the administrative act of control. There is increased or decreased use of general and impersonal rules, resulting in lower or higher visibility of the power relations. Figure 6 illustrates the totality of the situation with both anticipated and unanticipated consequences of the administrative act.[18]

One must not assume that a knowledge of theory construction and a knowledge of standards for theory of educational administration insure

FIGURE 5
**Unanticipated consequences viewed in the context of an administrator's antici-
pated consequences**

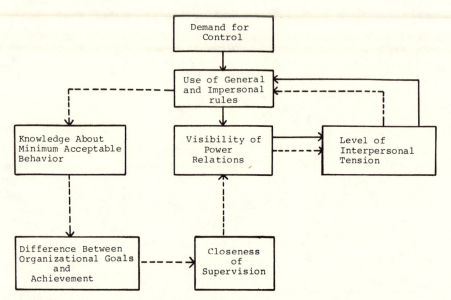

Griffiths, Daniel E., "The Nature and Meaning of Theory", p. 42.

FIGURE 6
Unanticipated consequences of administrative act 19

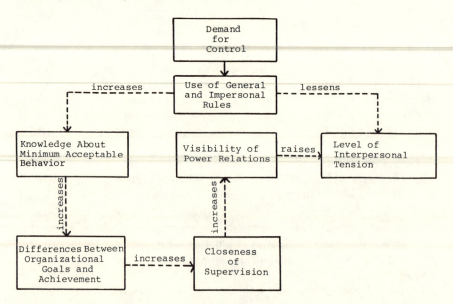

Daniel E. Griffiths, "The Nature and Meaning of Theory," Theory Development and
Educational Administration, p. 41.

that a complete body of knowledge called administration theory exists. Some say that it is in the initial stages of development, and others say that it does not exist. Most people will agree, however, that there have been and continue to be problems in the development of such a theory.

Andrew Halpin and Arthur Coladarci have identified such problems as lack of a common understanding of the meaning of theory, a tendency to be too preoccupied with taxonomic methods, and a lack of certainty about the "precise domain" of administrative theory.[19] Other problems identified are a commitment to "factualism," unwarranted respect for the authority of "experts" and "law," an inadequate professional language, a fear of theory, and emotional identification with personal views.[20]

SPECIFIC THEORIES OF ADMINISTRATION

Administrative theory has been classified in a variety of ways. William Lane and his associates contrast the rational models of organization with the conflict models.[21] A rational, systematically organized, controlled development of the institution is characteristic of a rational model. Efficiency, structure, and function are key words. Harmonious equilibrium based upon group consensus prevails. That which disrupts the harmony is abnormal.

In contrast to rational models, the conflict models have as a common base the recognition of the presence of conflict and its effects upon institutions. Conflict is considered normal; is an adjunct of power relationships. Power provides social order, not group consensus. The effective and efficient manager should be able to manage conflict and turn it into a positive operation.

Lane and his associates have stated the following premises of a conflict theory of organization: (1) conflict is a group phenomenon and extends beyond the subjective attitudes of persons as group members; (2) the problem is not which side is "good," but what the fight is all about; (3) an organization is a balance of power; (4) conflict between groups promotes cooperation within groups; (5) each side in a conflict must have some physical or symbolic identity; (6) symbolic identities have their highest expression in the statements of ideologies justifying the group's position in the conflict; and (7) conflict nourishes a diversity of organizational goals and unplanned cleavages between departments which further compromise the original goals.[22]

Conflicts are considered to be based upon group differences rather than individual ones. Differences may be racial, religious, goal-oriented, or even reflective of past group differences in viewpoint. Conflict does act as a stimulus, resulting in an effort to decrease the stimulus. Thus competition might occur with the ultimate result of achievement of institutional goals. Each group in the conflict must have an identifiable characteristic to give it visibility. When the characteristic disappears, the conflict disappears, even though it may not have been resolved. Conflict, in other words, must result in commonalities among members of the conflict group.

Griffiths uses a classification for administrative theory proposed by Frederick March and Herbert Simon which includes: (1) theories of conflict, that is, role conflict, personality conflict, and role-personality conflict; (2) theories of motivation in which the needs, drives, and motives of individuals are considered; and (3) theories of decision making in which man is considered as a rational being with certain limitations.[23] The concepts of motivational theories and decision making will also be discussed in other chapters in this book.

Motivational Theory

A specific theory of administration proposed by Chester I. Barnard considers organization as a cooperative system. This motivational type theory is representative of the rational model. It says that people act as they do because of their association with formal organizations, which may be defined as "that kind of cooperation among men that is conscious, deliberate, purposeful."[24] Most cooperation fails because of factors outside the formal organization, and "survival of the organization depends upon the maintenance of an equilibrium of complex character in a continuously fluctuating environment of physical, biological, and social materials, elements, and forces, which calls for readjustment of processes internal to the organization."[25]

The individual is a person and has properties which are: "(a) activities or behaviors arising from (b) psychological factors, to which are added (c) the limited power of choice, which results in (d) purpose."[26] This individual has the choice of entering into a cooperative system based upon his own goals and the alternatives available to him. The organization is the key element in Barnard's theory of administration.

Barnard distinguishes between *effective* and *efficient* action by saying that an action is effective if it accomplishes its specific objective aim while it is efficient if it satisfies the motive of that aim.[27] Individuals have biological characteristics which are limitations to be overcome by cooperation. From a sociological point of view, persons are regarded as "objects to be manipulated by changing the factors affecting them." Social factors in cooperation were identified by Barnard as (a) the interaction between individuals within a cooperative system; (b) the interaction between the individual and the group; (c) the individual as the object of cooperative influence; (d) social purpose and the effectiveness of cooperation; and (e) individual motives and cooperative efficiency.[28]

The basic assumptions upon which Barnard built his theory are (1) the human being possesses a limited power of choice; (2) among the most important limiting factors in the situation of each individual are his own biological factors; (3) cooperation is a social aspect of the total situation and the social factors arising from it; (4) the persistence of cooperation depends upon two conditions, (a) its effectiveness and (b) its efficiency; (5) the survival of cooperation, therefore, depends upon two interrelated and interdependent classes of processes, (a) those which relate to the system of cooperation as a whole in relation to the environment, and (b) those which relate to the creation or distribution of satisfactions among individuals; and (6) the instability and failures of cooperation arise from defects in each of these classes of processes separately, and then from defects in their combination. The functions of the executive are those of securing the effective adaption of these processes.[29]

There are two basic types of organization, formal and informal. A formal organization is a system of consciously coordinated activities of two or more persons. The elements of an organization are communication, willingness to serve, and common purpose. These elements serve to maintain internal equilibrium. Either effectiveness or efficiency is required for continued existence or maintenance of external equilibrium.

Informal organization is an "aggregate of the personal contacts and interactions and the associated groupings of people." Informal organizations are responsible for certain attitudes, habits, and institutions and also create conditions under which formal organizations may arise.[30]

Informal organizations are made up of interactions between persons for personal reasons. They precede and arise out of formal organizations. An important function of informal organizations is communication. Other functions are cohesion and maintenance of individual integrity. In the informal organization there is usually a "Company Grapevine" for all types of communication which are not handled by the formal organization.

Barnard defines authority as "another name for the willingness and capacity of individuals to submit to the necessities of cooperative systems."[31] Four conditons are to be met for the subordinate to assent to authority: (1) he can and does understand the communication; (2) at the time of his decision, he believes that it is not inconsistent with the purpose of the organization; (3) at the time of his decision he believes it to be compatible with his personal interest as a whole; and (4) he is able to mentally and physically comply with it.[32] The whole aspect appears to be: will all of these fit within the mission of the organization?

Barnard explained that organizations would function under this theory of authority because of the concept of *zones of indifference.* Each individual has a zone of indifference for orders which are neither acceptable nor unacceptable. These orders will be accepted according to the degree to which inducements exceed the "sacrifices which determine the individual's adhesion to the organization."[33]

Conflict Theory

A second specific theory of administration is Jacob W. Getzels's theory of administration as a social process. Getzels presents his theory in terms of a model of social behavior. This theory is representative of conflict theory.

Getzels views administration as the hierarchy of subordinate-superordinate relationships within a social system. Functionally, this hierarchy of relationships is the center for allocating and integrating roles and facilities in order to achieve the goals of the social system. The functions are the responsibility of the superordinate member of the hierarchy but only will be effective when accepted by the subordinate member. This interpersonal, social relationship is the core of the administrative process.[34]

The social system is composed of two sets of independent but interacting phenomena: institutions with roles and expectations, and individuals with personalities and need-dispositions. The result of the interactions is called social behavior. Institutions, roles, and expectations comprise the nomothetic, or normative, aspect of activity in a social system. Individuals, personalities, and need-dispositions comprise the idiographic, or personal, aspect of activity in a social system.[35] The interactions of behavior in a social system are illustrated in Figure 7.

Getzels uses the concept of selective interpersonal perception to account for the fact that some role incumbents understand very readily their mutual obligations and responsibilities, while others do so more slowly and sometimes not at all. When the two role incumbents understand each other, "their perceptions and private organizations of the

FIGURE 7
The interactions of behavior in a social system

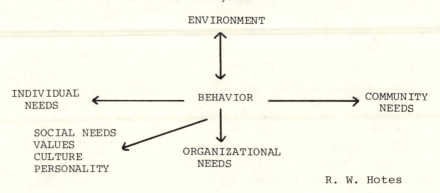

R. W. Hotes

prescribed complementary expectations are congruent." When the reverse is true, the term incongruent is used. Behavior, as seen in Getzels's model, is said to result from the individual's "attempt" to cope with an environment composed of patterns of expectations for his behavior in ways consistent with his own independent pattern of needs.[36] The interpretation of the concept conflict is based upon the idea that sources of conflict in the model are role-personality, role, and personality. The entire concept that people are dealing with people generally forms the subordinate-superordinate relationships.

Decision-Making Theory

The third specific administrative theory is identified as the decision-making theory. Such theories often make up a part of theories placed in other categories. Decision making also is a concept in leadership theory. For the purposes of this discussion of administration theory, only a brief consideration will be given to decision-making theory.

Daniel Wren discusses Barnard's inclusion of decision-making theory under the "third executive function." He describes Barnard as viewing delegation as a decision involving ends and means to ends. The two facets to decisions are (1) analysis, or the search for "strategic factors" which would create the set or system of conditions necessary to accomplish the organization's purpose; and (2) synthesis, or the recognition of the interrelationships between elements or parts which together make up the whole system.[37]

Several administration theorists equate decision making with the problem-solving process. Decision making is the process that one goes through in order to be able to pass judgement, solve a problem, and terminate a controversy. It is apparent that decision making can be called problem solving or other terms with the same connotation or relational meaning.

Robert Presthus describes organizations as miniature societies in which traditional social controls over the individual appear in sharp focus.[38] He uses an interdisciplinary approach in his theory, relying on Harry Stack Sullivan's interpersonal theory of psychiatry.

Presthus views large organizations as causing anxiety in their members. He defines large organization on the basis of Max Weber's model, the theory of bureaucracy, in which members tend to work with speed, precision, discretion, and technical know-how, without ambiguity or friction.[39]

Presthus says that the large organization induces anxiety in its members simply because of its fundamental characteristics such as size, specialization, ordering by one's hierarchical position, attitude toward status, and amount of power in the hands of a few. Members accommodate the demands of the organization in three ways: upward mobility, indifference, and ambivalence. Those with upward mobility "enjoy organized life and have little difficulty making decisions in conflict situations because they accept the organization's values as decisives." The indifferent member does not compete for organization favors and develops his interests outside of the organization. His anxiety lessens because he is not involved in the "race for rewards." The ambivalent member cannot get along with authority and "cannot play the organization game." He gives priority to individual friendships above the good of the organization. This theory of organization considers man a rational being and discusses behavior within an organizational context. It includes consideration of conflict and motivation.[40]

If a member utilizes much of his energies on the outside of the organization in a "moon lighting situation," there is little question about this activity being harmful to the organization; thus one of the administrative tasks is to analyze what is happening in the situation and try to avoid loss of important energies.

Systems Theory

A fourth theory of administration, the systems theory, is defined as a system of a complex of elements in mutual interaction. Systems theory is an organized manner of accomplishing objectives and goals. For example, in constructing a building one must start with the foundation before proceeding to assemble the walls and finally the roof.

Management theory deals with open systems which have many characteristics, including (1) having input and output; (2) having a tendency to maintain a steady state; (3) being self-regulating; (4) displaying equifinality (obtaining the same results from different initial conditions); (5) maintaining a steady state through "the dynamic interplay of subsystems operating as functional processes"; (6) maintaining a steady state partly through feedback; and (7) displaying progressive segregation. The system divides into a hierarchical order of subsystems which gain a degree of independence from each other.[41]

A number of derived propositions regarding conditions affecting change emanate from the systems theory model. The major impetus for change in organizations is from the outside. The degree and duration of change is directly proportional to the intensity of the stimulus from the suprasystem. Change in an organization is more likely to occur if the successor to the chief administrator is from outside the organization than if he is from inside the organization. When change in an organization does occur, it will tend to occur from the top down, not from the bottom up. "Living systems" respond to continuously increasing stress first by a lag in response, then by an overcompensatory response, and finally by catastrophic collapse of the system. The number of innovations expected is inversely proportional to the tenure of the chief administrator. This is one argument to change chief and other administrators over a period of years; for example, every five years. The more hierarchical the structure of an organization, the less the possibility of change. The more functional the dynamic interplay of subsystems, the less the change in organization.[42]

ADMINISTRATIVE LEADERSHIP THEORIES

A major component of administration is leadership. From the viewpoint of systems theory, leadership might be considered as a subsystem of systems administration. It could also be considered as a concept which becomes a part of the conceptual framework of administration theory. Leadership styles are definitely an important part of administrative theory.

Traditionally, the dimensions of leadership theory have been two in number, authoritarian and democratic. A third has been called laissez-faire. Authoritarian leadership is that which is associated with the bureaucratic organizational structure. Authority comes downward from the leader. He initiates decisions. He is the superordinate and does not consult with the subordinates. The exact opposite dimension is the laissez-faire, or free-rein, type. This type is one in which the individual member is independent of the group and the leader. He makes his own decisions. He acts outside of the organizational structure.

The most favored dimension for some administrators is democratic leadership. This type is seen in a participative type of organization. Authority stems from the group. Group members participate in the decision-making process. Ralph Stogdill summarizes leadership types as follows: (1) "authoritative (dominator)," (2) "persuasive (crowd arouser)," (3) "democratic (group developer)," (4) "intellectual (eminent man)," (5) "executive (administrator)," and (6) "representative (spokesman)."[43] The first three styles are extreme in nature, the more modern type of leadership style being that of situational leadership contingency management.

Stogdill surveyed the research done on leadership over the past forty years and categorized the definitions of leadership: (1) a focus of group processes, (2) personality and its effects, (3) the art of inducing compliance, (4) the exercise of influence, (5) an act or behavior, (6) a form of persuasion, (7) an instrument of goal achievement, (8) an effect of interaction, (9) a differentiated role, and (10) the initiation of structure.[44]

A review of leadership theory indicates three phases in its development: scientific management, human relations, and revisionist. Three authors are named by Warren Bennis as revisionists—Robert McMurray, Chris Argyris, and Douglas McGregor. Although their specific approaches to leadership theory differ, "they all share a common concern for revising the naive, unsubstantiated, and unrealistic aspects of the human relations approach without sacrificing its radical departure from traditional theory."[45]

Bennis describes McMurray's theory as one which indicates that "bottom-up management" is ideal but not possible because of the characteristics of managers as well as those of the "bureaucratic personality." "Benevolent autocracy" works and "is a method for making the best out of the worst."[46] The individual's needs and the formal organization's demands (as they are presently defined) are basically incompatible. The outcome of this is frustration to the individual, manifested through defense mechanisms that ultimately lead to the attenuation of the organization's goals.

McGregor's theory, according to Bennis, contains two elements, "a collaborative relationship between superior and subordinate that takes full account of their interdependency and reality task considerations that focus on the work requirements.[47]

Leadership theories may or may not be theories, but are attempts to gain an increasingly more sophisticated understanding of the nature of leadership. It is believed that characteristics of the individual and demands of the situation interact in such a manner as to permit one, or perhaps a few, person(s) to rise to leadership status. Groups become structured in terms of positions and roles during the course of member interaction. A group is organized to the extent that it acquires differentiated positions and roles. Leadership represents one or more of the differentiated positions in a group. The occupant of a leadership position is expected to play a role that differs from the roles of other group members. The expectancy reinforcement models seem best designed to explain the emergence and persistence of leadership in initially unstructured groups. They attempt to explain what leadership is and how it comes into existence. They do not explain who will emerge as a leader in any particular kind of situation.[48]

Paul Hersey and Kenneth Blanchard have proposed a life-cycle theory of leadership in response to theories proposed by the Ohio State Leadership Studies of 1945 and in the "Managerial Grid" of Blake and Mouton. They feel that there is no one best leadership style, but that, since situations differ, so must leadership style.[49] A three-dimensional model (relationship, task, effectiveness) was developed as a modification of the Ohio State two-dimensional model. The three-dimensional model illustrates the interaction between leadership style and the situation. When the style is appropriate to the situation, it is considered effective. Since effectiveness is determined by the interaction, there is no one best style, as the situation constantly changes.[50]

The life-cycle theory of leadership attempts to provide the leader with some understanding of the relationship between an effective style of leadership and the level of maturity of one's followers. The emphasis will be on the followers. The theory states that as the level of maturity of one's followers continues to increase, appropriate leader behavior not only requires less structure (tasks) but also less and less socio-emotional support (relationships).

Two final points must be made. First, the domain of administration is considered general rather than specific. The theories discussed can be viewed from the aspect of administration in higher education as well as from the aspect of management in industry. Second, there is no one unified theory of administration at this time. Theories have been proposed from a variety of perspectives and, certainly, some are more scientific than others. At least theories are being suggested to provide a framework for the discipline of administration, thereby providing a research orientation.

NOTES

1. Peter F. Drucker, *Management: Tasks, Responsibilities, Practices* (New York: Harper and Row, 1977), p. 6.

2. Andrew W. Halpin, "Administrative Theory: The Fumbled Torch," in *Issues in American Education*, ed. Arthur M. Kroll (New York: Oxford University Press, 1970), p. 157.

3. Jacob W. Getzels, James M. Lipham, and Ronald F. Campbell, *Educational Administration as a Social Process: Theory, Research, Practice* (New York: Harper and Row, 1968), pp. 1–5.

4. Halpin, "Administrative Theory," p. 162.

5. Ibid., p. 161.

6. James D. Thompson, "Modern Approaches to Theory in Administration," in *Administrative Theory in Education*, ed. Andrew W. Halpin (New York: Macmillan, 1958), pp. 22–24.

7. Halpin, "Administrative Theory," pp. 162–63.

8. Ibid., pp. 163–66.

9. Ibid., pp. 167–71.

10. Drucker, *Management: Tasks, Responsibilities, Practices*, p. xi.

11. Richard C. Williams, "Administrative Theory and Higher Education Administration," in *Handbook of College and University Administration, Academic Administration*, ed. Asa Knowles (New York: McGraw-Hill), pp. 54–55.

12. Jacob W. Getzels, "Administration as a Social Process," in *Administrative Theory in Education*, ed. Andrew W. Halpin (New York: Macmillan, 1958), p. 29.

13. Getzels, Lipham, and Campbell, *Educational Administration as a Social Process*, p. 8.

14. Daniel E. Griffiths, "The Nature and Meaning of Theory," in *Theory*

Development and Educational Administration, ed. Eddy J. Van Meter (New York: MSS Information Corporation, 1973), p. 37.

15. Ibid., p. 35.

16. Ibid., pp. 34–36.

17. Ibid., pp. 40–42.

18. Ibid., pp. 42–43.

19. Andrew W. Halpin, "The Development of Theory in Educational Administration," in *Administrative Theory in Education,* ed. Andrew W. Halpin (New York: Macmillan, 1958), pp. 7–9; Arthur P. Coladarci and Jacob W. Getzels, *The Use of Theory in Educational Administration* (Stanford, Calif.: Stanford University Press, 1955), pp. 10–14.

20. Coladarci and Getzels, *Use of Theory,* pp. 10–14.

21. Willard R. Lane, Ronald G. Corwin, and William G. Monahan, *Foundations of Educational Administration: A Behavioral Analysis* (New York: Macmillan, 1967), p. 40.

22. Ibid., pp. 42–46.

23. Griffiths, "Nature and Meaning of Theory," p. 43.

24. Chester I. Barnard, *The Functions of the Executive* (Cambridge, Mass.: Harvard University Press, 1938), p. 4.

25. Ibid., p. 6.

26. Ibid., p. 13.

27. Ibid., p. 20.

28. Ibid., p. 40.

29. Ibid., pp. 60–61.

30. Ibid., pp. 115–16.

31. Ibid., p. 184.

32. Ibid., p. 165.

33. Ibid., p. 169.

34. Getzels, "Administration as a Social Process, " *Administrative Theory in Education,* pp. 150–51.

35. Ibid., p. 152.

36. Ibid., pp. 156; 157.

37. Daniel A. Wren, *The Evolution of Management Thought* (New York: Ronald Press Company, 1972), p. 318.

38. Robert Presthus, *The Organizational Society: An Analysis and a Theory* (New York: Vintage Books, 1965), p. 93.

39. Ibid., p. 5.

40. Ibid., pp. 8–9.

41. Ibid., p. 48.

42. Ibid., pp. 48–49.

43. Ralph M. Stogdill, *Handbook of Leadership: A Survey of Theory and Research* (New York: Free Press, 1974), p. 27.

44. Ibid., pp. 7–16.

45. Warren B. Bennis, "Leadership Theory and Administrative Behavior: The Problem of Authority," *Administrative Science Quarterly* 4 (December 1959), p. 273.

46. Ibid., pp. 274–75.

47. Ibid., pp. 284–85.

48. Stogdill, *Handbook of Leadership*, p. 23.

49. Paul Hersey and Kenneth H. Blanchard, "Life Cycle Theory of Leadership," in *Readings in Management*, ed. Max D. Richards and William A. Neilander, 4th ed. (Dallas: South-Western Publishing Company, 1974), p. 480.

50. Ibid., pp. 480–81.

3

The Administrator's Task in Goal Setting, Planning, Programming, Budgeting, and Decision Making

The Scientific Decision-Making Process as a Basis for Planning and Problem Solving

RON HUGHES AND BOB W. MILLER

One theory of administration discussed in the previous chapter was the decision-making theory. This chapter will explore the relationship among several models of planning and decision making. The thrust of the chapter will be toward the understanding and application of the scientific decision-making process in institutions of higher education. Since so much of management in higher education is connected to proper decision making, an adequate discussion of this management principle is vital.

DEFINITIONS

Goals forecasting—Includes an element of flexibility in predicting the educational and institutional needs of the organization.

Goals setting—Three dimensions in the planning process: priority, time, structure.

MBO (Management by Objectives)—A system of management that requires the formulation of goals and the construction of objectives to meet those goals. This includes a "grass roots" approach at the faculty levels.

PPBS (Planning, Programming, Budgeting System)—Developed by the Department of Defense in 1961. Designed to provide a systematic process to identify commonalities in programs with similar objectives.

Planning system—Functional organization of the planning sequences into a super- and subsystem designed to effectuate the planning process.

Scientific decision-making process—The logical ordered exploration of any problem in a systematic approach to management.

ZBB (Zero-Based Budgeting)—A budget control system with "decision packages" which relate goals and objectives to budgeting priorities and needs.

THE SCIENTIFIC METHOD OF DECISION MAKING

The scientific method of decision making is the logical, ordered exploration of any problem in a systematic approach to management. The model presented in Figure 8 is similar to models offered by other authors, with the addition of specific evaluation and feedback paths which reflect the theories of creative problem-solving techniques presented elsewhere in this book. It is assumed that some perception of a problem situation exists. This model may be applied to almost any situation at any level. This universality of application is the central theme of the comparisons of the models to the decision-making process. This concept should be the central point of analysis as we look at the samples of the various models of planning. In the model presented, the major steps in the process are: (1) Suspect that a problem exists, (2) define the problem, (3) gather data, (if necessary return to step 2), (4) develop and list all discernable alternative solutions to the problem, (5) choose alternative with most advantages and fewest disadvantages, (6) develop strategies for implementing the chosen alternative, (7) implement the alternative, and (8) evaluate effectiveness.

It is important to follow the lines of flow very carefully. These lines define the procedures that must be followed in order to provide the climate for creativity that is implicit in this particular model. It is critical to realize that there is no evaluative feedback at the first four levels of the model. This lack of feedback as an aid to creative problem solving is described in the next section of this chapter.

The reader must make several assumptions about the operation of this model. First, an assumption must be made that the organization is committed to the concept of continuous evaluation as indicated by the model. The lines interrelating the evaluative process with the organizational system encompass the entire process of decision making. The unbroken flow is indicative of an ongoing process. The lines from the evaluation stage interconnect with the stages of choosing alternatives and developing strategies and indicate that the process of evaluation is also an ongoing process in these steps.

The second assumption is that the organization is familiar with the conditions necessary for creativity in problem solving. (There are not many opportunities for creativity in problem solving, as most problems are routine in nature.)

A third assumption is that one of the alternatives must be that no problem exists. This is represented on the model as part of the stage of choosing alternatives for implementation. The idea of "no problem" may result from the evaluation of the alternatives and would therefore result in the suspension of the remainder of the process. There are two possible routes after the choice of "no problem." One may simply return to the original organizational structure, or one may return to the defini-

FIGURE 8
Model for the scientific decision making process

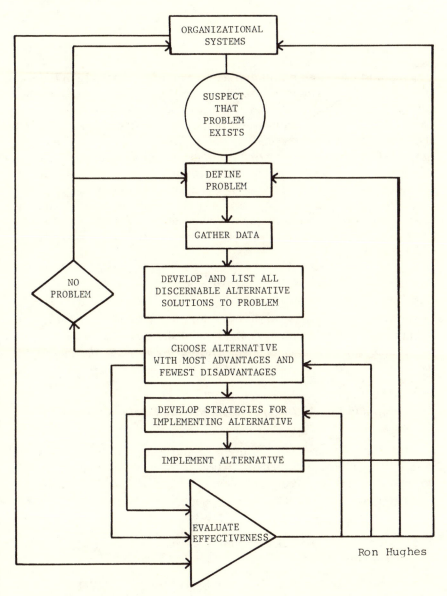

Ron Hughes

tion-of-problem stage and redefine the problem. The model takes into consideration the fact that one might erroneously return to the organization with the perception that there was no problem when in reality a problem was not recognized. Since we are in the mode of continuous evaluation, it is assumed that the symptoms will persist and that the entire process will be regenerated. The principle of this regeneration is inherent in the process of "feedback" in the form of continuous evaluation.

Define the Problem

The most crucial step in the process of arriving at a decision is defining the problem. While it is possible to reach an incorrect decision when the problem is accurately described, it is almost totally impossible to reach an accurate decision when the problem is not properly defined. For example: *A university professor calls the campus television station to complain that a film which is being transmitted to his classroom via the closed-circuit system is not being received properly. He demands that the technical quality be checked at the station and the situation be corrected immediately!*

Let us assume that the professor is correct in his assumption that the problem was poor technical quality from the television station. We have now defined the problem—poor technical quality—and proceed to the next step.

Gather Data

In order to begin to try to find solutions to the problem, we must first gather data about the situation. *Ask the professor to describe the nature of the technical problems. Check to see if those problems are present on the equipment at the station. We find that there is no trouble at the point of origin.*

Develop and List All Discernable Alternative Solutions to the Problem

After the data has been gathered, we must begin to formulate some solutions or alternative plans of action to solve the problem. *Assign a technician to check the transmission line to the classroom. Cancel the presentation and reschedule. No problem exists.*

Choose the Alternative with the Most Advantages and Fewest Disadvantages

Once all the discernable alternatives have been listed, the "best" one must be selected for implementation. The first alternative, testing the transmission line, is a sound proposition but will not solve the most critical problem of what to do about the class presentation. The second alternative, cancelling and rescheduling the film, is the best decision because it allows the professor to turn his attention to other matters in

FIGURE 9
Feedback in a communications system.

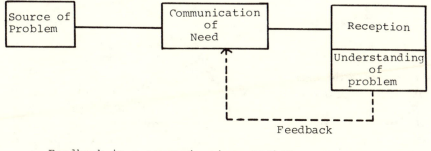

Feedback in a communications system.   R. W. Hotes

the class and still present the film at a later date. This alternative is selected for implementation.

Let us assume, however, that the third choice, "no problem," was chosen in this case. Imagine that the professor has a reputation for being a "crank," and that it is a common practice for him to call others and blame them for his problems. We might be tempted to assume that this is just another of those situations. We pacify the professor and assume that there is no problem. In fact, there is a problem, which interferes with operation of the class (the organization). Following the process of evaluation, we will find the same symptoms recurring the next time the professor requests that a film be shown via the television system. At this point we reenter the process. The necessary feedback has taken place, and the system is trying to correct itself, as shown in Figure 9.

Develop Strategies for Implementing the Alternative

What is needed to implement the alternative? The professor must now communicate to the station a new date and time for presentation of the film. He must also rearrange his teaching plan to accommodate change. The station must test the transmission line to insure that the situation is corrected before the new date. Many mistakes are made in choosing the correct strategy for the specific situation. One may choose the correct alternative and yet remain unsuccessful in implementing the decision if the appropriate strategy is not chosen.

Implement the Alternative

Operating under the assumption that all of the preceding steps have been carried out properly, we are now ready to carry out the plan and implement the decision. The professor reschedules the film and the transmission line is tested.

Evaluate Effectiveness

The evaluation stage of the decision-making process is one that often receives little attention, yet this evaluation is the essential ingredient in the success of the decision-making process. It is no great sin to fail to carry out any of the preceding steps correctly, but it is disaster to fail to evaluate the effectiveness of the decision in order to discover any mistake. In our example, the professor and his problem with the technical quality of the film, it would be disastrous for us to assume the problem had been solved. The tests of the transmission line revealed that the line was operating correctly, so the problem in the signal quality must be caused by some other malfunction in the system. We have already stated that there was no problem at the point of origin. The only other possibility was the improper operation of the receiving sets in the classroom. Upon investigation it was discovered that the sets were not properly fine-tuned. One set had been operating with a good picture and bad sound and the other with good sound and a bad picture.

In this example the problem had been improperly defined, resulting in a faulty decision. The real problem, the improperly tuned television sets, could have been corrected immediately in the classroom by the professor. *If you agree with this statement, you have made another bad decision.* The problem at the base of this situation is the lack of faculty understanding of the technical characteristics involved in the utilization of the television system in the classroom. The decisions made in the first steps of this example treated only the symptoms of the problem. The symptoms were dealt with and the central problem was corrected by giving in-service training in the operational characteristics of the television system to all faculty.

While the example presented above makes the process of scientific decision making seem simple, it is only because the example is a bit simplistic. The process of decision making was carried out in each step of the process itself. The ability to use the process is like that of developing skills in any other area of human endeavor. Practice is essential in developing decision-making skills. Begin with simple situations such as the one presented in our example and develop the ability to reduce more and more complex problems to their essential elements. The ability of a computer to solve complex problems is dependent on its ability to apply yes or no values to pyramids of increasingly complex combinations of information. Once the techniques of reducing the problem to its basic components have been mastered, then we may begin to develop solutions by the same process. But we must be as positive as possible that we are treating the real problem and not just the symptoms.

The act of decision making obviously involves the generation of ideas, at least in the listing of alternatives and the development of strategies for implementation. The next section deals with some techniques for developing creative ideas rather than standard "tried and true" solutions.

CREATIVE PROBLEM SOLVING

Funk and Wagnalls's *International Dictionary* defines creativity as "the quality of being able to produce original works or ideas." Amended for our purposes, the definition might read: The quality of being able to analyze, reconstruct, evaluate, and apply existing or original works or ideas in new combinations. This definition allows for the concept that the new application of a thought or idea is as creative as the original thought. A popular saying is that there is nothing new in the world, only new applications of old ideas. Creativity, then, must be the rearrangement of elements to give new meanings or modifications to ideas.

Why should we be so concerned with creativity? In this age of technological innovation that progresses in geometric leaps, we are facing more and more incredibly complex problems. One example reflecting our urgent needs for creativity is as follows: Relating to change in individuals, groups, nations, and the world, creativity is becoming a most important and unique area in connection with complex changes. Man must be able to adapt to new situations in his environment as rapidly as technology changes the environment. If we do not change as science progresses, mankind will be destroyed. Consequently, creativity is of the utmost importance to modern decision making.

The models presented in the following sections are designed to aid us in our decision making and planning for the futures of our organizations. We must provide the climate and conditions within these models of operation that will encourage and nurture the development of creativity.

Adherence to the scientific model of decision making will not insure that creativity will ensue. Indeed it is in the very process of decision making that creativity suffers most. In the stage of generating alternative solutions to a problem there is great danger that premature criticism and negativeness toward suggestions will smother any creative embers that are smouldering. It is recommended that the study of the systems of NGT (Nominal Group Technique) developed by Andre Delbecq and his associates, and of the Delphi Technique, be explored not only for their value in facilitating the decision-making process, but also for their common features of lending themselves to creating the climate for creativity.[1] This climate is available in their steps of idea generation and is preserved by limitations of the stages of criticism and evaluation in the process of decision making. These systems of decision making are only examples of the types of interaction that may take place in the decision-making process, but they encompass current thought patterns in common use today. They are also common techniques employed as subsystems in the approaches to management and budgeting presented elsewhere in this book.

This seeming emphasis on the group techniques of NGT and Delphi Technique is by no means meant to suggest that creativity can be developed only by group activity. On the contrary, individual creativity is one of the most important elements in any problem-solving or decision-making situation. The point is that individuals make up groups and that group decision making has a propensity for stifling creativity by premature criticism of ideas that are new or seemingly too radical. This tendency of groups has been shown in Irving Janis's work with the theory of "Groupthink" and by the research that was done in the development of the systems of NGT and the Delphi Technique. It would serve the creative person well to become familiar with the actions of group dynamics and their effects on the decision-making and, therefore, on the creative processes.

PLANNING SYSTEMS

The critical need for creativity in all phases of contemporary life has been well documented, but nowhere is creativity more essential than in the process of planning for the modern institutions of man. Society today is characterized by the numbers and nature of the institutions that man has created to serve him. Entire cultures are identified by their organizations and institutions: Socialists, Communists, capitalists, and so forth. These are not categories descriptive of the men that inhabit this planet. They are labels given those men by nature of the institutions that they have created for their own purposes. If we do not exercise the greatest care in planning the goals and objectives of these institutions, the danger is imminent that the institutions will not serve us, but that we will serve them.

The need for planning in an organization has been well documented. Our purpose is to look at some examples of planning models and endeavor to understand them in terms of the overall concept of scientific decision-making processes. The essential elements of three currently popular systems of planning are presented below. Each system has been proven effective in many different settings, and each deserves study on its own merit.

PPBS: Planning, Programming, Budgeting System

PPBS was initiated by the Department of Defense under Robert McNamara in 1961 and was implemented in all other federal agencies in

1965 by presidential directive. PPBS was designed to provide a systematic process to identify commonalities in programs with similar objectives, to analyze the performance and impact of programs, and to connect these objectives with the current year's budget. PPBS is directed primarily at defining the broad economic picture of policy decisions and desired results rather than the ins and outs of detailed planning and implementation, and therefore relates most directly to the areas of short- and long-range planning.

PPBS was not as successful as was hoped because it contained what critics have labeled as "critical gaps" in the system. The most notable gaps are:

1. PPBS focuses on what will be done, not how to do it.
2. Budgeting as defined by PPBS is a cost calculation based on the decisions made in the planning and programming steps (or long-range planning phase), whereas there are in reality many policy decisions and alternatives to be evaluated during the actual budget preparation.
3. PPBS does not provide an operating tool for line managers to implement policy and program decisions.
4. PPBS does not provide a mechanism to evaluate the impact of various funding levels on each program and program element, or to establish priorities among the programs and varying levels of program effort.
5. PPBS focuses primarily on new programs or major revision in existing programs.

Several critical gaps usually exist in ZBB (Zero Based Budgeting) and programmed based budgeting. Figure 10 illustrates important elements of PPBS with the addition of problem solving, or filling in the gaps. The important areas that fill in these gaps are: analyzing, decision making, evaluating, and recycling. This is the PPBADERS (Planning, Programming, Budgeting, Analyzing, Deciding, Evaluating, Recycling System) cycle of activities. This system will be discussed in the section dealing with comparisons with the scientific decision-making model.

MBO: Management by Objectives

Most writers agree that MBO means Management by Objectives. The applications of the principles of the system, however, redefine the original concept. Other systems based on the MBO idea may be called "Management by Results" or "Management-Personnel Evaluation by Objectives."[2] No matter what label we put on it, the system is one that requires

FIGURE 10
Program based budgeting

Planning
Includes short and long
range planning. These
goals and objectives
should tie into
mission statements.

Programming
One of the most significant
areas of concern. These
are actual educational programs arranged to meet the
goals of the institution.
Specific objectives on
courses and programs should
mesh with these goals.
These objectives and goals
are the basis of developing
operational plans.

Budgeting
Based upon goals and objectives
of the educational programs.
These program aspects can now
be translated into financial
terms.

Recycling
This section is where
one would modify
according to feedback
any problem areas or
"soft spots" in con-
nection with any part
of the program.

Evaluating
Did you achieve the goals
and objectives which were
set forth within your
expectation.
(Measuring final outcome)

Deciding
Making the final
decision for each
goal and objective
as related to each
individual alter-
native.

Analyzing
Data is analyzed,
environmental
analysis is required
to determine if ade-
quate resources are
available, what are
the consequences of
each alternative,
and setting priori-
ties for the final
decisions to be
made.

Miller, Bob W., *Program Based Budgeting*

the formulation of goals and the construction of objective activities to meet those specific goals. Generally, the goals are determined by top management, and the objectives are stated by successive layers of management down to the lowest level in the organization. These objectives are evaluated and approved by determining their effectiveness in achievement of the goals.[3] The MBO system is described in Table 2. This general model of the MBO system may be adapted for use in many organizational structures. A high priority is placed on communicating goals throughout the organization and on the process of feedback in the form of objectives generated to achieve those goals. The objectives form the basis for evaluation of the performance of the organization and its effectiveness as a whole.

TABLE 2
General MBO model

1. Mission Statement of Organization

    12. Set objectives and goals for the next year. Begin a new cycle of MBO's.

2. Professional Development for each Manager on MBO's

    11. At the end of year evaluate each objective with both subordinate and superordinate involvement.

    10. Monitor each objective of each individual subordinate three times per year.

3. Goal Statements by Chief Executive Officer (should be based upon "soft spots" or innovative ideas.)

    9. Each level of management has communication and modification with each subordinate for the purpose of modification and objectives agreeing.

4. Goal Statements which mesh with the chief executive. Goal statements should be made at each managerial level.

    8. Communication and Modification Session - Agree on final objective by each superordinate with each subordinate.

5. Professional development for each worker on MBO's

    7. Write each MBO Using the following sequence
        1. State Objective clearly
        2. Environmental Analysis
        3. Plan of Action
        4. Deadline for completion
        5. Evaluation of each objective
        6. Consider difficulty of each objective
        7. Tie in with goals and mission statements

6. Each member at the worker's level set MBO's Objective

    A   B   C   D   E   F

ZBB: Zero-Based Budgeting

Zero-Based Budgeting was introduced primarily as a budget control system but may be expanded to serve as a planning system as well. This is possible because it is inherent in the process of determining the "decision packages" that decisions be formulated relating to the goals and objectives of the organization. The formulation of the decision packages is the first step in the process of Zero-Based Budgeting. The manager is forced to determine the current level of activity in order to plan the package. A decision package identifies activities, functions, or operations in such a manner that management can evaluate and compare them with other packages for the purpose of determining priorities for the overall operation. The packages contain descriptions of the purpose (goals and objectives), the consequences of not performing the activity, measures of performance, alternative courses of action, and costs and benefits. (See Figures 11 and 12.)

Decision packages are formulated for different levels of performing each function. Each package builds upon the information provided in the previous level and allows management to select levels of activity that are consistent with the overall goals of the organization. The decision packages are then ranked according to priority at each level of management beginning with the lowest level and working up to top management. Evaluation of the effectiveness of the process is provided in the form of funding. The packages with the most cost-benefits, best planning, and so forth, receive budgets, while all others are dropped.

THE SCIENTIFIC DECISION-MAKING PROCESS AND SYSTEMS ANALYSIS

Systems analysis is the process of designing, specifying, and selecting the elements that make up a system. The systems analyst must fuse all the parts into a coordinated, cohesive, functioning whole.[4] In this age of proliferation of systems and technology, and of such rapid and continuous change, is there any one common denominator that will allow us to divide the complexities into workable proportions? Fortunately, the answer is, emphatically, yes! The scientific method of decision making presented earlier should be the primary tool of the systems analyst. In an effort to demonstrate the applicability of the scientific method of decision making as it functions in systems analysis, let us apply the model to the management systems described at the beginning of this chapter. Those eight steps in the decision-making process may be applied directly to the models of planning and budgeting.

FIGURE 11
Procedure for formulating decision packages, a

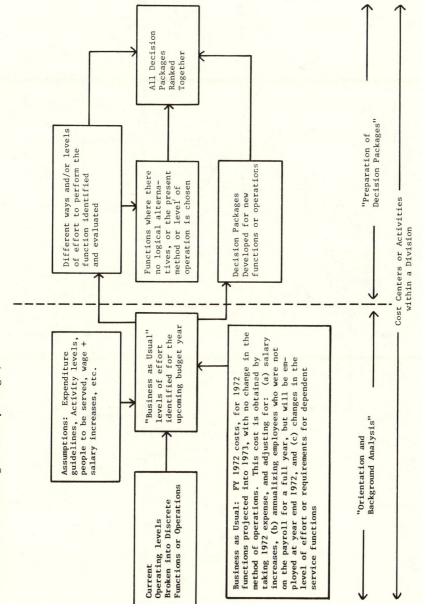

Peter Pyhrr, *Zero Based Budgeting* (New York, John Wiley and Sons, 1973), p. 200.

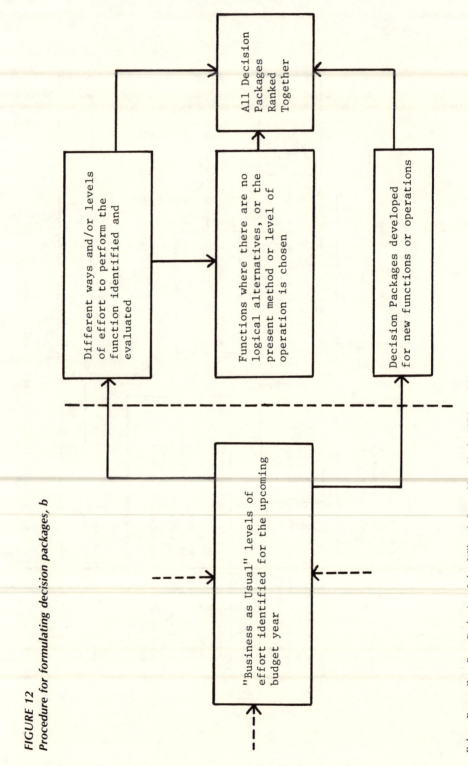

FIGURE 12
Procedure for formulating decision packages, b

Pyhrr, Peter, *Zero-Base Budgeting*, John Wiley & Sons, New York, 1973, p. 200.

Define the Problem

The area "define the problem" may be listed in several terms. By referring to the three models, PPBADERS, MBO, and ZBB, we may compare this area directly. The terminology is different in each case, but the relationship to definition of the problem is evident. Goals, issues, and the present condition of "business as usual" translate easily into the definition of the problem stage.

Gather Data

This function is not as readily identified from the models because it is assumed for PPBADERS and MBO that data will be generated in order to specify objectives/decision packages and in defining the issues. The ZBB model, however, requires specific data gathering as a prerequisite for determining business as usual.

Develop and List All Discernable Alternative Solutions to the Problem

This area is easily distinguishable in all three models. The requirement for listing the alternatives without regard to evaluation is essential for the creation of the proper climate for creative problem solving detailed earlier. The alternatives are developed in stage two of the PPBADERS, in the determination of objectives for achievement of goals in the MBO, and in the formulation of the decision packages in the ZBB.

Choose Alternative with Most Advantages and Fewest Disadvantages

The choice of the "best" alternative is defined by the bias of the system being considered. In the case of the PPBADERS system, the choice of the best alternative involves steps four and five, analyzing and deciding, because the steps share two decision functions. Rank ordering of the alternatives is included in step four, while the actual determination of the optimum alternative is included in step five. The MBO system relates directly to our decision-making model in that there is a specific step for determination of alternative strategies for attainment of objectives. There are several alternatives possible here because of the specification of many separate objectives to meet the organizational goals. The directing of all objectives toward meeting these goals determines that bias in this system. In the ZBB model, the function of choosing alternatives is contained in the function of ranking all decision packages. The process of ranking provides the priority of alternatives, and the funding level determines which alternatives are rejected. The process of selecting alternatives in relation to funding or budget levels biases this system toward financial emphasis.

Develop Strategies for Implementing the Chosen Alternative

Once we have selected the alternatives we must consider the process of implementing the strategy. The use of the term "strategy" is not without importance, as the term relates to the idea of carefully planned and conceived methods for achieving an end. Indeed, this very idea is central to this step in the process. In the PPBADERS model this approach is included in step five as "determining the optimum course of action." The model for MBO is equally clear in its inclusion of the idea by specifying a step to "Select operational strategy." The ZBB model does not appear to have this step spelled out. Closer examination, however, will reveal that the idea of planning strategies is included in the process of formulating decision packages. In each decision package, the methods for achieving the stated objectives must be described in detail.

Implement the Alternative

One might assume that the implementation step would be carried out as a matter of the natural course of events in the process. Yet none of the models presented list implementation as a distinct step in the process. Many goods ideas and plans have failed because it was assumed that they were being used as they were designed to operate. To be effective, an idea must be utilized properly. We must spell out clearly that we intend to implement the ideas developed and specified as ways of achieving goals and objectives. We must follow the operation of those ideas through a process of monitoring and evaluation.

Evaluate Effectiveness

All the models presented specify some system of evaluation or monitoring. The PPBADERS model and the MBO model both indicate high priorities for the evaluation process, as well as indicating a further emphasis on the continuous evaluation of the process through a formal "recycling" procedure. The ZBB model does not spell out this formal process of evaluation, but it is implied that evaluation is given through the levels of funding achieved. The model might be improved through the addition of a formal feedback and evaluation pattern.

IMPLICATIONS FOR THE PLANNER

Systems analysis is a process that has been developed to meet the need for understanding and application of the complex systems common in modern organizations. We have demonstrated the usefulness of the scientific method of decision making in the analysis mode, but what are the implications for using this approach in other areas of planning?

The application of the scientific decision-making process allows us to analyze systems for several different but related purposes. We may use the process for analysis and isolation of problem areas within a system. If any of the steps in the decision-making process are not functioning properly or are not present at all, we may suspect that area as the source of the problem.

One may use the decision-making process as the model for designing or generating new systems. By modeling new systems on the scientific decision-making model, we form our ideas in the mold of a proven system, and we automatically provide a format for future systems analysis of the new model in operation.

One may use similarities in models based on the scientific method as a basis for generating "supersystems." A supersystem is an overall approach to management and budget planning that incorporates several complex systems into the total operation. For example, we may wish to use three of the models presented in this chapter as a supersystem. The PPBADERS model would provide the system for long-range planning, while the MBO model is best suited for short-range planning, and the ZBB model may provide a format and system for the budgeting of the overall operation. These systems have this potential because they all have common properties and requirements.

A further implication is apparent. Since we have been able through systems analysis to identify common needs in all three systems, we should investigate the feasibility of establishing a Management Information System (MIS). The MIS is a supersystem of another genre. The MIS is usually a central computer system including a data filing and data output format that may be utilized by several different areas. Because there are common areas in the models, data needs and formats can be programmed in such a manner that all information needs in data gathering and evaluation may be served through one computer system. The common sources of data approach may eliminate much duplication of effort and make the implementation and evaluation of the overall supersystems approach more practical.

Setting Goals for Planning, Programming, and Budgeting

RUTH J. WATKINS AND BOB W. MILLER

At least three dimensions to goals must be considered in the planning process—priority, time, and structure. Each person must work on behalf of the total organization. Often goals are written by administrators and their content is never communicated through the organization. Therefore, the first dimension, priority of goals, should be established, communicated, and accepted by all the members of the organization.

Priority of Goals

At a given point in time the accomplishment of one goal is relatively more important than others. The establishment of priorities is also important in that the resources of any organization must be allocated by rational means. At all points in time, administrators are confronted with alternative goals which must be evaluated and placed in order of priority. Educational institutions are particularly concerned with the priority of seemingly independent goals. For example, a college president must determine the relative importance of implementing new teaching strategies, adding new programs, or establishing and expanding the service area goals. In addition to budgetary implications, the effort and time involved to implement the goal must be carefully considered.

PPBS (Planning, Programming, Budgeting System) is a system that not only establishes short- and long-range goals but serves as an analytical tool to compare organizational/program goals and determine priority based on short- long-term benefits.[5]

Timing of Goals

The second dimension to establishing and setting priorities of goals is their timing. The organization's activities are guided by different objectives depending upon the duration of the action, that is, short-term, intermediate, and long-term goals. Personal plans of action or activities are established to achieve short-term goals, which are stated as objectives to be accomplished to realize the ultimate organizational goals.[6]

Structure of Goals

The third dimension of goals is structure. For example, each division or department is given the responsibility for attaining an assigned goal, minimizing goal conflict. The process of goal setting must also recognize the relative importance of interest groups, and plans must incorporate and integrate their interests.[7]

Goals should be defined in terms that are understandable and acceptable to those who must produce the effort required to achieve them. All levels within an organization must support all other goal-setting levels. For example, the faculty and staff must support the department chairperson, who must support the division chairperson, who must support the administration.

To be successful, not just paperwork, goals must be implemented. The critical step in the implementation of goals is that of forecasting the future, the second phase of the planning process. Two basic issues must be resolved through forecasting: What level of activity can be expected during the planning period, and what level of resources will be available to support the projected activity.

Developing information about the future is a difficult and uncertain business that places a heavy premium on the judgment of the people involved. The use of committees of experts is a common way to develop information but has a large judgmental element. An example of this is advisory committees for technical/occupational programs. Such groups, despite the status of their members, are still subject to socio-psychological influences, and those influences are likely to affect the content of their recommendations.

A common problem in education, due to pressures of accountability and decreased funding, is the "bandwagon" effect. Educators sometimes rush to fund and participate in an emerging philosophy or system without fully weighing the merits reflected in the activity. It is vital to education that an increase in the area of formal research come about, to benefit students and institutions and to prevent nonproductive approaches. If this research is taken seriously, some degree of forecasting is possible in educational planning.

Forecasting for Goal Setting

Forecasting must include an element of flexibility, as the accelerated tempo of technological development, which influences the consumers of education, has greatly compressed the interval between the long-range plan and its implementation. Research on forecasting techniques for education in our modern society is in the stage of infancy.[8] Dale Mann offers five tactical hints that deal with planning for uncertainty:

1. *Work on uncertainty separately and directly.* Educators too often let their attraction to a highly valued outcome inflate the estimate that it will indeed take place, i.e., programs are adapted as a panacea because of the strong desirability for something to happen. The flaw is that other alternatives are not explored or ignored and therefore too many resources are expended and fatal flaws in the curriculum may exist.

2. *Be certain that the problem is stated accurately.* Decompose a complex problem into simpler ones. Attempt to get thinking straight in these simpler areas, paste the analysis together with logical glue, and come out with a plan for the complex problem.

3. *Look for precedents.* Very few of the problems educators face are so new that they have no precedents. Of course, none of this should be taken to mean that practices that were responsive to one set of circumstances can be taken off the shelf and bolted onto a similar, yet different situation. Modifications, adjustments, and tinkering are always necessary.

4. *In the absence of a precedent, create one.* Where precedents cannot readily be located, and where uncertainty is extreme, then the greatest assistance to calculation may come from establishing pilot programs or experiments.

5. *Begin.* Uncertainty is an extraordinarily pervasive and slippery business. No sooner is it reduced in one area of a problem than it crops up in another, usually critical, spot.[9]

In many institutions, estimates of future performance are matched against present or past performance. This can be a valid criterion for planning; however, it may become necessary to develop supportive data for more comprehensive, knowledgeable forecasting for educational programming and budgeting.

Operational Budgeting

The third phase of planning is the process of making the plans operational through budgeting for each element of the organization.[10] A considerable body of literature exists dealing with budgeting techniques. The usefulness of financial budgets depends mainly on the degree to which data are based upon certain premises or assumptions regarding the future.

To refer back to PPBS, whereby plans and budgets should be devised in terms of goals, it is not possible to develop a complete description here. However, the important point is to recognize that the logic of planning, from goals to resource allocation, is well established in business management. This logic is applicable to and is being adapted in the management of educational institutions.

The principal means by which management implements plans through procedures and policy making is the fourth and final phase of the planning process.[11] Policies and procedures, like plans, are both specific and general; abstract and concrete; short-term and long-term. Policy making is an important management tool for assuring that action is goal oriented. Management should explain how the goals are to be achieved; they thus direct the behavior and performance of persons charged with carrying out individual goals, divisional goals, and, ultimately, organizational goals. The test of the effectiveness of a policy or

TABLE 3
Managerial planning issues

Planning Phase	Key Management decisions
Goal setting	1. What goals will be sought?
	2. What is the relative importance of each goal?
	3. What are the relationships among the goals?
	4. At what points in time should each goal be achieved?
	5. How can each goal be measured?
	6. What person or organizational unit should accountable for achieving the goal?
Forecasting	1. What are the important variables which bear on the successful achievement of goals?
	2. What information exists regarding each variable?
	3. What is the appropriate technique for forecasting the future movement of each important variable?
	4. What person or organizational unit should be accountable for the forecasts?
Budgeting	1. What resource components should be included in the budget?
	2. What are the interrelationships among the various budgeted components?
	3. What budgeting technique should be used?
	4. Who or what organizational unit should be accountable for the preparation of the budget?
Policy making	1. What policy statements are necessary to implement the overall plan?
	2. To what extent are the policy statements comprehensive, flexible, coordinative, ethical, and clearly written?
	3. Who or what organizational units should authorize and prepare policy statements?
	4. Who or what organizational units are to be affected by the policy statements?

Donnely, *Fundamentals of Management*, p. 62.

procedure is whether the intended objective is attained. If the policy does not lead to the goal, it should be revised.

One can readily appreciate the fact that the planning function will be undertaken differently by a small private college, a large university, or a multicampus community college district. James Donnelly suggests that fundamental questions are appropriate for planning regardless of the type and size of the organization. (See Table 3.) There are no universally applicable planning approaches, but the necessity for "advance thinking as a basis for doing" is universal.[12]

The administrator's approach to planning must be eclectic as well as pragmatic. A borrowing of the best of past and present coupled with innovative actions is the source of success at every level of planning in an organization.

PROBLEM SOLVING

Problems will occur within any organization. The more comprehensive the planning functions, however, the fewer the problems that should occur. A number of problem-solving techniques are outlined for study and utilization in the research and management literature. Problem solving as a process is much discussed and little understood according to Edgar Schein. He insists that there is not one ultimately valid model, but that the steps or stages available to analyze problems are applicable to any kind of problem-solving process, whether it occurs in an individual, a two-person group, a large committee, or a total organization.

The Schein model presented in Figure 13 is an elaboration of the steps or stages in the problem-solving process opposed to a static model indicating a process. This model distinguishes two basic cycles of activity—one which occurs prior to any decision or action, and one which occurs after a decision to act has been taken.[13]

By all odds the most difficult step in the problem-solving process is the first one—defining and stating the problem. Correctly stating the problem does not always lead to a right answer, but incorrectly stating a problem practically guarantees a wrong answer. The difficulty sometimes arises because of a confusion between symptoms and a situation in which someone brings something to a person's or group's attention, or the person or group discovers something which is not as it should be. For example, an angry student wants to see the president; the faculty complain about a lack of administrative support; an employee is consistently late for work, or a faculty member for his or her classes; an employee circumvents his immediate supervisor; or two departments refuse to cooperate on a related project. It should be noted that none of the examples mentioned are really the problems to be worked on—they are

FIGURE 13
The stages of problem solving

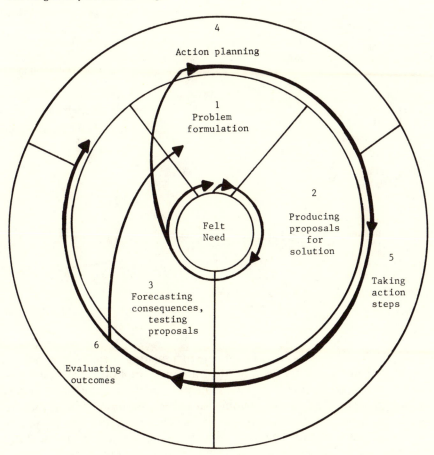

Edgar H. Scheim, *Process Consultation*, The Role of Organization. p. 46

the symptoms to be removed. Before the administrator or group can begin to solve the problem, they must identify or find it. This is the crucial and often most difficult stage of the problem-solving process.

By going over the incidents in detail and trying to identify what was going on which actually triggered the frustration, it is often possible to generalize the problem. Once the problem has been adequately formulated, move on to producing ideas or courses of action that might solve it.

Traditionally, problems are tackled on an individual basis. However, when there is need for input from more than one person (which frequently occurs), group techniques should be considered. Some potential advantages of group problem-solving are presented in Figure 14.

FIGURE 14
Counterbalancing positive and negative factors in group decision making.

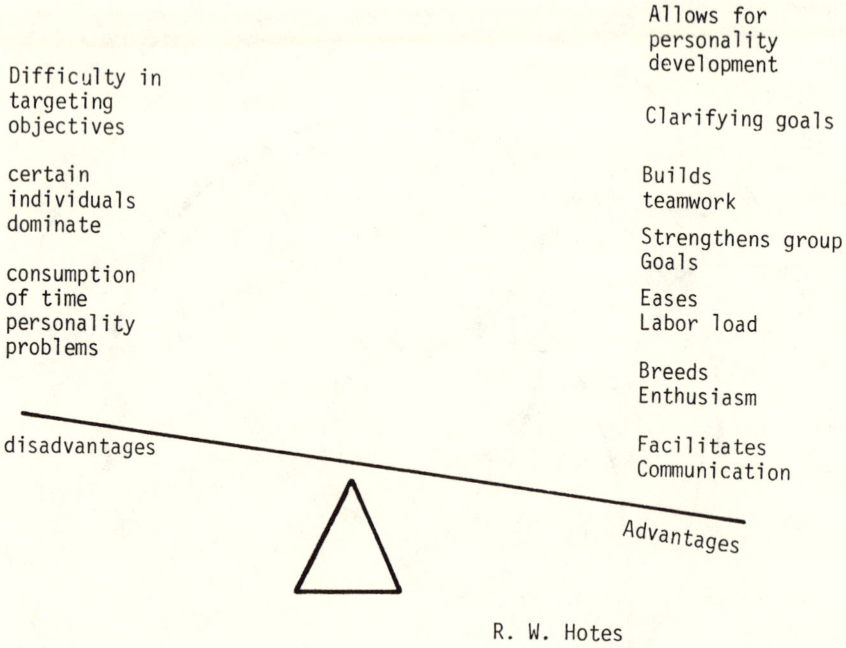

```
                                          Allows for
                                          personality
                                          development
          Difficulty in
          targeting
          objectives                      Clarifying goals

          certain                         Builds
          individuals                     teamwork
          dominate
                                          Strengthens group
          consumption                     Goals
          of time                         Eases
          personality                     Labor load
          problems
                                          Breeds
                                          Enthusiasm

          disadvantages                   Facilitates
                                          Communication

                                          Advantages
```

R. W. Hotes

A pitfall likely to occur in a group formulating ideas or courses of action to solve a problem is that ideas are evaluated one at a time; thus the group is never permitted to gain perspective on the problem by looking at a whole array of possible ideas for a solution. It is important when working in groups to not pass judgment prematurely when someone proposes a solution, moving immediately to the next proposal. This threatens not only the first idea but the person who proposed that second solution. Members whose ideas have been rejected early may feel less inclined to give ideas at a later stage.

The technique of brainstorming is built on the rule that no evaluation of ideas should occur during the idea production phase. This is a helpful technique to keep in mind to prevent premature evaluation and stifle good idea production.

Group problem solving also introduces various criteria into the evaluation of ideas; for example, personal experiences. It must be considered—at the stage of determining the consequences of various alternative solutions—that other methods of validation are available. Though more time-consuming, surveys and research are valid methods to employ. When these methodologies are used, they often may reveal new information which might lead to a reformulation of the problem. In group decision making, recycling—from initial formulation through idea production and idea evaluation to reformulation of the problem—is a very sound way to solve a problem. As the group reaches concensus of a proposed solution and makes a decision to act, it moves into cycle two of Schein's model.[14]

The phase of action planning can be treated as a new problem requiring its own problem formulation; that is, what are our problems in implementing the proposal we have decided on? What are alternative ways to implement the proposal? Which of our alternatives is the best way to implement the proposal? If these stages are short-circuited or avoided, it is quite possible that a good proposal will be inadequately carried out and the individual or group will draw the erroneous conclusion that the proposal was deficient, instead of recognizing the defect as insufficient action planning.[15]

Problem solving by individuals or groups can, then, be thought of as consisting of two cycles or phases, one of which primarily involves discussion, and the other primarily action. One of the key steps in any problem-solving technique or process utilized is the making of decisions. Of course, decisions are involved at every stage of the process but are only highly visible when an individual or group commits itself to trying out a proposal for action.

DECISION MAKING

In reviewing the plethora of decision-making processes and techniques, it becomes apparent that no one method should be judged as better than another. The important factor in decision making is to utilize a process and to understand the consequences of that process well enough to be able to choose the method appropriate to the amount of time available; the kind of task being worked on; the climate one wants to establish; and the history or background of the organization that will be impacted or influenced, or that will influence the ultimate decision. Many years ago the Hawthorne study established the premise "we support what we help to create." With this statement in mind, an exploration into decision-making processes is appropriate.

Colin Eden and John Harris take the view that all decision makers use procedures, but that the procedures may not have been explained although they are potentially capable of explanation. They recognize that there is more to decision making than just making a decision: before that stage is reached, decision makers collect data, arrange and process that data into information and, with this, conduct further analysis. Some administrators carry out this procedure informally, that is, without making explicit statements; others do so without consciously being aware of it and call this procedure "flair" or "judgment" or "intuition." What is important here is not what the procedure is called, but the recognition that every decision maker must use a procedure.[16]

David Borland indicates that for half of the decisions made, no one cares; half of the decisions made are either yes or no options; and only one out of four decisions remains complex. In these few decisions of complexity, a more formal procedure should perhaps be utilized.[17]

Decisions have been classified two ways, evaluative and developmental.[18] The former concerns those decisions in which the alternative courses were completely specified in advance and the solution consisted of selecting the best of these, however that "best" is defined. The developmental decision involves the search for a course of action better than any previously available.

A different perspective is that there are many features to decisions and, therefore, they can be classified in many ways. Before discussing these classifications, it is useful to highlight that there are two major attributes to decision making: understanding, and change. With these two attributes, decisions can fall into four quadrants of classification, as shown in Figure 15.

FIGURE 15
Major attributes in decision making

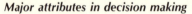

High understanding

1   2

Small
incremental   Large
change   change

4   3

Low understanding

Eden Collins, John Harris, *Management Decision and Decision Analysis*, (New York, John Wiley and Sons 1975), p. 32.

The four quadrants represent four different types of decision making. Quadrant 1, for example, represents most of the problems in administrative and technical decision making. Since problems in these areas occur frequently and are fairly easily brought to the attention of management, administrators have developed a high understanding of these problems. Because of this, these problems usually result in small changes.[19]

Quadrant 2 represents those problems where, although the administrator has a high understanding of the problem, its solution involves large changes. This may mean changing the underlying philosophy of an organization through reformulation of some of its objectives.[20]

The third quadrant is the area of crisis, where there is low understanding of the problem but the decision maker is nevertheless anticipating making major changes. This is the quadrant of the gambler or the opportunist aiming for high stakes since the risk involved in operating in quadrant 3 is high.

Finally, quadrant 4 represents that area in which there is low understanding of the problem and the decision maker is preparing to move slowly, changing in small increments and perhaps in a disjointed manner.

This classification of decisions lends clarity to the range of decisions that might be made at any level of administration. Certain levels of authority in an organization operate predominantly in quadrant 3 while totally delegating the placement of the decisions in other quadrants to other divisions or subunits. Regardless of the complexity of the decisions to be made, a successful administrator gains input from all areas of the organization that might be affected or required to implement the decision.

This concept also brings to the fore a related dilemma closely associated with decision making within an organization. Quick results in one-person decisions are desirable. However, it has been proven that shared responsibility in decision making results in better and longer lasting solutions. The dilemma in delegating responsibility for decision making is keyed to the question, "How democratic or autocratic can an administrator be in his delegation of this process?"

This question may be viewed in terms of a continuum developed by Tannebaum and Schmidt. If the continuum is extended at either extreme, the result is autocracy or abdication. Either extreme creates pressure and frustration. The autocrat violates our traditional values and our image of people who are open and sensitive. The abdicator is irresponsible and violates the concepts of leadership, inhibiting effective work and the accomplishment of goals.[21]

Another basic dilemma in current employee relations may be a discrepancy between what we believe to be right and desirable and what we do in practice in our relationships with employees. Administrators are under pressure to get the job done; to be efficient while pressed for time; believe that all points of view should be heard; and believe that participation in decision making is more effective, although it takes much more time. With these statements, one might ask again, how democratic can managers be? How autocratic must they be?

Offered below is a matrix that might be utilized as a tool to ease the consequences of the previously stated dilemma of democracy and autocracy in decision making by quickly determining the necessity for input and areas where input is required before arriving at any decision. The use of this matrix in itself requires making decisions. In terms of being costly in time, this holds equally true for members of an organization who would not be affected by a decision. A manager must decide the consequences of a decision to some degree before taking the time of other persons to provide input and determining the parameters or guidelines for those providing input. Indeed, if a manager requests participative decision making, he or she must be willing to accept this input and utilize the alternative before arriving at a final decision.

A similar matrix might be developed for any department, division, or unit within the organization for those decisions where participation is necessary within that unit, and where the results of the decision impact other persons within that unit. It is the purpose of a simplified or comprehensive matrix of this nature to encourage the decision maker to initially think through the impact and relationships of the proposed decision to be made prior to beginning the process of actually making the decision.

An example of one use of such a matrix would be the proposal to add a course to the curriculum with one section to be offered in a self-paced learning mode. The relationships or impacted areas are designated in a similar matrix in Figure 16. This example is based on an organization belonging to a multicampus district community college.

A list of questions for the individual decision-maker to minimize risks and suggestions to sharpen an administrator's concept of decision making is outlined below.

1. Have I defined the problem properly?
2. Are my basic premises valid?
3. Am I quantifying where possible?
4. Should I accept data limitations?
5. What are the cost, time and human factors?
6. What are the organizational factors?
7. Have all the individuals who should have been heard given input?
8. What are the alternative solutions?

FIGURE 16
Factors/areas for decision making

Factors for Consideration	District	Campus	Instruction/curriculum	Student Development	Business/Budget Division	Support service	Physical plant	Individual Staff/Faculty	Students	Community
Expectations/desirability		X	X		X				X	X
Political feasibility	X	X							X	
Technical feasibility				X	X		X	X		
Staff restraints						X	X	X		
Material restraints	X	X			X	X	X			
Positive consequences	X	X	X			X			X	X
Negative consequences					X	X				
Implementation						X	X	X		

Ruth Watkins

9. What are the evaluation criteria and procedures?
10. Can I build a model and make a case?[22]

Of itself, decision making isn't difficult; it's a matter of doing the obvious. The difficulty lies in defining the obvious. Directed effort is the basic ingredient in effective decision making. To define the obvious for decision-making purposes, decision makers must turn aimless activity into effort directed at developing a realistic pattern of needs. Phillip R. Marvin gives four steps to developing skills in formulating a realistic pattern of needs and to sharpening an administrator's decision-making efforts.[23]

Develop a decision-making profile. A decision-making profile eliminates impulse buying in decision making; for example, when you go to the supermarket without a shopping list, you generally come back with some of the things required, things you don't want, things bought on impulse. The development of a profile requires a careful scrutiny of four factors: (1) specific needs to be met, (2) new things to be achieved, (3) the consumer climate, and (4) consideration of capabilities.

A sharply structured decision-making profile provides the frame of reference for decision making. It is a dynamic frame of reference, not a static one. Needs, goals, consumers and competition, capabilities, all change with time and must be continually reviewed and redefined to keep decision-making profiles current.

Define targets, timetables and tactics. To sharpen decision-making targets, a manager must adequately define timetables and tactics. Target definition for decision-making purposes should encompass: (1) overall objectives, (2) resource allocations, (3) phase objectives, (4) review and appraisal points, (5) cost commitments, (6) byproduct benefits, and (7) probability of success.[24]

What is the decision expected to accomplish? To be on the safe side, a manager doesn't just ask the question; he or she must test the answer. Raise the question, "If this objective is achieved, will those involved be 100 percent satisfied?" If the answer is an unqualified yes, the manager can do something that will deliver this need.

Develop a meeting of minds. The concensus of those concerned as to the decision to be made; those sponsoring proposals; those responsible for action areas; and those who will apply the end products of a decision should be brought into focus. This gives all concerned an opportunity to reflect specific interests for which each is individually responsible. Equally important is the desirability of maintaining a balance between specific interests. Time taken to arrive at a meeting of minds is time saved many times over. False starts are eliminated and second guessing is avoided.[25]

Good decisions are managed, not made. Good decisions are based on the involvement of those concerned with the outcome of decisions; those concerned with carrying out the steps needed to turn decisions into action; those affected by the decisions themselves; and those initiating proposals. For the most part, failure is the result of not doing what was wanted because someone didn't know what was wanted. Good decisions reflect the thinking of those involved and define what is wanted and what is considered feasible by those involved in the outcome.

The obvious essence of a decision is that it is an event of choice; that is, to do one thing or another, to select a specific course of action from among a number of alternatives. A less obvious feature of decisions is that they are governed by standards extrinsic to the situation. If, for example, one alternative within a set has such compelling and attractive features that there is no point in comparing it with other alternatives, then there is really no "choice." In that case, the perceived excellence of one course of action forecloses any necessity to make a decision. There are many examples in which excellence or inevitability or compulsion vitiates the need for decision. It does not require a decision to take a clearly superior course of action, to accept an unavoidable event, or to "choose" to do what is necessary.

In education, too often there has been a disruption by major shifting to a full-fledged system in response to relatively minor consumer or administrative problems. In so doing, an institution or district has traded the minor irrationalities of their previous procedures or problems for major disruptions.

If a decision maker gathers information about alternatives, the likely future conditions in which the alternatives will operate, and the consequences of the alternative in those future states, more practical, sound, and long lasting decisions can be made.

Decision making is a process synonymous with the whole process of management. Decision making comprises three chief stages: finding reasons for making a decision; finding feasible courses of action; and choosing among courses of action. A decision is a moment in the ongoing process of evaluating alternatives related to setting goals, solving problems, and implementing and evaluating programs in any educational organization or program.

Today's and tomorrow's managers must evaluate and apply the principles presented above to generate and implement new ideas and systems for coping with the ever increasing complexities of modern higher education institutional management. Many of the subsystems presented are but parts of the supersystem, and will be discussed in other chapters of this book. Scientific decision making based upon a systematic analysis of the task to be done will develop a creative management procedure for dealing with problems of colleges and universities.

NOTES

1. Andre Delbecq, *Group Techniques for Program Planning: A Guide to Nominal Group and Delphi Processes* (Glenview, Ill.: Scott Foresman, 1975), p. 25.

2. Peter A. Pyhrr, *Zero Based Budgeting* (New York: John Wiley and Sons, 1973), p. 200.

3. Stephen J. Knezevich, *Program Budgeting (PPBS)* (Berkeley, Calif.: McCutchan, 1973), pp. 14–17.

4. Gerald A. Silver and Joan G. Silver, *Introduction to Systems Analysis* (Englewood Cliffs, N.J.: Prentice Hall, 1976), p. 14.

5. R. N. Anthony, *Planning and Control Systems* (Cambridge: Harvard University Press, 1965), pp. 57–58.

6. Ibid.

7. Knezevich, *Program Budgeting (PPBS)*, pp. 60–62.

8. James H. Donnelly, *Fundamentals of Management* (Homewood, Ill.: Business Publications, 1975), p. 67.

9. Dale Mann, *Policy Decisionmaking in Education* (New York: Teachers College Press, 1975), pp. 139–42.

10. Donelly, *Fundamentals of Management*, p. 63.

11. Ibid.

12. Ibid., p. 185.

13. Edgar H. Schein, *Process Consultation: The Role of Organization Development* (Boston: Addison Wesley, 1969), pp. 45–46.

14. Ibid., p. 46.

15. Albert H. Rubenstein, *Participative Problem Solving: How to Increase Organization Effectiveness* (New York: John Wiley and Sons, 1977).

16. Colin Edin and John Harris, *Management Decision and Decision Analysis* (New York: John Wiley and Sons, 1975), p. 5.

17. David Borland, unpublished lecture notes, EdHE 673, North Texas State University (Denton, Texas, Spring 1977).

18. Edmund Harris, *Management Decision and Decision Analysis*, p. 32.

19. Ibid., pp. 33–35.

20. Ibid.

21. Robert Tannenbaum and Warren H. Schmidt, "How to Choose a Leadership Pattern," *Paths Toward Personal Progress: Leaders are Made, Not Born* (Reprints from the *Harvard Business Review*), (Boston, Mass.: President and Fellows of Harvard College, 1980), pp. 8–17.

22. Borland, unpublished lecture notes.

23. Phillip Marvin, *Product Planning Simplified: Sharpening Up Decision Making* (New York: American Management Association, 1960), pp. 7–19.

24. Eden and Harris, *Management Decision and Decision Analysis*, p. 17.

25. Pyhrr, *Zero Based Budgeting;* pp. 5–8.

4

Organizational Design and Management

MARLENE H. BREWER

Today there is much discussion concerning what comprises the characteristics of an effective and efficient operation in organizational design and management in higher education administration. Historically, higher education has viewed teaching as its major purpose and function. Being involved with this "ivory tower" viewpoint precluded the perception by the university and education of achieving this goal in an organizational setting. However, during the past four decades, the education community has become increasingly conscious of the similarities and advantages of applying the principles being utilized in the business enterprise. This increasing concern with operational efficiency has been provoked by the conflicting goals of teaching, research, public service and the achievement of an ideal democratic community within the university which the education organization is attempting to meet. Six different approaches to organizational design and management contain significant tenets from which the main elements of modern administration techniques were derived. These six approaches will be examined and discussed. The most adaptable approach to higher education will be identified and its facets explored in detail.

DEFINITIONS

Contingency management—A process stressing the effectiveness of a leader according to the type of industry he/she is in as well as his/her personal style of leadership.

Design approach—The basic elements of the management process including long- and short-range planning, organizing, staffing, directing, and controlling.

Scientific management—The traditional or classical approach which is concerned more with the measurement of work than with the workman or the description of the organization.

Structuralistic management—A bureaucratic organization which is equated with rules and expectations flowing from superordinates downward.

Theory X management—Views the work group from the classical or scientific approach and directs and controls through authority exercised. Hard management techniques are embraced.

Theory Y management—Views the work group from the human element standpoint. The process is the integration of the worker into the organization to achieve his own goals and within those to achieve the organization's goals.

Theory Z management—A recirculating type of process capable of some degree of corrective action either as a result of internal changes within the system or in answer to environmental changes. This concept depends on the situation in which decisions and leadership styles exist within the organization structure.

DESIGN APPROACHES

A discussion of organizational design resembles the story of seven blind men touching and describing an elephant. In the story each blind man works with limited data and reaches a divergent conclusion. Each researcher and concomitant theory reflect that person's particular background. This individual background explains the rigid or structural orientation, the human behavior orientation, and the systems orientation. Involved in the analysis of organizational design are the basic elements of management and the awareness of the existence of a formal and informal group of social relationships.

The management process consists of the basic elements of short- and long-range planning, organizing, staffing, directing, and controlling. These elements, considered along with the assumptions and principles of the six approaches to management, provide a cohesive picture of organizational design.

When viewed as a total social group, the organization has both a formal and informal set of relationships. The formal organization is that group formed as a result of its structure. The informal organization represents a pattern of social relationships which is not recognized by the formal structure. Both these patterns have great influence upon the behavior of individuals within the group.[1]

Universal Principles of Management Approach

This approach is characterized by an authoritarian management approach to the group situation. There is one best method of accomplishing or doing, and the worker is considered in the same category as machinery. Henri Fayol has identified the following principles of management.[2]

1. *Division of work.* The specialization of workers, including management, to improve efficiency and increase output.
2. *Authority and responsibility.* "The right to give orders, and power to exact obedience." Responsibility occurs as a direct result of authority.
3. *Discipline.* In essence, "obedience, application, energy, behavior" given to the organization, which depends on the worthiness of the leaders.
4. *Unity of command.* The principle that no one should have more than one boss.
5. *Unity of direction.* Specifies that in addition to having only one boss, there should be only one plan for accomplishing goals.
6. *Subordination of individual interest to general interest.* The organization's concerns should be placed ahead of individual concerns.
7. *Remuneration (pay) of personnel.* Specified fair pay arrangements, satisfactory to all, whereby competence is rewarded, but not overrewarded.
8. *Centralization.* Consolidation of the management function should be done according to the circumstances surrounding the organization.
9. *Scalar chain.* The chain of command which can sometimes have several tracks. Persons at parallel levels down the tracks may be authorized to solve problems with the superior's knowledge.
10. *Order.* The principle that everyone has a position; similarly, all materials should have, and be in, a certain place.
11. *Equity.* Loyalty should be encouraged by kindliness and justice, but does not exclude sternness and forcefulness when needed.
12. *Stability of tenure of personnel.* High turnover of personnel both causes and is the result of inefficiency; better organizations have stable managerial personnel.
13. *Initiative.* The necessity for "thinking out a plan and ensuring its success."
14. *Esprit de corps.* Morale and team feeling are enhanced by keeping teams together and having good face-to-face communication.

These principles clearly delineate the rights of management. They do not recognize the rights of the worker or the nature of social interaction in a group situation along the formal line of organization or informal social behavior. These principles identify efficiency and increased output as the rationale for division of tasks in an organization.

The essence of the principles of esprit de corps and unity of command are still found in a modified form in current management practice. In evaluating this approach in relationship to higher education, application of these principles in their pure form would not be found in higher education administration since they represent a very limited approach to the understanding of the processes which occur in a group situation.

Structuralist Approach

The structuralist approach observes a bureaucratic organization in its current condition and is concerned with a comparative analysis. It does not concern descriptions or judgments about what should be. Max Weber, one of the founders of this approach, discusses illegitimate and legitimate power. Alienation of the worker results from the use of illegitimate power, whereas the use of legitimate power coincides with worker expectations, thus producing an internalization of rules by the worker.[3] Weber characterized bureaucratic structure as:

1. An organization with continuity which operates according to rules.
2. An area, or domain, of competence in which the persons involved share the work toward specified goals under predetermined leaders.
3. An organization with scalar (hierarchical) principles.
4. An organization with rules which are either norms or technical rules.
5. An organization in which administrative staff is separated from ownership of production devices or administration, and private belongings and the organization's equipment are separated.
6. An organization whose resources are free of outside control, and in which no administrator can monopolize personnel positions.
7. An organization in which any administrative acts, rules, policies, etc., must be stated in writing.[4]

The above descriptions of the characteristics of an organization remain, for the most part, valid today. Although these observations view the enterprise solely in terms of its functions, they are perceptive. This type of analysis also ignores the individual, his values, concerns, communications, and participation in the group situation.

If the structuralist approach were applied to the administration of higher education, the complexities represented by conflicting goals, overlapping group functions, and intricate communication channels would be completely ignored. The modern administrator often ignores this type of arrangement.

Scientific Management Approach

The scientific management approach, also known as the traditional or classical approach, is concerned with the measurement of work. It does not concern itself with the description of the organization, nor does it look at the principles of the organization. Frederick W. Taylor founded this approach to management, which reflected the two following assumptions: Man is machinelike. A man's feelings, personality, and work group are relatively unimportant.[5]

Weaknesses in this approach are readily apparent. Although it is directed toward the measurement of work and thus to an objective of the enterprise, it completely ignores the worker as a human being. This theory also fails to recognize that many other variables may exist in the assessment of an organization.

During the second and third decades of the twentieth century, when this approach was born and put into practice, it was quite effective since it was applied in the limited situation of a largely immigrant labor force and a large number of tasks that required only unskilled labor. A modern day opposite of this approach is called Management by Objectives (MBO). Peter Drucker has called this "management by objectives and self-control."[6] This process involves tying in the objectives of each manager or professional worker and his area into the goals of the total organization. The basic steps in this process have been identified as:

1. The manager sits down with the subordinate and the two of them determine the subordinate's specific areas of responsibility for the end results desired. This step is necessary to ensure that both agree on the specifics of the task to be accomplished.

2. The manager and his subordinate must agree on the standard of performance for each area of responsibility.

3. The manager and his subordinate must agree on a work plan for achieving the desired results in each area of responsibility, always in accordance with the overall goals of the company.[7]

Applying the scientific management approach to higher education administration in the form that Taylor originally developed would not be feasible. However, MBO is used in many educational settings. The advantages of this approach are the necessity for a base of understanding and communication in both vertical directions, and the necessity for basic agreement about the goals of the total institution. The disadvantage of applying this to the educational setting is the multiplicity of conflicting goals embraced by education and the lack of agreement on these goals even by the various disciplines within a given college or university.

Traditionally, structure was viewed in only one mode. This was the hierarchical line and staff concept, which was advanced by the universal, structuralist, and scientific management approaches. The chain of command followed the direction of a pyramid, with the top person at the apex of the pyramid. The line and staff concept was borrowed from military organization, with the line as the primary chain of command and the staff activities being considered purely advisory. This concept has undergone revision, with research and other departments being given equal importance with line functions. The line staff concept is still current.[8]

Theory X Approach

Theory X represents the first of three approaches involving the work group viewed from the human element standpoint. It views the work group from the classical or scientific approach and directs and controls through authority exercise. Douglas McGregor identified these assumptions as: (1) The average human being has an inherent dislike of work and will avoid it if he can; (2) Because of this human characteristic of dislike of work, most people must be coerced, controlled, directed, threatened with punishment to get them to put forth adequate effort toward the achievement of organizational goals; and (3) the average human being prefers to be directed, wishes to avoid responsibility, has relatively little ambition, wants security above all.[9]

Theory X is a work-oriented approach to groups operating in a production situation. The "hard" management technique embraces these assumptions. The mass, or workers, are viewed at a very mediocre level. Certainly, this viewpoint has little to recommend it. Management may give lip service to the individual value of every person while privately giving support to the above identified assumptions. This support is exhibited through practices and policies of paternalism.[10]

If Theory X assumptions were applied to higher education administration, there would develop, very shortly, high levels of dissatisfaction and conflict within the college or university. Since professors are high-level intellectual workers, they would immediately identify this management philosophy and resist it.

Theory Y Approach

Theory Y represents the second of three approaches involving the work group viewed from the human element standpoint. By the process of integration the worker can achieve his own objectives best by meeting organizational goals. This must be done by the creation of favorable conditions, making possible the achievement of these goals. The assumptions underlying this theory are: (1) The expenditure of physical and mental effort in work is as natural as play or rest; (2) External control and the threat of punishment are not the only means for bringing about effort toward organizational objectives. Man will exercise self-direction and self-control in the service of objectives to which he is committed; (3) Commitment to objectives is a function of the rewards associated with their achievement; (4) The average human being learns, under proper conditions, not only to accept, but to seek responsibility; (5) The capacity to exercise a relatively high degree of imagination, ingenuity, and creativity in the solution of organizational problems is widely, not narrowly, distributed in the population; and (6) Under the conditions of modern industrial life, the intellectual potentialities of the average human being are only partially utilized.[11]

The Theory Y approach to organizational design views the worker as having only positive facets to his personality in the work situation. Although this represents a philosophy at the opposite end of the continuum from Theory X, it by no means describes or allows for individual variations such as motivation, capacity, and adaptability in the work arena.

Although Theory Y may be too broad a generalization of the total enterprise, it is a marked improvement from the view of the worker as a mere extension of the machine. The possibility of increased worker cooperation and participation remains a definite plus. The improved quantity and quality of communication inherent in this philosophy is also beneficial.

From the Theory Y approach descriptive terms for the style of management utilized have developed. The first of these is the participative management concept. This management concept suggests that participation in decision making by the worker helps to better integrate his objectives with those of the organization. In other words, decision making should occur at the lowest possible point in the structure. This increased participation in turn increases productivity. Research seems to confirm the validity of this type of management.[12]

Another descriptive term for the Theory Y approach to management is "soft management." In many instances this term is used in conjunction with or in place of "participative management." Soft management embraces the concepts described in the preceding paragraph and also postulates that lower-level decision making will increase productivity by facilitating the integration of employee objectives with organizational goals. Research has found conflicting results in this area.[13]

The application of this style of management would be appropriate in higher education. Since the worker in this situation is a highly skilled "mind-worker," his or her productivity would be increased by participation in decision making. This type of worker will most assuredly resent an authoritarian style of management with the inference being he or she is only a machine.

The disadvantage in applying the assumptions of Theory Y in higher education is the generalization that work and the characteristics of human beings are the same in all situations. A second generalization not substantiated by research is the causal relationship between specific changes "in organization structure or process and the resultant output, productivity, or attitudes and feelings on the part of workers."[14] Applying this theory without modification for the worker and situation would be unrealistic.

Theory Z Approach

An alternate approach which perhaps can best describe and accommodate the infinite variables and factors in an organizational setting is a "systems," or Theory Z, approach. This approach can be defined as a "recirculating type of process and is capable of some degree of corrective action either as the result of internal changes within the system or in answer to external environmental changes."[15]

Various concepts and their application to management in higher education will be discussed here. A problem in describing a system is determining the parameters. The following variables are factors that can determine the "appropriateness of any given organizational structure or process."

1. *Size of Organization.* As size (defined as number of people) increases, organizational structure becomes more formal and complex, with the result that the appropriate processes of motivating employees toward the achievement of organizational goals become more authoritarian, rather than participative, in nature.

2. *Degree of Interaction.* As the need for interaction between members of an organization increases in order to accomplish the prescribed work, the organizational structure should permit a free flow of information and ideas, and the accompanying processes of motivation should become more participative and informal in nature.

3. *Personality of Members.* Effective organizational structure and processes conform to the personality and the expectations of subordinates. Subordinates who do not expect participation and who are dependent upon others for motivation react best to

authoritarian patterns of structure and motivation, while those who expect participation and are motivated largely from within react best to participative organizational processes and less formality in organizational structure.

4. *Congruence of Goals.* When the goals of the organization and those of its members are congruent, participative processes and a less formal structure are appropriate; but when organizational goals and members' goals are divergent, greater reliance must be placed upon authoritative processes and formal structure so that adequate control is assured.

5. *Level of Decision Making.* When decision-making functions are retained within a work group of an organization, participative processes and informal structure are effective. As the decision-making processes move upward in the organization and away from the work group affected by those decisions, formal structure and authoritative processes are more effective.

6. *State of the System.* When the performance of an organization is relatively poor in achieving organizational goals, authoritative processes of motivation and structure may be necessary to initiate corrective action; however, as the organization achieves expected goals, participative patterns of organization become more effective and are expected by the members of the organization.

7. *Departmentalization.* Structural organization, to be effective, must create manageable work units.

8. *Span of Management.* Structural organization, to be effective, must group people and work into an effective span of management.

The enumeration of these variables reveals the inclusion of the process, product, and person. However, this approach assumes a static situation. If one variable is changed, then appropriate alteration must occur within the system.[16]

The advantages of applying the systems approach to higher education management is obvious. It allows for alternative structure, decision making, and leadership. It provides an allowance for infinite variables and combination of the basic elements of management which are short- and long-range planning, organizing, staffing, directing, and controlling.

Higher education has several conflicting purposes. In utilizing the systems approach, agreement on one or all of these must be accomplished to produce a valid and useful analysis. Education reacts to multiple pressures internally and externally in redefining its purposes, and change in definition of purposes must be recognized in analyzing a higher education organization.

OPERATIONS RESEARCH

An early type of systems approach was that of operations research. It was originally considered to be an integration of the behavioral, social, and physical sciences. However, since mathematicians dominate this approach, it has not been as broad in its consideration as it might have been. Operations research is considered to be the total approach to a problem. A mathematical model is used to describe the problem. This model recognizes capabilities in men or groups but does not usually recognize a difference in performance level.[17] C. W. Churchman describes the phases of operations research as: (1) Formulating the problem; (2) constructing a mathematical model to represent the system under study; (3) deriving a solution from the model; (4) testing the model and the solution derived from it; (5) establishing controls over the situation; and (6) putting the solution to work—implementation.[18]

The operations research approach represents a precise method of looking at organizations. Since a model is a concept of reality, it should reflect reality as much as possible. An organization is never static, so a mathematical model cannot give a precise and accurate description of the infinite number of variables which are changing in their relationship to a given situation. The operations research approach, using a mathematical model, can be limited to such variables as inventory, equipment, and money, which do not change in their relationship to the total situation. In applying the operations research approach to higher education administration, these limitations need to be recognized.

Involved in applying the systems approach to management are several components, which for the sake of discussion are considered separately. These factors are contingency management, Management Information Systems, Management by Objectives, and Program Evaluation Review Technique.

CONTINGENCY MANAGEMENT

Contingency management can be defined as "the importance of stressing the effectiveness of a leader according to the type of industry he/she is in as well as his/her personal style of leadership."[19] This merely incorporates part of the systems approach—that part which states that a theory of leadership must be studied in connection with the design of the organization. The pertinence of these factors and their application were discussed earlier in this chapter.

MANAGEMENT INFORMATION SYSTEMS

Management Information Systems (MIS) can be defined as the use of the computer to provide integrated data through various levels of management in an organization.[20] MIS is designed to cut across vertical organization lines. Therefore its optimum utilization can only occur when the organizational structure is not along vertical, classical lines.

In an organization with a classical structure, there are varying degrees of resistance to this informational flow from department to department. In higher education, a vertical, hierarchical structure is found in most instances. Therefore, the use of MIS as a total system might be impractical.

MANAGEMENT BY OBJECTIVES

Management by Objectives (MBO) was discussed earlier in this chapter, in the section dealing with the scientific approach. Its integration into a systems approach should be explored. As it was defined earlier, MBO is a process which involves tying in the objectives of each manager and his area to the goals of the total organization.[21] This process can further be defined to say goals to be achieved "must be accompanied by a decision as to the means of reaching those goals. This set of means, in turn, becomes a set of subgoals and some means of attaining them must be established."[22] General goals of an organization are communicated downward from the top and are incorporated into the individual objectives of the lowest ranked worker in the organizational structure. These worker objectives are discussed with the appropriate superior and communicated in an upward vertical direction.

PROGRAM EVALUATION REVIEW TECHNIQUE

Program Evaluation Review Technique (PERT) was developed to meet the requirements of a complex production system by the Special Projects Office of the U.S. Navy's Bureau of Ordinance. It is one of two "time-event-network" analysis techniques. The other technique is called the Critical Path Method (CPM) and was developed by Du Pont. In order to use network analysis for purposes of planning and control, several conditions must be met.[23]

1. *A clearly recognizable end point or objective.* One-of-a-kind projects, such as developing and building the first prototype of the Polaris missile or constructing a shopping center, meet this requirement. The installation of a data processing system, the construction of a highway interchange, or the building of a piece of special machinery all have clearly definable and recognizable end points. In contrast, the 100,000th car from an assembly line is difficult to distinguish from its immediate predecessor or successor.

2. *A series of events.* There should be a series of clearly defined, separate but interrelated events leading up to the completion of the final project. In constructing a highway interchange, temporary routes must be built, bridges constructed, drainage facilities installed, service roads prepared, and many other distinct subprojects completed before the interchange is ready for use.

3. *Time for each activity.* The time required for the completion of the work or activity preceding each event must be calculated. Herein lies one of the major differences between PERT and CPM. PERT employs a method of estimating probable time, even though there has been no prior experience to serve as a basis for estimating time. CPM implies some prior experience or knowledge of the time needed for the completion of activities leading to each event.

4. *A starting point.* There must be a recognizable starting point—the issuance of a sales order for a piece of special machinery; notification from the government to begin the development of a weapons system; or the date of a scheduled plant shutdown as the beginning of an annual maintenance program.

These components of management in the systems approach—contingency management, MIS, MBO, and PERT—are all readily adaptable to organizational design in higher education. However, due to the multiple and conflicting goals or objectives of higher education, caution is advised in applying any organizational design concept from industry to education. An identification of similarities of facets in industry and education must be determined before application can be valid and useful.

NOTES

1. Edgar F. Huse and James L. Bowditch, *Behavior in Organizations: A Systems Approach to Managing* (Reading, Mass.: Addison-Wesley, 1973), p. 110.

2. H. Fayol, *General and Industrial Management*, trans. C. Storrs (London: Sir Isaac Pitman and Sons, 1949), pp. 21–22.

3. Max Weber, *The Theory of Social and Economic Organization*, trans. A. M. Henderson and T. Parson (New York: Oxford University Press, 1947), pp. 20–21.

4. Ibid., p. 22.

5. F. W. Taylor, *Scientific Management* (New York: Harper and Row, 1911), p. 75.

6. Peter F. Drucker, *The Practice of Management* (New York: Harper and Brothers, 1954), p. 62.

7. Huse and Bowditch, *Behavior in Organizations*, pp. 194–96.

8. Ibid., pp. 172–246.

9. Douglas McGregor, *The Human Side of Enterprise* (New York: McGraw-Hill, 1960), pp. 33–34.

10. Ibid., p. 34.

11. Ibid., pp. 47–48.

12. Henry L. Sisk, *Principles of Management: A Systems Approach to the Management Process* (Cincinnati: South-Western Publishing Co., 1969), pp. 253–54.

13. Ibid., pp. 252–53.

14. Ibid., p. 254.

15. Ibid., pp. 255–56.

16. Ibid., p. 254.

17. Huse and Bowditch, *Behavior in Organizations,* pp. 16–17.

18. C. W. Churchman, R. L. Askoff, and E. L. Askoff, *Introduction to Operations Research* (New York: John Wiley and Sons, 1957), p. 24.

19. Huse and Bowditch, *Behavior in Organizations,* p. 149.

20. Ibid., p. 273.

21. Ibid., pp. 194–96.

22. J. C. March and H. A. Simon, *Organizations* (New York: John Wiley and Sons, 1958), pp. 194–95.

23. Sisk, *Principles of Management,* pp. 640–41.

5

Leadership in Implementing Organizational Design and Defining Administrative Roles

Implementation of Organizational Design and Management

BOB W. MILLER

Much has been written about organizational design management; however, not enough has been said about its implementation and practical aspects. American institutions of higher education cannot function effectively and efficiently in teaching, research, and service if the management and leadership processes are not attended to on a proportionate basis. In providing leadership for the future for educational institutions, many attributes of management in business and industry should be utilized for organizational design and management. Administration of a college or university, from the trustees to the department chairpersons, has specific roles and responsibilities in organizational design and management of the institution.

No definitions of the terms utilized in this chapter are included here, since all of the roles and functions are discussed in the context of the chapter.

IMPLEMENTATION OF SPECIFIC ORGANIZATIONAL DESIGNS

Both formal and informal management involve social relationships. This implies that leadership is a "people process." Therefore, everything we do in the management enterprise affects other individuals and groups as well as ourselves.

When we consider some of the basic elements of the management function, such as short- and long-range planning, organizing, staffing, directing, coordinating, and controlling, we become involved with two major components: the organization, and the individual or groups within the organization.

The organization and organizational goals are the most important items to be considered in management. (An example of an organizational goal would be to provide the best education possible for each individual student.) Often the faculty, students, administration, and community are not made aware of this factor. Any individual within the organization can be replaced and the organization will survive. This is not to say that individuals and their motivation are unimportant. The happier and more satisfied the individual, the more likely he is to accomplish an effective and efficient job. This is the reason that professional development—job enrichment, motivation, communication, and group processes—are most important to individuals in the organization.

In implementing organizational design in educational institutions, it is vital that everyone within the organization have a job description and defined role. This should begin with the definition of the organization, utilizing such devices as planning assumptions, mission statements, organizational goals, purposes, and philosophy. Groups and individuals in the institution can not know where they are going if information of this nature is not provided. Once this information has been provided to each employee, it is necessary that each division, department, and individual develop job or role descriptions. Study after study has indicated that employees are much happier, better satisfied, have higher morale and esprit de corps when roles have been clarified. Thus, in implementing any organizational design, it is necessary to define goals of the organization and to define job descriptions of employees within the organization.

Short-Range Planning

The setting of short-range objectives is necessary to make any organization successful. These short-range objectives should be designed to meet long-range goals of the institution. One method to make this effective is a system of Management by Objectives (MBO), or management by results. This specific process begins by having both oral and written goal statements from the chief administrator. These goals must be communicated to each level of the organization, including faculty, students, and support staff members. In turn, the faculty and support staff members should write individual objectives which will enhance the organizational goals as well as provide input at the "grass roots" level. (MBOs are briefly discussed in Chapter 4, "Organizational Design and Management.")

The objective-writing process for faculty members should go above and beyond the regular classroom syllabus. Generally, these objectives are classified as *maintenance, problem solving,* and *innovative* in nature. In most cases, these objectives should be written in the early part of the school year and evaluated by the end of the school year. An example or process which has been effectively utilized in writing MBOs follows.

1. Statement of specific objectives.
2. Environmental analysis. (Do you have the appropriate staff, finances, time, resources, etc? Is the objective realistic and feasible?)
3. Statement of one or more plans of action to accomplish each objective.
4. Deadline for the objective to be completed.
5. Self-evaluation process to determine to what extent the objective was completed.
6. Difficulty in achieving the objective (very difficult, difficult, average, etc.).

The process begins with the writing of specific objectives. Next, immediate superordinate and subordinate discuss each objective and how it fits in with organizational goals. This is the stage when modification or adjustment occurs. Both parties should agree on what the individual is trying to accomplish. After adaptations are made, both parties should sign the objectives statement as a commitment to the other party and to the organization. The superordinate should analyze and synthesize objectives within the department or division for commonalities with other employees. This process will cause combined cooperation when synthesis occurs across all campus areas. The same process is followed by everyone from the department or division chairperson to the deans, vice presidents, and president. In the spring, or late part of the school year, the same type of communication process occurs; only at this stage there is an evaluation process which is initiated at each faculty and administrative level with each subordinate and superordinate involved. The purpose of each evaluation is to determine how effective and efficient each person has been in achieving each individual objective in connection with organizational goals. Many of the following year's objectives will result from this evaluation process.

Long-Range Planning

Business and industry executives claim that they would "go broke" without planning for a minimum of ten years in advance. Major cities have planned to the year 2000. One can imagine what a mess a city could be in if it did not accomplish long-range planning in connection with highways, sewer systems, and electrical power and telephone systems. Educational institutions also cannot exist on a quality basis without long-range planning. Planning must occur to acquire building sites, facilities, staffs, programs, hardware, and software. When a freshman enters a four-year B.A. or B.S. degree program, a four-year time frame is involved. For other types of programs, especially at the doctoral level, from two to ten years are involved. Therefore, students are affected by long-range planning even in the curriculum arena.

How should we go about implementing long-range planning? A systems approach should be utilized to assure quality control in the educational process. When considering how to obtain quality control, the space industry should be analyzed. A paper model spanning an entire wall of a building is ordinarily utilized. Every time a portion of the spacecraft is installed, the representative area within the model is colored in to indicate that the section is complete. All parts, bolts, screws, and sections are installed on the paper model as well as in the spacecraft. This process eliminates duplication of parts as well as preventing omission of items, thus insuring quality control for that specific spacecraft.

In the educational field in past years, quality control had not occurred often, so that there have been many repetitions and omissions in the curriculum. The major reason for lack of quality control is lack of short- and long-range planning.

How then should the process of systematic long-range planning be implemented? One specific technique which has worked in higher educational institutions follows.

First, analyze the past to determine former strengths and weaknesses of the organization. State these strengths and weaknesses in writing. These items can be isolated in the framework in which they functioned.

The second phase consists of determining what exists in the educational institution at the present time. Again, strengths and weaknesses exist in the present model, and suggestions for improvement should be made for the future. Each basic concept of strengths, weaknesses, and suggestions for improvement should be isolated, and a written statement should be made about how the organization is at present operating. The first two stages should be set forth in the form of a model in order that each segment may be analyzed.

The third phase consists of reviewing all planning assumptions, mission statements, organizational goals, purposes, and the institutional philosophy. These should project toward the future as far as possible. A model should be presented to all members of the staff by the board of trustees and the president. Vice presidents, deans, and division and department chairpersons should build models of their areas similar to the model presented by the president. Chief administrators should not expect subordinates to project toward the future without having projected the future of the institution themselves. Areas which should be projected for the future are: programs, curriculum and courses for each program, financing, staffing, buildings, site selection, number of students to be served, type of students to be served, software, hardware, maintenance needs, problem-solving projections, innovative projections, and professional development projections.

The fourth phase consists of *all* division or department chairpersons, deans, vice presidents, business management, research, and planning personnel (top level), and the president of the institution conferring to present and discuss programs. The first meeting should be scheduled on a one- to two-hour basis, with the president presenting his overall projection model. Only one or two presentations should be made in a day, in order that adequate time may be utilized for discussion and setting of priorities. Presentations are enhanced by the use of audiovisuals and typed materials to be given to each participant. Nine or ten working days will normally suffice for presentations. In each session questions should be asked and discussion should result in definite priorities agreed upon by the specific parties involved.

The purpose of these meetings is to inform individuals in leadership and support roles across the campus about educational planning and to bring about cooperation where commonalities do exist. In addition, major purposes are agreed upon involving priorities as a part of the programming in long-range planning. The planning process should involve faculty and staff members in the various divisions and departments. Once modifications and agreements have been made by subordinates and superordinates, they should be indicated on each division's basic model. These models should be discussed and displayed on the institution's walls in order that people in the community and the institution may be aware of long-range plans and projections. A pocket may be made on each model to hold a detailed monograph of the long-range plan. Each year, it is important for faculty and staff to remember that short-range objectives should be written in relation to the long-range plan. Educators should always keep in mind that conditions will change and that a flexible plan must always be in operation. The long-range plan should be updated at least every two years.

ORGANIZING THE INSTITUTION

When an institution is originally organized or is reorganized after having been in operation for several years, future organization and design depends a great deal upon the leadership of the chief administrator and controlling board. Either or both may feel that the old organization will suffice, or that change should occur in the institution.

If the leader is extremely autocratic then a structured line and staff organization should be implemented, as illustrated in Figure 17. In this model, most information and decisions are presented from the top down. Most decisions are made by the superordinate, and each level below may become "pseudoleadership" or "figurehead administration."

FIGURE 17
Line staff

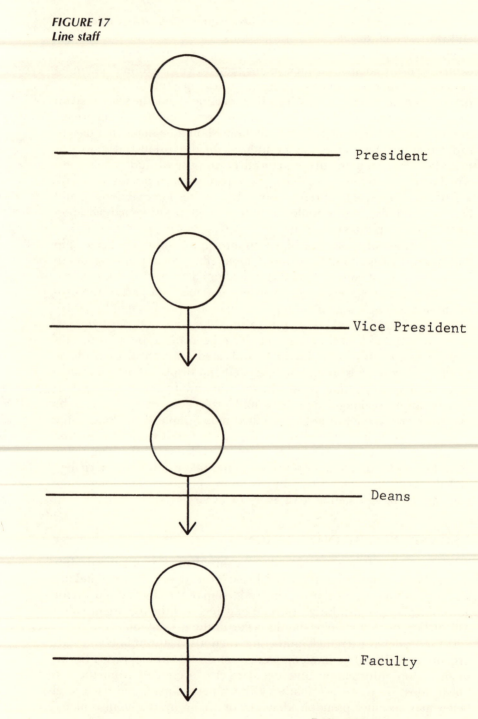

President

Vice President

Deans

Faculty

Bob Miller

FIGURE 18
The leadership constantly changes

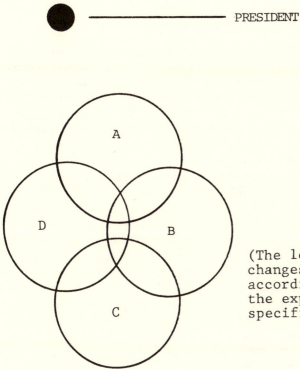

PRESIDENT

(The leadership
changes constantly
according to who has
the expertise at that
specific moment)

Bob Miller

This type of "Theory X" administration in its extreme form seldom exists in modern educational institutions.

Another type of extremism which seldom exists in its true form is "Theory Y" democratic leadership. This type of administration totally involves all faculty and staff. Voting occurs constantly, with committee work expected in *all* decisions. Chairpersons, deans, and vice presidents might constantly be elected, with persons in these administrative slots acting in a temporary capacity. The organization would consist of emerging leadership, as depicted in Figure 18.

An effective administrator almost always has to answer the questions, When does the individual make the decision, and when does the group make the decision? Where and with whom does the buck stop for the final decision?

A third type of extremism consists of free reign or laissez-faire administration. The only decision made by the chief executive is not to make a decision. The administration's basic philosophy is basically "wishy-washy" in relation to the decision-making process. This can cause leadership to emerge from anywhere within the organization.

A NEW MODEL FOR CONSIDERATION

Figure 19 presents various alternative approaches to organizational operation. Since our first three models were too extremist, these alternatives will work better for most administrators and faculty in actual practice. (One may lean toward autocratic, democratic, or laissez-faire administration, but not totally.) Most of us could operate with the *scientific decision-making* approach, where individuals or groups make decisions. This process consists of: (1) defining the problems, (2) listing all alternatives, (3) listing the consequences or advantages and disadvantages of each alternative, (4) making the decision, (5) selecting the best strategy to implement the decision, (6) implementing the decision, and (7) evaluating the decision.

One may wish to organize, operate, and make decisions in terms of innovations on a day-to-day, yearly, and long-range basis. This would be a *creative leadership* approach, one of constantly coming up with new ideas or modifications of old ideas. This approach involves constant reconstruction at each faculty and administrative level.

Another leadership approach is the *humanistic* operational style. This strategy has as its major concern the "people element." This approach begins with the student and has concern for faculty and other administrators. It is more concerned with interaction and self-concept than with subject matter and production.

A fourth leadership concept is *organismic*. This is the gestalt approach, whereby the administrative leadership is concerned with the "big picture"—the whole student, the whole organization. The organization and organizational goals are of the highest priority. Each individual is hired because he is "gung ho" for the organization or is considered to be an "organization man."

These styles of operational design are realistic in nature. They resemble "Theory Z," which was described in the previous chapter. A leader can operate in action terms using one or all four of these concepts.

Organization charts should be designed according to the leadership style of the chief administrator and the overall philosophy and mission of the institution. No matter what the organization, one should remember that the final decision always rests with the chief administrator and controlling board.

A number of studies show that no one type of leadership style, generally speaking, is more effective than another. Therefore, situational leadership, depending upon an institution's philosophy, becomes the important consideration.

FIGURE 19
Extreme philosophies of organizational operation

Individual Objectives	Individual Objectives	Individual Objectives	Individual Objectives	Individual Objectives	Organizational Goals	
Objective 1	1	1	1	1	S	New
Objective 2	2	2	2	2	U	objective
Objective 3	3	3	3	3	C	setting,
Objective 4	4	4	4	4	C	to
Objective 5	5	5	5	5	E	meet
Objective 6	5	6		6	S	long
Objective 7	6	7		7	S	range
Objective		8				goals
First Year	Second Year	Third Year	Fourth Year	Fifth Year	Sixth Year	Seventh - Twelfth Year

DIRECTING THE ORGANIZATION

Consideration of the basic philosophy and mission statement of an educational institution should be the primary concern of the executives in directing its organization. The organization must be directed on a goals and objectives format at each level of the institution. Other considerations related to the mission statement, philosophy, goals, and objectives are: What causes *motivation* within the organization? How are problems solved and decisions made within the organization? How will positive change take place within the organization? How will communication (formal and informal) take place within the organization? How will professional development take place within the organization?

Motivation

Motivation is a process that affects the emotions, objectives, and attitudes of each employee. This factor concerns the needs, wants, and actions of each employee. Part of the process of motivation in an organization concerns productivity. In order to achieve productivity, the individual must work toward organizational goals that relate to achievement of personal needs with a minimum amount of conflict. In operational terms, the executive must match commonalities of individual and organizational needs.

Effective motivation is basically internal, but external motivation can cause internal motivation. Some work in any organization is basically boring or unattractive. One task of the executive in an educational institution is to assist in making the work less boring and more challenging. An effective way to cause this to occur is to make the task objective in nature and goal directed. Supervisors vary tremendously in their basic assumptions about employee expectations and practices. All executives must consider motivation a high priority in meeting the needs of the organization and its employees. Leadership styles are an important factor in determining the type of motivation utilized.

To motivate employees, the executive must consider changing the behavior of individuals. This may involve establishing payoffs or rewards for positive changes on the job. The process will probably include the establishment of goals, objectives, and timetables for change. In addition, follow-up and reinforcement programs for change must be included for each employee. In considering behavior change, keep in mind that each person has individual differences which are most variable and complex in nature. Basically, people search for a variety of activities on each job. Keep in mind also that people react differently to each situation, thus making job satisfaction a most difficult area to deal with.

The motivation process involves group differences as well as individual differences. Each individual in the group has developed attitudes, beliefs, values, and value systems since birth. These factors will affect the sociopolitical and economic value systems of each group. In addition, the experiential background, educational experience, and loyalty values will affect group performance within the organization. The directive function of the executive in this context is to enable both the individuals and the group to grow professionally, to achieve reward for performance, to encourage participation, and to provide support services. To be effective and efficient in the motivational process, the leader must diagnose and analyze individuals and groups as well as counsel individuals.

Characteristics of effective direction in the organization are supportive supervision, open communication, high expectations, performance analysis, measurement of goals and objectives, encouragement of initiative and involvement, and effective teamwork. Many factors or variables must be combined in directing an institution.

The executive must constantly keep in mind the basic human needs: self-realization; self-esteem; social, security, and life support. In addition, specific ideas such as employee input, feasibility, commitment, role definition, challenge, and perception are important. Most of these have been discussed in detail by Frederick Herzberg in various books on human needs. Each individual has energy and wants to produce; the question is how to direct this specified energy toward the objectives and goals of the educational institution.

Managing Change

In directing the organization, positive change may or may not occur. The type of change necessary to meet the philosophy of the organization is a major factor in what the institution will become in the future. Most professionals in educational institutions have difficulty understanding change; most executives have not studied how to handle change with employees and have not considered problem solving as involved with change.

To consider how change occurs, look at the task to be performed, the structure of the organization, the employee involved with the task, and the leader who is trying to bring about a change. An administrator should also remember that he or she is considering a problem within the organization. To deal with the problem, one must be able to state the problem specifically on paper. The second thing to consider is that for any change which affects the employees of the organization there will be *restraining forces* as well as *driving forces*. When these two powerful forces push against each other, an *equilibrium*, or balance, usually results. This process, called a *force field of balance or analysis,* is illustrated in Figure 20.

FIGURE 20
Force field of balance

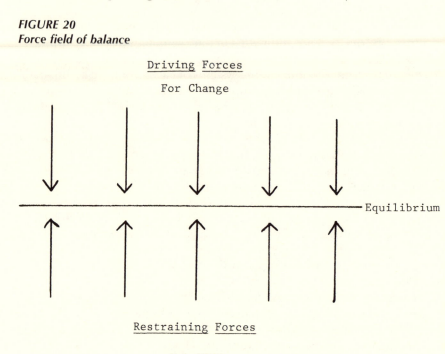

Driving Forces

For Change

Equilibrium

Restraining Forces

Bob Miller

In problem solving and in bringing about change, list all of the driving forces and then list all of the restraining forces. Look at the predominant driving and restraining forces involved. There are basic steps in change to become aware of when participating in this process. (1) The person involved in the change becomes aware of imbalance in connection with the situation; (2) the person involved becomes knowledgeable about the different alternatives or of other ways of acting and performing; (3) the person involved becomes psychologically ready to change, in that he or she now is choosing to change; and (4) once the change occurs on a positive basis, habit patterns are involved; therefore, the leader should assist the employee in "cementing in" the new behavior.

In cementing in the new behavior, the positive change with individuals and the principle of reinforcement become important. We know from theories of learning that positive reinforcement strengthens behavior. We also know that negative reinforcement suppresses a behavior. Therefore, in the change process, we want to: (1) zero in on the desired behavior, (2) assist the individual in determining any responsibility desired and what performance level is acceptable, (3) make sure the employee understands what has happened and be totally aware of the process utilized in making the event occur, (4) reward improvement of the positive act, and (5) utilize self-evaluation of effectiveness and efficiency of the changes involved.

To maintain a positive change in behavior for the future, the consequences of the changes brought about must be strongly influenced. Rewarded behavior more easily causes new habit patterns to be made. To discontinue bad habit patterns, unwanted behavior must consistently be punished.

In the process of change, the executive has the task of problem solving with the group. Before a problem in an institution can be solved, the group must know the total situation; therefore, it is the job of the leader to communicate the specific situation to the group. To accomplish the task at hand, the leader should assist the group in setting specific objectives relating to organization goals. Once a climate for change is established, another major task is to motivate change. Remember that people in the organization will be the individuals making the change work.

In summary, to cause change, leadership should utilize the following steps:

1. Describe the problem as you as an executive perceive it.

2. List the restraining and driving forces. (List anything that comes to mind, without being critical or selective. You can weed out the irrelevant items later.)

3. Now review the two lists (restraining and driving forces). Underline those forces that seem to be the most important and that you think you might be able to affect on a constructive basis.

4. Now, for each *restraining force* you have underlined, list the possible action steps that you might be able to plan and carry out to reduce the effect of the force or to eliminate it completely. *Brainstorm.* List as many action steps as possible, without worrying about how effective or practical they might be. You will later have a chance to decide which are the most appropriate.

5. Now do the same with each *driving force* underlined. List all of the action steps that come to mind which would *increase the effect* of each driving force.

6. Remember, the place to begin change is where stress and strain exists. Increased stress may lead to increased dissatisfaction, which probably will be a motivation for change. Consider whether the change could be more easily managed by reducing a restraining force.

7. Review the steps you have listed and underline the best alternatives.

8. List the steps you have *underlined.* Then, for each action step, list the resources that are available to you for carrying out the desired action.

9. Now review the list of action steps and resources and think about how they might fit into a total action plan. Eliminate all items that do not fit into the overall plan. At this time, add any new steps and resources that will round out the plan. Think about sequences and strategies for action.

10. Plan a way to evaluate the effectiveness of your action program as you implement the plan. What evaluation plan will you use?

11. The final step in the whole process is to implement your plan. Good luck!

Decision Making and Problem Solving

The best decision makers are only accurate, over a period of time, with a 51 percent average. Problems need to be solved; this is accomplished through decision making procedures. The scientific method of decision making is discussed elsewhere in this book.

Another way of analyzing the problem-solving process is to: (1) gather the basic facts, (2) define the exact problem specifically, (3) find the basic cause of the problem, (4) list all of the alternatives and decide on the best alternative (this process includes analyzing the consequences of each alternative), (5) select the best strategy for implementation, (6) implement the decision, and, finally, (7) evaluate the decision.

During the problem-solving process one should ask oneself: What? When? Where? How? Who? How Much? Also watch out for faulty basic assumptions, opinions, and hasty conclusions. It is also possible to analyze through observation, as in the question, "Is the problem one of people, or is it a technological problem?"

In problem solving, the most effective decision makers list all alternatives possible, then select those that are most appropriate for the specific situation. If the problem involves other employees, be sure they have input in the decision-making process. *Consistency* with the type of decision-making process, involving people, and the philosophical base are important to the organization and subordinates. The *strategy* and *timing* of implementing the process is also important. How permanent the decision will be, the cost of the decision, the practicality of the decision, and whether the decision will be acceptable to the organization must constantly be reviewed. How will the decision affect subordinates, superordinates, and colleagues?

When a decision is to be implemented, it is the responsibility of leadership to communicate the decision to those affected. If the decision affects others and tasks are involved, role responsibilities must be assigned, and the final step is to be sure that each person understands and is committed. Once this has been done, the decision as well as the process should be evaluated. The question becomes, Has the problem of the initial phase been solved? If not, the problem-solving or decision-making process has not been successful.

Staffing

Staffing the organization consists of selecting the most competent individual or individuals to meet organizational goals. To accomplish this task, recruiting, interviewing, processing credentials and other papers, and selection are important. Staffing requires recruiting, interviewing, and selecting from a number of potential candidates. The leadership cannot afford to hire the second or third best candidate for each position, but must hire the best educator. Because of this factor, many candidates must be recruited and interviewed to make the alternative selection process possible. For example, twenty-four or twenty-five interviews may be required to employ the best candidate for a specific position.

In the recruitment and interviewing process, the interviewer should analyze each individual in terms of his or her present abilities as well as potentialities for the future. In addition, the interviewer must look for the candidates' own satisfaction factors, as well as at how the candidates have performed in past situations. Candidates should be employed for their ability to relate to and perform within the basic philosophy, mission, and goals of the institution. The question posed to the candidate should be directly concerned with how the institution operates, from both teaching and administrative constraints and potentials.

A strong leader will want to be surrounded with capable personnel who have expertise in setting objectives and performing tasks to meet organization goals. No one person can have all types of expertise; therefore, other personnel should be employed with competency in all areas of concern for the institution.

Once an individual has been employed, he must be oriented to the job and the total institution. An interview or a policy handbook will not accomplish the complete task of orientation. One approach which has been successfully utilized, other than the opening week orientation, is a packaged approach during the first month of school. This approach has new employees go through packaged activities at their own rate (this can apply to part-time employees also). Slide-tape presentations, filmstrips, videotapes, and other media can convey effectively the messages of the president, deans, and division chairpersons. They can give instruction in record keeping, the use of audiovisual materials, library operations, and departmental guidelines. After a "new" professional educator goes through each segment of the package, he or she checks each item on a departmental checklist to signify that a specific activity has been completed. The department chairperson and the new employee both sign

the completed checklist. The final checklist with signatures is forwarded
to the immediate superordinate to complete the accountability process.

Once the individual has been employed and oriented, then the process
of training (in-service or professional development), becomes a necessity. No higher education institution can provide all in-service training to
meet organizational goals of each individual and group. No employee in
any organization, however, will progress or advance fully on the job
without effective and efficient in-service training. Professional development programs should be effectively planned around the needs of the
faculty and administration. These programs revolve around the needs
of students, individual employees, and organizational goals; therefore
professional development programs must develop the person as an individual and the individual as a team member. To accomplish this, counseling on a personal basis is important to meeting individual objectives
and organizational activities.

In addition to the above activities, employing officials must adhere to
and keep up to date with affirmative action requirements. All individuals within the organization must be made aware of governmental
updates and changes. The organization will want to employ the best-
qualified employees, while meeting affirmative action requirements.
(Additional material on this subject can be found in the chapters dealing
with personnel.)

Controlling

Controlling involves insuring progress toward goals according to the
plan of the organization. Specific factors important in the quality control
of a program are: (1) establishing reporting systems, (2) developing
performance standards, (3) measuring results, (4) taking corrective action where problems exist, and (5) rewarding performance.

Roles of Administrative Personnel

JO LYNN LOYD

Imagine, if you will, a university run solely by a president. He would teach, raise money, collect fees, prepare goals for the institution, coordinate the learning resource center, and handle student problems in addition to numerous other activities. Although this omnipotent president is almost impossible to imagine, in the past these were common tasks for college presidents. However, colleges many years ago were less complex, and all these tasks could be handled by one person. This trend was drastically altered as a result of specialization and expansion of knowledge, the development of research, the addition of multifarious service, as well as increased size and wealth of institutions. As a result of this complexity, "a proliferation of administrative officials" has emerged to share the load of the president.[1]

BOARD OF TRUSTEES

Within the hierarchical structure of institutions of higher education, as illustrated in Figure 21, the top policy-making body is a group of laymen, usually appointed by either the president of the institution or the governor of the state. These groups have various titles: board of trustees, regents, governors, visitors, overseers, and so forth.[2] For the purpose of simplification, they will be referred to throughout this chapter as the board of trustees. The specific duties of these members vary from one institution to another; however, some generalities can be drawn from their most common duties, which involve the trustees' role in purposes, budget and financing, interpretation, evaluation, facilities, staffing, and programs of the institution.

Purposes

The board of trustees is primarily a policy-making body. Within the realm of policy making, the most important duty of the board is to adopt

FIGURE 21
Organization

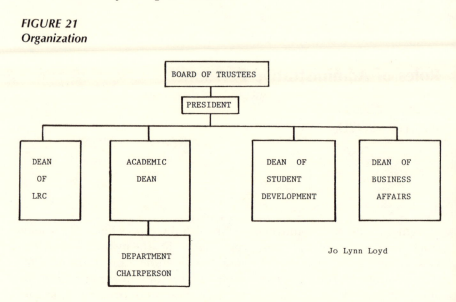

Jo Lynn Loyd

a statement of purposes for the institution.[3] Purposes establish the character of an institution, and they do not happen by accident. Through careful planning, the board of trustees formulates a statement of purpose that will become the image of the institution to the public. The framework for purposes is derived from the following rationale: the goals the institution wants to accomplish, the population the institution wishes to serve, and the means whereby the goals are to be achieved.[4] Without this definite direction for achievement, an institution will merely become a hodgepodge of programs with little or no cohesion or direction.

Budget and Financing

The second important duty of the board of trustees involves budget and finance. Appropriate procurement, conservation, and management of funds is the foundation whereby the purposes of the institution can be accomplished. Without competent handling of funds, the academic work of the institution will be impaired.[5] Board policy concerning funding needs to follow a thorough short- and long-range plan to be most effective. This will greatly facilitate policies concerning investments in addition to the selection of securities in which funds will be placed.[6]

Interpretation of Institution

The third important duty of the board of trustees involves the interpretation of the institution to the public.[7] Board members become "public relations messengers" for the institution and in doing so should maintain a two-way contact with the adult community and neighboring schools.[8] In short, board members are responsible for the reputation of the institution; consequently, they should always maintain a strict code of ethics. Within this code, members should desire to be objective and unbiased. They should also agree not to exert unnecessary pressure on the president of the institution and never to accept favors from the business community. The board of trustees should at all times enhance the image of the institution in the community.[9] Board members should remember however that they are not legal board members outside of official board meetings.

Evaluation

The fourth duty of the board of trustees involves the ongoing process of discovering how effectively institutional goals and purposes are being achieved. In this area the board acts not as the processors, but as the overseers. Their duty is to see that evaluation occurs by the regular staff or college specialists and then to objectively review results. Examples of areas that should be evaluated include: (1) acquisition of accreditation of the institution or of programs offered by the institution, (2) examination of the credit status of the institution for purposes of justification in the area of seeking a loan or issuing bonds, (3) appraisal of the demand level of students for admission into the college or university, and (4) efficiency or inefficiency of methods for recruiting, hiring, and holding a competent faculty.[10]

Proper evaluation measures acquired in these as well as other areas of the institution will not only facilitate objective decision making for board members, it will also serve to perpetuate and improve the institution through objective analysis in order to eliminate or modify weak areas. The individual institution will be no better than the decision makers on the board of trustees.

Facilities

The fifth function of the board of trustees is to provide and maintain an educationally efficient physical plant.[11] In this area, board members are responsible not only for the short-range, day-to-day upkeep of physical properties and facilities but also for the long-range needs, such as classrooms, labs, libraries, new equipment, and any new facilities needed for new methods of instruction.[12] In order to best serve this duty, the board should perform the following functions:

1. Board members should make sure that a clear and thorough assessment of building and equipment needs of the institution is prepared and kept current.

2. Board members must decide on the appropriate governing techniques whereby needed facilities will be acquired and the time plan for these acquisitions will be set.

3. Once facilities are obtained, the board accepts the legal ownership for the facilities; this involves seeing that the facilities are used, maintained, and properly protected.[13]

The importance of adequate facilities cannot be understated. This is the area of work which the board does that is most obvious to the public. When visitors come to the campus, they do not see whether or not good instruction occurs; instead, they see the conditions of the buildings and how conducive they are to learning. On the other hand, if facilities are too extravagant, the public may feel that funds are being carelessly appropriated. The point here is that the board must have sound policies for planning, financing, use, and preservation of properties and then delegate the implementation of these policies to the appropriate professional staff.[14]

Staffing

The sixth important duty of the board of trustees is not only to provide personnel for staffing the institution but also to approve personnel policies in relation to employment practices, salary schedules, working conditions, and fringe benefits.[15] Trustees are very simply employers; therefore, they must realize good personnel policies not only attract a qualified staff but also serve to facilitate retention. However, it is not enough merely to have good salary schedules and fringe benefits; trustees must also be willing to stand behind an innovative instructor even in the face of opposition.[16]

In regard to staffing, one final point needs to be made. Since the board approves all staff members, it should be realized that they are the body which selects and appoints the chief executive officer, the college or university president.[17] This is an extremely important task because the president is the chief liaison between the institution and the board. A further elaboration of the duties of the president appears in the next section.

Programs

The final all-encompassing role of the institutional trustee is to develop and constantly improve the education program of the organization.[18] In order to accomplish this goal, the board should be concerned with the following three areas designated by Martorana.

1. Board members must maintain a sense of direction and balance in course offerings consistent with the educational purposes and goals of the institution.

2. They must recognize and preserve the ideals of academic freedom in the areas of instruction, research, service as well as faculty participation in developing policies within these designates.

3. Finally, board members must encourage and permit changes and innovations in course offerings as conditions change.[19]

In order for institutions to progress, board members have to be flexible and foresighted. Rigidity of program policy will stagnate the institution. Very simply, board members must be gamblers. They must carefully analyze, approve, and implement novel programs that are unique and untested.

Evaluation of the Board

It is easy to see that the role of the trustee is vital to the college or university. Board members must have their hand in every phase of the education pot. They establish the purposes of the institution wherein the very foundations of the school are rooted. Furthermore, board members must direct the appropriation of funds in budgeting; become public relations messengers in the interpretation of the institution to the public; play a major role in seeing that goals are being met through evaluation; maintain and provide for the physical plant and facilities; direct all staffing for the institution; and direct and approve education programs that will serve to perpetuate the university. Yet the board does not operate the institution. They should hire the most competent man or woman possible as president.

PRESIDENT

The chief executive officer of a college or university is the president or chancellor. Within the hierarchical structure (see Figure 21) of the institution, he or she is usually located just under the board of trustees. The president is usually appointed by the board of trustees and his primary function is to preside in such a way as to lead the institution toward the fulfillment of its objectives and goals. The specific duties of the president vary from one institution to another; however, some generalities can be drawn from his most common duties, which involve the president's role in finance, physical facilities, public relations, student affairs, education programs, and faculty selection.[20]

Finance

The president is the most prominent figure when it comes to questions concerning short- and long-range financial planning for the institution. Although the president will usually delegate this responsibility down the chain of command, it is still his formal responsibility to see that the annual budget is prepared and presented to the board of trustees. In some cases in public institutions, the president also must present the final budget to the legislative body of the state for its approval. Although the president is formally responsible for the budget, he actually has little control over it. If his administrators are doing their job, the budget is in final form when the president receives it. Few if any revisions will need to be made. The majority of expenses for institutions are fairly fixed and there is rarely any opportunity to "play" with finances.[21]

Faculty

Another duty in relation to the budget for which the president is responsible relates to fund raising. Naturally, this duty is more important in private than in public institutions, but it is part of the president's role, either directly or indirectly, to make contacts with prospective donors.[22] This role can be visualized more clearly by examining the section on the public relations role of the president.

Physical Facilities

The president also plays an important role in the development of physical facilities. He will usually have a principal influence on the priority ranking of the physical facilities of the institution. If he is an effective president, he may receive input from a faculty committee that will help him to make his decisions. He will probably have to contend with factions on all sides in support of one building or another. However, the president must weather the storm and objectively assess the needs of the campus before presenting recommendations to the board of trustees. Once the board has approved a facility, the president will usually delegate the details to other administrators. However, he should be continually informed since he will need to make periodic progress reports to the board.[23]

Public Relations

The bulk of the president's time is spent in public relations. This responsibility ranges from making specific contacts to soothing ruffled egos, entertaining, and keeping up appearances. Since the president is considered to be the "voice of the institution," he must be very careful in taking positions. In a sense, the president can voice no personal opinion because any stand he takes will automatically be considered to be the position of the school. Therefore, he must "reconcile through his decisions and statements the emerging norms of a new generation and the prevailing norms of the establishment."[24] In every sense of the word, a college president must be a diplomat. He should meet with his constituents on an equal basis as well as cater to the needs of faculty, students, and administrators.[25] The president should also be willing to stay in the public limelight. Unfortunately, he and his family will live in a veritable fishbowl as a result of constant phone calls, entertaining, and, in instances, pranks.[26] The president will, however, speak up in terms of his value and value systems as they relate to organizational goals. This is all a part of leadership, and the president should be a leader, not a figurehead administrator.

Another important area within the realm of public relations is public speaking. If the president is an effective speaker, he will be bombarded with invitations. A firm rule of choice for a president is never to accept an invitation to speak on a topic of which he has little knowledge.[27]

Student Affairs

One constant complaint is that the president does not have enough time to directly work with students. However, this is the primary job of the dean of students, who is under the constant surveillance of the president. In this way, the president becomes an indirect influence on students. However, as primary decision maker for the institution, when conflict arises the president has the final authority.[28] More information on the specifics of student affairs is discussed elsewhere in this book.

Education Program

One of the priority decision areas for the president is in connection with the educational program. The president has the central responsibility to establish an institutional environment conducive to learning. Naturally he does not do this through the force of his own personality. The best results will be obtained from setting an example in the ways he works with his staff officers and other constituents of the institution.[29] In his own way, the president guides the various interests of the institution so that it will hold its own creditably among sister institutions and, if possible, show advances in many areas.[30]

Although many presidents do not feel that they control as much of the education program as they would like, they do act as overseers for top administrators of the institution. The president and the academic dean (the chief officer for instruction) should work closely in aligning programs and curriculum with institutional goals.[31]

Finally, the president is responsible for seeing that proper evaluation of programs and curriculum of the institution is completed. These evaluations should be made at all levels and program revision should be made based on their results.[32] One of the president's priorities should be to see that "quality control" exists in the educational program and that all students receive the finest education possible.

Faculty Selection

In most cases, the president has little to do with the selection of faculty members. He will usually perform a perfunctory interview, but if he has effective and efficient administrators he can trust them to make recommendations based on the goals of the institution.[33]

On the other hand, the president does play a role in faculty concerns. He should influence the faculty and in turn be influenced by them in the achievement of institutional goals. In so doing, a reciprocation of philosophies occurs which creates a better learning environment.[34]

Evaluation of the President

As the chief executive officer in a college or university, a president must have a tough mind and a tough body. In the words of M. A. F. Ritchie, "A timid soul with a fragile frame won't last very long."[35] The president is the primary decision maker in matters concerning finance, physical facilities, public relations, student affairs, and the education program. In coordinating the above areas, the president will probably supervise three or probably four chief administrators. Since these people are of high abilities, he must constantly strive to always be one step ahead of them in order for the team to work effectively. This requires skill and diplomacy as well as regular share sessions of intimate institutional problems. The president must also implement and integrate the board of trustees' action with the college operation in addition to keeping the board informed of school activities. In summary, he or she must think, act, and most of all, care. A president must be able to give above and beyond the specific duties of the office.[36]

ACADEMIC DEAN OR VICE PRESIDENT OF INSTRUCTION

The individual in the institution with his hand on the pulse of the education program is called by a variety of titles, including dean of instruction, vice president of academic affairs, academic officer, and academic dean. The term academic dean will be used here. This individual should be the "strong right arm" of the president.[37] His or her primary duties involve the education program, faculty, planning, staffing, organizing, leading, evaluation, and coordination.

Education Program

As noted in Figure 22, the most extensive duties of the academic dean involve the education program. In this area, he works in a variety of ways to achieve one comprehensive goal—to see that programs of the institution reflect its purposes. One way the dean seeks to accomplish this goal is by promoting instructional improvement. This is accomplished by coordinating supervision on all levels. Supervision and evaluation at all levels are important.

FIGURE 22
The role of the academic dean

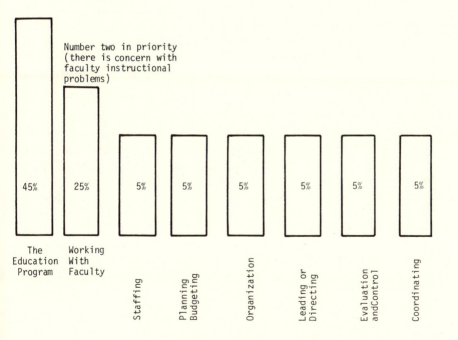

The number one activity
is this individual

Number two in priority
(there is concern with
faculty instructional
problems)

| 45% | 25% | 5% | 5% | 5% | 5% | 5% | 5% |

The Education Program | Working With Faculty | Staffing | Planning Budgeting | Organization | Leading or Directing | Evaluation and Control | Coordinating

(All should be related to educational program).

Miller, Bob W.
Priorities in the Academic Dean's Role

Coordination

The academic dean is also responsible for seeing that the curriculum of the institution reflects its admissions policy. As a prime example, the community college offers an "open door" admission which, in essence, states that anyone may enter. However, this type of policy attracts a diverse student population and, consequently, there must be programs on all levels for these students. Another important duty of the academic dean is to see that there is a clearly defined general education and liberal arts program. Specific courses should be listed for this program, and it should have requirements that are distinctly different from occupational curriculums. The academic dean is also responsible for seeing that the curriculum is "tight" and that the courses are well organized. Whenever possible, "excess baggage" courses that have been continued despite lack of interest should be removed. Once the curriculum is tight, the dean should check to see that the offered courses are organized in the most efficient and effective manner. Since the academic dean maintains files of course syllabi, he or she should review and/or suggest revision of these syllabi and then discuss the revisions with the individual faculty members. This may be delegated to a department chairperson. At the university level where graduate programs exist the dean must be sure that there are adequate curricula, staffing, financing, communications, and operations with governmental boards and support services. Finally, the academic dean must promote innovation. He or she should always be on the lookout for new teaching strategies and be encouraging when faculty members initiate such activities.[38]

Faculty

The academic dean, on one level or another, is involved with all facets of the faculty. Several of his duties involve checking qualifications of prospective faculty members before they are hired, promoting professional growth, committing them to purposes, and making schedules for faculty after they are hired. As personnel administrator on the campus, the academic dean houses files of all staff members. These files should be maintained and kept current, primarily for merit promotions. An effective academic dean promotes involvement of his faculty members in all areas of institutional policy.[39] Many of these areas are delegated to lower-level administrators.

Budget Planning

The academic dean guides and regulates the growth and development of academic programs in terms of funding. The dean reviews all the budget requests before sending them to the president for approval. If he or she is a top administrator, the president will receive a budget that is reasonable and justified. Programs need financing and they live or die depending on how much money the dean can provide for.[40]

Planning

Since the academic dean is most concerned with the growth and improvement of education, he must be involved in long-range planning. Striving for effectiveness and improvement of education will serve to motivate the dean to stay abreast of new programs for future implementation.[41]

Coordinating

The academic dean is a coordinator in two different areas: faculty and curriculum. He or she is a faculty coordinator striving to create a congenial learning environment with all departments working in harmony. The academic dean is also the voice of the faculty, and, in this capacity, he must provide guidance when possible. The goal in conflict between faculty and administration is to initiate creative consensus rather than poor compromise.[42]

The academic dean is also the curriculum coordinator. He schedules classes and final exams, makes classroom assignments, assists in preparing course outlines and selecting instructional materials. Since he is the chief academic officer, his counsel is often sought in all areas concerning the curriculum program.[43] In many cases there are deans of several colleges and schools in between the academic dean and the department chairperson. These divisions are usually colleges of education, business, arts and sciences, music, continuing education, and so forth. When these administrative officers are referred to as deans, the academic dean is usually classified as vice president.

Evaluation of the Academic Dean

The chief academic officer of the institution is the academic dean, who is most concerned with supporting institutional purposes with a strong education program. He works to improve the education program through coordination of evaluation, development of a strong liberal arts program, analysis of curriculum offerings, perusal of course organization, and encouragement of innovation.

The academic dean is also heavily involved in his role with faculty at all levels of professional growth and development. In hiring, he must take a comprehensive view of the needs of the whole institution as well as examine specific qualifications of the individual applicant. The academic dean is very concerned with faculty morale, so he strives through organization of departments, faculty loads, commitment to purposes, and professional growth to establish a working climate of balance and variety. In addition to these duties, the dean is also instrumental in the coordination of the annual budget for the academic areas, is heavily involved in short- and long-range planning, and is a coordinator of faculty and instructional specifics. At his disposal at any time is a complete supply of faculty members as well as course offerings.

DEAN OF THE LEARNING RESOURCE CENTER

The traditional library of yesterday has been replaced by comprehensive instructional media centers, called a learning resource center (LRC). This evolution has called for a new dean with comprehensive duties and specialties. These duties include the education program, personnel administration, facilities, budget, and evaluation. (See Figure 23.)

FIGURE 23
The role of the dean of the Learning Resource Center

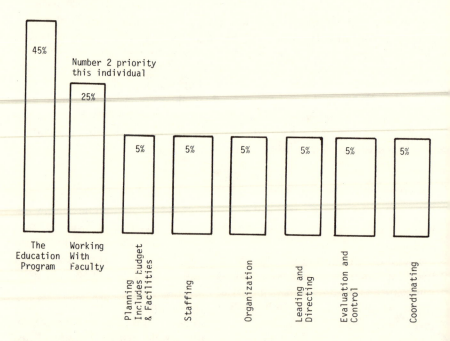

Miller, Bob W.
Priorities of the Dean of Learning Resource Center

Education Program

The LRC is the foundation for any education program. Research as well as techniques for improved instruction are located in this facility. The task of the dean is to effectively and efficiently *support* the education program through the LRC. He is also responsible for the preparation and dissemination of information to administration, faculty, and students regarding activities, services, and materials.[44]

Staffing and Personnel Administration

Since LRCs are complex, they require an administrator who is able to manage a large professional staff. The dean of the LRC must coordinate the hardware and software areas so that both work as a smooth total operation. Within the auspices of his job, the dean is responsible not only for hiring a professional staff but also for acquainting all staff with the specific duties of their jobs.[45]

Facilities

The dean of the LRC should be a primary consultant for planning of any new or expanded facilities. He is responsible for space utilization as well as arrangement of facilities to create the most conducive atmosphere for learning.[46]

Budget

The dean of the LRC is also responsible for the preparation of the LRC budget. His prime emphasis in this area involves the coordination of the budget in all areas with the goals of the institution. In order to do this, the dean should not only consult with the other professional staff to ascertain their needs but should present and justify the final budget to the administration.[47]

Evaluation

Another important duty of the dean of the LRC is systematically to evaluate LRC materials and services. Day-to-day pressures tend to make administrators lose sight of long-range goals. Systematic evaluation occurs at the following levels: dean's report, faculty questionnaire, student questionnaire, and visiting consultants' suggestions. This type of evaluation serves to promote the operation of the LRC for peak efficiency.[48]

Evaluation of the Dean of the LRC

The goal of the LRC is the *support* of the education program in the most efficient manner. This goal is best achieved under the direction of a competent LRC administrator, a dean who hires and directs a professional staff, plans and utilizes space well in facilities, prepares a feasible budget, and supports the education program in theory and fact.

DEAN OF STUDENT DEVELOPMENT

The most recent dean's level position to be added to the hierarchical structure of the college or university is that of the dean of student development. This title is so new that in many institutions it is still under the auspices of the student personnel administrator. However, the trend of the future is toward the development of the total individual and, therefore, in years to come, the student personnel administrator will most assuredly be replaced by a dean of student development. His specific duties will include student growth through the education program, reporting and planning, personnel, evaluation, and budget. (See Figure 24.) Additional chapters of this book emphasize student development.

Education Program

The primary responsibility of the dean is to coordinate an office of student development that is congruent with the purposes of the school. Within these purposes is the assumption that institutions are committed to the total development of the student, not just his intellectual development. Several primary areas that the dean of student development coordinates include counseling, psychological, and health service responsibilities; advising international students; academic advisory and tutorial programs; testing, measurement, and research; freshman orientation; and special programs. The dean of student development is responsible for the cohesion of all these and other areas as they relate to the student and the educational program.[49] He is responsible with the academic dean for all educational programs to see that each educational activity is integrated.

Reporting and Planning

Unfortunately, many new programs in institutions come and go without anyone's knowledge of their existence. The dean must make certain that this does not happen with the student development program. He is the person who must report and inform the campus of his activities and, in essence, draw a commitment from the entire campus. The dean of

FIGURE 24
The role of the dean of student development

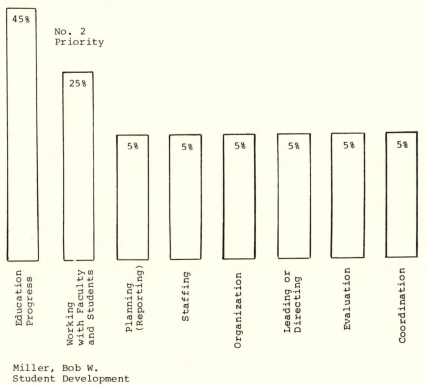

No.1
Priority
(Interpreting
of Student
Services and
Academic Programs)

45%

No. 2
Priority

25%

5%   5%   5%   5%   5%   5%

Education
Progress

Working
with Faculty
and Students

Planning
(Reporting)

Staffing

Organization

Leading or
Directing

Evaluation

Coordination

Miller, Bob W.
Student Development
Administrator's Role

student development is immersed in short- and long-range planning and therefore must report continuously on his activities to the entire faculty and administration. Utilization of formal and informal means of communication will greatly enhance the success of new plans if the dean of student development makes his actions widely known.[50]

Personnel

The student development dean is also responsible for staffing his department. Although student development is a relatively new field, programs in this area are now being offered from which he can draw qualified personnel. This eliminates the necessity for orienting student personnel graduates into student development practices. Because the concept of student development as an enrichment program for the total student is a new concept, graduates of student personnel programs would need philosophic orientation in order to be able to work in this type of position. The conscientious student development dean will hold miniworkshops and meetings for other faculty members to educate them in the areas of student development.[51]

Evaluation

The dean of student development is the prime instigator for evaluation within his area. Systematic evaluation of his department should exist to test theory, implementation of plans, the staff's effectiveness, and for goal outcomes. By promoting evaluation to achieve these goals, the student development dean will be able to revise departmental procedures to increase efficiency.[52]

Budget

Paralleling the responsibilities of other top administrators, the dean of student development must prepare a budget for his department. Evaluation results and planning will greatly facilitate this duty. They will establish the guidelines for future programs and procedures in addition to providing justification for budget needs. Results of evaluation measures supply concrete support for the dean of student development to use when he presents his budget to the appropriate administrator.[53]

Evaluation of the Dean of Student Development

Although all the administrators of a college or university are concerned about the student, the dean of student development has as his duty the enrichment of the total student. All the duties he is delegated, including the student education program, reporting and planning, staffing, evaluation, and budget, are supportive of this end.

DEAN OF BUSINESS AFFAIRS

The role of the business manager in an institution of higher education is no longer merely bookkeeping for the institution. Just as the president's role has changed throughout the years, so has the role of the dean of business affairs. These changes are normally attributed to the increase in immense campuses, huge student bodies, and diversity of educational programs.[54] The dean of business affairs today plays a major role in the management of all functions relating to buildings and grounds, student services, and goals of the education program.

Finance

As noted in Figure 25, the bulk of the duties of the dean of business affairs centers around finance. Part of his role is to supervise a staff that keeps up departmental accounts; to figure obsolescence, cost of materials, and insurance policies; to maintain inventories of facilities; and to report on income and expenditures at least once a month. In addition to

FIGURE 25
The role of the dean of business affairs

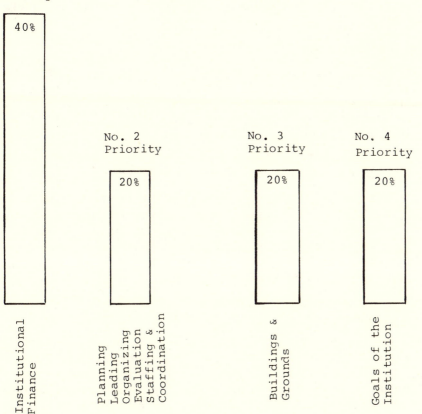

monthly reports he is also responsible for preparing a thorough and understandable annual financial report which he presents to the president.[55]

Generally, this dean is also the treasurer of institution. In this capacity he is responsible for the receipt, disbursement, and custody of funds. If endowment funds exist, he will probably also be responsible for their investment.[56]

Building and Grounds

Another important responsibility of the dean of business affairs is the department of buildings and grounds. This includes responsibility for the maintenance of plant facilities—utilities maintenance, minor and major building repairs, cleaning of facilities, allocation of space (both public and institutional), as well as aesthetic maintenance. Also included in this area is the business manager's responsibility for the safety of the institution. He executes this duty by supervising the security office. Therefore, any problems with allocation of space, maintenance or security of facilities, are handled directly by the dean of business affairs.[57]

Student Services

Through financial support, the business manager makes available various student services. He usually has supervision over dormitories and housing, food services, bookstore operations, and student accounts.[58] Without the business manager to act as accountant, these services would have difficulty remaining solvent.

Goals of the Institution

Although the business manager is not an education officer, he can and does influence policy making. He must work very closely with the academic dean to relate his activities to the education program that they are to serve.[59] The accounting regulations he imposes may affect departmental expenditures, which in turn affect the goals of the institution as achieved through its educational activities.

Evaluation of the Dean of Business Affairs

The primary role of the business affairs dean involves finance. This role through the years has increased in complexity due to the diverse growth of higher education. As a result the dean of business affairs will usually supervise a large staff to handle receipts, payments, accounts, purchases, and various other financial tasks. He must also maintain the physical facilities of the institution, coordinate the accounts for student services, and relate finances to the purposes and goals of the institution.

DEPARTMENT CHAIRPERSON

The next person in the hierarchical structure of the institution is usually either the department or division chairperson. Although there is some difference in these roles, parallels can be drawn from a discussion of the department chairperson. The tasks of the department chairperson vary considerably; however, major tasks include responsibility for an education program, budget, faculty, planning, and reporting.

Education Program

The chief responsibility of the department chairperson is to coordinate a department that will best enhance the education program of the institution. Some specific duties he performs to achieve this usually involve curriculum revision, scheduling of classes and sections, arranging teacher programs, and turning grades in to the registrar. In addition to these tasks, he may also teach courses in his own discipline.[60]

Budget

Education programs cannot exist without appropriate funds, and it is the department chairperson's job to try to obtain these funds. If he is an effective budget planner, he will ask his faculty to itemize and justify their needs. The chairperson can then objectively evaluate this data and prepare a feasible budget for the entire department. Once this budget is prepared, it is the chairperson's responsibility to present and justify it to the academic dean.[61]

Faculty

Within the area of faculty responsibility, the department chairperson is instrumental in interviewing and recommending new faculty for employment. He continues this role through staff development, new faculty orientation, productivity assessment, and handling faculty conflict. The department chairperson must also be skillful in facilitating interpersonal relations. Coordinating harmonious and efficient operations within a department requires a good diplomat.[62]

Planning

The department chairperson is concerned with his specific area of planning. In this area, he must plan the best possible programs to complement the goals and objectives of the department. This task should involve short- and long-range planning in which evaluation by students and faculty is considered.[63]

Reporting

In the area of reporting, the chairperson is responsible for two-way communication. He must report to administrators superior to him and faculty members subordinate to him. By reporting to administrators, the chairperson keeps superiors informed of his department's activities. Together, the department chairperson and the administrator may also be able to work out any small discord which might possibly become a major conflict. Therefore, if the chairperson has input from his faculty, he can work with administrators to solve any of these problems.[64]

Evaluation of the Department Chairperson

At the lower administrative levels, department chairpersons are the middlemen who serve to tie the faculty and administration together. These people are also instrumental in building the foundations of a strong education program. They do this by working with faculty members in hiring and development, devising short- and long-range planning, and reporting activities through appropriate communication channels.

MAJOR DIFFERENCES BETWEEN PUBLIC SCHOOL GOVERNANCE AND COLLEGE AND UNIVERSITY GOVERNANCE

Even though college and universities are interested in parents, spouses, and lay citizens, they are probably not as close to these individuals as are the public schools. Parents see their offspring each and every day at home, while many college students live away from home. In addition, most parents and lay citizens have learned the "Three Rs"; therefore they are more expert in these areas than they are in complex, specialized college subjects.

Students are not required to attend colleges and universities, whereas there is generally a compulsory education requirement at the public school level. Because of this factor there are more disciplinary problems in the public schools. This does not mean that colleges and universities have no disciplinary problems. It does mean that they do not have to put up with most problems, because students may be dismissed from class if they do not conform to basic policies.

In a similar manner, the public schools attempt to educate the masses; colleges and universities educate a more elite group.

The public school student does not have the freedom of movement of the college or university students. The college student may attend classes on Monday, Wednesday, and Friday, on Tuesday and Thursday, or perhaps only during the evening or weekend. The public school student attends classes Monday through Friday, usually during regular hours.

The teacher in a college or university also has more freedom than the public school teacher. The public school teacher works daily, while the college or university faculty member has more flexible hours. Their preparation hours may be very similar, however. Generally speaking, the university faculty member has to be concerned not only with effective teaching, but with publication, research, and services.

The public school teacher is involved in much routine classroom activity, while the college or university professor is involved with more internships and research experiences.

The college or university professor in most cases requires more education than his public school counterpart. He usually needs a doctoral degree and in many cases has the public school educator as his student.

What is the major difference between public school and university administration? Both administrative groups are charged with the five basic functions of management, planning, organization, directing or leading, controlling, and coordination. The major difference is that public school administrators deal more with the community, the public and parents. The college administrator deals with state agencies, lobbying, the instructional and student development programs. They also deal with issues of tenure, academic freedom, and faculty senates, and with many faculty and administrative meetings.

Although the hierarchical power structure of institutions indicates that some administrators are more powerful than others, it would be difficult for any of them to achieve efficient operation without the rest of the team. Each administrator, no matter how lowly, contributes to the operation of the institution and, in so doing, provides input that facilitates the smooth, efficient, and effective operation of a strong education program.

NOTES

1. Francis H. Horn, "The Organization of Colleges and Universities," in *Administrators in Higher Education,* ed. Gerald P. Burns, (New York: Harper and Brothers, 1962), p. 56.

2. S. V. Martorana, *College Boards of Trustees* (Washington, D.C.: The Center for Applied Research in Education, 1963), pp. 78–80.

3. James W. Thornton, *The Community Junior College* (New York: John Wiley and Sons, 1960), p. 118.

4. Martorana, *College Boards of Trustees,* pp. 78–80.

5. Harry J. Carman, "Boards of Trustees and Regents," in *Administrators in*

Higher Education, ed. Gerald P. Burns (New York: Harper and Brothers, 1962), p. 90.

   6. Martorana, *College Boards of Trustees,* pp. 85–86.
   7. Ibid., p. 86.
   8. Thornton, *Community Junior College,* p. 117.
   9. Carman, "Boards of Trustees and Regents," pp. 93–94.
   10. Martorana, *College Boards of Trustees,* p. 88.
   11. Thornton, *Community Junior College,* p. 117.
   12. Carman, "Boards of Trustees and Regents," p. 90.
   13. Thornton, *Community Junior College,* p. 84.
   14. Ibid.
   15. Ibid., p. 118.
   16. Ibid., pp. 82–83.
   17. Carman, "Boards of Trustees and Regents," p. 88.
   18. Thornton, *Community Junior College,* p. 116.
   19. Martorana, *College Boards of Trustees,* pp. 63–66.
   20. Louis T. Benezet, "The Office of the President," in *Administrators in Higher Education,* ed. Gerald P. Burns (New York: Harper and Brothers, 1962), p. 99.
   21. John J. Corson, *Governance of Colleges and Universities* (New York: McGraw-Hill, 1960), p. 65.
   22. M.A.F. Ritchie, *The College Presidency: Initiation into the Order of the Turtle* (New York: Philosophical Library, 1970), p. 17.
   23. Corson, *Governance of Colleges and Universities,* pp. 66–67.
   24. Richard C. Richardson, Jr., Clyde E. Blocker, and Louis W. Bender, *Governance for the Two-Year College* (Englewood Cliffs, N.J., Prentice-Hall, 1972), pp. 131–32.
   25. Richardson, Blocker, and Bender, *Governance for the Two-Year College,* p. 130.
   26. Ritchie, *College Presidency,* p. 57.
   27. Ibid., p. 43.
   28. Corson, *Governance for Colleges and Universities,* p. 64.
   29. Richardson, Blocker, and Bender, *Governance for the Two-Year College,* p. 127.
   30. Frank L. McVey and Raymond M. Hughes, *Problems of College and University Administration* (Ames, Iowa: Iowa State College Press, 1952), p. 8.
   31. Richardson, Blocker, and Bender, *Governance for the Two-Year College,* p. 128.
   32. Ibid., p. 133.
   33. Corson, *Governance for Colleges and Universities,* p. 63.
   34. Richardson, Blocker, and Bender, *Governance for the Two-Year College,* p. 130.
   35. Ritchie, *College Presidency,* p. 16.
   36. Benezet, "Office of the President," pp. 101–3; 108.
   37. Harold Enarson, "The Academic Vice-President or Dean," in *Administrators in Higher Education,* ed. Gerald P. Burns (New York: Harper and Brothers, 1962), p. 111.
   38. Raymond E. Schultz, "Judging an Academic Dean—The Dean's Role," in *Perspectives on the Community-Junior College,* eds. William K. Ogilvie and Max R. Raines (New York: Appleton-Century-Crofts, 1971), pp. 325–28.

39. Ibid., pp. 321–29.

40. Enarson, "Academic Vice-President or Dean," p. 112–13.

41. Ibid., p. 116.

42. Ibid., pp. 117–20.

43. Richardson, Blocker, and Bender, *Governance for the Two-Year College*, p. 158.

44. American Library Association, American Association of Community and Junior Colleges, and the Association for Educational Communications and Technology, "Guidelines for Two-Year College Learning Resources Programs," *Audiovisual Instruction* 18 (January 1973), pp. 50–61.

45. Ibid., pp. 55–57.

46. Ibid., p. 58.

47. Ibid., p. 56.

48. Carlton W. H. Erickson, *Administrating Instructional Media Programs* (New York: Macmillan, 1968), pp. 599–601.

49. Theodore K. Miller and Judith S. Prince, *The Future of Student Affairs* (San Francisco: Jossey-Bass, 1977), p. 159.

50. Ibid., p. 148.

51. Ibid., pp. 155–56.

52. Ibid., pp. 134–47.

53. Ibid., pp. 108–33.

54. McVey and Hughes, *Problems of College and University Administration*, p. 89.

55. Ibid., pp. 89–92.

56. Kenneth R. Erfft, "The Vice-President for Business Affairs," in *Administrators in Higher Education*, ed. Gerald P. Burns (New York: Harper and Brothers, 1962), p. 134.

57. McVey and Hughes, *Problems of College and University Administration*, p. 92.

58. Erfft, "Vice-President for Business Affairs," pp. 127–32.

59. Ibid., pp. 133–34.

60. McVey and Hughes, *Problems of College and University Administration*, p. 107.

61. James H. L. Roach, "The Academic Department Chairperson: Function and Responsibilities," *Educational Record* 57 (Winter 1976), p. 15.

62. Ibid., p. 23.

63. Ibid., p. 15.

64. Ibid., pp. 16–17.

6

Systems Planning in Higher Education Administration

A Case Study of Systems Approach in Administration

BOB W. MILLER

The primary purpose of systems utilization in administration is for futuristic planning, finding effective solutions to problems, bringing about quality control, avoiding repetitions and omissions in management and curriculum, and preventing crisis operation.

The process of systems administration is centered on a basic philosophy of administration, leadership styles and techniques, and mission of the institution. The process emphasizes that the institution will accomplish organizational goals by utilizing basic planning assumptions, objectives and goals, implementation processes, evaluation feedback, and modification or revision processes when necessary.

To initiate a systems approach to administration, an analytical approach must be utilized. This approach basically concerns analyzing the past and present strengths and weaknesses of the institution. A look at the past and present is necessary in order to plan effectively for the future. In addition, the process includes graphic portrayal (all items written or illustrated on paper) and checks and balances and is usually interdisciplinary. Any given part of futuristic planning involves predictions and should be researchable, to determine if the planning and predictions are effective and efficient.

Further involved in the systems approach to administration are the following. The process should involve a "people approach" instead of a "mathematical approach," especially since administrators are working with students and individual professionals in an educational organization. The process will result in the teaming of people in the management leadership aspects. No one person has the expertise to do all of the planning for one organization. To accomplish planning processes, research, surveys, group meetings, interviews, and analysis of behavior of individuals will become involved. The process will require external and internal motivation of both subordinates and superordinates in planning, implementation, and evaluation tasks. The process of modeling, common flowcharting, PERT, and other graphic designs will be utilized to illustrate basic planning documents. The process will require continuous evaluation to determine effectiveness and efficiency factors of the plan, and "recycling" or modification where the plan has been inadequate. The process will include constant projecting and planning toward the future.

DEFINITIONS

Curriculum flow chart—An administrative flowchart for curriculum revisions. Suggestions gathered throughout the campus from students, department chairpersons, division chairpersons, deans, academic and administrative vice presidents form a planning cycle which imparts the system design to improve and assure proper operation and procedure. It keeps the process on target.

Quality control programs—A program of checks and balances along the system design to check the quality of the present administrative flow and project the quality of the future process. Brings the programs together for flow analysis.

Recycling—A function in systems design that returns the process to a given point in the system to pick up an inadequate procedure and cycle that procedure back through the flow of the system.

System—An analysis of the past and present strengths and weaknesses designed into an administrative flow developed on goals and objectives for the future success of the administrative procedure.

Systems approach to administration—A planning approach to administrative procedure that analyzes problems, organizes past and present processes, analyzes present priorities, writes general statements of goals and objectives in long-range terms, and states short-range objectives in order that long-range goals can be reached.

INITIATING THE SYSTEMS APPROACH TO ADMINISTRATION

The important variables to initiate a long-range planning approach that involves quality control in an educational institution are: (1) analysis of past and present problems on a systematic basis; (2) analysis of the successes of past and present programs, concepts, individuals, groups, and organization; (3) analysis of past and present repetitions and omissions in any portion of the educational programs; (4) analysis of priorities for future planning in the educational organization; (5) writing general statements of goals defined as long-range priority items to be planned, implemented, accomplished, and evaluated; and (6) stating short-range objectives in order that long-range goals may be reached. (See Table 4.)

TABLE 4
One-year objectives to accomplish long-range goals.

Laissez Faire

Democratic

Autocratic

Scientific

Humanistic

Creative

Organismic

Other Styles

Administrative Theories
Bob Miller

HISTORICAL PERSPECTIVE ON A STRUCTURE TO PROMOTE PLANNING AND IMPLEMENTING CHANGES ON A SYSTEMATIC BASIS

During the 1970s, in a large college in the southwestern part of the United States, an academic dean, who was the chief instructional administrator of the entire college promoted leadership when introducing his "Systems Approach to Administration." A model was first designed in connection with the campus and, more specifically, with the academic dean's position. This process was followed by involvement of division chairpersons, then department chairpersons, and finally involved faculty members. The dean had served in prior administrative positions in the college and on other campuses throughout the state and nation; he had given a great deal of thought and planning in regards to designing and implementing this Systems Approach to Administration model. Once the academic dean had been on the campus for about two months he began the process of putting the plan in action. Several systems approaches had been utilized previously in business and industry and had been implemented from the classroom teaching standpoint (a systems approach to instruction); however, such an approach had not been accomplished from an overall campus or administrative point of view. This specific college had not been involved in total long-range planning, which is a part of the systems approach. In fact, few systems approaches to administration are likely ever to be thoroughly completed in the educational domain. Generally speaking, administrative leaders are not well enough educated in management, not well enough organized, or will not take the effort to devise a complete system for planning. Until this type of process is accomplished it is doubtful whether most institutions will be successful in meeting organizational goals.

An aspect important to the entire Systems Approach to Administration is the need for flexibility at all stages of the process in order for programs to progress effectively. During initiation of the project the academic dean secured the services of a professional systems specialist. Together the two educators developed a model for an "Administrative Systems Approach." They felt that it was important to analyze the past in order to plan steps for the future. In addition, they must know how far they had progressed in order to project five or ten years in advance. Executives in business and industry believe that an organization cannot really be successful unless projections are made a minimum of ten years in advance. Although education institutions cannot plan to this extent, they can project a number of years in advance.

The concensus of recent administrative thinking is that if we project at least five years in advance, education will probably be moving in the right direction. There have been too many "hit and miss" programs in education. Somebody designing curricula or programs grabs an idea here and another there, never analyzing the overall picture of the educational program. This is what the Systems Approach to Administration and "Quality Control Programs" attempt to do. These approaches assist in bringing instructional items, concepts, generalizations, programs management, and organizational goals together. Several years ago at Cape Canaveral, Florida, the academic dean spent two weeks watching scientists construct space vehicles, using the quality control system described earlier in this book.

On the campus of most modern colleges and universities there has been much discussion about long-range planning, quality control, development of priorities (especially for curriculum programs), staffing, facilities, financing, and innovations, as far as the five- to ten-year approach is concerned. Unfortunately, there has been very little successful action or implementation.

The aforementioned southwestern college had, as an objective and goal, prevention of gaps or omissions, repetition, and duplication in the curriculum. Using the systems approach, or long-range planning, many attempts were made to influence students, instructors, department and division chairpersons, deans, the president, the chancellor and the community. If professionals are not familiar with the philosophy of the administration and institution, it is not likely that they will all be headed in the same direction to benefit the students. A complete analysis was attempted in this area or context of planning. Once educators and students know where they are trying to go and what they are trying to accomplish, they are more likely to reach their destination. Important to the "Systems Approach to Administration" are:

1. Assisting the instructor in the facilitation of learning with students. (Which is what the instructional program is all about.)
2. Assisting the faculty member with learning spaces for students.
3. Assisting the faculty member with learning resources. (What delivery system does it take to get the teaching job done effectively?)
4. Assisting the faculty member with instructional design.

Anything concerned with the Systems Approach to Administration should connect directly with the instructional design and learning of students, whether it be buildings, staff, budgets, or programs. A problem which exists in most institutions is the utilization of what is already on campus, for example materials, laboratory equipment, and technological devices. The use of community resources is also important. Educational institutions will probably never attain full utilization of all facilities and equipment on each campus and in the community; however, this is something that educators should constantly strive for in the systems approach.

Any project planned or implemented by a college or university should revolve around the student, whether it be evaluation, communicating program objectives, defining faculty responsibilities, resources and resource staff, off- or on-campus facilities. Colleges should be organized to meet the needs of the community, state, and nation, whether they involve industry, business, education, culture, or recreation. Again, the number one concern should be the student. This concept cannot be overemphasized.

Another aspect important to this philosophy is the correlation of instructional and student service programs. Programs under the academic dean and the dean of student services usually are not teamed together in most institutions. Both areas should integrate and complement each other. Complete correlation of instructional and student service programs is important for total educational development of the student.

Instructors should do their utmost to relate to the individual student. The instructor should know each student personally and vice versa. This prime objective provides for a most effective and efficient learning process.

This leads us back to the Systems Approach to Administration. The approach should involve people, not mathematical models. An effective and efficient administrator will delegate, trust, and hold accountable his subordinates. The program as stated previously was started by developing a model that took into account the past, present, and future of the college. For the past, the decision was made that the items of high priority were program analysis, content of subject area, organization of the institution, goals of the institution, individual faculty-administration conferences, departmental meetings, division meetings, and potential professional improvement areas. Need analyses of teaching techniques and resources employed, and need assessment for the students were conducted. Also analyzed to some extent were the resources available to the college. Several research studies had been made of instructional costs per student, per semester, and per year. Short- and long-range objectives and goals were analyzed. Progress had been made in regards to instructional effectiveness, faculty evaluation procedures, and campus evaluation. None of these items were developed in any depth at that particular time.

The next task became, then, to analyze what was occurring at the present time in the educational process. A start was made by analyzing community and college programs, faculty objectives, division chairpersons roles, budgets, department chairpersons commonalities and relationships, faculty roles, materials requisitioned, materials needed, and materials that had been received and inventoried, in addition to those items which had been accomplished in the past. It became apparent that to progress the organization would have to project toward the future. Items that had to be analyzed in depth for the future were: (1) educational programs by subject areas; (2) faculty evaluation procedures; (3) total organization of faculty and their relationships with students and administration; (4) faculty, student, and administrators strengths, weaknesses, and potentials; (5) program and institutions evaluation procedures being utilized at the time and modifications needed to implement merit pay; (6) buildings and facilities; and (7) soft spots in management and leadership. (See Figures 26–28.)

The Systems Approach to Administration as it was perceived in this plan is a device which prevents omissions as well as repetition in the curriculum and programs. It is believed that this plan influenced students, teachers, department and division chairpersons, district administrators, and the entire community. The systems approach also involved long-range planning, quality control, priorities, staffing, facilities, programs, financing, and innovations. To accomplish specific goals, the decision was made to define roles for personnel and staff. Objectives of the educational programs on the campus also had to be defined in detail. Therefore, the question was asked, What are the goals and objectives of the campus? Samples of the answers received are: an open-door policy; university parallel programs; technical occupational programs; continuing education or adult education; instructor and professional counseling of students; students do not become numbers on a computer; each instructor should know the students personally; the college should meet the needs of business, industry, education, cultural development, and recreational activities; and the student is number one in priority.

A sample of campus program goals and objectives involved such items as meeting the individual needs of students, correlating instructional and student services programs, utilizing campus and community resources, and having the instructor do his best to relate to each individual student no matter what the student's potential might be. The job of educators was to provide the most effective and efficient instruction possible. Next the academic dean had to define his role in relation to the president, division and department chairpersons, and instructional faculty. The whole process can be reduced to the basic areas described below.

Academic dean (role or job description): (1) supervises the total instructional program of the campus through leadership of division and department chairpersons and faculty members; (2) constantly evaluates the total instructional program; and (3) constantly feels the pulse of all facets involving faculty and programs. This is accomplished in three basic ways: delegate, trust, and hold these same individuals accountable for results.

The next area for task definition is that of the division chairpersons.

FIGURE 26
Systems approach to administration: past

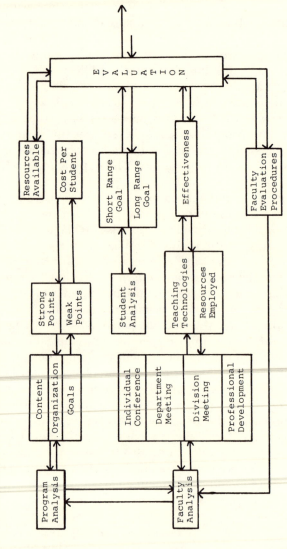

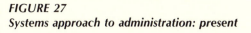

FIGURE 27
Systems approach to administration: present

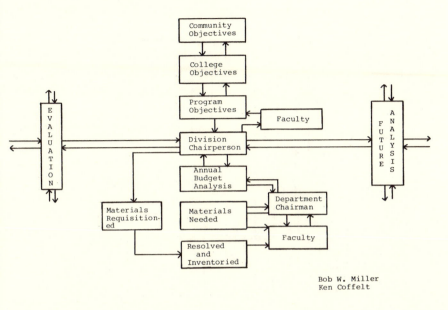

Bob W. Miller
Ken Coffelt

The academic dean cannot delegate away his responsibility on a legal basis. Even though many tasks are delegated, the dean still is legally responsible for these tasks.

Division chairpersons (role or job description): (1) supervise the total instructional programs of all departments within the division (includes planning, organization, supervision, administration, implementation, and evaluation) for department chairpersons, instructors, and students; and (2) provide leadership in production of effective and efficient syllabi.

Supervision and evaluation include visitation in classrooms; two-way, positive communication with instructors; student evaluation, and self-evaluation. Additional included items were: evaluation by video- and audiotapes; interaction analysis; staff development in evaluation procedures; professional development; continual evaluation of classroom instruction; curriculum revision; flexible scheduling; correlation of all subject materials and instruction; advanced placement with credit; the "teacher and staff" concept (which involves the master teacher, instructor, teacher assistant, teacher aids, and media technician); interdivisional team teaching; team teaching (modified/nonmodified programs); and released time for instructors for innovative educational programs (reduced load).

Thirty department chairpersons worked on the campus, and their

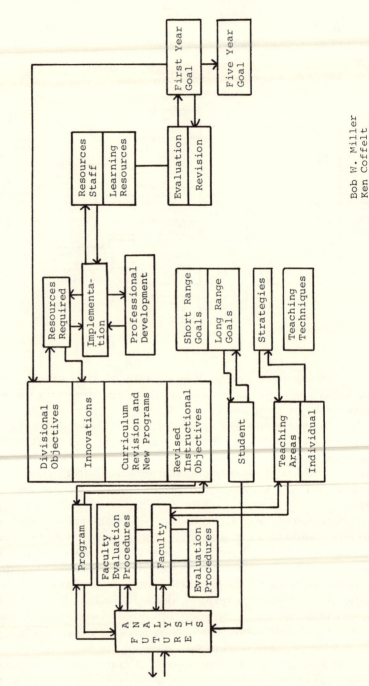

FIGURE 28
Systems approach to administration: future

Bob W. Miller
Ken Coffelt

roles differed from that of the division chairpersons and the academic dean.

Department chairpersons (roles or job description): (1) assist in preparation of the college catalog, curriculum brochures, faculty policies and procedures manual; (2) assist in planning professional development programs for the department faculty; (3) coordinate work with the bursar, registrar, bookstore, and student service personnel that applies to the department; (4) assist in the selection of department full- and part-time staff; (5) recommend policy to the division chairperson; (6) conduct departmental long-range planning; and (7) constantly feel pulse of students and faculty within the department.

Sample faculty responsibilities also were defined on the campus.

Faculty (role or job description): (1) utilize community activities and facilities; (2) place less emphasis on textbook teaching than on supplementary and learn-by-doing techniques; (3) emphasize meaning and understanding of concepts (involves and stresses understanding of structure and purposes of the disciplines for students); (4) curriculum design emphasizing the student, society, community-centered/general education, different levels of achievement (present as well as future); (5) stress importance of creativity in learning; (6) place more emphasis on "learning theory," or how students learn; (7) emphasize quality in teaching as well as innovative practical research which makes for improved programs and teaching; (8) place more emphasis on understanding and evaluation of self-concept (who am I? where am I going? how do I get there? what is my role in society?); and (9) place more emphasis on contributions to students' value systems.

In addition, for futuristic planning the following examples are listed to inform the reader of the types of items that should be included in long-range planning. No single area that involves organizational goals should be omitted in the Systems Approach to Administration. A sample of occupational programs projected for five to ten years includes: dental hygiene, dental assisting, operating room technician, dental laboratory technician, inhalation therapy technician, medical laboratory technician, occupational therapy assistant, sanitation technician, teacher aide technician, media library technician, child care, and photography technician.

Professional development and vehicle development include items that improve classroom utilization and software production for the learning of students. Samples are: educational television—two-way communication; videotape; dial access instruction; rearview projection; 8 mm single-concept cartridges; film strips and movies; slides, overhead, opaque, and visual software; and autotutorial approaches to instruction.

Projected sample methods and techniques of instruction include: inquiry development, miniteaching, microteaching, dyadic interaction, involvement of all students in class discussion, and problem-solving techniques.

Sample buildings and facilities that have been developed on the drawing board include: academic classroom building, auditorium, pods for team teaching, remedial diagnostic center for learning disorders, multimedia center, addition to faculty office building, technical-vocational building, model child-care center, and learning styles mall.

Another part of the systematic approach developed for the campus is a curriculum flowchart or curriculum revision process. Curriculum and instruction revision begins in October on the campus. Students and faculty make suggestions or recommendations in written form for further consideration during the revision process. The recommendations then go to the department chairperson, who modifies changes, makes additions to, or approves the proposal. This process is continued at each administrative level in the curriculum development sequences. Forms developed by campus and district officials for curriculum approval contain questions such as: What is the cost for staffing, multimedia classrooms, and other items required of the budget? What is the rationale or justification for the course or particular program? What do community environmental needs require for the future? How many students will be enrolled each semester?

From the department chairperson, the proposals go to the division chairperson. In this system an "open hearing," the date for which is set by the academic dean, is scheduled once the division chairpersons have accumulated all proposals from the department chairpersons. All interested students or faculty members are invited to this hearing, and anyone in the community may attend. The deans and president are not present at this conference because they do not want to influence decisions related to curriculum at this time. During these hearings, no one complains about other divisions' curriculum changes. Participants may make points, ask questions, have general discussions; but if anyone opposes some curriculum change that affects his or her division or department, he or she submits a written protest to the academic dean. The academic dean invites this person to the hearing of the division chairperson who proposed the curriculum change. The division chairperson and the academic dean converse on a one-to-one basis and go over all the proposals for the division. Division chairpersons justify proposals with rationales. The educator making the written protest is invited to present his or her argument and rationale before the academic dean. A number of questions are asked, and a defense of the proposals is carried on. The academic dean invites the dean of student development and the dean of learning resources to these hearings so that they may be informed regarding any programs that affect their administrative areas.

After these curriculum proposals are approved or rejected by the academic dean, the two or more academic deans of the different district campuses meet with the campus presidents and make their recommendations to the presidents on a face-to-face basis. Once the proposals are given to the presidents, the presidents modify (with approval of the academic dean) and submit them to the chancellor. The chancellor then makes recommendations to the board of trustees and to the various state agencies involved in the approval process. The entire process is illustrated in Figure 29.

STRATEGIES FOR WORKING WITHIN THE SYSTEM TO SELL THE SYSTEMS APPROACH TO ADMINISTRATION

In the process of selling the Systems Approach to Administration to subordinate division chairpersons, an unusual technique or strategy was utilized. It was stated earlier in this chapter that steps taken included: studying the quality control system and engineering of space vehicles at Cape Canaveral, Florida; hiring a consultant and building a past, present, and future model; and explaining the model and selling the concept to the campus president.

The past, present, and future model was then presented by the academic dean and the consultant to division chairpersons for their consideration. After the presentation, there was considerable pro and con discussion of the major concepts involved. Three of the division chairpersons were convinced this was an excellent plan. Two or three of the chairpersons were definitely against the Systems Approach to Administration model. Several other administrators attended these division meetings on a weekly basis. Those attending and participating in the meetings included the dean of student services, dean of learning resources, registrar, bursar, and director of the computer center. The purpose for their attendance was to integrate all aspects of the organization, especially for support services of the educational program.

Since two or three division chairpersons were opposed to the systems approach model for long-range planning, the dean and the consultant knew that additional strategies must be planned. The method they utilized is described below.

Convincing the Chancellor

The president of the campus was contacted and his permission sought for the academic dean to inquire as to whether or not the chancellor would be interested in long-range planning. The president agreed that the dean should contact the chancellor and present the overall plan to him. The dean appeared before the chancellor and presented the plan in detail. The chancellor was positive toward the entire planning model. The dean then asked if the chancellor would be willing to spend seven to nine days on the campus to have the long-range plans presented orally

FIGURE 29

Sample of flowchart curriculum revision

DEADLINE DATES

CURRICULUM AND INSTRUCTION PROPOSALS
(Steps in Making Changes)

STEP (1)
Faculty Members & Students
(Discussion & Recommendation)

STEP (2)
Department Chairmen (Discussion &
Recommendation) (Correlate with
other campuses)

STEP (3) - Nov. 20
Division Chairman - Should submit
material to all interested parties
beginning on this date and far
enough in advance of open hearings
to permit study

STEP (4) - Nov. 20
Open Hearings with Division Chairmen (Should point out changes, deletions, additions, implication to
other divisions (Adacemic Dean to
set calendar dates) Dean and President not to attend meeting (All
interested parties invited) Completed
by December 1

STEP (5) - Dec. 5
Comments, protests, objections to
Dean in writing in relation to
open hearings

STEP (6)
Deans & Division Chairmen
(Final report & discussion)
(Invitation issued to others at
request of Academic Dean)

STEP (7)
Academic Deans
Correlation Conference

STEP (8)
Recommendations from Deans to
Presidents (Catalogue changes
other than curriculum changes
due to coordinators of catalogue)

STEP (9)
District C & I Committee (2 Presidents
and 2 Deans) Resolvement Purposes

STEP (10)
Revision of forms on changes made by
Division Chairmen (Return to Deans)
(Return to President)

STEP (11)
Recommendation from President
to Chancellor

STEP (12)
Return of documents to campus
tration (Indicating
, deletions, approvals,
ons in writing from
lor's office; should
reasons for action

c Dean to coordinate all changes with Division
n in final form. Deans to correlate campus to
(Dean in charge to submit final recommendation
ows:

STEP (13) - Mar. 1
All catalogue curriculum changes due to Director of
Community Relations. Chancellor, Vice Chancellor for
Research Development, and Campus Presidents coordinate
reports to Coordinative Board and Texas Education
Agency

Advisory Committee must meet and
advise on proposed changes prior
to November 20

Bob W. Miller

and visually to him. Models to be presented were those of the academic deans, the president, and six division chairpersons. The chancellor agreed to this, and to bring along the vice chancellor for financial affairs, the vice president for research and development, and any other staff members that he might deem appropriate.

Facing the Division Chairpersons

The academic dean returned to the campus and related the information to the president. The next week during the division meeting, the chairpersons were given the following notice.

Six months from now the Chancellor, the Vice Chancellors and their staffs will come to the campus for seven to nine days to analyze your "Systems Approach to Administration," (long-range planning models) as well as the models of the President and the Academic Dean. The models will be presented by each administrator, both orally and visually. For the first time in each of our lives, we will have the opportunity to present total information on the past, present and future of education for students on this campus. The Chancellor will react to those things he sees as strength and weaknesses of our plans, and will make suggestions for future improvement.

Samples of items which will be projected for the future are as follows:

1. Educational Programs
   a. University Parallel
   b. Occupational
   c. Adult and Continuing Education
   d. Community Services
2. Professional development and inservice
3. Methods and techniques for instruction
4. Buildings and facilities to house education programs
5. Staffing for educational programs
6. Cost of financing educational programs
7. Curriculum flowcharts
8. How programs will be evaluated
9. Software and hardware for educational programs

Needless to say, when the division chairpersons found out that the chancellor and president were willing to participate and provide leadership for the plan, a new emergence of motivation took place.

After the division meeting, specific instructions and information were given to each division and the president in regard to time frame, support services for media, and printing. It was also pointed out that a model of each division's plan would be placed along with those of the president and academic deans, for display in the foyer of the administration building. Each division would write its plans and place the written plans in a pocket on its specific model.

Developing Individual Models

During the next six months, planning and production occurred everywhere from the president's office all the way down to each division office. Because departments and faculty were involved, the fever of planning became contagious. Even department and faculty members began to place long-range planning charts on bulletin boards and walls in their buildings. Everyone throughout the campus seemed to be in on the planning process. Eventually the time came for the appearance of the chancellor and his staff.

The next section presents an historical example of an actual systems model developed by a division of general studies in this southwestern college. This model describes by example the procedures explained in this chapter.

The System: A Look to the Future

MICHAEL M. MAYALL

Education should cause a student to know what he has not known before, to think about facts or ideas he hitherto has not contemplated, and to develop certain new attitudes, abilities, and modes of behavior. Unless education brings about some or all of these changes, it serves no real purpose. In the field of education, therefore, a system should serve the function of more effectively and more efficiently bringing about change in students.[1]

THE SYSTEMS APPROACH TO INSTRUCTION

A course or program must meet the needs of society and/or the individual. Needs are in a state of flux, therefore, the program must adapt to reflect this constant change. A developmental mode and delivery system must be utilized to assure that the product of the program is trained to perform in a changing societal situation.

The four basic elements of a systems approach, as shown in Figure 30, are: *input*—the capacity and interest of the student, plus the needs of industry; *output*—the student's terminal behavior; *resources*—institutional personnel, media, texts, etc.; and *operations*—the course or program. Attached to each of these elements and relating all four elements is *feedback*.

FIGURE 30
Basic elements of a systems approach

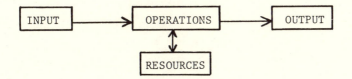

COMPONENTS OF THE SYSTEM

This section describes in detail the components of the system illustrated in Figure 31.

Society. Society establishes, controls through an elected board, and provides the funds for the educational institution.

Resources. Other institutions of society and industry are resources for the educational program. These resources provide facilities for work experience, consultant and advisory personnel, and an economics input.

Institutional management. Management is the professional staff selected by the controlling agent to administer the policies and goals of the educational institution. The institutional management contributes to the education model by: (1) establishing institutional goals and objectives based on its educational philosophy; (2) providing the educational facilities, auxiliary services, and financial support for programs; and (3) appointing qualified faculty and staff who reflect the goals and objectives of the institution.

Faculty. The faculty is the professional staff whose responsibility is to analyze and develop the various components of the model. They serve as the managers of learning.

Learner. The learner is the consumer of the model and is its expected product.

Learner capacities and competence. Characteristics of the learner consist of knowledge, skills, abilities, attitudes, motivations, and so forth.

Needs.

1. Needs of the learner. The student's needs should be considered in developing programs in terms of his or her interest, capacities, and competence.

2. Societal needs. The need for a course or program can be assessed in terms of national, state, and community manpower demands. An additional need could be for fulfilling the general education or cultural interest of society. The educational institution must constantly assist society in assessing its own needs.

A positive answer to the following questions is necessary before a decision about curriculum development is made.

Can well-qualified faculty be obtained?

Will suitable space for classrooms, laboratories, and shops be available?

Can tools, instruments, and specialized equipment of high quality be provided in sufficient quantity?

FIGURE 31

An educational model systems approach to instruction

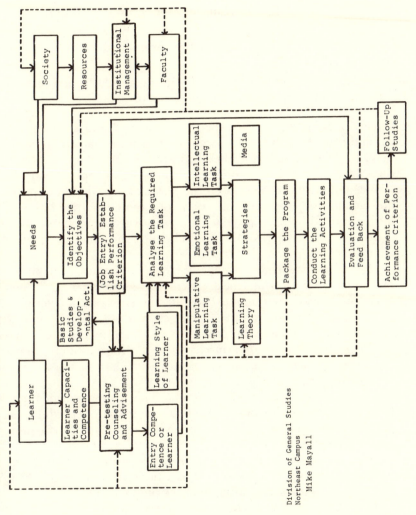

Division of General Studies
Northeast Campus
Mike Mayall

Will the budget permit expenditures for replacement of worn-out and obsolescent equipment?

Can coordinating, placement, and guidance services be provided?

Are students with the necessary ability and interest available in sufficient numbers?

Will all these factors result in a program that will satisfy student and community needs at a reasonable unit cost?

Can the institution sustain the program for a five- or ten-year period?

Can the manpower demand not adequately be accomplished by other programs in the region, state, or nation?

Identify the objectives. The specific knowledge and skills required to fulfill the needs of the course or program are ascertained in this component. In occupational education the instructional personnel should work directly with an advisory committee consisting of representatives of industry and business to establish the terminal behavioral objectives. Requirements for employees in entry jobs should be determined. This information should be provided by the advisory committee; however, the design of the curriculum should be the function of the professional educators.

The common learning or general education required for success and promotion on the job must be assessed. The educational requirements of the occupational program must be stated in terms of exit behavior objectives. These objectives refer to visible activity displayed or demonstrated by a learner at the time the program's formal influence over him ends.

(Job entry) establish performance criterion. Performance criterion is the conversion of behavioral objectives into a standard or test which evaluates the terminal behavior.

Pre-testing, counseling, and advisement. This component of the educational model provides information for the learner regarding the program of study and the opportunities associated with the curriculum. The two components, entry competence of learner, and learning style of learner, are established from data produced in the pre-testing, counseling, and advisement component. This component also interacts with the basic studies and/or developmental activities component.

Basic studies and/or developmental activities. Data may indicate that a learner has a general educational weakness and should be counseled into the basic studies program as an attempt to strengthen his or her general competence and improve his or her learning style. If the learner demonstrates a weakness in a particular area (mathematics, English, reading, and so on), remedial or developmental activities should be provided for repairing that area.

Entry competence of learner. Pre-testing reveals the input, or entry, capabilities of the learner. These capabilities are then utilized in determining the learning task required by the program. The entry competence also provides information pertaining to the starting point for the learner in the program and may lead to advanced standing or course waiver in the curriculum.

Learning style of learner. Additional data indicated by pre-testing is the learning style of the learner. This information is useful in studying the learning task.

Analyze the required learning task. The performance criterion is what the learner is expected to exhibit in the output component (achievement of performance criterion). Analysis of learning tasks identifies the learning required to enable the learner to demonstrate the performance task.

Intellectual learning task. The behavior objectives in the cognitive domain are analyzed as the intellectual learning tasks. These tasks involve mental and intellectual processes (memory, understanding, problem-solving generalization, concept, and so forth).

Emotional learning task. Emotional learning tasks stem from the affective domain of behavioral objectives. These learning tasks are associated with the feelings and attitudes of the learner.

Manipulative learning task. Manipulative learning tasks are those requiring motor skills that primarily utilize muscular coordination. These tasks stem from the behavioral objectives in the psychomotor domain.

Learning Theory—Strategies—Media. The concern in these components is the identification of everything that must be done by the components to attain the learning task. One must consider the various theories of learning; the strategies, methods, media, and other resource materials that can be utilized in accomplishing the learning tasks. In this phase our interest is in the organization and selection of program content along with the various alternatives to accomplishing the learning experiences.

Package the program. Packaging the program is the final organization of the program content into different courses along with the selection of instructional approaches and resource materials from the various alternatives. In this component catalog course descriptions are written, detailed course syllabi are constructed, and software materials are developed.

Conduct the learning activities. Scheduling the learning activities involves the decision of when (dates and time), where (location), and by whom (assignment of instructor) these activities will occur. Students must be enrolled and formal instruction be conducted.

Evaluation and feedback. Evaluations are made for the purpose of determining if the objectives of the model are being achieved and if any adjustments to the model are required to improve the achievement of those objectives. If a learner is able to demonstrate proficiency with performance criterion, then he moves into the achievement of performance criterion component and becomes a product of the model. Feedback, or quality control, in the model assists the designer in adjusting or reassessing: (1) needs of the learner and society; (2) inputs of societal resources, institutional management, and faculty; (3) objectives of the program and the job entry performance criterion; (4) entry competence and learning style of the learner resulting from the pre-testing and counseling; and (5) required learning task of the course or program along with the selection of the most effective and economical instructional approach in meeting these tasks.

Achievement of performance criterion. The learner reaches this component by being able to exhibit an output performance relative to the terminal behavior objectives of the course or program. The learner is thus a product of the educational model.

Follow-up studies. Follow-up studies provide feedback into the model after a product has graduated or completed the course or program. Studies should be conducted at specific intervals after the project's completion date.

DEPARTMENT OF BASIC STUDIES

Philosophy

General

1. The Basic Studies program attempts to combine remedial skill education with college level cognitive and affective curricula.
2. The Basic Studies program may be viewed as a service department for the campus insofar as it prepares some of its students for success in A.A. and A.S. programs.
3. The Basic Studies program fosters the philosophy of the open door by providing a success niche for students who may find little success (initially at least) in other programs and courses.

Specific. Basic Studies allows students to:

1. realistically assess themselves.
2. enrich their interpersonal experiences.
3. have a successful educational experience, especially where Basic Studies is the student's educational experience.
4. obtain a general educational foundation.

Five-Year Projection (Case Study)

Basic Studies is five content areas plus reading. It tries to take the relevant and make a general education for its students.

1. Greater emphasis on reading skills in the content areas; this emphasis will continue if it is found by evaluation in the succeeding years to be effective.

2. Greater cognizance of the affective content of our teaching; this emphasis will continue in the direction of humanizing education if it is found beneficial for our students and program.

3. Summer program to be evaluated for continuation or expansion.

4. Greater ecological emphasis in the content areas; this will continue until the environment is safe.

5. By the end of the second year portions of all the content areas will be packaged; further packaging will depend on evaluation of the packaging concept and of the individual packages themselves.

6. By the end of the second year, we will have prepared pre- and post-tests for a majority of the content areas. The data gathered from this will be used as a partial basis of program evaluation which will become continuous as soon as we have the measuring instruments and time. These should be refined in the future.

7. Development of a public relations program to reach students, community, and college, to continue through the life of Basic Studies.

8. We will try to refine the criteria for selection of Basic Studies students; hopefully, by better identification techniques we should increase the enrollment to a number approaching 180–200. This would of course mean that we should need two Basic Studies teams by the second academic year. Like so many of the items in this list, refinement of screening techniques is an ongoing process, as it has been in the past.

9. We would like to see the possibility of scheduling one large lecture period per week per class; this desire continues through the years until it is fulfilled, or perceived as no longer necessary.

10. A progress report should be written at the end of the first year; then, every two years.

11. By the third year, a two-year general education program should be instituted as part of the continuing search for the successful placement of our students here at the college.

12. After the first academic year, the emphasis in this document will be none save for the note that most, if not all, of items 1–11 are merely ways of defining what should be done in the Basic

Studies program. Items 1–11 are thus continuous in that evaluation, and feedback will take place with respect to them in the second through fifth years and beyond.

DEPARTMENT OF BEHAVIORAL OCCUPATIONS

Purpose

Improvement of instruction is basic to the rationale for the establishment of programs within the Department of Behavioral Occupations. Our role is to train paraprofessionals for an educational setting or for organizations that give full- or part-time care of children. This may be in a public or private setting or in the educational program of business or industry.

The use of paraprofessionals in educational settings is in its infant stage, and indications are that we are witnessing the beginning of a booming era. Emphasis on individualized instruction, early childhood education, new state legislation, the U.S. president's call for adequate care for children of working mothers, new dimensions in education such as differentiated staffing, plus a growing shortage of money present a convincing picture for training people to meet these manpower needs, as shown in Figure 32.

FIGURE 32
Department of behavioral occupations

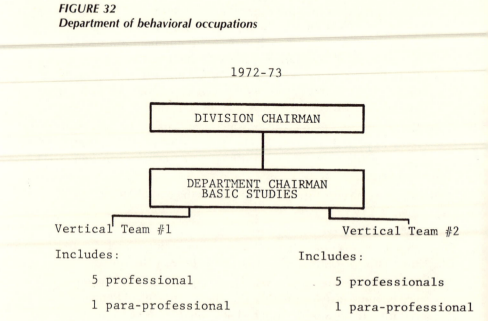

1972-73

DIVISION CHAIRMAN

DEPARTMENT CHAIRMAN
BASIC STUDIES

Vertical Team #1   Vertical Team #2

Includes: Includes:

   5 professional   5 professionals

   1 para-professional   1 para-professional

If we are to properly train our students, we must have adequate space, equipment, supplies, and staff. Otherwise we will only continue the mediocrity that is all too prevalent in our current educational settings.

This department shall strive to provide the maximum in learning and to develop within the student:

1. An understanding of the basic philosophy of modern education.

2. Knowledge and understanding of child growth and development including the physical and psychological needs of all children.

3. Knowledge and understanding of the importance of the family and parent-child relationships and interaction: the place of the young person in his family and culture.

4. Knowledge and understanding of a desirable working relationship as a member of a team.

5. A true understanding of the role of the paraprofessional.

Objectives

The following specific objectives have been adopted and will apply to the named program which operates within the Department of Behavioral Occupations.

Child Development Programs.

1. To provide the student with an understanding of his role and responsibilities as a primary caring person on the child development team in a day-care facility or a full-time care facility.

2. To familiarize the student with the basic qualities desired in an ideal child development person.

3. To teach the student proper methods of job management as related to the structure and service provided by the particular child development facility.

Teacher Assistant Program.

1. To enable student to be proficient in performing routine clerical tasks common to a classroom teaching situation.

2. To instruct the student in techniques and methods of assisting the teacher in classroom activities.

3. To instruct the student in the preparation and reproduction of instructional materials.

4. To familiarize the student with audio-visual equipment com-

mon to classroom instruction; to teach the student how to properly use the equipment.

5. To familiarize the student with routine library skills associated with the acquisition, organization, preparation, and preservation of library materials.

6. To provide instruction in the supervision of pupil activities outside the classroom.

Instructional Media Technician.

1. Exhibit appropriate utilization techniques and operating procedures for the various types of equipment.

2. Develop administrative skills in the various functions of an educational media program.

3. Prepare graphics, transparencies, still and motion pictures.

4. Exhibit appropriate utilization techniques associated with the acquisition, organization, preparation, distribution, and preservation of different types of media.

Department Goals

The first departmental goal is to develop curricula in the occupations that will be effective in the training of personnel to meet future certification requirements of state agencies.

1. Programs within this department have been established to train paraprofessionals either for an educational setting, residential homes, or for educational programs in business and industry.

2. As the curriculum continues to be developed, methods for effective teaching will have to be determined.

3. Liaison with state agencies, local agencies, and business and industry has been and must continue to be established. Personnel from these agencies must be utilized in planning curricula. Likewise, we should consider proper utilization of students we train and work with these agencies in effectively utilizing paraprofessionals.

To fully implement our behavioral occupations programs, plans must be formulated. Public schools, private day-care centers, residential homes, and business and industrial settings are and will continue to be utilized. However, the college will have to furnish adequate facilities for its part of the training.

1. Special day-care facilities will be needed in addition to classroom space.
2. Equipment for such a facility will be needed.
3. Additional laboratory space will be needed for the Instructional Media Technician Program.
4. Equipment—in addition to that utilized by the Learning Resource Center—will be needed.
5. A model day-care preschool program must be planned and implemented.
6. Additional teaching materials will need to be developed and/or commercially purchased.

To fully meet the needs of the community, it will be necessary to go into the inner city so that we may also train parents of the children that the paraprofessionals will be serving.

Five-Year Projection

A. Proposed Projects:

1. Further development of program for teacher assistants.
   a. Completing syllabi for courses in this program.
   b. Evaluating courses which have been taught.
   c. Exploring the possibility of redirecting one course in program and allowing it to be used as a practicum.
   d. Exploring possibilities of providing an opportunity for students to do further branching in program; allowing them to specialize in particular areas so that they might be better equipped to serve as assistants. Areas of specialization might include: Serving as assistants to counselors, special education, English, math, business, foreign language, and so forth.
   e. Planning and conducting a summer workshop for aides, assistants, teachers, and administrators from area schools. The purpose of such a workshop would be to promote the effective utilization of aids and assistants.
   f. Developing selective type criteria for admitting students to program.
   g. Contracting with students for work in particular courses.

2. Further development of program in child development (child care).
   a. Completing syllabi for courses in this program.
   b. Evaluating courses that have been taught.

    c. Exploring avenues for recruitment of students.
    d. Developing guidelines for a model day-care preschool program which would be operated in the Child Development Center.
    e. Contracting with students for work in particular courses.

3. Further development of Instructional Media Technician Program.
    a. Developing syllabi for courses taught in this program.
    b. Evaluating courses which have been taught.
    c. Exploring possibilities for recruitment of students; developing selective type criteria for admitting students to program.
    d. Adding additional equipment this year to update present laboratory.
    e. Packaging portions of some of the courses required in program.
    f. To attempt to have an open lab so that students may utilize equipment and facilities at their convenience.
    g. To contract with students for work in particular courses.

Additional Staff Requirements

First Year

1. 1 FTE (Full-Time Equivalent) coordinator of Instructional Media Technician Program.
2. 1 FTE paraprofessional—to be used to man openlab as well as to help in other areas.

A. Proposed Projects:
    1. To provide training for people of the inner cities in the areas of child and family management. (Initially, we would go into the inner city to do this training.)
    2. To begin concentrated effort of software development for all three programs within the department. This would be in the form of audiotapes, slides, transparencies, videotapes, films, printed materials, etc.
    3. To explore possibilities of adding another program for training paraprofessionals. This program would be added for the purpose of training auxiliary personnel in social casework. This would necessitate a study conducted by the Office of Program Development to determine the feasibility of such a program.

4. To study the possibility of a core curriculum for the three programs now in operation in the Behavioral Science Department. Studies currently being conducted by the Texas Education Agency indicate there is some thought being given to including Early Childhood Education under education rather than home economics.

Additional Staff Requirements

Second Year

1. 1 FTE instructor who should qualify to teach in two of the three programs (Teacher Assistant and Child Development).
2. 1 FTE paraprofessional to be used in Teacher Assistant and Child Development programs.
3. 1 FTE secretary.

Third Year

A. Proposed Projects:
   1. To design and equip a media laboratory in a facility that would provide adequate space for a class of twenty-five students.
      a. Cost: approximately $50,000.
      b. Size: 2,200 square feet plus 200 square feet for office and storage: (1) 900 square feet classroom space, (2) 600 square feet equipment lab, (3) 1,200 square feet production lab, (4) 2,000 square feet TV studio, (5) 400 square feet individualized space for preview and recording (10' × 10' cubicles), and (6) 3 offices and conference room.
      c. Cost of supplies would depend to a large degree on the number of students involved in programs.

Additional Staff Requirements

Third Year

1. 1 FTE instructor who would qualify to teach in Teacher Assistant and Media Technician programs.
2. 1 FTE paraprofessional.

Fourth Year

A. Proposed Projects:
   1. To build and equip a child development laboratory that would provide adequate space for caring for thirty children.

(1,000 square feet indoors,
2,500 square feet outdoors.)
B. Additional Staff Requirements
1. 2 FTE instructors.
2. 3 FTE paraprofessionals

Fifth Year

A. Proposed Projects:
1. To conduct a pilot project on nutritional needs of children.
2. To fully implement child development laboratory.
3. To develop criteria for ongoing evaluation of child development laboratory.
4. To do additional packaging where studies have indicated a need.
B. Additional Staff Requirements
1. 1 FTE instructor.

DEPARTMENT OF DEVELOPMENTAL STUDIES

Purpose

1. To reinforce skills (such as reading comprehension, vocabulary development, study skills, basic writing skills, and written com-

FIGURE 33
Organizational changes: 1971–1972

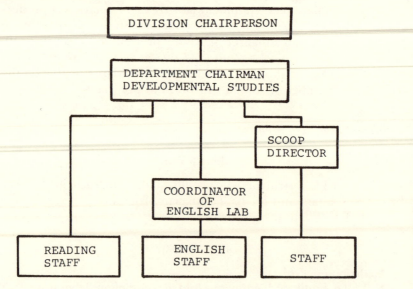

FIGURE 34
Organizational changes: 1972–1973

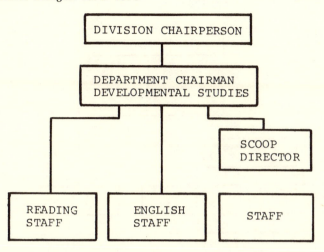

FIGURE 35
Organizational changes: 1973–1974

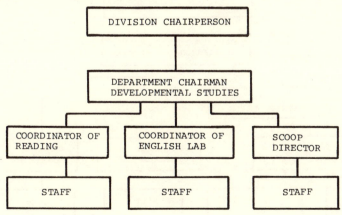

FIGURE 36
Organizational changes: 1974–1975

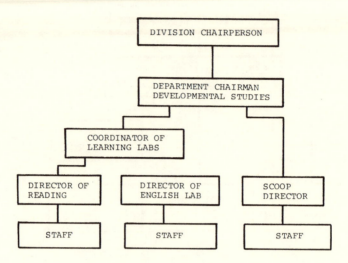

FIGURE 37
Organizational changes: 1975–1976

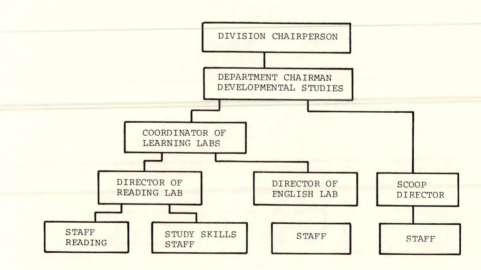

position) that are needed in order for the student to succeed in every area of college work.

2. To give the physically handicapped student an equal opportunity to succeed in college on a par with the average student; for example, to act as liaison between the student and faculty members who have such students in their classes; to supply whatever is necessary in special equipment and tutoring; to make their learning effective; to make them an integral part of campus life rather than isolate them in a separate area.

3. To help students who have been out of school for a number of years to regain confidence in their ability to succeed in college as they improve their reading and language skills.

4. To provide for students who are not working toward a degree or certificate but who are interested in improving their reading and language skills.

Programs and/or Projects

1. Learning center for physically handicapped.
2. On and/or off campus head-start classes.
3. English-language laboratory.
4. Saturday classes.
5. Study skills open laboratory.

ORGANIZATIONAL CHANGES

Figures 33 through 37 and Tables 5 through 8 illustrate organizational changes over the five-year period.

TABLE 5
Projected number of students

Year	Reading	English
1971-72	275	180
1972-73	325	270
1973-74	375	300
1974-75	425	330
1975-76	475	360

TABLE 6
Projected faculty needs

Subject	Year	Professional	Para-professional
Reading	1971-72	2+ (Equivalent)	
English	1971-72	1+ (Equivalent)	
SCOOP	1971-72	3	7 (Equivalent)
Reading	1972-73	3 (Equivalent)	
English	1972-73	2 (Equivalent)	
SCOOP	1972-73	3	7 (Equivalent)
Reading	1973-74	3 (Equivalent)	1
English	1973-74	2 (Equivalent)	2
SCOOP	1973-74	4	8 (Equivalent)
Reading	1974-75	3 (Equivalent)	2
English	1974-75	2 (Equivalent)	3
SCOOP	1974-75	4	8 (Equivalent)
Reading	1975-76	3 (Equivalent)	3
English	1975-76	2 (Equivalent)	3
SCOOP	1975-76	4	8 (Equivalent)

TABLE 7
Facilities, equipment, etc.

```
1971-72       Same plus space for SCOOP core.

1972-73       Room for English Lab

1973-74       Enlarged Reading Room and additional equipment;
              1 classroom available at all hours near the
              Reading Room; additional classroom for

                   Developmental English.

1974-75       Same

1975-76       Same
```

Changes in Content (New Courses)

1. Report writing.
2. Mini speed-reading course—two hours for eight weeks—one semester-hour credit.

Changes in Types of Students

There will be a greater number of students who are not in the university parallel program but who are interested in the certificate and technical programs and in self-improvement. (Development of the regional airport will bring large numbers of skilled and semiskilled workers and their families into the area.)

Changes in Methodology

1. Increasing the use of instructional packages and programmed materials in English 1203.
2. Allowing students to contract for a grade and/or credit, thus enabling them to finish the course prior to semester's end or allowing them to continue the course beyond the semester's end if need be.

TABLE 8
Staffing summary (full-time only)

	BASIC STUDIES	BEHAVIORAL OCCUPATIONS	DEVELOPMENTAL STUDIES
Present Staff	5	2	2
1971 Additional Staff	0	1 Professional 1 Para-Professional	3 Professional 5 Para-Professional 2 Clerical
1972 Additional Staff	5 Professional 1 Para-Professional	1 Professional 1 Para-Professional 1 Clerical	2 Professional
1973 Additional Staff	0	1 Professional 1 Para-Professional	1 Professional 1 Para-Professional
1974 Additional Staff	0	2 Professionals 3 Para-Professionals	0
1975 Additional Staff	0	1 Professional	0
Total Professional	10	7	8
Total Para-Professional	1	5	6
Total Clerical	0	1	2

3. Permitting students to indicate their preference for the following methods of grading: credit or noncredit, pass or fail, letter grade.

4. Recommending students with unusually high performance records for advanced placement in English 1613.

NOTE

1. Stephen J. Knexevich, Program Budgeting (PPBS), (Berkeley: McCutchen Publishing Corporation, 1973), p. 330.

7

Personnelling in Higher Education

Staffing, Recruiting, and Evaluating

MARY J. OSENTOWSKI

The primary reason students attend college is to gain an education. In order for this goal to be reached, it is essential that the college have competent personnel who will help those students receive an education. When 70 to 80 percent of a college's budget is allocated for faculty and administrative personnel, a competent staff is essential for a public that demands the most for its tax dollar.

DEFINITIONS

Affirmative action—The use of selection procedures which have been validated to assure equal employment opportunity for all in order that discrimination may be avoided.

EEOC—The Equal Employment Opportunity Commission is a federal agency named to monitor instances of discrimination in all processes involving a minority constituency.

Equal Pay Act—Prohibits discrimination in pay on basis of sex.

Tenure—A provision offered teachers in educational institutions that provides for job continuance, academic freedom, protection of their constitutional rights, and the right to be employed.

FACULTY STAFFING

In situations where a new college or campus is formed, the staffing of personnel is a tremendous task, one that is handled primarily by a few top level administrators with the assistance of a personnel director. If a new campus is opened within an existing district, then some core personnel can be drawn from faculty members on established campuses. Personnel familiar with district policy may help the opening of a new facility run smoothly. Using experienced faculty members on a new campus provides those faculty members with new challenges and, in some situations, the opportunity for a change of role: instructor to dean, dean to vice president, or division chairperson to instructor.

The blending of experienced teachers with new personnel can provide the best of two worlds. The new personnel may bring innovative ideas to the campus; the experienced personnel may be able to assist in implementing the innovative ideas more expediently because of their familiarity with their institution's policy.

Hiring personnel for a new college also demands some priority setting. Should very specialized instructors be hired in order to build a strong program in one particular area, or should instructors with a wider range of capabilities be hired initially to serve the needs of a wide spectrum of students? This question can be answered by looking carefully at the school's philosophy and expectations as well as by undertaking a needs-assessment survey in the area the college will be serving.

Although hiring an entire staff for a new college may be a responsibility of some administrators in higher education, most administrators are faced with adding a few additional staff members each year. Whether hiring an entire staff or one new member, it is important that the philosophy and expectations of the school balance with the background, experience, and capabilities of the prospective employees. If the school's needs and the employees' needs are both met, the chances are excellent that the most-qualified candidates will be hired and the learning institution will reap the reward.

Guidelines for the Hiring Process

Guidelines have been established by most colleges to facilitate the hiring of new employees. Richard Kaplowitz has contributed a model which can be followed in hiring academic administrators.[1] His model, with some adaptations, can be followed in the hiring of faculty members as well as academic administrators.

As soon as a vacancy exists on a campus, steps should be taken to hire someone to fill it. One procedure that may help in filling the vacancy is the formation of a search committee. The makeup of this committee will depend on the position to be filled. If the position is one of faculty status, it would be logical that students as well as other faculty members and administrators serve on the committee. The use of a search committee not only provides a broader view for evaluating applicants, but it also incorporates the participative management approach; that is, allowing representatives of various segments of the campus to have a voice in the selection of an individual who will directly or indirectly affect those various segments.

Once the search committee is formed and the job description agreed upon, it becomes necessary to advertise the opening. Various methods can be incorporated: advertising in professional journals, contacting placement services of professional organizations, and contacting graduate schools. Another means of recruiting prospective employees is by contacting presently employed personnel. One college states in its policy manual that faculty members are encouraged to work with division chairpersons and other administrators to recruit superior instructors. A personal endorsement or recommendation by a respected faculty member should be given some attention by the search committee. This process may be utilized in the university as well as the community college.

Shortly after a position is advertised, applications will be received by the search committee. It is important that applications be acknowledged; those applicants who lack necessary qualifications for the vacated position should be sent letters indicating this, and those who pass careful review by the search committee should be contacted for additional reference material. Ideally, written correspondence with prospective employees should be in the form of a personal letter. If a form letter must be used, it is advisable to use a typewriter that types individualized form letters.

After additional credentials are sent by prospective employees, the search committee will review the material. At this point rejection letters may be sent to those individuals who do not have the needed qualifications for the job; a list of possible reserve candidates is compiled; and those with the strongest qualifications are contacted and asked to meet with the search committee for an interview. When a rejection letter is written it should be of a positive nature.

Ideally, travel and lodging expenses for prospective employees who visit the campus for an interview should be paid by the educational institution. The candidate will be more favorably impressed by the sincerity of the school's interest in him or her as a future employee if the school pays the expenses. If the college is on a limited budget, fewer candidates should be invited to the campus for interviews. An established faculty member or administrator could serve as a host for the prospective employee and provide lodging. This not only can make the candidate feel more at ease, but college personnel may have an opportunity to get acquainted in a less formal setting. The formal interview should not be eliminated, but in addition to the formal interview, an informal session may in this way be arranged by the host.

After the interviews, it will be necessary for the search committee to do some additional research. Telephone calls may be made to previous or present employers with the candidate's permission. The advantages of phone calls probably outweigh any disadvantages. Phone calls offer instant information about a candidate. Those giving information may feel freer to be candid in a telephone conversation than in written correspondence. Specific questions to be asked should be prepared before the call is made. A disadvantage of phone calls is their expense, and therefore this method of gathering information should be used only for the strongest candidates rather than for all applicants who, on paper, have the qualifications for the job.

It is now the time for the search committee to select the top two or three candidates and recommend these candidates to an upper level administrator depending on the vacancy to be filled. The search committee may give these candidates equal endorsement, or perhaps rank them according to the committee's evaluation. Again, depending on the position, additional interviews involving the candidates and upper level administrators may occur at this time.

If the search committee has carefully searched and screened candidates, at this point a job offer will be made by the institution. However, if none of the top candidates are acceptable, the committee may have to go back to review some of the applicants or to reopen applications for the position.

When a job offer is made to a candidate, the other candidates must be notified immediately. It is poor public relations for those candidates who are not offered a position to hear via the grapevine that they have not been hired.

EFFECTIVE RECRUITING

In staffing a new college or in hiring even one individual for a position, it is important that equal employment opportunity guidelines be followed. Compliance with federal laws and orders dealing with affirmative action in employment can make the difference between thousands of dollars in federal funds for grants and student scholarships or an investigation and lawsuits. The scope of this chapter will not permit detailed discussion of federal legislation, but a brief review of various laws and orders follows.

1. Title VII of the Civil Rights Act of 1964 (as amended by the Equal Employment Opportunity Act of 1972) prohibits discrimination in employment because of race, color, religion, sex or, national origin. The 1972 amendment strengthened the powers of the Equal Employment Opportunity Commission in enforcing this law.

2. Executive Order No. 11246 (as amended by Executive Order No. 11375) requires that all federal contractors or subcontractors with contracts over $50,000 or with over 50 employees develop and implement written Affirmative Action programs.

3. Revised order No. 4 (1970) as amended (1974) established the

steps involved in constructing a written Affirmative Action plan under Executive Order No. 11246 and included women as one of the groups to be considered in establishing any Affirmative Action plan.

4. The Equal Pay Act of 1963 prohibits discrimination in pay on the basis of sex.

5. Title IX of the Educational Amendments Act of 1972 extended the coverage of the Equal Pay Act and prohibits discrimination on the basis of sex against employees or students of educational institutions receiving federal aid.

6. The Age Discrimination in Employment Act of 1967 prohibits discrimination against persons aged forty through sixty-five in any area of employment.

7. The Vocational Rehabilitation Act of 1973 as amended prohibits discrimination against the mentally or physically handicapped.

8. Affirmative Action is also required under the Vietnam Era Veterans Readjustment Assistance Act of 1974.

There have been and are cases in the courts testing the government guidelines for these employment practices. Among the cases have been some of reverse discrimination, involving the white male candidate. An institution must advertise widely in order to gather many qualified applicants and then base its selection of an employee on the ability of that individual to meet the responsibilities of the job. Affirmative Action demands that the employer must make additional efforts to recruit minorities and women, groups that have been discriminated against in the past.

Educational institutions should, in their search for the most talented candidates, take the suggestion that has been offered to business firms by John Iacobelli and Jan Musczyk—to actively recruit minority and female candidates by selective advertising.[2] In addition to advertising in the regular media, publications directed toward the special groups should also be utilized; these may include the *Ladies Home Journal*, *Redbook*, *Ebony*, and *Jet*. Another suggestion encourages a program of flexihours and job sharing. This has been used in some educational institutions but could be encouraged even more.

In-house training programs also are used to encourage minority and female employees as well as the white male to broaden their educational training. According to Jane Rosenthal and Arlys Gessner, "Offering a degree of training which you are reasonably able to undertake as a means of making all job classes available to women and minorities will enlarge the pool of qualified people and bring about equity in employment."[3] In some educational institutions an internship program has been provided for individuals interested in administrative positions. Employees can apply to work for a semester as an "assistant" to the president or vice president. This provides not only excellent experience and training but an incentive for those individuals who think they might be interested in becoming administrators. This program could be an ideal training ground for women and minorities whose representation in administrative positions has been minimal.

Affirmative Action and equal employment issues are concerns that institutions of higher learning must be knowledgeable about. Numerous court cases in the last few years indicate how important it is that administrators be attuned to current legislation. Administrators and personnel directors must be aware of Affirmative Action guidelines not only in advertising vacancies but also in interviewing prospective employees. This will be discussed in more detail in the following section of this chapter.

INTERVIEWING

The interview is a vital part of the staffing process, and for this reason it is given a separate area for discussion in this chapter. Too often little time or effort is given to learning good interview techniques. The penalty for this may be the loss of the most qualified candidate or an unhappy employee who leaves the organization within a short time. If this occurs the educational institution will also lose money, because of the expense of recruiting qualified candidates. In addition to the cost of replacing discontented employees, poor interview techniques may also result in lawsuits from the federal government, for there are specific questions which may not be asked of prospective employees.

There are several reasons for conducting an interview. One reason, of course, is to become better acquainted with the candidate. The information on an application can be verified and expanded. If there seem to be areas of weakness on the written application, these can be probed and perhaps dispelled. It is also possible to gather new information that does not appear on the written application. Perhaps volunteer work with which a candidate has been involved could serve as excellent preparation for the position to be filled. If the application did not ask for experience other than employment records, the volunteer work experience may never be mentioned.

In addition to verifying facts and gaining new information, the interview also provides the institution an opportunity to sell itself to the candidate. At a time when there is a buyer's market in education, this may seem unreasonable. But outstanding candidates may have several job offers, and the impression the school presents to the prospective employee is important.

The interview is important from the candidate's point of view also, for he or she wants to learn all that is possible about the expectations and philosophy of the institution as well as the personnel and actual job requirements. It is important that the administrator or search committee, whoever is conducting the interview, realize that the format is not "we ask the questions/candidate gives the answers." The interview session is a two-way communication process, with information going from the candidate to institution representatives and also from college personnel to the candidate.

At the time of the actual interview, when the candidate arrives at the administrator's office, several considerations should be given. The interviewer should meet the candidate outside of the room where the interview is to take place. This less-formal setting may help the candidate relax before the interview begins. The interviewer should then escort the candidate into the interview room.

Environment can play an important part in any communication exchange, so it is important that no environmental conditions distract from the interview. The room temperature should be comfortable; there should be adequate air circulation, and sufficient light so that nonverbal cues can be viewed easily. The room should be reasonably quiet and there should be no telephone interruptions. Hopefully, the room for the interview can be arranged in such a way that a desk is not located between the interviewer and interviewee. Large desks may act as a barrier in the communication process. It is better if comfortable chairs can be arranged in a conversational arrangement.

Objectives of the Interview

In an effective interview several objectives should be met. The competent interviewer wants to secure sufficient information, but at the same time have a "pleasant talk."[4] It is also important to avoid any discriminatory questions. One way to do this is to ask questions directly relating to the job description. This will also help the general organization of the interview and help avoid the pitfall of asking personal, irrelevant questions. Questions that ask who, what, when, where, and how are also encouraged. The use of "probe" questions can add to the value of the information secured in the interview.[5] The interviewer has the responsibility of getting the needed information from the candidate and controlling the actual length of the interview. Some digression is acceptable, for it is possible that more can be learned about the candidate during one of these moments.

Kaplowitz offers some specific basic concerns that might be considered in an interview session.

1. Has the candidate troubled to learn at least something about the institution and the role to be filled? Were the materials that were mailed to the candidate read?

2. Why is the candidate interested in this specific position?

3. What strengths does the candidate believe he or she can bring to the position?

4. Does the candidate have broad concerns about the field of higher education?

5. Why has the candidate left previous positions? If changes were frequent, were they a reflection of good upward mobility, personal instability, or a series of unfortunate experiences? What is the candidate's time perspective for his or her next position? Why is the candidate currently seeking a change of position?[6]

In addition to the general concerns which should be considered in the interview setting, any person involved in an interview must be aware of lawful and unlawful question. As mentioned previously, questions that relate directly to the job description are the safest if the job description includes sound objectives for the position. Some general questions that may be asked can be garnered from those used in the business field:

1. In your most recent position, what would you say are some of your important accomplishments?

2. Considering these accomplishments, what are some of the reasons for your success?

3. What did you particularly like about the position?

4. There are always a few negatives about a position. What would you say you liked the least?[7]

The above questions could be repeated in referring to other positions the candidate had held. Depending on the position for which an employee is sought, questions may be asked about planning and decision making.

1. How do you do your planning; that is, what processes have you found useful?

2. How have you improved your planning in the last few years?

3. What are some examples of important decisions you have made?[8]

Other open-ended questions might be taken from the following list.

1. Some individuals keep a very close watch over their personnel, others are loose in control. How would you describe your style of control?
2. Would you describe your relationship with your last three superordinates?
3. Give an example of a situation in which you have been very effective relating to others.
4. Describe one idea that you implemented that you are proud of.[9]

Some areas should not be discussed in an interview unless the subject matter is directly job related. These include national origin, marital status, sex, race, religion, and age. Educational institutions and all personnel involved in interviewing should be aware of questions to avoid in these areas. Questions to be avoided are as follows:

Sex and Marital Status.
1. Does your husband depend on you for finances?
2. Who will baby-sit your children while you are working?
3. Are you a believer in ERA principles?
4. Are you married?

Race.
1. Do you like having to work with members of a different race?
2. Are "you as a minority" good at working with numbers?
3. What are your feelings about militancy?
4. What do your parents do?

National Origin.
1. You don't mind Polish and Irish jokes, do you?
2. What nationality are you?
3. Were you born in the United States?
4. Do you have people in the "old country"?

Unfortunately, little attention is paid to interviewing techniques in too many educational institutions. Interview techniques and behavior of the personnel conducting such interviews are being judged by all those who are interviewed. If the prospective employees are getting a negative impression, the college should strive to improve its image. One way to improve the interviewing process is to incorporate several sessions of interviewing techniques in the staff development program at a college or university. This would not only benefit the college's image, but it would also enable college personnel to gather information that would help them improve their communication skills in an interview setting. If interview skills are excellent, chances will be even greater that the candidates with the most to offer an educational institution will be hired.

THE HIRING PROCESS

The exact procedure an institution of higher education utilizes to interview and hire new personnel can vary greatly. Some institutions allow the interviewing administrator to make unilateral decisions to present to the board. Others use a personnel committee including the building administrator affected. Many institutions have a multistage process where two or three interviews are conducted, with the number of candidates decreasing with each succeeding stage. Quite often school board members, faculty committees, and lay citizen advisory groups take an active part in the initial interviewing stages.

Whatever the system in a particular situation matters very little; there is probably little one can do about it. The point is to know the system you have and use it to the best advantage for both your institution and students. One should set up a system or method of accepting, processing, and evaluating inquiries for positions at your institution. The initial step for someone seeking a position in your institution would be resumes and cover letters. What you expect and what you get may be two different things.

Complete information in the cover letter and resume gives the employer the chance to make an informal judgment and saves time for both the applicant and the institution or company. The cover letter should indicate a special interest in the company; however, receipt of a run-of-the-mill resume and letter gives the impression that the applicant distributed these indiscriminately, like baiting a hook and hoping that some kind of fish will bite. Neatness and clarity are essential. Too many letters follow a "canned" professional format. An honest, forthright, individual approach is not only effective, it is refreshing.

It may well be that the only introduction you have to a prospective employee is the job application form. As stated above, recent laws have a lot to say about what kinds of questions you or your personnel director can ask an applicant; what kinds of tests you give; and what kinds of information you can request from previous employers. While these tough restrictions may help protect job applicants from discrimination, they also make it difficult for school employers to be discriminating. Yet if disregarded, the regulations in fact can land your school board in court.[10]

Application Forms

New applicant and testing requirements place institutions in a tough position. Since the product we all deal in is students, we should try to find out as much about an applicant as possible. Regulations concerning inquiries and tests are enforced federally through the EEOC (Equal Employment Opportunity Commission).

Institutions are finding that their job application forms are outdated—in some instances downright illegal—and that information once routinely requested of job applicants now no longer can be asked. Much of the push for revised application procedures can be traced to the 1964 U.S. Civil Rights Act which outlawed employment discrimination on the basis of race, color, religion, sex, or national origin. In 1972 this law was amended to include state and local government employees.

Again, what kinds of prehiring questions are illegal? "Have you ever been arrested, convicted, or spent time in jail?" According to EEOC, this kind of question never should show up on an application form. The courts agree. The legal explanation was offered by the judge in the *Gregory* v. *Litton Systems, Inc.* case. Said he: "Negroes are arrested substantially more frequently than whites in proportion to their numbers. Thus any policy that disqualifies prospective employees because of having been arrested once, or more than once, discriminates in fact against Negro applicants. The discrimination exists even though such a policy is objectively and fairly applied as between applicants of various races."

Another example: For some time, many institutions asked prospective employees, "What is the lowest salary you will accept?" Now such a question is taboo, and the reason has to do with sex discrimination. For many years, says EEOC, more women than men have been stuck with low paying jobs. Even when performing the same job, women have been paid less. Conditioned by this history of discrimination, women might still be willing to work for less money. In order to do away with the last vestiges of unequal pay, school districts and other potential employers are better off not asking this question.

Other types of inquiries considered standard just a few years ago, today are not allowed. Questions of a personal nature—such as sex, age, marital status, and number of children—cannot be solicited unless they constitute bona fide occupational qualifications (BFOQs). To illustrate, the sex of an applicant may be asked when hiring a gym teacher who will be in charge of supervising shower and locker room facilities. It is considered a BFOQ. The obvious lesson, therefore, is to be ultracautious when seeking sex definition from an applicant.

Other questionable inquiries include: "Do you have children under age 18? If so, what arrangements will be made for their care while you work?" If you ask this of women and not men, that's discrimination. If you ask it at all you may be guilty of discrimination against Catholics and minorities who, on the average, have larger families. "Color of eyes, color of hair?" It has never been proven that eyes or hair are bona fide occupational qualifications. "Friends or relatives working in school district?" This may be construed to reflect a preference given for friends or relatives of current employees. "Have your wages ever been garnisheed?" Garnishment records don't affect a worker's ability to do a job. Statistics show that blacks have their wages garnisheed more frequently than do whites, and refusing to hire a worker because of garnishment history may reflect a racist hiring practice. If an applicant is to be denied employment because of a criminal record, school boards first must demonstrate a relationship between the crime committed and the responsibilities of the position to be filled.

Look at your institution's employment application form. Anything contained in it (whether intentional or not) that would tend to disqualify a person on the basis of sex, race, or age from holding any job can be considered a violation of antidiscrimination laws.

To fill certain positions, an institution will need more information than can be gleaned from a standard application form. In such instances, the institution may wish to administer a test to measure an applicant's skills. Fine. But be advised that testing also falls under the watchful eye of EEOC, and the agency has much to say on that subject. For example, all applicants must be administered a similar test which must be related to the position.

EEOC published a set of guidelines concerning testing. Hence, the rules now say in general that tests have to be designed to measure a specific skill. No longer will an applicant for a typist's position pass the typing test only to be rejected because of failure to pass tests measuring general skills. This means that a typist applicant must be hired for a typist job if that person can demonstrate the needed skills; it also means that the applicant cannot be rejected because of an inability to answer questions correctly about mathematics, geography, or current events.

Telephone calls to references and former employers are perfectly acceptable, but these over-the-phone conversations can pose headaches of their own. The courts are saying that employers—including institutions of higher education—have no right to ask, and no right to give out, information that is hostile, reckless, or abusive. When you seek information about a teacher, it's okay to ask whether he has been denied renewal of his teaching contract. Make sure that the information you get is acquired from employment records, and is not just someone's personal opinion.

The first step in hiring is to have the candidate fill out a simple application form that asks only a few questions: name, position desired, social security number, education, employment history, job skills, certification, and so forth. Subjective questions such as, "What do you like most about your present job, and what do you like least?" also can be included.

After an applicant has filled out the preliminary form, presented the names of previous employers and personal references, and been interviewed, he or she is either hired or turned away. Once the position is offered, however, a second set of questions can be asked of the new employee—questions that might be improper if asked before that person was offered the job. These subsequent questions include information regarding marital status, names and ages of children (for insurance purposes), and physical data (including a possible requirement that the new employee complete a physical examination).

In reviewing the applications, the initial step must be to ascertain the presence of a valid educational credential. This requirement of a fair, reasonable, and nondiscriminatory evaluation is based upon the due process and equal protection clauses of the Fourteenth Amendment.

Loyalty oaths have been viewed by the courts as suspect when they restrict academic freedom and First Amendment rights. A court declared that an instructor could not be denied public employment merely because of his "knowing" membership in a "subversive" organization. In order for an instructor to be dismissed on the basis of association with subversive organizations, it must be shown that the teacher actually intends to overthrow the government or is attempting to proselytize his or her students to such ideas. This showing must conform to the requirements of due process.

It would be beneficial if the credentials evaluation process could be made more exacting so as to help school officials hire the most competent teachers. But how this might be done in light of the EEOC regulations is baffling. The regulations were adopted to make sure that people have an even chance at landing jobs, and to that extent the laws are good. Institutions of higher education are in a difficult position because they serve the public; if they make a mistake and hire the wrong person, the effects can be extremely serious.

Filing Applications and Preparing for Interviews

Once a file of applicants has been accumulated, whether or not a position is available is of little concern. Though there is presently an instructor surplus, interviewers must remember that the best applicants will be in demand with a number of organizations. Some small institutions in rural or remote areas remain involved in recruitment to obtain their instructors. Therefore interviewers must strive to sell their institution to the applicant. All of the applicant's questions should be answered honestly with major emphasis placed on the unique strong points that every institution possesses.

The key to successful interviewing is a united effort on the part of all interviewers to hire the best candidate available for the position. Care must be taken to insure that all applicants are treated equally. Once the initial screening process is completed and candidates are called in for personal interviews, the institution has the responsibility to interview each candidate using a consistent set of evaluative criteria. Every administrator realizes that care must be taken during the interviewing of prospective staff members. A mistake made during this process may have severe implications which can haunt an administrator and an institution for years. Therefore a comprehensive set of guidelines should be utilized by the interviewer to help insure that the school district's needs are being fulfilled. These guidelines can be found in the first part of this chapter.

Just what do administrators look for when interviewing instructors? Neat physical appearance, a favorable letter of recommendation from the aspirant's institution instructors, and clearly stated professional goals head the list of desirable qualifications. According to most institutional personnel managers, physical appearance, neatness, a strong desire to work, good verbal skills and command of the English language, as well as confidence and enthusiasm are valuable.

For the applicant with no experience, a letter of reference written by the applicant's university instructors, college or university supervisor, and administrators where the instruction took place, as well as teaching methods courses completed, a clear idea about professional goals, high enthusiasm, ability to provide for individual differences in classes, and a sound educational philosophy are important.

Questioning the Applicant

Other questions to consider asking a prospective candidate during an interview include: the candidate's background related to teaching; descriptions of teachers he or she admired while a student; areas of teaching expertise, successful classroom activities he or she directed, grading procedures, and experience with educational innovation.

Questions dealing with teachers the candidate admired in high school or college can be helpful. Look for answers that center on organization, strict discipline, and "really knew the material." These responses may give some clues as to how the candidate might act in the classroom. Next have the candidate list in order those subjects he or she most wants to teach. This may give a clue that the candidate wants to teach only a specialized course. One might also ask which ability levels the individual wishes to work with so that you can sense his or her commitment to handling all students.

Another sound idea is to have the interviewee describe the most successful classroom activity he or she has supervised in the last two weeks, assuming the candidate is teaching elsewhere. The point is to have the person describe an event within a fairly restricted time frame with the intent of ascertaining his or her sense of variety or creativity as a classroom teacher. Such a question tends to put the lecturer or drab, routine-oriented person on the spot.

One of the most controversial areas of inquiry for an administrator is that of the candidate's grading philosophy and practice. For example, "Could a low ability student get an A or B in your class?" "On the average, about how many students would you probably fail each year?" Ask the candidate to go over the actual grade distribution of his or her classes at the last marking period. Inquire fully into the ability level of each class and ask how typical these classes seemed to be. Inquire as to the components of a student's grade, trying to ascertain if the candidate sees tests as the sole criterion upon which grades are based.

As a follow-up to the question about the most successful activity the candidate had in the class during the previous two weeks, ask how the activity was graded. In this way some teachers kill a perfectly exciting activity.

Another important category of questions should deal with knowledge of or experience with educational innovation, for example: Who are the big names in your teaching specialty these days? What do they advocate? Who are a few of the national leaders in educational change? Who are some of the critics of American education and what specifically is their concern? What are the four or five leading trends developing in your subject area or field?

Another area of inquiry is what the candidate views himself doing in the future. A response of "working in industry," or even "going back to law school," or "being a travel agent" might be evidence of weak commitment to teaching, and hence a good reason for terminating the interview quickly. Ask also what the candidate sees as his or her unique or personal contribution to education and what his or her strongest drawback might likely be.

Ask what the candidate perceives to be the problem with today's college young people. Look for a condescending or haughty view of youth. During any interviewing session, the applicant should be given ample time to ask questions. The applicant should be shown a job description if available, a copy of the current teaching contract, a faculty manual, and the student handbook. This is by no means a checklist for each and every interview, but rather just a few suggestions. You must develop your own style to meet your own needs in staffing your institution with the best possible personnel.[11]

Making the Applicant Decision

Now you are ready to make your decision as to whom to hire. You have all the facts, you've interviewed, but there's one thing you have to consider seriously, and that has to do with tenure. One of the most misunderstood terms in teaching today is tenure. It's been charged that tenure protects incompetent teachers. Some believe that tenure equals "permanent employment regardless." Once a teacher has gained tenure, he or she has gained assurance that he will not be deprived of his livelihood without due process of law.[12]

When the tenure movement first swept North America at the turn of the century, it was sold as a tool needed to clean up public education. School systems were rife with bossism and political influence, and teaching jobs often were handed out like so many cigars as rewards for hard work during partisan political campaigns. Teachers, in short, had little protection from the ravages of political expediency. Just as the civil service was needed in the United States to protect federal workers from overt political pressure, so too were state tenure laws passed to protect the jobs of teachers. The purpose of the laws: To ensure that teachers, once they had proven their competency in the classroom, could not be removed except for just cause.

Among the forty-six states that have tenure or continuing contract laws, each has different provisions for dismissal. In general, most states permit the firing of tenured teachers found guilty of acts ranging from insubordination, immorality, cruelty, neglect of duty, and incompetency. Other state statutes contain hazy provisions that permit removal of a tenured teacher only for "just cause." In order to fire a tenured teacher an institution first must tread a maze of complex hearings. Teachers conceivably can drag an institution through a local hearing, a meeting of the state's professional practices commission, and then a hearing before the college or university's board of trustees or regents. And if one party isn't satisfied with the outcome, the teacher or institution then can launch a judicial process that begins in the lower courts and ultimately can reach the state supreme court. Everyone suffers—the trustees, the college administration, the teacher, and all the other teachers too. It's difficult, time-consuming, and expensive, and as a result not many tenured teachers are discharged.

Where the state has a collective bargaining law that includes a limited right to strike, an unsatisfactory outcome of the appeals process can culminate in a teacher strike. We can get rid of incompetent teachers, but it's expensive, difficult, and extremely trying. The individual teacher must sit and hear the board of trustees and faculty senate present reams of testimony about that teacher's abilities. It's often a thoroughly degrading personal experience, many university administrators agree, and find that many truly incompetent teachers resign before the dismissal process goes very far.

Tenure isn't really the problem. The problem is one of protecting teacher rights. Four elements, according to due process, are essential to the fair handling of teacher dismissals: specific written charges capable of verification must be presented to the teacher; there must be a hearing with counsel, if desired; there must be assurance that no new charges will be introduced at the hearing; and there must be provision for appeal.

Institutions must learn to adopt a workable process that rids the district of incompetent teachers. The twin keys to such a process are record keeping and evaluation. Record keeping and evaluation must be more than a grade card of failure. Evaluation of teacher performance used solely to judge whether a certain personnel action should be taken does not contribute substantially to improving the educational process. If improvements in teacher performance are needed, an effective evaluative system must present a time schedule that will allow improvements to be made. Time to improve, as well as knowledge of what improvements are needed, is an essential part of equitable and useful evaluation.[13]

A teacher under scrutiny and the observers must be advised beforehand what criteria are to be used in the evaluation and that all information is to be made available to the teacher. When the review is completed, reviewers and the teacher must sign the evaluation form. What is important is that the teacher's due process rights are spelled out and guaranteed. Teacher evaluation should be used as a way to strengthen education and build professionalism. If a teacher has been educated, certified, interviewed, employed, and has served for several years satisfactorily, surely that person is worthy of due consideration in job continuance. The instructor must be protected from arbitrary and capricious actions of irresponsible trustee members, pressure groups, or careless evaluators.

Some have said, "The good teacher doesn't need protection." It would be wonderful if that were true. Too many good teachers have been fired because they were "too old" or "too highly paid," or to make a place for someone's friend. Improving instruction and keeping competent teachers are the purposes of tenure. Of the teachers who achieved tenure and promotion under the old system, many have been productive and continue to excel in teaching. Others, however, have achieved status quo and are resting comfortably in a well-paid, semi-retired holding pattern, believing their positions secure.

Tenure has affected teachers' rights to be employed, their academic freedom in the classroom, protection of their constitutional rights both in and out of the school, and their right to continued employment. Teachers, however, may not invoke the Fifth Amendment privilege when questions are asked by institutional administrators concerning their competence.

Speaking or writing as a citizen outside the confines of the institution, the teacher should at all times be accurate, should exercise appropriate restraint, should show respect for the opinions of others and should make every effort to indicate that he is not an institutional spokesman. While academic freedom is a protected right, the teacher in a classroom should "avoid persistently introducing material which has no relation to his subject." In other words, academic freedom is not a shield to protect a teacher from being dismissed for persistently discussing in mathematics class ways to rid the campus of military recruiters. Attainment of tenure usually requires that a probationary period be satisfactorily completed.

Tenure laws for public college and university instructors differ from campus to campus, and it is extremely important to be familiar with the policies of your particular institution. Most regulations provide for a probationary period prior to the granting of tenure. Tenured teachers can be dismissed if it can be shown at a hearing conforming to the rudiments of due process that the teacher is incompetent, immoral, insubordinant, neglecting duty, or for what the courts have termed "other good cause."[14]

Nontenured teachers, on the other hand, are employed on an annual contract which must be executed anew each year. Since nontenured teachers are hired on an annual basis, their dismissal generally is a matter of not renewing their contracts for the succeeding year. These teachers, under normal circumstances, have no right to due process procedures prior to dismissal or nonrenewal. Due process may be required, however, in instances where the teacher is dismissed, or the annual contract is not renewed, based upon the exercise of constitutional rights.

Teachers whether tenured or nontenured have the same constitutional rights as do all citizens, and they may not be censured, dismissed, or fail to have their contracts renewed for the exercise of their constitutional rights. Probably the reason most often given for dismissing a tenured teacher is incompetence. The term has been used, however, to include not only conduct inside the classroom but also conduct external to the campus which can be shown to impinge upon the professional competence of an individual to teach.

Neglect of duty is usually stipulated in the tenure statutes as a cause for the dismissal of tenured teachers. All teachers have three general duties in addition to those specifically assigned by the institutional administrators at the time of appointment. Teachers must: (1) provide proper classroom supervision, (2) provide proper instruction in the use of appliances or equipment, and (3) maintain equipment in a proper state of repair. Negligence in the discharge of any of these or other specific duties assigned could be cause for dismissal. But what is negligence? It is defined as an act of omission or commission which a reasonably prudent person would or would not do. Negligence is a relative term which depends upon time, place, and circumstance.

Employers must be aware that their choices may influence the lives of individuals for years to come. Once you have made your decision on a candidate for a position, it is your job to enlighten that person on the many unique opportunities and benefits afforded by your institution. Sometimes this general orientation is done for all new teachers at a meeting before the new school year begins. Take a personal interest in new teaching personnel and localize it for your own institution. For example, one thing you might want to discuss is salary. If you are on the simple education experience pay schedule, there may be little to explain. However, in a merit-based system, there would be much to explain. Be sure the candidate fully understands the remuneration system.

Teaching loads are another area of concern. Usually the schedule is the standard—number of off periods, preparation, remedial classes, advanced classes, and so forth. The expected number of teaching hours each semester should be explained. Contracts should be explained for the period of teaching (nine-month contract, twelve-month contract). Summer school teaching opportunities should also be explained to the new instructor.

Fringe benefits are fairly standard, but be sure that the new teacher is aware of everything from the credit union to the dental plan and has every opportunity to take advantage of them. Benefits also include sick leave, vacation schedules, time away from class for personal matters, and release time for publications. Leave policy varies from school system to school system. Let the new teacher know from the beginning what your policy is—accumulation, forfeiture, buy-back, professional, or sabbatical leaves.

In education most leaves are granted for vertical growth, for degrees, and for professional advancement. Leaves are granted for additional study, travel, sickness, funerals, attendance at educational conferences, union representation, military service, and pregnancy. Such regulations confine educators to vertical growth in their own fields. Too often educators take leaves to study what they already know. The practice in effect tends to narrow their knowledge as they move vertically in a concentrated single field of study. While competency in a specific field is admirable, instructors live in a world where the quality of life and service increases as one broadens his knowledge of the things that influence his life as well as that of others. Reevaluation of sabbatical leaves for educators to include horizontal growth may open lines of communication, eliminate suspicions, and bring long-range benefits to our institutions and society. Sabbatical leaves could be granted by college districts and universities on an exchange basis with all facets of the community. Upon completion, institutions would have resource persons with firsthand knowledge of the business and industry communities and vice versa. Criticism could be lessened and community support strengthened if institutions provided horizontal growth opportunities for their faculty.

EVALUATION

After a candidate has been selected for a position, supervision and evaluation of the individual should continue. Supervision is, of course, the day by day activity of assisting a subordinate; this should not be seen by a faculty member as a threat. The goals of effective supervision and teaching should be the same, that is, the improvement of instruction.

An administrator in a supervisory capacity, whether division or department chairperson, dean or vice president, should serve as a resource person who can offer advice in handling problems. The supervisor should be able to help in budgeting money for specific programs or equipment and should provide contacts with experts in the field. These contacts may take the form of staff development sessions or of allowing subordinates to attend workshops or state and national conventions.

A supervisor has the responsibility of matching the goals and needs of an institution with the goals and abilities of the faculty member. If the supervisor has established good rapport with faculty members, then evaluation, which involves judgment and is a part of the supervisor's responsibility, should be handled smoothly.

Evaluation is important for several reasons, but the most important is probably the improvement of instruction. If educational institutions are student oriented and stress the value of learning, the improvement of teaching must be a vital concern. Evaluation may also be used for the purpose of granting tenure, ranking, or merit pay.

Reasons for Evaluation

Extensive work has been done in the area of evaluation in higher education. Several specific purposes of faculty evaluation are:

1. Helping faculty to improve their performance.
2. Making decisions on retention, tenure, salary and promotion.
3. Guiding students in their selection of courses and instructors.
4. Keeping an inventory of personnel resources for reassignment and retraining.
5. Evaluating curricula, sequences, programs, departments, and units.
6. Informing external audiences of faculty performances.
7. Conducting research on factors related to faculty performance.

Three reasons why evaluation of instruction is necessary concern the improvement of the educational process.

1. Evaluation is required for the recognition and reward of good instruction.
2. Evaluation will provide knowledge which can be used to improve instruction.
3. Evaluation can involve research on instruction.

One important prerequisite for a successful evaluation process is that faculty and supervisor agree as to what will be evaluated. Faculty members must also understand that the supervisor aims to work with them to improve instruction rather than as an adversary. (See Figure 38.)

Various Means of Evaluating Teaching

Evaluation can be based on a wide range of activities depending on the emphasis and philosophy of an educational institution. In institutions where faculty members are expected to spend the major portion of their working time with students and student related problems, the student will provide input in the evaluation process. (See Figure 39.) Usually this student input takes the form of rating scales which are distributed to classes for completion. Many acceptable standard forms, or instruments, are available, although some institutions use an in-house instrument that has been developed by a committee of representatives from faculty, student, and administrative groups. Often an institution will use portions of a standard form and add some specific questions that are relevant to the particular college or university.

In using rating scales in the classroom, two factors must be considered: the time at which the evaluation form is completed, and the actual length of the form. Conditions surrounding completion of the form must be uniform if the rating scale is to have high validity. At some schools the rating scales are given during the last few weeks of a semester; at others the rating scales are administered early in the semester so that instructors can make adjustments for the benefit of current students.

Students who are asked to participate in rating faculty members should receive feedback. This can present a problem, because faculty members often feel it an invasion of their privacy to have student rating scores published. One institution solved this dilemma by having faculty members sign release forms, allowing results of the rating scales to be released only to certain groups.

Students evaluating instruction should also have the opportunity to write some narrative concerning their learning experience. Instructors

FIGURE 38
Evaluation session

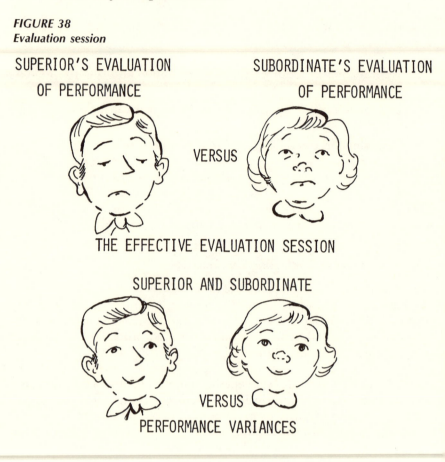

SUPERIOR'S EVALUATION
OF PERFORMANCE

SUBORDINATE'S EVALUATION
OF PERFORMANCE

VERSUS

THE EFFECTIVE EVALUATION SESSION

SUPERIOR AND SUBORDINATE

VERSUS

PERFORMANCE VARIANCES

1. BOTH PARTIES DISCUSS THEIR OWN EVALUATIONS
2. DIFFERENCES ARE RESOLVED
3. CAUSES FOR NEGATIVE VARIANCES ARE EXPLORED
4. APPROPRIATE ACTION PLANS ARE PREPARED
5. SUBSEQUENTLY, SATISFACTORY PERFORMANCE IS SECURED

Osentowski

should encourage students to write comments and assure them that suggestions will be seriously considered. Faculty members should then oblige by looking carefully at all suggestions and, if possible, implementing the suggestions in course revision.

Another area for evaluation is class visitation, either by a division

FIGURE 39
Teacher evaluation

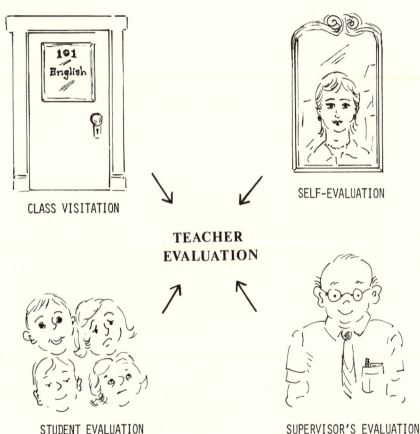

CLASS VISITATION

SELF-EVALUATION

**TEACHER
EVALUATION**

STUDENT EVALUATION

SUPERVISOR'S EVALUATION

Osentowski

chairperson or by a team of evaluators. This is sometimes considered a threat by some faculty members, but if a good supervisor-faculty member relationship has developed during the year and if faculty members see the supervisor as an ally, the threat should be reduced. The supervisor should arrive for the class visitation before the class actually begins and should try to observe the entire class proceedings inobtrusively. Depending on the class atmosphere, a supervisor may or may not be introduced.

Another area of evaluation is self-evaluation. Many faculty members rate themselves more highly than do students or administrators. One method of self-evaluation involves having faculty members complete the same rating scale that students use, then completing the scale again as they think the students would complete it. Faculty members then have several viewpoints to consider when looking at the results.

Self-evaluation may also include a personal plan of action. A faculty member establishes several goals for the year; these may be in the area of teaching improvement, professional growth, or service. These plans should be considered by the supervisor when making evaluations and recommendations.

Still another area a faculty member may investigate for self-evaluation is the use of videotape equipment. It would probably be most convenient to have someone from the media department come into an actual classroom and tape the instructor conducting a class. Student feedback and discussion can be a part of the tape, and an instructor can evaluate this as well as his or her own communication skills. It is recommended that the instructor wait at least one or two days after the taping session to evaluate it, enabling more objectivity. The videotape may also be used by a supervisor if he or she is unable actually to visit the classroom. The process is called micro-teaching.

The supervisor or division chairperson in making his or her evaluation should take into consideration the evaluation methods discussed: student evaluation, self-evaluation, and class visitation. The supervisor should also take into consideration the faculty member's committee work within the division, professional growth, and service offered the college and community in the area in which the faculty member has expertise.

The above areas for evaluation should be considered on all campuses. However, at some institutions where tenure, merit pay, and ranking prevail, other considerations such as peer evaluation and research must also be taken into account.

Eugene Meyer and Charles Smith, in a recent survey of U.S. teacher education institutions, found that 87 percent of governing boards viewed faculty evaluation as mandatory. Their survey, which investigated faculty evaluation practices, indicated that a merit plan was most often used for salary, tenure, promotion, and retention decision .

The merit rating usually takes into consideration the various evaluation segments discussed in this chapter. Whatever the factors considered for merit ranking or salary increase, it is important that faculty members as well as administrators have influence on included factors. According to John Bolin and John Muir, "A merit plan can succeed only as a cooperative endeavor of the administration and the faculty."[15]

At a time when accountability is demanded of educational institutions, when the educational field is a buyer's market, and when job insecurity for faculty is becoming a reality, it becomes essential that educational institutions recruit and hire the strongest candidates, following federal government guidelines. The instructors must then be evaluated carefully so that the instructional process can be improved continuously. The chief beneficiaries of all this are the students and the instructional process, and that is what the education business is, or should be, about.

Higher education, as we know it today, cannot survive in isolation. This is evidenced by the many defeats of tax increases and bond proposals, and by the lack of community participation. Participation usually happens in crisis situations, but public education needs more than hysterical support. It can exist, however, when it becomes an integral part and an active participant in the political, social, and economic life of the community, state, and nation that it serves. The whole concept of education as a separate entity administered by a separate board functioning under its own laws must change if total public support is expected.

Institutions must be accountable to the community and state that they serve. The processes developed in staffing, recruiting, hiring, and evaluating must follow acceptable guidelines approved by local and state adjudicators. Institutions that have consciously adhered to these guidelines appear to have continued as effective servants of the community or state. Effective processes of staffing must have enough integrity with the various boards and agencies who evaluate the institution to satisfy these constituencies. Continued effectiveness in staffing generally assures continued funding and trust by promoting agencies.

NOTES

1. Richard A. Kaplowitz, *Selecting Academic Administrators: The Search Committee* (Washington, D.C.: American Council on Education, 1973), pp. 14–15.

2. John L. Iacobelli and Jan P. Musczyk, "Overlooked Talent Sources and Corporate Strategies for Affirmative Action, Part II," *Personnel Journal* 54 (November 1975), pp. 575–77, 587.

3. S. F. Lynem, "An Old Dimension With New Emphasis," *NASSP Bulletin* 60 (November 1976), pp. 103–6.

4. Marcus Gillespie, "The New Rules for Interviewing Job Applicants: Schools Ignore Them at Their Peril," *American School Board Journal* 164 (March 1977), pp. 27–30.

5. Ibid.

6. Kaplowitz, *Selecting Academic Administrators: The Search Committee*, pp. 14–15.

7. Gillespie, "New Rules for Interviewing Job Applicants," p. 28.

8. Ibid., p. 29.

9. Ibid., p. 30.

10. Dixie R. Crase and Darrell Crase, "New Tenure and Promotion Guidelines Produce Growth Pains," *Peabody Journal of Education* 54, 1 (October 1976), pp. 56–59.

11. Jerome Cramer, "How Would Your Faucets Work if Plumbers were

Shielded by Tenure Laws?" *American School Board Journal* 163 (October 1976), pp. 22–24.

12. Crase and Crase, "New Tenure and Promotion Guidelines Produce Growth Pains," p. 58.

13. John G. Bolin and John W. Muir, *Merit Rating for Salary Increases and Promotions* (Athens, Ga.: Institute of Higher Education, University of Georgia, 1966), p. 28.

14. Kaplowitz, *Selecting Academic Administrators.*

15. Bolin and Muir, *Merit Rating,* p. 29.

8

Personnel Management: Faculty and Staff Evaluation Process

JACK D. TERRY, JR.

One of the major problems associated with personnel management in higher education is the faculty and staff evaluation process. Personnel managers consistently search for evaluation processes to determine guidelines for promotion, tenure, and remuneration of faculty and staff. In the past, effectiveness of faculty personnel has been determined on a highly subjective evaluation which was more an observation of personal qualities and research and publication abilities than a scientific evaluation process predicated upon multiple factors from all sectors of academic performance. Evaluation of institutional performance requires evaluation of personnel performance in an institutional context. If the social responsibilities of the university require evaluation of the faculty, then evaluation efforts must be so supported by administration and the students that the faculty cannot ignore them.

Generally, faculty members find evaluation acceptable if it leads to satisfaction, to suggestion for improvement, or reward. An analysis of these considerations provides further insight into faculty priorities and reaction to evaluation. Research productivity is both objective and tangible. Sending a manuscript to a publisher generally yields a note of thanks. Public service takes the professor into social, business, governmental, and industrial scenes, where being "the expert" is a heady experience, productive of numerous impressive anecdotes to recount upon returning to the campus, as well as a handsome financial reward. Likewise, participation in campus governance brings the faculty member a sense of involvement and power, contact with administrators, and public recognition. However, teaching and advising just do not offer the same measure of satisfaction and reward. Since teaching and advising are expected of every professor, whereas the other considerations are not, it is more difficult to achieve distinction as a teacher and therefore personal satisfaction as well as promotion and tenure are less likely.

DEFINITIONS

Administrative evaluation—Performed by area persons using hard data concerning individual faculty members which evidence improvement of instruction, professionalism, publications, classroom skills, classroom management, etc. The area from which professionalism in teaching can be evaluated.

Colleague evaluation—The use of peers to determine their colleagues' comprehensiveness; up-to-dateness of course content, textbooks, and assignments; grapevine feedback; and grading procedure.

Evaluation of teaching—A process of determining the efficiency, professionalism, classroom skills, goals, and outcomes of faculty members through the use of objective evaluation instruments (professionally prepared or personally developed). The main purpose of evaluation of teaching is to improve instruction and holistic self concept of the faculty member.

Faculty development—A program for continuing professionalism for faculty members, either individually developed by the professor with support from the institution or through an individually funded program at a regional development center. Faculty development provisions are often an enticement in faculty recruitment.

Merit—An additional monetary increment or advance in rank or tenure for the demonstration of professionalism through local, state, or national recognition, expertise in the classroom, or publications and services.

Promotion—A criterion-based process for the purpose of progressing professionally through the academic ranks of an institution on a clearly stated schedule.

Student evaluation—National testing instruments or personally prepared instruments that allow the clientele of the classroom—the student—to judge a multiplicity of classroom skills first hand. Though many would disagree, data demonstrates that the most accurate evaluation of teaching probably comes from the student.

Tenure—The granting of permanent employment, rank, and salary by the institution following a stated probationary period.

PURPOSE OF EVALUATING PERFORMANCE

The most general stated purposes of faculty evaluation include improvement of teaching; improvement in learning in reference to behavioral objectives; provision of bases for selection, recognition, and reward of effective teachers; research contributions to understanding teaching and learning; and assurance to students and the public that teaching is regarded as important.

Because teacher evaluation is a complex problem, effective evaluation must have its foundation in certain principles. Evaluation of teaching incorporates multiple variables, so that no one method of evaluation is in and of itself adequate. Evaluation must employ the best possible procedures and be an integral part of the teaching-learning process, not a distraction which detracts and interferes with learning rather than reinforcing it. The collecting of data for the evaluation process must be based upon observation and well-defined behavior that is acceptable to both students and teachers. Evaluation procedures must be a maturing process for the student and the teacher, with each accepting their responsibilities for assessing the extent and adequacy of their own positions.

Efforts in evaluation of faculty performance have been sporadic, limited in perspective, and largely ineffective. The widespread assumption seems to be that faculty research is adequately evaluated, but except for members of a few elite departments of major universities even this is not true. Publication rather than quality of instruction and student services is the criterion of most institutions. Advising and various forms of campus and noncampus service are virtually never adequately evaluated except when these areas are someone's particular responsibility. Only when efforts in faculty evaluation are turned to analyzing the strengths and weaknesses in the performance of all faculty activities, plus providing for improvement and capitalization of performance and changes in assignment commensurate with strengths, will faculty evaluation become productive.

However small the present impact of faculty evaluation, this must not become a deterrent in assessing faculty performance or in establishing a process for objective evaluation. The movement toward objective-based faculty evaluation is an attempt by educators to look positively at themselves. The question no longer is how much research notoriety can be gained or public service ventures be performed, but rather how are professors functioning in classroom leadership roles and how the personal goals of research and public service can become meshed with the goals of the institution and its students.

EVALUATION OF COLLEGE TEACHING

Pressure has been developing to provide evaluative data on college teaching. This pressure has come from the teaching faculty, from students, and from administrators. The major reasons for the pressure seem to be that teaching faculty want information that will aid in the improvement of instruction, students want information that will guide them in course and instructor selection, and administrators want information to guide them in pay and promotional decisions.

F. Costin, S. J. Greenough, and R. J. Menges have done considerable research which has centered in the development of specific rating forms and identifying attributes that are important components of effective teaching.[1] However, less attention has been given to the systematic selection, collection, and use of evaluative data. Any evaluation system must have basic validity and its rating forms must provide the validation. The teaching faculty should see the system as an opportunity to provide them with helpful information. Students must feel their part to be worthwhile input for improved instruction as well as professor-course selection. Likewise, the administration must have confidence in the information in order to make positive administrative decisions which verify that the evaluation program is useful as well as necessary to the continued growth of the institution. An essential condition of the process must be a flexibility of construct acceptable by users as appropriate to a great variety of instructional methods and situations.

In addition to satisfying a basic reliability postulate a faculty evaluation program must also consider three major variables—who does the evaluation, what type of evaluation data is to be collected, and who receives and examines the results. While students are a vital input resource in the instructional process, a complete evaluation should include information from other sources as well.

Colleague Evaluation

Colleagues are often appropriate judges of the quality and appropriateness of curriculum development, student advisement, and such related matters. Departmental administrators are usually in the best position to judge how well a faculty member fulfills administrative responsibilities related to course improvement and to evaluate contributions made by faculty members serving on committees, boards, and search groups. That colleagues are an important source of evaluation information about instruction is an important consideration. Colleague evaluation of the appropriateness, comprehensiveness, and up-to-dateness of course content, textbook assignments, examinations, feedback and grading is useful. These are justifiably concerns of colleagues interested in the quality of instruction and are aspects of the teaching process which may be judged more clearly by a fellow expert than by a student.

Department Administrator Evaluation

An additional input to aid the evaluation of college teaching is the information obtained from the departmental administrator. Thus, leaders' number one priority should be to assist the teacher in the improvement of instruction. In the evaluative capacity the administrator acts as a summarizer and organizer of information to be forwarded to higher levels of administration.

The combination of several variables in the evaluation of college faculty begins to reduce the threat of a one-method evaluation process and places improvement of the instructional procedure at the heart of the evaluation program. The use of evaluative data is the pivotal concern of a teaching faculty; its assists and improves instructional expertise.

The prime consumer of the data of teaching evaluation is the individual faculty member. Evaluation for the sole purpose of reward or punishment is the source of severe tension and seems to indicate that the evaluation process offers little prospect for improvement or advancement. On the contrary, evaluation of teaching should be used to promote improvement and development plus a sense of growth in the faculty member. Identification of instructional problems through evaluation assists the instructor in an improved design of course content. Likewise, if problem areas are present, the evaluation will isolate these and provide the instructor an opportunity to develop a process of correction. Classroom expertise and operational modes are vastly improved by identifying the instructor problem areas. To ignore evaluation results is to suggest a lack of professionalism and a disdain for self-improvement.

From a student's perspective, the evaluative material will assist in the selection of courses as well as give a detailed description of the operational procedure of the professor in the classroom. Since current course descriptions in catalogs are often outdated and give little indication as to the instructor's classroom habits, a data information sheet for students could be a valuable tool for course and instructor selection.

The department head, nonetheless, is by far the most important user of the evaluation data. He has considerable decision-making responsibility and is usually the person who will organize and summarize the available materials for submission to higher levels of administration. In making decisions the department head should have all the data and should take into account evidence of improvement in instructional problem areas. The information forwarded to higher administrative levels should be an organization and summation developed from all data, students, colleagues, and department heads.

The institutional administrator will review all summary of data in order to make the proper decisions concerning an individual faculty member. Note that the information does not stand on one isolated element, such as student evaluation or peer evaluation, but rests on a composited summary of data gathered from multiple levels of institutional activity. This composite data summation is usable because it is developed through a three-cycle process which allows all who are in close contact with the faculty member to make positive and negative judgments. The information is then organized and a summation overview is prepared for use in decision-making. The total process is developmental and improvement oriented. No decision should be made concerning the fate of an instructor based on half the available data. Less tension and fear would accompany teacher evaluation if guidelines as identified in this chapter were adopted.

Student Evaluation

Student evaluation of faculty is usually rejected unless the faculty feels the evaluation is specific to the discipline or content of the course. Many faculty members discount the idea that students can evaluate the quality and fairness of an examination or the justifications of specific course requirements. According to Norman Eagle, administrators on the other hand, accustomed to hearing the complaints of students, generally take a more broad view than do the faculty of what might be evaluated by the students. Students are capable of evaluating much more than is often supposed. However, they evaluate what they are allowed to evaluate, and faculty members tend to eliminate from student evaluations any aspects that might require a change in their teaching concept.[2]

STUDENT RATING FORMS

The past several years have witnessed an increased attempt to evaluate college teaching through student rating systems for faculty instruction. Several years ago a study was done by J. W. Gustad which surveyed the methods of teacher evaluation used by 584 colleges and universities. In most cases the survey revealed that the evaluation cited most often was an analysis of student ratings. More recently, however, Gustad noted a substantial decrease in the systematic use of student ratings in favor of informal student opinion polls of teaching along with an increase of evaluations by deans and department chairs. Perhaps, Gustad concludes, this decrease is related to the lack of convincing validity data. On the other hand, a perceived threat to faculty because of a strong desire on the part of students to be actively engaged in the use of student rating forms for teaching evaluation may be an important clue to the decline of the rating instruments.[3] (See Appendix 1, Student Evaluation Form at the end of this chapter.)

Faculty resistance to the use of student rating forms may come primarily from the fact that many rating scales have been prepared by individuals not qualified to construct such instruments. Some faculty members will challenge the administration on the use of student rating instruments, no matter who prepares the forms or organizes the data into national and regional norms. The claim generally is that student ratings are unreliable and that the forms favor the entertainer over the professional researcher who gets the information across with less pomp and fanfare. Also, teachers correlate grade expectations with the rating scores. According to Gordon Greenwood, the teacher who grades easier will have the higher scores, whereas the difficult teacher with higher expectations will have lower scores.[4] Another reaction is that students are not competent judges of instructional procedures since the majority of these procedures are spent on long-term objectives, and only experience provides adequate competence in determining whether the instruction was effective. Where pay, promotion, or tenure are the major criteria there are many teachers who claim that effective teaching and research go hand in hand. It is more feasible to evaluate the research since this eliminates all the variables of the classroom experience and allows an objective evaluation of tangible rather than intangible elements.

RATING CRITERIA

Costin, Greenough, and Menges suggest five criteria upon which student rating proves its ability to strengthen and improve instruction as well as a teacher's self-knowledge.

1. Such ratings could provide feedback which the instructor might not be able to elicit from students on a face to face basis. (This information alone, with no sanctions contingent, could improve teaching.)

2. They could provide departmental and college-wide norms against which an individual faculty rating could be judged.

3. They could provide a way in which a faculty member could, if he desired, demonstrate his undergraduate teaching effectiveness to those who have expressed an interest in evaluating this parameter for salary increase.

4. They could provide information to the department and college on areas of relative strength or weakness of undergraduate teaching, suggest directions for the development of new courses and programs, and provide evaluation information and norms on the various new programs which are implemented.

5. They could provide the student with a source of information to aid in the selection of courses.[5]

It is obvious that these benefits can exist only to the extent ratings represent accurate and valid appraisals of classroom instruction. What of reliability?

In some of the earliest studies of student opinions of college teaching, E. R. Guthrie (1949) found correlations of 0.87 and 0.89 between students' ranking of their teachers from one year to the next.[6] G. D. Lovell and C. F. Haner (1955) used forced-choice rating to obtain opinions with a correlation between ratings made two weeks apart of 0.89.[7]

More recent surveys found moderate to high correlations between mid-semester and end-of-semester evaluation. It would appear that students can rate classroom instruction with some degree of reliability, according to Greenwood and his associates (1973). In fact, the evidence concerning the stability of students' ratings argues against the contention that students' ratings are difficult to interpret since they may be conducted after a good or bad classroom experience.[8]

The charge of inadequate validity in student rating of teaching because of the subjective nature of the classroom experience has been refuted most assuredly by the "consumer" of the classroom, the student. Many faculty members would judge the ratings as valid to the extent that the students' criteria match the faculty members' goals in teaching.

W. J. McKeachie (1969) discovered that students evaluating teaching on various aspects of critical thinking performed particularly well and rated their instructors as "more effective" than did those students who did poorly on examinations.[9] In a more recent study by McKeachie with Y. Lin, and W. Mann (1979), students who rated teachers high in "student rapport" tended to be more effective at "critical thinking."[10]

S. A. Cohen and W. G. Berger (1970) discovered a significant correlation between the performance of a class section of students on an objective examination and the ratings they gave their professors in the area of "student interest" and "student-faculty interaction."[11] R. G. Lathrop and C. Richmond (1967) and Lathrop in 1968 identified positive correlations between high ratings of instruction and the degree to which the students felt they had achieved the course objectives.[12]

There appears to be justification for the belief students are partially capable of rating certain qualities of instruction which have a tendency to increase their accumulation of factual information or provide a motivational experience. Since these isolates can be reliably evaluated, it is reasonable to assume that students who understand course objectives are capable of evaluating whether those course objectives were in truth fulfilled during the learning experience.

STUDENT-IDENTIFIED TEACHING EFFECTIVENESS

Students identify certain characteristics with teaching effectiveness. French (1957) from an experiment at the University of Washington, identified the following characteristics of teaching effectiveness: (a) interprets abstract ideas and theories clearly, (b) gets students interested in the subject, (c) increases skill in thinking, (d) helps broaden interests, (e) stresses important material, (f) makes good use of examples and illustrations, (g) motivated to do outstanding work, (h) inspires class confidence in his knowledge of the subject, (i) has given new viewpoints or appreciations, (j) is clear and understandable in his explanations.[13]

P. L. Crawford and H. L. Bradshaw asked students to describe the most effective college teacher they ever had. The most frequently mentioned characteristics were: thorough knowledge of the subject matter; well-planned and organized lectures; enthusiastic, energetic, lively interest in teaching; and student oriented, friendly, willing to help students.[14]

Student opinions of the criteria of "good teachers" as revealed by several other studies are consistent with those found by French. D. Musella and R. Rush surveyed seniors at the State University of New York at Albany and many of these same criteria were listed.[15] In a survey of 16,000 students at Washington State University, N. W. Downie found similarly listed characteristics of teachers.[16] A randomly selected sample of students were asked to state their views of an "ideal professor." The foremost criteria were knowledge of the subject, interest in the subject, flexibility, and preparation. Costin asked over 200 graduate and undergraduate students to rate their best professor. Items that received high ratings were: well prepared, used relevant examples, followed the logical sequence of thought, and explained clearly.[17]

Many argue that students lack the introspection and long-term perspective to evaluate and judge good teaching. A. I. Drucker and H. H. Remmers supplied evidence which refutes this concept. Asking alumni ten years out of college what they thought the important qualities of an effective instructor were, and comparing their answers to a present undergraduate group, they found that both groups agreed on the ranking of these criteria: (a) adequacy of preparation, (b) interests, (c) stimulation and intellectual curiosity, and (d) progressive attitude. They also found out that present students' ratings correlated positively with alumni ratings of the same professors.[18]

STUDENT ABILITY TO JUDGE EFFECTIVE TEACHING

Another frequent argument against the validity of student ratings is that the student is apt to judge the instructional period more on the basis of entertainment than on the quality of information received, learning, or long-term usefulness. J. D. Royce (1956) concluded that high student ratings were to a large degree the function of popularity.[19] Guthrie (1954) in a broad survey at the University of Washington found that teachers who received the highest ratings were substance teachers and not merely entertainment oriented. In fact, he concluded that popularity of a teacher may well be an index of effective and substantial teaching and that student ratings may reflect both.[20]

The entertainment accusation is a possible farce. A better question might be to see if a professor's interest in the subject makes him or her enthusiastic enough to be entertaining as well. Guthrie found that students were particularly fond of instructors who seemed to be highly interested in their courses.

There is an additional concept that hostile students may assign poor ratings simply as a function of their need for independence beyond the instructor or as a sheer act of hostility. Many students probably felt the rating results would have no effect on the faculty member anyway. There is need for a definitive study of the development of student hostility and faculty evaluation.

Consensus is that the most widely used instrument of evaluation for faculty performance is the student rating scale. Research has provided sufficient proof that these rating scales can supply reliable and valid information on the quality of courses of instruction. This information can be used, though not in isolation, with other evaluation materials in constructing normative data for the evaluation of teaching and may aid an individual instructor in improving teaching effectiveness.

The students' ratings of teaching, though valid and reliable, fall far short of a complete assessment of an instructor's teaching contribution. There are other obvious factors which should be taken into account in any overall measure of instruction. These include participation in committee and institutional service responsibilities, direction of graduate theses and research, teaching awards given by the students, individual innovative classroom instruction, departmental colloquia, participation as a guest lecturer, development of new courses, improving the methodology and material content of a course, plus many other systematic observations of the daily work style of the instructor. However, if teaching performance is to be evaluated for the purpose of individual improvement or for purposes of pay and promotion, the systematic measure of student attitudes, opinions, and observations can hardly be ignored. The use of formal student ratings provides a reasonable way of measuring student reaction.

USEFUL TOOLS FOR FACULTY EVALUATION

Current college teaching evaluation instruments require the student to indicate the degree to which any statement is characteristic of an instructor. Instruments like the widely used Purdue Instructor Performance Indicator usually employ a forced-choice format that asks the student to make somewhat global assessments of the instructor's characteristics. This approach has somewhat severe limitations in terms of student response sets and instructor halo effects. Any instrument that attempts to overcome this problem should permit the student to assess the instructor only on those items that the student considers relevant to that course and that instructor and be composed of items describing specific teaching behaviors. Neither the institution nor the instructor should require the student to make inferences beyond observable behavior as most current evaluation instruments do. A multiplicity of rating instruments presently on the market could be used beneficially in evaluating faculty performance.

Manuals have been developed to help teachers prepare their own evaluation instruments. Likewise, R. R. Perry has developed a "criterion behavior" list of sixty items which can be used in formulating an evaluation instrument.[21] Gadzella and C. E. Gray also have developed extensive lists of criteria which can be useful in the construction of a rating scale.[22]

To make evaluation of teaching as meaningful as possible, W. F. Farrar suggested using the "critical incidents" approach. He suggested that faculty collect critical incidents of faculty behavior from both their peers and students, classify them, and then have the students judge the frequency with which they occur in the classroom.[23]

The use to which student rating instruments results are put depends heavily on the confidence that faculty and administration have in them. Problems are encountered by students and faculty as well when comparisons among courses differ widely in the level, content, and format. Students at different levels rate their courses differently, and required and elective courses may be rated differently. If these ratings are to be used as part of an evaluation of the instructor's ability, then courses should be compared with others of the same general classification and level.

Instructors are more likely to react negatively to ratings (regardless of the end use of the data) if the system is forced on them or handled blindly, statistically, or administratively. However, given choice in the matter, the instructor is likely to accept student ratings as a source of personal evaluation and guidance.

FACULTY DEVELOPMENT PROGRAMS: THE MAJOR THRUST OF EVALUATION

It's not a new idea to start evaluation programs. They are initiated by the dozens each year in colleges and universities. However, it is a new idea to accrue all the benefits possible from an evaluation program, a process often overlooked in the argumentation and noise of rating scales and evaluation forms. Too many say, "I don't mind your attempt at evaluation, but I will not tolerate your pointing a finger at me." Too many evaluated faculty members scan only the present horizon without seeing any immediate impact and do not realize that the eventual success is in the pipeline and coming their way.

Institutional Development

One benefit of faculty evaluations should be individual and institutional development. In-service education and organizational development are a must in solving the widespread dilemma of inadequate performance and preparation. The emphasis is not dismissal but development, not a pink slip but an individual program of development to make a more adequate faculty person.

James Hammons and Robert Simerly suggest accountability through institutional training and development. Hammons cites needs and funds for planned activity and measurable objectives to insure a program of continued development. Simerly identifies the establishment of 400 to 500 faculty development programs instituted in the last several years. His study examines the major approaches to faculty development through the service of an institutional researcher. The thesis in the role of the researcher is to create a reliable data base about each faculty member in order to influence the decision-making process of the power elite in the institution. The researcher would develop programs for each faculty person to follow in an upgrading of his professional excellence.[24]

Regional Centers for Faculty Development

In addition to the institutional research, there have arisen regional centers for faculty development predicated upon gathered data summarized from evaluative resources. Faculty Development Centers assist with the development of nontraditional approaches in undergraduate education throughout regional areas. These centers assist institutions in considering constructive changes within the context of their purposes, goals, and resources. The growth of these centers represent a trend toward translating the traditional institutional verbal commitment to teaching into formal arrangements and budgetary support for genuine and professional efforts to stimulate effective instruction. Such centers could assist the institution in a developmental program for faculty in order to extend their effectiveness and influence in a more direct program of instruction.

I. M. Cook and R. F. Neville and others identify the growth of the faculty development program. Program items listed include personnel development as a priority; new dimensions of personnel development programs; attitudes of a new college or university professor; and the role of a faculty development program in a two-year community college, a four-year college, and in graduate education programs. Other subjects include courts decisions affecting faculty evaluation; faculty evaluations—what do they mean; a model for implementing competency-based programs; the on-campus teaching consultant; preparing faculty members through preservice programs; teaching strategies for postsecondary institutions; career development for faculty personnel; and career development for administration.[25]

Thomas Martin and K. J. Berry as well as John R. Hayes critically analyze the symbolic relationship between a professor's academic and professional roles. Because of this relationship modern universities accept a faculty member's professional accomplishments in the form of research and publications as an index of academic excellence. There is a need for teaching developmental programs for a number of research oriented professors.[26]

TENURE, PROMOTION AND MERIT

After the expiration of a probationary period of appointment, a teacher is accorded faculty status on an indefinite basis better identified as *tenure*. This appointment, generally by regular election of the board of regents or trustees, is to the rank and salary to which a person is entitled by his or her experience, evaluation, teaching skills, and professionalism. The probation period varies by institution from three to seven years. Exceptions can be made to this probation period by the president, president of the faculty, or board of regents or trustees for experienced teachers from other colleges or universities.

During the last year of probation the teacher will be reviewed and a decision relative to continuance and tenure are made. Generally several means of evaluation are used: colleague evaluation, department evaluation, student evaluation, professionalism, publications, and so forth. All of these are taken to form a picture of the faculty members and judgments are determined by these evaluation criteria. No one criterion should determine tenure. A combination of many evaluation instruments and evaluations should be considered.

All *promotions* should be determined using the same evaluative criteria as tenure. An acceptable battery of evaluation instruments by colleagues, students and administrative heads should be identified to the teacher before hiring as the basis upon which future promotions will depend. A criterion for evaluating faculty should be a predetermined part of the tenure-promotion process for the college or university. All incoming teachers should clearly understand the level of competence required for retaining faculty status as well as that required for promotion.

Promotions within a step of faculty positions and promotions between steps (that is, associate professor to full professor) should be determined on an objective criterion as well as by administrative adjudication. The more clear the criteria for promotion the less the confusion when pro-motion does or does not take place.

It is most difficult to explain a promotion criterion without discussing a merit advancement program. *Merit* is a part of any promotional pro-cedure that honors its members beyond the normal modus operandi of the system. Merit often involves an additional increment or progress within a professional rank because of outstanding service or profes-sionalism. Often public service, consultation, publications, national rec-ognition and so forth are part of the criterion for merit.

A college or university should develop a program that can end in a merit advance but should be careful to make the criteria commensurate in some form of accomplishment for every professor. Merit criteria could include classroom expertise, campus service, community service, national service, awards and recognitions, research, publication, and consultations. The institution should set firm policies as to the nature of the reward and the process by which that reward will be given. If all criteria are thoroughly understood and merit is available for all who would want to strive for it, then when a merit promotion or increment is awarded all faculty and staff members will know the basis upon which it was awarded.

Many institutions include merit as part of the promotion and salary increment process. Some increase a professional step by number of dol-lars as a merit increment. The amount is clearly identified to all faculty and staff members so that a merit achievement is not secret. When merit is associated with tenure or rank the achievement may include an incre-ment by virtue of a change in rank or status. For instance, an outstand-ing professor may be in the fourth year of a five-year tenure program and because of outstanding recognition be given tenure a year in advance.

Likewise, a professor might be in an eight-year step as an associate professor and because of a merit opportunity for publishing be ad-vanced to full professor before the promotion is due as a reward for outstanding scholarship. Any of these provisions clearly spelled out to all faculty and staff members are windfall profits appreciated by all in-volved. Merit is a marvelous means of honoring achievers by tangible means.

Faculty evaluation will fall far short if a complete assessment of an instructor's total contribution is not evaluated. Multiple factors must be taken into account in any overall measure of instruction. If teaching performance is to be evaluated for pay or promotion, a complex system-atic process of evaluation must be carefully examined and inputs can be ignored. Student ratings, peer evaluations, and administrative evalua-tions should all be included in the total assessment.

When faculty members make an impact on students and this impact can be objectively evaluated, hiring, retaining, promoting, and tenuring become a more exact process. The process of evaluation should be a growth process for the individual, the students, faculty peers, and the institution as a whole. When faculty members, students, and administrators apply all available knowledge gleaned from evaluative criterion about faculty impact, the parameters of each experience become a developmental growth pattern.

Evaluation is the process to growth. All academicians recognize the necessity for evaluation at the course level. What about the professional instructor level? Does continued growth prevail there? Faculty evaluation should center its thrust in personal improvement. Developmental programs presently available for faculty members indicate a new dimension in academia: a retooling or retraining process for the advancement of the person, the student, the institution. If faculty evaluation can retain this lofty concept rather than its mundane threat aspect, what may happen to academics might astound us all.

NOTES

1. F. Costin, W. J. Greenough, and R. J. Menges, "Student Ratings of College Teaching: Reliability, Validity, and Usefulness," *Review of Educational Research* 41 (1971):511–35.

2. Norman Eagle, "Validity of Student Ratings: A Reaction," *Community and Junior College Journal* 46 (1975):6–8.

3. J. W. Gustad, "Policies and Practices in Faculty Evaluation," *Educational Record* 42 (1961):194–211.

4. Gordon E. Greenwood, Charles M. Bridges, William B. Ware, and James E. McLean, "Student Evaluation of College Teaching Behaviors," *Journal of Higher Education*, November 1973, pp. 596–604.

5. Costin, Greenough, and Menges, "Student Ratings of College Teaching," p. 515.

6. E. R. Guthrie, "The Evaluation of Teaching," *Educational Record* 30 (1949):109–15.

7. G. D. Lovell and C. F. Haner, "Forced-Choice Applied to College Faculty Rating," *Educational and Psychological Measurement* 15 (1955):291–304.

8. Guthrie, "Evaluation of Teaching," p. 113.

9. W. J. McKeachie, "Student Ratings of Faculty," *AAUP Bulletin* 55 (1969):439–44.

10. W. J. McKeachie, Y. Lin, and W. Mann, "Student Ratings of Teacher Effectiveness: Validity Studies," *American Educational Research Journal* 8 (1971):435–45.

11. S. A. Cohen and W. G. Berger, "Dimensions of Students' Ratings of College Instructors Underlying Subsequent Achievement on Course Examinations," *Proceedings of the 178th Annual Convention of the America Psychological Association* 5 (1970):605–6.

12. R. G. Lathrop, "Unit Factorial Ratings by College Students of Courses and Instructors," mimeographed (Chico, Calif.: State University, 1968).

13. G. M. French, "College Students' Concept of Effective Teaching Determined by Analysis of Teacher Ratings," *Dissertation Abstracts* 17 (1957):4585.

14. P. L. Crawford and H. L. Bradshaw, "Perception of Characteristics of Effective University Teachers: A Scaling Analysis," *Educational and Psychological Measurement* 28 (1968):1079–85.

15. S. Musella and R. Rush, "Student Opinion on College Teaching," *Improving College and University Teaching* 17 (1968):137–40.

16. N. W. Downie, "Student Evaluation of Faculty," *Journal of Higher Education,* Vol. 23, 1952, pp. 495–96, 503.

17. F. Costin, "Intercorrelations Between Students and Course Chairmen's Ratings of Instructors," mimeographed (University of Illinois, Division of General Studies, 1966).

18. A. J. Drucker and H. H. Remmers, "Do Alumni and Students Differ in Their Attitudes Toward Instructors?" *Purdue University Studies in Higher Education* 70 (1950): pp. 62–64.

19. J. D. Royce, "Popularity and the Teacher," *Education* 77 (1956):233-37.

20. Guthrie, "Evaluation of Teaching," p. 110.

21. R. R. Perry, "Evaluation of Teaching Behavior Seeks to Measure Effectiveness," *College and University Business* 47 (1969):18–22.

22. Gadzella, "College Student Views and Ratings," pp. 89–96.

23. W. E. Farrar, "Dimensions of Faculty Performance as Perceived by Faculty," *Dissertation Abstracts* 29 (1969):3458.

24. James D. Hammons, "Suggestions Concerning Institutional Training of New Faculty," *Community College Review* 1 no. 2, pp. 49–60; Robert G. Simerly, "Improving Institutional Accountability Through Faculty Development: Reacting to Conflicting Pressures in Post-Secondary Education," (a paper presented at the Annual Conference of the Association for Institutional Research, May 1976).

25. J. M. Cook and R. F. Neville, *The Faculty as Teachers: A Perspective on Evaluation* (Washington, D.C.: ERIC Clearing-house on Higher Education, George Washington University, 1971), pp. 147–65.

26. Thomas W. Martin and K. J. Berry, "The Teaching Research Dilemma: Its Sources in the University Setting," *Journal of Higher Education* 40 (December 1969):691–703; John R. Hayes, "Research, Teaching, and Faculty Fate," *Science* 1, 2 (April 1971):227–30.

Student Evaluation Form

SAMPLE

Course Title: _____ Course No.: _____ Section (if any): _____

Course Instructor: _____

This is a confidential questionnaire; you need not sign your name.

Your thoughtful answers to the items on this form will provide helpful information for your instructor.

Instructions: 1. For each item or statement please circle the number which best represents your thinking. Be sure to circle only one number for each statement. If you circle more than one number for any single item your response for that item cannot be used.

2. If any particular item does not apply to this course, skip that item and move to the next one.

Section I

Rate the frequency of your instructor's procedures in this course in the following areas, using this code:

       1 -- Never
       2 -- Seldom or hardly ever
       3 -- Sometimes
       4 -- Frequently
       5 -- Always or almost always

The instructor:

		Never	Seldom or hardly ever	Sometimes	Frequently	Always or almost always
1.	Evidenced a thorough knowledge of the subject.	1	2	3	4	5
2.	Was well prepared for each class session.	1	2	3	4	5
3.	Encouraged class participation.	1	2	3	4	5
4.	Stimulated students to think.	1	2	3	4	5
5.	Demonstrated the importance and significance of the subject.	1	2	3	4	5
6.	Respected students' comments and views.	1	2	3	4	5
7.	Gave assignments that related to the course objectives.	1	2	3	4	5

Copyright © 1978 by Dallas Theological Seminary: Reproduced by permission.

8. Used teaching methods that were suitable to the subject matter.   1   2   3   4   5

9. Gave helpful insights on the subject.   1   2   3   4   5

10. Had self-confidence.   1   2   3   4   5

11. Required an amount of work throughout the semester that was appropriate for the credit hours received.   1   2   3   4   5

	Never	Seldom or hardly ever	Sometimes	Frequently	Always or almost always
	1	2	3	4	5

12. Provided meaningful assignments to involve the students in the learning process.   1   2   3   4   5

13. Related the subject matter to life situations (or theory to practice).   1   2   3   4   5

14. Was actively helpful when students had problems.   1   2   3   4   5

15. Was available to meet with students outside of class.   1   2   3   4   5

16. Gave quizzes and/or exams that were free from ambiguity. (Skip this item if no exams or quizzes were given.)   1   2   3   4   5

17. Answered students' questions competently.   1   2   3   4   5

18. Was clear and easy to follow.   1   2   3   4   5

19. Gave quizzes and/or exams that accurately assessed what was learned in the course. (Skip this item if no exams or quizzes were given.)   1   2   3   4   5

20. Motivated students to do their best work.   1   2   3   4   5

21. Controlled class discussions to prevent rambling and confusion.   1   2   3   4   5

22. Showed friendly concern for the students as individuals.   1   2   3   4   5

23. Seemed enthusiastic about the subject.   1   2   3   4   5

24. Assigned grades that were fair and impartial.   1   2   3   4   5

25. Responded to students' questions in a friendly manner.   1   2   3   4   5

Section II

Rate your agreement/disagreement with items 26-35, using this code:

1 -- Strongly disagree
2 -- Disagree
3 -- No strong feeling either way
4 -- Agree
5 -- Strongly agree

	Strongly disagree	Disagree	No strong feeling either way	Agree	Strongly agree

26. The instructor prepared a helpful course syllabus.   1   2   3   4   5

27. The instructor gave course objectives that were meaningful and were relevant to the subject.   1   2   3   4   5

©1977, 1978 by Dallas Theological Seminary. All rights reserved.

		Strongly disagree	Disagree	No strong feeling either way	Agree	Strongly agree

28. The instructor accomplished the objectives stated for this course.   1   2   3   4   5

29. The instructor made the assignments and grading clear.   1   2   3   4   5

30. The instructor usually seemed well organized.   1   2   3   4   5

31. I gained much factual information on the subject of this course.   1   2   3   4   5

32. I gained a better understanding of problems and issues in the subject.   1   2   3   4   5

33. I greatly increased in my appreciation for the subject.   1   2   3   4   5

34. I often applied (or was motivated to apply) course material to my life situations.   1   2   3   4   5

35. I developed skills and competencies needed in this field.   1   2   3   4   5

Section III (To be filled in only by students in preaching groups, practicums, seminars, and other group situations. If this course did not include such a group, skip this section and go on to page 4.) Do not fill in this section to evaluate student assistants.

Use the following code:

     1 -- Never
     2 -- Seldom or hardly ever
     3 -- Sometimes
     4 -- Frequently
     5 -- Always or almost always

The instructor:

	Never	Seldom or hardly ever	Sometimes	Frequently	Always or almost always

36. Made helpful analyses of the students' techniques, in preaching, teaching, or other group situations.   1   2   3   4   5

37. Suggested specific ways students can improve, in preaching, teaching, or other group work.   1   2   3   4   5

38. Encouraged students to develop their own technique, in preaching, teaching, or other group work.   1   2   3   4   5

39. Seemed genuinely interested in helping each student progress, in his preaching, teaching, or other group work.   1   2   3   4   5

40. Was openminded and objective in evaluating the students' work, in their preaching, teaching, or other group work.   1   2   3   4   5

Section IV

Indicate your overall rating of this course, using the following code:

     1 -- Unsatisfactory
     2 -- Poor
     3 -- Acceptable

4 -- Good
5 -- Outstanding

	Unsatisfactory	Poor	Acceptable	Good	Outstanding
41. My overall rating of the <u>course content</u>:	1	2	3	4	5
42. My rating of the instructor's overall <u>teaching effectiveness</u>:	1	2	3	4	5
43. My rating of the overall <u>value of the course</u> to me:	1	2	3	4	5

Section V

What features of the course were strengths which should be repeated in future classes?

_____

_____

_____

_____

How can the course be improved?

_____

_____

_____

_____

Additional comments.

_____

_____

_____

_____

Rev. 9/77, 1/78

9

Faculty Unionism: The Campus Crisis

RHEY NOLAN AND BOB W. MILLER

Academia, like most vibrant institutions, is continually faced with new and challenging issues. But, perhaps, the academic world is least able to handle these issues in an efficient and satisfactory manner because of the divergent goals and objectives of those involved. Most institutions or businesses are controlled by an administrative staff united towards a common goal: maximum profits. Academia, however, is not united on just what "maximum profits" constitutes in higher education. And so the main issue of the 1980s and 1990s in higher education, unionism, may create discord within any college or university.

The thesis of this chapter concerns administrative leadership power and responsibility within the unionized campus. Without a doubt, the most affected group on the unionized campus is the administrators. Studies to date show a difference of perceptions when examining the loss of administrative "power" on the unionized campus. Frank Kemerer and J. Victor Baldridge found that "presidents on unionized campuses feel they have lost power to unionized faculty, and foresee a steady erosion of the administrative capacity by faculty unions." While they concede that college and university presidents feel a loss of power, they also believe that, "Despite the president's feelings of vulnerability, evidence indicates that there is actually a shift toward greater administrative power. Internally, more and more decisions are forced upward, away from departments to the central administration."[1]

DEFINITIONS

Academic freedom—Exists in a community of teaching and learning where freedom of the mind and spirit are accepted as fundamental privileges which cannot be directed through administrative or coercive channels.

Commonalities—A system of rewards which are available to all staff personnel without regard to rank, tenure, race, sex, or national origin. Faculty have objectives in common.

Due process and tenure—The process of arbitration which is given a faculty person in danger of losing a job. Sets forth the conditions under which that arbitration may take place.

Line management—Administrators who are in the administrative vertical positions in relation to the president or chancellor, through whom all materials, both beneficial and detrimental, should flow in due process.

Merit ratings—A criterion system for recognizing faculty achievers based on a nonbiased set of standards available to all faculty and staff personnel.

Mirror image—Persons hired in a division or department who have feelings, beliefs, and life-styles similar to the department or division head.

Reward system—Incentive program available to all personnel, constructed on a criterion basis and not biased in its administration. May include increased pay, release time from teaching responsibilities, sabbatical leave, national recognition, etc.

Tripartite—The three parts of the administrative process: administrator, professor, student.

UNIONIZATION

While accepting Kemerer and Baldridge as authorities in the field of faculty unionization, one must certainly question the validity of their evidence. We have only to observe the executive in a unionized private industry to realize the usurpation of power and responsibilities by the union. Determination of wage rates, whom to hire and fire, and working conditions are all areas that suffer removal of executive power and discretion by unionization. Leaders in education generally realize that the advent of campus unionization does create additional personnel or administrative responsibilities, but it is perhaps questionable that this "is actually a shift toward greater administrative power." Kemerer and Baldridge do seem to be aware of this point, for they noted:

The burdens of negotiating and administering the complex provisions of contracts compound the difficulties of administration. Campuses are increasingly balkanized into "Veto groups," and administrative discretion to respond to campus problems is increasingly circumscribed by contractual provisions, particularly in personnel areas.[2]

Others who take the position that administrative authority will increase on the unionized campus include Caesar Naples, who concludes that

Written contracts and binding arbitration are not the threat to managerial authority feared by many. Rather, collective bargaining presents management with the opportunity to delineate areas of managerial freedom of action which were cloudy and unclear under traditional governance. The negotiation and administration of contracts will tend to require that managers develop resources and skills essential to effective management. Yet traditional faculty governance mechanisms add significantly to the process of decision making and should continue to exist, at least for the time being.[3]

The farsighted college or university administrator must be cognizant of the fact that unionization, if it hasn't already occurred on his campus, will likely take place. Therefore, Naples makes a significant point in advising that the continuation of mechanisms will bridge the gap created in faculty-administrative relations as the result of campus unionization.

The administrator must also bear in mind the possibility that the faculty will utilize the union to enhance their strength and power in the decision-making process. Kemerer and Baldridge feel that "Faculties will use unions to establish stronger faculty participation in decision making in institutions that have never had a strong tradition of faculty governance and to preserve their role in governance where it is being challenged."[4] Increased participation in the decision-making process by faculty could produce excellent results. Every progressive educator is a proponent of increased involvement by faculty in most phases of the decision-making process. How beneficial increasing faculty roles will be depends largely upon the attitude taken by the administration. The administration will either gracefully accept the new faculty role, or it will adopt an adversary attitude. The role of adversary can, and usually does, work two ways.

One main area of concern for administrators involves due process and tenure. When the American Association of University Professors (AAUP) organized, its first major task was to insure the protection of academic freedom in higher education. Later the association promoted the idea of "academic due process." Everett Carl Ladd, Jr., and Seymour Martin Lipset note that "Over the years, it [AAUP] demanded, and in large measure secured, the institutionalization of academic 'due process,' with respect to safeguards governing the conditions under which professors might lose their job."[5] Such "academic due process" creates a dilemma for the administrator. Most administrators at all leadership levels of a college or university want the finest, most distinguished, most diversified faculty members possible. With the institutionalization of academic due process and tenure, an administrator is forced to resort to what many would perhaps consider "unethical" means of upgrading weak departments. Many high level administrators will confidentially seek advice from outside the college or university to aid in preventing lower echelon administrators from staffing their departments with their "mirror image" faculty members. A political science department full of Henry Kissingers would not be a strong political science department.

Under unionization the only way for the upper echelon administrator to have any control over the diversification of faculty is to have a hand in the hiring process, for once faculty are hired, even if on probation, they are usually here to stay.

The tendency of unions to try to reduce or eliminate the power of "management" to differentially reward employees appears also with respect to the issue of job security, or tenure. Unions seek to have new job appointments defined as "probationary" ones, which implies a claim to permanency for anyone who demonstrates that he can handle the job. Once appointed, a person should have a superior claim to a permanent position, even if a more able candidate should subsequently appear.[6]

The "sharp administrator" must do his utmost to insure faculty quality, for unions tend to encourage promotions and tenure by default. Many tenured or to be tenured faculty are not truly tenure material, at least in terms of the quality we expect in exchange for tenure.

HOW DOES UNIONISM COME ABOUT?

If all personnel in educational institutions had been treated fairly in past years, it is likely that unionization would not have occurred or at least would have been slowed down. Items of concern from the faculty viewpoint include treatment by immediate supervisors, delegation, trust, accountability, fringe benefits, salary, working conditions, discrimination, and the administrator's leadership style.

Most effective faculty members want administrators who understand how to work with people effectively and efficiently, who know how to lead, who can and will make decisions when necessary, and who on appropriate occasions will delegate trust and hold employees accountable. Teachers also want administrators who know about reward systems and can bring about rewards when they are deserved.

When individual faculty members *cannot* obtain the above-mentioned items they begin to seek other alternatives. These faculty members discover that they can more nearly secure the items they need and want by working with large numbers of people. Where do you find large numbers of people with common goals and objectives? Teachers find them in either professional organizations or unions. Formerly teachers and administrators belonged to the same professional organizations. Both groups found that enough commonalities did not exist for them to remain in the same organizations. Thus, administrators formed professional administrators' organizations while faculty stayed with faculty professional organizations. Both groups moved in separate directions, causing splits between teachers, administrations, and boards of trustees.

To combat the splitting or division type of problems all groups must find commonalities in the educational domain involving effective and efficient education for students. Educators and boards must concentrate more on what is good for students. If common areas of concern are not found by all groups, administrators, teachers, board members, students, and education will all continue to lose. Each problem area will then be negotiated or go through the collective bargaining process. In the long run, all groups will suffer, especially students.

WHERE DO MERIT RATINGS FIT INTO THE PICTURE?

Previous ideas of tenure dealt with the idea of "merit." Individual salaries for faculty members likewise dealt with merit. But Kenneth P. Mortimer and G. Gregory Lozier note that today in higher education,

> . . . bargaining agreements tend to substitute the "objective" standards of seniority and time in rank for the principle of merit. The agreement is that faculty members of equal rank and longevity are entitled to equal pay. While a few clauses are found which allow for merit raises above and beyond the minimum salaries provided for by the contract, pressure upon the administration to abide by the scale may inhibit the free distribution of merit increments.[7]

Hence, we find another administrative discretion or responsibility assumed by the union. Merit salary increases have always been a way for the administrator to reward outstanding, meritorious service by individual faculty members. But according to Ladd and Lipset,

> More important, perhaps, than the limitations on merit increases is the fact that the union contract has shifted the decision power for such individual raises from the administrative structure to "peer judgement." This eliminates the power of administrators to implement the so-called "star" system, the emphasizing of "quality" or prestige distinctions among the faculty.[8]

If administrators are not able to use the "star" system of merit pay and tenure, are we then correct in assuming that academic and faculty quality are declining under unionization? Or do we accept the notion, expressed by many, that "professionalism" will maintain that quality? If the latter is true then we must all, someday, agree upon a definition of professionalism.

Another administrative concern is faculty bypassing the "line management" and going directly to the state legislature for its needs and desires. Occasionally unionized faculty will try to justify their union associations by reminding executives of the outside forces that threaten higher education. "The forces that threaten higher education come primarily from outside the academy, and collective bargaining is a positive response to those threats—an attempt to preserve certain important values in face of escalating external pressures."9

It is safe to say that these outside forces are, most notably, the state legislatures. While it is true that state legislatures can exert considerable pressure, especially by threatening to withhold appropriations, the administrator must be aware of and prepared to deal with unions and unionized faculty members who meet and "negotiate" directly with the state legislature. *Time* magazine, in an article entitled "Unionized Professors," stated that

> Professor Donald Percy, a vice-president of the University of Wisconsin, fears that unionization could well result in the end of academic autonomy for state-supported universities as faculties "leapfrog" their administrations to negotiate directly with legislatures. "What is there to prevent the legislatures from negotiating tenure or curriculum?"10

Thus, another area in which administration could see power units removed. The following case study demonstrates why unionism begins to appeal to many faculty members.

THE FACULTY SENATE TO CONSIDER BARGAINING

Professors seek greater influence—a case study at a major university: (North Texas State University, Denton, Texas).

A resolution establishing a committee to study collective bargaining for the faculty will be considered Wednesday by the Faculty Senate.

The resolution is sponsored by Dr. Larry Brown and Dr. Robert Smith of the history faculty.

"Collective bargaining could be a cooperative venture between the faculty and administrators—another means of communication to achieve an acceptable disbursement of funds," Dr. Brown said. "It doesn't have to be an adversary relationship."

"I want to know if collective bargaining appeals to the faculty. It was brought up several years ago and the faculty was indifferent to it. Maybe the time has come to ask the question again."

Dr. Smith said a collective bargaining agent might increase the amount of faculty input into the budgetary process.

"I am interested in a collective bargaining agent for the faculty discussing with administrators how university funds are disbursed," Dr. Smith said. "We don't have any say-so in how much money the deans appropriate to the departments. Maybe with a collective bargaining agent we could have some input into the distribution of funds."

Both faculty members said although the resolution was triggered by recently published reports on administrative and faculty pay raises in the budget, the main reason for the resolution is the decline of faculty real income in the last decade because of inflation.

"We are losing to inflation year after year," Dr. Smith said. "We can't blame the administration for that. It's the legislature. Then again, maybe a collective bargaining agent, not just for this university but for all universities, would have a better arrangement worked out with the legislature."

The Association of College Teachers released a study this year indicating that faculty salaries in public universities have decreased 16 percent in purchasing power since 1969.

"The faculty have been very passive in the matter of salary allocations, and collective bargaining might give us a position to take to the administration and the legislature," Dr. Brown said.

"I'm not saying the faculty ought to say how much money should be allocated, but a collective bargaining agent could communicate to the persons who make the division of funds what our needs are," he said.

"Neither of us is advocating unionism," Dr. Smith said. "With collective bargaining, we could have a little more control over our fate."

Some state laws prohibit state agencies from entering into collective bargaining agreements with state employees represented by a labor organization, but allow state employees to present grievances concerning wages, hours of work or conditions of employment either individually or through a representative that does not claim the right to strike.

Also some state laws further prohibit state employees from engaging in strikes or organized work stoppages against the state.

Dr. Brown said recent public statements by the vice president for administrative affairs, that faculty members could increase their teaching load and eliminate faculty positions in order to receive "whopping raises" were "sophomoric and asinine."

"It's not just the teaching load we have," Dr. Brown said. "We have committee work, writing for publication and research."

Dr. Smith said many faculty members carry more than a nine-hour load. "The criteria for promotion in the College of Arts and Sciences is publication," Dr. Smith said.

"If we had a collective bargaining agent, there wouldn't be as many irresponsible statements by administrators," he said.

In the past year's budget, faculty members averaged a 5.1 percent increase, including promotions, and 4.9 percent excluding promotions.

Salaries for the president, vice presidents and persons reporting directly to them increased 12.1 percent overall from last year's budget.

Full professors received a 4.2 percent salary increase university-wide, associate professors received 5 percent and assistant professors averaged 5.5 percent.

Instructors averaged a 5.3 percent salary increase and lecturers received a 5.4 percent increase. The President said no raises were granted to teaching assistants.

Individual faculty salary increases ranged between 0 and 22.3 percent.

The faculty salary increases were calculated by comparing the previous years salary of each member with what the same person receives in the new budget. It does not include faculty members hired after last year's budget was prepared or unfilled positions for which money was allocated.

Dr. Smith said he taught at Purdue University and "their philosophy toward the faculty was expressly opposite of the philosophy here in the South."

"The administrative attitude was that without a faculty, you don't have an administration. When there's a financial crunch, they take care of the faculty first. So when money was tight, they did without capital improvements."

STUDENTS AND THE UNIONIZATION PROCESS

Naturally, the administration, the union, and everyone else involved in higher education policies and procedures must be aware of the *students*, for it is their needs that should dictate the functioning of the institution. But another faculty justification for unionizing is the existing, supposed, or assumed power and influence of the student in the university. The campus demonstrations of the late 1960s and early 1970s led to the administration's courting of student opinion, and, to some extent, approval, in certain operations of the college or university. Such increased student involvement has aided, in some cases, the rise of certain unionized faculties. John Hepler, cited in Ladd and Lipset's book, indicated that "A report by a Central Michigan faculty member of the background of the NEA victory there in September, 1969, contends that the faculty were discontented with the new president's concern for students, at the expense of faculty interest. They supported collective bargaining as a way of restricting an overly pro-student administration."[11]

Attitudes and actions such as this may cause the students caught in the middle, between the administration and the faculty unions. Surprising as it may seem, it is quite possible that students will begin to side with the administration. The students begin to tire of a multitude of faculty rules and requirements, of the impersonality of the professor/student relationship, and of the lack of faculty concern with actual teaching as perceived by the students. T. R. McConnell predicts that students will demand and get a review of the total work load of faculty members and of the distribution of faculty time and that collective bargaining will rapidly become tripartite rather than just bilateral negotiation. He says that it is easy to see why administrators and students may find it advantageous to combine against the faculty, not only in the distribution of the fundament, but also in moving toward evaluation of faculty services and in establishing standards for appointment, promotion, and tenure. McConnell feels it is not inconceivable that on many of these questions students may ultimately acquire the balance of power.[12]

Are we viewing another area of declining administrative power and responsibility? Does the future hold an administrative hierarchy concerned only with the payment of bills, assignment of custodial duties, and other caretaker responsibilities? The possibility definitely exists. Whether a unionized campus will dictate this caretaker status is left to the discretion of American educators.

It is fitting that this chapter should discuss students and their future role under unionism, for the student is often the forgotten segment of the tripartite. It is certainly correct to assume that students will not be involved in labor-management negotiations. According to F. M. Brandes, "Since student interests are not represented at negotiations, it is student interests that must eventually suffer."[13]

How, then, will the student suffer from something that does not directly affect him? Alan Shark states that "When faculty demand more money, fringe benefits and reduced teaching loads, student tuition and fees may rise or essential student services will be cut. Course offerings will be reduced or programs phased out."[14]

It is necessary to realize that the student *is* directly affected by faculty/union demands. Shark, in another treatise, points out that students do constitute one of the primary memberships in the college or university community, yet they have failed in their efforts to acquire negotiation rights. He concludes that "truly sharing in a community of interests" requires that students, faculty, and administration be able to sit together at the bargaining table.

Figure 40 questions where the student will find his niche in faculty union-administration negotiations. Will the student sit at the top of the

FIGURE 40
Student pyramid

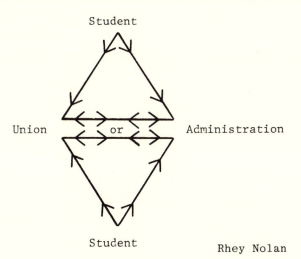

Student

Union   or   Administration

Student   Rhey Nolan

triangular bargaining table, giving significant input to both labor and management, or at the bottom of the inverted triangle, with one-way communication coming from both labor and management and no provision for student input? These experts will not speculate the eventual outcome, but offer a model for study.

Figure 41 suggests the student at the top of a triangle *providing input* to both the faculty union and the administration. The student also is at the bottom of a connecting inverted triangle *accepting input* from the faculty union and the administration. All the while negotiations are continuing between the faculty union and the administration. The important aspect of this model is the involvement of the student in the negotiation process. (The negotiation process is viewed here as a continuing activity, not operable only during periods of contract renewal.)

The faculty union and the administration must keep in mind the idea that in economic terms the student is the "buyer," while everyone else in the tripartite is the "seller." As with any buyer, if students are not satisfied with the product and the means by which they gain the product, they can and will go elsewhere. It is relatively safe to conclude that not all colleges and universities in a given geographic area are going to unionize, and if nonunionized facilities provide superior services and at the same time accept student input, then the student may exercise his option to enroll at such a facility. The benefits of being unionized then become moot.

FIGURE 41
Student pyramid

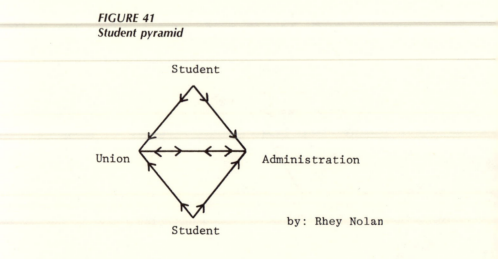

by: Rhey Nolan

NOTES

1. Frank R. Kemerer and Victor J. Baldridge, *Unions on the Campus* (San Francisco: Jossey-Bass 1975), p. 9.

2. Ibid., p. 10.

3. Caesar Naples, Jr., "Collective Bargaining: Opportunities for Management," in Jack H. Schuster, *Encountering the Unionized University* (San Francisco:Jossey-Bass 1974), p. 59.

4. Kemerer and Baldridge, *Unions on the Campus*, p. 11.

5. Everett Carl Ladd, Jr., and Seymour Martin Lipset, *Professors, Unions, and American Higher Education* (Washington, D.C.: American Enterprise Institute for Public Policy Research, 1973), p. 5.

6. Ibid., pp. 71–72.

7. Kenneth P. Mortimer and Gregory G. Lozier, *Collective Bargaining: Implications for Governance* (University Park, Pa.: Center for the Study of Higher Education, Pennsylvania State University, 1972), p. 27.

8. Ladd and Lipset, *Professors, Unions, and American Higher Education*, p. 71.

9. Ellis Katz, "Faculty Stakes in Collective Bargaining: Expectations and Realities," in Jack H. Schuster, *Encountering the Unionized University* (San Francisco: Jossey-Bass, 1974), p. 27.

10. "Unionized Professors," *Time*, 6 November 1972, pp. 74–76.

11. Ladd and Lipset, *Professors, Unions, and American Higher Education*, p. 92.

12. T. R. McConnell, *The Redistribution of Power in Higher Education: Changing Patterns of Internal Governance* (Berkeley: Center for Research and Development in Higher Education, University of California, 1971), p. 137.

13. F. M. Brandes, "Point of View," *Chronicle of Higher Education*, 16 April 1973, p. 12.

14. Alan Shark, "A Student's Collective Thoughts on Bargaining," *Journal of Higher Education* 43 (October 1972), p. 558.

10

Collective Bargaining: A Winner or a Loser for Educational Personnel?

HAZEL M. JAY AND BOB W. MILLER

Recent developments in collective bargaining are not entirely new. Some have their roots very deeply in the past; others have had false starts many times over the years and are now beginning anew. Fundamentally, the emergence of organizations of employees arose because it is in the nature of modern industrial society to organize. Employees also organize when employers do not provide appropriate salaries, fringe benefits, job enrichment, or working conditions. When there are large-scale operations, large sums of money, large numbers of people, the only way individuals seem to have an impact is through organized effort.

DEFINITIONS

American Association of University Professors (AAUP)—Organized in 1915, AAUP has been involved in protecting academic freedom, tenure, and due process, advancing faculty salaries, and gaining faculty involvement in the governance of the college or university.

American Federation of Teachers (AFT)—Organized in 1916, AFT is a part of the American Federation of Labor. Is the most aggressive organization for teacher rights.

Arbitration—A process of negotiation between a professional negotiator and an employment group. All decisions from this process are binding on the collective group.

Bureaucracy—Academic governance in which the faculty has little to say about the implementation of the school enterprise but are handed down decisions and determination from above.

Campus autonomy—Each campus has the privilege of interpreting broad state guidelines under the direction of its president and board of trustees. Each campus is a separate entity to be dealt with individually.

Collective bargaining—A process of joining persons with common needs to bargain with an employing agency for specific physical or spatial needs. Commonly used by unions to achieve desired ends.

Collegial governance—Academic governance in which faculty has a strong voice in the implementation of the school enterprise.

Grievance citation—A petition which may be presented to an institution by the representatives of a collective union. Represents the needs and interests of all under the umbrella of that particular collective union.

Morale or esprit de corps—A feeling of togetherness and companionship usually generated by a common cause.

National Education Association (NEA)—Effective at state and federal levels and has its strength in community colleges and public school districts.

Negotiation—A due process carried on with a school employer by delegated representatives of a teachers union for the purpose of reconciling a grievance or personnel problem.

Non-resolvement—A collective bargaining request that cannot be resolved and is turned over to a professional negotiator. In most union organizations all decision-making processes are forfeited to the negotiator and all decisions are binding on the members of the collective union.

Political governance—Academic governance in which faculty and administration have little to say about the implementation of the school enterprise, which is determined by the political system that governs the institution. In this context the assumption is that the political force is the state government.

Strike—A process whereby members of a union stop work in a collective fashion, none performing their assigned task until the grievance issues are settled or clarified.

Superordinate—A supervisor immediately above a particular person in line supervision. Supervises all activities of that person including all academic privileges.

Union—A collection of persons employed in a common enterprise joined together for the purpose of exerting collective pressure on the employer.

HISTORICAL DEVELOPMENT

Three major periods of union development can be delineated, with the first lasting from 1900 to the mid-1930s. This was the era in which skilled craftsmen unionized. The second period, from the mid-1930s to the mid-1950s, was characterized by the unionization of semiskilled workers. The third period began in 1960, when unions began to make inroads with the white-collar worker employed in the public sector.

Teachers began to unionize and strike during this period. Since 1962 employees in public education are seen as an emerging sector of collective bargaining and have developed negotiation procedures with over 1,500 school boards. Teacher negotiations have taken place in many states, and strikes have been numerous.

In the years since the collective bargaining process began, a series of strategies and tactics consisting of diplomacy, politics, and poker have developed. On occasion the process has been backed by coercive pressure. Generally collective bargaining has been viewed as a system of representative government. Members participate in the decision-making process concerning their working environment, salaries, terms and conditions of employment, and other matters related to their interests as an occupational group. Three principal characteristics of collective bargaining are: the representative has the authority to make decisions; the organization representative speaks only for the members; the bargained-out decisions are contracted by majority vote.[1]

Three organizations have made a decided impact on the direction of collective bargaining and have position statements relative to their mission. The American Federation of Teachers (AFT), organized in 1916, is an affiliate of the American Federation of Labor. It is the most militant, aggressive organization and has more members than the other two organizations. It also has the dedication and organizational talents of activist supporters. The American Association of University Professors (AAUP), founded in 1915, has been more involved in protecting academic freedom, tenure, and due process, advancing faculty salaries, and gaining faculty involvement with university governance. Since 1974 its membership has dropped, and there are indications that more emphasis will be on shared authority, collegiality, peer control, academic freedom, and responsibility. The National Education Association (NEA) organizational structure is influential at the national and state level and has its strength in community colleges and public school districts. The future of the NEA is dependent upon its success in negotiating coalition mergers and alliances with other groups.[2]

Other organizations may become effective in representing faculty, particularly where there are law school units in close proximity. Faculty senates, councils, and associations are dependent upon institutional approval. Since administrators are members of the academic organizations, they can not take part in the bargaining process. The improvement of faculty employment conditions certainly falls within their province, but the nature of collective bargaining does not allow for their participation. Joseph Hankin reported that when a union was formed on a campus, the campus organizations ceased to exist. It is believed that in-house representation would have difficulty putting forth the faculty cause before the public.[3]

WHY COLLECTIVE BARGAINING?

It is generally conceded that unionization occurs as a response to changes in the environment of education and in the structure and function of individual institutions and systems of institutions. Additionally, faculty desire effective administration and a voice in determining the conditions under which they function. As the economic, political, and demographic climate changes, it becomes more essential that appropriate methods are developed to allow for communication and negotiation in an environment conducive to resolution of the issues. In times of inflation, when the legislature and government control salary and fringe benefits for educators, the threat of strikes may increase.

As greater internal power has become concentrated in university/college administrators, and as the collective bargaining movement has grown, a change has occurred in faculty. Faculty feel threatened and there are concomitant changes in their sense of security. Faculty members today approach this issue as craftsmen did fifty or sixty years ago.

Externally the American system of education has changed, in the size of its institutions and with the growth of multicampus institutions, consolidation of systems, and increased demands for accountability. Additionally, faculties have had to do more, class enrollments have increased, and tenure has been more difficult to obtain. Threats to faculty positions and differences arising among faculty have brought about many unresolved issues, including policies that foster open admissions, special treatment considerations for minority students, and undue expectation of faculty participation in the total program. More specialized departments serving as support services are part of the growing numbers that want a voice in the operations of the college.

Does campus autonomy exist when collective bargaining occurs? There is no single point of view. It depends on the size of the institution; the philosophy and type of administration. Many faculties see the bargaining process as a method to protect faculty prerogatives. The administrative point of view is somewhat different, in that the administration and board of an institution should be able to determine its priorities within broad state requirements. The commissioner must represent the campus and remain an advocate of education in the arenas of the public, taxpayer, legislature, and governor. The board of trustees has relationships similar to the commissioner plus the responsibility for optimizing access and quality of education.[4] Furthermore, the board must protect the idea of enough campus autonomy to maintain faculty quality, fiscal integrity, and student affairs programs.

The literature describes at least three traditional academic governance concepts: collegial, bureaucratic, and political. All three may support academic collective bargaining, but the bureaucratic and political models would be less likely to support the negotiation process. It is doubtful that the collegial perspective reflects governance today. However, there are indications that faculty unionization supports the beliefs and principles of the collegial model. The bureaucratic and political models reflect an undercurrent of purpose that would support the drive for unionization, contract negotiation, and contract administration. Regardless of the chosen position or stance, the choices are few. The decisions of all groups have been and will continue to be difficult to make.[5]

NEGOTIATION ISSUES

Faculty workload has been discussed frequently in the last few years, particularly at state supported institutions. Grievances concerning teaching work loads or the allocation of the work load among faculty may have a greater impact than differences with a department chairperson. However, some industrial studies have indicated that relations with the immediate superordinate may be the most important area of concern for the individual employee. The philosophical views of faculty must be considered and, if unresolved, a grievance citation may be instituted. Regardless of who hears the petition, there are limitations, one from the institution and the other in the language of the collective bargaining contract.

Concerns about wages, benefits, and job security are considered important issues and frequently cause faculty to seek help from union-type organizations. Additional dimensions that cause fear among faculty include fear of budget cuts, problems of teacher surplus, and lack of input in governance. The influx of unions is a protective reaction against external economic pressures as well as a reflection of the desire to be more involved in the decision making of the college. If enrollments and reward systems decrease, chances are greater that union affiliation will take place.[6]

The AAUP has been concerned with the problems of maintaining academic standards as well as with developing evaluative procedures that would allow peer group discretionary privileges to make tenure recommendations and to prevent abuses of the evaluative process. Other emerging patterns indicate that students, faculty, and administration are more likely to keep this issue directed toward evaluation and promotion and make explicit the departmental procedures for tenure.

Pressure from legislators, state coordinating agencies, and boards of trustees for retrenchment and accountability has accelerated the trend to adopt management techniques in the operations of the colleges and universities. A new style of operation is emerging which, unlike the old one, relies mainly on control, planning, evaluation, and reallocation to promote institutional strength within fiscal constraints. The reaction by faculty is predictable in that there is confusion, resentment, and general resistance.[7]

WINNING OR LOSING THE BATTLE

Who wins or loses in the battle of collective bargaining? Even though teachers may have no other way to successfully achieve increased benefits, the group that usually gets hurt the most is the students of an institution. The reason is that divisions occur, between faculty and administration, faculty and the board, and sometimes even between faculty and students. The concept of working for the organizational goals of quality control in the educational program is lost.

When faculty, administration, and boards of trustees are on separate sides, the element of trust is lost and, therefore, morale and esprit de corps suffer. Also, when this split among professional educators occurs professional organizations decline in numbers. If a professional organization declines from 200,000 to 125,000 members, the result will be a loss of impact on state and federal legislative bodies.

In addition, everyone seems to lose when faculty members, administration, and boards lose control of their own political negotiation powers. Once an item of non-resolvement is turned over to a lawyer or a professional negotiator, some of the educational groups lose all decision-making powers. The arbitration is binding on all educational groups. The educators' hands are tied. In other words, the education profession would be much better off playing on the same team and resolving issues on their own instead of bringing in an outside agent.

There is a tradition in education that recognizes excellence in teaching and community service. Unions, as they have developed in the United States, have concentrated on obtaining benefits for their membership. If true unionization is the form which characterizes collective bargaining in higher education, a decrease in professional attitude and motivation among faculty members may be the result. By subordinating professional status to economic expediency, faculty members may lose academic freedom. Differences brought about by collective bargaining movements on individual campuses may bring about changes in faculty work loads, curricular organization, and instructional staffing patterns.

Collective bargaining is not likely to lie dormant in most state legislatures. Several sources indicate that many teachers view strikes as distasteful; however, the balance of power may swing toward the unions once teachers realize that negotiation and other elements of the collective bargaining process might help them gain more inroads into the overall decision-making processes of their respective educational institutions.

NOTES

1. Joseph W. Garbarino and Bill Aussiecker, *Faculty Bargaining: Change and Conflict* (New York: McGraw-Hill, 1975), pp. 27–36.

2. Joseph N. Hankin, "What's Past Is Prologue," in *Adjusting to Collective Bargaining*, ed. Richard J. Ernst (San Francisco: Jossey-Bass, 1975), pp. 13–22.

3. Ibid., p. 14.

4. Frank R. Kemerer and Victor J. Baldridge, *Unions on the Campus* (San Francisco: Jossey-Bass, 1975), p. 224.

5. Ibid., pp. 3, 15.

6. Ibid., pp. 64–65.

7. Ibid., p. 219.

11

Women Administrators in Higher Education: Cooperation or Conflict?

BOB W. MILLER AND CAROLYN K. SCHROEDER

In order to discuss how men and women can work together more effectively, a number of specific items will be presented with solutions proposed for the specific problem.

Daily operation in the office and social activities associated with the job. Questions such as the following are frequently asked: Can a man act as he has in the past with men when a woman manager is present? Must he give up his pipe and cigar and have two sets of language? Should he open doors and pull out chairs for the woman? Will a small amount of flirtation help build the working relationship?

There are no basic rules, policies, or guidelines for men and women managers to follow in this area. Problems are not generally solved when people are afraid to discuss the issues; therefore, sessions can and should be held to bring the issues out into the open to be dealt with freely.

DEFINITIONS

Conflict resolvement strategies—Field-tested strategies to resolve specific conflict situations.

Leadership models—Differing types of leadership styles (Theory X, Theory Y, Theory Z, Contigency Theory, Management by Objectives). The behavior consistency exerted by the person in a superordinate or emerging role.

Performance appraisal—Scientific evaluation instruments for the purpose of evaluating and appraising performance.

Problem-solving and decision-making techniques—Differing types of models for solving specific problems or making specific decisions.

Team management concept—A concept of management which considers the total strength of the entire management team and uses each member's strength rather than one member's weakness.

TRAINING PROGRAMS DEALING WITH MEN/WOMEN ISSUES

In regard to training programs of various types, much of the education process depends upon a psychological approach. For example, one executive held a meeting on "How to shorten meetings and how to cut down the number of meetings." The managers who participated came up with twenty guidelines in each area for improvement factors. The guidelines were important but not nearly as important as the psychological impact on the subordinates which came from being involved in the discussion of guidelines for implementation purposes. Likewise, if there are to be sessions on such topics as "How to bridge the gap between men and women executives," an awareness exists which in itself has a psychological impact on the men and women who participate.

In addition to the male/female awareness issues, other items which should be discussed between the two groups are leadership approaches, problem-solving and decision-making techniques, conflict resolvement strategies, team management concepts, group concerns, communications, and so forth. Several major corporations have held such awareness sessions for their executives and managers and have found the sessions helpful in bringing out hidden feelings about women.[1]

PERFORMANCE APPRAISAL AND THE EXECUTIVE

One of the primary guidelines that a manager should utilize is that of evaluating the tasks rather than the individual attributes of the subordinate. Of course, personality and other personal attributes do make a difference in the task performed; however, performance appraisal must be consistently fair. The manager should also evaluate in terms of the goals and objectives set forth by the organization.

All too often managers, whether female or male, want to play the role of the "good ole boy or girl" during the evaluation process. They will evaluate a subordinate's performance as being in the top 10 to 25 percent of all employees and six months later they want to fire the same subordinate for incompetence. The evaluation has not been consistent.

No one likes to be involved in the firing process, although it is sometimes necessary for the sake of the organization. It is important that manager and superordinates stand together on the data gathered when this process becomes necessary, and it is just as important that the employees be told the same "story" by everyone involved.

THE INTERVIEW PROCESS

An old adage important at this stage for the woman executive is, "An ounce of prevention is worth a pound of cure." More specifically, the executive should interview for the role of the given job to be filled and should interview for specific relationships with colleagues. For example, will men and women be working together as a team or as superordinates and subordinate?

If the roles in connection with male and female relationships are defined in the initial interview, many future problems may be avoided. The interview is an excellent time to teach what is expected from both the male and female executives.

DRESS AND APPEARANCE OF THE "SOPHISTICATED EXECUTIVE"

Appropriate attire is important for the male and female executive alike. However, this does not imply that the "IBM Gray Flannel Suit" image is necessary for the woman to be effective and efficient. On the other hand, a woman in a management role cannot afford to wear Levi's or cheap pantsuits which give a "thrown together" image.

The woman executive can be feminine in her role and dress accordingly but a mistake is made when she tries to dress like and otherwise emulate the male. Above all, caution stresses avoidance of extremism in any form by female or male executives. The rule of thumb is that an executive, male or female, should dress as if there were an important appointment every day. Recently a state higher education task force was having lunch at a private club. All male and female managers were dressed on a sophisticated basis, with the exception of one male manager who wore a sloppy but clean golf shirt. During the meal, the lieutenant governor of the state joined the group and, needless to say, the underdressed manager was most embarrassed.

WOMEN MUST MAKE THEIR OWN DECISIONS IN RELATION TO THEIR POSITIONS

Women must be allowed to make the tough decisions as well as the easy ones. They should be trusted and held accountable for the tasks and areas assigned as their jobs. To be effective decision makers, women must learn how to define problems, gather appropriate information, list alternatives, analyze the consequences of alternatives through advantages and disadvantages of each, make decisions, utilize appropriate strategies to implement those decisions, and evaluate the decisions.

One problem that college presidents and business executives have in the area of administration and learning is not to be defensive when they throw out recommendations or ideas to a board or an executive staff. Women managers must also be aware that this is a tremendous conflict area and that more managers and executives get fired over this item than all other combined.

WOMEN AND EQUALITY

Women must make a unified effort to express what they really want as a group of managers or executives. At the present time, there is no concensus on these needs or desires. The National Association of Bank Women has conducted seminars for male managers. At one session the men were divided into two groups. One group was asked to list adjectives describing a good manager; the other, to list adjectives describing the "ideal woman." The lists follow. *Good manager:* intelligent, aggressive, objective, decisive, reliable, flexible, motivated, pressurized, sensitive, responsible, trustworthy, considerate, imaginative, goal-oriented. *Ideal Woman:* attractive, wealthy, educated, supportive, flexible, intelligent, mature, tolerant, decisive, open-minded, frugal, loving, gentle, soft-spoken, conversationalist.

Only three adjectives—flexible, intelligent, and decisive—appeared on both lists. These factors could lead to conclusions such as, male managers do not want to take directions from their ideal woman, the ideal woman is not the effective manager, or, men do not want the same characteristics in girlfriends or spouses that they want in effective superordinates.

The question is, what would women managers have listed if they had the same opportunity of responding to the two lists? Another question is, why were female executives not given the same chance to respond as the male managers?[2]

RESPECT DIFFERENCES AND EMPHASIZE COMMONALITIES

All of us have individual differences, otherwise our jobs would not be exciting and we would not have different types of automobiles, clothing, products, or entertainment. But to work in an institution or corporation, it is important that our philosophical beliefs and organizational goals be similar in nature. The major concern is that managers must work cooperatively and turn conflict of individual differences into resolvement through teamwork or compromise.

In connection with respect of differences and emphasizing commonalities between men and women managers, the following questions often arise.

1. What will a man's wife think if he has a female boss? She will have to adjust, as men have for years.

2. How does a man cope with a woman who cries? "Toughness" is a loaded word in the executive domain. Men consider toughness as a priority element in the management world. It is important

for women to develop this skill, yet not be misinterpreted as a "cynical female manager."

3. Is the woman with no skill, experience, or education made a boss just to fill a quota for affirmative action? Sometimes, and this probably does more harm to other aspiring women executives than any other single factor. This is also true for incompetent men who are promoted.

4. Will the woman's lack of clout hold the man who is her subordinate back from future promotion? This is similar to situations involving holding back women; the fact of the matter is that it depends on the woman or man involved.

THE WOMAN EXECUTIVE: A VICTIM OF STEREOTYPES

Women have been stereotyped in our society. Some of the more prominent examples follow, along with debate.

Women Managers Lack Education, Training, and Experience

Both women and men must exhibit expertise in management and leadership if they are to be given the opportunity to fill the role of executive. The statement that women lack education and training is becoming more and more untrue as many women presently training for management and executive roles receive much the same training that male leaders have undergone to obtain their present situations.

It has also been said that women are less willing to seek additional education, to take on extra work, to work overtime or travel. In reality, women are going back to school to update their knowledge, have the same intrinsic motivation as men to do extra work, and involve themselves in overtime and travel.

The women executive must be competent if she is to be an effective manager. Studies have indicated that the competent woman manager with appropriate education, experience, and training will have fewer problems dealing with male executives. On the other hand, when a woman without these essentials is placed in a management position, reverse discrimination may be charged. Thus, men become resentful.[3]

Women Managers Are Tied to Family

This statement is partially true, in that some women may be reluctant to leave their families for purposes of travel. However, this statement is also applicable to some men. The single person, male or female, has definite advantages in relocation and travel as an executive. The question is *if* the single woman plans to raise a family after achieving her executive position. After she is married, how long will she wait to do so and will it conflict with her position? In defense of women in this area, it should be pointed out that absentee rates are similar for men and women and there is no greater job turnover for women than for men.[4]

Women Are the Weaker Sex

Due to set roles and activities in the past, women have become known as the weaker, softer, more sympathetic and emotional sex. They handled what many men thought to be the "easy" tasks in life such as cooking, cleaning, grocery shopping, and rearing the children. Thus women have become stereotyped as being capable of handling only these duties, and deviation therefrom has caused the present day problem of men and women working together on the same level.

Medical studies show that women live longer, are tougher physically, and can endure more pain and disease than men. The woman in her capacity as cook, housekeeper, and shopper must be an organizer, to prepare meals; a manager of funds, while shopping and hunting for bargains; and meticulous in carrying out her cleaning chores in addition to being a diplomat, when handling children and sometimes acting in the role of arbitrator. The woman in her capacity as "domestic engineer" has many of the same qualifications as the male manager or executive who handles the everyday problems of running a business.[5]

The Sex Factor

This is generally considered a taboo issue, not to be discussed between men and women. The general guideline in relation to sexuality and female and male executives is that both men and women use their charm and charisma to obtain favorable decisions. Some men and women use them as a strategy in working with the opposite sex. It is important that this topic be discussed during the interviewing process in order to avoid any future conflict in this area, A point to consider, however, is that while some men and women may use this sexuality to achieve desired results, many men in the executive world may use their friendships or "buddy system" in much the same way.

Emotional Factors Affect Women as Managers

Another problem that men and women must deal with daily is stress. This topic has been discussed more in connection with women than men. Women must get their feelings under control so as not to precipitate emotional battles when working with other managers. When a woman loses her temper and control, she is said to be emotional; when a man loses his temper, he is said to be an effective, tough executive who can make the difficult decision.[6]

Men and Women Are Not Equal and Should Not Receive Equal Pay

The following statement was made by the benefits administrator of the Johnson and Johnson Corporation. "The woman executive has equal competence, experience, and education with the male manager at the same level but still does not receive equal pay." This statement becomes more important each day due to the fact that women at present make up a proximately 40 percent of the total work force. More and more women have moved up as far as executive status is concerned. It is reported that women's salaries and fringe benefits have increased; however, the reports do *not* show that salaries and fringe benefits are equal to those of men with similar training, education, and experience.

Effective and efficient superordinates will obtain the best possible salaries, fringe benefits, and working conditions for all employees. It has been said that we can tell how great the manager is by how much he lifts his people up, not by how much he holds them back. How, then, can we afford to accomplish less than the best for female managers?

Fear of the Unknown

There are men in any field that feel insecure around competent subordinate managers. There is an insecurity in the male that causes him to fear that he may not be as good as another and, thus, feel his position may be threatened. This situation is amplified when the "threat" is in the form of a woman, because of the common belief of men that they are stronger and more capable of handling the more difficult decisions in life. When the "weaker, less competent sex" achieves, it is a blow to the male ego. It is evident that in some cases a male prejudice against women exists. Male managers, on a whole, do not want to admit that a woman might be as capable and sometimes more capable than themselves. Cutting down on these insecurities and prejudices can solve some of the problems of female managers working with male executives.

One should recognize the fact that people, male or female, differ from one another. Characteristics such as emotions, skills, education, and competence vary not only from man to woman but also from man to man and woman to woman. When filling an executive position, an individual's strengths and weaknesses, not gender, should be the basis upon which the final decision is made.

NOTES

1. Marilin Bender, *"When the Boss is a Woman," Esquire,* 28 March 1978, pp. 35–41.

2. Ibid., pp. 35–41.

3. Darrel Long Tiller and Robert Maidment, "Effective Women Managers: Fact and Fantasy," *Forum* 5 (May 1978), pp. 6–7.

4. Ibid.

5. Ibid.

6. Ibid.

12

Motivational Theories Applied to Higher Education

Motivational Theories

PAULA S. BRIN

Our society is dominated by organizations. Most people spend over half of their waking hours in work organizations. Because increased productivity and effectiveness is a major objective of any organization, whether it be an educational or business enterprise, motivation becomes a major area of concern. In discussing motivation, two key questions arise: (1) How can an individual within any organization be continually motivated to work at his optimum performance? (2) How can an underperformer be motivated to increase his productivity? In order to propose possible solutions to these questions, it is necessary first to examine three major leadership theories which enjoy widespread acceptance and utilization in work organizations today. We will then examine various motivational factors, and finish by reviewing possible causes for underperformance that need consideration.

DEFINITIONS

Hygiene theory—Developed by Frederick Herzberg, this theory identifies motivational factors in terms of satisfiers and dis-satisfiers. These likewise are developed from lower needs to higher related needs producing genuine personal satisfaction.

Maslow's Hierarchy of Needs—A compendium of elevated levels which describe a progression from base needs (physiological) to achievement needs (self-actualization) with descriptive indicators as achievement success.

Motivation—A conscious and unconscious effort to stimulate efficient productivity by meeting a taxonomy of human needs—biological, sociological, and sociocultural.

Theory X—Authoritative style of management with a work-centered approach to structure and productivity and an external force as an authority figure.

Theory Y—Participative style of leadership with all members of a group integral contributing partners in the enterprise.

Theory Z—Systems management designed to allow prediction of effects of organizational change with some degree of correctional action as a result of external or internal change. A type of situational motivation and leadership.

LEADERSHIP THEORIES

Although a myriad of leadership theories exists today, two major leadership styles encompass the extremes in management technique: authoritative leadership and participative leadership. A third leadership style which has gained widespread acceptance in the personnel management realm, often referred to as "contingency leadership," is an attempt to utilize a system encompassing both extremes of the authoritative and participative leadership styles, depending on situational environments to determine which is most effective.

A brief analysis of each of these three leadership theories will provide an overall understanding of how motivational techniques are used by leaders (supervisors or managers) in each of these organizational structures. A more complete explanation of the authoritative, participative, and systems management styles may be found in Chapter 4, Organizational Design and Management.

Theory X: Authoritative Style of Leadership

Douglas McGregor, of the Massachusets Institute of Technology and author of *The Human Side of Enterprise*, believes that management's traditional assumptions about people were unrealistic and that management's methods of implementing those assumptions often led to the failure of many well-laid plans. He coined the term "Theory X" to describe this authoritative style of leadership in an organization.[1]

Theory X is a work-centered approach to organizational structure and productivity, operating under the theory that an external force, specifically an authority figure, is needed to motivate workers to achieve goals. It rests on the philosophy that complete authority is the key motivating force directing the course of an organization. Three basic assumptions on the nature of work and human behavior in work situations are inherent in Theory X: (1) The average human has an inherent dislike of work and will avoid it if possible; (2) because humans dislike work, most must be forced, controlled, supervised, and threatened with punishment to get them to work; and (3) the average human being prefers to be told what to do, avoids responsibility, has minimal ambition, and desires security above all else.[2]

The Theory X organizational system is one of strict hierarchal power. Decision making is highly centralized and located at the apex of the organization; thus, the nominal head of the organization is the locus of the decision-making process. The supervisor is merely an agent of higher authority whose function is optimizing goals of the organization to the rank and file (work force). In addition, since work is assumed to be distasteful and people are assumed to tend to avoid work, the supervisor's efforts must be oriented toward production.[3]

The worker in Theory X is regarded as an individual unit directly responsible to his supervisor; he is a cog in a machine to be directed, coerced, and controlled in order to achieve organizational goals. His function is to perform only his present job. "Hired hand" is an appropriate term to use in this situation in that only the hands seem to be useful; the nature of this system disallows any interest in the complete man. Little room for self-improvement or self-advancement exist.[4]

The major motivational force in Theory X is punishment—the threat of discharge, which might keep the employee from fulfilling his financial obligations. There is minimal or no intrinsic satisfaction or fulfillment in work. Likewise, the worker possesses little or no ambition or creativity since the organizational structure does not facilitate acknowledgement of such traits.

In evaluating Theory X, research in many but not all cases indicates low production, not because of an inability to perform, but as a result of a deliberate restriction of output. Any attempt to increase output aggravates the situation. Conflicts arise between workers and supervisors; consequently, worker morale is low and little job satisfaction exists. Because of this theory's stifling effect, workers withhold creative ideas to avoid possible conflict.[5]

Theory Y: Participative Style of Leadership

Research by social scientists in the human relations field caused McGregor at a later date to establish a new set of assumptions on the nature of work and human behavior in work situations. Theory Y is a people-centered approach to organizational structure and leadership. The extreme opposite of Theory X on the continuum, Theory Y emphasizes human relations and is characterized as "participative." Six basic assumptions underlie Theory Y.

1. Utilization of physical and mental efforts in work is as normal as play or rest. The average person does not dislike work. Attitude depends on controllable conditions.
2. External control and threat of punishment are not the only

means for achieving organizational objectives. Man will exercise self-direction and self-control in the service of objectives to which he is committed.

3. Commitment to objectives is a function of the rewards associated with their achievement. The most significant of such rewards, such as the satisfaction of ego and self-actualization needs, can be direct products of efforts directed toward organizational goals.

4. The average human being learns, under proper conditions, not only to accept, but to seek responsibility. Avoidance is generally an effort of experience, not an inherent human characteristic.

5. The capacity to exercise a relatively high degree of imagination and creativity in solving organizational problems is widely distributed in the population.

6. Under the present conditions of modern industrialization, intellectual human potentialities are only partially utilized.[6]

Decision making in Theory Y is widespread and diffuse, based on the premise that the average man has the capacity to exercise a relatively high degree of creativity, imagination, and ingenuity. The role of the supervisor, consequently, is one of acceptance. He replaces the authority and power of Theory X with the persuasion and participation tactics. He is no longer dealing with individual units, but with a group of which he is a member. His intragroup function is to serve as a leader; his intergroup function is coordinating the efforts of the two groups to which he belongs.[7]

The individual in the participative organizational structure of Theory Y is an integral member of a group. He has a need to maximize the contribution of each member of the group by encouraging individual growth and self development.

Motivation in Theory Y is derived from satisfying the ego, and the self-participation process, though difficult to handle, offers the opportunity for unity and loyalty among workers. If such group loyalty can be propagated, the following positive effects can be realized by the individual. He will (1) have a greater identification with the group and greater feelings of belonging, (2) have more friends in the group and the company than outside, (3) have better interpersonal relations among members of the work group, (4) have a more favorable attitude about his job, and (5) have a higher production with less sense of strain or pressure.[8]

Theory Y espouses the view that man is a rational being, intelligent and capable of making his own decisions. He is willing to work and needs work to satisfy deep-seated psychological needs. The acceptance of authority rather than the right of authority is one of the major differences between Theory Y and Theory X.[9]

The major drawback to Theory Y is that it is not easily implemented. First, management must give up some of its traditional authority. Second, when it becomes necessary to use certain controls, workers must be given reasons for the option. Third, Theory Y does not let the manager remain aloof. It requires competent interaction with the group. Fourth, workers must know their personal goals, be informed of organizational goals in terms that are easily understood, and, in consultation with them, methods must be found to make the two congruous.[10] An equally important problem is the fact that participative management will not work unless employees are trained to be self-motivated, self-directed, and responsible for their individual assignments.[11]

Both theories X and Y are too sweeping and are based on too many generalizations. Neither theory is in accord with current research discoveries. They assume a consistent relationship between: (1) job satisfaction and productivity, (2) degree of participation and productivity, and (3) type of supervisor and productivity.[12] Human behavior cannot be so neatly parceled and controlled. Theory Z is an attempt to propose a more middle-of-the-road approach, trying to take into account the diversity of human nature.

Theory Z: Systems Management

Theory Z is a systems approach to management designed to allow prediction of effects of organizational change with considerable accuracy. For our purposes, a "system" will be defined as a recirculating type of process capable of some degree of corrective action. This corrective action can result from internal change in the system or external environmental changes. A system is usually made up of one or more subsystems on which the entire system is dependent and vice versa since variable and interdependent situational factors make it impossible to establish a single system. One fact to keep in mind is that what works for one organization may be a total failure for another.[13]

The Theory Z contingency management concept operates under the following philosophy. When the performance of an organization is relatively poor in achieving organizational goals, authoritative processes of motivation and structure may be necessary to initiate corrective action. However, as the organization achieves expected goals, participative patterns of organization become more effective and are expected by the members of the organization.

In Theory Z, the level of decision making varies with the degree of participation at which the organization is functioning at a given time. When decision-making functions are retained within the work group, a participative organization structure is feasible; but as decision-making processes experience an upward movement, away from the work group affected by those decisions, formal structure and authoritative processes are more effective. The role of a supervisor, then, varies with the situation. He must be able to operate at various times either as an authority figure or as a participative member, depending on the circumstances. Usually, the larger the organization, the more formal and complex its structure, with the processes appropriate to motivate workers becoming more authoritarian than participative.[14]

The role of the individual worker, like that of the supervisor, is subject to fluctuation in Theory Z. Participative processes may work when goals of the organization and individual are consistent, but a more authoritative system is required when organizational goals and individual goals are divergent. However, Theory Z requires that as the need for interaction increases, the organizational structure should accommodate, allowing a free flow of information and ideas. Likewise, accompanying motivational process should become more participative and informal in nature.[15]

The main problem with Theory Z lies in determining the nature of the system. If it is to operate effectively, the organizational structure must reflect the personalities and expectations of its employees. Those who expect authoritarianism and who are dependent on those around them for motivation react best to an authoritarian system of structure and motivation. Those who expect interaction and participation are largely motivated from within and react best to participative organizational processes and less rigidity.

Theory X and Theory Y operate on opposite ends of the organizational structure continuum. Theory Z is a more flexible structure which demands a systems approach whereby an organization can alter its management processes to accommodate its employees' personalities and individual traits to effect more successful management and supervision. It is important to remember that increased productivity is the goal of any organizational system, and all three of the aforementioned management styles have proved successful in various situations.[16] The next section will deal with various motivational methods that may be employed to increase productivity.

MOTIVATIONAL METHODS

Until recent years, the area of worker motivation was almost totally ignored as a method for increased productivity; instead, the research emphasis was directed mainly at the organizational structure as the primary means for increasing production. The worker's attitude was considered only incidently in relation to the structure. The Institute of Social Research of the University of Michigan, however, has been conducting systematic research on the principles of organizational structure and the principles and practices of leadership that result in high productivity and job satisfaction. The basic concept under which the Institute of Social Research operates is the philosophy that no matter how varied the task nor in what phase of business, common fundamental principles can be applied to effective organization of human activity. It postulates that scientifically valid data can be obtained which allow for these statements of general principles and that these principles can then be transferred to various situations.

In order to understand a worker and know how to effectively motivate him, several key principles for understanding individual personalities must be considered.[17]

1. Personality is a product of heredity, environment, and learning experiences in life.

2. Complexes are an interrelated system of charged emotional ideas.

3. Humans possess several common traits, such as intellect, goal setting, tool design, and communication skills.

4. Training activities should use these common traits to enhance the learning experiences of personnel in terms of motivation and supervisory effectiveness.

5. Observing individual differences through personnel records, job observation, and social contacts enhances a supervisor's ability to utilize all organizational aspirations.[18]

Virgil Rowland notes, "There are four areas of knowledge which the management (or supervisory) person needs to be familiar with if he is to direct his people adequately: (1) He needs to know what he is supposed to do as a manager (or supervisor). (2) He needs to know to what degree he is expected to perform on certain parts of his job. (3) He needs to know how well he is expected to perform on the job segments, and (4) He needs to know how well he is actually performing them."[19]

A supervisor must be able to employ certain leadership techniques to facilitate motivation. First, he must set a personal example for his subordinates to follow. Second, he must be able to utilize persuasion tactics to instigate change or acceptance. Third, he must have consistency in his own behavior. Fourth, he should maintain a system of regular rewards, emphasizing the positive and deemphasizing the negative whenever possible. And finally, he should set and maintain a challenging work pace for himself and his subordinates.[20]

One of the major problems encountered in establishing an organizational structure that encourages a desire for increased productivity on the part of the worker is the confusion and lack of insight as to what factors are motivators. Abraham Maslow's "need hierarchy" theorem can be applied to aid in clarification. Maslow's Need Heirarchy is pyramidal in the shape, with the satisfaction of physiological needs at the bottom. These physiological needs, which include rest, food, clothing, and shelter, are the first needs an individual must meet, but are also the lowest-level needs. Once the physiological needs are met, man begins to strive for security, or protection against deprivation. The third level in the hierarchy deals with the social aspect of mankind, his need for association, a sense of belonging, giving and receiving love, and identification. After these first three levels of needs are achieved, man begins to strive for status, recognition, and respect. The highest level of development in the Need Hierarchy is that of self-realization, self-actualization, and self-fulfillment. Maslow concludes that a man cannot and will not progress to the next highest level until the lower one has been achieved.[21] In organizational management, it is important to be aware that man has an inherent desire to continually strive for the highest level in the pyramid.

With Maslow's hierarchy in mind, most experts in organizational design agree that hygienic factors (maintenance needs) do not serve as motivators. The following hygienic factors, therefore, are not important in themselves, but their absence may create unrest or dissatisfaction; consequently, they are significant in that they must be maintained at competitive levels in order to retain present employees and attract new employees.

1. Physical needs—work layout, job demands, rules, equipment, location, grounds, parking facilities, aesthetics.

2. Social needs—work groups, coffee groups, lunch groups, social groups, interest groups.

3. Status needs—job classification, title, furnishings, location, privileges, relationships, company status.

4. Orientation needs—job instruction, work rules, group meetings, shop talk, newspapers, bulletins, handbooks, letters, bulletin boards, grapevine.

5. Security needs—fairness, consistency, reassurance, friendliness, seniority, rights, grievance procedures.

6. Economic needs—wages and salary, automatic increases, profit sharing, social security, workmen's compensation, unemployment compensation, and retirement, paid leave, insurance, tuition, discounts.[22]

Because money is vital to our society, it is interesting to note that money is considered a hygienic factor. That is not to say that it is unimportant, but according to research done by Frederick Herzberg and others of the Psychological Service of Pittsburgh, it does not serve as a motivator. It can, however, be considered a measurement of success. Factors intrinsic to the job itself serve as motivators. Consequently, opportunities for advancement and the way a supervisor performs his job are important as motivators.[23]

Once hygienic factors have been identified and eliminated as true motivators, the problem becomes one of human dynamics. A supervisor must try to design job situations that create experiences leading to positive attitudes toward work and the job itself. True motivational factors involve incidents associated with feelings of self-improvement, achievement, the desire for an acceptance of greater responsibility, and recognition for achievements. Because job design is fundamental to the satisfaction of such needs, it is important to any motivational system. For the professional worker, minor changes in organizational policies and administration often permit these motivators to operate more effectively.[24] Masterson states: "After a person has experienced the deep job of satisfying the higher needs, he becomes more or less insatiable as regards his need for prestige, reputation, self-actualization, and the like. Hence, these needs serve as powerful motivating forces within an individual."[25]

The following factors have been delineated as motivators with respect to increased productivity.

1. Delegation of duties, access to information, freedom to act, atmosphere to approve.
2. Personal growth and achievement.
3. Merit increases, discretionary awards, profit sharing.
4. Company growth, promotions, transfers and rotations, education, professional memberships.
5. Utilized aptitudes, work itself.
6. Responsibility, recognition.
7. Involvement, goal setting, planning, problem solving, work simplification, performance appraisal.[26]

A person with high achievement needs requires a variety of stimuli. He enjoys the responsibility of problem solving and demonstrates in repetitive situations the desire to set goals that are challenging. He is willing to take reasonable risks. Likewise, he desires to know how well he is performing in his work.[27] "People seek to achieve a sense of importance from doing difficult but important tasks which help to implement goals which they and their friends seek."[28] Self-realization is a powerful motivating force in successful men. This explains why they continue to take on arduous tasks and responsibilities again and again.

Equally important to high achievement needs is the need for recognition. Managers and professionals are usually willing to dedicate great amounts of time, energy, and enthusiam to their contributions if they feel those contributions will be sufficiently recognized.

Mobility is also considered to be an important motivational factor. An individual may be motivated when opportunity for mobility within the organization exists, due to a need for growth, achievement, increased responsibility, and recognition. Oftentimes a person will stagnate for too long a time. Most people desire variety in job demands. Mobility allows for new experiences, whether a move is lateral or vertical. Promotion, strictly defined as a vertical movement upward in organizational hierarchy and usually associated with pay increase, is a common mobility technique. Inherent to the idea of promotion are increased responsibilities.[29]

Up to this point, the emphasis has been primarily to focus on positive methods of motivation, minimizing the negative aspects of motivation—discipline. But negative aspects cannot always completely be eliminated. As next to the last resort, fear psychology may be introduced. If a supervisor has tried every technique at his disposal and still has failed to motivate an underperformer, he needs to ask himself the following questions: Have I really tried hard enough? Should I try one more time? He should be sure never to transfer or promote individual problems. This does not rule out the possibility of transfer if a manager is satisfied that all other alternatives are inadequate. Thus, the fear psychology used would be the threat of transfer to an undesirable job situation.[30]

Termination or discharge is the ultimate alternative. If all other possibilities have been exhausted, discharge is the last resort. Just as an internist sometimes exhausts all his medicinal cures and turns to a surgeon, an organization must sometimes do the same. There is no point in retaining a cancerous toe that will eventually destroy a healthy leg and perhaps cause death. In such a case, losing a toe is a bargain, because the patient is saved. For the healthy, smooth operation of an organization, termination of an underperformer who is not interested in changing may be the only answer.[31]

Even after the decision to terminate an employee has been made, four alternatives for discharge may still be considered. One is disability leave of absence. This is less than total separation. The underperformer knows he has to reconstitute his channels of energy utilization if he is to return. This alternative gives him the opportunity to look for another job without the stigma of being fired. A second alternative is early retirement. If the individual is of an appropriate age, this would be a less jarring experience. Third is the possibility of forced resignation. Man's work is a central part of his life. If his higher needs are not being satisfied at this position, he might be more satisfied elsewhere. Also, because of the possible negative effects on other members in the department of other alternatives—tolerating his unsatisfactory work, disability leave of absence, or premature retirement—this may be the healthiest for all concerned. The final alternative is discharge. It is ultimate and final. Opportunity no longer exists for developmental action. This move "requires guts," as Frederick Haas puts it.[32]

Although hygienic factors are important to consider in organizational design because they can serve as dissatisfiers in a work situation, it is the motivational factors of responsibility, recognition, achievement, and mobility that will encourage increased productivity. To implement and administrate procedures that are designed to fulfill these needs requires a skillful and trained supervisor. Therefore, the next section in this chapter is devoted to identifying the role of a supervisor in motivating his subordinates.

THE SUPERVISOR'S ROLE IN THE MOTIVATIONAL PROCESS

A distinct correlation exists between the role of the supervisor and productivity. Consequently, the role of the supervisor is a key factor in any motivational system. A supervisor's skill in overseeing his subordinates as a group is an important variable in success: the greater a supervisor's skill in using group methods, the greater the productivity and job satisfaction of the work group.[33]

The following four major factors determine the effectiveness of the supervisor as a motivating force.

1. *Organizational climate.* Policy area is a major concern.
2. *Style of management.* The most effective style is when a high concern for the needs and goals of the individual is expressed. In other words, the management is oriented to people as well as production.
3. *Delegation of authority.* The supervisor's role must be clearly delineated from those being supervised.
4. *Use of participative methods.* Evidence indicates that participation contributes strongly to motivation of employees.[34]

Consideration, however, must be given to the fact that even though the supervisor's role is a distinct element in the motivation of employees, effective supervision is heavily dependent upon organizational climate.

Given the proper organizational climate, the supervisor must develop a sensitivity to his subordinates and be aware of whom to motivate, how to motivate, when to motivate, and when to use alternative motivational tools.[35] An effective supervisor is able to identify with his employees and stay psychologically close to them.

Open channels of communication become extremely important to the supervisor. He is aware that he needs a combination of efforts organized to get a task accomplished through people. If there is no human interchange and the employee feels he is only an instrument of production, he is likely to be a low producer. Therefore, it is important for a supervisor to show an interest in an employee's problems both off and on the job. Research indicates a high correlation between the kind of supervision and the productivity and satisfaction an employee derives from work.[36]

Mobility is also vital in the motivational factors for the supervisor. An effective supervisor trains his employees for their present job as well as the next higher job. In this way, the employee is aware that if he performs his present job well, he may have a chance for promotion and a new challenge. In addition, the supervisor should attempt to restructure an individual's work so that it will become more challenging, and thus also satisfy higher level needs.

Decision making is another technique in which a supervisor can train his subordinates. This will give the worker a sense of responsibility and relieve some of the supervisor's burden. To do this, a supervisor must require his subordinate to make his own decisions by having him list alternatives to a problem and then select one. After selection, the individual should be prepared to support his decision.[37]

Continuous reinforcement is the most valuable technique a supervisor can utilize to motivate his subordinates. In order to do this, the supervisor must learn to observe from the background. He must have a clear idea of what satisfactory performance is and let his people know what they have to do to measure up to these standards. In addition, he must be prepared to demonstrate the right technique if it becomes necessary. Finally, he must look upon training as a continuous process and nurture it with continual evaluation and feedback. In attempting to raise levels of aspiration, in a positive appraisal interview he must tell his subordinate what presently exists and what potential there is for increased responsibility.

Once an individual has been given a chance to demonstrate his worth on the job and when he has earned the right to it, a supervisor should give him full recognition. Recognition reinforces a positive self-concept and usually motivates a person to strive for higher goals in order to acquire additional recognition. If an employee feels his supervisor is interested in his well-being and recognizes his achievements, he will more likely be a high producer.

To be a good supervisor, a person has to have a variety of ways to manage and motivate subordinates. He has to know his people and what is important to each. He must listen to them and encourage them to talk, building a sense of importance concerning them and their work. High but not impossible standards should be set for the group. A supervisor must be considerate and consistent in his behavior. He has to have established objectives and a sense of direction for himself and his subordinates. Whenever possible, he should give orders in the form of suggestions or requests. He must delegate responsiblity for details, showing his staff that he has faith in them and expects them to do their best. He must maintain open channels of communication, keeping subordinates informed and asking them for their opinions and suggestions. When one is offered, he should let the individual know what action is taken. This gives the subordinate a chance to participate in the decision-making process. In addition, a supervisor should let his people know where they stand. If criticism or reproval is in order, it should be taken care of privately and constructively. Any praise, however, should be done publicly. All of these items are important for a supervisor to consider as he deals with the problem of motivating individuals. If an employee feels his supervisor is interested in him as a person, he will generally produce for him.[38]

LOW MOTIVATION FACTORS

Certain low motivation factors need to be clearly defined. A major reason for this is that the cause of underperformance may be one of perception. The worker may perceive objective reality as one thing while his supervisor may perceive it as another. For example, a supervisor may see a task as a challenge, but his employee may view it as a threat. At this point, the worker's second-level needs of security go into operation; the supervisor's third and fourth levels do. In other words, the supervisor perceives the task as a positive, but the worker may view it as a negative.[39]

Another possible cause for underperformance is that the worker may be satisfying his first- and second-level needs (physiological and security) on the job, while higher level (affiliative and egoistic) needs are being satisfied off the job.[40] The supervisor's job, then, is to challenge the worker to strive for higher levels on the job by creating more challenging job situations.

A final area of concern when evaluating the underperformer is the question of interpretation. A supervisor should not say "soon." He must be definite. He should always talk in terms that are meaningful to him and his subordinate.

Administration in higher education demands consideration of human motivation and the factors that produce maximum performance. In order to produce desired changes in students in the form of learning behavior, administrators may need to pay closer attention to the needs of faculty members. Like other workers, faculty members may be thought of as "human capital," in the sense that they are the means through which value is produced in the form of learning. Following this analogy, students may be thought of as "raw materials" in relation to the production of learning outcomes.

In a real sense, then, attention to the human needs of faculty members is an investment in higher education which can be justified in terms of real productivity in higher education. Unfortunately, however, the light shed upon motivation of professional and managerial employees by Chris Argyris, Robert Mager, and others has often shone somewhat dimly in the halls of academe. Some reasons for the lack of application of motivational theories to higher education faculties are as follows.

1. Many top-level administrators in American colleges and universities have not been trained as administrators. They have been chosen, in many cases, from the ranks of outstanding professional scholars in such disciplines as physics and chemistry, and find such topics as motivational theories too "insubstantial" from their professional frame of reference.

2. Boards of regents and boards of trustees often feel that academics are overpaid for the actual work performed. They view the professor as an instructor, accountable for eight hours of classroom teaching each day. Rewards for publication and research scholarship do not enter into their value system and the relationship between teaching and scholarship is not clear to them.

3. Implementation of motivational theories through such strategies as Management by Objectives can require significant effort and allocation of resources. Some administrators are afraid to rock the boat.

4. Finally, college and university faculty members themselves often have been reluctant to accept a system of rewards based on production. The traditional model of the tenured professor with his or her independence from the world of political pressure has appeal to many who seek careers in higher education. It has been customary to relegate the decision-making process in promotion and tenure to departmental and peer evaluation, without trying increased rewards to increase production.

Although some major business enterprises have instituted merit incentive plans for professional and managerial employees, higher education has been slow to implement such procedures. Some professors and administrators argue that it is impossible to institute completely fair and effective merit reward systems in a public-service bureaucracy such as public education. The potential rewards in increased effectiveness and efficiency seem to make the effort worthwhile, however.

Faculty Motivation

ROSE NIESWODOMY

Any study of motivation brings to mind the old caricature of the donkey alternately led by the promise of an extended carrot and prodded by a stick. Although these concepts still have merit, they no longer are satisfactory explanations for human behavior. Knowledge derived from the behavioral sciences has significantly increased understanding of human motivation. Faculty members are concerned with motivation of students and educational administrators are involved with motivation of faculty. Therefore, it seems essential in any study of educational administration to examine motivational concepts. Insights into the manner in which people respond to particular conditions and the ability to make effective motivational decisions require knowledge of the motives that bring about human behavior.

THE NATURE OF MOTIVATION

Motivation begins the day a baby is born (or perhaps even during prenatal life). All human behavior is stimulated by unsatisfied needs, both conscious and unconscious. There is a basic core of needs that must be met if an individual is to grow and function normally. This basic core includes both biological and psychological needs and is strongly influenced by society.

All living organisms have inborn tendencies for maintenance or survival and for growth or actualization. Scientists have been able to explain most of these tendencies on the biological level, but the psychological level is not as well understood. Behavioral scientists have yet to develop a theory that is general enough to apply to all forms of behavior and can be verified scientifically.

There are similarities as well as differences in human motives. Cultural anthropologists have determined universal needs from which cultural norms appear to have evolved. Psychologists have also prepared listings of basic needs that result in human activities. For example, hunger motivates an individual to seek food whether he lives in the United States or in Timbuktu. Thirst is another of these basic needs. However, these seemingly simple needs can become complex when examined in light of social learning, folklore, and ritual.

The biological needs that appear most relevant to human behavior include (1) visceral needs, (2) the need for safety and avoidance of pain, (3) the need for stimulation and activity, and (4) the need for sexual gratification. Psychological needs are not as readily identifiable, but generally psychologists agree on the following broad needs: (1) order, understanding, and predictability; (2) adequacy, competency, and security; (3) love and affiliation; (4) belonging, acceptance, and approval; (5) self-esteem and identity; and (6) value, meaning, and hope.

Cultural variations give rise to wide differences in human motives. Americans would not respond to motivation in the same manner as Australian aborigines, and vice versa. There may also be differences in the motives of people from the same cultural groups. Studies in a large metropolitan area in the United States indicate that underprivileged people have widely different motives from those found among people of middle-class background. A study of executives showed significant differences between executives from lower-class backgrounds and those born into high positions.[41]

Individual human motives are likely to differ greatly in societies with freedom of speech, press, and religion. For example, the cultural heritage of Americans makes them more reluctant to accept authoritarianism than individuals in many other countries of the world. Physiological needs also can be modified by the customs and norms of society. Babies are frequently fed on a schedule that has been culturally determined, and this schedule modifies the "natural" hunger pangs of the infant.

The level of need and the fulfillment of that need may be dependent on many factors, such as age and mental maturity. Not all individuals have the same capacity or desire to fulfill their needs or attach importance to them. Frequently the more difficult it becomes to satisfy a need, the more important the need becomes. If no food is available and an individual is only moderately hungry, he may do nothing at that moment. However, if he is starving he may run ten miles to the closest food store and even steal the food if necessary. The closer he gets to the food store the faster he will run.

Man may choose to be a nonconformist, developing matters of behavior that differ from the predominant patterns of the society or group. Some uniformity in human motives can bring about harmony in social living. However, there is also need for diversity in society. Armies, hospitals, and universities cannot all be staffed by the same type of individuals. In education it is hoped that each teacher fits into his or her role and that their motives are in harmony with those of the educational institution.

CURRENT MOTIVATIONAL THEORIES

Man has always been interested in his own behavior. Drawings by cavemen depict the behavior of mankind at their time in history. Theories of motivation probably developed long before anyone ever heard the word "theory." Numerous systems have been developed for the classification of human needs, ranging from those that attempt to explain all human motivation as the result of satisfying one basic need or drive to classifications that list many separate needs. Among those who have sought to explain behavior in terms of a single need is Sigmund Freud, who stressed the libido—a broad concept of the sex drive—as the basic motivator of man. Two of his students, Alfred Adler and Carl Jung, also postulated single motives. Adler believed that the desire for power was the primary motivator, while Jung was concerned with the desire for individuality as the basis of motivation. There is probably no universal motivator for all mankind, nor is there a single motivational force for any one individual. Most current motivational theories see motivation as a complex process involving many needs or drives.

Maslow's Hierarchy of Needs

Abraham Maslow has developed a theory of human motivation in which human needs are arranged in the form of a hierarchy.[42] Maslow contends that basic physical needs are the most potent of all needs. Educators usually do not have to be concerned with this level of need, although adequate salary might belong at this level.

The next level of need involves safety. Man has a need for security. Job tenure and benefits, such as life insurance, would fulfill needs in this category. In this area, faculty members would also have need for undisturbed routine, predictability, and orderliness.

Needs of the next level are related to love and belongingness. Man likes to be part of a group in which there are shared interests. Faculty members at an educational institution certainly have shared interests, but this does not necessarily mean that all faculty members can become part of the group. Unfortunately, cliques and "in-crowds" exist in learned institutions just as they do in other groups in society.

The next higher level of need is for esteem. Man has a need for recognition, respect, self-confidence. He must feel that whatever he is doing is useful. There are many ways this need can be met in an educational institution. A word of praise from the department chair can go a long way toward raising the self-esteem of a faculty member.

The highest level of need is for self-actualization. Man has a need for self-fulfillment—that tendency to become what one *must* be. Maslow believes it is difficult for young people to reach this plateau. Senior faculty members may realize this self-actualization process since many of their lower-level needs have already been fulfilled.

Maslow contends that once needs at a certain level have been fulfilled they are no longer motivating forces. However, a sudden threat to a prior level of satisfied need can cause regression back to that level. Need gratification leads only to temporary happiness, which tends to be succeeded by another discontent. Love stories traditionally end, "and they lived happily ever after," but Maslow does not see perfect happiness as ever being achieved.

Although it may be difficult to categorize human motives into five neat categories, all of the needs in Maslow's hierarchy should be taken into account in planning a motivational system. Educational leaders should consider the higher needs as well as the more obvious lower-level ones.

Hygiene Theory

Another motivational theory closely related to Maslow's theory is the Hygiene Theory of Frederick Herzberg.[43] Herzberg identified factors that he called satisfiers and dis-satisfiers. His research indicated that factors which surround the job, including salary and working conditions, are important but are essentially hygiene matters which tend to prevent dissatisfaction but do not lead to satisfaction. Hygienic factors are important for two reasons. First, when absent or not present in sufficient quantity they become a source of unrest. Second, hygienic factors must be maintained at competitive levels in order both to retain present employees and attract new employees. Faculty members may possess altruism, but they have to eat like everyone else. Money will nearly always be a consideration in any job.

Once these lower-level needs are met, satisfiers of the job become prominent. Herzberg found that the good feelings associated with a job are related to personal satisfaction, the accomplishment involved in the job, and the potential for growth and peer recognition. Opportunities for responsibility and challenge in the work itself are the motivators that really fire up a person and make him want to work to achieve self-fulfillment. The road to effective motivation, according to Herzberg's theory, is to make the job more meaningful and satisfying.

MOTIVATION IN EDUCATIONAL ADMINISTRATION

A review of current motivational theories indicates that there are no hard and fast rules on how to motivate individuals. However, it is generally accepted today that the stick is not the best motivating force in most cases. Work and the products of this activity may become sources of satisfaction. The world would be a sad place if work were actually the burden is it so often assumed to be. The idea that work is a burden is stressed from early childhood on. People hesitate to admit they like work for much the same reason that most children will not admit they like school. A distinction should be made between what people say about work and the actual satisfaction that follows their efforts. A relationship between job satisfaction and productivity appears to be a function of the level of skill required by the job. For jobs that are highly routine and require a low level of skill, there is an inverse relationship between satisfaction and productivity, but in professional occupations where the level of skills is high, productivity on the job is positively related to the individual's satisfaction with his job.[44]

Motivation of a professional employee should be viewed differently than motivation of a factory worker, for example. Intrinsic motivation is extremely important. Unless faculty members perceive teaching as a means of meeting their inmost personal needs, they will rarely have the commitment necessary for creativity and excellence in their teaching. Most faculty in some conscious or unconscious way have discovered that teaching has the potential for satisfying their important needs.

Educational administrators can make use of many of the motivational theories that have been developed. An eclectic blending of motivational theories may be beneficial. It is also important to remember that professionals such as educators need a large degree of individual responsibility and authority, challenging and diversified assignments, and advancement in status and recognition. The largest influence educational administration can have on external motivation of faculty members is in the shaping of goals, objectives, and rewards. Goals determine the probability that faculty members will focus their behavior in a certain direction to satisfy their needs, and rewards are tangible elements of the environment that help satisfy needs. When the needs and goals of the individual are in harmony with the rewards and goals of the institution, an environment is present that will enhance high quality performance and productivity in the educational institution.

New Faculty Members

Most new faculty begin their teaching careers with enthusiasm and a desire to become superior teachers. Their dream is often shattered in the classroom when students fail to respond in the desired manner. However, the eagerness and ambition of new faculty members can also be dulled by an educational leader that fails to foster the essential external motivation. New faculty members need a great deal of encouragement, praise and positive "strokes" for their teaching performance.

Since their basic needs, such as salary and good working environment, are probably being met, they now are trying to meet their need for self-esteem.

Educational leaders can help meet the needs of new faculty members in many ways. The following are some of the more important approaches to motivation of new faculty members.

1. *Thorough orientation.* Make the new faculty member feel he or she is needed and wanted. His role must be defined and he should be given a clear-cut description of his responsibilities. This involves more than handing him a copy of the faculty handbook and the course syllabus from which he is to teach.

2. *Provide a "buddy" system.* Each new faculty member should be paired with a faculty member in his department who has been with the institution for at least two years. This one-to-one approach helps to acquaint the new faculty member with the institution much sooner.

3. *Make them feel like a member of the team.* It is easy for faculty members to form cliques just as other groups in society do. Senior faculty members should try to help the "new kid on the block" feel like part of the team. To be asked to go to coffee by one of the professors in the department will greatly increase the self-esteem of a new faculty member.

4. *Allow autonomy.* Encourage new faculty member to gradually gain independence. Give them freedom to teach in ways which are best suited to them.

5. *Have patience with the new faculty member.* New faculty members will make mistakes. In one educational institution a new faculty member diligently put his entire lecture on overhead transparencies only to find a malfunctioning projector in the room at class time. Anyone who has to give an entire lecture holding his transparencies up to the light needs no reprimand from his superior.

6. *Tell them when they have done a good job.* For some reason it seems to be easier for leaders to tell a subordinates what they have done wrong than to compliment them on a job well done.

7. *Be interested in them as individuals.* Show them you are concerned with their needs, ambitions and fears. Identify what level of need the faculty member is attempting to satisfy.

8. *Keep them well informed.* Keep faculty members informed of their performance and also of any changes that may affect them. If students have registered complaints about a new faculty mem-

ber, it is better to inform him of this fact than to let the grievances build up.

9. *Be willing to learn from new faculty members.* When a new faculty
member has ideas and suggestions for change, listen to him. Let
him know that his ideas and opinions are welcomed and his
efforts are appreciated. A new idea of his just may be the shot in
the arm that the department needs.

Tenured Faculty

Educational administrators may find themselves wishing for a carrot
when trying to motivate faculty members who are full professors with
tenure. The stick does not hold as much power with these individuals as
it might with other faculty members and deadwood is not as easily removed. However, external motivation of these individuals is possible.
They still have needs—to create, to be fulfilled. Since most of their
lower-level needs have been met, they can now concentrate their energies on self-actualization. They have reached the apex of their careers
and the time in their life when more energy can be devoted to research
and publication.

A study was conducted to determine who wrote the most articles from
1962–1971 in six well-known mass communication journals was reported by James L. Bess. The authors of these articles for the most part
were found to hold the rank of associate or full professor. When these
authors were asked to cite reasons for their success as mass communication scholars and researchers, they cited what might be termed personal
motivation factors. Typical responses included "personal satisfaction in
opening new areas of scholarly interest" and "my own drive and per-
sistance." However, other responses included "free time to conduct research" and "support from the university."[45] This university support
served as an important external motivator.

Despite the many difficulties and frustrations in teaching, most faculty
claim to enjoy it and would not choose to give it up. Recent research
shows that even if given the opportunity, university faculty, on the average, would reduce their weekly hours devoted to teaching by only about
5 percent. Most of the motivation of faculty members at this time in their
lives is intrinsic. However, educational administrators can provide the
climate to help them reach their full potential. Monetary support and
release time to work on new plans and developments in which faculty
members are interested are only two ways administrators can help provide the climate for these master teachers to reach their maximum potential. Educational administrators must keep in mind that all individuals have needs and drives as long as they live.

MEASURING FACULTY OUTPUT THROUGH ASSESSMENT AND RATING SCALES

Measuring the output of faculty members in universities and colleges may require the assessment of qualities that are peculiar to the field of higher education. Motivating professionals in higher education may require the consideration of factors different than those that might be considered in business and industry. Many instruments have been developed by individual institutions for the purpose of rating faculty performance.

Table 9, Department Chairperson's Rating of Instructor—Form B,

TABLE 9
Department chairperson's rating of instructor—Form B

```
DEPARTMENT CHAIRPERSON'S RATING OF INSTRUCTOR - FORM B

INSTRUCTOR_____ SUPERVISOR _____ DATE_____
```

Being as objective and impartial as possible, rate each Instructor by circling the number which you feel most aptly expresses your evaluation, remembering that 3 denotes expected performance and that each department is entitled to choose its own criteria under each major area with the consent of the Division Chairperson and the Dean of Instruction.

A.   Common areas of contribution:

		Unsatisfactory Performance		Expected Performance	Exceptional Performance	
1.	SKILL IN PRESENTING SUBJECT					
	Departmental Criteria:	1	2	3	4	5

1.
2.
3.

:
:

Sample criteria that may be considered: (observes classroom instructional techniques, reviews student performance in related areas, etc.)

Rationale for ratings other than 3:

2. PROFESSIONAL CAPABILITIES

Departmental Criteria:	1	2	3	4	5

1.
2.
3.

:
:

Sample criteria that may be considered: (exhibits knowledge of subject, understands course objectives, contributes to achieving goals of the institutions, etc.)

Rationale for rating other than 3:

illustrates criteria for faculty performance appropriate for a two-year institution. Faculty members in a senior college or university may have to fulfill other expectations as well.

EVALUATING SERVICE

Although teaching and publication/research activities are primary areas of faculty responsibility, college of education faculty must be expected to be actively involved in service to the division, college, university, and professional community.

Faculty members often give exceptional service to the college or university. For example, they prepare incisive, important reports as members or chairpersons of time-consuming committees or task forces. The important developmental work of a division, college, or university often is done by such a group. Those who serve lengthy and unusually demanding assignments should be given credit for professional service. Careful documentation must be made in the candidate's dossier of the extent of responsibility, time requirements, and products of such assignments.

Prestige is brought to the university and college by those who assume positions of leadership in professional organizations. Recognition by one's peers may include election or appointment to offices or directorships in national, regional, or state organizations. Other organizational positions of responsibility are in areas such as journal editing, and refereeing. The extent of such involvement and responsibility should be evident from the list of professional activities submitted by faculty candidates for promotion and/or tenure. The divisional committee will be responsible for assessing the degree to which service credit is merited by the faculty member.

Papers presented at professional meetings should be considered in the criteria for promotion and tenure. Consideration should be given to whether the paper is eventually published, the prestige of the convention, whether the paper is an "invited" presentation or not, and whether the presentation was selected in competition with significant proposals of other members. Papers and speeches of national magnitude may be considered in lieu of some publications.

Recognition for service contributions should be given to those who share their unique expertise. For example, a few faculty are specially qualified to advise advanced students in areas such as research design and statistics. Most faculty members spend inordinate amounts of time in such advisory tasks. This represents a type of service to the college and university that should be recognized.

Other faculty make extensive contributions to efforts to broaden the scope of the college or university. Those faculty who devote themselves to the development and, in some instances, funding of programs and innovations make an invaluable contribution to program development. To assess the value of such contributions the responsible committee and administrators should examine the extent of commitment of the involved faculty and the quality, scope, and visibility of the program developed.

These criteria also should be applied to the procurement of funding and subsequent development of innovations and programs. The procurement of needed outside funding for developmental support of new programs is an important opportunity for faculty service. Those faculty securing substantial amounts of funding should submit evidence of their developmental work as manifestations of service to the college and university.

Faculty who supervise students and interns in the various programs typically spend considerable time traveling and in making outside contacts. Those who do an outstanding job of meeting this responsibility perform a service for the college and university. The visibility provided the university through this type of fieldwork often results in the recruitment of new students, both at the graduate and undergraduate levels. Faculty candidates for promotion and tenure should furnish evidence of excellent performance through the procedures adopted by their respective divisions. The mere fact of a supervisory assignment should not be taken as evidence of outstanding service. Data and/or information should be supplied indicating that the faculty member has done an excellent job in such an assignment.

Intensive interaction and contact with field practitioners is crucial for a professional school such as a college of education. Another important role through which this crucial function may be met is that of consulting. The extent and type of consulting that a faculty member is asked to do perhaps is an indication of professional reputation and effectiveness. Within divisions, because the nature of faculty expertise is very specialized and the demands from the field may differ, the opportunities for consultant work will undoubtedly vary. Therefore it is possible that a substantial part of a faculty member's service might be in this area. It is also quite appropriate that in some specialties little consulting would be expected. In areas with large numbers of field constituents, such as elementary or secondary education, the faculty member would be expected to be asked to consult. The candidate for promotion and/or tenure would be expected to furnish evidence not only of the scope but also of the quality of consultant work done. Feedback from program participants would be one example of such evidence.[46]

Every person represents a motivational universe. Regardless of the motivational theory used, the faculty member is going to respond in one way or another. Although common motivational factors exists, every individual is unique in his response to a given environment. It would be more simple if educators could determine the most effective means of motivating faculty members. This, however, is an impossible task. Every educational institution has its goals and objectives. Likewise every individual faculty member must be taken into consideration. Personal needs must be met.

Motivational strategies employed to stimulate tenured and non-tenured faculty members may differ. As a general assumption, it may be correct to state that tenured faculty members should be self-motivated in a professional sense. On the other hand, because faculty members are human, reward systems such as merit pay and bonuses may lead to increased efficiency. The difficulty in applying such formulas equitably and in avoiding rivalries and jealousies has been a major problem, leading to a reluctance on the part of administration to try such systems. Yet motivation is the key to growth. Growth of all faculty and staff is the key to institutional success. They are like hand and glove.

NOTES

1. Jay L. Todes, John McKinney, and Wendell Ferguson, Jr., *Management and Motivation: An Introduction to Supervision* (New York: Harper and Row, 1977), p. 25.

2. Thomas R. Masterson and Thomas G. Mara, *Motivating the Underperformer* (New York: American Management Association, 1969), pp. 33–34.

3. Henry Sisk, *Principles of Management: A Systems Approach to the Management Process,* (Cincinnati: South-Western Publishing Company, 1969), pp. 241–44.

4. Ibid., p. 244.

5. Ibid., p. 251.

6. Todes, McKinney, and Ferguson, *Management and Motivation,* pp. 25–26.

7. Sisk, *Principles of Management,* pp. 248–49.

8. Allison Davis, "The Motivation of the Underprivileged Worker," in William Footewhyte, *Industry and Society* (New York: McGraw-Hill, 1946), p. 556.

9. Sisk, *Principles of Management,* p. 246.

10. Todes, McKinney, and Ferguson, *Management and Motivation,* pp. 26–27.

11. Ibid., p. 169.

12. Sisk, *Principles of Management,* p. 251.

13. Ibid., pp. 254–55.

14. Ibid., p. 256.

15. Ibid., p. 255.

16. Ibid., p. 255–57.

17. Ibid., p. 256.

Ibid., pp. 550–51.

18. Todes, McKinney, and Ferguson, *Management and Motivation,* p. 177.

19. Virgil K. Rowland, *Managerial Performance Standards* (New York: American Management Association, 1960), p. 25.

20. Masterson and Mara, *Motivating the Underperformer,* pp. 11–12.

21. Ibid., p. 4.

22. Sisk, *Principles of Management,* pp. 545–66.

23. Ibid., pp. 545; 462.

24. Sisk, *Principles of Management,* pp. 249–462.

25. Masterson and Mara, *Motivating the Underperformer,* p. 4.

26. Todes, McKinney, and Ferguson, *Management and Motivation,* figure 67, pp. 242–45.

27. Masterson and Mara, *Motivating the Underperformer,* pp. 2–3.

28. Rensis Likert, "Motivation: The Core of Management," in *Management: A Book of Readings,* eds. Harold Kootz and Cyril O'Donnell (New York: McGraw-Hill, 1972), p. 558.

29. Sisk, *Principles of Management,* pp. 550–51.

30. Masterson and Mara, *Motivating the Underperformer,* p. 14.

31. Ibid.

32. Frederick C. Haas, *Executive Obsolescence: Research Study No. 90* (New York: American Management Association, 1968), p. 57.

33. Likert, "Motivation: The Core of Management," p. 554.

34. Sisk, *Principles of Management,* p. 552.

35. Todes, McKinney, and Ferguson, *Management and Motivation,* p. 183.

36. Likert, "Motivation: The Core of Management," p. 552.

37. Ibid.

38. Masterson and Mara, *Motivating the Underperformer,* p. 12.

39. Ibid., p. 6.

40. Ibid., pp. 4–5.

41. Haas, *Executive Obsolescence,* p. 58.

42. A. H. Maslow, *Motivation and Personality* (New York: Harper and Row, 1954), pp. 80–106.

43. Frederick Herzberg, *The Motivation to Work,* 2d ed. (New York: John Wiley and Sons, 1959), p. 252.

44. Todes, McKinney, and Ferguson, *Management and Motivation,* pp. 243–45.

45. James L. Bess, "The Motivation to Teach," *Journal of Higher Education* 48 (May/June 1977), pp. 233–56.

46. North Texas State University, *Faculty Tenure and Promotion Policy,* 1978, p. 5.

13

Techniques and Strategies for Program Development and Evaluation

S. JAMES CORVEY AND BOB W. MILLER

As with planning, problem solving, and decision making, the planning, organizing, development, implementation, and evaluation of programs in higher education is a process that involves a major portion of the administrative energies available to an institution. It is through this process that an institution grows to reach its potential or fails to achieve its objectives and goals. Throughout higher education the "waxing and waning" of the fortune of institutions, of branches of institutions, of particular departments, and of individuals depend upon sound program development.

Although it is difficult to generalize a model for the various possible programs that might be developed in all of the public and private universities, junior/community colleges, and post-secondary technical schools, common elements and accepted techniques are useful in most developmental situations. The first of these is the institutional examination and information-gathering technique necessary to preplanning. The second involves the development of the program itself, the marshalling of resources and personnel leading to the writing of program elements of curriculum. The third component of program development involves the implementation of program elements, usually in a pilot phase. Often this period is one of adjustment and refining of materials and techniques.

A fourth, and often neglected, element of program development focuses on evaluation. This element emphasizes an objective examination of the program elements and outcomes. From this evaluation answers can be found to questions such as, Should this program be integrated into the institution in its present form? Are the outcomes congruent with the stated objectives of the program? And, most important, Do students benefit from this program?

Program development and implementation is a systematic process involving analysis of the key elements of need, desirability, and the ability to carry out the program. This is an intensive development and implementation phase with evaluation and assessment forming the final step in a process leading to the adaption of a particular program.

The following in-depth examination of the steps outlined in this chapter will necessarily cite particular examples, incidents and details regarding what various educators have said about program development and evaluation. However, it is important to note that although professional educators are in general agreement on the major elements involved, the order that these elements take and the weight given to the elements vary to a considerable degree from situation to situation and institution to institution.

DEFINITIONS

Cost analysis—A process which may be employed through three kinds of costs: research and development, investment, and operating costs. These are placed on physical qualities such as time, space, equipment, and supplies.

Free choice model—A planning model to develop projections predicated on the number of students expected to exit from a particular discipline and the number of faculty expected to teach in that discipline.

Manpower planning model—Projects manpower needs, then develops projections of the number of individuals needed to fill those requirements.

Program development—A systematic process involving analysis of the key elements of need, desirability, and the ability to carry out the program.

IDENTIFYING EDUCATIONAL NEEDS

The impetus for developing educational programs can arise at virtually any level in an institution from the individual instructor through the president or board of trustees. It also may arise from regional, state, or federal suggestions or mandates, or from community or student pressures. Among these multiple points for generating possible program development, Dorothy Knoell and Charles McIntyre cite a natural division between those programs that operate on a laissez-faire or free choice philosophy and those that operate on the manpower planning model.[1] In general, the free choice model includes general education, nonvocational programs and attempts to "supply the right amount and kind of education predicated upon existing and anticipated student demand." The manpower planning model projects manpower needs and then develops projections of the number of individuals required to fill those needs. For example, if you allow too many dental programs in one state you can quickly flood the market. The point of departure in these two models is the relative role the state or federal government plays in determining the need for specific programs. The two governmental agencies greatly influence programs of colleges and universities, especially in connection to funding. This concept is within its basic right since "education is a function of each state and since the federal government gets involved in the matter of 'educational welfare.'" In general, the manpower planning model derives from extensive surveying of manpower needs in broad geographic areas and in numerous occupations. This type of surveying goes beyond simply determining the demand for manpower to also estimate the supply. D. Kent Halstead identifies the following formula for supply-demand analysis for developing manpower needs through state surveys. Manpower Planning Model (Demand − Supply = Manpower Requirements).

Demand for manpower is created by: (1) New jobs due to growth and technology; (2) Death and retirement; (3) Transfers and promotions to other occupations.

Supply for manpower is created by: (1) New entrants from training programs; (2) Unemployed workers seeking work in the occupation; (3) Entrants from other occupations; (4) Immigrants.[2]

Obviously, this type of extensive and intensive surveying is beyond the scope of individual institutions. From these and numerous other state surveys, however, broad areas of need can be identified as possible areas for program development by individual institutions. The size and mission of the institution will determine whether further surveying is necessary to answer questions concerning the development of a new program. For example, a major university drawing students from across the nation might contemplate developing a program if multistate regional manpower needs dictate. A community college, however, with its localized clientele, would have difficulty in identifying which programs would be needed in its restricted geographic area by using state and regional surveys alone. In order to determine local manpower needs it is necessary for community colleges to turn to more localized assessments of manpower needs. A community college usually has several sources for local surveys. The U.S. Census Bureau is a major source which maintains statistics for area industries as well as detailed demographic data. In addition, many cities and counties maintain extensive data concerning occupations, including projections for future growth. Chambers of commerce and business organizations are also sources for information about growth and need in a community.

Most institutions, however, would not rely solely on surveys conducted by outside agencies. Instead, these surveys are indicators which tend to focus the institution on areas most likely to be candidates for program development. N. Dean Evans and Russ L. Neagley identity six components, including several local surveys that should be conducted to determine needs for new colleges. These include (1) County or regional population projections for the area to be served by potential colleges; (2) County or regional resources and development surveys; (3) Business-industry surveys; (4) Professional surveys; (5) Student-parent surveys; (6) Enrollment studies to predict potential student enrollments in the college.[3] Although these are cited as elements of a feasibility study, the same considerations must be taken into account when developing new programs or expanding existing programs to encompass new elements. Examples of a business-industry and a student-parent surveys can be found in Appendix 2 and Appendix 3.

As with the manpower planning model, the free choice model can be analyzed in terms of need. It is interesting to note, however, that the free choice model is based not solely on the numbers of students expected to exit from a particular discipline, but also on the number of faculty expected to be employed to teach that discipline. Halstead states that "the two most critical assumptions—because they vary and are subject to error—are the expected student-faculty ratio and the trend in total enrollment."[4] The problem of projecting total enrollment is highlighted by Donald Norris when he cites several competent but varying projections for enrollments through the year 2000.[5] The extremely complicated, and admittedly imprecise, process identified by Halstead for determining student-faculty ratio in the free choice model at the state level is illustrated as follows.

Free choice model.

1. Obtain for at least the past 5-year period the number of student credit hours classified by level of instruction (lower division, upper division, master's and doctor's), type of institution (junior community college, senior college, university), and field of study.

2. Convert the number of student credit hours in each field of study and at each level of instruction to percentages of the total instruction at each type of institution. Thus for one year at all senior colleges, 10,000 credit hours of English instruction at the lower division level might equal 5 percent of the total instruction (200,000 credit hours) offered.

3. On the basis of past trends and stated assumptions, project the future share (percentage) of total instruction expected in each field-level combination. For the example in step 2, the past trend in lower division English instruction may warrant a 6- or 7-percent increase in the future.

4. For each type of institution, project total enrollment during each year of the projection period. Convert to full-time-equivalent [FTE] students and, in turn, to total instructional load in

student credit hours (one FTE student is usually equal to 12 to 15 credit hours).

5. To determine projected instruction loads, apply the projected share percentages in each field-level combination (as determined in step 3) to projections of total instruction load.

6. For each type of institution, subject field, and level of instruction, determine planned future student-faculty ratios in terms of student credit hours or instruction per FTE teaching faculty member.

7. The number of FTE teaching faculty required in each discipline, by level of instruction and type of institution, can now be determined by applying the student-faculty ratios to the number of student credit hour instructional loads predicted in step 5.

8. New annual staff requirements can be expected to equal new additional staff requirements based on enrollments as calculated in step 7, plus replacement of yearly staff losses through resignation, retirement, or death.[6]

The above process is useful for determining statewide enrollments in general studies free choice curriculums at the state level. This process would apply especially to senior colleges and universities. However, individual institutions can gain much useful information from conducting student-parent surveys as identified by Evans and Neagley,[7] and by analyzing population trends in areas and target populations served by the institution.

Although external stimuli provided by need surveys are a major factor in program development, they are by no means the only influences that stimulate development. A commentary by experts in the field concerning internal influences that affect curriculum change of universities (see Figure 42), lists (1) academic departments, (2) the college or other academic division, (3) the president and academic deans, (4) individual faculty members, (5) the students, and (6) the extracurriculum. These are major areas within the college or university that generate curriculum change, and with slight modification they may be applied to community colleges as well.

Additional internal forces that spawn curriculum change and modification are discussed by Lewis Mayhew and Patrick Ford. They state that analysis "suggests that discussion, political actions, judgement of experts, and search for social needs are the prevailing methods of curriculum analysis and development."[8] Among the specific methods discussed, and the most used for analyzing curriculum, is administrative review. The administrative review process is defined as the ongoing process of

FIGURE 42
Internal changes that affect curriculum

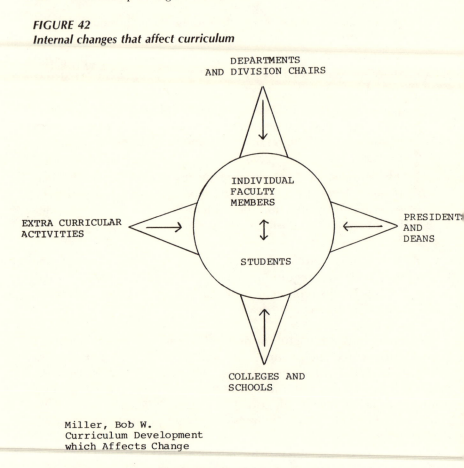

DEPARTMENTS
AND DIVISION CHAIRS

INDIVIDUAL
FACULTY
MEMBERS

EXTRA CURRICULAR
ACTIVITIES

PRESIDENT
AND
DEANS

STUDENTS

COLLEGES AND
SCHOOLS

Miller, Bob W.
Curriculum Development
which Affects Change

accepting new courses into the curriculum on an annual basis. Generally, this is an organized process of review and expansion of existing programs. A more in-depth review of curriculum is gained through self-study. The process of self-study may be a product of the accrediting process or may arise from the desire of an institution to examine its curricular offerings. At times a modified study will be used to examine the curriculum. This type of self-study is done by using a short-lived committees that recommend changes to the administration and faculty for consideration. These changes in curriculum usually involve state agency and regional accreditation association approval.

In community colleges the role of advisory committees in curriculum change is important. Advisory committees are comprised of representatives from business and industry who may be considered experts in their respective fields. Their input is valuable because they can assess curricula, identify that which is outdated, and suggest modifications. Advisory committees are now utilized at senior college levels and in general education programs. This process likely will expand in the future.

Other less frequently used methods involve the use of a consultant or group of consultants to analyze an institution and suggest curriculum changes. Finally, in isolated cases, a governing board may form committees with the assistance of selected resource persons to review and suggest changes.

It is readily apparent that the identification of the need for curriculum change and the gathering of information to effect that change is a complex process. Dependent on the type of program to be developed and the scope of the institution, it may involve federal, state, and local educational groups as well as outside sources of information and expertise. The result can profoundly affect an institution's offerings, both immediate and long-term. All too often, however, much red tape is involved. An institution should have enough checks and balances to provide quality control in curriculum development.

FACTORS IN PROGRAM DEVELOPMENT

In a generalized system of development, needs assessment, goal setting, resource analysis, and evaluation are closely allied. It is useful, however, to analyze each element separately to form a clear understanding of the relationship each of the various elements has to the other. Perhaps the most comprehensive work in this area of analysis has been done by the Western Interstate Commission for Higher Education (WICHE) Planning and Management Systems Program.[9] This program is designed to develop common data elements and terminology in a number of planning areas across a variety of institutions of higher education. These elements may then be used by an individual institution for the purpose of program planning and resource allocation. Ben Lawrence discusses the numerous systems developed or being developed by WICHE.[10] The process module shown in Figure 43 illustrates a framework which could be used for subsystem development.

Within this framework, systems for developing goals and objectives, for calculating resources, for identifying alternative programs, and others are explored. Although it is outside the scope of this chapter to examine in-depth the WICHE program, it is suggested that the WICHE planning manuals be considered for use in program planning and development.

Role of the State in Planning

The role of the state in planning has been previously mentioned in the area of needs analysis. The state also plays a large role in the actual

FIGURE 43
A model of higher education management

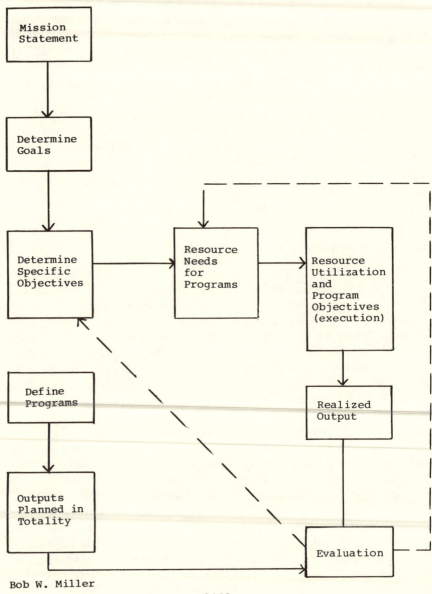

Bob W. Miller
Higher Education Management, 1982

development of programs. Halstead identifies eight areas in which the state has a planning function.

1. Delineating sharply and concretely the generally accepted broad educational objectives of the state and determining through analysis and assessment those objectives which should receive highest priority over a given period of time.

2. Preparing multiyear comprehensive plans designed to integrate the curriculum, research, and services of statewide higher education, to correct inadequacies, and to attain educational objectives.

3. Developing various program alternatives and, by systematic analysis and comparison, presenting for review specific recommendations.

4. Studying continuously and evaluating thoroughly existing state programs in order to determine their adequacy and compare benefits and costs.

5. Examining state and other sources of financial support in order to determine the potential for additional revenue, and developing legislative and other proposals which will take advantage of identified opportunities.

6. Collecting, interpreting, and managing descriptive and quantitative educational data in the state and nation—data which relate to and have implications for educational planning—then applying such data to the development of plans.

7. Conducting and supporting research activities to determine cause-and-effect relationships, testing and analyzing the effectiveness of specific plans proposed and adopted, and developing assessment instruments and techniques.

8. Establishing coordinated working relationships and effective communication with all organizations and individuals directly concerned with planning.[11]

These are broad areas of responsibility which in most cases do not extend to specific program elements. There are, however, exceptions in individual states. Texas, for example, controls individual curricular offerings through two state-level agencies. The Texas Education Agency has the primary responsibility in post-secondary education to approve instructors and courses in the occupational area. The Coordinating Board of Colleges and Universities, although it does pass on occupational programs, has the primary responsibility for approval of courses in the universities and in the academic offerings of community colleges.

Both agencies, as is the case in most states, fund occupational and university parallel programs; thus they influence courses and programs to a high degree.

On the institutional level, a great deal of work has been done relating to program development using simulation models. One application of simulation was PRIME, Planning Resources in Minnesota Education, as described by David Cordes.[12] This particular application took place at three educational institutions in the state of Minnesota. The three institutions, a state university, a community college, and a public school, utilized a computer simulation, CAMPUS, to analyze factors in program development that impact the development, implementation, and ongoing activities over a several-year period.

The data elements needed to run this simulation include: (1) staff and staff support, (2) space, (3) teaching equipment, (4) type of course, (5) staff specialization, (6) schedule time, and (7) success factors for students enrolled. This very sophisticated simulation was used to project program needs and cost factors for up to a ten-year period. In institutions with sufficient resources, this type of analysis has a distinct advantage and, though costly, provides invaluable planning information. For institutions unable to implement the sophisticated design characterized by CAMPUS, the problems of analysis are more difficult; however, the elements to be considered remain the same. Planning and projecting by institutions should constantly attempt to approach precision while remaining aware of the imprecise nature of these activities.

ANALYZING PROGRAM COSTS

Cost analysis, one of the areas identified in WICHE documents, is explored in a different manner by Emil J. Haller.[13] In his discussion Haller identifies "four basic types of resources that any administrator has available for allocation. The four types are: (1) Time (2) Space (3) Equipment and (4) Supplies." To these four types of resources Haller couples the three categories of "(1) Research and Development costs—necessary to develop a program to the stage it can be introduced into the system. (2) Investment costs—costs necessary to implement the program, and (3) Operating costs—costs necessary to operate the program" to form the following cost input structure.

R & D Costs	Investment Costs	Operating Costs
1.1 time	2.1 time	3.1 time
1.2 space	2.2 space	3.2 space
1.3 equipment	2.3 equipment	3.3 equipment
1.4 supplies	2.4 supplies	3.4 supplies

Haller points out that by utilizing this method of analyzing costs an institution can avoid a common error in cost analysis, described as the tendency to act as if the only important costs are those occurring in the first year. The following illustration is of a hypothetical projection of costs in the categories identified. Programs and costs go together to illustrate the following:

1. Comparing students' performance on comprehensive examinations administered by neutral agencies or institutions at the time students enter with performance on appropriate examinations at the time they graduate. (Not inexpensive, but a relatively uncomplicated procedure.)

2. Making an annual comparison of rates of student admission, retention, and attrition.

3. Collecting basic information concerning alumni:

   a. occupational choices

   b. participation in governmental, community, and voluntary activities

   c. admission to graduate schools

   d. publication of writings

   e. awards and honors received

   f. number of children and their educational status

   g. self-perceptions as to happiness and satisfaction with education

This checklist provides only a starting point in developing evaluative measures. Scarvia Anderson, Samuel Ball, and Richard Murphy list fifteen types of evaluative measures and approaches to evaluation encompassing literally hundreds of measurement instruments.[14]

Similarly, *Evaluation in Education,* edited by W. James Popham, identifies numerous measures ranging from summative evaluation at the local level through the use of standardized measures, criterion-referenced measure and matrix sampling, to the formative evaluation of instruction.[15]

The selection of appropriate measures and the application of these measures to the individual program are dependent on the size of the program, the intent (outcomes) desired of the program, the complexity and level of evaluation needed, and the cost of evaluation.

In the final analysis, evaluation is a mirror of program design. It must reflect an examination of a program from needs assessment through designing of goals and objectives to implementation and, finally, it must measure educational and instructional outcomes to determine the worth of a program to students and the institution.

It can readily be seen that research and development costs do not reflect the long-term expenses of operating a program. The same can be said of investment costs to a lesser extent, with replacement of equipment and retraining of personnel being the prime factors of continuing expense in this area.

Through the systematic development outlined, educational institutions attempt to approach precise measures of cost to implement new programs. The complexity of the factors involved has so far made precise measure elusive. Paul Dressel states that because of the number of complex variables involved "no institution or school system has carried out a systems analysis to the point of allowing and applying fully satisfactory models of prediction and control.[16] The fact remains that both short- and long-range projections of cost factors are important in curriculum planning.

PROGRAM EVALUATION

Program or curriculum evaluation, as with other steps in the overall development and implementation model, must find its root in the mission of an institution, its goals and general objectives, and the specific goals and objectives of the program. Many types of measures are available; however, the organization of these measures into a coherent framework is necessary if the institution is to have a retrieval base for making decisions about the successful individual program. One such framework is provided by a model, illustrated in Figure 44, developed at the EPIC Evaluation Center in Tucson, Arizona. This model deals with three variables of behavior, instruction, and population.

This particular model has advantages because it does not dictate the level of sophistication in evaluation, but instead provides a conceptual framework that can be used to provide evaluation information across a broad range of programs and program elements. With this framework an institution can address the key components of a program and utilize individual measures to address specific program elements. The Carnegie Foundation identifies measures that can be used by an individual institution as measures of effectiveness.[17]

Program development in post-secondary education is an extremely important and complex process. Complicating the process is the imprecise nature of projecting needs, enrollments, and finances beyond the short term. In order to approach program development with a semblance of certainty, it is necessary to employ systematic data-gathering techniques and scientific projection methods. This chapter has only touched on a few highlights and illustrations of the types of systems that might be employed. Each individual program development cycle will be

FIGURE 44
The epic evaluation model

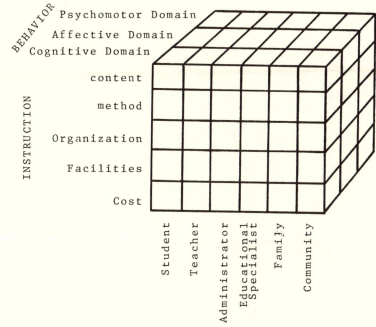

POPULATION

Phi Delta Kappa National Study Committee on Evaluation, *Educational Evaluation and Decision Making.* F. E. Peacock Publishers: Itasca, Ill., 1971, p. 242.

constructed utilizing needs survey instruments, program models, and evaluative techniques that are unique to the institution and program. The selection of these elements must be done with clear understanding of the strengths and weaknesses of each and should be employed in a manner that makes maximum use of the information generated. Only through this method can educational institutions expand programs and at the same time maintain viability in educational offerings and stability in financial affairs.

Program development and evaluation is a most difficult area which requires team effort and cooperation to obtain quality control in the curriculum and instruction elements in a college. By utilizing appropriate techniques and strategies, the results achieved can be most gratifying for the institution, the administration, faculty, and, most of all, students.

Appendix 2 and 3 follow at the end of this chapter. Appendix 2 is a survey instrument designed by the Delaware County Community College District as a means for analyzing the need for a community college. Appendix 3 is a community college needs assessment survey questionnaire of eleventh- and twelfth-grade students to determine post- high school needs.

NOTES

1. Dorothy Knoell and Charles McIntyre, *Planning Colleges for the Community* (San Francisco: Jossey-Bass, 1974), pp. 6–7.

2. D. Kent Halstead, *Statewide Planning in Higher Education,* (Washington, D.C.: Government Printing Office, 1974), p. 382.

3. N. Dean Evans and Russ L. Neagley, *Planning and Developing Innovative Community Colleges* (Englewood Cliffs, N.J.: Prentice-Hall, 1973), p. 121.

4. Halstead, *Statewide Planning in Higher Education,* p. 390.

5. Donald M. Norris, "Speculating on Enrollment," in *Individualizing the System,* ed. Dyckman W. Vermilye (San Francisco: Jossey-Bass, 1971), pp. 139–47.

6. Halstead, *Statewide Planning in Higher Education,* pp. 382–83.

7. Evans and Neagley, *Planning and Developing Innovative Community Colleges,* pp. 285–93.

8. Lewis B. Mayhew and Patrick J. Ford, *Changing the Curriculum* (San Francisco: Jossey-Bass, 1971), pp. 81–86.

9. Ben Lawrence, "The WICHE Planning and Management Systems Program: It's Nature, Scope, and Limitations," in *Managing the University: A Systems Approach,* ed. Paul W. Hamelman (New York: Praeger, 1972), p. 51.

10. Ibid., pp. 49–75.

11. Halstead, *Statewide Planning in Higher Education,* pp. 20–21.

12. David C. Cordes, "Project Prime: A Test Implementation of the Campus Simulation Model," in *Managing the University: A Systems Approach,* ed. Paul W. Hamelman (New York: Praeger, 1972), pp. 77–105.

13. Emil J. Haller, "Cost Analysis for Educational Program Evaluation," in *Evaluation in Education: Current Applications,* ed. W. James Popham (Berkeley: McCutchan, 1974), pp. 401–49.

14. Scarvia B. Anderson, Samuel Ball, and Richard T. Murphy, *Encyclopedia of Educational Evaluation: Concepts and Techniques for Evaluating Education and Training Programs* (San Francisco: Jossey-Bass, 1975), p. XV

15. James W. Popham, *Evaluation in Education: Current Applications,* (Berkeley: McCutchan, 1974), p. 145.

16. Paul L. Dressel, *Handbook of Academic Evaluation* (San Francisco: Jossey-Bass, 1976), p. 65.

17. Carnegie Foundation for the Advancement of Teaching, *Missions of the Curriculum: A Contemporary Review with Suggestions* (San Francisco: Jossey-Bass, 1977), p. 253.

Delaware County Council for Higher Education Business Industry Survey

Delaware County Council for Higher Education
Business Industry Survey

Name of Establishemnt or Firm_____
Kind of Business _____Person Reporting_____

This survey is being made to help determine the need for a community college in Delaware County. Its purpose is to secure information on the requirements of business, industry, and community services for trained people and the type of training that will best prepare them for these positions. You may rest assured that the information you give us will be confidential. Neither your firm nor specific information regarding it will be identified in any way in the reports. Your cooperation in answering this questionnaire is greatly appreciated.

* * * * * * * * * * * * * *

1. What is your a·erage number of regular employees?_____
2. What percentage of your employees are engaged in work which requires more than high school training but not neccessarily a college degree?
   _____
3. Will the proportion of your employees requiring training beyon⁴ high school increase during the next ten years?_____Yes _____No Don't know
   _____
4. Would there be opportunities for employment in your organization for people with two years of technical or semi-professional training beyond the high school? _____Yes _____No
5. If "Yes" would you check the types of training in the list below which, if

   offered by a local community college would be of value to your firm or organization

   _____1. Drafting and Blueprint Reading
   _____2. Management Development
   _____3. Labor Management Relations
   _____4. Instrumentation and Plant Control
   _____5. Laboratory Technician
   _____6. Metallurgy
   _____7. Business Management
   _____8. Agriculture (Economics, Engineering, etc.)

```
_____ 9.  Building Trades
_____ 10. Foreign Language
_____ 11. Economics and Government
_____ 12. English and Speech
_____ 13. Mathematics
_____ 14. Literature and History
_____ 15. Industrial Chemistry
_____ 16. Inspection and Quality Control
_____ 17. Engineering Aides
_____ 18. Mental Hygiene
_____ 19. Advertising
_____ 20. Product Design
_____ 21. Pruchasing
_____ 22. Law Enforcement and Related Occupations
_____ 23. Photographic Processes
_____ 24. Applied Science
_____ 25. Applied Mathematics
_____ 26. Machine Technology
_____ 27. Welding
_____ 28. Retailing Merchandising
_____ 29. Plant Protection
_____ 30. Secretarial
_____ 31. Clerical Practice
_____ 32. Business Machines
_____ 33. Business Machines
_____ 34. Bookkeeping and Accounting
_____ 35. Air Conditioning and Refrigeration
_____ 36. Electronics
_____ 37. Electric Wiring and Motors
_____ 38. Machine Shop Practice
_____ 39. Technical Writing and Reporting
_____ 40. Apprentice Training (Tool and Die, etc.)
_____ 41. Physics
_____ 42. Mechanics (auto, diesel)
```

Other_____   Other_____

_____   _____

6-A. Are some of your college graduate employees spending a significant portion of their time at less than college graduate level work? _____Yes _____No

6-B. If so, could employees having two years of training beyond high school replace some of the college graduates in your organization? _____Yes _____No

7-A. Is there an organized training program in your company of organization for less than college graduate level employees? _____Yes _____No

7-B. If so, could it be modified _____or eliminated_____by programs in a community college?

8.   Do existing educational facilities in the area meet the employment needs of your organization for less than college graduate level employees? _____Yes _____No

9.   If you have not attached a separate letter on this questionnaire, would you please comment here on your thoughts concerning the need or advisability of developing a local community college, which would include two-year terminal technical-vocational and/or semi-professional training programs.

Other Comments:

May we quote your comments in the letter or above? _____Yes
                                                  _____No

* * * * * * * * * * * * *

Delaware County Public Schools Community College Survey Questionnaire

DELAWARE COUNTY PUBLIC SCHOOLS
COMMUNITY COLLEGE SURVEY QUESTIONNAIRE

This survey of eleventh and twelfth grade students is part of a county-wide study to determine the post-high school educational needs of the Delaware County area.

DIRECTIONS: 1. Please qnswer all questions and statements.
DIRECTIONS: 2. Check all answers that apply to you. You may need to check more than one space to answer some of the questions.

High School _____   School District of Residence _____

Name of Student_____ Age_____ Sex M_____ Grade 11 _____
                                              F_____ Grade 12 _____

Occupation: Father_____
Occupation: Mother_____

Number of brothers and sisters: In elementary School (grades: kindergarten-6) _____, in junior high school (grades 7-9) _____, in senior high school (grades 10-12) _____.

I. If a two-year community college were available in Delaware County at a cost of $300 per year, would you be likely to attend? _____Yes _____No

II. If you answer to #1 is "yes", please answer these questions:
    A. Why would you choose to attend the community college?
        1. The low cost   _____
        2. To live at home   _____
        3. To keep a job while studying   _____
        4. To be near friend   _____
        5. To improve scholastic record   _____
        6. Other (Please explain)_____
        _____
        _____
        _____

    B. In what type program would you be most likely to enroll?
        1. Liberal arts program for transfer to a four-year college _____
            Technical training program. Exampes: Chemical, mechanical and electrical technology.

Terminal professional program. Examples: Nursing, lab
technician, dental or medical technician, legal or medical
secretary   _____
C. Which type of student would you be?
1. Full-time day student.
2. Part-time evening student.   _____

III. Please indicate the occupation in which you are:
A. Most interested _____
B. Somewhat interested_____

IV. If you would not go to college (Even if a community college
were available), please indicate your reason.
A. Getting married   _____
B. Want full-time job   _____
C. Entering armed forces   _____
D. Can't afford cost of college   _____
E. Not sure of future plans   _____
F. Other (please explain)   _____

_____

V. Do your parents want you to continue your education after high
school?   _____Yes _____No

VI. For seniors only:
A. Have you been accepted for college, university, or some other form
of post high school education for the fall of 1964? _____Yes _____No
B. Did you seriously consider one of the colleges or universities located
within commuting distance of your home? _____Yes _____No
If yes, which one?_____
If no, why not?_____

Student Signature_____
Parent's Signature_____

(Use reverse side of sheet for any comments you may have.)

14

A Systems Model for Program Development and Evaluation

MICHAEL ROSS AND BOB W. MILLER

The development of new programs in higher education is a significant administrative endeavor. The combined efforts of many people are required to do the job adequately. The coordinated efforts of these people operate together to create a program development process.

This chapter will explore a typical process of program development used by colleges and universities. The specific process that an institution uses may vary from college to college, although some elements will remain essentially the same.

Today there is a vast amount of program development activity taking place within colleges located in large metropolitan areas. Figure 45 depicts a community college district with five colleges and a district office. The various levels that will typically be involved during the development process of a particular program are shown. Throughout the chapter references will be made to the various levels of administration shown in this model.

DEFINITIONS

Assessed needs—A statistical data-based investigation via survey and other evaluation instruments to determine specific needs for a projected program.

Final authorization—An adjudicatory board to pass final judgment on the establishment of a particular program.

Implementation—A step-by-step process to achieve all stated objectives in the program development design to bring the program into full operational process.

Program idea—A creative idea for an educational program which may emanate from (1) manpower surveys, (2) publications, (3) advisory committees, (4) students, (5) faculty, (5) conferences, or (6) business and industry.

FIGURE 45
Program development activity in a large college

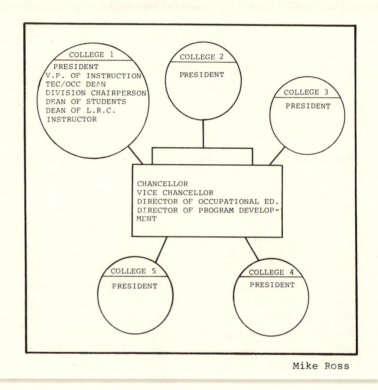

Mike Ross

Program evaluation—An on-going systematic process to determine the index of program success and the feasibility of continuing or dropping a program.

Task force feasibility study—A group of persons representative of all areas involved in new program development, including internal and external representatives to assess the feasibility of such program development.

PROGRAM IDEA

Figure 46 presents a graphic representation of the steps in the program development process. Each step will be described in detail in the paragraphs to follow. The process as depicted in this flowchart begins when the idea for a new program originates. Program ideas may arise from several possible sources, as shown in Figure 47. In a multicollege

FIGURE 46
Flowchart of steps in program development

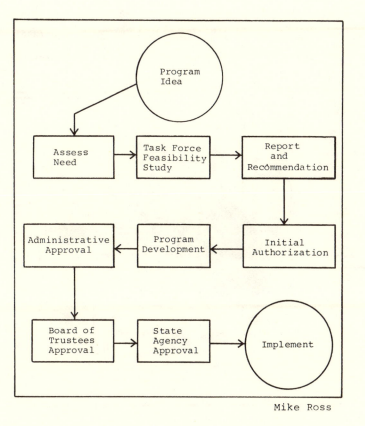

Mike Ross

Phi Delta Kappa National Study Committee on Evaluation, *Educational Evaluation and Decision Making.* F. E. Peacock Publishers: Itasca, Ill., 1971, p. 242.

district these ideas are normally funneled to the district office of program development. Sources of ideas are:

1. *Manpower projections.* State education agencies conduct periodic studies to determine the projected manpower needs in different occupational fields for various regions of each state. Many large metropolitan areas conduct manpower studies to determine needs in the local area. State employment agencies also provide

FIGURE 47
Program ideas may arise from several sources

Mike Ross

information regarding employer needs and manpower availability. An important concern in connection with needs assessment and manpower projections is that the United States has a
mobile population. The average person moves his home at least
six times during his lifespan. Because of this factor local, state,
regional, and national considerations must be kept in focus.

2. *Local associations and agencies,* or at times local professional
   groups, may request that certain programs be offered through
   the college district. For example, a local association of engineers
   may determine that nearly all of its member companies have
   personnel shortages in the design and drafting area. The association may submit a request to the college district office that a

program in design and drafting be implemented to increase the supply of available draftmen.

3. *Employers.* Individual employers may contact the district office indicating areas of need. This is an ideal way to develop a curriculum since these employers will have a certain commitment to employ these students after graduation.

4. *Conferences.* Some ideas are generated through attendance at conferences by district personnel. Here ideas can be shared with other colleges throughout the state and country.

5. *Publications.* Reading publications can sometimes stimulate ideas for program development. If, on the other hand, someone has created an excellent program in another institution and it fits your organization's objectives, you can implement those ideas.

6. *College faculty and staff members.* Program ideas also originate from faculty and staff members within a college. For example, an instructor in a food service program had a successful program that prepared students for careers as chefs and occasionally as managers or assistant managers of small restaurants. The instructor had an idea that a program in hotel-motel management could also be very successful and that the two programs would complement each other very well. His belief that this new program could be successful was strengthened because he knew that there was currently a local shortage of personnel with this type of training and that future projections for this career field were promising. Consequently, he submitted the idea and it successfully cycled through a program development process and was initiated. This type of program has advantages since there is a certain amount of commitment from faculty, thus the program probably will be easier to implement.

Assess Need

Once an idea for a new program has been submitted to the office of program development, a study should be conducted to determine the need for the proposed program. The initial step should be to check the manpower projection statistics from the various agencies previously mentioned. These statistics can provide data concerning projected needs for programs locally, regionally, and nationally. If a review of this information reveals that a particular program may be justifiable, a more in-depth study of needs may then ensue.

Perhaps the most reliable method of determining local needs of a specific program is through a survey instrument. An example of an instrument used by Dallas County Community College District is shown

TABLE 10
Survey of needs

The following questions concern the availability of entry
level optical lab technicians in the Dallas area. Please
answer the questions according to your personnel needs and
experiences:

Circle the letter of your response on the multiple choice
answers and check your answer on yes or no questions.

1. How many entry level optical lab technicians do
    you currently employ?

    A. 1 - 9
    B. 10 - 15
    C. 16 - 20
    D. More than 20

2. How many new optical lab technicians do you hire
    each year due to employee turnover or expanded
    growth?

    A. 1 - 3
    B. 4 - 6
    C. 7 - 10
    D. More than 10

3. Based on your firm's anticipated growth, how many
    new optical lab technicians do you expect to hire
    over the next five years?

    A. 1 - 9
    B. 10 - 15
    C. 16 - 20
    D. More than 20

4. Indicate the availability of trained optical lab
    technicians in the Dallas area.

    A. Ample optical lab technicians available.
    B. Some optical lab technicians available.
    C. Few optical lab technicians available.
    D. More job openings than there are persons
        available to fill them.

5. Have you had to recruit optical lab technicians from
    outside the Dallas area?

    Yes_____
    No _____

                    SURVEY OF NEEDS. DALLAS COUNTY COMMUNITY COLLEGE
                    DISTRICT

in Table 10. The survey ascertains the needs for a proposed new optical lab technician program. It was mailed to all known employers of optical lab technicians in the Dallas area. A review of the questions included in the survey will indicate the type of information that must be gathered. Careful analysis of this information will enhance the chances of making sound decisions with regard to program development.

Other information also is sought during the needs assessment phase of program development. It should be determined if there are other institutions in the area with identical or similar programs. Similar programs in other regions or states may be contacted to see how successful their efforts have been. Another important step is to determine and show evidence that a proposed program is compatible with the mission statement of the community college district. For example, consider a college district strongly committed to the philosophy that all students, including those in occupational programs, should take courses to stimulate social, aesthetic, and citizenship growth. Such a college district would probably reject a proposal for a one-year certificate program in welding technology that excluded academic support courses. On the other hand, a college district that had as its primary goal to meet the manpower demands of its community may consider such a program if a definite need could be established.

Task Force Feasibility Study

One of the most important groups in the program development process is the task force. A task force may be composed of the director of program development, appropriate technical/occupational dean(s), and representatives from business and industry of the occupational area to be studied. The business/industry representatives should be people in decision-making positions because they are able to provide supply and demand information. The task force reviews the information gathered during the needs assessment phase and then gathers other information necessary to complete an accurate feasibility study. Other information sought by the task force should be:

1. What types of instructional equipment and facilities are needed for the program? Are existing facilities and equipment available? If not, what will be the cost of obtaining needed facilities and equipment? Should these facilities be leased, or built on a permanent ownership basis?
2. What are the staffing requirements? How many instructors, paraprofessionals, adjunct professors, and staff personnel will be needed? What is the cost of providing necessary staff members?

3. How many students can be expected to enroll the first year, second year, and fifth year? What methods of recruiting will be used? Who will do the specific recruiting of students?

All information gathered by the task force is compiled and reflected in a written report. Included in this report is a recommendation by the task force on whether or not to continue with the development of the program. This report is submitted to the appropriate college administrative council for their authorization.

The members comprising this council will vary from college to college. It may be composed of the presidents from each college in the district, the chancellor or vice chancellor, and the district director of occupational programs. The council must include the top level administrators in the district, due to the critical nature of the final decision to be made. If initial authorization is given to proceed with the program this will constitute a significant commitment of time and money. Before a council will approve such a commitment it must be reasonably sure that there is a justifiable need for the program and that it will have a high probability of being successful.

If the council is in favor of the program it will then assign it to a particular college within the district. Several factors determine the choice of campus to be assigned the program. Some factors to be considered are, the interest of the college administration in the program, available facilities, existing related programs, and location of the college. Once a program is assigned to a college it is the responsibility of that college and of appropriate district and campus personnel to develop the program.

PROGRAM DEVELOPMENT

The key personnel involved in the program's development at this point are the vice president, dean of instruction, technical/occupational dean, and appropriate division chairperson from the assigned college. From the district office the director of occupational education and the director of program development are involved. If the program being developed is closely related to an existing program, an instructor or instructors from the related program may also be included.

An advisory committee with representatives from business and industry is also organized at this point. The advisory committee differs from the task force insofar as it is composed of people actually doing the work that the program will train people to do. These people need not be top-level members of their organizations. Their primary function is to suggest and evaluate curriculum and to relate changes and trends in technical and labor requirements. A major point to be made is that the educator in the institution will develop the final program. In other words, the advisory committee members make recommendations only.

It is wise at this point to also consider the use of a consultant. The consultant in this situation would be a person considered expert in the program area being developed. This person has usually invested many years in the area of his expertise and can provide valuable information relating to the program. Many dollars may be spent unnecessarily if a consultant is not utilized from the beginning.

Other key members of the college staff should be included during the program development stage. The dean of learning resources and the instructional development specialist can provide valuable insight into developing strategies to achieve objectives. The dean of students also should have input into program development. He has overall responsibility for some key functions related to instruction, such as counseling, placement, and student assessment.

Perhaps the most important step in planning the program at this point is the development of the curriculum. It is first necessary to identify the competencies that need to be learned by the student. When these are identified, course descriptions are written that cover the competencies. It is also necessary to explore possible support courses and to select those that are most appropriate. After all courses are identified and described, a proposed curriculum pattern is written which includes the program courses and support courses. The curriculum development phase is important and should be a thorough process which includes quality control.

Tasks other than curriculum development which must be undertaken during the program development phase are as follows. A budget should be planned which reflects the proposed cost of the program. The budget should include items of expense such as purchase of equipment, additional faculty and staff, operating expenses, and publicity. Facilities should be located to house the new program. These may include a classroom, office space for instructors, lab space, and storage space.

PROGRAM DEVELOPMENT IN GENERAL EDUCATION

This chapter has thus far dealt with the process of program development essentially for occupational programs. It is perhaps appropriate at this point to discuss briefly how this process relates to general education curriculum development and revision.

First, many varying definitions of general education may be given. Charles Monroe cites James W. Thornton's definition: "General education refers to programs of education specifically designed to afford young people more effective preparation for the responsibilities which they share in common as citizens in a free society and for wholesome and creative participation in a wide range of life activities."[1]

How is the general education curriculum to be determined? The methods are many. Some colleges simply review and adopt catalogues of other colleges. Many changes are initiated by the faculty and administration of colleges. Pressures from students and community members can lead to a revision of curriculum. Monroe believes that middle-class values serve as the controlling force for most general education curricula.[2] Student unrest during the past number of years has also resulted in curriculum revision.

Whatever the methods used for determining and revising curriculum, it is generally done in an effort to establish or maintain relevance. It has been suggested by a number of educators that advisory committees for general education courses would serve an appropriate purpose in this regard. Input from specialists and experts within a community is just as important for English, science, math, and history as it is for occupational programs.

The system that a college uses to develop or revise general education curricula may be similar to that model shown in this chapter. At the college level, essentially the same people would be involved in the development or revision of general curricula as are involved in occupational curricula. At the district level a curriculum committee would probably be involved instead of the occupational education department.

FINAL AUTHORIZATION

When program development is completed by the assigned college and appropriate district personnel, a report should be sent to the state agency for its initial reaction and back to the district council for final administrative approval. If the proposal is found to be deficient in any area it may be returned to the office of program development and to the college for corrective action. When final administrative approval is granted, the proposal is submitted to the board of trustees by the chancellor or president of the college or university for final authorization.

Upon receipt of final authorization from the board of trustees, final approval is sought from the appropriate state agencies. If this approval is given the program can be implemented.

Advisory committees should be utilized as well for continuing education. One educator making up a course or program by himself is not sufficient for quality control. The input of advisory committee members operates as a check and balance system which in turn assists in quality development.

IMPLEMENTATION

During the implementation process the program is actually brought into operation. Before the program is operational, facilities must be made ready and necessary equipment purchased. College maintenance personnel may or may not be able to accomplish the work required to prepare the facility. Major modifications to prepare the facility possibly could be subcontracted to outside companies.

The hiring of faculty for the program is an important aspect of the

TABLE 11
Summary of steps of program development process

STEP	ACTION TAKEN	PEOPLE INVOLVED
1. Program idea	Ideas sent to director of programs development	Originator of idea Director of Program Development
2. Assess need	Preliminary check to verify need	Director of Program Development
3. Task force feasibility study	Magnitude of demand is determined.	Task force Dir. of Prog. Dev Dir. of occ. ed. Tec/occ dean
4. Report and recommend	Submit report with recommendations	Dir. of Prog. Dev Dir. of Occ. Ed.
5. Initial Authorization	Grant initial approval and assign to college or deny approval.	Administrative council
6. Program development	Develop curriculum and all aspects of the program necessary for implementation. Submit reports as appropriate.	Dir. of Occ. Educ. Dir. of Prog. Dev. Dean of Instruction Tec/occ Dean Dean of Students Dean of L.R.C. Division Chairperson Faculty Advisory committee Consultant
7. Administrative approval	Final approval granted or returned for correction	Administrative council
8. Board of trustees	Grants final approval	Board members
9. State agency	Grants final approval	Appropriate agency officials
10. Implement	Program is put into operation.	Same as step 6

Mike Ross

implementation process. Recommendations may be sought from the advisory committee members. The position openings also are announced in local and national newspapers. Candidates are screened and the best possible prospects are identified. The interviewing process must be thorough to insure that the best possible person is chosen for the job.

Program publicity is also generated during the implementation stage. Brochures are printed which describe the program. Once again the advisory committee can be instrumental in helping to spread the word about the new program through professional meetings and other contacts. Local newspapers, radio, and television are key contacts for publicizing the program.

Recruitment of students should be a concern during program implementation. The publicity effort described is a complementary function to recruitment and should serve to stimulate interest in the program. All local high schools and community colleges also should be contacted and informed of the program.

When the program is in operation the actual program development process has temporarily achieved its objective. Each step in the process is shown in Table 11 to serve as a brief summary.

PROGRAM EVALUATION

Once a program is placed into operation its future success is dependent to a degree on a continuing and accurate evaluation process. Program evaluation is viewed by some as a threatening procedure; but it should not be, as its main functions are to improve program quality and instruction and to insure that the program is meeting institutional goals and objectives. Several evaluation procedures may be employed to determine a program's degree of success. A follow-up questionnaire may be mailed to graduates and to nongraduates who leave the program to determine what percentages are working in the field for which they were trained and how effective and efficient the training has been for those students employed.

Perhaps the most crucial index of program success today is enrollment. College funding in most states is based on enrollment. A program must enroll a certain number of students in order to cover the cost of operating the program. That is not to say that a program with a low enrollment necessarily is in danger of being closed, particularly if there is a manpower need for its graduates. However, a low enrollment will be a matter of concern to administration and recruitment efforts will probably be strengthened. In some cases leadership for the program will have to be evaluated where low enrollment exists on a continual basis.

Advisory committees may serve as a means for evaluating programs, particularly in the area of curriculum revision. They can often identify

FIGURE 48
Deadline dates
Curriculum and instruction proposals

Advisory Committee must meet and
advise on proposed changes prior
to November 20

(STEPS IN MAKING CHANGES)

STEP (1)
Faculty Members & Students
(Discussion & Recommendation)

STEP (2)
Department Chairmen
(Discussion & Recommendation)
(Correlate with other campuses)

STEP (3) – Nov. 20
Division Chairmen
Should submit material to all
interested parties beginning on
this date and far enough in advance
of open hearings to permit study

STEP (4) – Nov. 20
Open Hearings with Division Chairmen
(Should point out changes, deletions,
additions, implication to other
divisions)(Dean of Instruction to set
calendar dates) Dean and President not
to attend meeting (All interested parties
invited) Completed by December 1

STEP (5) – Dec. 5
Comments, protests, objections
to Dean in writing in relation
to open hearings

STEP (6) – Dec. 6
Deans & Division Chairman
(Final report & discussion)
(Invitation issued to others
at request of Dean of Instruction)

STEP (7) – Jan. 12
Deans of Instruction
Correlation Conference

STEP (8) – Jan. 19
Recommendations from Deans to
Presidents. (Catalogue changes
other than curriculum changes
due to coordinators of catalogue

STEP (9)
District C & I Committee (2 Presidents
and 2 Deans) Resolvement Purposes

STEP (10)
Revision of forms of changes made
by Division Chairmen (Return to
Deans) (Return to President)

STEP (11) – Feb. 15
Recommendations from President
to Chancellor

STEP (12)
Return of documents to campus
administration (Indicating changes,
deletions, approvals, rejections in
writing from chancellor's office;
should include reasons for action

Dean of Instruction to coordinate all changes
with Division Chairmen in final form. Deans
to correlate campus to campus (Dean in charge
to submit final recommendations as follows:

STEP (13) – Mar. 1
All catalogue curriculum changes
due to Director of Community
Relations. Chancellor, Vice
Chancellor for Research Development,
and Campus Presidents coordinate
reports to Coordinative Board and
Texas Education Agency

Bob W. Miller

curricula that should be revised to meet current practices in business and industry. In some cases they may even point out courses that have no current relevance or suggest new courses to keep up with advancements in a field. In too many institutions obsolete courses and programs are not deleted. This is an important decision-making area for the chief administrator.

National accrediting agencies for colleges and schools also serve as a means of evaluation for colleges and individual programs. For example, the Southern Association of Colleges and Schools requires a thorough self-study to be conducted by all colleges every ten years. The association evaluates all phases of the college operation including educational programs and faculty. This study identifies weaknesses and leads to recommendations for improving deficiencies within the college.

Students also serve as a vital means of program evaluation. Periodic teacher and course evaluation instruments completed by the students may indicate strengths and weaknesses of a program. Once a student has completed the program and is working, his or her input may be even more valuable. He can relate his education to his job and point out areas, if they exist, in which he was not as well prepared as expected. In several cases former students of programs are appointed to serve on these advisory committees.

Evaluation should be an ongoing, systematic process. There is too much at stake for evaluation to become haphazard and infrequent. Change in the business and industrial world is inevitable, and the only realistic, reliable method we have to identify and respond to that change is systematic evaluation.

Program development is an important administrative function in higher education today. The process of program development as described for a typical college or university in this chapter may serve as a model for implementing new programs. Whatever model is used, it is imperative that it be systematic, thorough, and accurate to insure successful implementation. Figure 48 depicts a quality control model for curriculum development within colleges and universities. Once a program has been implemented, the only realistic and accurate means of effectively conducting the program is through an ongoing process of evaluation.

NOTES

1. Charles R. Monroe, *Profile of the Community College* (San Francisco: Jossey-Bass, 1973), p. 67.

2. Ibid., p. 51.

15

External Groups, Communication, and Public Information

JAMES S. McELHANEY, JR., AND BOB W. MILLER

The complexities of higher education administration, as previously documented, are made no less complex by the administrators' need to carefully plan a program to communicate with external groups whose perception and/or image of the university can be critical to its success or failure.

Higher education and/or post-secondary education in recent years has taken on new dimensions and, as a result, administrators have found it necessary to alter the traditional image at many institutions. Elements leading to that image change include the increased demand for adult education and vocational-technical education and the subsidence of the postwar baby boom from which institutions could draw almost unlimited enrollment applications. Image changes have been necessitated by legislation. When a rash of civil rights legislation was enacted in the 1960s, many formerly all-black, all-white, all-male, all-female institutions discovered that their images were, if not terminal, at least tenuous. Administrators at these universities were then faced with the problem of effectively and delicately changing their institution's image in the minds of those external groups whose contributions to and support of the university is so critical. Vassar University, for example, world renowned as a woman's university, has been faced in recent years with the problem of becoming coeducational and hence requiring an image change while, like most universities, faced with decreasing enrollment applications. In order to successfully alter its traditional image and at the same time successfully compete for enrollment applications, Vassar implemented a concerted image change/recruiting campaign employing both traditional and innovative advertising and promotion methods, utilizing the expertise of a national, accredited advertising agency.[1]

The purpose of this chapter is to illustrate the elements that create a composite image of the institution and the value of advanced planning for that creation, and to identify external groups for whom the image is created and the methods of communicating with those groups.

DEFINITIONS

Alumni public—The most vocal and dependable external group dating back to the beginning of the education endeavor. Former students of a specific institution.

Community public—The most important yet delicate external group for the program of public relations because of the desired image with residents of a community.

External groups—Groups of individuals who are not closely associated with the institution by virtue of salary or governance responsibilities. Sometimes termed *publics*.

Institutional image—The concept of an institution held by a number of external groups that are not totally associated with the institution or its institutional life.

Media public—The "new kid on the block" in terms of external groups and potentially the most visible public. This group has the power to make or break the institution through the printed or mediated word.

Public information—The method or process of transmitting the image of the institution to the minds and consciousness of the various external groups.

Student public—The most significant internal group in the public relations program of the institution.

EXTERNAL GROUPS

It is most appropriate that the first element in the title of this chapter is the reference to external groups, since it is this identifiable entity which can have the greatest effect on the reputation and subsequent success of the university or college. More accurately stated, this groups's *perception* of the university or college can have a most profound effect on the institution's reputation. It is therefore critical that these external groups perceive the institution in a positive context.

External groups easily identified include civic organizations, local businesses and industry, governmental agencies, media, foundations, and other benefactors. Less easily and somewhat paradoxically identified as external groups are alumni, parents of the student body, and the institution's regents or governing board. On the face of it, it would seem that this latter group would be better described as internal, and certainly they are closely associated with the university, but their perception of the institution is equally significant in creating, establishing, and maintaining the institution's image and/or reputation.

In the final analysis, it would appear that the only internal groups affecting the university are the administration, students, faculty, and staff, and even these groups are not and cannot be defined as purely internal. The university and its image are a composite of the perceptions of all these groups and their perceptions of each other. As complex as this observation may seem, it is simple truth.

Broadly stated, the subject at hand is the institution's/administrator's concern with *positive* public relations, or relations with the institution's multiple publics. It is the chief administrator's responsibility to determine what image the institution shall have, how it shall be achieved, and what methods shall be used. Although simply stated, the responsibility cannot be carried out without very detailed planning, substantial expertise, and widespread commitment to the plan.

DETERMINATION OF PUBLICS

The chief administrative officer must determine in early planning what the university is and what he wants the diverse publics to think it is. Once these objectives are firm, he must then determine how to achieve the desired result. A positive public relations program will be of immeasurable assistance in accomplishing these goals. It is therefore equally important that the chief administrative officer formulate his concept of public relations. For instance, does he see public relations activities at his institution as an effort to embrace the entire relationship of higher education to the public? Is the public relations thrust to be directed at asserting intellectual leadership in the community? Is the public relations effort to be concerned with promoting those special activities that interpret the institution to the public in order to enhance its prestige and reputation? Or, does he regard public relations as a tool of persuasion and suggestion to accomplish certain specific objectives such as fund raising, securing better students or faculty, and other immediate aims?[2] The fact is, all of these purposes are valid and viable, but they do need to be put into a priority order, discussed with and subscribed to by subordinates, and, finally, administered by a competent, expert practitioner of public relations. This final admonition cannot be overemphasized. As President Carter Davidson of Union College wrote, "If a chief administrative officer fails in a college, it is largely due to the failure of his college public relations program."[3] To avoid that failure, President Herman B. Wells upon his retirement from Indiana University said, "Find a public relations counselor in whom you have confidence for your close associate, who has the ability and courage to tell you when you are wrong."[4]

Following determination of image, administrative concurrence, and interpretation and priorities of the public relations effort, it is then necessary to develop a profile of the groups at whom the public relations activity will be directed. As this facet develops, it becomes curiously apparent that the success or failure in achieving positive public relations with each group is greatly dependent on the relative success or failure with all other groups. To put it another way, the public relations chain is no stronger than its weakest link.

Student Public

Students are a most significant target, perhaps the most significant, in the public relations program. Not only are they the largest and most immediately available group, but after graduation they continue to be of prime concern as alumni. It is obvious that the need for quality instruction, facilities, counseling, and other student services not only be recognized and made available, but that a concerted effort be made to make the student aware of their availability and quality. Also important is providing students with an opportunity for input into the administration process and convincing them that their input is given full consideration. An unhappy student is one of three things, none of which is good for a public relations program. He or she is, or can be, a dropout, a negative spokesman for the university, or both. Integral to any public relations program directed at students must be public recognition for student accomplishments and contributions, and an awareness of the role they play in creating a positive image of the university.

Accepting the importance of positive public relations with the students, it then follows that parents of the students are a group of almost twice their size and, some may suggest, twice their importance. Their concerns are that their offspring be provided with a good home away from home, substantial personalized attention, and, in general, the same concerns as the student. It may be assumed that at least initially the university enjoyed a positive image with parents since they chose to entrust their children to the university. The concentration, then, for the public relations effort is to reinforce that image with a happy student, frequent communications from faculty and administrators, and ample invitations and opportunities to visit the campus.

Community Public

Possibly the most delicate public relations efforts will be required in establishing the desired image with the residents of the community in which the university is located. Initially, some of the problems are blatantly clear, such as traffic congestion near the campus, removal from the tax rolls of that property upon which the university is built, and, in many cases, reduced rates for public utilities provided the university by the community. The problem of "town-gown" relations was never more clearly detailed than by Jacques Barzun, dean of faculties at Columbia University.

> . . . [the community] can go out and see the university flaunting its greatness on the open street. And it is not only big, but hard to get at, . . . and harder to get into. It speaks of its admissions standards, which may well be a cloak for snobbish discrimination. When it encroaches on neighboring property, it speaks of necessary expansion. Where is the necessity? Isn't it big enough, strong enough, proud enough as it is? Most of these university people no doubt are pleasant-spoken when you meet them at the grocer's, but collectively they are stuck up, keep their children out of public school, and object to the run-down state of the neighborhood. They complain of crime, vice, drug peddling, and assaults on their girls and their professors. . . . Who do they think they are with their iron gates and gaudy costumes, and their names always in the papers? . . . The neighbors visit all manner of vague resentments on the place—it is "red" and reactionary; it is selfish when it takes, and patronizing when it gives. We need them and we don't want them. In short, it cannot do right and therefore cannot be right.[5]

Barzun's observation, although not succinct, is accurate. The solution, overly simplified, is a public relations effort that continually reinforces the positive contributions of the university to the community in terms of economics, cultural activities, and similar examples wherein the community and its citizens benefit.

Alumni Public

The tradition of maintaining positive relations with alumni is probably as old as education itself. There are, however, two contemporary tragic flaws in public relations efforts directed at alumni. The first flaw is that, generally speaking, the effort's success or failure is directly related to the success or failure of the football team or some other such single element. The second is the failure to recognize the value of a supportive alumnus until the student becomes an alumnus. It is critical that the university early on forge a bond between the student and future alumnus that is not only sentimental and social but, most importantly, intellectual. If this is accomplished, the institution is more likely to avoid a confrontation in the future with a self-serving alumni organization which may be inclined to mobilize in an effort to override sound educational policy. Emerson Reck put the alumni in perspective when he said:

> The alumni form the most important off-campus public of most colleges and universities, and there is no limit to the good they can do for their institutions, provided (1) the experiences of their undergraduate years can be recalled with appreciation and pleasure; (2) they are kept fully informed regarding the objectives, policies, progress and problems of their alma maters; (3) they are given an opportunity to perform challenging tasks for their institutions.[6]

The goal then in establishing positive public relations with the alumni is to get them as interested in education as they are in football.

Although the faculty and staff of a university might more logically be described as an internal group, the fact is that this group does not function solely on the campus. They have lives and interests outside of and separate from the university. For this reason, a well-conceived public relations effort needs to incorporate this element into its service plans. What the faculty and staff do off campus reflects directly on the university. To those not directly connected with the university, faculty and staff members are the university, as are the president, the regents, and, to a similar degree, the students. It therefore becomes abundantly clear that it is very important that faculty and staff members be kept adequately informed of the university's policies, programs, and problems. This requires a continuing internal information program which should also gently but persistently remind faculty and staff of their public relations responsibilities.

Media Public

A potentially critical portion of any public relations plan, which requires close attention, is that involving media relations. This external group, improperly attended, can destroy overnight, if not more quickly, years of effort spent in building an institution's image and, in its place, create an image that may well take more years of effort to overcome. This is not to imply a malicious element in the media or that a university needs to pander to it or to any other external group. It is, however, an admonition to recognize the tremendous influence, large audience, and widespread attention given information disseminated by the media. A public relations program that is at all derelict in keeping the media well informed on the university, its policies, programs, procedures, and goals is a program that very nearly contains an open invitation to disaster. The fact is that very few media representatives can be considered well informed or experts in the field of higher education. It is therefore mandatory that exacting measures be included in the media relations program to insure, insofar as possible, that inadvertent ignorance is never the cause for creating a distorted image of the university.

The pragmatics of administration at any college or university will almost certainly dictate the inclusion of a well-defined public relations plan for dealing with foundations and other potential donors, including federal agencies. It is inconceivable that any administrator would ignore potential sources of supportive funds for scholarships, buildings, research, and/or special projects. It is not uncommon for this activity to be assigned to a separate office normally entitled "Development." Concentration of attention on fund raising is generally considered to be of a higher priority at private institutions than at state institutions since, obviously, there is little support from state funds available to the private institutions.

Within the overall public relations plan there must be included programs designed to provide positive relations with legislators and regents or other governing bodies. These plans quite often require that the chief administrative officer assume the primary responsibility for their successful execution. Almost without exception, it is the president who represents the university to these two groups. He or she is, of course, supported by his staff but, in the final analysis, he alone will be the symbol of the university; its spokesperson and interpreter to legislators and regents. It is for this reason that in the early planning for a public relations program the chief administrative officer must fully consider the amount of time, effort, and support that will be required in order to properly handle this responsibility. Quite often activities such as legislative liaison between legislative sessions can be handled by administrative assistants. At any rate, it is apparent that substantial advance planning in this area is essential.

At this point there should be a clear understanding of the relationship between external groups and the university. It should also be apparent that to alienate any of these groups or to otherwise fail to keep them informed could result in the institution having to face great numbers of detractors unnecessarily. Certainly every college or university will always have critics, and well they should, but a properly conceived and executed public relations plan will go far to insure that the criticism leveled at the university is positive instead of negative. The task at hand for the administrator is to gather all the confidence and support for his institution that can be mustered through effective public relations.

COMMUNICATIONS AND PUBLIC INFORMATION

It does little good to identify external groups whose image of the university may bode ill or well for the institution if there is no plan for communicating with them or providing sufficient information with which they may formulate a positive and accurate image.

The lines of transmission or methods of communicating are manifold. They range from face-to-face, one-on-one, verbal, to utilization of the mass media. In any case, it is imperative to remember when disseminating information that the critical consideration is how the information will be interpreted by the recipient. If, after preparing information for dissemination, there is any discernible possibility that it might be adversely or erroneously interpreted, it is advisable to rewrite or otherwise restructure the communication to eliminate the possible misinterpretation.

It is generally accepted that the most effective way to communicate an idea or concept or image is by face-to-face personal contact. This type of contact will have greater impact over a longer period of time than any other form of communication. For this reason the public relations effort needs to be superlatively efficacious among the students, parents, alumni, staff, and faculty. These groups are the largest and most immediately aware, hence their personal contacts are substantially more numerous and of greater impact. If these five groups have a poor image of the institution, they can have a tremendous effect on subsequent recruiting efforts, community relations, development efforts, legislative relations, and many other areas that are significant to the university. It is critical, therefore, that those responsible for administering the public relations program provide for gathering feedback from the multiple groups related to the university. The most obvious method of obtaining this feedback is the systematic, formal or informal opinion survey. Information gained by such surveys provides indicators of possible problem areas, evidence of successful public relations efforts, early indications of developing needs on campus, and other trends which may or may not affect the university.

Substantially greater efficiency and effectiveness are attainable in that portion of the public relations program that deals with the production and dissemination of printed and broadcast material. Such material includes everything from media news releases and accompanying photographs to departmental brochures, college catalogs, pamphlets, recruiting films, displays, and annual reports. It must always be remembered that every piece of promotional or advertising material will have an effect on the image of the university. For this reason specific guidelines on design, style, reproduction, and distribution must be provided and followed with utmost diligence. Division, department, school, and college autonomy within the university is a generally accepted goal within all institutions. There must, however, exist among these entities and their administrators a concensus in terms of the university's image and the methods of maintaining and extending that image. This is not a difficult goal to attain if properly established in the initial planning for the public relations program, and if the faculty, staff, and administration have adequate confidence in the professionalism of those administering the public relations program.

Earlier paragraphs have alluded to the need for students, parents, alumni, faculty, and staff to have a positive image of the institution and confidence in its public relations programs and administrators. Early planning for the program and the inclusion of some of the groups in the planning function is, as stated, a significant element in providing the right image and confidence. The public relations program, however, must provide for continuing reinforcement of these desired attitudes. Effective reinforcement can be accomplished in many ways, including establishment of student/faculty/staff recognition programs, suggestion systems, creation of advisory committees, a speakers bureau, and initiation of internal and external publications and/or communications systems. A composite of these methods and/or others of a similar nature should also provide a two-way communications system and contribute substantially to the formation of a positive image of the university.

Unless a university is a private religious institution, there is obviously a substantial amount of contact between the community in which the university is located and the student body, faculty, and staff. The potential for poor relations between the university and the community, as cited earlier, is enormous. For this reason, the public relations program needs to include an ongoing program of activities designed to provide continuing contact of a positive nature. The primary activity designed for this purpose is the open house and/or tour program. It provides the community with an opportunity to see the university up close and wide open plus ample opportunity for the community to meet face-to-face with faculty, staff, and students. In addition to formal activities, a concerted effort must be made to encourage the community to attend other functions on campus, such as concerts and athletic events. These activities, coincidentally, may also be effective public relations efforts with parents, alumni, legislators, and regents. It is generally considered effective public relations to regularly include civic leaders in activities on campus, especially social activities, since the assumption is that if civic leaders have a favorable image of the university, so will their constituencies. This assumption is of course logical, but—one word of caution—community leaders can change, particularly in election years and at other unspecified times for any number of reasons. The point is that substantial effort should be exerted to involve the community as a whole with the university and its mission, not just the leaders in the community.

Generally speaking, a community places more confidence in its media than in its elected officials. It is therefore significant that a well-devised public relations program devotes a substantial amount of effort to creating the desired image with local media. This effort obviously includes supplying news releases. Pragmatically, however, it must include a great deal of personal contact between public relations personnel, media representatives, and university officials. It is true that "familiarity breeds contempt," but it is also true that lack of familiarity breeds suspicion, and suspicion in the media breeds speculation and worse. The public relations program must take every opportunity to insure that the media is informed *and understands* the university, its goals, procedures, and role in the community.

A university or college is not a freestanding obelisk. It is an institution supported by principles, ethics, emotions, and all sorts of intangibles and tangibles. The source of these supportive elements is people. These people, individually and in groups, are possessed of preconceived expectations. If the institution which they support fails to fulfill their expectations, they are inclined to withdraw their support, at which point the institution must fall. It therefore becomes the responsibility of those in whose hands the institution is entrusted to insure not only that the university fulfills their expectations but exceeds them and, further, that those who support the university are aware of the fulfillment. It is therefore imperative that a consistent and effective communications system be an integral part of the institution in order that the diverse groups supporting the institution are continually reassured of the value of their supportive efforts and of how those efforts are accruing to the benefit of all.

Lest the preceeding rationale appear too philosophical, included in the moral and spiritual support provided is the necessity for providing financial and economic support. However, in the most pragmatic sense, a university must have both or it can have neither.

NOTES

1. Jean Seligman, Lesa Dougherty, Richard Manning, Vern E. Smith, "The College Hustle,"*Newsweek*, April 3, 1978, p. 86.

2. Edward L. Bernays, *Public Relations* (Norman, Okla.: University of Oklahoma Press, 1963), p. 284.

3. Ibid., p. 284.

4. Scott M. Cutlip and Allen H. Center, *Effective Public Relations* (Englewood Cliffs, N.J.: Prentice-Hall, 1964), p. 411.

5. Jacques Barzun, *The American University* (New York: Harper and Row, 1968), pp. 161–62.

6. Emerson W. Reck, *Public Relations: A Program for Colleges and Universities* (New York: Harper and Row, 1946), pp. 161–62.

16

Public Relations: A Critical Administrative Function

ROBERT W. HOTES

Several of the preceding chapters have discussed various aspects of the communications process from the point of view of academic administration. Systems of internal communication have been identified as essential elements in the process of managing a complex educational or training organization. This chapter concerns the analysis of communications problems which involve the relationship of the institution with external publics; that is, individuals who are directly part of the college or university setting or who are potential customers for a proprietary training organization.

DEFINITIONS

External publics—Communication with the press and media within the service public and the private sector for the purpose of persuasion or motivation toward institutional goals and objectives.

Institutional public image—The process of communicating to the public the institution's view of itself and the view to be held by the public and private sectors.

Internal publics—Communication within the institution's boundaries for the purpose of persuasion or motivation toward institutional goals and objectives.

Mass media—The combination of all reporting devices (newspaper, radio, television, magazines, etc.) by private corporations to provide newsworthy items to the public for the purpose of informing the masses.

Press relationship—Working relationship with the media-producing agencies of a community for the purpose of presenting a positive image to the public.

Public relations—The methods and activities employed by an individual, organization, corporation, or institution to promote a favorable relationship with the public.

IDENTIFICATION OF PUBLIC RELATIONS FUNCTIONS

A variety of public relations problems may face the academic administrator in an educational or training organization. In general, however, such problems may be classified as belonging to the general categories described below.

Problems Dealing with Internal Publics

Points of conflict or miscommunication exist between the representatives of administration and institutional governance, and employees, students, and, most probably, the families of students and employees. All of the individuals in these groups are bound together through a bond of service. This service may be provided with the profit motive as chief incentive, as in an industrial training organization, or it may be provided as a public service, funded by tax revenues. In either case, one group of individuals serving the needs of another group may be identified.

Problems Dealing with External Publics

Relations with external publics include press and media relations as well as contact with groups within the service community or service target group. In many cases, both alumni relations and relations with potential students and their families may be classified as an integral part of external public relations. In the case of alumni relations, however, a case might be made for considering alumni relations as part of the internal public relations function. Quite probably, dealing with alumni involves both internal and external public relations functions.

While it is convenient for discussion to classify public relations functions in an educational or training institution as belonging either to the realm of internal or external public relations, the nature of organizational communications is such that the two functions cannot really be separated. An effective alumni relations program coupled with an honest attempt to work with faculty to develop their potential talents and abilities and to aid them to meet their aspirations can be an effective method of ensuring positive external communication and public relations. An association of alumni dedicated to the school and its programs can be as strong a factor in the continued effectiveness of an institution as its instructional programs. Likewise, a carefully chosen, competent faculty will serve as a link between the school and the community. Ways in which these can be fostered and strengthened will be discussed later in the chapter.

DEALING WITH EXTERNAL PUBLICS: SOME
IMPORTANT TOOLS AND CHANNELS

Many individuals within an organization may have responsibilities for the conduct of public relations. In the case of external public relations, especially press and media relations, most institutions find it expedient to select specialized personnel to handle particular tasks. It is important to remember, however, that the focus of responsibility for the conduct of public relations, both internal and external, is on the chief executive officer of the institution. Subordinate roles within the organizational structure may involve heavy contact with various elements of the school's publics and/or the mass media. But, by virtue of his or her office as chief executive, it is the president, chancellor, or manager who will be held responsible by the governing body for projecting and protecting an appropriate image of the educational or training institution.

Basically, there are two models or constructs according to which a public relations strategy for an institution may be formulated. The first is a centralized model, with the executive serving as a focal point through which information about the institution and its programs must pass before diffusion to the external public. The second is a decentralized model, with various levels of participation by individuals within the organization according to the position each holds within its structure and operation. Following this model, individuals within several subunits of the organization are delegated responsibilities relating to the public relations function insofar as the public information and communications role is a part of the overall responsibilities of their position or office.

Both models may be found in operation in American colleges and other institutions of higher education. In both models the chief executive of the school is a central figure in the public relations process. In the first model, the administrative head acts directly as a communicator with the press and other media. He is the spokesman of the institution and the most visible member of the school organization. In the second model, the administrator operates through others, through delegated authority. The administrator allows deans, department chairpersons, and instructors to represent the institution to the public, insofar as the public may be interested in the specific aspect of school operations with which the subordinates are concerned.

It is worthwhile to note that in both models the chief administrator of the school is still the individual directly responsible for the public relations function. In the present context of educational and training practice, presidents or chief executive officers are often effective representatives of the institution with regard to media relations and public exposure. Professional public information personnel are also employed for this purpose. Although in some cases board members and political figures have intervened in college or university affairs, in most cases observers have identified such a situation as purely a usurpation of function on the part of the trustee or politico. The general consensus of opinion and the force of current practice is to accept the chief executive officer of the institution as the legitimate representative of the institution in the public eye. Other individuals exercise public relations functions through delegation.

The choice of a model to fit the needs of a particular institution is made on the basis of a number of factors, including the size of the institution and the focus of its financial support. Small colleges and technical institutes usually find that it is most appropriate for the responsibilities for most public and media relations to be focused on the activities of the chief executive officer or president, while larger institutions often will have several individuals filling public relations functions. In certain cases, the apparent head of a college campus, the president, is in fact not the major decision maker, but a figurehead. In one large community college multicampus district, for example, the district's chancellor retains the real executive power while delegating many of the less important public relations duties to campus presidents. Because this individual has little real administrative authority, he may be thought of as primarily a public relations functionary.

In most cases, however, the administrator who has public relations responsibility must also bear major responsibility for his decisions as they affect the organization. In these cases, it is naturally the chief executive officer of the organization who will be chosen, by the board of trustees of the college or by the responsible administrative personnel of a business venture which operates a training organization, to represent that institution to the public. Naturally, many heads of public and private institutions of training or education have little experience in managing press relations, and for this reason they employ press officers or administrative assistants to aid them in dealing with the media.

THE WORKING PRESS: HOW TO USE PRESS RELATIONS TO AID THE SERVICE PUBLIC

The commodity called news is a report or series of reports about persons, places, or things. News is not simply an event, but a report of what has happened, is happening, or will happen. A person or event is newsworthy if there is a probability that others would like to know or need to know about that person or event. These are elementary explanations, but they are essential for the discussion which follows.

One of the major stumbling blocks to effective, healthy, productive relations between institutions of post-secondary education or training and the working press is the fact that many administrators do not understand the nature of news, its importance to our society, and the role that men and women who work in the mass media organizations play in the life of the community and the nation. Many college and university presidents or academic deans have been trained as "pure scientists" in the sense that their scholarly activities have been centered on a delimited, narrow field. While the progress of science and technology no doubt is benefited by such specialization, the narrow scope of training in chemistry or physics, or political science or English Literature, for that matter, provides little background experience in most cases for the college or university administrator who must deal with the very imprecise and contextual world of media relations. The following comments are intended to provide introductory aids to developing strategies for working with the media based on an understanding of how mass media functions and the characteristics of many of the individuals who work for news organizations.

Mass Media in Society—How They Affect Post-secondary Education

In the American political system, a free press is an essential part of the structure of society. We depend upon mass communication to provide the information needed for individuals to make free decisions regarding necessary choices for their own lives and for the public good. However, the press in the United States is not subject to governmental control. The Federal Communications Commission can and does provide regulating authority for many operations of the radio and television industry. This regulation is designed to insure public service and to protect the American public from abuse of the powerful tools of broadcast communications.

The administrator of an institution of post-secondary education will be more effective as a communicator on behalf of his organization if he remembers the essential differences between broadcast and press journalism. Both broadcast journalists and their counterparts working for newspapers and magazines have a high level of respect for their chosen calling. They would like to feel that others have the same level of respect for the working press. The administrator of a college, university, or technical school who is able communicate to members of the working press that he has a sincere respect for the role that journalists play in society will have an advantage in managing media relations.

The role of the mass media in American society is unique in that those who work in journalism are employed by organizations in the private economic sector. The major purpose of these institutions is not public service, but the production of profit. As private corporations, newspapers, magazines, and radio and television stations must operate to produce revenue for their owners—usually in the form of dividends paid to stockholders. On the other hand, those who work in the gathering and dissemination of news think of themselves as professionals, dedicated to the service of the common welfare. Journalists feel, by and large, that society cannot function without them. To a certain extent—journalists may be correct in their assessment of their own importance. Because the United States and other free societies depend on mass media to link consumer with producer through information, the role of the press and the broadcast industry is essential to the functioning of the free enterprise system. It should be noted that even totalitarian societies depend to a great extent on the mass media for the link between the forces of production and the points of consumption. A central difference, however, lies in the fact that in totalitarian societies such as the Soviet Union, the People's Republic of China, and East Germany, the government exercises close supervision of the press to "protect" individuals from error and to utilize the means of communication to enlist popular support.

The lack of governmental or social control of the media is a central aspect of media relations in the United States. Executive administrators who wish to make the best possible use of opportunities for successful media relations should understand that there is a large degree of freedom and autonomy granted to the press under the United States Constitution. First Amendment rights allow individual members of the press to exercise judgement as to which particular events are worthy of media treatment. College and university administrators sometimes are surprised that reporters and editors do not share their enthusiasm for particular school programs or activities. Ill will is sometimes generated through the actions of administrators who try to force newspeople to give free "publicity" to school events. The central point is that it is the representatives of the media themselves, not the school administrators, who are the arbiters of what is newsworthy and what is not newsworthy. News, as it appeals to public interest, is the stock in trade of journalists, and because the organizations for which they work are inspired by the profit motive, newspeople will be careful to select only those items for exposure that they feel are of general interest to a wide reading or viewing public.

The administrator who tries to force members of the press to publish certain stories concerning the college or university will often find that resentment develops in the relationships between the institution and reporters and editors. While it is beyond the scope of this chapter to discuss professional press ethics at any length, it should be noted that most members of the working press feel that they are doing the best, most professional job that they can under the circumstances. They are zealous defenders of the public's right to know, and any suggestion that they are not doing their duty in this regard will usually be taken as an insult. Administrators will bear in mind the fact that they cannot force a newspaper or radio or television station to give publicity to a particular event or program. But, if the program or event is really *newsworthy*—that is, if it is of interest to members of the community—the media will be anxious to give it coverage. An administrator who is respectful of the right of the members of the working press to act as judges of what is newsworthy will find that they are by and large anxious to have any leads about college or university activities. Education in the United States touches all levels of life—not only the scholastic institutional structure, but the home and family, church, club and organization. In the American news-gathering and dissemination system, news means public interest and public interest means profits. Good reporters will want to report a newsworthy story about the people involved in post-secondary education. Backgrounds and plans of students as well as what they are doing in the present are often of interest to the general public.

The Economic Basis of American Journalism

In order to make profits for their owners, American news professionals sell time and space. Broadcast stations, both radio and television, are primarily in the business of supplying audiences for advertisers, called sponsors. The stations get the attention of individuals by providing information and entertainment. There is an economic exchange, in other words, of the viewer's time for the advertiser's message. The medium of exchange for broadcast stations is time.

Newspapers have the same motivation. They exist primarily to make a profit for their owners. Secondarily, perhaps, they operate to serve the public good. Definitely, they are indispensible to the effective operation of the American economy.

There are differences between the two types of mass media, however. Readers are obliged in most cases to pay money for a subscription to a particular newspaper. They are therefore more selective of print media than they are of broadcast media. Those who buy a newspaper read it, in order to get value for their money. Newspaper buyers and readers are, therefore, a much more select target for communication than are the general audiences for radio and television broadcasts. But the news professionals who work for newspapers and magazines must also insure the attention of their readers. They do this by supplying news—especially local news—to individuals. This news is essential to the conduct of everyday affairs in the community. Newspapers also may provide features such as editorials, comics and advice columns. But their main goal is to supply news to readers who will also be interested in the advertisements which are placed in close proximity to the columns of news. In many cases the advertising that a newspaper carries may also be news. This is true for special sales and public notices, to cite two examples. And although newspapers have a more select audience than do the broadcast media of radio and television, that audience tends to be more economically productive and of greater interest to advertisers at the local level.

Few general interest magazines have survived the rapid development of television as the nation's major medium of news and information. But selected magazines may be effective for reaching particular audiences of interest to a college or university. Magazines may be effective in recruiting new students for particular new programs, for example, or effective for developing good will among members of a particularly influential group.

In order to work toward developing a favorable public opinion through press and media relations, educational administrators will find it useful to plan for effective management of news and information resources. The following steps may be useful in developing a systematic approach to media relations.

Determine the kind of public image that you think your school should have. This involves an analysis of how individuals in the community presently see your school and a determination of how they ought to see the school. Such an analysis naturally depends upon a close study of the goals and the mission of the organization and a formulation of an institutional philosophy. Only if there is a clear understanding of the mission and philosophy of the institution can an effective image be built. A concrete example may be useful in this context.

A comprehensive community college may be established as an institution of post-secondary education that can serve both individuals who desire to complete a four-year degree and those who wish to specialize in a two-year technical program. Because of long-standing assumptions on the part of many persons in the community, however, the prevailing image of the local community college may be that of an academically inferior institution where individuals who cannot meet the admission standards of colleges and universities are to be "brought up to standard" for entrance into a "real" college or university. In such a case, one of the major points of emphasis for efforts toward institutional image building would be the development of community understanding of the excellence of the academic programs of the community college. Although it is difficult and often impossible to change the opinions of individuals or groups, a gradual and persistent effort to emphasize the positive factors that surround any institution can produce results.

To the example of a community college faced with a lack of complete community understanding, we can also add the factor of the necessity of community support on a broad variety of levels. To a certain degree the effective college president and his staff will socially interact with community leaders. Generally this is advantageous to the development of positive public relations between the institution and the community. On a broader scale, however, the mass media may play an essential part in supplying information about the educational institution to the public. Administrators in education cannot afford to rely on the cultivation of a select group of supporters, no matter how influential they may be within the community. A broad base of public support is needed in the context of present day American educational practice.

STRUCTURING AN EFFECTIVE MEDIA POLICY

Each element of an effective media policy should be weighed in the light of the particular institution's mission and goals, and all of the elements involved should be considered in relationship to their functioning as a whole.

Determine who will have authority and responsibility for various aspects of the public relations program. As mentioned earlier in this chapter, the president of a college or university is generally given the principal responsibility for determining the scope and thrust of the public relations program of the school. This responsibility is delegated to him by the board of trustees. But within each organization a firm determination should be made as to which subordinates should handle various aspects of the public relations program. As in other aspects of administration in postsecondary education, delegation is a key to effective and efficient operation. This delegation must be real and not merely apparent, and it is essential to let individuals know that they will be expected to handle particular aspects of the public relations functions of leadership. Individuals should be able to talk freely about their programs with members of the working press where appropriate. They should be able to do so without fear that a chief administrator or his assistant will feel that they must have the right of prior censorship. In order for such delegation to become a reality without jeopardizing the operation of the college or university as a whole, individuals must be trained to be responsible.

Leaders in education should measure the impact and effects of public relations strategies in terms of results, not in terms of methods. If an administrator does not have confidence in the individual chosen to represent the college or university in a particular capacity, he has made a bad choice in delegating responsibility to that individual. Individuals in charge of particular programs should be specialists in their chosen fields, and administrators should be able to trust them to represent the activities of the college or university in those areas to the press. Because of human nature, mistakes will be made. Chief administrators should not expect perfection in public relations programs or in any of the institution's activities, but they do have the right to expect the maximum possible effort from individuals. This is essential if the institution's programs and policies are to be effective and if they are to be well received by the public.

In the case of the administration of media programs as well as other aspects of leadership, holding individuals accountable involves realistic assessments of goals and results. A program such as a Management by Objectives system might be one way to insure a realistic assessment of the success of a media relations program.

Establish criteria for measuring results. Much social research has been done on the impact of the mass media on various segments of the public. It is not the purpose of this chapter to present a digest of the research in this field. However, the college or university administrator should be aware of what research says about media influence on human behavior in a free society. In general, research evidence gathered through the last twenty years points to no definite conclusion with regard to the impact that the media have on the direct or indirect actions of individuals, although there has been a great deal of speculation since the early 1950s concerning the effect that television violence may have on certain classes of viewers, especially the young.

For the educational administrator, the problem of justifying expenditures for advertising in the mass media may revolve around the problem of demonstrating to a board of trustees or a state finance committee the need for an increased budget for paid radio and television ads to aid in the student recruiting effort or to overcome a negative image. In most cases, it would seem quite difficult to point to a certain number of students and claim without reservation that these individuals would not at present be attending the institution if it were not for a particular media effort.

One commonly used method of determining media effects is a questionnaire or response section on an enrollment form or other document which asks the individual student to indicate how he or she learned about the institution. Such a device may be useful to the extent that such reports reflect an accurate assessment by students of various influences on their enrollment.

A more difficult problem is the determination of changes in the image of an institution among members of its service public. A growing institution in the Southwest, for example, presently has a problem with changing its image from that of a second-rate subsidiary campus of a statewide system to a full-fledged graduate and undergraduate institution. Strategies chosen by the president and staff of this institution include increased emphasis on intercollegiate athletics and wide publicity relating to campus activities and special events. Not least among the devices employed by this school is a coordinated media package involving radio and television as well as the press. Both paid and "public service" messages are used. Surveys are taken from time to time by the student press to gain information on whether incoming students have been reached by these messages, but, by and large, expenditures for this kind of media compaign must rest on the assumption that such strategies ought to work, since undergraduate surveys concluded on college campuses are characteristically not dependable.

Because public and private colleges and universities and specialized vocational schools often do not have resources for intensive media research, media campaigns conducted by colleges and universities tend to be quite conservative, often involving an invitation by the president of the institution to investigate the services of the institution.

The effectiveness of such appeals in influencing eighteen- or forty-year-old prospective students to explore the educational possibilities of a particular institution has not been clearly demonstrated. It is difficult to determine whether or not such an approach is actually effective in marketing and the recruitment of students.

It has been said that education in the United States often follows when it should lead. This is probably the case with regard to utilizing the media in order to form a positive public image. Colleges and universities generally present their messages to the public in the same way that professionals and churches do. None of these groups are generally aggressive. There is no clear evidence that this approach is most effective in getting across the message of an educational institution. Furthermore, the college president or chancellor may not be the most attractive image of the institution to an eighteen or twenty year old. As a matter of fact, he may not be very appealing as a media image. The sophistocated leader in education administrator does not let himself develop an exaggerated feeling of importance and recognizes that others in the organization may be able to do a better job in specific areas.

Judging what is appropriate media publicity for a particular public institution may involve discretion and tact. No person and no institution can please all people all of the time. The institution's commitment to service should determine the target group to be served, and appropriate messages should be designed for that group. Television commercials for a public college featuring minorities may anger certain citizens in a community, but they may be the appropriate approach in light of a public college's mission to serve diverse members of the community.

Selecting Media for External Communication

Selection of media to communicate effectively involves determination of the message content, identification of a target audience for communication, and the selection of an appropriate level of communication.

Colleges and universities must be especially careful in choosing communications media, since the target audiences they wish to reach are changing constantly. New media strategies may be important factors in reaching individuals with messages concerning the institution and interesting them in its services. Increasingly, colleges and universities are seeking to use radio, television, and the press to bring their message to the public. In a time of financial constraint, it is essential that expenditures of public monies be justified in terms of approved societal goals. In the case of media publicity, such outcomes would be increased public awareness of the institution's programs and, hopefully, increased enrollments.

Considerations in Selecting Media

The following points may prove useful in selecting media for college or university public relations efforts.

The medium should suit the message. Messages advertising programs of interest to young adults will probably be effective on radio stations specializing in popular music. Ads for senior citizens programs or for financial backing will probably require stations with a different format. In certain cases, television commercials may be effective, but costs must be weighed against anticipated benefits.

Reliance on "free" promotional devices and public service announcements should be limited, since there is a great demand for such free publicity. Planned in conjunction with paid advertising, the free public service announcements provided by radio and television stations may be helpful. But they cannot be depended upon totally. In addition, radio and television stations are profit motivated and expect to be paid for their time. It is true that radio and television stations must, by law, devote a portion of their air time to public service. It is also true, however, that the form this public service takes is largely up to the station.

Newspapers are not under the same constraints as radio and television stations to provide free publicity for community groups and organizations. But they will be receptive to community news if it really is news, and not thinly disguised advertising.

Administrators should hire individuals who have connections and experience with the working press to assist them with media affairs. Media professionals resent the college president or dean who tries to force them to provide free publicity for a college or program. They want to be respected as professionals and prefer dealing with a representative who knows the pressures of the job.

Finding Resources for Effective Public Relations

Although it is usually wise for the university or college administrator to rely upon professional help in planning public relations campaigns and strategies, publicity and communications with the public are often delegated to department and division chairpersons. These individuals are called upon to contact the media on behalf of their individual programs and, at times, to schedule events which will bring the public into contact with the college or university as a whole. An example of this kind of responsibility would be the scheduling of a performance by a noted visiting musician, or a student music recital. In any case, it is often left up to students and faculty members, under the leadership of the department or division chairpersons involved, to arrange for appropriate publicity for these events. The following sources provide basic information concerning the public relations process for leaders who may be asked to solve public relations problems for the first time.

One of the most widely used and cited volumes in the Public Relations field is Scott Cutlip's and Allen Center's *Effective Public Relations*.[1] Long used as a public relations text in schools of business administration, this book gives theoretical foundations as well as practical information. Written from the point of view of corporate public relations, some consideration is given to the affairs of public organizations. Almost all of the information contained in the volume can be adapted to the needs of educational organizations.

One of the few books directed to the specific needs of public relations efforts in higher education is Sidney Kobre's *Successful Public Relations for Colleges and Universities*.[2] A comprehensive bibliography is provided in Scott Cutlip's *Public Relations Bibliography*.[3]

For general reading that provides a background in the field of public relations, Edward L. Bernays's *Public Relations* is a classic.[4] An excellent guide to the location of sources and services, for public relations use is Richard Weiner's *Professional's Guide to Public Relations Services*.[5]

There are several important journals in the public relations field. Since these deal primarily with research and case studies relating to public relations problems in the private sector and in the operation of governmental bureaucracies, they may not be of direct interest to the administrator who must serve as occasional publicist for his or her organization. It is the thesis of this chapter that administrators can use their time more effectively in choosing goals and directions for public relations efforts, than in acting as public relations agents working with the press and the community on a day-to-day basis. The administration and supervision of public relations efforts remains a significant and critical public relations function.

NOTES

1. Scott M. Cutlip and Allen H. Center, *Effective Public Relations* (Englewood Cliffs, N.J.: Prentice-Hall, 1978).

2. Sidney Kobre, *Successful Public Relations for Colleges and Universities* (New York: Hastings House, 1974).

3. Scott M. Cutlip, *A Public Relations Bibliography* (Madison, Wis.: University of Wisconsin Press, 1965).

4. Edward L. Bernays, *Public Relations* (Norman, Okla.: University of Oklahoma Press, 1963).

5. Richard Weiner, *Professional's Guide to Public Relations Services* (Englewood Cliffs, N.J.: Prentice-Hall, 1971).

17

Historical Aspects, Present Status, and Future Concepts for Student Services and Student Development

GARY R. BEAUCHAMP

An age-old adage states, "There is nothing new under the sun." While this holds true in nearly all facets of life, it is amazing to find this truism aptly applied to the general topic of higher education. It is particularly amazing to realize that student development, with its myriad of conflicts, has come round full circle to its inceptual position with a sophisticated twist. To realize this position as noteworthy, observe the beginning stages of higher education in America.

DEFINITIONS

Financial aid—The distribution of allocated funds, to students both federal, state, and institutional, based upon a predetermined dissemination formula or policy.

Guidance and counseling—Provisions ranging from information via printed materials to individual or group activities which determine decision making.

Health program—The provision of medical services and outpatient care on a limited or extended basis.

Placement—The process of identifying potential job opportunities in the public and private sectors and the assessment of students for placement in or recommendation for those job opportunities.

Proactive student development—A developmental plan that anticipates problems and difficulties in student life and provides objectives to meet those difficulties.

Reactive student development—A developmental plan that does not anticipate problems and difficulties in student life and provides management by crisis rather than management by objectives.

Resident life—The concern of housing is to be responsive to the total needs of students, which include comfort, safety, and a wholesome environment.

HISTORY OF DEVELOPMENT

The first colleges in America were founded upon the obsolete patterns of English universities. Their purpose deviated, however, to be singularly that of training young men for the ministry of the gospel. Harvard College was founded specifically for this purpose. Secondly, the colleges were to perform additional functions: to give students a fundamental training in morals and religion, to develop some of the social graces and ability to get along with one's peers and, after the Revolution, to educate and prepare citizens and leaders of the republic. In modern vernacular, the college was a system of total student development with the emphasis on the personality of the individual, especially the moral aspects of his life, as well as on the educating of the mind. The curriculum in this period was the limited facet of college life. It consisted of the classics, Latin, Greek, and philosophy, each of which was carefully pruned of anything that could taint the morals of the student. One of the first statements of educational philosophy was made by John Milton. "I call therefore a compleat and generous education that which fits a man to perform justly, skillfully and magnanimously all the offices both private and publick of Peace and War."[1]

For the next two hundred years higher education experienced severe growing pains. Church-oriented education was soon antiquated, and a progressive citizenry was demanding a curriculum more suited to the needs of the American student. The Morrill Act of 1862 granting lands and federal aid to state colleges; the Brown Report publishing a review of the past and crying for reform; literary societies promoting student debates on hallowed subjects—history, literature, philosophy, logic, religion, and current topics—all led to an improved and broadening educational system.

While educators were progressing in intellectual pursuits, they were less successful in finding proper outlets for extracurricular student time. These early colleges did not tolerate foolishness or unworthy activities and any function that occurred outside the classroom was placed in this category. The result of this notion was a lack of recreation and release for the students which led to eventual riot and disorder. The primitive living conditions in the schools and the lack of time-consuming challenges promoted a rampant destruction of property. The most frequent targets were privies, which were a constant source of trouble. Students would periodically burn these facilities in an attempt to force their renovation. In 1800 the Prudential Committee of Yale built three "Necessary Houses," eight feet square and divided into four separate compartments. Three years later, more were built, presumably because the others had been burned. The new ones were constructed of brick. The sophomores, however, tried to blow up the brick ones. Other forms of revolt included the smashing of doors and windows. The University of

North Carolina suffered from students riding horses through the dormitories. After the Revolution, Harvard students brought cannon balls from arsenals into their dorms, intent on rolling them down the halls, a practice soon imitated at other colleges.

History records a number of students and faculty who suffered serious injuries as a result of student riots. Reaching a climax in the renowned "Bread and Butter Rebellion" of 1828 and the "Firemen's Riots" during which a student shot and killed a fireman, the history of early colleges was written in riot, disorder, and discipline. Positive total student development during this time was obviously a failure.[2]

After the Civil War student rebellions were on the wane. Four factors are credited with this occurrance. Changes in the curriculum which created a new attitude on campuses; the decline of excessive college discipline systems; coeducation, with its moderating influence on the conduct of male students; and the rise of intercollegiate athletic sports all combined to absorb much of the superabundant youthful energies which had formerly gone into fomenting rebellion.

While one problem appeared to be solved, early twentieth-century observers of the American college felt that a deplorable gap was developing between instruction and out-of-class student activities. It was suggested that these two main aspects of the modern college—the intellectual and the socioathletic—worked at cross-purposes to produce a campus versus classroom war.

After the First World War, however, notable strides were made in producing a new synthesis of the principal needs of American college life. Educators began a serious examination of the flourishing extracurriculum and accepted it as a challenge rather than a threat. The debate changed from the dangers of various student activities to the ways in which an institution could constructively profit from them to the benefit of the student. Toward this end divergent personnel services surfaced to give attention to the student's problems of self-support, career identification, health and personal problems, academic guidance, and orientation within the university.

The characteristic title for this new concern came to be the "student personnel movement," today's "student development program." New though the title may be, the concept of cultivating the physical, social, and moral aspects of a student's life as well as the intellectual could be traced back to the early church-dominated American colleges.

PHILOSOPHY OF DEVELOPMENT IN CONFLICT

One might ascertain that the swell of enthusiasm for the development movement carried these programs to new heights of acceptance and success. In fact, student development continues to have an identity crisis and is still battling its way in today's universities. While on some campuses student personnel staff members have ascended to high institutional positions, there are signs that health and counseling as well as other services are seriously threatened.[3]

The University of Wisconsin at Madison closed its entire counseling service. Texas Tech closed all infirmary beds. Some institutions such as the University of Utah have combined mental health services with academic programs for budgetary considerations. In 1973, a $40,000 reduction in the budget for counseling and student health services at the University of Missouri caused the student health center to close as a separate department and be made part of the medical school. In California legislation was passed stating that no more psychotherapy would be given on state-funded campuses.

While budgetary problems have contributed to decline in services due to rising costs and heavily taxed educational dollars, budgetary problems alone do not explain the lack of support for student development programs. Many educators embrace the philosophy of the late Robert Maynard Hutchins, "A University is an intellectual community of people at various stages of development, physical, and intellectual, trying to understand major issues that confront and are likely to confront mankind." When asked how he would change modern universities, he replied, "At the lowest level. If a university is an intellectual community, it should get rid of everything that isn't intellectual."[4]

There is, therefore, a dilemma. A dilemma which will never be solved until the purpose of higher education is pronounced. What is the purpose of a college or university? To teach how to, or why? Lessons for society living or to make a living? Do they exist to pay homage to traditions of society, or to be avant-garde for the new world of the future? As long as the emphasis is on such lofty questions and ethereal concepts, it is no wonder there is an impasse. The purpose of higher education should be to assist the *student* in his striving for knowledge of his relationship to mankind and to the universe. To this end the university must seek to develop an integrated person—intellectually alert, socially adapted, and physically disciplined. It is a process of educating the whole man. More than concepts, more than philosophy, more than ideals, the object is flesh and blood—the student. While it may test and hire and promote and pay and research and program, there is still only one salable commodity—the student—and the only true measurement is how well the student functions, achieves, and lives a worthwhile life after leaving the institution.

John enters college at an earlier age than most students because he has an higher than average IQ and is promoted through secondary school in record time. In college John studies, prepares laboriously for difficult assignments, studies, and attends every class. He is considered a loner, eats meals only when convenient to his studies. John graduates magna cum laude having made few associations, and lives thereafter in a shell. Neurotic, uptight, and frustrated with a world that does not meet his expectations of perfection, he goes on a rampage and becomes a sniper, shooting at hundreds of people, killing fourteen.

Bill enters college, Mr. Average-Cool. Missing classes three-quarters of the time, Bill copies notes from classmates, manages to slip by grades by enrolling in heavily populated classes and "bulling" his way through most exams. Bill is involved in every social function on campus. He has many friends, and spends graduation night unconscious from too much booze, drugs, and song. Bill gains easy employment as a salesman because of his charismatic first impression, but his heavy addictive problems soon surface and he is a job-failure repeater.

These two young men represent opposite poles on the spectrum, but they are not exceptions. They are representative in one way or another of many college students today. While John experienced an exceptional intellectual experience in college, the total man was not developed. He lacked the social skills to enable him to function in a gregarious world. Bill excelled at social grace accomplishment but missed the value of life preparation, on both a vocational and a moral level. In neither case can we say the purpose of higher education was served.

An institution can exist only on the strength of its purpose for being. The programs of that institution are successful only when they enable the student to be fulfilled through those purposes. On the strength of such a philosophy, and toward the development of a total man or woman, the student development program at any institution of higher education is a paramount structure. See Figure 49, Objectives of Student Development.

THE STUDENT DEVELOPMENT PROGRAM

The diagram in Figure 50 depicts the totality of a student development program and the interaction of various elements within the system. The basic components of the system are the personnel, the processes, and the objects. The model presented depicts (a) the objects worked with, (b) the population from which the objects are derived, and (c) the processes utilized. These components must be examined in order to understand the complexity of such a program. The objects with which the student development staff works are individuals, groups, and nonpersons (facilities, equipment, ideas, residence, classrooms, and laboratories). The population with which development is concerned contains the student, his parents, the community in which he is schooled, and the staff (administrators, faculty, counselors, resident personnel, and so forth).

The student comes to the school already a complex individual, the

FIGURE 49
Objectives of student development

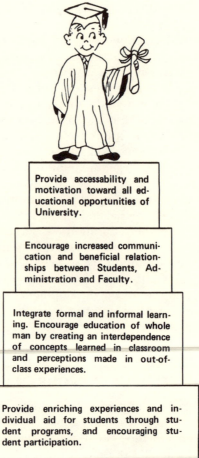

Provide accessability and motivation toward all educational opportunities of University.

Encourage increased communication and beneficial relationships between Students, Administration and Faculty.

Integrate formal and informal learning. Encourage education of whole man by creating an interdependence of concepts learned in classroom and perceptions made in out-of-class experiences.

Provide enriching experiences and individual aid for students through student programs, and encouraging student participation.

Provide atmosphere for self-discovery and expression.

Provide climate for challenge toward higher levels of intellectual pursuits, personal and moral maturity.

Gary Beauchamp

FIGURE 50
Student development model

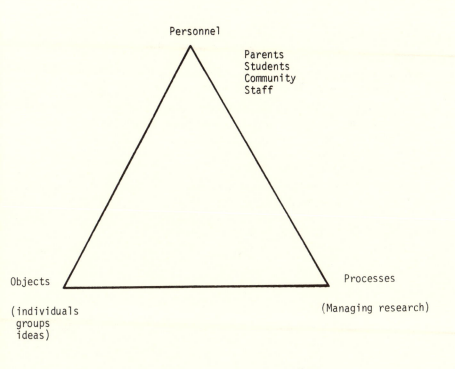

R. W. Hotes

product of a lifetime of character traits. He enters college in this initial state and is immediately besieged by the barrage of collegiate influences representative of the personality of the institution.

The Student

Who is the student of the 1980s? The student of today has evolved from the veterans of the 1940s, to the quiet generation of the 1950s, to the protesting activist of the 1960s, to the informed student of the 1980s. Today's student is not only different from the student of the past, he is new to the scene of higher education. While in the past 80 to 90 percent of high socioeconomic level youth attended a college or university, this decade has brought a sharp rise in students from lower socioeconomic levels.[5] Over 50 percent of low economic level students with high ability enter our colleges, usually junior or community colleges, while 20 percent of low ability, low economic level students also attend college. These figures are taken from a study of 10,000 high school graduates by James Trent and Leland Medsker of the Berkeley Center for Research and Development in Higher Education, University of California.[6]

The junior community college student attends school for multiple reasons. He is a student of practical considerations, with a desire for financial well-being and business success. 70 to 75 percent of community college students aspire to transfer to a four-year institution, although only 35 percent actually do make the transfer.

The four-year student chooses a college based on academic reputation and intellectual interests. This student is more likely to give importance to service-orientated activities. He is strongly influenced by political affairs, personal development, philosophy of life, and may likely aspire engage in community action.[7]

Today's student is highly aware of his world. He is a legal voter and politician and has developed a keen interest in the future of his world economically, ecologically, politically, religiously, and sexually, as well as intellectually. He is a person striving toward self-esteem, self-insight, self-assurance, and self-identity. To limit today's student would constitute a grave injustice, so divergent is the student of today. He is not the

FIGURE 51
Student development

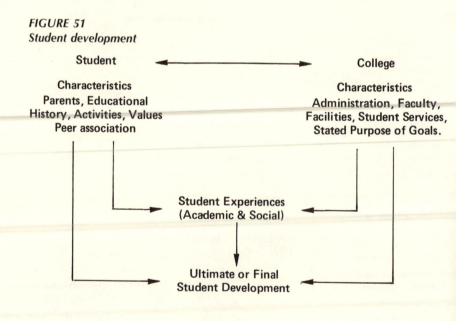

GRB, 1978

spoon-fed high school graduate born to educated parentage of yesteryear, but is likely to be a minority ghetto student pulling himself up the long haul, determined that his voice be heard.[8]

This student is a product of his home environment, his peer associates, his educational experiences, and his own self-concept, as illustrated in Figure 51. He brings these tools with him to college, where he is confronted with the college characteristics. The characteristics of an institution perhaps are best seen through the student services it provides, since academic pursuits are (with vocational exceptions) usually fairly standard.

STUDENT DEVELOPMENT SERVICES

The enabling process of a student development program has the primary functions of educating, guiding, stimulating, and helping. Within these areas are the individual compartments of the development program.

Educating

In all the rhetoric concerning the value of total student development, one must not overlook the initial reason for the student to be at the institution—to learn. While this whole realm of responsibility falls within the range of the academic departments of the university, every aspect of development must concentrate on facilitating the student's learning in a comfortable environment at his own individual peak ability level. A student development program that detracts from or conflicts with the educating process has lost sight of its purpose for existing.

Student services have profound effects on the educational experience by providing living arrangements, organizing enriching activities, and providing counseling and help for students with difficulties, both academic and in adjusting to the college setting.

The separateness of the functions of academic and developmental departments of universities is the greatest single negative factor in accomplishing the purpose of graduating a total man. Faculty who teach only in the classroom and whose influence ends at the doorstep miss the most creative periods in the learning process of the student. Most universities today have isolated departments which, if combined, could facilitate the total educational process. For example, there is a division of academia dealing with academic advising, and a division within development for student counseling. One is designed to help a student with intellectual pursuits while the other is available for emotional and other problems. Most often a student with an intellectual problem is also emotionally bothered by that problem.

If John is flunking statistics, he is most likely to become distraught, frustrated, disgruntled with his associates and the university as a whole. Susan has a hearing disability which causes extreme emotional discomfort and a general lack of confidence, displayed in the classroom as low achievement. Whom do these students see for help? Their academic adviser, to advise them how better to accomplish the tasks in the classroom, or their psychological counselor, to help them deal with these problems? This area is being handled on some campuses as a cooperative effort to the success and satisfaction of both departments.

Florida State University recently shifted the emphasis of its developmental division from extracurricular activities to innovative concern with the total development of students, academic and personal. Activities outside the classroom had been considered secondary, neither valued nor rewarded by the university and thereby taken lightly by faculty, administration, and students alike. The decision was made to bridge services and curriculum, removing the confusion and the distinction about what was being developed in the student.

The key to this program of "adaptive education" is continuous interaction. A unit is constructed to be responsible for guiding and evaluating the students' entire educational experience from orientation to graduation. To perform this function some aspects of services need to be considered part of the formal curriculum. This places faculty on a parallel line with developmental personnel, giving a positive ebb and flow between the two. The faculty has immediate knowledge and conceptual understanding of the needs of the students, while the developmental staff has a clear picture of the goals of the educational process, blending the best of both worlds. This is especially valuable in light of today's new students, who come from widely varying socioeconomical-intellectual levels. A number of learning environments are provided to meet the student at his entering level and draw him to the standards of the institution.

The concept of coordinating academia and development enables the student's progress to be measured accurately and to his greatest fulfillment. A student is tested in the classroom on factual attainment, but without enriching experiences facts can be soon forgotten, or the value thereof neglected. Therefore evaluation has the purpose of indicating to the student where he is now and how much farther he has to go to accomplish his goals.

The university is in the business of training professionals to go out into the world to accomplish tasks. While the student is learning these tasks, he is a storehouse of talent for the university to utilize.

The organizational unit of the counseling center at Florida State University is a good illustration of this student utilization. The center is designed to be a bridge between student affairs and academic affairs. It is manned by professionals employed full time by the student development department and by faculty from several departments in the university. Graduate and undergraduate students are hired to assist in the program, and receive both valuable training and credit for their work.

One program of weekly groups who develop competencies to handle persistent crises and conflicts involves an intense interaction between the student, faculty, and the professional or paraprofessional counselor. Another program deals with career identification. This program enables a student to view his chosen field not from a pure classroom base, but through brochures, slide presentations, career counseling, and referral to community professionals in his field to gain a closer look at the field both for evaluating purposes (whether I can live with this) and goal-setting purposes (where am I, and what do I need for where I am going?).[9]

The Center for Student Development at Kansas State University has attempted to coordinate operations within the campus, classroom, and community in its University Learning Network (ULN). Created in 1970, the ULN is a telephone information assistance and referral center (academic, campus life, and community) operated by a paid student staff, volunteers, and a faculty adviser. In addition, the staff has assumed coteaching assignments for designated developmental courses in the academic department. One such course is a study skills laboratory (1–3 credits), and another course is designed to train persons working in paraprofessional capacities within the institution.[10]

In researching the area of development coordinating with academia, two factors become readily apparent. First, any organization attempting this pattern is unique, and second, informative, counseling, and career-oriented staff members take the forefront in adapting academics and development. It seems conceivable that other departments within the university would do well to utilize the same plan.

Resident Life

The concern of housing personnel is to be responsive to the total needs of students, which include a comfortable, safe place to live and an adequate physical environment as well as opportunities for development.[11] Note in Figure 52, David DeCoster's and Phyllis Mable's "General Objectives for Student Housing," the steps utilized in achieving this function.

The objectives of a successful total housing program should be met level by level, one building upon the next, with mutual cooperation and support of management and educational personnel. While these five levels mesh and blend to form one continual flow, each level represents a

FIGURE 52
General objectives for college student housing

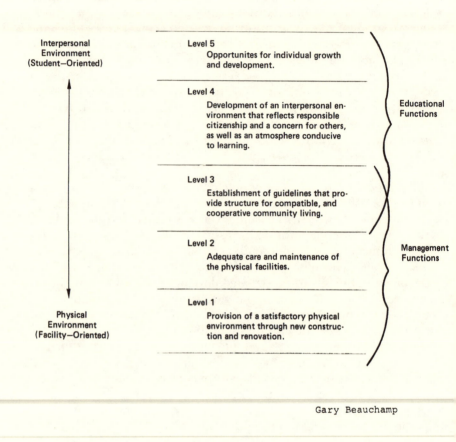

Gary Beauchamp

distinct set of student needs. Success at one level will depend on how well student needs are met at lower levels.

Dan may have extreme difficulty overcoming the distraction of preoccupying noise and excessive partying during study hours (level 3), and therefore be unable to pay adequate attention or interest in various educational or cultural programs (level 4). This figure demonstrates how the residence experience can be considered a complex area of student development and one that should be considered as a whole—the people, the facilities, and the program.

In light of a rising upsurge in community colleges and increasing building costs, educators are taking a second look at the values of residential life for the student. A 1973 study by Alexander Astin is worthy of note.[12] Data for the study was compiled by the Cooperative Institutional

Research Program of the American Council on Education. The study involved two million students in five hundred institutions. The sample included students who entered as freshmen in the fall and who were followed up in the following summer and fall.

Some 152 items in four major areas were covered on the questionnaire. Two groups of students were formed on the basis of their residence, either in the college dormitory or at home or another private residence. Results of these two areas were parallel.

The results for the first category, "Educational Progress," showed that living in a dormitory compared to living at home had positive benefits. Dormitory students were less likely to drop out and more likely than commuters to attain the baccalaureate in four years, to apply for admission to graduate school, and to earn a high grade point average. In the "Behavior" category, living in a dormitory seemed to stimulate responses generally associated with social life and interaction.

The category "Attitudes and Values" revealed that living in a dormitory had a consistently positive effect on students' perceptions of their own interpersonal competency, as indicated by their self-ratings of self-confidence and public speaking ability.

In the category "Ratings of the College," living in a dormitory clearly increased the incidence of students satisfied with the overall undergraduate experience, particularly in the area of interpersonal contacts with faculty and other students. Students who lived with their parents were more likely to rate facilities high, possibly because they were not as familiar with them as the resident students, and so were less likely to have become frustrated in using them.

The obvious high interest area for educators was in the ratio of students completing their education. The actual rate of degree completion among dormitory residents (60.6 percent) was more than 7 percent higher than expected, based on student input characteristics. Data for students who lived with parents or in other private residences showed actual rates of degree completion (30.1 percent) lower by 9.3 percent than expected.[13] The residential life staff plays an important role in the development process if through their programs the student is enabled to complete his education and gain social living skills in the process.

Many institutions today offer a wide variety of residence programs. Residential options in college residence halls offer students alternative educational and social opportunities for facilitating life-style and life preparation. A housing program, however, must fit within the framework of the overall atmosphere and fulfill the purposes of the institution in which it is placed.

Abilene Christian University, Abilene, Texas, is a politically and socially conservative institution of higher learning. The religious atmosphere and dedication to wholesomeness of development demands a housing program strictly segregated by sex. In loco parentis is the existent philosophy in mens' and womens' facilities, with strong expectation for the obeying of university rules and regulations including prohibition of drinking and smoking. Intervisitation rights do not exist in the residences, and all educational and social activities are conducted away from the living centers. The University of Texas, in Austin, Texas on the other hand, a comparatively liberal school, has a variety of living centers, both coed and segregated, depending on the student's choice. There is no student curfew, and visitation rights are accepted, with the hall council determining visitation hours. Alcoholic beverages are allowed in students' rooms. These activities are within the norm of educational experience on this campus. The philosophical impact on the student is felt in each case, as the purpose of each institution is symbolized and promoted by the standard established in the living community.

The concern of student development within residences is of growing interest. To integrate the whole educational process, the facility of living is a major factor. The residence can enhance the cultural and intellectual life of its students. By having classes taught and faculty offices placed in them; by scheduling lectures, musical events, and plays in the evenings; and by providing advisory, counseling, and library services in proximity to them the university can bridge the traditional separation between the concerns of the classroom and those of the residence hall.

Guidance and Counseling

Since the establishment of a counseling system in Washburn College, Topeka, Kansas by Karl Menninger in 1920, guidance services have become an integral part of the college scene. Even in institutions that consider their programs to be strictly intellectual there is the recognition that learning can best be achieved where disruptive forces are resolved. Some problem factors within the student himself require individual help. Some problems stem from interaction within a peer group, student-faculty conflict, or difficulty in orientation with the university.

Counseling activities vary from providing information via printed materials to being involved in individual confrontations or group activities attempting to resolve the more important problems and decisions faced by young people today. Most students need help in some area. They need to understand admission prerequisities or graduate requirements. Students may have to be disciplined or resolve a monetary concern. Career identification is a vital concern of every student. In each case a counselor can enable students to resolve questions and problems for themselves. The major job of the counselor is that of listening, attempting to evaluate the student's situation, and then trying to help the student cope with his problem and/or decision.

Guidance services contribute to the philosophy of educating the total man by giving him the skills and tools to grapple with and resolve problems both while a student and later in life. The most common model for the counseling staff is that of therapist. The counselor interacts as a psychotherapist, or psychologist. He or she has traditionally provided therapy for a selected few students with personal problems. According to O'Banion, the counselor of today needs to emerge from his cubicle and be at the disposal of all students.[14]

At Portland Community College, counselors are located where the students congregate: in the library, study areas, cafeterias, and office areas. Sessions are relatively open, with the counselor's desk placed in a large area, as opposed to the cubicle of the past. Private facilities are available for occasions that require privacy. Evaluation of this system indicates that the services are being used on a broader scope by students and faculty alike.

Some colleges offer counseling for special groups: the handicapped, women, academically deficient adults, minority students. Group counseling is widely popular. Called by nonguidance names, groups such as sensitivity training, basic encounter groups, and world in crisis provide stimulating settings for discussion and discovery of the students' relationship to mankind and to the world at large.

The commuting student especially needs the group experience to integrate him with the student body and broaden his association with the college, faculty, and so forth. In Illinois, Springfield Junior College has a special program for commuting students. During the semester staff members of the developmental program's counseling division select the names of students with whom they are unfamiliar. These students are invited in small groups to a one-hour session during which they are introduced to the student development program and to the other students and identify their area of study, future plans, and overall view of the college. They are encouraged to investigate ways of becoming more involved with college life.[15]

It is refreshing to discover that student counseling has broadened beyond the emotional problem area and branched into a network of enabling processes vital to the life of the student development program.

Financial Aid

Financial aid is a department of development services that frequently falls under the scope of the guidance program. This is due in part to the procedure for acquiring student aid. The federal government makes monies available to higher education on the basis of need and ability. The decision of who is an apt candidate for such funding must be made by a proper evaluating body. The business office is not equipped or inclined to decipher testing data, and faculty certainly should not be required to delve into the financial affairs of the institution, so the logical participants are developmental staff members—the financial aid personnel.

As the difficulties of financing a college education have increased and as society has recognized the growing importance of higher education, student loan programs have increased dramatically. It has been estimated that the amount of money borrowed annually by college students increased twenty times in the 1960s and has increased considerably to date. In 1965 it was estimated that approximately $800 million was outstanding in student loans. Federal money is available to students of low economic families who show adequate standards of ability. Serious gaps are left; however, State governments attempt to fill the gaps.[16]

In 1974 the federal government set up the State Student Incentive Grant Program, which gave states $19 million in matching funds to help them begin new need-based programs or expand old ones. In 1980 $69 million was put in this program.

The National Association of State Scholarship Programs stated that state funding of $746 million was available in October, 1977, a 14.5 percent increase over the previous year. While federal programs exist mainly for public institutions, state programs benefit strong public and private institutions. More than half of state aid goes to high-priced private institutions. State programs are reaching many more students than ever before. In 1969 only nineteen states had student aid programs, with $199.9 million serving 470,800 students. In 1977, 1,190,000 students in fifty-six states and trust territories received state awards. Alaska is the only state not providing student aid.[17]

An effective program of financial aid communicates important information to prospective students as well as to students already enrolled. Once applications for student aid have been received, financial need must be determined and the institution's resources considered. The types of assistance should be weighed against the needs of the student and available aid be distributed in the fairest manner. This funding may involve awarding loans, scholarships, work-study, and/or grants. The administration of such an activity is complex, and its complexity will increase as educational costs continue to rise and governmental conditions evolve and change from year to year.

Health Programs

A health program may or may not be considered a part of the student development program depending on the operation of the university. This service, however, does have a direct bearing on the condition of the student experience, and by the very nature of the growth of the individual concerns the total development of the student. A typical health program consists of required medical examinations for all incoming students, facilities for first aid, special examinations for participants in athletic events as required by state law, and treatment for varying degrees of illness and the correction of defects. The size and personality of the institution will determine the dimensions of this program.

On the Oral Roberts University campus an aerobically oriented doctor and staff are a permanent part of the program. All incoming students undergo a fitness test and are given weight and physical ability standards to which they must comply within the school semester. The facility for this program is a two-story, 116,000 square foot building housing equipment for the aerobics program, a health services center, the physical education department, and a human performance laboratory.[18] This health program is fully developed, but health programs on other campuses are no more than nurse's aide stations with first aid facilities and one bed. The student in this case is usually referred to a community doctor in cases of recurring illness.

Placement

As in the Middle Ages, universities today open doors to the professions, whether it be the clergy, law, medicine, finance, merchandising, science, or others. A student, however, needs assistance in finding the doors that will enable him to meet his specific goals or discover the right combination of education and talent. In order to wade efficiently through the myriad of opportunities, he needs a placement center whose staff can guide him into a worthwhile occupation.

The student expects the placement department to find him a job, one that pays well and is interesting. The placement department needs therefore to be an extension of the educational process which will equip the student for the proper job opportunity when it arises. This is a vital area for faculty involvement.

One major role of the placement office is to accurately acquaint the student with his career future so that placement is appropriate to interest and ability as well as occupational opportunity in his chosen field. A competent counseling unit can assist students in formulating job campaigns, make the proper job referrals, and serve as an effective liaison between the academic world of preparation and the world of business, industry and allied health.

Another vital service of the placement office is that of public relations for the college with the business world. The placement department needs to keep accurate records and prepare reports on where students have gone and how they have succeeded with their careers after graduation.

Student Life Activities

The student life activities area of extracurricular activity is occasionally placed under student government services, but still falls under the realm of development. Without such activities college existence would become routinized, automated, and void of pleasure and warmth. These activities will not be explained in detail, but a recognition of them is necessary to see the composite university setting. They include student government, entertainment (student productions and guest performers), campus publications, religious groups, academic clubs, social groups, intramural sporting events, campus radio stations, social functions, and intercollegiate sporting competition.

These activities broaden the student, his interests, his social abilities, and his associates. These nonacademic areas are highly important to the overall development of the total student.

ADMINISTRATION AND FACULTY

Every institution of higher education is a community of people. The effectiveness of the university or college depends entirely upon the structure of the organization of its management. The greater the involvement between departments within the institution, the greater the impact on the student and the better his total development needs will be met.

In many institutions the administration is based on highly structured and isolated pattern. This generally places the development department in a secondary position of importance within the structure. The students are often the losers as the services offered do not appear to integrate with requirements and so are expendable.

The trend in organization is changing on many campuses to include the director of student development on administrative staffs, occasionally on the vice-presidential level. He or she then is able to coordinate services with academics in a program productive for both students and the academic world.

Some doubters feel that although "an attempt has been made to clothe the student services dean with the trappings of status and authority, in practice he has less of both than the organization chart indicates."[19] Within the administration of the developmental program many patterns are emerging, and future evaluation will decide which is the most effective.

A low trust organization as illustrated in Figure 53 consists of head of department, division heads, counselors, residence managers, staff, and so forth. This is often desirable because of the ease of design, visible lines

FIGURE 53
High trust and low trust organizations

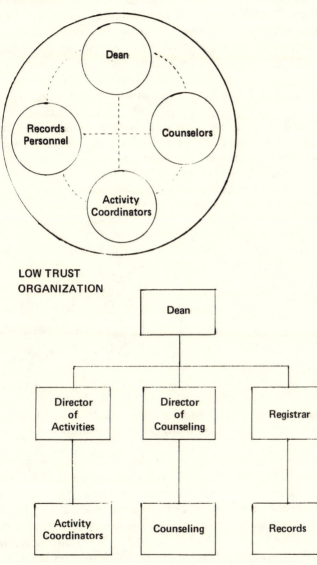

**HIGH TRUST
ORGANIZATION**

**LOW TRUST
ORGANIZATION**

Gary Beauchamp

of authority, and "top man" definition of roles. It lacks, however, inter-relational skills of problem solving, or blending of services.

A high trust organization consisting of the same personnel in a different pattern of organization tends to demonstrate group defined and accepted objectives, goal-setting structure, mutual respect of coordinating personnel, open communication, and tools for problem solving. This type of organization will be as effective and as functional as the quality of personnel involved.

In the developmental program effective administration of services must begin with good human relations within the organization of the institution, with the faculty, with the student, and within the ranks of the staff. To this end student developmental workers will not be able to relate to faculty if they work only as a closed society under the supervision of the vice president of student affairs. Development must continue to be coordinated with academics in order that the purpose of higher education—the educating of the total man—be served.

ACCOUNTABILITY AND BUDGETING

Two terms concerning higher education are appearing more often in this decade—accountability and budget model. On a cursory reading they do not seem to have much in common, but in fact one is highly dependent upon the other.

One problem student development personnel have had to overcome is that of justifying student services on the basis of an "invisible return." Research had to be based on nebulous, suppositive reactions, not concrete data. It has always been difficult for the student developmental professional to explain to external professions and the public in general just what this invisible return means to the student, institution, and society. To a business person looking for concrete data proving the effectiveness of a program, it is not enough.

A survey recently was taken by the Division of Research and Program Development of the National Association of Student Personnel Administration (NASPA) to help student development officers understand the nature of accountability demands. The questionnaire used in the survey placed emphasis on three areas of information: (1) the nature and source of demands for accountability data being experienced by student developmental programs, (2) initial voluntary responses being implemented within these developmental programs in response to these demands, and (3) proposed needs for assistance in responding to these demands.

Accountability demands were described as: (1) requests for program costs, (2) requests for data on program outcomes and impact, (3) requests for staff productivity data, and (4) requests for documentation of the legitimacy of student services offered.

The data clearly confirmed the feelings of most professionals that state agencies, governing boards, and institutional administrations are mostly interested in cost information related to the programs rather than their impact on students or the need for such services. Only 29.3 percent of the institutions had experienced requests for program impact data, while almost 42 percent were required to provide cost data on student developmental affairs.[20] This means that while lip service is given to the need for both cost and impact data by most funding agencies (state legislatures, state coordinating boards, governing boards, and so forth), there is a startling emphasis on, even a preoccupation with, cost data, and a tendency to make decisions based on the concept of "money to high priority departments." ˙

The problem exists in not getting the message to the proper channels that student development services are interested in serving the student, making an impact on lives, solving needs and problems, and enriching campus life—difficult concepts on which to place dollar and cents values.

An attempt to answer this problem by attaching imaginary fees for services based on hours of service, multiplied by number of students using the service, multiplied by the standard fee price, would facilitate a more precise analysis based on inputs and outputs. This unit of measurement is able to present accountability for noninstructional units. It serves two important functions: (1) a quantitative measure for internal evaluation of student programs, and (2) an understandable vehicle for resource allocations.

The basic premise is to assign a dollar figure to every service and function of a student service office. This is figured along with a head count of students using each service, which figure is used for justification of annual budget requests and for the survival of the service offered.

One obvious disadvantage of this system is that while it measures quantity, the quality of each service is still unmeasurable. However, the desirability, the need, of each service is readily seen by the number of students who avail themselves of the opportunity to use said service.[21]

Budget considerations for student development are varied, depending on the characteristic of the institution in question. One university might quote the figure of development requiring 15 percent of the budget, while other institutions would quote above or below this figure.

Cost is and always will be a large factor in the future of student services. As long as they are viewed as an expendable frill development programs will lie low on the totem pole of budget priorities. If a program must exist on meager finances and a slim staff, this will seriously affect its effectiveness.

It may be time to devise creative reallocation of funds within the program: utilize paraprofessionals in the place of professional counselors as training aids for routine tasks; use new media to take over routine information-giving jobs such as orientation, advising, transfer, vocational counseling, and use housing facilities as areas for offices, thereby saving building dollars and keeping the personnel close to the students.

NEEDS OF THE FUTURE

Educators must prepare today for tomorrow's needs. Waiting until tomorrow to make the necessary changes for an effective program will leave student development a dollar short and a day late. Some immediate recommendations are:

1. Higher education must reassess its purpose for existence.
2. Higher education must then reaffirm its commitment to developing a total student, an enabled adult person prepared for life as well as for making a living.
3. An integrated curriculum must be designed to have an impact on the student's life, not solely on his intellect.
4. A new curriculum should include courses that will enable a student to become skilled in problem solving.
5. College and university administrators should devise methods of involving professional student development staff with the academic personnel.
6. Student developers need to emphasize the curriculum as a priority over the extracurricular.
7. The student development department (especially in the community college) must find ways of involving a greater portion of the college community in its program.

Terry O'Banion describes the emerging model of the student development officer as that of a

human development facilitator. Facilitate is an encountering verb which means to free, to make way for, to open the door to. The human development facilitator does not limit his encounter to students; rather he is interested in facilitating the development of all groups in the educational community (faculty, secretaries, administrators, custodians, and other service workers and board members).[22]

This broadening concept of student development moves away from the narrow services which only solve problems into services based on the belief that every student is a gifted person with untapped potential, and that every person can live a fuller existence as a result of his educational experience. This is education at its apex.

The integrated model of total educational services involves the entire institution and all of its functions. The administrator in higher education who accepts this model no longer neatly can categorize the classic functions of the institution of higher learning—instruction, student personnel, and business services—as separate entities with clearly distinguishable outputs. If an administrator sees all of the functions of the institution providing post-secondary education as contributors to a single, valuable output, that of the total, mature, and educated individual, he or she is on the way to accepting an integrated system. Such acceptance will lead to the breaking down of administrative barriers which hinder the process of learning and personal development.

A practical example may be of use in this regard. American university and college students have often complained that hours established for the business office or the office of financial aid are set in favor of daytime students. Students who attend during evening hours are often unable to obtain any services besides instruction. Yet fees and requirements for the two groups of students are the same. Institutions which have recognized such problems have provided a full line of evening services, headed by evening deans and other administrators who have authority to direct the affairs of the college or university, to give approvals, and to make necessary decisions. This type of arrangement stems from a realization that a college or university education reflects efforts on a number of levels and is aimed at serving a variety of needs, both cognitive and social.

NOTES

1. Quoted in Ernest Earnest, *American Procession* (New York: Bobbs-Merrill, 1953), p. 11.

2. Ibid., pp. 36–62.

3. J. Roger Penn, Jewell Manspeaker, and Brian J. Millette, "The Model Merry-Go-Round," *National Association of Student Personnel Administration Journal* 12 (Spring 1975), pp. 222–24.

4. Phillip W. Semas, "Hutchins' View of the University," *Chronicle of Higher Education* 14 (23 May 1977), pp. 5–6.

5. Terry O'Banion and Alice Thurston, *Student Development Programs in the Community Junior College* (Englewood Cliffs, N.J.: Prentice-Hall, 1972), p. 29.

6. Ibid., pp. 26–34.

7. Oley R. Herron, ed., *New Dimentions in Student Personnel Administration* (Scranton, Pa.: International Textbook Company, 1970), pp. 29–42.

8. Joseph Katz, ed., *Services for Students* (San Francisco: Jossey-Bass, 1973), pp. 26–28.

9. Earl Nolting, "A Center for Student Development: Concept and Implementation," *National Association of Student Personnel Administration Journal* 13 (Fall 1975), pp. 46–49.

10. Jerry N. Boone, Clarence O. Hampton, and John D. Jones, "Student Affairs and Academics: A Team Approach," *National Association of Student Personnel Administration Journal* 13 (Fall 1975), pp. 43–45.

11. David A. DeCoster and Phyllis Mable, eds., *Student Development and Education in College Resident Halls* (Washington, D.C.: American College Personnel Association, 1974), p. 28.

12. Alexander W. Astin, "The Impact of Dormitory Living on Students," *Educational Record* 54 (Summer 1973), pp. 204–10.

13. O'Banion and Thurston, *Student Development Programs,* p. 202.

14. Ibid.

15. Max Siegel, ed., *Counseling of College Students* (New York: Free Press, 1968), p. 181.

16. Anne C. Roach, "State-Aid Programs," *Chronicle of Higher Education* 14 (31 October 1977), pp. 13–14.

17. O'Banion and Thurston, *Student Development Programs,* p. 140.

18. *Oral Roberts University Catalogue,* 1977–1978 (Tulsa, Okla.), pp. 42–43.

19. Richard L. Harpel, "Accountability: Current Demands on Student Personnel Programs," *National Association of Student Personnel Administration Journal* 13 (Winter 1975), p. 147.

20. Ronald P. Satryb, "A Budget Model for Student Personnel," *National Association of Student Personnel Administration Journal* 13 (Summer 1974), pp. 51–56.

21. Katz, *Services for Students,* p. vii.

22. O'Banion and Thurston, *Student Development Programs,* p. 204.

18

Student Development Administrative Concerns and Application Modes

BOB W. MILLER

The period since World War II has seen the college student awake from his 1950s sleep, expend his stored energies in myriad forms on varied causes, and enter the 1980s demanding a say in the direction of his education and the experiences and possibilities it offers him. The administrator who ignores this development and its ramifications has his head in the sand. It will, whether he likes it or not, send its shock waves throughout the institution of higher education. The administrators most affected, and therefore most in need of being in the thick of things, are the chief student personnel and instructional administrators. It is upon their shoulders that the tasks of dealing with these partnership demands will fall. They will be charged with finding ways of interfacing students with the institution in its various forms.

Several questions need consideration. Are these the same college students in different clothing or a new breed? Do they require the same institution in a new form or a truly changed institution? Do these questions require traditional ways of thought restated anew, or do they require new and therefore radical ways of thought?

A body of literature which portrays a quandary in the student personnel area has come into existence in the past decade. This literature generally questions and points directions for the future. This process is a necessary evil yet undoubtedly a healthy state of affairs. However, student personnel and instructional administrators and professionals alike must begin to act on these questions and recommendations, thereby setting their houses in order and providing leadership for the college as a whole.

Throughout this chapter, the term "student personnel" is used to indicate the whole area of work with the student, while "student development" will refer to the underlying philosophy of that work.

DEFINITIONS

Bureaucratic paradigm—Budgeting, facilities, design, and intraadministrative relations.

Counseling paradigm—Humanizing one-to-one relationships; administrative credibility based on personal credibility

Curriculum paradigm—Curriculum development with the student in mind.

Environmental paradigm—Helping students interface with their universe.

Ombudsman paradigm—Student and faculty problems facilitated.

THE EMERGENT PHILOSOPHY OF STUDENT DEVELOPMENT

Post–World War II philosophy in student personnel was based on a student services point of view. It anticipated and attempted preparation for individual student differences, it viewed the student as a whole person, and it started with the student where he was at any given moment.[1] While no one would quarrel with these tenets, it is instructive to see that they grew more out of expedience and coincidence than out of a true philosophy.[2] As needs were haphazardly uncovered, they were assigned to whomever had time for them, would accept them, or could be coerced into accepting responsibility for them. This last thought is essential. This coincidental approach leads to a philosophy of hindsight, an analysis that underwent periodic updating.

Even though these three tenets were sound, they were not interrelated in any way because of the nature of their development. Dispersion of student personnel tasks by expedience precluded input of a coordinated nature from the various divisions of the institution. The student personnel worker thus became a regulator, a serviceman, or a therapist. The student went to student services much as a patient goes to a doctor or pharmacy to have the appropriate remedy to his particular ill dispensed. With the advent of the 1960s, and an awakening student, the "doctors" started running out of diagnoses and prescriptions. The resulting quandary, which still exists, made us all uncomfortable, but it did bring about the start of a search for a real philosophy for student personnel. The student development point of view has been the result.

Student development assesses the student in terms of goals and objectives rather than needs. This is radically different from the student services point of view and requires new ways of thought. Student development brings the student to interface with the entire campus and involves all parties in developing objectives for the student. While student services is a service station, student development moves outward, is emergent; attempts to go to the student, not to wait for the problem to arise and then dispense a service. This requires a separation of the nature and attitude of the duties and functions involved.[3] Students at an institution with a student development program will be free to choose the direction of their learning and will be responsible for those choices.[4] This will remedy one of the major problems student personnel administrators faced with the student awakening of the 1960s. By its very nature, student services trapped student personnel staff into accepting responsibility for the student. When students began to develop on their own and student services were still dispensing prescriptions, the trap was sprung. Student service areas are generally thought of as: guidance and counseling, financial aid, placement, health, follow-up, student inventory, student activities, veterans' affairs, housing, intramurals and extramurals and various other services.

Students now enter into interpersonal relations with a development facilitator, a relationship that includes: challenge, stimulation, confrontation, and excitement; warmth, caring, understanding, acceptance, and support; and appreciation of individual differences.[5]

Student Development and Adminstrative Philosophy

What existed prior to student development was an involvement with student regulation or therapy. Student development calls for a behavioral climate of learning. This requires a new student personnel professional, one who is catalytic—what has been called a facilitator by counseling psychologists. This approach, which is still in transition, requires decentralization in some form of various student learning and counseling activities. It also requires support services from learning resources and business affairs.

Student services lacked integrative, institution-wide input. Student development strives to involve the whole campus community. The chief student personnel administrator must consider organization in a period of transition. Attitude is of utmost importance in this respect. Attitude will undoubtedly affect the success of this task of involving the institution with the student. Just as student personnel organization tends to be traditional and its staff passive, so other institutional areas most likely will be benign at best and myopic at worst in their attitude toward student development.[6]

An emergent philosophy would require a similar style of administration, never status quo but always changing, taking on new shape to meet new challenges. To begin with, the student personnel and instructional administrator must be offensive, as this yields complexity of control as well as rigidity of structure in direct proportion. He must have the strong self-concept necessary for effective leadership. This yields trust in subordinates and gives those levels of information interchange which frees an organization from the cycle of advance and decline. Open-mindedness will allow instructional and student personnel administrators to influence rather than control. The student personnel and instructional administrator must learn that effective management involves the movement of resources to dynamic organizational units which obtain their objectives to the satisfaction of the student while providing a sense of accomplishment for the instructional and student development professional.[7]

Some parallels in the world of business management merit consideration. Rensis Likert of the University of Michigan has conducted extensive research showing that the more participative the approach, the better the results, except for the autocratic type of leader. Figure 54 represents these findings in business terms, but the parallels for education are obvious. System 1 is described as "Exploitative Authoritative," system 2 as "Benevolent Authoritative," system 3 as "Consultative," and system 4 as "Participative Group."[8] They range from complete lack of trust to complete trust. Interestingly enough, Likert reports that when managers were asked what action was taken when costs were cut, increased productivity resulted, and improved earnings were desired, the answer was a move toward system 1, a system proven to achieve the opposite results. Likert suggests that faulty accounting procedures do not represent increased earnings in their true light; that is, cash income derived from even greater liquidation of business assets. All administrators must avoid falling into this trap.[9]

Student Development and Administrative Action

The administrator must view the tasks before him through a theory or philosophy, a way of thought, that has an emergent nature. People's relationships are the guiding nature of student development. People affect people in varied ways; they communicate both formally and informally in varied ways.[10] Student development is the membrane of interface between the student and the institution, and the student personnel and instructional administrator can begin to imagine organizations which bring institutional goals and objectives into focus in ways that are mutually supportive, compatible with the institution's character, and integrative.[11] This integration includes not only student personnel and instructional programs, but all support areas as well, such as business service and learning resources.

The administrator's first action then is to consider; what point of view, what way of thought sees an organization that is most responsive to the student development viewpoint. The administrator must imagine what the clientele, competencies, and roles in that organization will be.[12] Figure 55 puts this into perspective.

Student Development and Administrative Organization

In the organizational process the administrator will go from expansive conception to specific models in setting up an emergent organization.

FIGURE 54
The manager and his organization

CAUSAL VARIABLES

If a manager has:

Well-organized plan of operation

High performance goals

High technical competence
(manager or staff assistants)

and if the manager manages via:

SYSTEMS 1 or 2
e.g., uses
direct hierarchical pressure for
results, including the usual
contests and other practices of
the traditional systems.

SYSTEM 4
e.g., uses
principle of supportive relationships, group methods of supervision, and other principles
of system 4.

his organization will display:

INTERVENING VARIABLES

Less group loyalty
Lower performance goals
Greater conflict and less
    cooperation
Less technical assistance
    to peers
Greater feeling of unrea-
    sonable pressure
Less favorable attitudes
    toward manager
Lower motivation to produce

Greater group loyalty
Higher performance goals
Greater cooperation
More technical assistance
    to peers
Less feeling of unreasonable
    pressure
More favorable attitudes
    toward manager
Higher motivation to produce

and his organization will attain:

END-RESULT VARIABLES

Lower sales volume
Higher sales costs
Lower quality of business sold
Lower earnings by salesmen

Higher sales volume
Lower sales costs
Higher quality of business sold
Higher earnings by salesmen

R. Likert, *The Human Organization,* (New York, McGraw-Hill, 1967), p. 14.

FIGURE 55
Competencies

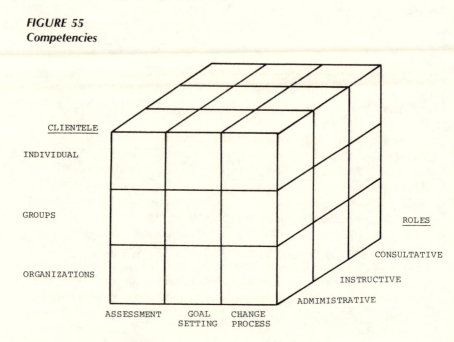

Terry O'Banion, A. J. Thurston and J. Gulden, "Student Personnel Work: An Emerging Model", Junior College Journal, pp. 89–90.

While this may seem contradictory, Figure 56 shows this concept more clearly. It is not a constricting process but an emerging one; and when various clientele, roles, and competencies enter the universe of thought, it is integrative and liberating.

In analyzing the work to be administered, three divisions appear: (1) the jobs to be done, (2) the optimum time for doing those jobs, and (3) the roles and relationships of the personnel employed to do those jobs. Jobs fall into categories of routine services best done by clerical staff, developmental functions performed by professional staff, and activities with students. Time analysis is a standard component of any organizational structure which is to function effectively. Roles and relationships must be organized in a dynamic, high trust manner. Student development will then become part of every job on campus. The following ideas must be kept in mind as the organization is built.

1. Effective student personnel work and instruction takes time and costs money.

2. Active involvement by students and faculty in an activity is a most effective motivator.

3. Some student personnel services and instruction are of a routine clerical character.

4. Most student personnel services necessitate a human-to-human relationship, or a group-to-group process.

5. Effective student personnel services and instruction require clear communication through both formal and informal channels.

6. Student control by rigid regulation and policy leads to evasion and rebellion.

7. The high trust principles of wide participation in decision making, face-to-face relationships, mutual confidence, open communication, and internal control of performance make for good management.[13]

Once the administrator has a grasp of functions and roles, models can become more specific. One possibility is to break down the organizational structure by functions and roles. This suggests the separation of development functions from those of a managerial or service nature. Figure 57 shows this breakdown.

FIGURE 56
Emergent organization

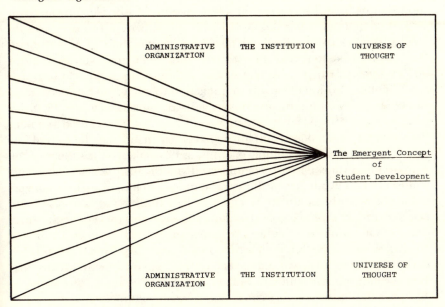

Terry O'Banion, A. J. Thurston and J. Gulden, "Student Personnel Work: An Emerging Model", Junior College Journal, Vol. 41, (1970), pp. 89–90.

FIGURE 57
Student personnel organization chart

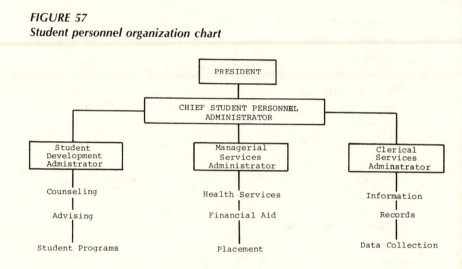

Bob Miller

The student development administrator will be a professional practitioner trained in the development area. (Such programs are now starting to develop in higher education.) The managerial services administrator could be a person of business/legal background adept at the managerial, control, and, most likely, disciplinary functions of his role. The student services managerial administrator must be familiar with the latest technology in data storage and retrieval.[14] This model frees the student development personnel to be full-time educators. This model applies only in the student personnel area.

Student development now is in a position to engage in the decentralization of both counseling and advising. The counselor will no longer be in a cluster of offices. He or she may be in the learning resources center, the student center; or may be found in each instructional division office or in the cafeteria. Individual counseling now takes on a supermarket approach. As the student goes up and down the institutional aisles, the counselor is there to guide his educational purchases. As institutional involvement with the individual grows, the counseling professional can become involved with group counseling, where students help each other, taking on leadership and responsibility. The thought of having a counselor housed within an instructional division is particularly enticing in terms of academic advisement. Faculty are nearby for expert consultation and at the same time are drawn to interface with the total student. The orientation has now become "how," not "when."[15]

With decentralization student personnel administration begins to merge with instructional administration. As employment time decreases continually in the development of society, leisure activities and quasi-volunteer activities will increase. Students must be prepared for this future. With the concept of in loco parentis dead for all practical purposes, student personnel can help higher educational institutions replace it with a concept of avuncularity, from parent to uncle as it were. This is especially possible with the faculty boom over. Faculty are more free to be involved along with the whole institution in student development paradigms, defined at the beginning of this chapter.

For this model to be realized, student personnel workers must be open to redefinition, scholars in the field must maintain a link with their professional heritage and develop desirable future alternatives for developmental programs, and education must anticipate needs and create student development practitioners with professional expertise and administrative skill.[16] Student personnel workers must master a body of knowledge, acquire skills and techniques, and pursue development and integration.

With goals now well clarified, the chief personnel administrator can involve his staff in a sound organizational technique. Management by Objectives, which has been proven sound in business, industry, and government, can easily be converted to administration by objectives, or administration by results. The administrator now has a system which will bring the emergent philosophy of student development to life. This may be seen in the following list of advantages.

1. Communication is improved.
2. Evaluation is stressed.
3. The importance of the student is emphasized.
4. Institutional objectives are clarified.
5. Relevant items are brought into focus.
6. Accountability is established.
7. Merit pay is objectified.
8. Planning is brought into focus.
9. Supervision is lessened and influence expanded.
10. Morale is improved.

There are, however, some disadvantages to administration by results or objectives. Administration by objectives does not measure methods (these are activities), and the administrator must insure the ethical accomplishment of objectives. Administration by objectives takes time, costs money, and is hard work. Arbitrary decisions must be made, so the administrator must have a positive self-concept. Last of all, administration by objective can be little more than paper shuffling without real commitment on the part of all concerned. This concern must start with the chief administrator and involve low level managers.[17]

Administration by objectives has obvious ramifications for budgeting given the current rise of program based budgeting systems and Zero-Based Budgeting. A student development program in an emerging posture and objective oriented program will be ready for these budgeting systems when they arrive. They may indeed be instrumental in the institution-wide development of these systems given the increased cost of student development, as opposed to student services, in dollars and cents. Student development budgets already will have been well justified. The institution's business manager must be cooperative and supportive if these budgeting processes are to work effectively.

STUDENT DEVELOPMENT ADMINISTRATION, STUDENTS, AND FACULTY

Higher education faces a new student today as the open door becomes the accepted admissions practice throughout higher education. This new student is characterized all too often by lower persistence, a lower degree of parental support, financial problems, a preoccupation with survival, poor self-image, and a nonacademic perception. The new student calls for new administrative designs and administrators who are willing to consider the possibility that traditional higher education could be wrong in some aspects.[18]

"In loco parentis seems to have gone the way of the academic gold standard." Administrators must strive for student development to help students enter into a shared search for values and value systems. The new student must be helped to accept uncertainty, to realize that values will be matters of import that will claim his attention and utilize his basic energies. He must learn to choose freely from alternatives, taking into consideration the consequences of those alternatives. This means that the student must become well versed in the problem-solving or decision-making process. As those choices are affirmed and cherished, they will form a basis for action and a pattern of social behavior by their repetition. This process must occur as the student encounters the real world through contemporary history, and most of all through the process of dealing with people.[19]

Student development faces several challenges in interaction with the new student. One is overcoming affective testing. Education is moving from cognitive to integration with the affective domain, and testing can be a useful device. The student must be assured that testing will not be used to pigeonhole him.

As student development progresses, the student may experience emotional problems in leaving his environment and heritage. We are still working with elements of future shock where many students are not ready to face a world of change. Cocurricular activities can be of help here in bringing the student's heritage to new light. Special studies, courses in human development, and so forth, are possible solutions. Cocurricular activities can also help alter an antiintellectual posture.

Low finances can be the cause of a surface appearance of lack of seriousness. Education must be made inexpensive, not cheap, for students. No student with academic or occupational abilities should be deprived of educational opportunity because of lack of financial support.

Plural admission criteria probably need to replace the "gold standard." This is not to be taken as a lowering of standards but as a new view of the possible competencies that traditional views may have ignored. The question might be asked, "Are we educating for the right things in life?"

Bringing students into the college community is perhaps the most difficult challenge. Minorities, foreign students, varied ages, commuters—how can these diversified elements be brought to some sort of unity? How can we provide an effective education to meet the needs of society?

STUDENT ROLES, FACULTY ROLES

As students mature and become more experienced, they should participate in direct proportion in the affairs that affect their lives. The college community should strive to be a microcosm of society. Faculty involvement in the student development process is a prerequisite for this. Who does the student come in contact with more often, excepting his peers, than the faculty? They must be the front line of any successful development program, suggesting again a need for the merging of student development and academic administration. In addition, this merging must occur up and down all levels and all ranks as illustrated in Figure 58, concerning student/faculty roles.[20] While these suggestions are offered within a community college format, they are equally applicable to the four-year college or university.

"Toward improved involvement"

1. Each community college should have a student organization with defined powers and responsibilities and an established place in the machinery for the development of institutional policies.

2. To improve communication between the student organization for policy formulation and the faculty organization for policy formulation, there should be representatives of each sent as

FIGURE 58

Flowchart for policy formulation administrative organization

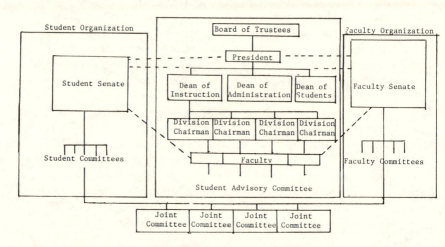

Richard C. Richardson, Jr., in Terry O'Banion, "Student Development Implementation Personnel Work: An Emerging Model," *Junior College Journal* Vol. 41 (1970), pp. 55–60, 64.

observers to the other. It would be the responsibility of such observers to comment on the point of view of their organization upon request and to keep their organization informed of the activities of its counterpart.

3. Joint faculty-student standing committees should be established to deliberate and make recommendations to the faculty and student policy-formulating bodies. Faculty members should predominate and there should be a faculty concern. Student members should predominate and there should be a student chairman of those committees involving matters of primary concern to the students.

4. An attempt should be made to ensure the representativeness of student policy-formulating organizations by the election of candidates from defined constituencies as opposed to the at-large elections which are frequently the case at present. It is suggested that the division or department might serve as a basic reference point in defining constituencies.

5. Divisions and departments should be urged to consider students majoring in their disciplines as viable sub-groups of the college and to create student advisory committees that would meet with

faculty members in these areas to foster communication and planning for improved student life. These advisory groups might also be involved in faculty meetings of the department or division whenever possible.

Several areas should be primarily or totally under student governance.

1. Student publications such as newspapers, bulletins and yearbooks.
2. Allocation of student activity fees to various students.
3. Assisting in student conduct and discipline unrelated to the classroom situation. (Example: student courts.)
4. Recognition of campus student organizations through chartering and approval of various clubs, fraternities, etc.
5. Approval of a variety of guest speakers invited by students.
6. Approval of distribution of student-initiated literature on campus.
7. Approval of distribution of off-campus literature on campus.

Areas which should be considered for some degree of student involvement are as follows:

1. Faculty reappointment, promotion to higher rank and tenure through faculty personnel committees.
2. Recommendations on admissions standards for curricula and courses.
3. Recommendations on class size.
4. Input into allocation of instructional funds.
5. Leadership given to curricula or course revision, addition, or deletion.
6. Ad hoc committees or task forces on administrative structure of the college.
7. Recommendations to the administration on staff salaries, fringe benefits.
8. Input on teaching loads.
9. Provision of services to the community.
10. Requirement for degrees and certificates.
11. Input and recommendations on the selection of a president.
12. Input on selection of college officers directly related to student life.

Student responsibilities include:

1. Compliance with and support of duly constituted civil authority as an individual student.

2. Respect for the rights of others and cooperation to ensure that such rights are guaranteed, whether or not the views of those exercising such rights are consistent with the views of the majority. Student documents should provide for both responsibilities and rights.

3. Cooperation to ensure that the will of the majority is implemented after due consideration has been given to contrary points of view. Such cooperation, however, does not include the suppression of minority points of view. The minority must be protected as well as the majority.

4. The exercise of dissent within a framework compatible with the resolution of difference. Constructive criticism is always helpful in improving an institution.

5. Knowledge of college regulations established through the joint efforts of students, faculty, and administration. Handbooks should be written in student language where students are involved.[21]

Faculty advising in the traditional sense is out of date. Faculty must be brought to an understanding of the complexity of human relations and aspirations needed to advise the new student. They must realize that all education does not happen in the classroom. Student personnel professionals need to realize that a great deal of learning does occur in the classroom. In student development, there should be a team aspect for advisement involving faculty, student development professionals, and paraprofessionals. They must help the student take an active part in his own educational experiences and assist the student in the synthesization and integration of those experiences. They must be concerned with the growth as well as the performance of students with whom they come in contact. Faculty must allow student personnel to assist them in a catalytic way with appropriate counseling and testing services. This again calls for faculty to hold a favorable opinion of student development and of their own teaching, for qualified student development personnel, and for student development administration organized for campus-wide permeation.[22] Both groups, faculty and student personnel workers, must assist each student in a teaming process which involves learning in the affective, psychomotor, and cognitive domains.

Considering student personnel professionals as educators in an administrative structure which allows for delineation of roles or paradigms holds great potential for catalytic activities. The student development professional is best suited to relate the cognitive and affective domains. He or she can aid in divisional organization and in scheduling, can serve as an interdisciplinary liaison, and teach developmental courses. Also, they can aid in the training of student assistants, work-study students, and paraprofessionals. In this educator role, they can be invaluable in bringing student development to life for the student and faculty to the benefit of both.

Student development must be emergent, dynamic, and organized in a climate of trust and support. It must permeate the institution, utilize all its resources, and thereby motivate it to become integrated in an interface with the student. Student development must be catalytic, a permeable membrane between the student and the institution. Student services must decentralize, seek out the student, anticipate his needs, and share in his hopes, goals, dreams, and joys. The faculty member will continue to be the content specialist but will team with the student personnel specialist in bringing the affective and values domains to the student.

What is the nature of the person who becomes involved in this field? That is perhaps the last remaining key to bring student development to fruition. Programs that attempt to train professional practitioners in the student developmental areas are now coming into being. These people oriented educators are the student development administrators of tomorrow, yet they generally have little administrative skill. To improve the system, there must be specific education for faculty, student development professionals, and administrators. Yet a combination of counseling and administration is probably not a sufficient base either.[23] Chief student personnel administrators, when surveyed, suggested the following areas in some combination as making up a student personnel curriculum.

1. Courses in Psychology and Sociology
2. Counseling principles and techniques
3. Practicums in student development work
4. An overview of student development work in higher education
5. A study of college students and their experiential background
6. Social psychology, anthropology and human relations
7. Higher education, the university, college and community college[24]

Not enough is known at this juncture to bring the behavioral and social sciences to the practitioner state. Therefore no foundation exists for the training of a student development professional as a behavioral scientist who is a student personnel practitioner. However, what is known is being passed along, and programs are moving in the professional practitioner direction.[25]

The student personnel administrator should constantly work toward the goal of eliminating his existence, for as student development reaches new heights, his services are needed less and less, if he does an effective and efficient job as student developer.

NOTES

1. David T. Borland and Russell E. Thomas, "Student Development Implementation Through Expanded Professional Skills," *Journal of College Student Personnel* 17 (1976), pp. 145–49.

2. H. Heiner and J. M. Nelson, eds., *A Manual for Student Service* (Olympia, Wash.: Washington State Board for Community College Education, 1977), pp. 243–47.

3. Borland and Thomas, "Student Development Implementation," pp. 145–49.

4. T. O'Banion, "A Program Proposal for Preparing College Student Personnel Workers,"*College Student Personnel Journal* 10 (1969), pp. 249–53.

5. Ibid.

6. Borland and Thomas, "Student Development Implementation," pp. 145–49.

7. J. Harvey, "Administration by Objectives in Student Personnel Programs," *Journal of College Student Personnel* 13 (1972), pp. 293–96.

8. Rensis Likert, *The Human Organization* (New York: McGraw-Hill, 1967), p. 14.

9. Ibid., pp. 11–12.

10. Ibid., p. 14

11. Ibid.

12. Ibid.

13. T. O'Banion, A. J. Thurston, and J. Gulden, "Student Personnel Work: An Emerging Model," *Junior College Journal* 41 (1970), pp. 89–90.

14. Harvey, "Administration by Objectives," pp. 293–96.

15. O'Banion, Thurston, and Gulden, "Student Personnel Work: An Emerging Model," pp. 180–93.

16. E. M. Chandler, "Student Affairs Administration in Transition," *Journal of College Student Personnel* 14 (1973), pp. 392–98.

17. Borland and Thomas, "Student Development Implementation," pp. 145–49.

18. O'Banion, Thurston, and Gulden, "Student Personnel Work: An Emerging Model," pp. 26–35.

19. Ibid., pp. 68–77.

20. Ibid., pp. 55–60, 64.

21. Ibid., pp. 59–60, 65.

22. Ibid., pp. 2–10.

23. K. P. Cross, "Student Personnel Work as a Profession," *Journal of College Student Personnel* 14 (1973), pp. 77–81.

24. O'Banion, "A Program Proposal," pp. 249–53.

25. Cross, "Student Personnel Work as a Profession", pp. 77–81.

Student Development Administration: The Leadership Task in Making the Process Work

BOB W. MILLER

Student services in the past and even at the present time have provided the following basic services: guidance and counseling, placement, financial aid, special services, student activities, student inventory, health services, extramurals and intramurals, veterans' affairs, registration and admissions, follow-up, housing, and security. How does an organization incorporate both student services instruction and the student development concept in actual practice? Some educators may not consider both areas to be important. In fact, some educators will not consider student services or student development to be important.

To be effective and efficient, the program must be integrated with the instructional learning resources, business affairs, and all other education programs. The rationale for a student development program involves all elements of the learning process. (See Figure 59.)

Student personnel administration or student service administration is a special area which has called for the management of basic areas for student services. In many cases the administrator has been an instructional person who adapted to managing these specific programs.

Many presidents have not held student services in high esteem because in most states those services have not received monies from state legislatures or coordinating boards, while the instructional areas has. Because of the financial conditions, student services have not been a high priority item.

DEFINITIONS

Quality control—The process of assuring the best possible environment in which learners may grow, make positive changes, and be active in student and public life.

Student development—An integrated process which includes all functions of the student services and instructional domains involving students, faculty, and student personnel professionals.

FIGURE 59
Organizational flow, student development concept

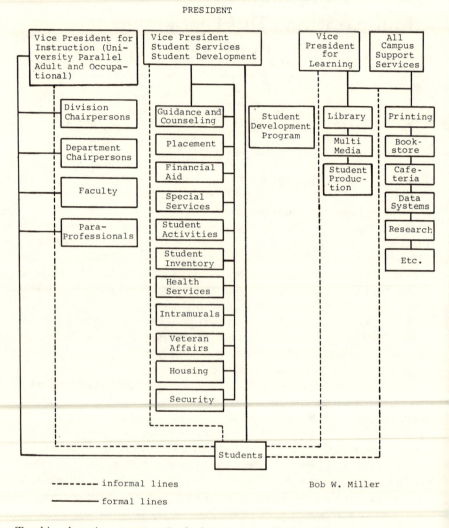

PRESIDENT

-------- informal lines   Bob W. Miller
———————— formal lines

Teaching-learning process—Includes the total educating environment of teaching values, social conflicts, goal and objective setting, synthesis process, teaching methods, and teaching strategies.

THE STUDENT SERVICE PROCESS

Student services have taken care of all types of tasks: record keeping, advisement, testing, placement, discipline, grants and loans, problem solving, counseling, testing, and other student needs. In too many situations, there has been very little quality control and the students who have needed the services have not availed themselves of such. The people who have provided the services have often had the attitude that students should come to them instead of their going to the students.

THE STUDENT DEVELOPMENT PROCESS

In the student development process, student personnel professionals must team or integrate with the instructional staff, or vice versa. To do this, a widespread redefinition of roles is needed. Many of these new roles will involve the learning processes and activities of students. In order to make this take place, there must be active involvement by students, faculty, and student personnel professionals.

The entire educational team must be concerned about the cognitive and psychomotor learning domains and even more about the affective domain. The team must be concerned with coping, self-concept, self-awareness, and self-direction on the part of all students.

What is student development and how can one implement the process into the educational system on a practical basis? In answering the first part of the question, we must be aware that the process involves human relations, tact, people relationships, and human development concepts. Further, we are concerned about positive human behavior factors. We also are bringing about a combination of the affective domain with the cognitive domain. Our priority becomes that of developing a self-directed person, a positive self-concept for the student which causes him or her to respond to everyday activities on a most positive basis. To accomplish all of this in one student or many, the mission for the campus or the institution must be a combination of all the prementioned ideas.

When we become concerned or we really care about the student development concept, our number one priority as professionals is that each staff member from the superordinate to the subordinate be involved in the integration or teaming of all the college resources (human, hardware, and software).

INTEGRATING STUDENT SERVICES AND STUDENT DEVELOPMENT

An assumption can be made for most collegiate institutions that student services will continue because most of these activities are needed by at least a portion of the students in an institution. If this assumption is true, then we must consider adding the student development concept. In fact, student development cannot be an add on; it must be an integrated concept to be effective and efficient.

To integrate the two concepts with the learning program of the college, we must look carefully at our present programs and activities and the total structure. What will it take now and in the future to meet the needs of the "new student"—commuting, evening, vocational-technical, minority, teen-aged, middle-aged, and married students. Most educational programs currently in operation do not meet the real concerns of many of our students.

Human resources within each institution especially need review. Professional personnel often are utilized for minutia. In the student service activities, paraprofessional personnel could often be utilized at much less cost with just as much effectiveness for the job performed. In addition, as in a Management by Objectives program where personnel must think objectives, we must now get professional staff members to think "student development." This requires much staff development for faculty, student personnel workers, paraprofessionals, and support personnel.

THE LEADERSHIP TASK IN STUDENT DEVELOPMENT IMPLEMENTATION

The task of the student development personnel professional will become that of facilitating an overall positive learning climate through teaming efforts with all faculty, administration, and support services. The leader will want to provide activities that promote the following types of experiences.

1. Positive learning experiences throughout the campus classroom and community. The classroom experience should interface with self-directed learning and behavior coordinated with various types of leadership programs.

2. Coordinated activities between instructional and student development personnel should be brought forth. These ventures should have a heavy emphasis on student development.

3. Both professional groups will need strong expertise in human relations, management, leadership, instructional methods, techniques and strategies, curriculum improvement, and instructional design development.

4. There should be an important facet of developmental aspects of human learning. In other words, how we develop in the post-secondary time frame and how we emphasize the positive change that should occur in individual students.

5. Facilities should be planned which cause all college and community resources to be utilized. The learning resource center staff should be totally involved in this process.

6. A total study should be made of the mission and objectives of the college with the purpose of teaming for the student in the developmental process. Each staff member should be made aware of this study when completed and develop the perception of the student development educational program.

Many tasks in student services can and should be accomplished by a paraprofessional. They include: fun and games activities, grading examinations, clerical and record keeping, advising student groups and individuals, student government direction, sponsorship of clubs, social and entertainment activities, planning and implementing intramural activities, and so forth.

To implement student development, the administrative leader must see to it that the professional student development educator changes his role to be and becomes a *learning specialist*. This person must develop expertise in "How Johnny learns and what are his learning styles?" He or she may use as a base student inventory items to begin with. He then must branch out into a learning process with other college faculty. He must learn to design activities that will promote learning by students. The attempt must be made to incorporate human development and behavior change in students. To do this, the learning specialist must influence instructors, administrators, and others to include learning activities that will affect the academic curriculum. This influence must bring about the inclusion of self-directed, self-concept types of activities or other special activities to meet the needs of students.

The student development professional must not be a threat to the faculty member; the faculty member is the content specialist. The task then becomes to deliver more than content to the student.

This learning student development specialist must be an ally, not an enemy. Assistance should be given in relation to individual learning management problems of the student. The whole process means teaming with colleagues; assisting in providing an organismic process of learning for students.

One task of this learning specialist is to get the mechanical, emotional blocks for the student and faculty member out of the way. This may mean providing additional facilities—resources from the communities, speakers, audiovisual aids—counseling, consulting with teachers about strategies or activities, arranging for enrichment activities, coordinating a series of workshops or clinics for faculty or students, bringing in outside consultants, arranging field trips, sharing the cost of certain activities, mapping students' learning styles, doing case studies on student learning problems, and focusing on emphasis of developmental programming through all aspects of the program.

HOW TO MAKE STUDENT DEVELOPMENT EVOLVE

How do we really get a student development program moving? Too often, educators only talk about the concept and then do nothing. To begin, roles must be defined for the academic, student service, business manager, and learning resource administrator positions. This definition should cause integration and teaming to occur. The teaming aspect then must be diffused at each level. Faculty members must realize that they have as much responsibility for teaming with student service personnel as student service personnel have for learning with faculty.

The chief administrators and middle management must communicate with each other on a daily basis. This communication process must include priority items to be taught in the classroom in connection with student development. Once priorities are set, classroom management styles and strategies should be discussed and implemented throughout the organization. Administration and middle management should be involved in this process, but the most important people to involve are faculty, student personnel professionals, and students.

Support services such as the learning resource center, the registrar, the printing office and others also should be involved in the initial formulation of the student development process. Job descriptions should be reviewed in these areas in order that support personnel will be able to fit into the student development process.

The tasks of support personnel will need to be reevaluated in order that they may successfully contribute to the operation. The business manager, registrar, and media and library personnel must organize and plan with the student personnel and academic staff in order to make the entire operation function effectively and efficiently.

One of the next phases should be a systems approach or blueprint to the step-by-step procedures and strategies that will be followed in implementing the student development process. This systems approach should be accompanied by a PERT and other charts specifying dates for completion of each phase.

PROFESSIONAL DEVELOPMENT OR INSERVICE FOR STUDENT DEVELOPMENT

One cannot assume that students, faculty, administration, or the community understand the student development process. If the process is to work, seminars and workshops must be provided on all levels, including students. Objectives should be set forth, and activities and strategies should be devised that will meet these objectives. Administrators, faculty, student service personnel, and students must understand the whole process and how to implement it. Knowledgeable consultants should be provided from inside and outside of the educational institution for this purpose. They should give assistance at each level about how this process should and will work.

Neither can one assume that this process will continue in the classroom after a one shot affair. Teachers will revert to the old system if updating, retreading, selling, and enthusiasm for the approach are not provided. New professional staff will be employed, new students will enter the campus, and these people must be oriented to the process. Another group of personnel who must understand the concept is non-classified staff such as secretaries. The new board of trustees and the community also should be informed about the new process.

FURTHER COMMENTS ABOUT THE STUDENT DEVELOPMENT APPROACH

The student development approach to education is new and will not succeed without leadership and promotion activities. Ideas that must be enthusiastically endorsed by the leadership are as follows:

1. Teachers, administration, student personnel workers, and students must be people centered and enjoy interacting with each other. The process should result in personalization and group interchange among each person in the educational institution.
2. A great amount of thought-provoking material and inquiry discussion must be provided about student development.
3. Educators must be genuinely interested, supportive, and really care about their students.
4. A number of teaching methods or strategies must be implemented to correlate with learning styles.
5. Opportunity must be provided for educators and students to get to know one another and to work closely together.
6. The educator must become totally knowledgeable about the student development process. He must develop experiences, examples, and analogies to draw from in order to teach effectively.
7. The instructor must plan and be well organized for the task at hand. This includes producing software to meet the educational objectives of the course.
8. Educators in the system must think positively and have high expectations of students.
9. The program must include thorough coverage of syllabi, development of speaking ability on the part of students (commu-

nication skills), stimulation in reasoning and actual thinking, encouragement of students to commit and defend themselves on important issues, and, most of all, a systems approach to building self-direction, confidence, positive self-concept, and a positive approach to life and living.

10. The educator should make use of student participation—an important experience for future leaders.

11. Attention must be given to how the student can be enlightened and motivated. How can he develop leadership and follower-ship characteristics and incorporate these skills into day-to-day encounters?

12. Concentration should be directed by learning how to evaluate the individual student's worth as a person. This analysis should be of the student's role in all relations with people.

13. Concentration should be placed on developing openness on the part of the educator as well as the student in the classroom. All must share themselves freely and without reservation.

14. Students should know from the beginning what course objectives are (including student development concepts) as well as expectations of instruction.

NEW LABELS FOR OLD BEHAVIORS OR AN OLD LABEL FOR NEW BEHAVIORS

Until recently, the student development concept has received attention as far as talk is concerned but very little action or implementation. In the past, student development was a theory. Student development must utilize the wholistic approach.

As we strive to implement student development as administrators, we need to remember that the true end of education is developmental, not teaching per se. We must also remember that quality control is important in the developmental process. Individual students interact within the environment. The climate for learning is important. Developmental education begins early in life, and no stages can be omitted. Therefore, we must influence kindergarten through grade twelve to begin this process in the primary grades. The experiences of the learner matter in life. Educators want learners to be active, to grow and make positive changes in the developmental process.

The two most important aspects in development are the cognitive and affective domains. In many situations the psychomotor domain complements the other two. The whole process is concerned with the development of value and value systems which beome involved with ego concepts in the individual.

In student development, we must be concerned with the teaching-learning process. Areas to be emphasized are: (1) the teaching of values; (2) social conflicts; (3) moving from goal setting to objective setting; (4) synthesis processing; (5) beginning with the student and ending with the student; (6) beginning with activities, content, and objectives that lead to self-direction for all students; and (7) teaching methods and strategies that involve students in a complete process relevant to life.

The contention of this author is that we will not be successful in implementation in higher education unless the academic community gets involved.

After support and professional development have been given from the top on down, then, the academic classroom teacher must implement through the development of syllabi, lesson plans and software. After this occurs, then the student personnel worker and learning resource personnel can be effective in supporting the content specialist. Until the academic community gets involved, student development will not be implemented on a successful basis. The academic specialist and the academic administrator must also take a leadership role in the entire process.

20

The Finance Support Program

JOE IBIOK AND JACK D. TERRY, JR.

Finance is one of the most important aspects of administration, and yet it is one of the least heeded and least understood. Leaders in educational administration find it more convenient to concentrate on programs, policies, organization, evaluation, and motivation and are content to give only a passing thought to finance. When discussing the quality of services and falling standards, they prefer to look elsewhere for the causes. This is not to say that all shortcomings of the educational system could be corrected simply by providing more money, but as in industries, so in education—available finances determine the quality of the end product. Any discussion of educational administration must necessarily include a clear understanding of the finance program. In this chapter an attempt shall be made to discuss income needs of the institution, securing of funds to meet those needs, allocation of the funds secured, and the budgeting process.

DEFINITIONS

Budget—A statement of the estimated income and authorized expenditures for a fixed period, usually one year.

Current operating fund—The income that is needed to finance the instructional programs, maintain the educational plant, and meet instructional costs.

Endowment capital—Gifts and donations received which form the endowment principle.

Fee—A one time or recurring request such as admissions filing fee, graduation fee, late examination fee, etc.

Formulas—A process of securing funds based on an equivalent student attendance on a full time basis. Sometimes called Full-Time Equivalent (FTE), Full-Time Teaching Equivalency Enrollment (FTEE), Fiscal Year Equated Students (FYES), Full-Time Equivalent Student) (FTES) or Average Daily Attendance (ADA).

General purpose tax—Tax for any authorized expenditure; used mainly for general operations.

Private donors—Includes philanthropic foundations, nonalumni individuals, alumni, business corporations, religious groups. Their gifts may be general or restricted to specific programs of particular interest to the donor.

Program budgeting—Called PPBS (Planning, Programming, Budgeting System. A management technique designed to merge the planning process with the allocation of funds.

Revenue bonds—Bonds issued to repay investors from receipts derived from the operation.

Student fees—May include tuition, student fees, and building usage fees.

Zero-Based Budgeting—A budget process that requires all cost center directors and department heads to defend every operation before funds are allocated. Each item is ranked in priority order so that if anything is dropped the last item is eliminated first.

INCOME NEEDS

The goals and the means of each institution of higher learning may differ. The proportion of income from each source also varies from college to college, with the result that a common pattern of financial administration in institutions of higher learning is lacking. However, four different income needs must be accommodated in any institution, namely, current operating income, endowment capital, physical plant funds, and scholarship funds.

Current Operating Income

Current operating income is vitally important to both private and public institutions. It is income needed to finance instructional programs, maintain the educational plant, and meet administrative costs. The size of this income determines the type and quality of programs, the type and quality of instructional materials, and the salaries of faculty and staff. It is common for the expenditures to differ according to the nature of the course or program. The federal government may fund a special program or a research project and demand that funds be used specifically for that purpose. The current operating needs of institutions tend to increase faster than other categories of needs and commonly constitute from one-half to three-fifths of total income.

Endowment Capital

Institutions receive gifts and donations which form the endowment principal. Efficient management of the endowment principal produces annual income for the institution. The size of the endowment income will depend upon the size of the endowment principal. Therefore, all institutions need and cherish gifts and endowments. While endowment income is important to both public and private colleges, private colleges seem to need it more than their public counterparts. In a sixty-college study, endowment income was found to vary from 8 to 70 percent of income.[1] It should be noted that endowment income is part of current operating income. This income often provides funds to encourage research in social science, to balance the heavy funding of natural science research by the government.

Physical Plant Funds

The physical facilities for instruction and for auxiliary enterprises need money to build and to maintain plant operations. Each institution meets these construction costs in a combination of different ways. The institution may borrow funds for the buildings or obtain funds from the government or private benefactors. Most state supported institutions have their physical plant fund needs cared for. For private institutions the type, size, and quality of facilities may be determined by the amount of physical funds available. The prevailing practice is for the institutions to issue revenue bonds and repay the investor from receipts derived from the operation.

Scholarship Funds

Increasing costs could keep many of our collegeworthy but impecunious young people from attending college. It therefore becomes important to all institutions that various kinds of student aid be available to needy students. The extent to which any institution can offer students aid depends upon the resources available to it and the amount of scholarship funds it has. The entire subject of student aid warrants more attention in light of the ever-increasing costs of education.

Higher education, like any other industry, needs money. Colleges, private or public, need money to support the faculty, supply the instructional materials, maintain the buildings, and provide assistance to needy students. Where is the money generated? American colleges and universities derive their income from many sources.

SECURING OF FUNDS

Any discussion of government aid to higher education precipitates such questions as, What are the commitments and responsibilities of government for higher education? How much should government provide? What are the consequences of reliance on government aid? While opinions may differ on these questions, there is a general consensus on the importance of education to the general welfare of the people. This recognition dates back to the North West Ordinance of 1787, when it was expressed that "Religion, morality and knowledge being necessary to good government and the happiness of mankind, schools and the means of education shall forever be encouraged." Education has been the responsibility of the state from early times. The federal government has no legal obligation to support education but has exercised a moral obligation to help the states and the people in this worthy cause. Of all three levels of government, it is the state that has exercised the preponderant influence upon higher education. Only a handful of universities are supported by local governments, and quite a few junior/community colleges have been created and supported by county governments. Except for one university and the military academies, the federal government has not chartered any institutions of higher learning. Up until the 1950s, as high as 73 percent of the total income of some liberal arts colleges came from state and local governments, but most state constitutions now prohibit appropriation of public funds to private institutions and even for those which do, support to private institutions is minimal.

Taxes

Every state, without exception, at present exempts all institutions of higher learning from state and local taxation. Private colleges are exempt from property taxes. This adds up to a substantial saving and is a form of support from the state to all colleges.

State Support of Public Institutions

The state legislature annually or biannually makes appropriations to state establishments of higher education. This forms the principal source of funds to the institutions, but no institution receives all its funds through appropriations. When the institution receives its appropriations bill, it then prepares a budget for the school year. In Texas the coordinating board which is charged with the responsibility of financial planning uses a formula to appropriate funds directly to several board general areas. Those elements of costs not specifically funded in the formula are to be requested by each institution on the basis of need. Those items of cost that cannot be paid for through appropriation are met internally. Most institutions operate with the state government on a similar basis.

Junior/Community Colleges

States also contribute to the support of community colleges, but the larger proportion of community college finances come from the local taxing unit (the county or junior college district). The proportions of the sources vary from community college to community college but Chambers suggests that on the average, a community college receives about one-third of its operating funds from the state, one-third from local taxation, and one-third from student fees.[2] The trend across America is for the state to provide more and more of the total community college funding.

Federal Aid to Higher Education

Even though the primary function of providing education rests with the states, federal participation in financing higher education dates back to the beginnings of the Republic when public lands were granted to states to support seminaries, colleges, and universities. Thereafter, federal aid has been in the form of direct loans and grants to institutions, fellowships, loans to students, research grants and contracts, and loans for plant construction. It should be noted that the federal government is not now aiding institutions in undergraduate programs, or paying staff and faculty salaries and other operational costs. The largest amounts of federal money now are awarded in the form of research contracts and grants. Emphasis of federal aid is on engineering, science, and graduate work. There are numerous different federal programs for which any institution of higher learning might qualify. In view of the complexities in the negotiations, some institutions delegate a vice-president or dean who is familiar with the intricacies to deal with the federal agencies concerned. The exact figures for federal aid to higher education are hard to come by, but it is estimated that higher education institutions receive close to $3 billion annually from the federal government and its agencies.

Federal aid to higher education is very controversial. One of the issues is the church-state relationship which makes federal aid unavailable equally to all students and institutions. The question of control always follows federal aid also. Some observers hold that "he who pays the piper calls the tune." Others, to the contrary, hold that even after more than one decade of federal support, federal control is still minimal and resulting benefits far outweigh the slight inconvenience of loss of control. Each institution has or should have a financial aids officer who should help students to secure federal loans, work-study, scholarships, and fellowships provided by federal agencies.

Income From Nontax Sources—Private Donors as a Source of Income

The private donor has always played a major role in providing operating income to colleges and universities. Some of the country's leading institutions were founded by private donors and benefactors who have continued to support higher education. One might expect that as government assumed a major role in funding higher education, private donation would decline. Available evidence indicates the reverse, and Roger Freeman reports that it is encouraging that voluntary giving in the United States has doubled over the past ten years and that education's share of the charity dollar climbed from 11 to 17 percent.[3] The Council for Financial Aid to Education reported in 1962 that 1,032 colleges and universities received about $803 million from private donors, and therefore one could estimate that today the total of private donations is well above $1 billion per year.

Private donors include philanthropic foundations, nonalumni individuals, alumni, business corporations, religious groups, and others. Gifts may be general or restricted to specific programs of particular interest to the donor. They are more important to private institutions than to public institutions. Each institution should actively seek to attract more donations from alumni and corporations to supplement its income. Donors are granted income tax credits for all contributions to educational institutions. (See Table 12.)

Student Tuition and Fees

Student tuition and fees has always been a controversial source of income, next only to federal aid. Some of the controversy centers around the question of who should bear the greater part of the cost of education—the student and his family or the state? The middle-of-the-road opinion is that while the student should not get something for nothing, fees should not be so high as to constitute a barrier to anyone adjudged to be physically and mentally capable of benefiting from a college education.

With few exceptions, institutions currently charge fees. The trend of fees is upward and is higher in private institutions than in public institutions, but in neither one are the fees charged equal to the educational service received by the student.

Fees are a major source of operating income to the institution. For some private colleges, between 55 and 65 percent of the total operating income comes from student fees. Public institutions as a group derive between 25 and 35 percent of their operating income from fees. In some states where state institutions by law provide free tuition, students pay nominal fees for other services. Fees are not uniform in any way, but colleges in similar situations tend to cost about the same, partly because no one wants to price himself out of the market and because the administrators and teachers belong to the same professional groups and consult each other informally in matters of this nature. In some states, a

TABLE 12

Example of a state-supported institution state appropriation bill for years ending

EXAMPLE OF A STATE SUPPORTED INSTITUTION
STATE APPROPRIATION BILL FOR YEARS ENDING

		AUGUST 31 19__	AUGUST 31 19__
1.	**General Administration:**		
	a. President (with home, utilities and private supplement of $14,000 from private sources)(other salary paid by alumi)	28,000	29,000
	b. All Other General Administration	1,522,059	1,522,059
2.	General Institutional Expense	374,649	374,649
3.	Staff Group Insurance Premium	177,450	177,450
4.	**Resident Instruction:**		
	a. Faculty Salaries (non-transferable)	12,458,879	12,882,481
	b. Departmental Operating Expense	2,338,513	2,338,513
	c. Organized Activities	7,097	7,097
5.	Vocational Teacher Training	12,925	12,925
6.	**Library (non-transferable)**		
	a. Books, Periodicals and Binding	423,363	423,363
	b. All Other Library Expense	820,833	820,833
7.	Organized Research	651,924	651,924
8.	Extension and Public Service	78,670	78,670
9.	**Physical Plant Operation**		
	a. General Services	129,885	129,885
	b. Campus Security	225,000	225,000
	c. Building Maintenance	709,611	709,611
	d. Custodial Services	505,758	772,111
	e. Grounds Maintenance	159,220	159,220
	f. Utilities (non-transferable)		
	(1) Purchased Utilities	814,120	919,824
	(2) All Other Utilities	12,605	12,605
10.	Non-Faculty Salary Increases	623,682	800,508
11.	**Special Items (non-transferable)**		
	a. Tuition Scholarships	15,000	37,800
	b. Historical Collection	32,282	31,472
	c. Oral History Collection	22,382	23,816
	d. University Centoer for Community Service	23,975	25,089
	e. Center for Social and Rehabilitative Sevice	22,391	33,576
	f. Center for Studies in Aging	15,170	15,170
	g. Council of the Federation of North Texas Area Universities	54,000	54,000
	.rs and Rehabilitation of Facilities	1,313,750	600,000
	) TOTAL, NORTH TEXAS STATE UNIVERSITY DENTON, TEXAS	23,593,193	15,758,316

coordinating board is responsible for the recommendation of tuition policies for institutions of higher learning. Three kinds of student fees may be identified—tuition, student service, and building use fees. Fees are charges per unit of credit hours taken in the institution.

Endowments and Grants

Endowments may be defined as "permanent funds held in trust, with only their income to be expended." A grant, on the other hand, is a property transferred by deed or writing.[4] In the United States both public and private institutions possess endowment funds which they hold inviolate and spend only the income from them as current operating income. With the acceptance of a gift or bequest for endowment, the governing board of the institution undertakes, to the best of its ability, to safeguard the principal by investing it according to the terms and deriving income compatible with its safety. It should be emphasized that the use of endowment principal for current expenses or for building is improper. Nor should invested funds be pledged as security on debts.[5] Endowment funds are generally invested in "farm lands, urban business properties, government bonds, utility bonds, the capital stock of business corporations and in other forms."[6] Unless the terms of the gift so stipulate, the endowment may not be invested separately or in any specific way.

Endowment income is an important source of income only to a few older private institutions as private giving no longer looms as large as it once did. Nevertheless, the importance of these contributions cannot be overlooked in a decade when costs are rising faster than income.

In theory, the governing board of the institution has final responsibility for the acceptance of funds and their management, but it is the practice to delegate the details of investment to a committee or to the chief financial officer of the institution.

Auxiliary Enterprises

Institutions are not legally required to operate dormitories, bookstores, laundries, or student union cafeterias. But these enterprises contribute to making the student's (and faculty's) environment conducive to learning. Auxiliary enterprises therefore are necessary and important to our institutions as they contribute to the achievement of the objectives of higher education. Almost all institutions operate one kind of auxiliary enterprise or another, both for the service provided to students and for additional income. The income of each enterprise is expected to cover all its incidental expenses as no tax appropriation may be used to subsidize it. Auxiliary enterprises are primarily service enterprises, not profit-making operations, but when they are well managed, they produce some income which can be ploughed back as current operating income for the institution. "Auxiliary enterprises account for more than 20 per cent of the total current operating expenditures of the institutions in the state of Texas," according to the Miller and Carter Report.[7] Auxiliary enterprises may be pledged or nonpledged. The income of pledged enterprises like school dormitories, student unions, food services, and bookstores must be used to retire bonds and meet interest expenses, and when the related bonds are retired, the enterprise reverts to a nonpledged status. A single account should be maintained for each enterprise so it can be singled out for attention if it incurs a deficit.

ALLOCATION OF FUNDS SECURED

In a single day of business, the institution's business office, where most of the financial aspects of the college take place, receives money from many sources. The bookstore sold books and art materials, a foreign government sent a check for tuition and living expenses of a sponsored student, interest was received on bonds and dividends on stock, a student repaid a loan plus interest, the government sent a check for research, and so forth. The key to ascertaining order in this type of confusion is the classification of funds. The business manager and his staff must be aware of his responsibility to any particular fund or class of funds.

Each institution may use its own classification system, depending on its size and type, but Thad L. Hungate suggests the following: (1) Endowment funds, (2) Funds temporarily functioning as endowment, (3) Funds subject to annuity agreements, (4) Student loan funds (loanable principal), (5) Plant funds, (6) Current funds (those applicable to program), (7) Agency funds.[8] The nature of the asset determines the class and often the financial officer has to make a judgment. Such judgment with respect to one fund group requires knowledge of the others.

How to Allocate Finances to the Various Areas of Internal and External Expenditure

The term "expense" is often used to denote the cost of services and materials used in a given period of time. Capital costs include the cost of acquiring capital assets like land, buildings, and equipment that will serve for periods longer than one year. That share of capital costs that may be fairly assigned as productive factors in carrying out the selected activity for the period considered is called use cost of capital. Use cost is only an estimate since the life of the capital cannot be known in advance. Expenditure is a broad term that includes expense and capital outlay.

Essential to allocation of funds is the identification of types of cost. Some institutions only have two types, total institutional cost and instructional salary cost, and all expenditures for these functions are obtained from the departments on a special form. In other institutions the cost elements are divided first into main headings to correspond to the formula areas and then are broken down in the budget.

After the necessary cost data is secured, the second step should be the application of suitable procedures for cost analysis. To determine average cost of a research project, determine the direct costs that are properly chargeable. To this, add indirect costs. For example, the cost of a research project is shown as follows:

	Direct cost..........................	XX
	Staff Benefit.........................	XX
	Imputed Use Value of Capital Asset	XX
Indirect	Physical Plant.......................	XX
Costs	Library..............................	XX
	General Administration................	XX
	TOTAL........................	XXX

The Budget—Plan and Instrument

Each institution of higher learning handles millions of dollars annually. They need planning and coordination at all levels. The financial plan for realizing the educational program as contained in the catalog is found in an instrument called the budget. The budget may be defined as "a statement of the estimated income and authorized expenditures for a fixed period, usually one year."9 The ultimate responsibility for the approval of the budget rests with the board of regents. The chief financial officer (usually the vice-president for fiscal affairs) is responsible for estimating the income and expenditure of the institution and for assisting in preparing the budget. Staff and faculty members, heads of departments and all related committees have responsibilities for contributing their thoughts to the improvement of the institution through budget planning.

Structure of the Budget

The arrangement of the estimated receipts and expenditures related to the teaching and research functions of the institution in a way that relates financial plans to fiscal policies is termed budget structure.

The two major elements in the budget structure are capital outlay (expenditures for land, buildings, and equipment) and current operations (expenditures for programs and the income that finances them).

Summary of Budget for X College 19__ to 19__

	Income	Expenditures
Current Operations	XX	XX
Capital Outlay	XXX	XXX
TOTAL	XXXX	XXXX

Budgetary procedure may be divided into three steps: preparation, adoption, and execution and control. The preparation should be completed prior to the beginning of that period. The president is the chief budget officer. Each department chairperson or other officer having a spending unit under him prepares an estimate of the amounts needed by his department and sends it to the president's office, usually through the chain of command. Such chairpersons are supposed to confer with their colleagues in the organizational unit and discuss the translation of their plans for service into financial terms. The requests received by the president's office are compiled after the president has an opportunity to meet with department heads to obtain justification for their requests. Usually requests exceed the estimated income and the budget has to be equalized. The next step is the adoption of the budget by the board of regents. The president has the responsibility of defending the budget at this stage. The board judges the soundness of the entire plan as represented in the budget. The budget must be controlled so that expenditures do not exceed estimates. During the year the budget must be revised to take care of unforeseen conditions and at the end of the year it is closed out. The budget is usually prepared on special forms that are designed to show comparative data. A surplus should always be maintained in case emergencies arise. All aspects of budgeting should follow the chain of command.

Zero-Based Budgets

Zero-Based Budgeting is a method of budgeting in which faculty members and departmental heads are forced to defend every operation under their control before any funds are allocated to them. The departmental head starts out with the assumption that he has no dollars at all (zero) to work with. From that zero point he breaks down and identifies every function or program under his jurisdiction. The program is evaluated in terms of cost and merit and the alternative decision packages proposed. Each decision package is ranked in priority order so that if anything is to be dropped the last item is dropped first.

Zero-Based Budgeting is a break with tradition in that traditionally the department head takes last year's budget as his starting point. To last year's figures he adds any new projects and estimated increases. Zero-Based Budgeting is causing some administrators headaches, but it is very suitable for educational budgeting. It is most suitable for items that come under headings of general and administrative costs. Also the soft areas of research, maintenance, and support operations can easily increase the budget size. By using zero base, a number of hidden factors can be revealed. Also, responsibilities for decisions and activities are pushed down to the lowest levels of the organization. In addition each faculty member and administrator becomes more accountable for objectives and financial concerns.

Program Budgeting

The concept of program budgeting called Planning, Programming, Budgeting System (PPBS) is comparatively new. It is managerial technique designed to merge the planning process with the allocation of funds by making it impossible to allocate funds without planning.[10] The emphasis is on accounting for achievement, rather than the dollar, in a situation where alternative programs are competing for the same resources. Briefly stated, the process consists of establishing objectives, developing alternate implementation programs to meet those objectives, estimating the resource requirements and possible benefits of each program, and selecting among the alternatives. K. E. Said divides the whole process into three phases. The first phase is the planning function which concerns itself with the institutional objectives and long-range plans. Questions arise such as, What programs should we develop? How shall the funds be allocated between programs? Are the programs consistent with each other? What goals and objectives should be attained through these programs? Who should benefit and who should pay for education? How many students should be educated by how many teachers and support personnel? What background should teachers have and where?

The second phase sets forth the institution's long-range plans more explicitly. Activities leading to the goals and objectives and the costs thereof are sorted and regrouped. This will provide alternate programs and program groups.

The third phase is the budget preparation and the actual allocation of resources to the various programs and program elements. Each program budget then becomes a display of information regarding the levels of activity and the costs thereof for several years ahead.[11]

Both Zero-Based Budgeting and program budgets can produce more accountability for achievements as well as dollar. They can help the institution to "improve its external relationships and achieve internal balance by promoting interaction among its academic units."[12] Since it cannot be implemented through the business office or the central budget office in isolation from the academic units, program budgeting ties decision to budgeting. However, neither Zero-Based Budgeting nor program budgeting has been totally accepted in institutions because of the human elements involved and because in practice institutions do not tend to perform the planning and budgeting function simultaneously.

The university or college doesn't wing its way into existence on shoestring budgets and happenstance financial planning. On the contrary, state subsidies, tuition and fees, and property taxes are the three major sources or revenues. Federal funding is increasing for vocational programs, facilities, and student assistance through grants and loans, but it still represents a small fraction of the income of the college. Most colleges depend upon the three abovementioned sources to account for 90 to 95 percent of their income.

State subvention for colleges and universities exist in patterns varying from no support, to shared effort with local community support, to full support minus tuition and/or federal funds. The patterns fall into three classifications: fixed amounts per full-time student, proportionate amount of costs of operations per full-time student, and full state support.

Formulas are usually based on Full-Time Equivalent Student (FTES), Full-Time Equivalent Enrollment (FTEE), Fiscal Year Equated Students (FYES), Full-Time Equivalent (FTE) which uses the credit hour as the unit, or Average Daily Attendance (ADA) which uses attendance hour as the unit. Reimbursement is usually based on current enrollment rather than that of a previous year. Almost universally, state formulas provide higher rates of reimbursement for technical-vocational programs than for academic programs, to offset their higher costs and to encourage colleges to offer more of them.

Some administrators believe that they can get more money from the combination of local taxes and state subventions than from either source alone. In the long run the logic of a uniform method of funding all higher education institutions, expediency, and property tax reform will have more influence on the patterns of support than all the argumentation and conservation.

Property taxes are a major source of revenue for colleges in all but a dozen states. For some they are the major source. Although property taxes are set by local boards of trustees, legislatures are deeply involved with the kind and amount of levy that may be made on property. Local boards must contend with a number of constitutional and legislative prescriptions and proscriptions on their taxing powers.

The three major property taxes common to most locally supported colleges are: the general purpose tax, which may be used for any authorized expenditure although it is used mainly for general operations; special purpose taxes, which are being levied with more frequency; and the capital-outlay tax, which can be used only for buildings and equipment. Among these three sources, the general purpose tax produces the largest amount of revenue. Generally, property taxes promote 20 to 50 percent of operating revenues. In the case of a few colleges, especially those having no or low tuition, this tax is the principal revenue, accounting for 60 percent or more of funds.

Legislatures set minimum and maximum rates that may be levied on property. For instance, California has a maximum of thirty-eight cents per hundred dollars of assessed valuation which may be increased only by a majority vote of the electorate or special legislative action.

Property taxes generally continue to rise wherever educators have the option to raise them. Educators may sympathize with the plight of property owners, but they feel that their first obligation is to keep the college operating at maximum strength. Though the property tax has been attacked (*Serrano* v. *Priest; Rodriquez* case) the emotional attachment to the principle of local control will assure its continuance. The stability, ready identification, and tremendous value of property, which make collection easy and returns high, and the inability of legislators and governors to agree on substitute sources of revenue will keep the property tax very much alive. If legislatures do not find a satisfactory solution for property tax relief, the electorate may force the issue by approving referendum measures to limit the rate and purposes for which tax funds can be used.

Most colleges resort to tuition and fees to help make up some of the differences between budget requirements and inadequate state and local revenues. Pronouncement of no tuition or low tuition attracts attention but does little to assist in balancing an already inadequately funded budget.

All colleges classify students for tuition purposes: in-district or resident; out-of-district; and out-of-state or nonresident. Occasionally a fourth classification, foreign, is used. A nonresident usually pays higher tuition. Likewise in-district tuition is lower than out-of-district and much lower than out-of-state.

Out-of-district tuition is not normally intended to be a source of revenue. Theoretically, it is a device to prevent a district from shifting its educational responsibility to other districts; force an area not in a college district to join or annex one; or prevent a student from attending a college outside his district except under special circumstances.

An examination of current tuition policies automatically involves some analysis of the practice of charging fees. Colleges generally make a distinction between a fee and tuition, though the terms are sometime used interchangeably. A few may be a one-time request such as an admission filing fee or graduation fee, a late examination fee, and so forth. Theoretically, tuition is a charge for instruction while a fee is a charge for service somehow related to instruction.

From all of this the conclusion must be made that even though tuition and fees probably contribute about 25 percent to the total operating revenue of the college, they are an important revenue for the college. There is a possibility that their revenue may approach one-third of total revenues in the next few years. In locally supported colleges tuition and fees may become the second most important source of revenue, below state aid and above property taxes.

A fourth source of financial assistance is federal aid. This aid comes in a variety of packages. Many colleges have an individual or staff whose primary function is to keep track of the kind of aid available and to prepare requests for funds the college is eligible to receive. Federal aid is available for many vocational programs, manpower programs, veterans education, elementary and secondary education, preschool educational aid, and gerontology aid.

There is additional federal aid for construction of facilities; purchase of materials, equipment, supplies; professional development staff; and program development. However, federal aid is still far from becoming a major source of income for colleges and universities. Present federal economic policy gives a strong indication that future aid may decrease rather than increase.

Additionally, colleges and universities may attract large donations earmarked for particular needs or programs. An auditorium, swimming pool, or other special purpose building may be given. Acquired real properties or business investments can be used as endowments or collateral for financial purposes. Short-term investments of temporary surplus funds accumulated from operating income, contingency accounts, or bond sales are small but welcome income producers. A district building or one or more campuses may have large unexpended funds to invest in short-term notes. Bond sales are a profitable means of acquiring investment income.

Investment income from bond funds (arbitrary bond profit), however, is restricted by the federal Treasury Department to 15 percent of the difference between the interest on the bonds and the profit on the reinvestment of temporarily unused proceeds from the sale of the bonds. In June 1972 the Treasury Department proposed to reduce the allowable difference to 0.125 percent. The penalty for violating this revision is withdrawal of the tax-exempt status of the bonds.

All these sources together still form only a small fraction of the income of a public college.

The subject of finance is most essential to the general administration of higher educational institutions, but it has not received an attention

FIGURE 60
Sources of income

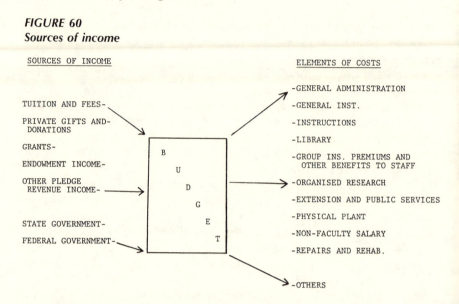

commensurate with its importance. Colleges and universities, like all other enterprises, have income needs. They must have money to meet instructional and administrative costs, endowment principal to invest, funds for physical facilities, and scholarships and student aid funds to help students meet the ever rising cost of obtaining higher education.

FIGURE 61
Elements of organization for management of Higher Education

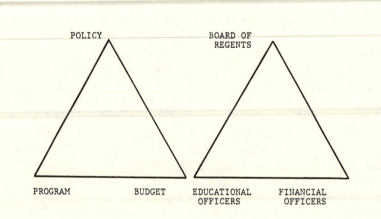

The objective of the institution being to approximate as nearly as possible an even balance between income and expenditure, it prepares and adopts a carefully planned budget. Figure 60 illustrates the sources of income that most public universities receive. The other information which is shown are the elements of cost that public higher education institutions normally expend monies for. Together, source of income and elements of cost, will make up the entire budget.

Figure 61 illustrated how institutional policy and educational programs are tied to the budget of each public university. The personnel of the organization who become involved in setting the budget include: the educational officers, the financial officers, and finally approval by the board of regents.

FIGURE 62
Organization of the business office (North Texas State University)

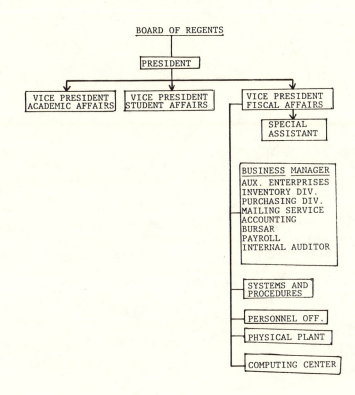

The truimvirate policy, program, and budget comprise the indispensable elements of management. No one of them moves without the other. *Policies* represent guides to planning and performance. They are the official views on the various aspects of management. The *program* is those organized experiences that advance the learning process. It is the primary medium through which institutions objectives are met, and it includes all educational, social, or recreational activities peculiar to student life. The *budget* is a financial plan of operation, usually for a fiscal year, showing the essential financial provisions for achieving the program. Figure 62 describes the organization of the business office.

It becomes apparent that institutions of higher learning are different from commercial enterprises. While commercial enterprises are profit oriented, colleges spend everything to produce educational services. However, the accounting systems used by the institutions seem so similar to those of commercial enterprises that the differences between the two are not always sufficiently reflected. The whole area of financial administration and financial accounting for educational institutions needs to be revisited.

NOTES

1. Dexter N. Keezer, *Financing Higher Education* (New York: McGraw-Hill, 1959), p. 70.

2. Edmund S. Boe and Harry S. Damp, "The Elements of Program Budgeting," *Journal of Accountancy,* April 1971, p. 41.

3. John D. Millet, *Financing Higher Education in the United States* (New York: Columbia University Press, 1952), p. 111.

4. The National Committee on Standard Reports for Institutions of Higher Education, *Financial Reports for Colleges and Universities* (Chicago: University of Chicago Press, 1935), p. 20.

5. Ibid., p. 30.

6. June A. O'Neill, *Sources of Funds to Colleges and Universities* (Washington, D.C.: Carnegie Commission on Higher Education, 1973), p. 30.

7. National Committee on Standard Reports, *Financial Reports for Colleges and Universities,* p. 68.

8. Thad L. Hungate, *Finance in Educational Management of Colleges and Universities* (New York: Columbia University, 1954), p. 19.

9. Ibid., p. 65.

10. Ibid.

11. K. E. Said, "A Goal Oriented Budgetary Process," *Management Accounting,* January 1975, pp. 31–36.

12. Ibid., p. 36.

Definitions of the Elements of Institutional Costs

The educational and general functions for which appropriations for the 1975–77 biennium are to be requested by the public senior colleges and universities in Texas are defined below. The listings of examples are not to be interpreted as necessarily meaning that each institution will have expenditures in all categories, but are intended only as illustrations of the named functions.

I. General Administration and Student Services (formula)
   A. General Administration—10XXX
      Definition: Salaries, wages, and all other costs for the following functions and activities.
      Note: Because funds to support the functions performed by governing boards and central administrative offices for certain public senior college and university systems having responsibility for more than one academic institution have historically been separately requested and appropriated, the costs for these boards and offices are excluded from the defined elements.
      1. Government of the institution.
         The costs incurred on behalf of the governing body in discharging its responsibilities.
         Example: governing board.
      2. Executive Direction and Control.
         The costs incurred in the executive direction, control and implementation of policies of the governing board and the chief executive officer.
         Examples: chief executive's office (president), chief academic officer's office, chief business officer's office, assistant(s) to the president.
         Excluded are costs of academic administrative functions defined in "Instructional Administration Expense."
      3. Business and Fiscal Management.
         The costs incurred in the attainment of financial goals through proper effective accounting records and procedures and budgetary and cost controls.

Examples: business office, fiscal office, comptroller's office, personnel services, purchasing office, property and inventory control, internal audit, systems and procedures.

B. Admissions and Registration.

The costs of administering undergraduate and graduate admission activities, processing and maintenance of the student records and reports, and the registration of students.

Examples: registrar's office, dean of admissions.

2. Other Student Services.

The costs of administering and coordinating the development and maintenance of the student life program including counseling with students on disciplinary and other non-academic problems, the guidance of foreign students, student and graduate placement, and student financial aids.

Examples: chief student affair's office, dean of men, dean of women, testing and guidance, student life, international office, placement, and student financial aids.

II. General Institutional Expense (formula)—12XXX

Definition: Expenses of a general nature which benefit the entire institution and are not related solely to any specific department or division. The definition of functions within this element should not be interpreted as implying that each institution should engage in all the activities defined. Included are salaries, wages, and all other costs for the following functions, services, or activities:

A. Public informational activities including bulletins, catalogues, publications, exhibits, and news service.

B. Institutional memberships.

C. Commencement exercises for the graduating classes. Included only are costs of speakers, arrangements, and caps and gowns for guests.

D. Convocations and public lectures.

E. Official functions.

F. Mail services, excluding the cost of postage.

G. Legal fees and expense required to protect the interests of the institutions and the state. In the case of public senior colleges and universities, these expenses must be authorized by the attorney general.

H. Development activities.

I. Student band.

J. The costs of maintaining and securing records pertaining to alumni of the institution for evaluation of the educational programs of the institution. (Note: For the 1974–75 biennium, the expenditure of educational and general constitutional funds by public senior colleges and universities to support alumni organizations or activities is prohibited under sec. 38, article IV, H. B. 139, acts of the sixty-third legislature, 1973.)

K. Telephone central office. Does not include long distance call charges nor cost of telephone instruments. These costs are to be charged to the using departments.

L. The cost of conducting studies for the improvement of the institution.

M. Insurance (other than property and those covered under staff benefits).

N. Other general institutional expense items, except as follows:

1. Service department charges (except for mail service and telephone central office) should be allocated to the users, e.g.: stenographic bureaus, central stores, central computer operation costs, printing shops, copy centers, supply centers, microfilm services, etc.

2. Any item of cost specifically identified within the definition of an element of institutional cost should be included in that cost element and not "General Institutional Expense."

III. Staff Benefits—13XXX

Definition: Premiums or costs toward staff benefits programs for employees. Examples of staff benefits authorized by the legislature are:

A. Staff group insurance premiums. (formula)

B. Faculty development leaves.

C. Old age and survivors insurance.

D. Workmen's compensation insurance.

IV. Resident Instruction

Definition: Resident instruction includes all functions directly related to teaching, classified as follows:

A. Faculty salaries (formula)—14XXX–25XXX

Definition: Salaries or wages of those engaged in the teaching function, including heads of teaching departments. Included also are laboratory assistants, teaching assistants, teaching fellows, and lecturers who are responsible for, or in charge of, a class or class section, or a quiz, drill, or laboratory section. Not included are the salaries or wages of guest lecturers or of student assistants, laboratory assistants, and graders whose duties involve grading, clerical functions, store keeping, and preparations of class or laboratory material or other subordinate functions.

B. Departmental operating expense (formula)—14XXX–25XXX

Definition: Salaries, wages, supplies, travel, office furniture, equipment, and incidental operating expense for the operation of instructional departments, other than faculty salaries. Included here are the salaries and wages or guest lecturers and of student assistants, laboratory assistants, and graders whose duties involve grading, clerical functions, store keeping, and preparation of class or laboratory material or experiments or other subordinate functions. Includes teaching equipment customarily assigned to teaching departments and provides for replacement and updating of teaching equipment as well as acquisition of new items. Also includes costs of practice teaching other than faculty salaries, and all direct or prorated computer costs related to resident instructional programs.

C. Instructional administration expense (formula)—26XXX
   Definition: Salaries, wages, supplies, travel, equipment, and incidental operating expense of the offices of academic deans or directors of major teaching department groupings into colleges, schools, or divisions, and the office of the dean or director of graduate studies. Examples of activities include, but are not limited to, the following: instructional budget planning; faculty recruitment, development, assignment, and utilization; curricular expansion and revision; student academic advisement; maintenance of scholastic and admission standards. Not included are the offices of the heads of teaching departments.
D. Organized activities related to instructional departments—28XXX
   Definition: All costs of activities or enterprises separately organized and operated in connection with instructional departments primarily for the purpose of giving professional training to students as a necessary part of the educational work of the related departments. Examples of such organized activities are college farms, creameries, poultry processing plants, veterinary hospitals, nursery schools, and home management houses. Does not include cost of practice teaching. Where these activities are not conducted primarily for educational purposes, they should be excluded from the definition of this element of cost.

V. Vocational Teacher Training Supplement—30XXX
   Definition: The matching part of salaries, wages, and such other costs as are required to finance the vocational teacher training program according to provisions of the Texas State Acceptance Act and the plan of the state board of vocational education for vocational teacher training under the Smith-Hughes and George Parden Acts.

VI. Library (formula)—32XXX
    Definition: Salaries, wages, other operating costs; books, periodicals, binding costs; and equipment of separately organized libraries (including archives).

VII. Organized Research (formula)—34XXX–35XXX
     Definition: Salaries, wages, and other costs of separately organized research divisions such as research bureaus, research institutes, and separately budgeted or financed research investigations. Departmental research not separately budgeted or financed and contract research and services are not included.

VIII. Extension and Public Service—36XXX
      Definition: All costs of activities designed primarily to serve the general public, including correspondence courses, adult study courses, public lectures, radio and television stations, institutes, workshops, demonstrations, package libraries, and similar activities.

IX. Physical Plant Operation and Maintenance
    A. Physical plant general services—38XXX
       Definition: Salaries, wages, supplies, travel, equipment, and other operating expenses to carry out the duties of physical

plant administration, planning, and general services. Examples of the activities included are:

1. Administration
   Salaries, wages, travel, equipment, and other operating costs required to administer one or more functional units of the physical plant.
2. Planning
   Salaries, wages, travel, equipment, and other costs required to prepare architectural and engineering plans and specifications, for the expansion, renovation, and rehabilitation of physical plant facilities, excluding fees for new construction.
3. Other general services, including:
   a. Acquisition and repair of general classroom and laboratory furniture. Does not include office furniture.
   b. Central receiving and storing of supplies and equipment.
   c. Safety, including fire, occupational, radiation, health and sanitation safety.
   d. Garbage and trash disposal.
   e. Hauling, moving, and storing.
   f. Property insurance.
   g. Truck and automobile expense in general service of the institution.

B. Campus security—39000
   Definition: Salaries, wages, supplies, travel, equipment, and other operating expenses to carry out the traffic and security services of the institution.
C. Building maintenance (formula)—39100
   Definition: Costs, including salaries, wages, supplies, materials, equipment, services, and other expenses necessary to keep each building in good appearance and usable condition and prevent the building from deterioration once it has been placed in first class condition for the type and age of building. Does not include auxiliary enterprise buildings. Building maintenance includes minor repairs and alterations, costs of materials, hire of personnel, and other necessary expenses for the repair and for the repair and/or painting of the following: roofs, exterior walls, foundations, flooring, ceilings, partitions, doors, windows, plaster, structural ironworks, screens, window shades, venetian blinds, plumbing, heating and air conditioning equipment within or a part of the building, electric wiring, light fixtures (including the replacement of lamps), washing of all outside window surfaces, built-in shelving, and other related items.
D. Custodial services (formula)—39200
   Definition: Costs including salaries, wages, supplies, materials, equipment, services, and other expenses necessary to keep the buildings in a clean and sanitary condition. Does not include auxiliary enterprise buildings. These services include care of

the floors, stairways and landings, and restrooms; cleaning chalkboards, inside of windows, walls, and room furniture and fixtures; assigned dusting, removal of waste paper and refuse, and other related duties. Common operations include: mopping, sweeping, waxing, renovating of floors (sanding and refinishing of floors are excluded); dusting, polishing of furniture and fixtures such as venetian blinds, partitions, pictures, mpas, radiators, etc.; cleaning and disinfecting commodes and urinals, cleaning and washing other fixtures, walls, and partitions, and replenishing supplies for restrooms; the emptying and cleaning of waste receptacles, and dusting and cleaning of windows and other glass surfaces; sweeping and cleaning of entrances; and opening and/or closing buildings, doors, and windows.

E. Grounds maintenance (formula)—39300

Definition: Costs including salaries, wages, supplies, materials, equipment, services, and other expenses relating to the upkeep of all lands designated as campus proper (improved and unimproved) not occupied by actual buildings, including any court, patio, and/or inner garden or court enclosed by buildings. Grounds maintenance begins after the site improvements are complete. Phases of grounds maintenance are:

1. Land improvements
    a. Permanent: lawns, trees, shrubs, etc.
    b. Seasonal: flowers, bulbs, etc.
2. Circulation systems
    a. Vehicular: streets and roads—improved and unimproved; parking areas—improved and unimproved; traffic controls—signal lights, signs, and barriers.
    b. Pedestrian. walks and paths—improved and unimproved.
3. Other activities
    a. Campus lighting: streets, campus.
    b. Irrigation systems.
    c. Non-structural improvements: walls, fences, fountains, campus furniture, others.
    d. Ancillary enterprises: nursery, greenhouse areas for special academic study.

F. Utilities—39400–39900

Definition: All costs of purchase, manufacture and delivery of utility services, including: electricity, steam heat, water (hot, cold, or chilled), storm sewers, sanitary sewer, compressed air, gas, clocks and bells, institutionally owned telephone systems (does not include switchboard operators and commercial telephone service), preventive maintenance, and repairs and minor alterations to production and distribution facilities. Does not include costs of utilities for auxiliary enterprises.

X. Special Items—40XXX

Definition: The costs of those items which are not included in any of the other elements, or, -he costs of those items which are peculiar to the particular institution.

XI. Major Repairs and Rehabilitation of Buildings and Facilities— 81XXX

Definition: This item includes major repairs, rehabilitation, and renovation of existing buildings and facilities (including repairs and alterations to production and distribution facilities for utilities where such facilities do not primarily serve auxiliary enterprises) including salaries, wages, and costs of materials for such items; but does not include routine, ordinary, annual, or periodic maintenance.

21

What Administrators Ought to Know about the Instructional Program

Objectives: Who Needs Them? You Do!

BOB W. MILLER AND CAROLYN K. SCHROEDER

An administrator may wish to relate a case study about the instructional process to his faculty members during an inservice session. The following is a specific case with which instructors can identify.

> Imagine that it's your first day of class. Your name is on the board along with the course number and textbooks needed.
>
> "I hope you are all in the right class. Are there any questions?
>
> "Yes, Mr. Smithers."
>
> "I want to know just what you are going to cover in this course. What can I expect to learn from it? Frankly, I don't see why I even have to take this course!"
>
> Somewhat shaken, you begin to explain to him what the course is about, how interesting it is, and why it is important. That look on his face though is telling you he is just not getting it.
>
> "Damn!" If you only had a written statement telling exactly what he is expected to learn, the conditions under which he will be expected to work, and the criteria by which he will be judged. Hopefully, after the course is over he would see the worth of it all. Possibly this student's attitude could even change!
>
> "Joe, let me put it another way. The objectives of this course are. . . ."
>
> Now you're on your way. You're spelling out exactly what the learner will accomplish when he completes his learning experience. In other words, you're explaining the behavioral objectives of your course. You're describing a proposed change in a learner—a statement of what the learner is to be like when he has successfully completed a learning experience.[1]

DEFINITIONS

Accountability—Responsibility for goals and objectives either developed individually or superimposed from above.

Achievement management—How well a student achieves and masters content at a given level.

Appropriate practice—(a) Equivalent appropriate practice occurs when the practice situation is essentially the same as that called for in the performance or behavioral objectives; (b) Analoguous appropriate practice provides practice activities that are similar but not identical to the performance or behavioral objective.

Comprehensive community colleges—Institutions in a community setting which offer a wide variety of services seemingly appropriate to the needs of a nontraditional education. Basically a two-year institution.

Conceptual areas—These can affect teaching either positively or negatively—lesson plans, course outlines, goals, objectives, individual differences, etc.

Continuing Education Units (CEUs)—Credit given in unit measures for nontraditional educational services.

Domains—(a) Cognitive domain involves intellectual process; (b) Affective domain involves the feelings or emotions; (c) Psychomotor domain involves the manipulative skills and values.

Enrichment management—Provision for in-depth study to allow a student to apply what has been learned.

En route behaviors—Any skills that are preliminary to the accomplishment of the stated objectives.

External degree—A degree achieved away from a college setting with little or no time spent in residence at the college.

Individualized instruction—An individualized system designed with goals and objectives developed in sequential steps leading to a particular predetermined outcome.

Instructional package—An organization of devices and other materials which presents a complete body of information and is largely self-supporting rather than supplementary to the teaching-learning process.

Maintenance management—Opportunity and review in the system to maintain skills and values learned.

Measurability model—A model that establishes specific performance objectives which the educator expects the learner to accomplish. A measurement of results obtained by the teacher in relation to the learner.

Modeling—A teaching tactic which allows the student to see those behaviors that he is expected to adopt.

Motivation management—Rewards built into the system to motivate the student to stay involved.

Needs assessment—An evaluation of the student's needs in order to develop objectives to reach new levels of learning.

New students—Include members of minority groups, students with previous military service, physical and so forth handicaps. Any student who normally would not have attended a college.

Nontraditional student—A student who attends college for a purpose not strictly academic. (Vocational/technical, noncredit, continuing education, etc.)

Prescriptive management—A plan developed from test and assessments for a student to master content learning.

Professional development—A process of upgrading all levels of educational administrative and teaching functions and prescribing additional studies or workshops to improve performance.

Teaching machines—Manipulative machines which have a body of materials available through a systems design for an individualized study approach.

Technical skill—The functioning area capabilities of an individual.

Terminal behavior—That final behavior designed to be performed in the performance or behavioral objective.

WRITING OBJECTIVES

Your *objectives* might well be: *written* in terms of student performance; *observable* by one or more of the five senses; *specific* enough to be meaningful; *measurable* in terms of (a) level of performance, and (b) conditions under which the performance is to take place; *sequential* in relation to prior and subsequent objectives; *relevant* in relation to prior and subsequent objectives; *attainable* within the time period allowed; *challenging* to each individual student.

Sounds like a lot of work, doesn't it? Yet your students have a right to know the educational objectives of your course. In the pick and choose marketplace of education you can't afford not to tell them. That's a portion of educational accountability.

If we are to be held accountable, we ought to know what objectives should include, how to select them, and the appropriate application to be made of them. First, let's look at what kinds of objectives we can use. There are three types or domains: *cognitive, affective,* and *psychomotor.*

The cognitive domain involves the intellectual process. These objectives range from simple recall of material to highly organized and creative ways of synthesizing new ideas.

The affective domain involves feelings or emotions. Responses in this domain can be labeled as interest, attitude, appreciation, and values.

The psychomotor domain involves manipulative skills. It is most often related to handwriting, speech, physical education, and vocational and technical courses.[2]

The first step in formulating objectives is dependent upon the answer to an important question, namely, "What do we want the learner to demonstrate after completing a learning experience?" Or, stated another way, "What do we want him to be able to do?"

Once this has been decided upon we must devise, in concrete terms, a specific statement of instructional intent. To do this, we must thoroughly understand the task at hand. The task should be broken down into smaller elements so that what is taught can readily be mastered in the proper sequence. Questions such as these need to be considered: What prior knowledge is required? What concepts or terminology must be known? What subtasks are necessary?

In selecting your course objectives, remember that they should be written in such a manner that the student knows what you expect him to do, under what conditions or circumstances, and to what degree of accuracy or skill. The student must have no doubt concerning what you expect. All too often objectives are written in a way that makes them vague and meaningless.

It is not sufficient merely to say that you want the student to "learn" or "know" something. Tell him precisely what he has to do with that knowledge. Use active words like "write," "recite," "solve," "list," "compare." Stay away from meaningless terms like "appreciate," "believe," "enjoy"—constructs that can't easily be measured to any significant degree. The affective domain can be measured if you know what you're trying to teach.

Tell the student that he has to solve "eight out of ten problems" in order to reach the appropriate skill level. State clearly your expectations. Do not simply say he must "solve subtraction problems." Indicate how many problems, and the number of problems that must be correct. He has the right to know.

Are you setting a time limit in which he has to answer the eight out of ten problems? Can he use his textbook to answer them? In other words, *specify the conditions* under which he must perform.

When we apply objectives, the question arises, Should they always be stated in the cognitive domain? What if a student learns to do eight out of ten problems but will never take another math course again because he hated every minute of it? What have you really achieved then? Will he remember that math if he really hates it?

Therefore, it is important also to consider *affective objectives* for your course. Do you really know how your students accept or respond to your course? Affective objectives range in acceptance from a low of simply receiving the instruction to a high degree of acceptance involving a change in values. Benjamin Bloom explains how one can rate affective behavior from lowest to highest.[3]

To measure affective objectives you must know the student's status before and after instruction. In other words, you must pre-test and post-test each student. There must be some kind of observational comparison. What about the student's attitudes toward your subject? His class attendance? Is he eager to do more than you expect him to do? Dos he seem to be attentively occupied during the class period? What does he say about your course? Is he eager to volunteer for extra work or additional reading?

Affective objectives are probably the most neglected, because many educators feel that affective behavior cannot be measured. Don't you believe it! There is not a single course in which affective objectives are inappropriate. Is there any point in teaching anything that is hated and soon forgotten? Obviously, the answer is no. But there *is* every reason to hope that your course will somehow influence values and the value system of a student and help him grow in ways that will be personally fulfilling.

When writing objectives, it is important to include objectives for each of the three domains. Include *affective* objectives simultaneously and on an equal basis with psychomotor and cognitive domain objectives. If you can hand your students a list of meaningful objectives and discuss those objectives the first day in class, you're on your way. Let the student know what is expected of him; precisely what he needs to learn. He may just learn it and like it, and you will then be more responsible and responsive.

Objectives are important. You had better start thinking about them. If you don't, the person who takes your job will.

Almost Everything an Administrator Wants to Know About Individualized Instruction

BOB W. MILLER and CAROLYN K. SCHROEDER

You have finally decided to take that daring step toward individualizing your courses. Now that you have committed yourself, what comes next? You've heard all the jargon—affective domain, behavioral objectives, appropriate practice, humanization, small group, large groups, rap groups, packages, *ad infinitum* and *ad nauseum.* How do you go about pulling it all together (or sorting it all out)?

INDIVIDUALIZED INSTRUCTION

Individualized instruction adds such a humanistic appeal to instruction that in today's currents of educational practices the question is not, "to individualize or not to individualize" but rather, "how can individualization be more effective?" Many attempts at individualized instruction have been and are being made. Teachers are concerned about a more individualized approach to teaching. They want to be able to meet the needs of each student individually instead of all students as a total group. Should a teacher attempt to meet the needs of each student? Maybe yes, maybe no, probably so, Let's entertain the possibilities. *No,* if he doesn't believe that all students can not, will not, and/or don't want to learn at the same rate. No, if he doesn't believe that students won't learn in the same way or for the same reasons. No, if he plans to arrive with his students, leave with his students or spend office hours involved in that committee report he needs to complete. An even further no, if he is limited in knowledge of behavioral objectives.

On the other hand . . . *yes,* if he believes none of the nos mentioned above are appropriate. The tie breaker could simply be to place ourselves in the student's shoes. Are there subjects that can be taught better to a large number of students? Are some subjects better-suited to small group instruction? What about subjects in which you would prefer independent help? Merely answering these questions may suggest a need for individualization. What then are some important factors in individualizing instruction effectively?

First, a good understanding of individualized instruction should be established with the faculty. Contrary to popular belief, definitions for individualized instruction have many facades, some of them doing the thought a considerable disservice. Ask any number of well-informed teachers what individualized instruction is. Practically all will respond with positive or negative comments.

However, more often than not they will describe a well-rehearsed circus of activities starring computers, programmed texts, teaching machines, isolated lonely students, and perhaps a "no teacher" situation. Individualized instruction isn't necessarily all or any of these things. It is no one specific way of instructing nor any one special program of instruction. It does expect and even influence the learner to take individual responsibility for his efforts in performance. This is done with consideration for many things: intelligence quotients, learning styles, entrance levels, and interests, to name a few. Instruction following evaluation of these factors, then, can not be limited to nonsocial, computerized, or one-of-a-kind activities mentioned previously.

Second, a teacher can be more successful if he or she is effective and efficient in writing accurate measurable behavioral objectives. Knowing where the student is going and being able to measure his success is of utmost importance. Writing behavioral objectives is important, yet no less important is the ability to apply appropriately the many different instructional procedures in accomplishing an objective. The variety of instructional procedures employed offers the student a choice in reaching an objective.

Third, individualization can take place in almost any teaching situation. Team teaching and nongraded arrangements are conducive to individualization. A self-contained classroom may be individualized. Large groups may be formed for "core" instruction, when lectures, demonstrations, and media can be used. Smaller groups may be formed for the purposes of discussion, projects, panels, and so forth. Individual tutoring, programmed materials, or other independent activities can be arranged when necessary. All of these approaches can be used effectively in team teaching, nongraded, or self-contained situations. The major emphasis is on the student. What is right for him as an individual should determine the program in which he works. This is a major part of the personalized approach.

Doll reminds us that "each of us is a slow learner at some time and for some reason."[4] Individualizing instruction is not an end, but is a means of alleviating this problem.

To individualize or not to individualize? The question is rather, How can I individualize more effectively? An administrator must be well versed in individualized instruction if he or she is to provide leadership in this type of educational strategy.

Appropriate Practices

An extremely important aspect of the learning process is the selection of appropriate practice opportunities. Therefore, once goals and specific behavioral objectives have been delineated for a particular learning situation, the next, vital step in the learning process is the choice of appropriate practice activities. According to W. James Popham, "appropriate practice occurs when the student is given the opportunity to practice the behavior called for in the performance objective."[5] There are primarily two types of appropriate practice: equivalent appropriate practice, and analogous appropriate practice.

Equivalent appropriate practice occurs when the practice situation is exactly the same as that called for in the performance on behavioral objectives. An example of this type of practice follows.

When the objective of a mathematics class is that the students will be able to "solve word problems of a particular type," and they are given opportunities to solve word problems of the same type during the instructional sequence, the equivalent appropriate practice activity has been utilized.[6]

The findings of educational studies dealing with equivalent appropriate practice have supported the effectiveness of using equivalent appropriate practice activities in the learning process. In one study conducted by Ross E. Fraub, the investigator discovered that sixth grade pupils who were permitted to practice on heterogeneous problems, as opposed to groups permitted to practice on homogeneous or irrelevant problems, performed significantly better on a complex mathematical task involving the solution of heterogeneous problems.[7]

The second type of practice, analogous appropriate practice, provides practice activities that are comparable but not identical to those called for in the performance objective.

If the terminal behavior called for in an objective requires the student to respond in writing to such written stimulus materials as test questions, a teacher might orally present comparable questions and ask for oral student response, thus, analogous appropriate practice would be utilized.[8]

In most learning situations and for most learners the use of equivalent appropriate practice seems to render better results. A study conducted by George L. Gropper contrasted the effects of giving "actual" or equivalent practice, and "recognition" or analogous practice opportunities to students learning to assemble a simple electrical motor. Both groups received instruction by videotape; the first group engaged in analogous practice activities of recognition, and the second group participated in "actual" or equivalent practice exercises. The error rate of the second group was only 2 percent, while that of the first group was 4 percent. From these findings, Gropper concluded that "actual" or equivalent appropriate practice was the better of the two practices for this particular learning situation.[9] The particular characteristics and abilities of the members of a given class and the nature of the subject to be learned will help to determine which type (or types) of appropriate practice to employ.[10] It is possible that the educator will find it advantageous to utilize both types of practice in given situations.

A factor for consideration before deciding on appropriate practice opportunities is prerequisite tasks, or en route behaviors. En route behaviors are any skills a student must master as preliminary or basic skills to enable him to accomplish the exit behavior stated in the objective.[11] For example, a Spanish class is studying the *Poem of El Cid*. The teacher wants the students to be able to read and analyze the style of writing of the twelfth-century Spanish ballad. The prerequisite skills, or en route behaviors, for this learning situation would be that the students be able to read and understand the Spanish language and be familiar with any new or difficult words appearing in the ballad.

Robert M. Gagne has devoted considerable attention to the question of task analysis and strongly suggests that once the exit skills of the behavioral objective are clearly in mind, one may proceed to the identification and sequencing of en route behaviors that will enable the student to accomplish the desired exit skill.[12]

In order to establish sequential and successful learning experiences, a behavioral objective must be delineated, en route behaviors considered, and appropriate practice opportunities provided. These points of consideration must be taken into account by the administrator if he or she is to make the faculty aware that utilization of these factors are important to students in the learning process.

Strategies for Achieving Affective Change

Teachers who thrive on challenge are finding plenty of overtime action in today's college classrooms. By noontime every teacher has faced, in the classroom, a conglomeration of society's best and society's worst. The challenges that these students present are innumerable and monumental. Yet, contrary to popular opinion, the most crucial of all these challenges lies not in course content, urban adjustment, or financial achievement. The critical challenge lies in the instructor's ability to help these students change their attitudes toward education, understand and control their emotions, and examine and evaluate their values.

Teachers have long recognized the important role played by attitudes and feelings in the process of learning. Yet for years teachers have been unable to change and deal effectively with attitudes and feelings as they exist in the classroom. Teachers have balked at attempting such changes for two reasons: they wondered if it was their responsibility, and they did not know how to bring such changes about. Times have changed. Today's teacher knows that he or she must take responsible action toward improving a student's attitudes and feelings. However, the nature of this responsible action, as in the past, continues to complicate the professor's day and may prove to be most frustrating.

Although the concern over teacher responsibility is of immense importance, it would be agonizing to spend hours in discussing this issue only to find that bringing such changes about in the classroom was impossible. We believe these changes are possible, so it is to the problem of causing and measuring attitudinal changes in the classroom that we will devote the remainder of this section.

DEALING WITH THE ABSTRACT

Attitudes, emotions, and concern for the student's total affective domain present a unique challenge in abstraction for the teacher. Changing attitudes, getting students to appreciate various subjects, and increasing student awareness, are all Pandora's box-like objectives found in many of today's lesson plans. However, dealing effectively in the real world of students requires teaching to be more concrete and objectives to be more useful. Herein lies the problem.

To be effective, we must reduce our abstract objectives to definite, observable behaviors. Perhaps an example from Robert Mager may help. Like the educator, the physician deals daily in an effective way with the abstract. How does he do it? He reduces his abstract, nonmeasurable terms to "indicator behaviors" that *are* measurable and changeable.[13] The physician does not measure health or illness. The physician measures body temperatures, heartbeat rates, blood pressures, and weights. Like the physician, educators must begin to view change in student attitude in small, observable, "indicator behaviors." This will provide teachers with demonstrable and measurable evidence that change is occurring. Instead of teachers striving to create an attitude of appreciation toward art, teachers should develop small measurable behaviors that they feel represent the student who possesses such an appreciation. Again, this is exactly what the physician does. Small specific behaviors are examined and analyzed and determination follows as to whether the patient is healthy or ill.

Mere determination of desired behaviors in the college classroom is not enough. Today's instructor needs help in the engineering of such behaviors. Encouragement alone, however, will not guarantee the adoption of student responses. Students cannot be expected to engage in activities reflective of affective change unless teachers provide sound principles from which to learn such behaviors. We are proposing nothing new. We only seek to remind educators of the most reliable and most valid strategies of current learning theory: modeling, contiguity, and reinforcement.

Modeling

The first strategy effective in changing student affect must involve modeling. Modeling is a tactic that allows the student to *see* those behaviors that he is expected to adopt. This learning by example places the burden of obligation on the teacher. He must prove a worthy example which students may model. Teachers must never ask of students what they are unable to do themselves. We would never expect someone who has never seen a football game to be a good football player; likewise, we must not expect students who have never experienced positive attitudes in the classroom to develop such attitudes accidentally.

Contiguity

The second strategy is a little more complex. The principle of contiguity suggests that any response accompanying a stimulus situation will tend to be repeated when that stimulus situation is repeated. This suggests that students learn best by doing.[14] Seeing the behavior of others is not enough to produce significant and long lasting changes in student behavior. Students should be allowed to *see* the behaviors expected of them, and they must then be given the opportunity and encouragement to *practice* such behaviors. Again, we would not expect a person to learn how to ride a bicycle only by watching; eventually, he must get on the bicycle and try for himself. Likewise, we must not be satisfied with the student's merely observing participatory behavior in the classroom. He must be encouraged to imitate such behavior on bis own before the truest learning takes place.

Reinforcement

The third strategy involves the principle of positive reinforcement. After we have allowed students to see the behaviors expected of them and given them the opportunity, at least temporarily, to exhibit these behaviors, we must attempt to increase the probability that these responses will occur again. This involved the principle of reinforcement. After the student exhibits the desired behavior, we must offer concrete rewards in order to insure permanent change. On the elementary level, these rewards most often take the form of green and gold stars, as well as candies, cakes, and cookies. The secondary level rewards range from grades, honors, and certificates to letter jackets. The nature of the reward seems of secondary importance. It is the recognition that students find most satisfying. Recognition is a reward that each teacher possesses in abundance; yet, how seldom do we choose to give it. Again, students learn best under conditions of praise and encouragement. A reward that says I like you and I like what you do is a reward that changes behavior even at the college level. If teachers would dare to move in this direction, they would soon become more than just teachers. Instructors may even make friends of students, and understand those they teach.

By using reinforcements, students will find new behaviors satisfying and teachers may finally begin to see change. Allow students to *see, do,* and *do* again. These sound learning principles are of proven worth when used by skilled hands. Leaders in the instructional program must provide professional development in these learning domains to encourage professors to utilize them daily in the classroom.

HUMANIZING INSTRUCTION

One of the objections raised by instructors to the use of a systems approach to instruction is that it is too mechanistic. Like a product on an assembly line, the student advances from station to station or from tape to tape, being removed as necessary for "recycling" or "repair" or occasionally being cast on the "seconds shelf" because he doesn't meet the standards of quality control.

One flagrant misunderstanding regarding the use and intent of objectives is the notion that students must become dehumanized by their encounter with objectives. Such a notion is of course untrue. How can we insure that humans will prevail in a system approach to instruction? One way to humanize the system is to make it responsive to the needs of the individual student. Any system that can be modified to adjust to the varying needs of individuals is a responsive or humanistic system. Any instructor who is willing to make the adjustments of modifications in the system is a "human" instructor, one who is sensitive to the needs of other humans and willing to respond humanistically to those needs. A system that insists that all students do all things at the same time is not a humanistic system; neither is the instructor behaving in a sensitive manner if he insists that all students progress in lockstep. Suppose an instructor wishes to humanize his system. How can he make the necessary modifications?

First, instead of proceeding with his instruction a priori, he can engage in a needs assessment procedure with his students. Needs can be assessed through such devices as surveys, tests, conferences, or small group discussions. Using the results of the needs assessment, the instructor then can make recommendations to his students for progressing through the system of instruction. Conferences among students on specific concepts should be built into the instructional process. Conferences with instructors on a personal basis also should be constructed in the educational format.

A second way to humanize instruction is to provide different objectives for different students. This strategy is commonly called *branching*. Using the results of the needs assessment process, the instructor and student can work out objectives suitable for the individual student. One student may need instruction to achieve entry-level requirements of the course, while another student might be able to challenge the first three units. It would be inhuman to ignore either student need.

An instructor who chooses to follow these procedures will likely find himself in the role of a manager of learning rather than that of a lecturer. Several kinds of management decisions must be made. For instance, a student's aspirations (his goals, both long- and short-range) will influence the setting of his individual objectives. Other management options which provide for personalized instruction with students are as follows.

1. *Achievement management.* How well a student achieves and masters content at a given level will determine his next step in the instructional process.

2. *Prescriptive management.* From tests, a student and instructor can decide the most effective and efficient way for the student to proceed with his learning—what it will require for the student to progress from point *A* to point *B*.

3. *Motivation management.* Rewards built into the system will motivate the student to remain involved in the learning process. The building of a positive self-concept is important to the entire learning encounter.

4. *Enrichment management.* Provision for in-depth study will allow a student to apply what be has learned to specific real world situations.

5. *Maintenance management.* Building into the system opportunity for review and/or use of skills learned will contribute to the learner's ability to maintain his skills at a useful level.

All these types of learning management encourage constant and frequent assessment and reassessment of the learner's goals and achievements.[15] Both teacher and student are involved each step of the way.

A third way to humanize instruction is to give attention to *how* a student learns as well as to *what* a student learns. If the system provides only for learning in isolated situations through the use of programs and autotutorial devices, there is little opportunity for human interaction. The instructor should provide frequent opportunities for students to work together in pairs or in small groups. Peer tutoring is another excellent procedure for bringing about learning under humanistic conditions. According to various studies, the majority of learning occurs directly or indirectly because of the peer group.

The instructor who creates an atmosphere of warmth and interest toward his students brings a humanizing influence to bear on a classroom even if the students are working individually. Whether or not a procedure for instruction is "human" largely depends upon the instructor who is implementing the procedure. A series of lectures can be cold and indifferent, or they can be warm and responsive. Likewise, a systems approach can be warm and responsive or it can be cold and indifferent. The option rests with the instructor.

Administrators have the responsibility to make faculty members aware of humanization of instruction in the classroom. It should not be assumed that this important process will occur automatically with teachers. Preservice education in colleges is not adequate. Inservice is a must.

New Services for New Students in Higher Education: An Administrative Challenge

ROBERT W. HOTES

The United States has entered a period of "educational inflation" in which the traditional value of a college education is being called into serious question. Because in most societies access to certain kinds of education has traditionally been associated with access to the power structure of society, the selection of those who will have access to the kinds of educational experiences which lead to an advanced level of social and economic preferment has often been an occasion for rivalry and contention. In contemporary America, perceptions of the nature and values to the individual of the liberal arts college education seem to be in the process of modification and change, although there is little evidence at the present time that the majority of Americans have ceased to look upon the college degree as something to be greatly desired.

The present concern regarding the nature and value of post-secondary education and the kinds of things that such an education can and should do for those who experience it happens at a time in which the services and benefits of post-secondary education are being extended to large numbers of nontraditional students. These students are nontraditional in the sense that they come from racial, social, ethnic, and other minority groups that have not previously provided large numbers of consumers for the services of higher education. Unfortunately, many individuals who previously have not had access to the benefits of post-secondary education are being granted opportunities to experience those benefits at a time when the system for providing such benefits is being called into question.

Comprehensive community colleges have been identified as institutions offering a wide variety of services seemingly appropriate to the needs of nontraditional or "new" students to higher education, but many public and private colleges and universities also are making innovative strides in this area. The assumption is that student development services are integrally related to the total personality of the student and closely connected to the kinds of instructional services provided. This chapter will review and synthesize some appropriate selections from literature dealing with student development and student services and utilize the resulting synthesis as a basis for the development of directions for providing development services to nontraditional students.

THE NEW STUDENTS

The acceptance and implementation of open door admissions policies by public colleges and universities in recent decades has been a major factor in changing the composition of the student bodies at American college campuses. Although policies adopted by both public and private four-year colleges and universities have played important roles in changing the profile of the "typical" American college student, K. Patricia Cross sees the difference between students at two-year public community colleges and students at universities as roughly comparable to the distinction between "new" students to higher education and "traditional" college students. According to Cross, a prime determinant in the classification of new students is high school academic performance. Only 37 percent of the two-year college students had high school grade averages of B or better in 1971, while the percentage of students with B or better high school grade averages in four-year colleges was 69 percent.[16]

Other factors important to the identification of new or nontraditional students are membership in minority groups, previous military service, physical handicaps, and sex. In the case of students who are enrolled in college while sentenced to penal institutions, restriction of freedom is a factor which might be added to the list of characteristics of new students.

In addition, new or nontraditional students are very often older than twenty-four, are typically married or divorced, may have children, and are very often employed. They also frequently commute to classes. New students have not only had less success in high school academic performance than traditional or typical students; they are also less likely to predict success for themselves in meeting the academic challenge of the post-secondary situation.

A survey of college freshmen conducted by the American Council of Education revealed that a larger proportion of the university students surveyed reported that they felt they could perform with success twenty-five of the thirty academically related activities listed on the instrument. In other words, students who had done well academically in high school were confident that they could also perform well academically in college. On the other hand, on questions dealing with nonacademic activities, such as the ability to mix martinis, typing skill, and the ability to do a certain number of push-ups, greater proportions of the two-year college students rated their potential high.

It seems clear that self-images of students who attend two-year colleges and those who attend four-year colleges and universities may be substantially different, and that "going to college" may have substantially different implications for students who attend the two-year schools. Because of perceptions of certain individuals of relatively lower prestige attached to enrollment at a community college, as well as the influence of a poor scholastic record in high school, nontraditional students may tend to look outside the college environment for activities in which they may have opportunities to excel or achieve at satisfactory performance and acceptance by a peer group.

Nontraditional Students

Nontraditional students may have reasons for attending college that differ significantly from those of most students at four-year colleges or universities. The values that they bring with them into the college setting also may bear little resemblance to those of their contemporaries enrolled at four-year colleges. Differences in social and family environment and levels of parental expectations may account for many of these differences. Because of the code of behavior dominant in a low-income neighborhood, for example, a college student from that neighborhood may have difficulty in conforming to the customary standards of performance and behavior expected on most college campuses. Lying and cheating may be perceived as arts rather than vices in many low-income communities, and students from low-income groups may see such behavior as a way to survive in a new and hostile college environment.

The fact that new students often commute to college may also influence their attitudes toward the college experience. The necessity for commuting will often influence scholastic performance as well, since commuting restricts the time available for use of learning resources on campus. Students who live at home are under a different set of social pressures than those who live on campus, and it is more difficult for them to change patterns of behavior which may be detrimental to academic performance at college.

Students attending community colleges and urban four-year colleges may often experience difficulty in establishing identities as college students and in making clear distinctions between past experiences, which may have been negative and threatening, and the present opportunities at the college. Commuting students may have difficulty in establishing social acquaintances or relating to established groups on the college campus.

Central problems are student boredom, indifference to ideas, and the irrelevance to their education of their associations and relationships with other students. These attitudes and feelings are attributable in part, at least, to the fact that many students from culturally poor backgrounds and with narrow vocational interests enter college as a step toward qualifying for jobs that call for a college diploma. But they do so without enthusiasm, curiosity, or involvement with ideas or learning.[17]

Traditionally, certain personality changes described by the term *maturation* have been expected to take place as a result of a student's experience with college. Attendance at college for young adults has been thought to provide the basis for an opportunity to metamorphose into cultured, mature persons. One means for bringing about this complex of changes has been identified as the opportunity for interpersonal contact among diverse individuals with similar goals. Opportunity for interaction among individuals with occasions for the discovery of mutual congeniality in various settings, academic and residential as well as recreational, are essential to the production of personal change.

Nonresident Students

Nonresidential colleges and universities can often provide little opportunity for interpersonal contact in a form suitable to the needs of commuting students. Students at these colleges are under the time pressure of travel from home to campus and often remain home oriented, particularly if they are mature adults with family responsibilities. They are often job oriented, but seldom have an opportunity to be college or campus oriented. Extracurricular and social activities sponsored by the college are not usually designed to serve the needs of full-time homemakers who happen to be part-time college students, or handicapped students who may depend on special transportation to and from campus.

Studies reported by Arthur Chickering indicate that students who attend college while living at home with their parents fall short of the kinds of learning and the levels of personal development typically expected by the colleges they attend, and which might reasonably be expected when their social backgrounds are taken into account.[18] Students who live in college dormitories exceed the learning and personal development levels that are predicted when their advantages in ability, in prior educational background and community and family backgrounds, are taken into account.

In comparison with students who live in college dormitories, students who live at home are typically less fully involved with academic, extracurricular, and social activities related to their college life. According to Chickering, the degree aspirations of commuting students diminish over a period of time, and they become less committed to a variety of long-range goals than their resident peers. Such students report a shrinking estimate of competence, and their estimates of their own abilities and personal characteristics tend to decrease. Significantly, their satisfaction with college decreases over a period of time, and they become less likely to return to college and to complete a degree. Ben Barger highlights disadvantages of nonresident students by describing how residence halls may be seen as components of a comprehensive model for educational and personal student development activities. He suggests that residence halls can be seen in an educational model as living laboratories (or laboratories for living) in which students can be helped to use their own needs and problems to develop an understanding of group process, social organization, communication, and leadership.[19]

L. Steven Zwerling suggests that some community colleges actually reinforce a predisposition to failure. In his opinion, the very fact of attending a community college rather than a four-year institution thwarts a student's academic chances, since many community colleges operate under the assumption that a large number of the students who enter college through the "open door" will inevitably fail to measure up to the standards set by the institution.[20]

As an example of what appears to be a concentrated and coordinated effort at the state level to practice social engineering through manipulation of access to higher education, Zwerling describes the California Master Plan for education. In Zwerling's interpretation, the plan makes recommendations on how to maintain and even further stratify the state's tripartite higher education system through "diversion" of students from the state's four-year colleges and universities to its public junior/community colleges. Paradoxically, the plan recommends diverting to community colleges those who are most in need of educational opportunities that will reinforce self-esteem. Yet the state provides less money per unit for education at the community college level than at the senior college or university level, since students diverted to the community colleges are thought to have less chance for success than higher-achieving peers. Accordingly, Zwerling makes the assertion that while the more selective colleges and universities are committed to the success of their students, the least selective—especially the community/junior colleges—are committed to the failure of their students.[21]

SOCIAL ADVANTAGE AND NEW STUDENTS

The low status of the college student who commutes as compared with the prestige of students at private and public four-year residential institutions may have an effect on his or her actual level of achievement, and the lack of opportunities for contact with a success oriented peer group may also place the student at a significant disadvantage. If the general equation made by Cross and others of the new student to higher education with the community college student is correct, then expectations on the part of nontraditional or new students that going to college will be a means of social advancement may not be fulfilled. Attendance at a community college may be for some simply a matter of marching in place.[22]

Many new students may be forced into attending college by societal pressures, since going to college has become the rule rather than the exception for high school graduates. But what do new students expect to gain from college? Apparently, they are not often interested in what might be called the "college experience." This may be particularly true of adult students—those beyond the generally accepted age for college attendance. On the other hand, many adult students may enroll precisely because they feel that they may have missed an opportunity for such an experience. They may wish to have an opportunity to find out what they have been missing.

Adult students may be influenced by various levels of social expectation, although they are most frequently characterized as being work oriented. A woman may feel that a college degree may have an influence on her acceptance by the wives of her husband's business associates. Or she may feel that college will provide her with the intellectually and socially liberating experiences necessary for her to play an appropriate role in business or public service. Husbands of professional and businesswomen may feel that a degree is necessary for self-esteem and acceptance as an equal partner in marriage.

Within the student body itself, social pressures have implications for the quality and purpose of student life and development and for the student's perception of his or her role and potentials as a college student.

Role and Skills Expectations

In general, the new student in higher education is interested in courses and skills that will enhance his or her life, lead to an upgrading of occupational status and salary level, or in programs tailored to a particular avocational need or desire. Because community/junior colleges are often comprehensive in their offerings, including occupational curricula as well as college or university parallel programs in their planning, they are attractive to many new students. There is, however, a large and identifiable, if not exceptionally profitable, market among adult learners for courses of the avocational or personal enrichment variety. And although some adult students may not express a strong interest in earning college credits applicable toward a degree, many desire to have some record of attendance at college.

To meet this need for credentials, colleges and universities have developed surrogate credit accounting systems for certifying attendance (and, presumably, learning) in non-college credit courses such as gardening, cake decoration, and belly dancing. The American college or university is vested with a credentialing role. The extension of this service or function to learning outside of a planned degree program seems to be a logical development, although as yet a qualified success.

Continuing Education

In order to meet the need for certification of non-college credit learning or college "enrichment" experience, institutions have developed accounting systems utilizing continuing education units (CEUs). The CEU concept is related both to an attempt to serve individual student needs through non-college credit experiences and to the pattern of academic administration of the institution. On the one hand, the CEU record is designed to provide the individual student with a personal measure of progress reported as a collection of CEUs in various noncredit course activities. On the other hand, the CEUs are a visible record, prepared and stored by the college and therefore invested with a degree of prestige, which may be presented to employers and others as documentation of educational experiences. Like any other credential, the record of CEUs may have whatever significance that is deemed appropriate by the student and those to whom it is presented as an indication of achievement.

While CEUs are an approach to meeting needs for documentation of non-college credit learning, the development and use of such a system points out some of the difficulties in relating the entire credentialing function of the college to the needs of nontraditional students. The face value of the college credit hour, like that of the CEU, is determined by the value it holds in the mind of the individual who earns it and the agreement that others in the society have as to its acceptability as a measure of performance or achievement. The new student may experience considerable frustration in his expectations for the value of the college credential in a period in which large numbers of highly credentialed individuals are unable to find employment at a level that matches their expectations.

Skills, Markets, and Opportunities

The "softness" in the market for the products of higher education may have negative implications for new students who have made significant sacrifices in time and foregone income as well to climb the academic ladder. Barton suggests that colleges should not concentrate on convincing students of the marketability of particular programs, but rather direct increased competitive efforts to improving the educational product and providing assistance in an orderly transition from college to employment. According to Barton, higher education has been party to the dividing of life into three "time traps," where only young people can learn, only adults can work, and the retired are allowed to do very little. Barton maintains that there should be a broader opportunity for development of human resources through a policy of mixing work, education, and leisure; producing "educated" individuals rather than technical specialists with occupational skills.[23]

Such theories involving assumptions concerning the ultimate goals and utility of post-secondary education are of slight use to the young people and adults who look upon the college degree as the key to a better job. Students in American colleges and universities by and large expect the credentials they earn at those institutions to have a market value, and new students in particular may find themselves ill equipped by previous experiences to handle the psychological and social competitiveness that develops among job hungry students. Often increased attempts at competition in the academic arena lead to frustration and a growing tendency to question the worth of prolonged exposure to higher education. Such frustration may be caused in part by temporary factors, particularly economic recessions, but a deep-seated and fundamental cause may be the failure of "compensatory" education to guarantee improved social and economic status.

In order for colleges to be successful credentialing agencies, they must build and maintain credibility with both clients and the prospective employers of college educated individuals. This credibility is especially critical if new students are not to be short-changed in the employment marketplace. College students, new and traditional, are both basic raw materials and the product of the education industry. Like other industries, education, despite philosophic and partriotic pretentions, has its own share of self-serving, unscrupulous, and insensitive entrepreneurs. In recent years higher education has become demythologized and recognizable as "edubusiness," involving risks on the part of consumers and entrepreneurs. New students to higher education are faced with special risks and deserve special protection and consideration.

NEW TERRITORIES FOR NEW SERVICES

The demand for access to higher education by individuals with diverse backgrounds and needs has spurred the development of external degree programs designed to tap unexplored markets for higher education. Four-year colleges and universities in particular are exploring ways of delivering educational services at locations far removed from the campus. Such programs are based on the theory that individual students who do not wish to attend classes on campus and those who are unable to do so can nevertheless have access to all of the experiences necessary for a college education.

An assumption underlying the development of external degree programs is that such factors as opportunities to participate in student organizations and association and identification with a campus community are not essential to higher education, although they may be quite useful. This assumption seems to be contradicted by evidence supplied by Chickering and others cited above.[24]

Because of the widespread belief that higher education can be used as a tool for social and economic advancement, however, there appears to be significant interest in such programs as the Nova University external doctor of education program and the Dallas County Community College District "telecourse" series. Both methods for offering off-campus academic work have proved relatively successful in addressing the needs of a select group of highly motivated adults. The idea of the external degree seems to have significant political support in several states, especially Florida and California.

External Degree Programs

Although there are obvious disadvantages to a degree program that is totally external, some experts see such programs as beneficial, not only in increasing options for individual students but also as developments which have fundamental implications for theory. Ideally, learning and personal development can be freed from dependence upon campus atmosphere and dormitory residence, allowing students in many situations and in many diverse circumstances to earn credits toward a degree. The question of whether or not the outcomes of such programs in terms of academic, personal, and social development will be judged satisfactory by students remains to be answered by longitudinal studies.

Two additional questions are also important in this context: What kinds of specialized services in addition to instruction should and can be provided for adult students in such new learning situations, and how can such services be effectively and efficiently provided to produce the maximum beneficial effect on student development?

Continuing Adult Learning

A major difficulty in providing guidance for adult students, particularly in those institutions with special staffs to provide services to adults, is the establishment of an appropriate interpersonal relationship between counselor and client. Working with adults may offer special challenges to the counselor in higher education because adults may have needs which are often quite difficult to define and to address.

Adults turn to higher education for various reasons including frustration and the need for social acceptance, or what may be characterized as a need for renewed growth. Other adults turn to higher education in order to reassess their individual value systems or to gain contact with new and contrasting value systems. Providing for guidance services that can help in identifying and meeting such needs and desires is problematic even in an on-campus situation and becomes extremely difficult when students have little or no contact with campus facilities and campus life.

In addition, an educational program for adult learners, whether conducted on campus or off campus, must generally be subordinated to a preexisting life pattern. Adults must make decisions with serious implications in order to find the time and the place for study. Education always replaces something else in the life of the adult learner. It is not simply added to the activities of a life, and the effects of that replacement must be considered both when the educational activity is planned and throughout its duration. Problems can be anticipated not only with regard to the scheduling of learning activities, but especially in connection with providing opportunities for nonclassroom learning experiences and guidance services.[25]

If external degree programs are to become more important and acceptable alternatives within the framework of American higher education, the off-campus delivery of counseling and human development services as well as the provision of instructional services will have to be carefully planned. When applied to the particular needs of new or nontraditional students, especially to the needs of those students who earn college credits through televised instruction or other forms of external instructional delivery, many traditional student services seem inadequate. How appropriate, for example, is the extension of the opportunity to participate in campus student government or intramural atheletics as a tool for the human development of men and women who enroll in college courses via television? On the other hand, many such students may be faced with problems that may be addressed through traditional student services delivered in nontraditional forms. Services which fall into this category include admissions, the record-keeping function, and career planning. A prime consideration in arranging for the delivery of these services to off-campus students is provision for adequate contact between college personnel and the clients whom they serve.

Off-Campus Delivery of Services

One direction which might be further explored in planning to meet the challenge of off-campus delivery of services involves the perception of higher educational services as community based activities. Max Raines has suggested that community based college services may be thought of as "outdoor student personnel work." According to Raines, traditionally accepted community services and student personnel work share important commonalities. They share a concern for human development; they seek to adapt activities to the needs and interests of the clientele; they both acknowledge the importance of the whole person, and recognize the importance of creative environments that are conducive to individual and group development.[26]

In Raines's view, differences between community services and student personnel services are more operational than conceptual. Student personnel programs traditionally focus on campus life and a relatively homogeneous student target group, while community service programs focus on community life and a diverse clientele. For community based colleges and universities, however, the boundaries between these two service populations have become blurred. The campus of a comprehensive community college, for example, is identifiably part of the community the college serves and, in a real sense, the community is the college campus.

As Benjamin Wygal has noted, the financing of such community based educational activities poses serious financial problems for many colleges, due in part to the fact that the public and legislators do not at present clearly identify a number of these services—community based counseling, for example—as part of the college mission. And, as presently identified, community based, performance oriented education often seems to be too narrowly identified, to the point of being synonymous in the minds of many with off-campus activities centering on avocational pursuits, recreation, citizenship, and community services. According to Wygal, in its truest sense community based education is basically the institution joining hands with the community to define and serve community needs.[27]

Such a joining of college and community may pose administrative as well as financial problems. It may, however, offer the best opportunity available under present circumstances to extend the influence of the college to new students throughout the total campus of the community college—the community itself.

As a leader in the college or university and in the community as a whole, the administrator is expected to take positive steps in serving the needs of a wide variety of students. The leader in higher education may be called upon to make the first, innovative efforts within the community served by the institution to meet the needs of nontraditional students. A particular challenge to the abilities of administrators in the coming decades will be the presence of thousands of international students on American campuses. Meeting the needs of these students while preserving the relationship of the college or university to the community may become one of the major factors in providing services to nontraditional students in the years to come.

Accountability in Education: An Inevitable Step

BOB W. MILLER

The systems approach to education based on behavioral objectives, Management by Objectives, and long-range planning has aroused much opposition within the education profession. The term *accountability* evokes shudders of fear within the hearts of many educators. The very thought of having to prove convincingly that an individual is doing what he professes to be doing in measurable terms is inconceivable to a majority of today's educators. Although most individuals in the education profession would agree that a salesperson should be rewarded for performance and that an assembly line worker should be evaluated on the basis of productivity, these same individuals back off when it is suggested that the output of one engaged in producing the intangible service of learning should be rated and compensated on the basis of output. Not only does such a practice appear to be impossible, but it also smacks of dehumanization.

In this day of rapidly rising costs due to inflationary pressures, the education industry finds itself in a position of having to call upon the reluctant public that supports it for more and more financial resources. Education, like individuals, businesses, and industries, must operate on a relatively fixed income that does not inflate with the rest of the economy, thus finding it difficult to maintain the same level of performance, much less make improvements. Current conditions dictate that education must accomplish more results with less resources than in the past.

THE PROBLEM EXAMINED

To analyze the problem the education industry faces, the basics of inflation first must be examined. Economists look upon inflation as a condition in which the supply of money in the economy exceeds the supply of goods and services. Therefore, the consuming public attempts to outbid each other for the available goods, forcing prices upward. The problem is made worse when the productive factors in the economy receive increased payments in excess of increases in their output. For example, if a factory worker, a productive factor, receives a wage increase in excess of increases he has achieved in producing goods, more is added to the money supply than to the supply of goods and services.

Factors Involved

In examining the multiple factors contributing to the inflationary pressures our economy has faced in the past decade, one factor stands out. For industries engaged in the production of tangible goods such as manufacturing and construction, increases in output or productivity have generally exceeded increases in payments such as wages. However, *in the service industries, of which education is one of the largest, increases in productivity have been low while increases in payments have been exceedingly high.* In other words, much of our current inflation can be attributed to a lack of increased productivity in the service sector of the economy. Within this specific perspective members of the education profession have little justification for cost-of-living increases, much less anything more.

Add to the above economic condition the fact that in general the public upon whom the education industry depends for financial support is losing its confidence in the capabilities of the educational system, and you see the industry facing a compounded problem. This lack of confidence is demonstrated in complaints and attitudes expressed in various ways and even more dramatically in the negative response across the nation given bond and tax proposals in recent years. The only meaning that can be derived from these conditions is that the education profession suddenly finds itself in a position of having to prove not only that it is doing what it claims to be doing, but that it is continually doing it better.

SYSTEMS APPROACH TO EDUCATION

It is in answer to this need that the systems approach to education and the accountability it involves enters the picture. Educators are faced with increasing productivity and verifying those increases in measurable terms. These increases in productivity must be accountable in three areas: personal, professional, and public. The systems approach, therefore, places responsibility for increased productivity on the individual educator in the classroom, on the professional as a whole, and on the general public which both supports the industry and benefits from its services.

Measurability Model

An individual instructor who claims to teach must be capable of proving it. Such an achievement can be accomplished through the "measurability model" incorporated within the systems approach. This model establishes specific performance objectives which the educator expects his learners to learn, accomplish, and demonstrate. Once these objectives have been identified, defined, and selected, the necessary learning activities needed to accomplish these objectives must be chosen. Measurement criteria must be determined to account for the achievement desired.

Once the model is developed, the learners involved must be subjected to a pre-test on the performance objectives. The results of the pre-test not only determine the status of the student but also indicate the learning activities needed to accomplish the objectives. Upon completion of the prescribed activities, a post-test is administered and the degree to which the objectives have been accomplished can be measured. Through means of recycling and reevaluation, learning can be practically guaranteed.

A measurability model applied to the classroom not only measures the achievement of the learners involved but also can be a valid measurement for improving the educator's ability and productivity. By subjecting the model and its results to constant evaluation, better methods and strategies can be employed which will increase the educator's effectiveness in measurable terms. Improvement can be shown through teaching more in less time. A major contributing factor to increased productivity in any industry is the elimination of waste, especially wasted time.

Productivity in education in the past was based upon the assumption that the more education and experience an instructor had, the more productive he became. An examination of the structure of salary schedules in the education profession easily shows this assumption to be a common practice. The systems approach to education and its accountability can verify the accuracy of this assumption and also establish a means by which increased productivity can be measured in more accurate terms.

Management Systems

The systems approach does not limit itself to the classroom in the educational industry any more than it limits itself to the assembly line in the manufacturing industry. Professional accountability requires that members of the education profession in administrative and supportive service activities also must prove their value. A measurability model based on behavioral objectives, Management by Objectives, and a long-range planning system provides the criteria for evaluating the contribution made to the total educational process necessary to determine the productivity that occurs within this area. It requires this segment of education to identify their contribution by establishing what they are achieving in terms of performance objectives. Through predetermined evaluative processes the degree to which they succeed can be measured.

Once the education profession becomes capable of proving its ability in measured results, the accountability then shifts to the general public. At that time the industry can justify bond issues and tax increases to increase the level of educational performance to that desired by the public. When educational output can be measured and related to dollar costs, then the only limits placed upon its capabilities will be the standards established by society. The accountability responsibility then rests with society, since educators will be capable of providing any level and quality of education that the public deem satisfactory and is willing to support.

The threat of accountability procedures should not generate fear within the heart of the professional educator. Rather, it should offer a welcome opportunity to prove what is being accomplished to the general public, the profession, and the educator himself. At that time the education industry will be justified in calling for increased support for the most vital and essential production within a free society.

The question which will be asked of most educators in the future will be: What do you do? Answer: I teach; or, I am an educational administrator. The next comment from some public citizen will be, Prove it.

We predict that classroom instructors will be required, through a measurability model, to demonstrate in writing that they have accomplished a specific amount of results (for example, 90 percent results for 90 percent of students) in each college section that they manage or teach. The responsibility for accomplishing this goal should belong to service and administrative personnel as well as instructors. The team effort of media, library, printing, and administrative support will be necessary to achieve accountability factors.

Quality control is as important in the educational setting as it is for the production of materials and products by business and industry. We can no longer afford hit-and-miss tactics in education. The systems approach assists in preventing gaps or omissions and repetitions in the curriculum. It also assures that the student must master a subject area before going on to the next unit of learning.

In the past the student has been held accountable for what he or she learned or did not learn. The student will continue to be held accountable in the future, but the time has arrived when the faculty member and administrator also will be held responsible for learning under prescribed conditions.

Professional Development: The Missing Ingredient in Improving Instruction

BOB W. MILLER AND NAOMI WARREN

Have you ever seen a cake that looked mouth watering and tasty, but upon taking a bite realized that salt had been omitted? Or, have you worked a 1,000-piece puzzle in anticipation of the breathtaking picture that would result, but found only 999 pieces? Or better yet, have you tried to drive a car with only three tires in place? You're probably thinking, "Now that's silly; everyone knows it is better to 'get it together' before attempting to bake a cake, work a puzzle, or drive a car!" And you are right. Yet how many times have you seen teachers and administrators attempting to run a well-organized educational program without an equally well-organized professional development program?

WHY PROFESSIONAL DEVELOPMENT FOR FACULTY?

What is the primary objective of the teacher? To teach or manage students. Therefore, any teacher with the appropriate degrees and teaching certificates has adequate knowledge to achieve this goal. Wrong! How can that be wrong? Before attempting an explanation, answer the following questions. Have any new teaching methods and/or ideas been introduced to you since you received your last degree? Has any social change occurred in that same period of time? If you answered yes, then you realize that degrees do not provide the final answer. There is no way that preservice education can teach all an instructor needs to know for the remainder of his professional teaching career. It is only the first step toward reaching the goal of master teaching. The second, third, and fourth steps are professional development. If you answered no, then you might need to consider professional development as a means of adjusting to the changing world in which we live. Remember that effective professional development is a must. Professional development occurs because the administrator makes it occur on an effective and efficient basis by means of thorough planning and coordination.

Considering the importance placed on knowledge and training in the educational system, educators for too long have been content to take a back seat in the areas of professional and staff development. As a result, those who should be leading the way are content merely to amble along hoping for the best. What has caused this lackadaisical attitude toward professional development? The culprit may be poor planning and lack of coordination between organizational objectives and individual goals and interests. Any program without well-developed plans and stated goals and objectives is doomed to failure. It generally breeds boring sessions and irrelevant activities, which in turn lead to an attitude of "Oh, brother!" whenever the next activity is announced.

Before professional development can take its proper role in the educational system, three changes must take place: attitude changes on the parts of both administrators and teachers; process changes in the way professional development is planned and conducted; and structure changes as to where professional development fits in the total picture. Development must be seen as a part of the educational system's total operation, not as an isolated activity. It must become a routine aspect of professional life.

A PHILOSOPHY OF PROFESSIONAL DEVELOPMENT

Any professional development or inservice education program must be based upon institutional goals if it is to be effective. The planning process should include professional administrators, faculty, and other staff members representing all aspects of the organization. Short- and long-range objectives should be constructed. An example follows for a new college or district.

	Themes
1st year	Philosophy on operation of the new district or college
2nd year	Campus operations (vice presidents', deans' and president's areas)
3rd year	Various division or department operations
4th year	Individual subject areas operation
5th year	Individual instructors

The above-mentioned items are long-range planning themes for each of five years. These long-range goals do not preclude inservice or professional development for each teacher, administrator, department, or college on a yearly basis or on a personalized basis.

Professional development plans must be based upon the needs of individuals within the organization. Assessments should be made as to what each professional feels will make him a more effective and efficient instructor or administrator. Once the assessment is made, the information should be utilized, not just put aside or placed in a file.

After a campus, institution, or department makes a decision about topics or subjects to be presented, a further decision should be made as to who the consultant will be; who can effectively implement the objectives to be taught to the professional staff. Once the best person has been selected, the objectives (preferably behavioral) should be presented to him or her both orally and in writing, to assure that he or she speaks to the issues that were presented by the group. Other decisions which need to be made are as follows.

1. Where will the session be held—in a large school auditorium; in small group sessions in a classroom; off campus, where interruptions will not occur; or should the sessions be individualized in a learning laboratory?

2. Who will attend—administrators, faculty, or both; all departments or selected departments; new faculty members or experienced faculty? (Experienced faculty often are given unnecessary repeat sessions.) Many types of inservice activities are effective for one type of professional and ineffective for others.

3. What support services are necessary for the professional development sessions? If you are writing and producing educational packages, for example, you may wish media and print support.

4. Who will coordinate the sessions?

5. Who will make up evaluation forms and conduct the evaluation?

There are decisions to be made depending on the type of workshop, consultant, location, and so forth. It is important to be sure that the inservice flows smoothly from beginning to end. Each area or item must be planned and coordinated in detail.

Do administrators need professional development? Yes. If they are to lead professional teachers, counselors, and other staff members, they must be out in front of their subordinates. Often administrators wonder why boards or trustees do not promote them to chief administrative positions. Two major reasons generally are involved: hiring practices, such as not employing the most competent person initially; and administrators who have not received appropriate professional development.

If a leader expects his faculty to participate in professional development, he or she should be involved in their specific inservice if at all possible. In addition, he should stay ahead of his subordinates in such areas as planning, evaluation, directing, controlling, leadership, and so forth. He may acquire these skills through university courses, workshops, reading, conferences, lectures, visitation to other institutions, or a combination of several activities.

WHAT IS PROFESSIONAL DEVELOPMENT?

What then *is* professional development? It is a program—formal or informal—that provides the learner with the tools necessary to conceptualize, experience, and reach insights that alter his perception of his role and task. It is continual development, training, or growth to avoid stagnation. Professional development programs require long-range planning and coordination, an appropriate sequence of activities, evaluation, and support of change efforts.

Evaluation of professional development is a critical area. Without it no one knows whether goals and objectives were obtained and development becomes isolated learning rather than a planned developmental sequence. With the proper utilization of evaluation techniques, steps can be taken to correct defects and/or make adjustments in the program and at the same time determine if the next level of development can be attempted.

AREAS OF PROFESSIONAL DEVELOPMENT

When planning professional development activities, the program developer must remember that in order for development to take place the individual must see a need for it, and must desire to be developed. With this in mind, let us look briefly at three crucial areas of development for the teacher and the administrator: technical, conceptual, and human relations skills.

Technical skill by definition is the functioning area capabilities of an individual. Those needed by the educator relate to both subject knowledge and teaching expertise. With the barrage of knowledge confronting the teacher, is it any wonder that continual development is needed in this area? Is it surprising to find that the administrator must upgrade and refine his leadership abilities and receive training in how to make professional and staff development work for him and his staff?

An educator is lost if he cannot function in the *conceptual* areas of planning and organizing. Consider the many ways these can affect the teacher either positively or negatively: lesson plans, course outlines, goals and objectives on a daily or semester basis, individual differences and how to plan for them, and the paper shuffling that must be handled. It almost goes without saying that the leader must be an authority in the field of planning and organization if he is to operate as effectively as possible. Who, then, could object to development which makes the job easier to perform?

The third skill, *human relations,* is probably the most important to the instructor and the administrator. Think of the persons with whom the educator deals: students, teachers, administrators, parents, and the general public. Although development in this area is most beneficial, it is one of the most neglected areas of training. More attention must be given to the attitudes, values, and beliefs that influence the individual's behavior and relationships with others if teachers and administrators are to operate at their fullest potential.

All training and development can be slotted into one of the three areas mentioned, but it is important to remember that all individuals do not require the same level of training at the same time. By not following this principle, those who implement a developmental program are planning for failure before they even begin.

Professional development should be considered a vital part of an educational institution. To be effective, it must be well-planned, well-organized, and individualized. The areas of technical, conceptual, and human relations skills cover the significant aspects of training that must consistently and continually be upgraded. As programs are implemented based upon individual goals and objectives compatible with those of the educational organization, professional development will take its proper place in the educational system.

Quality Control in Packaging Instructional Materials: An Administrative Concern and Commitment

RUTH WATKINS AND BOB W. MILLER

An administrator who accepts the challenge of heading the production of packaging self-instructional materials will be greatly helped if he or she is aware of all aspects of packaging, from inception to the completed product. Each part of an instructional package performs an important function and cannot be eliminated from use without in some way impairing the thoroughness of the overall plan.

WHAT IS AN INSTRUCTIONAL PACKAGE?

Throughout this section, the following definition of an instructional package will be used: The organization of devices and other materials which presents a complete body of information and is largely self-supporting rather than supplementary in the teaching-learning process.

Various approaches to packaging have been validated for use in different situations. Certainly, instructional packages can be effective without the use of media equipment and software. This section deals specifically with those packages that utilize various pieces of media equipment and software for the students' acquisition of knowledge. No matter what format is selected to communicate this knowledge to the students, the basic design process for the development of the package and its components remain the same.

Components of the Instructional Package

There are three components in every effective instructional package: (1) *objectives,* which precisely express how the student will perform after using the material, (2) *learning activities,* which name the devices, instructional materials, and/or direct experiences that will be needed to achieve the desired behavior as stated in the objectives, and (3) *evaluative procedures* indicating how the student must demonstrate his comprehension of the information presented. This third component also includes modifications that must be made by the content specialist and learning resource staff to make the package more effective and efficient.

These three basic components can be exemplified in a self-instructional package developed for a physical science course. It is a four-hour source arranged so that the entire class can meet every Monday for a lecture period, while the students arrange for their own lab periods. Then the instructor meets with small groups for discussion on Fridays. The self-instructional package is used by the student during the lab period. The student is given a study guide or written package which includes a statement of information to be studied and the reason for its importance. Following this, the instructional or behavioral objectives are stated, so that the student is fully aware of what he or she is expected to know or be able to do after completing the lab unit. The format utilized to present this body of information, in this case, is a slide-tape presentation. As the student works through the package, the tape requires him to stop the presentation from time to time and respond to questions and statements in the report form. During the dialogue of information, the student may also be asked to stop and conduct an experiment and record his results.

After completion of the report form, the student may elect to repeat the package. The lab instructor also is available for consultation. A written exam is taken by the student to evaluate his or her acquisition of this information. Recycling may take place if necessary. Further evaluation of the student's understanding of the information is conducted during small group discussions and individual conferences with the instructor. Throughout the units, discussion of objectives with the peer group is important. It is also necessary to plan individual conferences with instructors on various concepts. According to studies, the humanization of instruction is most important. Students must not be left to learn with only a package or a teaching machine. This approach to packaging instructional materials has been validated as an efficient and effective instructional strategy.

Development of the Instructional Package

A systematic approach is essential to the development and production of instructional packages to insure that each unit has all the features necessary to produce maximum results. Developmental steps include giving the rationale for the unit, formulating objectives, designing evaluative measures, specifying learning activities, constructing a prototype, field-testing the prototype, revision, and implementation. All these steps are important to insure "quality control" in the learning process.

In determining the rationale for studying the information, the student should be informed of why it is important that he master the material in the instructional package. Many instructors fail to realize that extrinsic motivation leads to intrinsic motivation with students.

Perhaps the most difficult stage in development is that of determining the specific objectives to be reached. Toward this end, the instructor needs a complete specification of what it is that the student should be able to do after the instruction occurs. Once a set of instructional objectives has been selected, procedures must be developed to gather evidence or produce criteria to determine whether or not the objectives have been achieved.

After the required competencies are clearly defined, the next task is to design appropriate learning activities through which these competencies can be achieved. The activities should be as varied as possible. In some situations "branching," or alternative learning activities, techniques utilize software at different levels of difficulty. Instructors, being the most sensitive determiners of their own needs in instructional communications, may only need to present a single concept within the context of the course in a packaged format.

Packaging Self-Instructional Materials

Packaging self-instructional materials is a monumental task requiring large amounts of time, energy, ideas, and resources. In the earliest stages, in addition to the task of content development, other aspects should be considered simultaneously rather than sequentially. For example, media hardware selection may generally consist of more or less standard equipment. However, exploration of the unique capabilities of various presentation formats is advantageous in determining the appropriate selection. To accomplish specific learning objectives, assistance should be sought in this area from learning resource staff members. Facilities for storage and the packaged materials' accessibility to students also must be considered. If other than commercially prepared software is to be used, production capabilities and the time required for production must be considered. After such considerations have been explored and decisions made, the designing and construction of the prototype begins.

The production procedure for the software is dictated by the format selected to present this unit. Storyboarding or script writing is the initial step in production. This is done by writing and analyzing each unit of the prepared script, identifying essential visuals needed to highlight the key points, and providing for examples to emphasize key concepts. It is also used to clarify and enrich the discussion. It may include original illustrations, locational and outside sources, or photographs from commercially produced illustrations and examples. From this visual story-board the art work is created; slides, film, filmstrips, or videotapes may then be produced.

The audio portion of the package is the major source of information. Since the narration assumes the tutorial responsibility in the absence of an instructor, a quality recording is desirable and should be done in a soundproof studio. It is important to remember that audio by itself can become very boring to the student. Quality visuals enhance the learning process.

When motion is necessary to explain or demonstrate the content of the instructional package being produced, a videotape format might be selected. This is a versatile format because several visual sources may be mixed into the program. It is possible to transfer location footage from 8 or 16 mm film or 35 mm slides.

After all necessary materials are produced and assembled, appropri-ate facilities organized, and complete course directions incorporated in a syllabus for the students, it is time to field-test the package. One pro-cedure might be to select groups of student volunteers to test the pack-age and help to determine its effectiveness and practicality. Following their completion of the prototype, each student should be interviewed extensively concerning reaction to this way of learning, difficulties which may have been encountered, and suggestions for improvement. From these interviews deficiencies are determined and any necessary revisions may be made. It should be remembered, however, that this may not be the specific "learning style" of all students. Duplicate copies are pro-duced from the prototype as needed. The development process is com-pleted and the instructional package is available for implementation.

The use of media makes possible the meeting of a much wider range of objectives than previously was possible. The mere fact that many instructional items involving several media are put together in a single package does not necessarily result in a truly integrated instructional unit. In order to qualify in this connection, the prescribed use of a coordinated instructional package must result in the mastery on the part of the learner of the information or skills, or in attitude shaping or specific educational and instructional goals.

In order to be effective and efficient, the content specialist (the in-structor) remains in control of the total learning process of each indi-vidual student. Quality control is also necessary from the learning re-source staff, the printing staff, and other support areas. Too often, poorly prepared software in the learning process turns students off. Today's student should receive nothing but the best when it comes to individualized instruction.

NOTES

1. Robert F. Mager, *Preparing Instructional Objectives* (Palo Alto, Calif.: Fearon Publishers, 1962), p. 3.

2. Stuart R. Johnson, *Developing Individualized Instructional Material* (Palo Alto, Calif.: Westinghouse Learning Press, 1970), pp. 10–16.

3. Benjamin S. Bloom, *Taxonomy of Educational Objectives: Affective Domain* (New York: David McKay, 1974), pp. 21–23.

4. Maurice Gibbons, *Individualized Instruction* (New York: Teachers College Press, 1971), p. 9.

5. James W. Popham, Elliot W. Eisner, Howard J. Sullivan, and Lousie L. Tyler, *The Influence of Objectives in Institutional Decision Making* (Chicago: Rand McNally, 1969), p. 41.

6. Ibid., p. 42.

7. Ross E. Fraub, "Importance of Problem Heterogeneity to Program Instruction," *Journal of Educational Psychology*, pp. 54–60.

8. W. James Popham, AERA Monograph Series on Curriculum Evaluation, Washington, D.C.: American Educational Research Association, 1964, p. 42.

9. George L. Gropper, "Programming Visual Presentation for Procedure Learning," *AV Communications Review*, pp. 33–56.

10. Popham, AERA Monograph Series on Curriculum Evaluation, p. 42.

11. James W. Popham, "Appropriate Practices," Behavioral Objectives Filmstrip Series, (Los Angeles: Vimset Associates, 1967).

12. Robert M. Gagne, *The Conditions of Learning* (New York: Holt, Rinehart and Winston, 1965, 1970), pp. 65–66.

13. Robert Mager, *Goal Analysis* (Belmont, Calif.: Fearon Publishing, 1972), p. 16.

14. Earnest R. Hilgard, *Theories in Learning* (Los Angeles: Meredith Publishing, 1966), p. 77.

15. Sidney R. Wilson and Donald T. Tosti, *Learning is Getting Easier; Classrooms are Becoming More Responsive to Individual Student Needs*, (San Rafael, Calif.: Individual Learning Systems, 1972), pp. 27–28.

16. K. Patricia Cross, *Beyond the Open Door* (San Francisco: Jossey-Bass, 1976), pp. 185–190.

17. Burton R. Clark and Martin Trow, "The Organizational Context" in *Peer Groups, Problems and Perspectives for Research*, eds. Theodore M. Newcomb and Everett K. Willson (Chicago: Aldine Publishing, 1966), pp. 34–36.

18. Arthur W. Chickering, "College Advising for the 1970's," *New Directions for Higher Education* 1, no. 3 (Autum 1973), pp. 69–80.

19. Ben Barger and Ann Q. Lynch, "University Housing: A Healthy Learning Laboratory," *New Directions in Higher Education* 1 (Autumn 1973), pp. 5–17.

20. L. Steven Zwerling, "Second Class Education at the Community College," *New Directions for Community Colleges* 7 (Autumn 1974), pp. 23–37.

21. Ibid.

22. Ibid.

23. Paul E. Barton, "Human Resources: The Changing Labor Market and Undergraduate Education," *Liberal Education* 61 (May 1975), pp. 275–84.

24. Chickering, "College Advising for the 1970's."

25. Ibid.

26. Max R. Raines and Gunder A. Myran, "Community Services: Goals for 1980," *Junior College Journal* 42 (April 1972), pp. 12–16.

27. Benjamin R. Wygal, "Will the Economy Crunch the Community-Based Movement?" *Junior College Journal* 46 (November 1975), pp. 12–13.

22

Protecting the Right to Learn: Selected Legal Problems Controlling the Quality of the Learning Environment

ROBERT W. HOTES

Faced with increasing pressure from the various publics of American post-secondary education, college and university administrators may in the coming decades find that both new statements of institutional policy and existing rules and regulations must meet standards of efficiency and reasonableness in relation to institutional purposes and goals.

Administrators of public colleges and universities may be presumed in many cases to act for the state in formulating policies and rules governing specified activities of those who attend or work for such institutions. It seems essential, therefore, that administrators avoid arbitrariness and exercise both caution and reason in formulating and promulgating rules and regulations affecting the lives of individuals within the academic community, or in some way related to it. As Professor Graham Hughes has noted, law and policy often depend upon similar principles and have similar effects upon those whom they are intended to govern.[1]

In an era in which the preservation of human rights has become a major focal point of concern, college and university leaders must carefully avoid adopting policies that may infringe on individuals' First Amendment rights.

DEFINITIONS

Adversary hearing—The process of allowing a person of divergent views (political, social, sectarian, religious) the freedom and privilege of speech in opposition to a popular view.

Clear and present danger—Clear and convincing proof that the speech and speaker would cause danger to the orderly functions of the institution.

Clear and present danger doctrine—A person cannot be restrained from speaking or the audience prevented from listening merely because the presence may constitute a possible danger.

Due process protection—Allowing an individual to give fair notice of conduct as required by civil statutes.

Ex parte restraining order—A restraining order which allows for a partisan presentation only.

Proactive—A proactive stance anticipates problems or difficulties rather than reacting to them.

BASIC PRINCIPLES AND CASES

According to Professor Henry P. Monagen, two basic principles can be distilled from court cases involving the protection of First Amendment rights. The first principle is that a judicial body, following an adversary hearing, must decide on the protected character of the speech for which privilege under the First Amendment is claimed. The second principle is that judicial determination must either precede or immediately follow any government action that restricts speech. In Monagen's view, these two broad principles should limit any governmental activity that affects freedom of speech, no matter how indirectly.[2] It would seem imperative that college and university leaders be cognizant of these principles as they formulate regulations dealing with off-campus or "outside" speakers.

In describing the evolution of judicial opinion regarding the exercise of "civil rights" by students, David Schimmel and Louis Fisher state that until the decision reached by the court in the *Tinker* v. *Des Moines Independent School District* case, courts generally used the "reasonableness test" in judging whether school rules were constitutional. In general, a rule would usually be upheld if a reasonable relationship between it and the goals of the school could be established, since judges felt that the courts should not substitute their judgment for that of school officials who were presumed to be experts in the field of education. In the *Tinker* case, however, the court ruled that individuals who enroll in school do not thereby forego the exercise of constitutionally protected rights.[3] In light of the *Tinker* decision and decisions in subsequent cases, it seems clear that those who administer the operations of American colleges and universities must steer a cautious policy course between the Scylla of institutional anarchy and the Charybdis of virtually endless challenges to legally indefensible regulations.

The notion that colleges and universities can and should be free marketplaces in which ideas can be examined and shared has gained wide acceptance in the United States. Maintaining an educational climate in which divergent ideas and philosophies can be studied and debated is a necessary activity for administrators of institutions whose aim is to produce "educated" citizens who can become leaders of society. Tension often arises, however, from efforts to implement the ideal of the collegiate atmosphere as a free marketplace for ideas and an arena for philosophic debate while exercising levels of authority sufficient to insure the smooth functioning of complex institutions such as colleges and universities. Individual freedoms necessary for the discovery and creation of knowledge may at times conflict with rules and regulations designed to make the teaching/learning environment possible.

In a number of colleges and universities, appearances by off-campus speakers have presented challenges to the conduct of educational functions. Although some of the social and political ferment which made college and university campuses focal points for the activities of militant groups has subsided in the last few years, the actions of off-campus speakers remain a matter of concern to administrators.

According to policies developed at many post-secondary institutions in recent years, student organizations that have obtained official recognition by the school administration are permitted to invite guest speakers to appear on campus. General practice involves the filing of an application requesting the use of campus facilities on a particular date. Because campus facilities are involved, the freedom of college students to hear particular points of view is not the only issue. Administrators may consider denying applications for permission to host off-campus speakers for various reasons related to the general welfare of the institution and the conduct of its activities, such as anticipated violence or serious disruption of classes. Courts have held, however, that if a denial is based on the political or ideological persuasion of the speaker or on the nature of the speech per se, denial of permission may constitute an abridgement of the rights of the students.

In considering the authority of universities and colleges to restrict or prohibit the assembly of students to hear particular speakers on campus, courts have applied the "clear and present danger" criterion, with the interpretation that the First Amendment guarantees free speech except where the absence of limitation on speech will create a clear and present danger that such speech will contribute to the overthrow of the government by force and violence (*Dennis* v. *U.S.*). In determining whether there is a justifiable reason for limiting speech, the court "must inquire in each case whether the grave nature of the evil, 'discounted by its improbability,' justifies such invasion of free speech as is necessary to avoid the danger."[4]

In the case of educational administrators attempting to prevent disruption of campus learning activities through restrictions on particular off-campus speakers, it is necessary that they have sufficient evidence that disruption would probably occur if the individual or individuals were allowed to speak on a stated occasion. Thus, in *Stacy* v. *Williams* the court stated that a university administrative authority may deny an invitation to a guest speaker requested by a campus group if it reasonably appears that the speaker would advocate the violent overthrow of the government of the United States, or of the state or a political subdivision of the state, willful destruction of the institution's buildings or other property, or the disruption of educational functions. A college or university administration may also deny permission for an off-campus speaker to appear if it seems reasonably probable that the speaker's actions would be a cause of physical harm, coercion, intimidation, or "other invasion of lawful rights of the institution's officials, faculty members or students," or of "some other campus disorder of a violent nature."[5]

In drafting speaker regulations, the administrator must make it clear that the advocacy prohibited is "of a kind which prepared the group addressed for imminent action, steels it to such action and gives rise to reasonable apprehension of imminent danger to essential functions and purposes of the institution, including the safety of its officials, faculty and students."[6] From the opinion of the court in *Stacy* v. *Williams* it is evident that administrators must be prepared to give specific reasons for believing that a particular speaker would constitute a "clear and present danger" to the educational functions of the institution.

In *Stacy* v. *Williams* the Fifth District Court provided a detailed model for a speakers policy which has served as a guide in subsequent actions. The case is thought to be unusual in that the court actually spelled out a policy, rather than restricting its actions to the explanation of principles upon which educational authorities might act. The case arose in Mississippi in 1968 from the denial by the University of Mississippi of permission to the University of Mississippi Young Democrats to invite Charles Evers, a well-known black activist, to campus to speak in support of the Democratic presidential ticket. Student members of the Young Democrats believed that some of the regulations promulgated by the Board of Trustees of Mississippi's Institutions of Higher Learning were unconstitutional and challenged the following in court:

No speaker shall be invited or permitted to speak on any campus without first having been investigated and approved by the head of the institution involved. . . . No person may be permitted to speak . . . who has announced as a political candidate for public office.

No person shall be permitted to use the facilities of the state institutions of higher learning whose presence will constitute a clear and present danger of inciting a riot.

No person shall be invited or permitted to speak . . . who advocates the violent overthrow of the government.

Any person feeling aggrieved at any adverse ruling . . . may file an appeal within five days (to the Board of Trustees) for a hearing at their next succeeding regular Board meeting.[7]

The court affirmed that although some notification and approval requirements to maintain adequate security, avoid scheduling conflicts, and allow administrators to rule on proposed speakers according to careful standards were constitutional, educational administrators do not have "unbridled discretion" in determining who may speak on campus. In the court's opinion, there must be a fair review procedure allowing students to challenge administrative decisions and requiring a ruling within a reasonable period of time. The regulations of the Mississippi Board of Trustees did not provide such procedures and they also failed to provide that requests for speakers might be initiated by students. In the opinion of the court the university could not arbitrarily withhold such permission from a particular student group, since there was adequate evidence that outside speakers had appeared on occasions at the request of other campus groups and the administration itself.

The court also saw no grounds for withholding permission on the basis that the speakers were campaigning for candidates for political office. As with other speakers, the court said, political candidates or their representatives may not be barred unless through application of the clear and present danger criterion. Specifically the court said that "any classification which bans political speeches is arbitrary and unreasonable," frustrating a major purpose of the First Amendment.

With regard to the prohibition of persons whose presence may constitute a disruption, Judge Keady noted that allowing a person to be barred from campus merely because his or her presence constitutes a danger reflects a misconception of the clear and present danger doctrine. A person cannot be restrained from speaking or the audience prevented from listening merely because of the speaker's presence and identity. Grounds for refusing permission must be based on apprehension that the speaker will say or do something that will lead to serious disorder, and law enforcement officers must "quell the mob, not the speaker." Even though a speaker may hold views that are not acceptable to the majority of the members of the campus community, this fact in itself is not a permissible basis for a denial of the students' right to hear that speaker. In addition, the court made a distinction between "the mere abstract teaching of the moral propriety for a resort to force" and preparing a group for violent action. There must be an urging to do something, rather than a mere exhortation to believe something, and this advocacy must produce a "reasonable apprehension of imminent danger."[8]

The court also held the Mississippi Board of Trustees regulations to be unconstitutional in failing to make provision for prompt review of an adverse decision regarding a particular outside speaker. Scheduling opportunities for appeal at the next regularly appointed board meeting did not, in the opinion of the court, provide the sort of prompt, fair, and efficient review necessary to satisfy the students' right to due process. The sponsoring student group should have an opportunity to have a hearing before the proposed speaking engagement so that there might exist a reasonable possibility of reversing the administration's decision in the case at hand. Delaying the appeal process until the next regular board meeting might in effect make the question moot.

Because it felt that the Mississippi Board of Trustees had failed to develop adequate rules, the court provided guidelines in the form of a code of its own. The principle points of this set of regulations are as follows:

1. Requests to invite speakers will be considered only when made by a recognized student organization.

2. No invitation shall be issued by an organization without prior written concurrence by the head of the institution or his designee. Any request not acted upon will be considered granted.

3. A request may be denied only if the institution determines that the "proposed speech will constitute a clear and present danger to the institution's orderly operation by the speaker's advocacy" of such actions as the violent overthrow of the government; the willful destruction or seizure of the institution's buildings; the forcible interference with classes or other educational functions; the physical harm, intimidation, or invasion of the rights of faculty, students, or administrators; or other campus disorders of a violent nature.

4. When an organization's request for an outside speaker is denied, the organization may appeal and obtain a hearing within two days before a campus review committee composed of three faculty members appointed by the Board of Trustees plus the president and the secretary of the student body.

5. When the request for an outside speaker is granted, the administration may require that the meeting be chaired by a faculty member or administrator and that a statement be made that the views presented are not necessarily those of the institution.[9]

Although courts generally refrain from the kind of educational decision making exemplified by actions in the *Stacy* case, these guidelines have been used to evaluate the appropriateness of speakers policies at other institutions of higher education. In a 1971 Texas case, for example, two "non-students" sought injunctive and declaratory relief from a ban on their proposed appearance and activities at North Texas State University. The Fifth District Court held that where First Amendment principles were involved and where the state and the university knew of a scheduled rally one week in advance and were aware of the probability that no student or off-campus speakers would appear at the rally, an ex parte restraining order against the nonstudents was not justifiable.[10]

The court felt that the university's regulations regarding outside speakers were deficient because they lacked certain provisions as articulated by the court in *Stacy* v. *Williams*. In particular, the court in the *Duke* v. *State of Texas* case felt that North Texas State University's policy should have provided that a request for an outside speaker not acted upon by the administration in four days be considered granted. In the opinion of the court, the policy then in effect at the university did not define permissible advocacy in an adequate manner and suggested the creation of a student-faculty review committee which in fact was not extant.

Another problem area identified by the court centered on the placing of responsibility on the sponsoring organizations for law violations arising from meetings with outside speakers. The court maintained that such responsibility should fall upon the shoulders of the speakers themselves, not upon the shoulders of members of the sponsoring organization. In addition, the court felt that the university's policy was deficient in not specifically identifying the administrative official whose responsibility it was to approve the invitation extended to an outside speaker. The court had reference to *Vernon's Annotated Texas Civil Statutes* to locate the authority for a Texas university to regulate conditions with regard to the presence and performance of off-campus speakers (Articles 2651a, 2919j), finding that the language of the university's policy, incorporating that of the state statute regarding "persons having no legitimate business" on campus and "any undesirable person," failed to give "fair notice of proscribed conduct" as required by the due process protection extended to rights guaranteed under the federal Constitution.[11]

From the judicial opinion in the *Duke* case, it is evident that college and university administrators must be cautious in their employment of language in policies and regulations restricting the appearance and activities of off-campus speakers. Vague language might be considered to allow unwarranted interference with the exercise of individual liberties guaranteed under the Constitution. In the *Duke* case, the university regulation and the statute on which it was based were judged to not sufficiently guard against ambiguity and arbitrariness in the use of the term "undesirable person." The determination of who might be an undesirable person would depend on subjective factors and would be considered differently by administrators and student groups in various circumstances. In addition, administrators might be able to exercise the kind of "unbridled judgement" disapproved in the *Stacy* v. *Williams* case in determining what might be considered "legitimate business" on a college campus.

In *Dickson* v. *Sitterson* (1968) the court found that standards of permissible statutory vagueness are particularly strict when First Amendment rights are involved. In this case certain students at the University of North Carolina and other individuals brought action against the Board of Trustees of that university, challenging the statutes of the state dealing with speakers at state universities and colleges as these statutes were reflected in the policies of the University of North Carolina. The statutes provided that the boards of trustees of state institutions of higher education (those institutions receiving state funds) must adopt regulations controlling the use of facilities for speaking purposes by any person who was a known member of the Communist Party, was known to advocate the overthrow of the federal or the state government, or who had pleaded the Fifth Amendment with respect to Communist or subversive activities. The language of these designations was judged by the court to be too vague, since the broad classifications made violation of the due process provision of the Fourteenth Amendment possible. The court also held that a prohibition based upon the invited speaker's exercise of a Fifth Amendment privilege would not be, in itself, valid cause for administrative action to prevent his or her speech.[12]

The nature of the clear and present danger criterion appropriate for use in prohibiting speech on campus can be seen in the decision of the U.S. District Court in the *Molpus* v. *Fortune* case. The court affirmed that nothing less than clear and convincing proof that the speech of the person sought by the student group would cause a clear and present danger to the orderly functioning of the university would be sufficient to meet this criterion for limitation of constitutionally protected freedom of speech. In this 1970 case evidence was provided which indicated that the speaker proposed to limit his speech to discussion of a particular crisis at a state college as viewed by him as a student leader. The speaker's presence per se was not held to pose a clear and present danger to the educational operations of the institution and the administrators therefore were required to approve the request.[13]

The college or university administrator reacting to the cases discussed above might be led to several useful conclusions regarding formulation of policies for outside speakers. First, the courts have generally followed the principle that educators have the right and the duty to make reasonable policies to safeguard the fulfillment of the institution's mission. No unnecessary or unenforceable policies should be made, but administrators should be proactive in formulating policies to cover the important areas of college or university life. Rational, well-articulated policies can be useful tools in the administrator's arsenal and are probably indispensable to the functioning of the contemporary educational enterprise.

Secondly, such policies and rules as are formulated must be written in careful language. Each component part of a policy or regulation must be specific and guard against infringement of constitutionally protected rights. Prohibitions may not be overly broad or vague in limiting First

Amendment freedoms. Even word-for-word incorporation of state statutes into the policies of educational institutions may fail in the face of
Fourteenth Amendment guarantees.

Policies and regulations should be reviewed regularly to keep them in
line with changing human needs and with changes in the law. Administrators should not be immobilized by fear in the face of possible legal
challenges, but should, with the help of competent legal counsel, seek
reasonable and creative solutions to such challenges under the guidance
of a sound educational philosophy.

Following is a model speakers policy based on the procedures of several colleges and universities. It is presented as a policy formulated at a
fictitious community college. Also included are brief notes on some pertinent cases which influenced the formulation of particular aspects of
the policy statement.

OUTSIDE SPEAKERS POLICY—EREHWON
COMMUNITY COLLEGE, UTOPIA, USA

Erehwon Community College seeks to provide broad and deep learning experiences for its students in an atmosphere conducive to academic
achievement. Accordingly, it is appropriate that students and the entire
campus community be afforded opportunities to learn from outside
speakers as well as from the college faculty and staff. In order to preserve the quality of the academic atmosphere at the college and to allow
full attention of faculty and students to their respective responsibilities
for teaching and learning, the following policy has been adopted by the
college.

1. Requests to invite speakers who are not Erehwon College faculty
   or staff members or currently enrolled students at the college to
   speak to any convocation on campus will be considered only
   when made by a student or faculty organization recognized by
   the president of the college. In cases in which a speaker is to be
   scheduled to address a regularly scheduled class session or sessions on campus, the appropriate requesting organization will
   be the academic department through which the course or
   courses are offered.

2. Written requests for the appearance of off-campus speakers
   specifying college facilities and space needs for the planned
   event must be submitted to the president of the college or
   his/her designee(s) at least five (5) class days prior to the date of
   the proposed event. Requests will be made on forms designed
   for such purposes, available through the Office of Student
   Services.

3. The issuance of invitations to outside speakers by members of the college community may be limited by the availability of suitable facilities. In particular and unusual circumstances, an invitation may be cancelled by the president of the college or his/her authorized designee(s) if in his/her opinion the proposed event or speech constitutes a clear and present danger to the academic functioning of the college by the speaker's advocacy of such actions as the violent overthrow of the federal or state government; the willful destruction or seizure of the institution's buildings; the forcible interference with classes or other educational functions; the physical harm, intimidation, or invasion of the rights of faculty, students, or administrators; or other violent acts which would lead to campus disorder.

4. If an organization's request for an outside speaker is denied, it may appeal and obtain a hearing within three (3) regular class days before a Campus Facilities Use Review Committee composed of three faculty members appointed by the Board of Trustees of the College District plus the president and the secretary of the campus Student Government Association. (The three faculty members of the Campus Facilities Use Review Committee will be appointed for a term of one year beginning September 1 of each calendar year. Appointments will be made by the Board of Trustees of the College District, acting upon a list of nominees proposed to the board by the campus faculty senate.) The appealed request will be considered granted if not denied by the committee within three (3) class days of the sponsoring organization's initial filing for review through the president or his/her designee(s). When the request for an outside speaker is granted, the administration may require that the meeting be chaired by a faculty member or administrator and that a statement be made that the views presented by the speaker are not necessarily those of the institution.

5. Any requests not acted upon by the president of the college or his/her authorized designee(s) within four (4) class days after submission may be considered granted.

DISCIPLINE AND STUDENT CONDUCT

Some of the classical issues dealing with student conduct revolve around issues related to the ability of students to exercise their rights as American citizens while they are enrolled at a college or university. A more recent development in the protection of the learning climate is the disruption of the campus's normal activities by students who are not American citizens. Because the nation's colleges and technical schools are enrolling increasing numbers of foreign nationals, the potential for further disruption is strong.

The right of academic institutions to regulate the quality of the learning experiences they provide for their students has not always been accepted without question. The purpose of academic institutions is the transmission of knowledge and the pursuit of truth. Truth, however, is subject to varying definitions and must always be subject to interpretation within a societal context. In other words, there is a temptation on the part of many individuals within a society to attempt to control the definition of truth and to influence the quality of the learning experiences to which the youth of the society are exposed. Although the goal of a society may be freedom of inquiry, rules must be established and maintained for the orderly conduct of affairs and for the assurance of progress in both life and learning.

In cases dealing with student conduct on college and university campuses, the courts have maintained that they are not concerned with specifying the rules and regulations which a particular school should maintain in force, but rather that it is their intent to intervene only in cases where there is a clear violation of the law or arbitrary, capricious, or unreasonable action on the part of the administration.

An important case dealing with student conduct served as a vehicle for an enunciation of this standpoint by the court:

Historically, the academic community has been unique in having its own standards, rewards and punishments. Its members have been allowed to go about their business of teaching and learning largely free of outside interference. To compel such a community to recognize and enforce precisely the same standards and penalties that prevail in the broader social community would serve neither the special needs and interests of the educational institution, nor the ultimate advantages that society derives therefrom. Thus, in an academic community, greater freedoms may prevail than in society at large, and the subtle fixing of these limits should in a large measure, be left to the educational institution itself.[14]

On the other hand, the court clearly saw a duty to intervene where the rights of students are abridged.

A second aspect of the behavior of the courts in dealing with matters of student discipline is their tenacity in asserting that due process must be exercised in matters affecting the punishment of student behavior while attending a college or university. A major case in this instance was *Dixon* v. *Alabama State Board of Education*, in which offending students were expelled without due process after an informal interview. The Fifth Circuit Court of Appeals reversed a ruling by a lower court which had supported the expulsion. According to the Appeals Court ruling, the elements of fair play were not present in the dealings of the university with the students. Because the concept of due process in procedures dealing with student conduct had not been adequately clarified, the court took steps to define the concept of due process as it applied in cases of student discipline and conduct.

Both notice and hearing are required by due process prior to expulsion from a state college or university. . . . The notice should contain a statement of specific charges and grounds which, if proven, would justify expulsions under the regulations of the Board of Education. The nature of the hearing should vary upon the circumstances of the particular case. A hearing which gives the administration of the college the opportunity to hear both sides in considerable detail is best suited to protect the rights of all involved. . . . The rudiments of an adversary proceeding may be preserved without encroaching upon the interests of the college. . . . The student should be given the names of witnesses against him and an oral or written report on the facts to which each witness testifies. He should also be given the opportunity to present his own defense against the charges and to produce either oral testimony or written affidavits of witnesses in his behalf.[15]

From this opinion of the court the three basic elements of due process—notice of the charges, a chance to examine the evidence and/or witnesses, and a chance to respond to the charges—are clearly applied to student conduct. It is important to note that a court trial is not required, although the elements of due process cited by the court are in fact the underpinnings of the Anglo-American legal trial system. Another important aspect to note is that where academic institutions have allowed themselves to be exposed to charges of violation of student's rights and where the procedures necessary for protection of such rights have not been made explicit in the particular context of the facts, the courts often will provide an ad hoc set of guidelines or principles which will then serve as the basis for the development of other decisions.

In the cases cited above and other cases such as *Stricklin* v. *Regents of the University of Wisconsin,* which dealt with the issue of temporary suspension of students,[16] the concept of a fair hearing is clearly delineated. In the *Stricklin* case, the court reinstated suspended students who were accused of participating in a violent campus disruption. The students were suspended pending a full hearing, and the court held that the regents did not prove that a temporary or preliminary hearing was not possible.

The attitude of the courts in preserving student's First Amendment rights led to a *Joint Statement of Rights and Freedom of Students,* which states the following concerns regarding the status of students who may be subject to disciplinary action during the period when they are awaiting final action:

Pending action on the charges, the status of a student should not be altered, or his right to be present on the campus and to attend classes suspended, except for reasons relating to his physical or emotional safety and well-being, or for reasons relating to the safety and well-being of students, faculty, or university property.[17]

In cases dealing with the possible violation of student rights by academic officials, the courts have been concerned that regulations concerning student conduct and discipline be in written form and distributed to all students. In addition, the wording of such statements of required student conduct is important. In *Camp* v. *Board of Public Instruction*, the students argued that the standards which they were supposed to have violated were vague, and the court was in agreement. The court in this case indicated that institutions of post-secondary education could not require conduct so vague that men of intelligence necessarily must guess at its meanings. An institution has an "obligation to clarify those standards of behavior which it considers essential to its educational mission and its community life."[18]

In addition to stipulating that students accused of misconduct of a serious nature be given a hearing, the courts have mentioned specific characteristics of appropriate hearings in such cases. The hearing should be before a regularly constituted hearing committee and should consist of both students and faculty members. None of the members of the hearing committee should be directly involved in the case at issue (*Jones* v. *Tennessee State Board*).[19] In the hearing the student has the right to confront his or her accuser (*Jones* v. *Tennessee State Board*; *Esteban* v. *Central University*; *Joint Statement*). The court also maintained, however, that the right to cross-examine is extended to the student only and not to his or her attorney, if the student is so represented.[20]

An important factor to note in this context is that the due process procedure as specified by the courts in the cases cited above seems in many particulars to resemble a full-fledged trial. This is not the case, however. It does not seem to be the intention of the court to require a legal trial in all cases involving student conduct. What the courts seem to have in mind is a system that will guarantee to students the free exercise of First Amendment rights and provide machinery for resolution of problems revolving around alleged use or abuse of those rights, without recourse to a court of law in the majority of instances. Again, it seems to be the mind of the court that academics should be able to resolve most of the issues pertaining to school government, and the courts are reluctant to provide specific directives unless a need for such action is manifest.

IMMUNITY DOCTRINES

For many centuries, governmental agencies have been protected from suits by the individuals they protect, govern, and serve through so-called immunity doctrines. The idea underlying immunity doctrines stems from the concept that the state can do no wrong. This concept was originally articulated as the principle that "the king can do no wrong." As the courts have seen it, the state cannot sue itself. Because the king represented the entire body politic, it was felt that he, and the government which was under his control, should be immune from suits by any member of the state. The king and the government represented the powers of the people and, accordingly, it was felt that the people were not able to sue themselves for abuse of such powers. In principle, educational institutions, both public and private, are considered to be institutions acting in behalf of the state and the people through the services provided. In general, immunity from suit in the context of this discussion can be classified as either governmental immunity or charitable immunity.

Governmental Immunity

As applied to educational enterprises, governmental immunity refers to those institutions conducted with state funds for the educational benefit of the public. These educational institutions are viewed as tools of the sovereign power of government, exercising a necessary function of government. They therefore should be free from tort liability.

The rationale for governmental immunity centers around funds for payment of suits. The taxpayers would have to bear the brunt of judgments since the only funds available to public organizations are tax funds. A similar rationale is based on the idea that money appropriated for governmental operations should not be expended in the payment of damages arising out of tort claims.

In recent years, however, legal experts have expressed the opinion that governmental immunity is becoming a thing of the past. Increasingly, the courts have searched for remedies for individuals who have been injured through the neglect of public institutions and officials. At the present time, however, the administrator in post-secondary education should be aware that his or her institution may be open to liability for specific kinds of damages.

Charitable Immunity

A second kind of legal immunity which may apply to educational organizations is termed *charitable immunity*. The rationale for charitable immunity rests upon the fact that educational institutions are in general viewed as public trusts. Both public and private institutions are viewed as providing essential, beneficial services to the individuals within the body politic. The central principle is that charities should not be held liable for a negligible act, since for charitable institutions to be required to pay for damages incurred because of negligence or other torts would frustrate the purposes of the trust, that is, the public good. Although the doctrine of sovereign immunity still stands in several states, the trend is clearly away from dependence on it as an iron-class legal protection from suit by individuals for compensation for personal injury.

ADDITIONAL TOPICS

This chapter has given a brief overview of some of the principles that influence the direction of the law and of which administrators in post-secondary education should be aware. Many additional topics should be mentioned because of their timeliness for the practice of educational administration.

The Bakke case in California was of interest to administrators who must tread the narrow path between fulfillment of the letter and the spirit of the law in regard to admissions policies and equal opportunity employment practices. The ultimate decision of the Supreme Court seems to have left the final answer to many problematic questions in the area of student recruiting and the employment of members of "protected" groups in abeyance. Administrators who hope to find clear and easy solutions or general norms which can be applied to all cases of a particular genre will be disappointed to find that no clearly delineated solutions to problems can be discerned from the decisions of the court. In matters involving legal difficulties, academic administrators in post-secondary education will find that the following principles may be of use:

1. The general administrator should develop a sense of legal propriety. He or she should be aware of basic areas of exposure arising from the activities in which the institution is engaged. The educational administrator who is able to look ahead and to avoid problems due to his or her proactive stance will have an advantage.

2. The administrator should make use of professional expertise when problems arise. General administrators should make use of legal counsel when necessary. Legal counsel should be consulted in the development of policies involving personnel matters, admission, student conduct, and other areas of potential legal involvement.

3. Always attempt to exercise good faith in dealing with both students and the general public. Academic administration has been called "the art of the possible," and, unfortunately, some practitioners have gained reputations as manipulators of public opinion, and slick public relations operators.

Faithfulness to the mission of the institution and honest uprightness in dealing with students will generally provide a sound footing for conducting the activities of the academic enterprise.

In the preceding discussion, the problem of protecting student rights was examined from the point of view of administrators who are faced with conflict arising from activities of students and/or staff. An additional problem in contemporary higher education deals with the presence on campus of individuals who are not citizens of the United States. In recent years some of these individuals have engaged in disruptive activities revolving around events in their home countries. Administrators are faced with the dilemma of protecting the rights of United States citizens who are attending the institution in order to secure an education and the problems of dealing with foreign nationals.

In general, citizens of other nations who are resident in the United States for any purpose and who do not have diplomatic immunity are subject to enforcement of the same laws as are United States citizens. They are also protected by the same guarantees of freedom extended to citizens who attend institutions of post-secondary education. At the present time, there is little precedent to aid the college administrator in determining the exact measures to be taken in dealing with such disorders. In certain cases, international students who become subject to academic discipline because of conduct may be subject to deportation.

The entire question of the increasing presence of foreign nationals as students on American college and university campuses and in United States technical training centers deserves comprehensive study, both from the point of view of providing more efficient services and from the point of view of legal exposure on the part of colleges and universities. The crisis in American-Iranian relations pinpointed the relationship of higher education services to American foreign policy. Educational and training services have become important products of American society, and the issues centering on the rights of citizens of other nations to benefit from these services will no doubt be a subject of discussion and inquiry in the future. A major responsibility of educational administrators is the creation of a climate in which learning can take place and the protection of the rights of students to profit from learning experiences.

NOTES

1. Graham Hughes, "Rules, Policy and Decision Making", *Yale Law Journal* 77 (January 1968): 411–38.

2. Henry P. Monagen, "First Amendment 'Due Process'", *Harvard Law Review* 83 (January 1970): 518–51.

3. Tinker v. Des Moines Independent School District, 309 U.S. 503.

4. Dennis v. U.S., N.J., 71 S.Ct. 857, 865, 868.

5. Stacy v. Williams, 306 F. Supp. 963 (1968).

6. Ibid.

7. Ibid.

8. Ibid.

9. Ibid.

10. Duke v. State of Texas, 327 F. Supp. 1218.

11. Ibid.

12. Dickson v. Sitterson, 250 F. Supp. 486.

13. Molpus v. Fortune, 311 F. Supp. 240.

14. Zanders v. Louisiana State Board of Education, 281 F. Supp. 747.

15. Dixon v. Alabama State Board of Education, 294, F. 2nd. 150.

16. Stricklin v. Regents of the University of Wisconsin, 297 F. Supp. 416.

17. Ibid.

18. Camp v. Board of Public Instruction, 82ct. 245.

19. Jones v. Tennessee State Board, 90 Supp. ct. 79.

20. Jones v. Tennessee; Esteban v. Central University, 415 R. 2nd 1077.

23

Managing Affirmative Action in Higher Education Administration

ROBERT W. HOTES

The administrator in higher education will be faced with many challenges in the decades ahead. For the most part these will be reflections of the challenges that confront the society as a whole. A major concern in American society in the future will be the effective and efficient utilization of the human resources at its disposal. These resources include many individuals in need of specialized educational services and with particular needs which are not presently being met by the nation's colleges. Some of these individuals belong to identifiable groups now protected by a system of laws and regulations related to the provision of equal educational opportunity.

The body of case law that deals with the provision of equal educational opportunities for all American citizens is already large and is steadily growing. As more of the individuals who belong to the so-called protected groups begin to understand their rights under the existing laws, there will be increased pressure on educational institutions to provide additional services and facilities which will ensure an equal access to all important learning experiences.

Underlying the movement toward the provision of equal opportunities for education at the post-secondary level is a set of important assumptions which may be said to permeate the entire fabric of American life. The notion that equality is a necessary factor in the American democratic experience and that such equality is an appropriate and achievable goal for the American society is not of recent origin. The notion that the American political experience can provide an environment in which the majority of its citizens might experience a fundamental degree of equality is not to be found with any certainty in the works of the founding fathers. At the same time, the thrust of the American experience toward the development of basic equality for all American citizens was so great that the Frenchman Alexis de Toqueville, writing in the early part of the nineteenth century, was able to affirm that the fundamental quality or aspect of the American political experience was a basic equality among all of the citizens.

In addition to the philosophical problems involved with the possibility of achieving any real measure of equality in a diverse population, the educational administrator in the coming decades is confronted by many interfacing and at times contradictory rules and regulations which restrict the free operation of the college or university in the achievement of its goals. There is no doubt that some federal laws and regulations relating to equal opportunity are confusing to both educational administrators and the educational public. There is a tradition of judicial response to questions involving equal opportunity in education, but, for the most part, this tradition deals with the primary and secondary education setting, not with higher education. The development of measures providing equal educational opportunity for all Americans may be seen as a logical outgrowth of programs that were developed for primary and secondary schools.

DEFINITIONS

Affirmative action—A series of positive measures to make opportunities available to individuals belonging to groups that have been discriminated against in the past.

Antinepotism—Restrictions against more than one member of the family being employed by the college or university within the same work team, division, or department. If this law discriminates against a woman or minority by denying employment it can be termed unfair.

Discriminatory conditions—Conditions that are the results of unintentional biases which have been reflected in certain personnel policies; or, they may be the reflections of personal biases on the part of individual administrators, faculty members, and the college or university as a whole.

Equal educational opportunity—The development of measures and procedures providing equal educational opportunity for all Americans without considering race, creed, color, or national origin.

Feudal patronage—Discrimination in job placement preferring those persons who graduated from particular colleges or universities or were related to or closely associated with college or university alumni for the purpose of job prospecting.

Minorities—Specifically defined by the Department of Labor as Negros, persons with Spanish surnames, American Indians, and Orientals.

Nondiscrimination requirements—These requirements apply to all persons including citizens of the United States and those who enjoy the benefits of citizenship through legal or temporary residence. No discrimination shall be placed upon these persons though not members of a legal minority.

Positive action—The process employed to overcome the systematic exclusion of members of various minority groups from access to career opportunities and advancement tracks available to other citizens.

Systematic exclusion—A process of systematically excluding particular persons from professional or occupational advancement or training because of race, creed, color, or national origin.

Following is a discussion of major concerns of the academic administrator relating to laws and regulations involved in equal opportunity.

HIGHER EDUCATION GUIDELINES: EXECUTIVE ORDER 11246

In 1972 the Director of the Office for Civil Rights of the Department of Health, Education and Welfare issued a set of guidelines to college and university administrative personnel in the matter of compliance with Executive Order 11246, "Nondiscrimination Under Federal Contracts." This document was a major source of information on the concepts of equal opportunity and affirmative action as they apply to higher education.

Nondiscrimination and Affirmative Action

As explained in Executive Order 11246, the obligations facing institutions of higher education and the administrators who are responsible for their activities fall into two categories: nondiscrimination and affirmative action. Nondiscrimination requires the elimination of all existing discriminatory conditions. These conditions may be the results of unintentional biases which have been reflected in certain personnel policies, or they may be the reflections of personal biases on the part of individual administrators, faculty members, and the college or university as a whole. In the light of the law and of the executive order, the origin of the alleged discrimination is not of prime importance, although the moral factors involved in discrimination practiced by an educational institution cannot be completely ignored. A college or university contractor, that is, an institution that receives federal funding must "carefully and systematically" examine its employment policies to insure that they do not hinder the opportunities of any persons on the grounds of race, color, sex, or national origin. The contractor must also insure that the practices of those who are in a position to make recommendations for employment, and to supervise the activities of employees, and to make recommendations for advancement are nondiscriminatory.

Affirmative action, on the other hand, requires the college or university to take positive measures to make opportunities available to individuals belonging to groups that have been discriminated against in the past. These measures may involve a variety of actions, including additional efforts to identify, employ, and promote qualified members of groups formerly excluded. The premise or concept behind affirmative action is that positive action must be undertaken in order to overcome the difficulties of "systematic" exclusion of members of various minority groups from access to career opportunities and advancement tracks available to other citizens. The college or university administrator should realize that this obligation is imposed without regard to whether there has been any active discriminatory activity on the part of the institution in the past. Affirmative action implies a positive approach to the problem of inequity through inequality of opportunity; the assumption is that unless positive action is undertaken to overcome the effects of systematic exclusion and discrimination, the status quo will tend to prevail, even if it is deplored by administrators and other members of the academic community.

Who Is Protected?

In considering the protection of certain individuals under the law as implemented by Executive Order 11246, a distinction is made between the nondiscrimination requirements of the law and the affirmative action requirements which are dependent upon the law. The nondiscrimination requirements of the executive order apply to all persons, including citizens of the United States and those who enjoy the benefits of citizenship through legal temporary residence. This presumably would include foreign nationals with student visas. The individual need not be a member of a conventionally defined minority group.

Affirmative action programs which require assessing needs in the form of estimates of underutilization of individuals in target groups, setting goals, and establishing time-frameworks for the achievement of goals are directed in particular towards minorities and women. Minorities are specifically defined by the Department of Labor as Negros, Spanish-surnamed, American Indians, and Orientals.[1] Other groups may consider themselves to be minorities, and it is clearly against the law for colleges and universities to deny consideration for employment or advancement within employment on the basis of membership in any particular ethnic or religious group. But affirmative action programs as such are directed at specific elements within the general population.[2]

What Is to Be Done to Comply?

Part of the establishment of affirmative action programs involves the establishment of goals and timetables for minority and female employment. It is necessary to determine if women and minorities are underutilized within the work force of a particular institution, and if that is the case, specific timetables and goals must be developed by the organization to remedy that underutilization. The term *underutilization* means that there are fewer members of minority groups or women present in the work force than would be expected in light of their availability in the employment marketplace. If, for example, the ratio of available men and women with doctoral degrees is 40 percent female and 60 percent male, the expectation would be that approximately 40 percent of a university's professional staff with that academic credential should be female. This particular conception has been the subject of controversy and can cause difficulty within the academic community and the imposition of obstacles to the success of the affirmative action program in a college or university. Nothing in the executive order or the law which it is intended to implement requires that a college or university contractor eliminate or dilute standards that are necessary for the conduct of the institution's functions.[3] The affirmative action concept does not require that an institution hire an individual who is unqualified. But a particular burden of proof is placed upon the employer. The employer must prove or demonstrate that a selection for employment is made on the basis of legitimate job related qualifications.

The development of an affirmative action plan is similar in several ways to the development of various forms of Management by Objectives programs. The college or university contractor must set particular goals for the recruitment and hiring of minorities. The achievement of these goals is not considered to be the sole measurement of compliance with the executive order and the law concerning equal employment opportunity. But as in the case of other systems or programs in which goals are set and used as a means to determine performance, failure to meet a goal requires a determination of the causes of such a failure. If the educational institution falls short of an affirmative action goal that it has set, this does not automatically mean that a conclusion of noncompliance with the executive order would be reached. Failure to reach the goal does require, however, a statement from the institution as to why the goals were not reached.

If, on the other hand, it appears that the cause for failure of the affirmative action program was a lack of attention to the nondiscrimination and affirmative action policies and procedures set by the institution itself, then the institution (contractor) may be found to be out of compliance with the law and the provisions of affirmative action. Goals are required, but *quotas are not required or permitted* by the executive order. Goals are designed to be a means of evaluating progress and achievement, not a rigid measure of legal compliance.

Executive Order 11246 should not be construed to mean that standards should be lowered or diluted. It is recognized that standards must be set and maintained in order to retain the integrity of the college or university and the excellence of its academic programs. The affirmative action concept does not require the promotion or hiring of unqualified personnel. What it does do is to require a serious effort at making opportunities available to qualified individuals who may be targets of discrimination. The institution is required to demonstrate its good faith in setting goals for its own behavior and to demonstrate accountability in reaching those goals. In this regard, the type of activity required for the establishment of a program of affirmative action and the maintenance of compliance with such a program is similar to activities in developing and maintaining a Management by Objectives program in a university or college administration, or the setting of learning goals and objectives in any course of instruction. The concept of equality of opportunity requires that any standards or criteria for employment or advancement that may have had the effect of excluding women or minorities or of limiting their access to opportunities must be eliminated, unless it can be shown that such criteria are conditions of successful performance in the particular position involved.

In order to comply with the provisions of Executive Order 11246, the institution involved must establish procedures to be used in employment and related practices which govern all procedures involved with the employment of individuals in particular units. This includes a description of any tests which may be used to evaluate preparation for the position and the criteria by which a candidate is considered either for initial employment or for promotion.[4] It is up to the contracting college or university to demonstrate that the standards and criteria to be used in employment selection are valid predictors of job success. These criteria must be demonstrated to have some direct relation to the duties of the position involved.[5]

The requirement that only performance related criteria be used in the selection of candidates for employment or advancement in employment brings up several related questions. For an occupation such as college teaching, the requirement of an appropriate academic degree seems to be a reasonable prerequisite. But is the holder of an advanced degree granted by an external degree program as well prepared for service as an instructor who graduated from a public or private university of the traditional type? Should a minority candidate with an advanced degree from an external degree program be given equal or preferential consideration in comparison with those who hold degrees from programs requiring on-campus residence? The answers to such questions will be based upon the goals and responsibilities outlined in the school's affirmative action plan. It is a fact of academic life that all programs and all degrees are not equal in quality. On the other hand, competent educational leaders have traditionally looked for the proper person to fill a particular position, with the source of academic credential being of secondary importance. Because the principal commitment of colleges and universities traditionally has been to the individual student, institutions have been primarily interested in obtaining the services of the best-qualified individual for a particular position. It is generally accepted that the process of selection of applicants for academic positions has in many cases in the past been discriminatory toward women and minorities. This situation has resulted in an imbalance of composition of the staffs of American colleges and universities in favor of white males. In light of the condition of oversupply in the academic job market of today, there is little excuse for administrators to claim that qualified women and minority applicants are not available. In any case, the executive order makes it clear that institutions must take the initiative in identifying opportunities that may be highly desirable to minority job candidates and in seeking applicants from minority groups who are qualified to fill such positions.

What about Recruitment?

In the past, universities and colleges may not have expended much effort to recruit females and minorities as employees. According to Executive Order 11246, universities and colleges now must recruit both women and minorities as actively as they have recruited white males in the past.[6] If, for example, some universities have tended to recruit primarily from a few schools which traditionally produce mostly white male candidates, they must take measures to insure contacts with other schools which may be producing minority and female candidates who are qualified for the available positions. Advertising in media that reach female and minority candidates is another step that can be taken to insure compliance with the law and the executive order. Traditional methods of staffing in the academic areas, principally the reliance on the word of mouth system for advertising position vacancies, and the buddy system, in which department chairpersons and administrators rely upon external professional contacts for informal recommendations in the matter of hiring professional personnel, have come under especially severe criticism. Before enactment of the civil rights legislation that has been directed toward reducing and eliminating inequities in the composition of university and college faculties, a standard practice was to allow department chairpersons to recruit and select personnel for their own departments. Often these individuals would utilize contacts at the universities from which they graduated or to which they felt the strongest ties. An informal advertisement of the position or positions to be filled would be made by letters or perhaps by telephone calls to a select number of friends and associates at other institutions. These individuals often would be able to recommend qualified candidates for the position under discussion or make a referral to another source. This was a type of feudal patronage system which had both limitations and advantages for maintaining academic quality control. Although there have been some positive results from such a system, in many cases women and minority candidates are not in the same word of mouth channel, and their candidacies may not be advanced with the same effectiveness. On the other hand, in some cases the word of mouth system was able to serve as a control mechanism, since colleagues felt that their personal reputation was involved in each endorsement. Under the present laws, however, the word of mouth system is clearly precluded as a major means of recruitment. The university or college contractor must examine the activities and policies of each unit that has responsibility for recruiting and hiring. If the applicant pool reveals a significantly lower number of women or minorities than would reasonably be expected from their availability in the work force, the contractor must modify or supplement its recruiting policies. This supplemental action may take several forms. Where there is evidence of any practice that is discriminatory against qualified women and minorities, these practices must be eliminated.

It is recommended that an expanded search network include not only the traditional avenue through which candidates have been located (for example, letters to academic departments at other institutions in the case of academic appointments, and advertisements in newspapers in the case of other jobs, often termed "classified positions"), but whatever nontraditional means are liable to produce results. Some means and areas of recruitment are:

a. Advertisements in appropriate professional journals and other periodicals which list openings for the professional positions of the type or types required.

b. Unsolicited applications or inquiries.

c. Women and minorities teaching at colleges and universities which aim at serving minorities or women as a special student target group. (So-called Black or women's colleges.)

d. Minorities or women who have professional preparation and status but who are working in other areas—that is, areas other than the area of post secondary education. These areas include government, industry, law, hospitals, etc.

e. Professional minorities and women who have received grants or professional recognition.

f. Minority and female doctoral recipients from the contractor's own institution and from other institutions who are not presently utilizing their professional training.

g. Women and members of other protected groups who show what seems to be outstanding promise for achievement in the future. Some institutions have set up programs where an opportunity to work on a terminal degree is provided for these individuals, along with a promise of possible employment related to the completion of the degree. While such a program may be useful in providing candidates who reflect the philosophy desired by a particular institution, the practice would seem to leave the institution open to problems at a later date. Such problems relate to a perceived "guarantee of employment."

h. Minorities and women who have been listed in data banks, especially those which have made a conscientious effort to locate minority and women talent.[7]

Specific Areas of Responsibility

Under the provisions and directions of Executive Order 11246, the institution is required to make explicit its commitments to equal opportunity employment in all recruiting announcements or advertisements. It is not permissible for a prospective employer to eliminate from consideration any individuals on the basis of sex or minority group status. It is a violation of the executive order for an employing institution to state that only candidates from minority or protected groups will be considered.

One of the alleged problems which has been encountered in the recruiting of faculty members from institutions that employ primarily minorities or women is the problem of so-called raiding of these faculty members by more prestigious, predominantly white universities and colleges. By and large, the executive order does not take this problem into consideration. The needs of so-called minority colleges and universities would seem to be considered as secondary to the overall process of education in the public sector. It would thus appear permissible for predominantly white public institutions to use their advantages of prestige and ability to offer economic incentives to secure the best talent from the faculties at minority institutions.

The availability of large numbers of unemployed or underemployed academics may mitigate this problem to a degree. Many individuals are willing to accept positions at a relatively low rate of pay in order to secure an academic appointment in a market in which oversupply conditions at times exist. Unfortunately many of these individuals are not of the first rank in academic preparation and scholarly skill. There is a possibility that minority students attending institutions who employ these persons are thus being shortchanged since they are not able to come into contact with appropriate standards and criteria of excellence. The perception that the predominantly minority institutions are second rate and inferior is accordingly enhanced and perpetuated.

DISCRIMINATION IN THE HIRING PROCESS

After a suitable talent pool of applicants for relevant positions has been established, standards for selecting candidates from that pool and assigning specific salary levels and positions must be established in a nondiscriminatory manner. Specific procedures must be formulated and made explicit in order to insure nondiscrimination. Since a major complaint among female academic professionals has been that they have been assigned to and kept at lower ranks than their male counterparts, care must be taken to avoid this practice. Assumptions often were made that female employees, regardless of their professional preparation and stature, would be likely to marry and raise a family. It was thus assumed by personnel officers that these individuals would see their work at the university or college as secondary to their family career responsibilities. This assumption often produced an attempted justification of lower salaries and restricted job advancement opportunities offered to female applicants and employees.

It has been the policy of some major universities and colleges to discourage applications for instructional positions from individuals who have received their terminal degrees at that particular university. Executive Order 11246 precludes the restriction of women and minority candidates on this basis if they are otherwise qualified. Unless the institution does not hire any of its own graduates at all, it must give equal consideration to its own students who are women and minorities. In other words, the fact that they are graduates of a particular institution should not be used to justify excluding qualified women and minority students from positions at that same institution on the pretext of avoiding "inbreeding."[8]

Official commentators on Executive Order 11246 point out that in the area of academic appointments a nondiscriminatory selection process does not require or permit a process of "reverse discrimination" through which unqualified individuals will be given the preference over qualified individuals. Employees are not to be fired, demoted, or displaced on the grounds of race, color, or national origin in order to fulfill an affirmative action goal. It is theoretically not permissible, for example, to refuse to renew the contract of a qualified white male instructor after the first year merely in order to replace him with a female with equal qualifications. It is possible that replacement with a female or minority faculty member with *superior* qualifications would be permitted, however, on the grounds that the institution has the right to plan for its own future development. Such a substitution might be made if the particular faculty member to be replaced did not meet performance requirements, or did not meet tenure requirements. In any case, principles of justice and equity should be guiding forces in all personnel decisions. Replacement of competent individuals is not the intention of the executive order.

There is nothing in the law or in Executive Order 11246 that justifies dismissals, job transfers, alterations of job descriptions, or changes in line of promotion or fringe benefits on the basis of achieving a particular quota of women and minorities in a particular institution. Administrators may adopt such practices and attempt to justify them in light of the executive order, but this is clearly a contradiction of both the letter and the spirit of the law.[9]

Several other areas of the personneling process that may be troublesome to the administrator formulating and implementing affirmative action policies include:

training to ensure that employees receive opportunities to upgrade their skills and work potentials without reference to their sex, race, or religious faith. Training programs should be constructed and designed so as to assure opportunities for staff development and effective human resources utilization. This is especially important in light of the emphasis which will be required in the future on the upgrading of skills of professional workers. In the college and university setting, training programs for academic workers are often confined to occasional opportunities to attend conferences and meetings of professional groups and associations. Naturally, there must be no discrimination in allocating these opportunities to qualified individuals.[10]

An equally important aspect of a training program established by a college or university should be classes and opportunities provided for nonteaching personnel. Secretaries and other employees, including janitorial and maintenance personnel, should have opportunities for developing their skills. Institutions of higher education are in a particularly advantageous position in providing these opportunities to their staff members. Tuition waivers for so-called classified personnel may allow workers with modest incomes to attend classes during their free time. Some institutions allow staff members released time during the day in order to attend particular classes that are related to job advancement and job skills. If an institution has democratic ideals, it is not inconceivable that employment in a nonprofessional capacity might be a step on the path to eventual professional qualifications. Unfortunately, employers are not accustomed to think of staff development in terms of value produced for the operation of the institution. Usually, the sole criterion for job performance assessment utilized by those who are in charge of employment at colleges and universities is whether or not an individual performs his present task. Little thought is given to what the potential of the individual within the organization might be if sufficient opportunities were provided for developing skills and personal resources. This narrowness of vision is wasteful of the energies both of the individual and of the organization.

Institutional Antinepotism Policies

In order to correct certain abuses in the control and distribution of employment opportunities, some colleges and universities established so-called antinepotism practices or procedures. Because of employment patterns in the past, stated or implied restrictions against the employment of more than one member of the same family by the institution or within the same academic department tends to limit opportunities available to women. If an antinepotism rule has led to the denial of opportunity for employment of a minority individual, that restriction is discriminatory and not permitted under the terms of Executive Order 11246.[11]

Placement and Job Classification

Certain job classifications have tended to include a disproportionate number of women and minorities. In institutions of higher education, these categories include secretarial positions in the case of females and janitorial positions in the case of black and Hispanic females and males. Care must be exercised by the administration of colleges and universities to insure that where no valid or substantial differences in duties exist, artificial classifications are not made that tend to segregate employees by race or sex. An example is the classification "administrative aid" or "administrative assistant." If there are no valid distinctions in the duties performed the classifications should be combined so as to avoid a two-tiered structure.[12]

Promotion and Termination

One major requirement of all personnel policies and practices which may be expected to stand a test of justice under the law is that policies must be made explicit and administered in such a way as to insure that women and minorities are not subject to discrimination. In the case of promotion, Executive Order 11246 implies that an employer must make every effort to insure equal promotion opportunities for women and minorities. It is important to note that special efforts must be made to provide such opportunities where required. Job training and job counseling are two ways in which such requirements may be met.

One area related to affirmative action programs and the legislation behind Executive Order 11246 involves actions to be taken when terminations of employment are necessary. In situations in which terminations are necessary, the employer must be able to demonstrate that the decision to terminate is unrelated to race or sex, religion, color, or national origin. Seniority may be used as a basis for making decisions on terminations. But if it can be demonstrated that an individual would have had more seniority had it not been for discriminatory actions, seniority must be eliminated as a consideration, or the individual must be presumed to have the seniority required or which she or he would have had if there had been no discrimination.[13]

An example may be helpful. Let us suppose that because of a drop in student enrollments and poor administrative planning it is necessary for a particular department at a major university to reduce its staff by two individuals. Naturally, the department chair and the dean of the college will be reluctant to attempt to make a decision on particular individuals whose contracts will not be renewed. But since they know that they cannot avoid doing so, they establish a decision-making process based on an assessment of the following characteristics. The order of the list does not necessarily reflect priority: (1) Holding of tenure; (2) length of service with the institution; (3) productivity in scholarly publications and research efforts; and (4) teaching effectiveness, as evidenced by student and chairperson assessment of teaching skill.

In order to make the selection of individuals who must leave the institution more equitable, the university president and the dean of the division affected by the reduction in strength decide to establish a special task force to make recommendations. After suitable deliberation, this task force narrows its selection to two individuals. Both have attained the rank of assistant professor and, naturally, both have earned the terminal degree. While there is some difference in the publishing and research histories of these two individuals, the task force has determined that there can be said to be a "rough parity" in their achievements in research and publication, and also a "rough parity" in their ratings by students, faculty members, and administrators in the area of teaching effectiveness and overall performance. Professor Johnson, a woman, has held the rank of assistant professor for one year, while Professor Adamson, a man, has held the rank of assistant professor for two years. Each of the two faculty members has served at the university for five years. Professor Johnson, however received her appointment as assistant professor one year after Professor Adamson. On the basis of these facts, the special task force or group appointed to determine which faculty member should be terminated recommends that Professor Adamson be retained on the basis of longer service in the rank of assistant professor. It should be remembered that both individuals have identical overall time in service with the university.

After the task force has submitted its recommendation to the dean and president, Professor Johnson contacts the University Faculty Grievance Committee to indicate that she will contest the decision. It is her contention that she was not elevated to the rank of assistant professor at the same time as Professor Adamson because the university administration had discriminated against her on the basis of sex. She indicates that if consideration is not given to her case at the university level, she will consider filing an action with the Office of Civil Rights of the Department of Education.[14] If her argument is upheld, Professor Johnson may be successful in removing time of appointment to the rank of assistant professor as a consideration in determining which of the two faculty members will be subject to severance of employment, and another criterion for making the decision will have to be found.

Conditions of Work and Related Benefits

The terms of Executive Order 11246 and the provision of the law require that employers, including university and college employers, insure nondiscrimination in working conditions for all employees. Aspects of work that may be especially pertinent to the university situation include the opportunity to do research, selection of assignments, and training opportunities in the form of inservice training and professional conventions. Assignment of office space and access to clerical and paraprofessional services also may be included in these considerations.

For all employees, access to eating facilities such as dining halls or faculty clubs must be open to all individuals within grade of employment. No discrimination on the basis of race or sex may be permitted. In addition, where any services are a part of the ordinary benefits of employment for certain classes of employees, no members of such classifications can be denied on a discriminatory basis. A strong argument could also be made that as a part of the democratic structure a publicly supported college or university would not feel comfortable with its mission while denying access to service facilities to any member of its work force, regardless of job classification.

In the past, members of minority groups have been denied access on the basis of race or sex to housing made available to faculty members at a reduced rate. Such practices are openly discriminatory and may not be continued.

Executive Order 11246 also requires that college and university employers adhere strictly to the concept of equal pay for equal work. A university or college must set forth in sufficient detail guidelines for determining the pay scales within each job classification, and these guidelines must be made available to present and prospective employees.[15] The applicant's level of pay must be determined on the basis of capability and record of performance, not former salary. If a minority or female applicant applies for a position as an associate professor at a state university, and the starting salary range for individuals entering employment at that level is $24,000 to $30,000, the fact that at her former institution she earned significantly less for a similar position can not be used as a reason for denying her equal pay with others at her new institution who hold similar rank.

Back Pay

Under the Civil Rights Act of 1964 (Title VII), the Equal Pay Act, and the National Labor Relations Act, universities and colleges may be required to make up discrepancies in pay to female and minority employees in the form of back pay. Evidence of discrimination that requires back pay as a remedy may be referred to the Office of Civil Rights for negotiation of a voluntary settlement. If this effort is not successful, the appropriate federal enforcement agency may be involved in a dispute involving back pay.[16]

Leave and Fringe Benefits

Women are afforded particular protection from employment discrimination in the areas of leaves related to pregnancy and childbirth. Basically, Executive Order 11246 specifies that women may not be penalized in their working conditions on the basis of requiring time away from work for the purpose of childbearing. Pregnancy and childbirth are to be considered reasonable causes for a leave of absence for all female employees, disregarding marital status, and following childbirth they must be reinstated without loss of benefits. Leave for reasons related to pregnancy must be treated in the same way as other medical leave, without additional conditions. Mandatory lengths for leaves should not be stipulated, since the principle is that the leave should be related to the medical need involved. The length of time required for such leaves should be dictated by individual health, not by arbitrary policy. Following the end of a leave related to childbirth, a female employee must be reinstated to her position or one of similar status and pay without loss of seniority and benefits. Any leave related to pregnancy must be in accord with the employer's general leave policy.[17]

Grievance Procedures

In hearing complaints of matters dealing with discrimination in employment in universities and colleges, the Office of Civil Rights and the Equal Employment Opportunity Commission (EEOC) share responsibilities. The EEOC has jurisdiction over individual complaints of discrimination by academic as well as nonacademic employees of educational institutions.

As a result of a formal agreement between EEOC and the Office of Civil Rights, individual complaints of discrimination are investigated by EEOC, while class complaints and information involving possible patterns of discrimination—for example, a consistent policy of excluding Spanish-surnamed applicants from employment consideration—are within the jurisdiction of the Office of Civil Rights. In general, the Office of Civil Rights of the Department of Health and Human Services is concerned with patterns of discrimination, and the EEOC is the appropriate agency to deal with individual complaints. However, institutional grievance procedures which are written and effectively promulgated remain the first step in discussing alleged discrimination. The requisite elements for such a procedure are discussed in another chapter in this volume.

Developing Affirmative Action Programs

The following points are suggested for consideration as part of an affirmative action program:

1. *Development or reaffirmation of the equal opportunity employment policy.* This is a necessary first step, and involves goal setting by each organization and subunit. The statement of goals should take into consideration the mission of the college or university as well as its overall commitment to eliminate discrimination in employment on the basis of sex, race, religion, or national origin.

2. *Dissemination of the policy.* This step is vital to the effective formulation and administration of all policies. It is essential that all individuals with responsibilities in relation to employment and promotion understand their responsibilities in light of the law and the institutional policy. The policy should be made available to all employees.

3. *Responsibilities for implementation.* An administrative procedure must be set up to organize the institution's efforts and to monitor progress. It is suggested that an individual be delegated to direct EEO programs and that this individual be given the requisite top level support to execute the assignment. Some colleges and universities combine EEO functions with other duties, while others create a special office at the directorial or vice-presidential level. Some institutions appoint the director of personnel to oversee this function. This would seem to be a less suitable

approach than appointing a special officer who is free to devote major efforts to the success of the program. In some institutions the EEO officer has been assisted by one or more task forces comprised primarily of women and minority faculty members. While such a task force may aid in the identification of problems and the establishment of positive goals, it also may lead to factionalism and lowered morale within the institution.

4. *Internal audit and reporting systems.* An integral part of the affirmative action program of each institution must be a system for auditing and monitoring progress. Systems will vary from institution to institution. It is important, however, that all such systems be sufficiently planned and developed so that a proper evaluation may be made. The institution must report at least once per year to the Office of Civil Rights on the results of its program. In the majority of cases, an effort to locate and appoint women and minorities must be in evidence. Reporting systems should include a method of evaluating applicants, referral and retention rate, and a system for retaining and evaluating applications.

5. *Publication of affirmative action plan.* Affirmative action plans that are accepted by the Office of Civil Rights are subject to disclosure under the Freedom of Information Act, 5 U.S.C. 552. Certain areas of an affirmative action plan may be exempt from disclosure, however. Any information about employees that may be considered an invasion of privacy, information that may be considered to be a part of trade secrets, and certain confidential commercial and financial information may be excluded from disclosure. The major point to remember is that the bulk of the institution's affirmative action plan is subject to disclosure.

6. *Development of an affirmative action plan.* Because responsibility for personnel decisions may be more decentralized at many colleges and universities than at the majority of private businesses, the chief administrator of the institution will need to enlist cooperation from a broad spectrum of individuals and subunits within the campus organization in the formulation and implementation of an effective affirmative action plan. It is suggested that administrators attempt to involve faculty members as well as other administrative personnel in implementing the provisions of an affirmative action program which will involve individuals throughout the institution and the entire academic community. It is especially important that those individuals who have responsibilities in personnel function areas—including

such "first-line" leadership personnel as department chairpersons—be involved as much as possible not only in enforcing the provisions of an affirmative action program, but in formulating the strategies for implementation. It is also important that all members of the administrative team and the academic community understand the philosophic and legal background and implications of the affirmative action program so that they can cooperate fully with it.

NONDISCRIMINATION ON THE BASIS OF HANDICAP

The responsibilities of college and university employers with regard to handicapped individuals deserve a separate treatment from a discussion of the federal regulations that preclude discrimination on the basis of sex, race, or national origin. The regulations issued by the federal government, governing nondiscrimination on the basis of handicap are designed to implement Section 504 of the Rehabilitation Act of 1973, 29 U.S.C. 706, as amended. Section 504 states that "no otherwise qualified handicapped individual shall solely by reason by his handicap, be excluded from the participation in, be denied the benefits of, or be subject to discrimination under any program or activity receiving federal financial assistance."[18]

Unless proof of undue hardship can be furnished, recipients of federal funds must make reasonable accommodation to the handicaps of both applicants for positions and employees. In addition, universities and colleges must make efforts to provide equal services to handicapped students. In order to provide such services, administrators must make sure that new facilities which are constructed are accessible to handicapped individuals and that all programs are operated in a nondiscriminatory manner. The administrator in higher education should remember that the major principle is that no agency or institution receiving federal funds may discriminate against a person solely on the basis of a handicap. The essential concept here is that the discrimination must not be *only* on the basis of the handicap. It is *not* necessary to offer employment to individuals who are unable to perform work at a desired level, but it is illegal to refuse consideration for employment in a certain position to an individual merely on the basis of a particular handicap.

While the concept of affirmative action does not apply precisely to the actions that must be undertaken to insure nondiscrimination against handicapped individuals, institutions are nontheless required to take positive steps to insure that programs and facilities are made accessible to handicapped students, and that handicapped individuals are not discriminated against in employment or promotion on the basis of their handicap.

Definition of a Handicapped Individual

Section 84.3(j) of Section 504 of the Rehabilitation Act of 1973 defines handicapped persons as those who fall under the following categories:

1. Individuals with physical or mental impairment which substancially limits one or more major life activities (i.e., walking or speech).
2. Individuals who have a record of such impairment or who are regarded as having such an impairment. For example, an individual who has been in the past committed to an institution for the mentally impaired would be covered under the provisions of the Act, even though the person has never actually been mentally impaired.

To insure that recipients of federal funds are aware of the law, they are required to submit a letter of assurance to the Director of the Office for Civil Rights. Some of the types of disabilities covered by the law include visual, speech, and hearing impairments; diseases such as cancer and diabetes; mental retardation; and alcohol and drug addiction. The inclusion of individuals with histories of drug and/or alcohol addiction in the category of those who are considered as handicapped individuals is troubling to some administrators and faculty members. The concern is that the law may require individuals who are unable to perform the needed tasks to be hired in place of individuals who can and will perform. The spirit of the law is, however, that no job should be denied to an individual merely because that individual has a handicap unrelated to job performance. If the individual cannot perform the work to a satisfactory level, the job need not be offered.

The major fact for administrators to remember is that their prime goal remains the filling of positions with *qualified* personnel. The purpose of the federal legislation is to insure that there will be no discrimination against qualified individuals who are able to perform the job functions simply because of a handicap or disability that does not affect job performance. Administrators in colleges and universities cannot afford to be ignorant of the provisions of the law regarding equal opportunity in employment and services provided to individuals with handicaps.

Because of the function of higher education within the fabric of American society, administrators must be aware of their responsibilities with regard to the laws affecting equal opportunities in employment and education for women, minorities, and the handicapped. In addition, administrators should be aware that it also is illegal to discriminate against persons between the ages of forty and seventy in terms of employment. The laws and regulations which relate to equal opportunity are sometimes perceived by educators as restraints upon the ability of the institution in the making of personnel decisions. In addition, some administrators may utilize federal regulations in an unethical manner to achieve goals and ends that are not related to the intent of the law. College administrators may restrict hiring of full-time instructors, for example, claiming that the laws relating to equal opportunity require the filling of certain posts with minority applicants. In this way, instructor overloads and part-time instructors may be utilized at a considerable savings to the institution in salaries and fringe benefits.

It seems essential to rely upon the principles of justice and equity in all the operations of an institution dedicated to public service. The administrator who can view the application of the principles of equal opportunity and affirmative action as challenges requiring positive action will aid the institution in meeting its leadership obligations in society.

NOTES

1. U.S. Department of Health, Education and Welfare, *Higher Education Guidelines: Executive Order 11246* (Washington, D.C.: Department of Health, Education and Welfare, 1972), p. 3.

2. Ibid.

3. Ibid., p. 4.

4. Ibid., p. 8.

5. Ibid., p. 4.

6. Ibid., p. 5.

7. Ibid., p. 7.

8. Ibid., pp. 7–8.

9. Ibid., p. 4.

10. Ibid.

11. Ibid., p. 8.

12. Ibid., p. 9.

13. Ibid., p. 10.

14. Ibid., p. 14.

15. Ibid., p. 11.

16. Ibid., p. 12.

17. Ibid., p. 14.

18. U.S. Equal Opportunity Commission, *Affirmative Action and Equal Employment: A Guidebook for Employers*, vols. 1 and 2, (Washington, D.C.: U.S. Equal Opportunity Commission, January 1974), p. 3.

24

Voluntary Cooperation in Post-Secondary Education: The Promise for the Future

ROBERT W. HOTES

Because of the pressures and constraints that are being focused on post-secondary education in the United States, many authors suggest that individual institutions explore means of cooperation to meet challenges on various levels. This chapter will review some of the progress that has been made in voluntary interinstitutional cooperation by certain groups of post-secondary institutions and explore suggested patterns for further efforts.

DEFINITIONS

Centralization—Institutional or consortial involvement is vested in one central office or administrative cluster.

Consortium—Formal arrangement for cooperation in one or more areas of activity among two or more institutions.

Coordinating boards—Elected institutional bodies set up by the state legislature to coordinate the work of the various institutions within the learning cluster.

Proactive—Initiative taken by the administration or faculty before the fact rather than relating to the situation after the fact.

THE NEED FOR COOPERATION

One characteristic of American institutions of higher education and post-secondary training has been pluralism. The American institution of post-secondary education is unique in many ways. Perhaps one of the most outstanding qualities that mark the higher education institutions of the United States as unique is the fact that there is no single institutional type "typical" of the contemporary American college or university.

Although the basic classifications *public* and *private* are valid and useful as general categories, the relations between all institutions of higher learning and the various levels of government are presently so complex as to prevent a simple dichotomy. The basic characteristic of sources of major funding—public dispersal of funds or private donation—still remains the most useful classification.

The impact of federal legislation on funding of both private and public colleges and universities has produced a change in the structure of American post-secondary education. However, few institutions can claim to be entirely independent of the influence of governmental regulation and control, since almost all institutions depend in one way or another on forms of governmental aid for their existence and survival. At the present time, dependence upon federal aid is merely a matter of degree. In most cases, public institutions are more highly dependent upon sources of revenue controlled by the federal government than are the privately supported colleges. The level of involvement of the federal government in privately funded institutions is on the rise, however. Such involvement may take a variety of forms, including aid to various groups within the student body, such as women and veterans, or supplementary funding for certain programs to attract particular interest groups to the campus. A notable example of the latter kind of funding is the efforts in recent years to provide access to all college and university services and programs to those who are handicapped.

In all of the cases mentioned previously, governmental agencies provide funding for activities and programs, enabling the affected institutions to initiate or maintain programs that would not otherwise be economically feasible. It is generally true, however, that funding by governmental agencies also involves degrees of governmental control and/or regulation at various levels. Acceptance of federally dispersed funds opens an institution to various levels of control by federal bureaucracies. Some leaders in higher education administration today suggest that increasing governmental control on both the federal and the state level is inevitable, and that the best that administrators can do is to fight a "delaying action" to retain some of their prerogatives. In the view of these individuals, governmental control of post-secondary education will become a fact of life in the United States, as it is a fact of life in many other nations. A major problem seen by those who feel that state and federal control of higher education is inevitable because of the increasing financial problems involved in operating schools and colleges is the fact that where there is control by a centralized agency, innovation in curricula and programs to meet the needs of a local constitutency may be curtailed. In one state, for example, certification of all programs must be handled through a special board for higher education operating in the state capitol. Programs must be submitted to the board for approval before final implementation, and changes in the curricula already established also must be approved at the state level. In such a situation, administrators sometimes may be apprehensive that the ability of the institution to create and implement innovative programs may be impaired. In the particular example cited, standard practice in proposing additional programs for college and university campuses around the state has degenerated into a comparison of the proposed course or program with a similar offering by the major state university system. Agreement with the programs approved by this university system means almost proforma approval by the state governing board for post-secondary education.

Under a set of procedures such as the one described above, it is not too difficult to envision a monolithic structure for higher education, with programs being determined almost entirely by a small group of academics operating under the aegis of and often in close proximity to the center of political power in the state. In turn, state policies and practices probably would be most heavily influenced by restraints originating in the federal government. With an increasing portion of the revenues of both public and private institutions of post-secondary education deriving from federal sources, the influence of the federal government seems destined to increase. One indication of such a trend is the recent government movement to establish a special office for higher education at the federal level.

Increasing government control of American post-secondary education has many educators concerned for several reasons. First, the American tradition in educational control is clearly established in favor of pluralism and decentralization. There is no specific constitutional delegation to the federal government for the conduct of education. Matters concerning educational practice are reserved to the individual states, along with other aspects of government for which there is no specific provision.

Second, there is a growing resentment on the part of American taxpayers of the machinations of "big government" at every level. Evidence indicates that Americans prefer to have local control of their educational system. State and federal governments presently intervene in many areas, especially in primary and secondary systems. Although this involvement has been gradual and generally is accepted for areas such as school lunch programs and supplementary funds used to purchase learning aids such as textbooks and audiovisual equipment, there is no evidence that Americans would favor control of higher education by the federal government. As a matter of fact, the success of recent tax-limitation proposals in various states would seem to provide indications to the contrary.

PROBLEMS IN LOCAL CONTROL: WHY CENTRALIZATION IS ATTRACTIVE

Although there is little evidence that American post-secondary education is ready to move toward centralization in a form similar to that of Great Britain and most of her former dominions, present problems make the need for increased efficiency in the operation of post-secondary institutions apparent. Increasingly, colleges and universities and other forms of post-secondary education such as vocational training centers are turning to federal funding agencies for assistance in meeting the pressures of inflation and the subsequent rises in operating costs.

The rapid expansion of post-secondary education in the 1960s produced a rapid growth of collegiate-level institutions, both public and private. At the present time and for the foreseeable future, many of the traditional markets for post-secondary educational services seem close to being exhausted. Administrators in educational institutions will face a different and unique set of challenges entering the closing decades of this century. The skills and capabilities that have been most serviceable in meeting the challenges of rapid expansion in the field of post-secondary education may not be most appropriate for a steady state or a period of decline.

In addition to the personal challenges to administrators, there will be new challenges to the economic basis upon which the American system of higher education is built. Administrators who are unable to explore novel paths leading to solutions to such problems as recruiting students in a depleted market area may be tempted to turn to government aid in order to survive. The question of survival will depend upon the forward-looking proactive initiative of their faculties and administrations.

In brief, many writers in the field of higher education would see contemporary problems facing American institutions as posed in the form of a dilemma: colleges and universities may retain individual control of their own destinies and suffer the consequences of reduced support and financial curtailment; or they can look to government for salvation in the form of supplementary funding and accept the concomitant centralized governmental control.

Other educators who feel that neither of the two solutions is viable have suggested that institutions engage in cooperation to share and maximize available resources. Such sharing and conservation of scarce educational resources may be undertaken by directive through involuntary state control and coordination, or individual institutions may initiate efforts for voluntary cooperation among themselves.

STATE REGULATED COOPERATION

Due to pressure from voters, state legislators have moved in recent years to establish governing boards on the statewide level to regulate institutions of post-secondary education within their borders. In large states such as California, New York, and Texas, state coordinating boards have varying powers. Due to the unfortunate rise of unscrupulousness and fraud on the part of some who work within the framework of higher education institutions, there has been an erosion of public confidence and trust in post-secondary education and a concomitant demand for increased supervision and oversight on the part of state authorities to protect the public interests. Such developments as the spurious degree, often offered by mail, and the proliferation of small colleges sponsored by certain religious sects have moved state legislatures to take action to protect their citizens against chaos in the field of post-secondary education. The measures taken to prevent this chaos generally have been in the direction of coordination, leading to eventual state control.

VOLUNTARY COOPERATION

In recent years, voluntary cooperation among collegiate-level institutions has received significant attention. Several authors, notably Lewis D. Patterson and Fritz Grupe, have done extensive work on the development of plans for cooperative efforts in post-secondary education and have analyzed some of the advantages and disadvantages of such cooperation.

According to Patterson, the number of national higher education organizations that are beginning to show an interest in furthering the voluntary cooperative approach is growing. He notes, however, that there is a tendency for many of these associations to give mere lip service to the concept of cooperation. The decisions to commit dollars and personnel to such programs are few and far between. Patterson identifies two particularly wasteful areas:

1. The scheduling of meetings, workshops, and seminars at the local, state, regional, and national levels without proper articulation and coordination.
2. Lack of planning and coordination in publications.

He also suggests that a national center to plan and coordinate efforts on building consortia would be useful.[1]

Major media are devoting increased attention to the formation and development of academic consortia. Patterson, who has been one of the major figures in the development of the theory and practice of consortia in post-secondary education, says that the concept of a "consortium has changed from a narrowly defined phenomenon to what might be considered an approach or technique for dealing with problems and changes in college and university education."[2]

CONSORTIA: WHAT THEY ARE AND WHAT THEY CAN DO

Loosely defined, consortia are formal arrangements for cooperation in one or more areas of activity among two or more institutions. In the focus of our discussion, we are considering consortia in post-secondary education. In this context the term consortium has come to denote a wide variety of cooperative associations and affiliations. Consortia have been formed to offer students in a given area more variety in course offerings than is available at any of the individual institutions. Other consortia have been formed to focus on enriching cultural opportunities by providing for joint activities and guest speakers. Consortia also have concentrated on the development of a pool of learning resources which can be shared by member institutions.

The possibilities for combinations of effort and talent among post-secondary institutions are practically numberless. In almost any situation in which there is a need for improvement or expansion of a particular activity conducted by collegiate institutions, there are possibilities for shared effort. The fact that such possibilities exist does not mean that individuals or institutions will take advantage of them. In many cases attempts at bringing about cooperation between institutions meet formidable obstacles from several quarters. Following are problems which may confront innovative individuals who are interested in establishing interinstitutional cooperation.

1. *Caution on the part of chief administrators.* Presidents, deans, and others often are reluctant to surrender any element of control over institutions or programs to counterparts at other institutions. This is especially true when an attempt is made effecting cooperation between institutions that have some historic rivalry or that have been in competition in the same student market for some time.

2. *Lack of clear-cut formulations of the objectives of consortial cooperation.* Cooperation among institutions of higher and post-secondary education is often easier to talk about than to put into effect. Implementation of plans and programs for cooperation in such areas as the sharing of learning resources (library and nonprint media collections, for example) can only take place where there is a solid commitment to real action on specific measures. Vague generalities produce a situation in which time may be wasted without significant results.

3. All individuals who are involved in making the cooperative effort work must be aware of what is to be accomplished and what methods and strategies are to be used to accomplish the

goals. Once there is sufficient understanding on the part of all individuals involved, a firm commitment to action can be formed.

AUTONOMY: CAN IT BE MAINTAINED?

One of the major fears on the part of many administrators confronted with plans for cooperation is that their institutions will lose autonomy, and therefore some aspects of freedom, by involvement in cooperative activities with other colleges and/or universities.

For those who have had success in the establishment of consortia among institutions offering higher education, a distrust of those who seek to protect institutional autonomy may seem natural. In many cases, initial resistance to consortial arrangements on the part of chief administrators has been overcome. Those who have established unsuccessful consortia will, in turn, be distrustful of situations that might limit the effectiveness of consortia. Experience has indicated, however, that responsible institutional autonomy can make cooperative interdependence successful.

According to Lloyd Averill, institutions participating in consortia have a customary distrust of institutional autonomy. They must face the fact, however, that only responsible institutional independence can serve the legitimate interests of the state and the people represented by the state. In Averill's view, institutional autonomy is an essential value in the context of effective cooperation. Consortia should perpetuate and protect this value, Averill maintains. "Voluntary consortia must now become centers of open and unabashed advocacy for the autonomy of institutions of higher education."[3]

Averill and others point out the fact that excessive coordination at the state level can limit the efforts of both public and private universities and colleges to form useful patterns of innovation in curricula. As noted earlier, a major concern of many educators is that state coordination will limit the ability of institutions to respond to the needs of their communities with innovative curricula and programs.

ADVANTAGES OF COOPERATIVE EFFORT

One of the major assumptions behind movements toward interinstitutional cooperation in post-secondary education is that there will be distinct advantages in cooperation. Some of the advantages cited by theorists and practitioners in educational administration for voluntary cooperation among colleges and universities are as follows:

1. Duplication of essential services can be avoided. In some cases colleges and universities that serve overlapping geographical

areas can combine efforts and reduce costs to member institutions through the use of consortial arrangements.

2. Resources, including key personnel, can be shared, leading to financial savings for the individual institutions. Care must be taken to practice strict accountability in assessing potential savings to institutions, since savings may be more apparent than real. In certain cases, for example, formulation of a workable system of sharing educational or training resources perhaps would entail more expense than reliance on the traditional pattern of insularity. It has been said that "administration is the 'art of the possible.'" Before proposals are made for interinstitutional cooperation, studies should be made to insure feasibility.

3. Use of consortial or other cooperative arrangements may increase the ability of individual institutions to meet challenges of variable enrollment and reduced financial resources through sharing of costs for research and development activities and other functions that may be financially burdensome for individual institutions.

The brief discussion of interinstitutional cooperation in the preceding pages gives only a partial overview of the possibilities for innovation using consortial arrangements. The bibliography in Appendix 5 at the end of this chapter includes references which may be useful to individuals interested in pursuing further study or research in the area. Many forms of cooperative effort among colleges and universities remain to be explored. The experiences of groups of institutions that have been involved in consortia have underscored the fact that several factors are essential to the effectiveness of cooperation:

1. The purposes and goals of the voluntary consortium must be clearly established and understood by key personnel at all institutions involved. Confusion of goals and purposes often breeds mistrust on the part of those who will be responsible for the success or failure of the consortium.

2. No consortium will be effective without the support of the chief administrators and key personnel at all institutions involved.

3. Consortia are not panaceas. They will not solve all problems relating to academic administration and governance in postsecondary education. Consortia can be effective in meeting specific needs and helping to solve particular problems.

Finally, the creation of the federal Department of Education will have significant impact for the decades to come. It has been estimated that nearly 70 percent of the decisions made by educational administrators are influenced either directly or indirectly by federal legislation or control. As the Department of Education develops and matures, its impact on higher education is certain to have an effect on possibilities available for voluntary cooperation.

NOTES

1. Lewis D. Patterson, "Introduction: National Cooperative Trends," *Institutional Interface: Making the Right Connection: Trends and Issues in Cooperation* (Washington, D.C.: American Association for Higher Education, 1974), pp. 1–4.

2. Ibid.

3. Lloyd J. Averill, "Autonomy: Myth and Reality," *Trends and Issues in Cooperation* (Washington, D.C.: The American Association for Higher Education, 8 Fall 1973), pp. 10–16.

Selected Bibliography on Consortia

Andrew W. W. *Cooperation Within American Higher Education*. Washington, D.C.: Association of American Colleges, 1964.

Anzalone, J. S. *An Interinstitutional Admissions Program for the State University of Florida*. Tallahassee, Fla.: State University System of Florida, 1967.

Associated Colleges of the Midwest, *ACM: Associated Colleges of the Midwest Faculty Handbook, 1970–71*. Chicago: 1971.

Averill, Lloyd J. "Autonomy: Myth and Reality." *Trends and Issues in Cooperation*. (Washington, D.C.: American Association for Higher Education, Fall 1973), pp. 10–16.

Bradley, A. P. "Academic Consortium Effectiveness: An Investigation of Criteria." Ph.D. dissertation, University of Michigan, 1971.

Breneman, D. W. "Selected Aspects of the Economics of the Five College Cooperation." Mimeographed. Amherst, Mass.: Amherst College, 1971.

Burnett, H. J., ed. *Institutional Cooperation in Higher Education*. Corning, N.Y.: College Center of the Finger Tahres, 1970.

Carnegie Commission on Higher Education. *The More Effective Use of Resources: An Imperative for Higher Education*. New York: McGraw-Hill, 1972.

Central Steering Committee of the CCFL Self Study and Long-Range Plan. *Patterns for Voluntary Cooperation*. Self-Study Report of the College Center of the Finger Tahres. Corning, N.Y.: College Center of the Finger Tahres, 1971.

Council of the Clairmont Colleges. *The Constitution of the Clairmont Colleges*. Clairmont, Calif.: 1970.

Donoar, G. T., ed. *College and University Interinstitutional Cooperation*. Washington, D.C.: Catholic University of America Press, 1965.

Eko, E. V. "Voluntary Academic Consortia: The Impact of Multiple Memberships on Private Colleges and Universities." Ph.D. dissertation, Union of Experimenting Colleges and Universities, 1972.

Five College Long-Range Planning Committee. *Five College Cooperation: Directions for the Future*. Amherst, Mass.: University of Massachusetts Press, 1969.

Fox, L. E. "Putting Cooperation into Purchasing Yields Savings." *College and University Business*, 1972, 53 2.

Frederick, E. and O'ostdan, B. L., comps. *Directory: The Marine Science, Inc.* Millersville, Pa.: Millersville State College, 1972.

Grupe, Fritz H., "Consortia and Institutional Change," *Trends and Issues in Cooperation,* Spring 1974.

_____. *Undergraduate Cross Registration.* Report of the Associated Colleges of the Saint Lawrence Valley and the Office of Higher Education Management Services of the New York State Education Department. Albany, N.Y.: 1975.

Grupe, F. A. "The Establishment of Collegiate Cooperative Centers." Ph.D. dissertation, State University of New York, 1969.

Halerston, W. "Early Attempts at Cooperation Among Member Colleges of Colleges of Mid-America, Incorporated." Mimeographed. Sioux City, Ia.: Colleges of Mid-America, 1972.

Hodghmanson, H. T. "Import of Consortia on Institutional Vitality." Mimeographed. Berkeley: Center for Research and Development in Higher Education, 1972.

Kilgour, Frederick G. "Library Networks: What to Expect." *Institutional Interface: Making the Right Connection,* Spring 1974, pp. 22–28.

Paltridge, J. G. "Urban Higher Education Consortia." Berkeley: Center for Research and Development in Higher Education, 1971.

Parlminson, R. D. "Selected Voluntary Consortia in Higher Education: Financial Aspects." Ph.D. dissertation, University of Indiana, 1972.

Patterson, Lewis D. "A Descriptive Study of the Governing of Selected Voluntary Academic Cooperative Arrangements in Higher Education," Ph.D. Dissertation, University of Missouri, 1971.

_____. "Evolving Patterns of Cooperation." *ERIC Higher Education Research Currents,* June 1975, p. 3.

_____, ed. *Consortium Directory: Voluntary Academic Cooperative Arrangements in Higher Education.* 5th ed. Kansas City, Mo.: Kansas City Regional Council for Higher Education, 1971.

_____. *Comprehensive Bibliography on Interinstitutional Cooperation with Special Emphasis on Voluntary Academic Consortia in Higher Education.* 5th ed. Kansas City, Mo.: Regional Council for Higher Education, 1971.

Provo, J. L. "A Change Process Model for Bilateral Interinstitutional Cooperation in Higher Education." Ph.D. dissertation, Kansas State University, 1971.

Sagen, E. L. "A Network Model of Steps for the Implementation of the Planning and Establishing of Higher Education Consortiums." Ph.D. dissertation, Ohio State University, 1969.

Silverman, R. J. "Toward an Inter-Organizational Theory in Higher Education." Ph.D. dissertation, Cornell University, 1969.

Swerdlow, K. G. "Selected Voluntary Academic Consortia in Higher Education: Academic Program." Ph.D. dissertation, University of Indiana, 1972.

Trendler, C. A. "Institutional Cooperation for Academic Development Among Small Church-Related Liberal Arts Colleges." Ph.d. dissertation, Indiana University, 1967.

Tront, W. E. "The Kentuckian Metrouniversity: Case Study of a Consortium."
    Master's thesis, University of Tonisville, 1972.
Zimmerman, W. D. "A Foundation Executive's Assessment of the College Con-
    sortia Movement." In Papers of the Academic Consortia Seminar on As-
    sessing the Consortium Movement. Edited by L. D. Patterson. Mim-
    eographed. Kansas City, Mo.: Kansas City Regional Council for Higher
    Education, 1968.

25

Learning Resources in Higher Education

The Learning Resource Center: Support Service or Change Agent

THEODORE R. LAABS

Over the past ten years, the development of the learning resources concept has occurred haphazardly. There appears to be little uniformity in the application of the title "learning resource center" to the various operations within post-secondary institutions, including colleges and universities. In one institution the library might be called the "LRC"; in another it is a remedial laboratory. Still another may have an instructional materials center that is separate from the library, the audiovisual center, as well as any special or remedial lab. The instructional materials center would be called the learning resource center to differentiate it from the library.

When asked to define the library as a learning resource center (LRC), the definition usually proceeds in terms of items or entities including services housed in the library or whatever facility is designated the LRC. The aggregation of parts is considered as a support service which supplies the teacher, student, and staff with materials and information as requested. Occasionally the complaint is raised concerning the lack of involvement in the instructional process. Or perhaps when a financial crunch hits an institution the business office will tighten up on purchases, forcing the LRC staff, supported by faculty, to justify the quantity of requisitions in terms of items expended. Cost usually plays a significant factor in this exchange. What then is LRC, and how does it become involved in the instructional process?

DEFINITIONS

Audiovisual department—That department which develops and maintains all audiovisual equipment for classroom support and for LRC usage.

Automation department—That department which develops the material that can be automated for learning system use.

Data processing department—That department which catalogues all materials in the LRC on a computer. The data is immediately retrievable for update, future acquisition, present acquisition, and inventory.

Learning resource center—A more broad concept than library, which generally means books or printed material alone. This center houses all the materials, print or nonprint, that are used for instructional and research purposes. Includes both the mediated center as well as the library.

Learning systems—The software used in the learning process and playable on the equipment maintained by the audiovisual department.

Library department—The department of the LRC which concerns itself with the oversight of the entire LRC operations.

Nonprint material—Any material for use in LRCs that is not traditionally considered print material.

Print material—Books, magazines, abstracts—any material whose primary delivery system is printed.

THE ROLE OF THE LEARNING RESOURCE CENTER

The role of the LRC is determined by the way it is perceived by the institution, the chief administrator, and the vice president. Role perception further determines the organizational structure. In the final analysis it is role perception that affects the expected results of the organization.

If the LRC is perceived as a support service, the relationship of the service will be ancillary. If the LRC is perceived as a change agent, its influence will be on the learning taking place as a result of the instructional process. Both support services and change agents are qualities present in an LRC. The difference is in the emphasis and degree of emphasis stemming from the role expectation of the institution.

The problem with most definitions of an LRC is that they concentrate on the support aspect of the LRC and neglect the change agent. The overemphasis of the support service can be determined by reading any set of standards, description of functions, or role definitions. The elements that illustrate the support characteristics are a "laundry list" of entities: materials, equipment, facilities, staff, tasks, activities, and services.

The assumption is that if all the entities are included, the purpose of the operation is defined and the operation is identified. Therefore the role of the organization is established through the enumeration of the parts. The whole is considered the sum of the parts. The whole can be modified by changing or rearranging the parts without destroying or diminishing the integrity of the whole—in this case, the organization of the LRC. The question then becomes, is the totality of the LRC an aggregate of parts or is the whole greater than the sum of its parts? The answer to this question reveals the manner in which the role of the LRC is perceived by the administration. The expectations of the institution determine the efficacy of the LRC within the institution. Stated another way, is the LRC plugged into the instructional process?

The LRC as Support Service

As a support service, the functions of the LRC are tacked on or added to the instructional process. Teachers call the media center and complain that the equipment is malfunctioning. The library may receive complaints that certain books or magazines are not available. Students may complain that the fine regulations are unfair or the circulation policy does not allow them to keep materials longer. The LRC is considered in terms of the objects it provides.

Budget rationales usually concern specific acquisitions or categories of items. The necessity of a collection of books is assumed. Certain formats are regularly requested by instructors. The need according to the previous year's use is based upon an enumeration of items, people using the facility, and the dollar amount expended. With a base established, increments are added as the budget is developed. Inflation, expansion, and maintenance of status are the primary budget criteria. Services performed stop short of the learning results. Educational specifications are seldom considered. The emphasis is on technical specifications. The quality of the item for the lowest cost as reflected in the bid procedure is the primary concern. The business office reviews the allocations and sets the parameters. There are, of course, exceptions. But for the most part, especially in smaller institutions, budgets are established according to the dollars available, with different departments competing. Determinations of allocations are made according to the most persuasive individual. Persuasion is in terms of perceived needs.

When libraries compete for the budget dollar, a comparison is usually made with other libraries in terms of collection size and number of volumes against what the institution can afford. The more volumes, the better the library. Evaluation is in terms of collection growth.

When the library is called an LRC and considered as a support service, a split function develops. The support is split between the students' needs and the needs of the instructional areas. In serving the students the library strives to meet their requests, which may include library material for personal enrichment or independent study. Community use of the college library also may be a factor, depending on the college's concern for public relations in the community.

The other part of the split function is the teacher's needs. The instructor uses the library for professional development as well as for assisting the student through a reserve system which limits the circulation of materials to insure a greater number of students access to a limited number of copies. The instructor may draw upon the library to provide materials for class assignments.

Unlike the library, the audiovisual services support the teacher rather than the student by providing him or her with requested instructional aids. Approval of department chairpersons may be required, but approval is generally in terms of funds and materials available, and the ability of the media staff to produce the desired aid within a stipulated period.

THE IDENTITY PROBLEM

What is a learning resource center? In some institutions it is a library with a name change. A university with a strong library will have an LRC, but it might really be the remedial reading lab. Still others might combine library and audiovisual services under one administrator to more efficiently control the budget and administrative functions.

Why is it necessary to change the name of the library or remedial reading center to learning resource center when the function of the roles of these centers is not changed to correspond with the new designation? It appears that the name change occurs when a new format or service is added to an existing organizational unit.

A Definition of the LRC

Since there appear to be a variety of entities called learning resource centers, a definition is in order to establish a frame of reference: *The learning resource center is a centralized administrative configuration which systematically integrates four primary components: library, audiovisual, instructional development and alternate instructional modes into an operational unit which functions as a change agent for the learning process.* The above definition is based upon Gary Peterson's conceptualization of the learning resources center.[1]

Key Elements of the LRC

The key elements of the definition are illustrated in Figure 63. These five elements provide an alternative to the listing of parts and set the stage for an organization in which the whole is greater than its parts.

The centralized administrative configuration means that instead of having two or more persons report to the dean or vice-president, one person is responsible for the operation. That is, the administrative con-

FIGURE 63
Key elements of the learning Resources definition

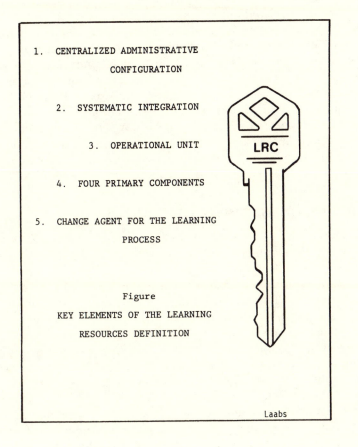

1. CENTRALIZED ADMINISTRATIVE
         CONFIGURATION

   2. SYSTEMATIC INTEGRATION

      3. OPERATIONAL UNIT

   4. FOUR PRIMARY COMPONENTS

5. CHANGE AGENT FOR THE LEARNING
              PROCESS

              Figure
KEY ELEMENTS OF THE LEARNING
    RESOURCES DEFINITION

LRC

Laabs

figuration of the LRC is not localized. It need not be in the center but can be anywhere. Apart from the span of control, the administrative configuration provides for a unified planning structure. Objectives may be set which encompass the entire LRC. Unified direction and allocation of fiscal resources is obtainable. The expertise of several professional staff members may be pooled to work as a team rather than functioning as independent departments competing among each other and with other departments.

Systematic integration takes the components out of the aggregate concept of parts enumeration and establishes relationships. Stephen Knesevich in *Program Budgeting* (PPBS) defines this system: "An array of components designed to accomplish a particular objective according to plan: a cluster of interactive and interdependent components that focus on one or more related objectives."[2]

The totality is greater than the sum of the parts in this definition, since the results are determined by the objectives. Moreover, the components are interactive and interdependent. Thus the relationship of the parts is established. The systems definition goes beyond an enumeration of parts and provides a cohesiveness which suggests internal monitoring. Systematic integration does not occur, for example, if two independent departments report to the same administrator. The components must be interrelated. A library and audiovisual center each forming their own separate function but reporting to the vice president of academic affairs are not systematically integrated and therefore are not an LRC.

FOUR COMPONENTS OF THE LRC

The four components of the LRC are library, audiovisual services, instructional development, and alternate instructional modes. (See Figure 64.)

The library. A quality of the first component, the library, is that it is student centered. The primary clientele of the library, the student, uses its collection for a variety of reasons. The services and items provided have been listed elsewhere. In the traditional library the collection was of paramount importance. More recently services expanded from collecting to include access to the collection through reference assistance and bibliographic instruction. In educational institutions an instructional program regarding library utilization is usually developed informally. A library orientation program recognizes the students' need for additional skills in using the library. The orientation is extended still further to include study habits and borders on the edge of alternative instruction modes. These extensions carry the library into the learning resources arena.

Audiovisual services. Audiovisual services, unlike library services, are teacher centered. The teacher requests and prescribes the instructional aids for the student. Production, an important function of the services provided, responds to the instructional requirements, if teachers cannot acquire the mediated material desired for class presentations. They turn to local production either to produce the materials themselves under the guidance of the audiovisual specialist or ask the audiovisual staff to

FIGURE 64
Four components of the learning resources center

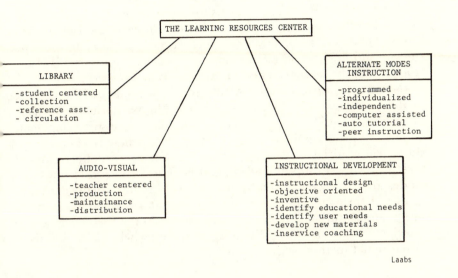

Laabs

produce the required items, often with little concern for technical refinements.

Mobility distinguishes the media specialist from the librarian. The librarian waits for the user to come to the library, while the audiovisual specialist cultivates a clientele among the teachers and delivers the materials. The media center is not always localized but may be decentralized among the departments. The audiovisual budget also may be allocated by department. The library on the other hand has an easily recognized profile and a specified budget.

Instructional development. Instructional development refers to the development of instructional designs and strategies that concentrate on learning results. Instructional development is a part of instructional technology that is explained in a 1970 report.[3] The report referred to a systematic way of designing, carrying out, and evaluating the learning process as a total process. It emphasized combining human and nonhuman resources for greater instructional efficacy.[4]

Media selection as well as production is contained in the instructional development mode. The mode goes beyond the provision of media in that it considers the objectives of the instructional process as determined by the instructor as well as the learning resulting from the objectives. The learning results must be observable and measurable; that is, there should be an identifiable change in behavior resulting from the employment of resources, including mediated resources as well as print materials from the library collection.

The difficulty with the instructional development mode lies in the perceived role of the teacher versus that of the instructional developer. Here a possible conflict can occur if the developer is not diplomatically astute. Qualities of the developer include tact, persuasion, influence, finesse, and integrity in identifying and meeting the needs of both the teacher and the learner. There must be a team approach.

Alternate instructional modes. Alternate instructional modes are those modes currently not being used or practiced by a majority of the faculty in an institution. They could include the following instructional methodologies: programmed, individualized, independent, computer assisted, autotutorial, and peer instruction. Unlike teaching techniques such as lecture, group discussion, and laboratory demonstration, these modes are readily enhanced by and in some instances dependent upon mediated formats. Their acceptance varies and may be experimental within an institution. The term nontraditional is not used because of its growing overuse and the difficulty of defining what is traditional in instructional methodology.

CHANGE AGENCY AND THE LRC

The LRC as change agent refers to the perceptible change that occurs in the learner as a result of the instructional design implemented through a planned set of instructional strategies. Change does not necessarily mean the destruction of the institution or its organization. Role expectations could be changed by the LRC, but that is not the primary concern. The primary concern is the measurable, demonstrable, or perceptible result which occurs when learning resources are employed by the learner. (See Figure 65.)

The evaluation of the LRC as a change agent should be based on the learning that takes place because of mediated resources or LRC objectives as they are implemented in the instructional process. The effectiveness of the LRC is judged by what it accomplishes in the learning situation, not by how many books it hands out. The static collection warehouse or museum concept of the library in higher education does not address itself to the learning needs of the student population.

Change objectives, if they are to be effective, should be written not in terms of the standard enumeration of parts or components but in terms or what happens as a result of the utilization of the resources in the learning process. The adoption of a new format or piece of equipment in itself is not change. The increase in a student's criterion test score as a

FIGURE 65
The learning resources center as change agent

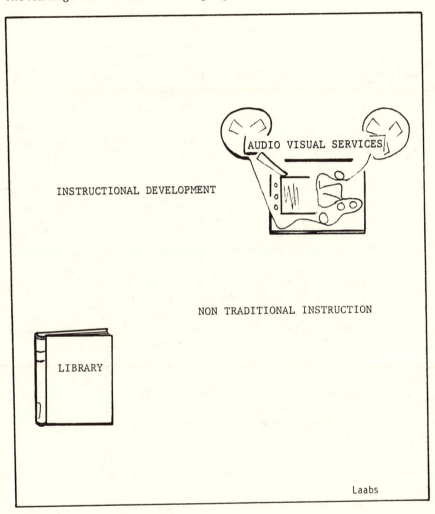

result of using a particular book or mediated format may be an indicator of change.

AN ELECTRONIC CHANGE AGENT

The Learning Resources Center functions as an electronic change agent through the introduction of technological developments in video, computers, and the transmission of instructional information, visual, audio, electronically rather than manually. The change agent role occurs when the LRC is able to take the initiative introducing new, innovative or experimental concepts through the addition of hardware, software as well as new titles to the print collection.

While there are other ways in which the LRC may function as a change agent, the reference here is to the influence of recent developments on the instructional support role of the LRC, namely the effect of the microcomputer, video in relatively inexpensive but quality formats, video discs and the interaction of the computer with the video forms.

The interaction of video with computer control revives the concepts of individualized self paced instruction. Using a video disc with its large storage capacity and random access, the computer is able to present practice and drill, tutorial, simulations and games. The computer can also perform a variety of functions from frequency counts to correlations, monitoring the student's progress through the lesson. The instructor is able to diagnose the student problems, success, attempts, and failures in an item-by-item analysis and is in a better position to give the student detailed assistance with minimum routine administrative effort expended.

The change agent function occurs when the LRC provides not only the space but assists in the development of interactive video. The media branch of the LRC may combine a microcomputer with a video recorder, a ½ inch Beta format. In this case the access and storage may be less than that of the disc, but on the other hand locally produced programs can occur. The video recorder-player now commands as it sets up exercise, but with the attachment of a video camera can record a situation for play back comparison and evaluation by the student. Such an application has a variety of possibilities in art, science experiments, speech, drama, police safety simulations, and any where the student actively participates in learning skills.

The Learning Resources Center as a service, a total program, rather than a place, supports the instructional program, not as a passive responder but actually as a change agent. As a change agent the responsibility, both administrative and instructional, includes providing access to new technologies for faculty and student utilization. Access to microcomputers in the LRC is an example. Software support for the equipment, orientation search strategies, electronic distribution, and access.

To fulfill the role of change agent the LRC participates actively in instructional design and development. Unlike the involvement of some libraries which occurs after the course has been established and faculty or students request the books available, to be effective, the LRC must be involved in the course design process. The introduction of instructional technology concepts as well as the anticipation of new technologies and electronic service can best be explored at this point without major fund

committment. Needed experimentation, and trial periods can be initiated. Once the course is established it is difficult to introduce change.

ATTRIBUTES OF THE LRC COMPONENTS

When the components of the LRC are discussed individually they are
referred to in terms of objects or tangible entities. The attributes are the
intangible relationships that not only bind the components together but
also differentiate one component from another. Librarians claim that
they are different from audiovisual specialists because of the uniqueness
of books. This claim varies from librarian to librarian, but there are
those who hold the book sacred. Such a love affair with books has no
place in an instructionally oriented institution. The attribute here is that
of a collector or a museum curator, not one of instructional utilization of
books. The educational institution looks at books with a learning emphasis, for the information they contain and the impact that information has
through the instructional design on the observable or perceived learning
that takes place.

The primary attribute of the librarian should not be love of books but
concern for the student, specifically the librarian's concern with providing the student with information and showing the student the skills and
search strategies needed to find that information. The librarian's contribution to the learning process is developing the self-sufficiency of the
student in obtaining information regardless of content or form.

The audiovisual specialist approaches the instructional process
through production and design of learning materials. The creation of
learning materials or units, regardless of the format, identifies the audiovisual specialist.

The instructional developer concentrates on the design element in the
learning process. The design is the unifying matrix that pulls together
the information-gathering and production modes to form a unit. This
unit may be implemented through a variety of strategies depending
upon the instructional objectives and the teacher's choice of methodology and techniques to facilitate the learning process. The developer also
is concerned with monitoring results to determine the extent to which
learning has taken place and the efficacy of units presented for future
use, reuse, or modification.

Alternate instructional modes are a set of instructional techniques that
are used as required by the uniqueness of the student's learning pattern
or style. Additional techniques may be prescribed as a need is diagnosed.
Their use depends upon the planning that is involved in the learning
objectives as well as the appropriateness to the learner's need. As a set
they should not be indiscriminately used.

The attributes of the components form the attributes of the LRC concerned with the uniqueness of the student. Thus materials are selected, processed, and employed to match the learner's style, but at the same time a learning-oriented change is introduced in the student.

By combining components into a learning resource center, the configuration should have a measurable impact on the learner. The LRC as a single unit will shuffle the components to facilitate that impact. This may mean combining all circulation procedures in an access mode rather than separating them between library and audiovisual departments. But, more important, the components as a group have a measurable effect on the learner. The evaluation of that effect is what justifies the existence of the LRC and its components. The presence of collections, facilities, or equipment alone is of little instructional value unless it is introduced in a planned and meaningful manner into the learning process.

As a support service the components and the LRC cannot be justified apart in terms of the learning process. The justification of the support service lies in its auxiliary characteristics and holdings. Until the impact of the support service is perceived in the learner, the service is not an integral part of the instructional process.

The LRC is greater than its parts if it becomes involved in the learning activity by facilitating change in the learner. This can only occur if its role is perceived as a change agent as well as a support service incorporating evaluative techniques extending beyond the support function.

Support Services through Learning Resources

FLOYD T. KING, JR., BOB W. MILLER, AND
THEODORE R. LAABS

The traditional library is disappearing, along with separate facilities for library and audiovisual activities. Combined library and audiovisual services are not always harmonious within institutions, but they must become so if institutions of higher education are to meet the needs of students and faculty within a changing environment. Students live in a complex and media oriented society, and no one particular format for communication can be considered best for all. When print and nonprint materials and services are coordinated into one center, under one objective, they are most accessible, providing greater potential for use and greater potential for learning. A recent survey of community colleges indicated that three-fourths were administering the library and audiovisual services as a single unit. Guidelines for learning resource centers are being modified and rewritten to reflect the unified media concept.[5]

This unified concept is fairly new on the educational scene. Many institutions of higher education are located in facilities over fifty years old. Most of these institutions, through tradition, have separate locations and administrations for their library and audiovisual services and are not making enough effort to move toward any kind of consolidation of services and/or administration.

IMPLEMENTATION OF LEARNING RESOURCE CENTERS

The disadvantage of a poorly planned library building is not only its awkwardness for users and staff members, but also its excessive operating costs which serve as a continuous annual burden on the parent institution and, ultimately, on the taxpayers.[6]

Architect Harry F. Anderson states that the primary basis for successful architecture is a statement of the functional needs of a program. One important distinction which must be recognized is that there are two kinds of program: functional and architectural. Each has the same goal—a library facility, of whatever name, that will reflect the method of operation, the kind of work and service to be offered, and the functional requirements of the institution. The functional program is prepared by those who are going to use the building and the architectural program by those responsible for its design. Some specifications for the development of the functional needs program should include the following:

1. It is written and is an "official document."
2. It tells how the building is to be used.
3. It establishes the goals, the policy and philosophic framework.
4. It separates needs from wants.
5. It establishes a priority of needs.
6. It defines the challenge.
7. It helps establish the character of the building.
8. It defines the relationship of the major parts of the building.[7]

Who prepares the functional needs program? Ideally it should be a team effort headed by a responsible, open-minded, dedicated librarian. Other team members might include a library consultant, someone from administration (perhaps the officer for development), a trustee, and appropriate representatives from the faculty and the student body.

The preparation of this functional needs program will be difficult, especially in this day of continual and profound change. Concepts are changing. The sophistication of communications media, the daily improvement of mechanical and electronic devices, the changing nature of the kinds of materials available, and the dynamic state of colleges are all factors which compound the task. It is a responsibility, however, which cannot be avoided.[8]

Anderson expresses some general thoughts on the building itself. It must be:

1. Comprehensible, understandable, friendly.
2. Efficiently planned whereby the librarian and staff are so located that as much time as possible can be spent with the users.
3. Human in scale and in the use of materials.
4. In harmony with its natural setting.
5. Capable of providing privacy.
6. Capable of exterior expansion and interior change.
7. Expressive of the philosophy of the college.
8. Centrally located and within the framework of a flexible and adaptable campus master plan.

9. Agreeably quiet, possessing good acoustic qualities.
10. Well lit, with quality of light more important than quantity.
11. Well ventilated, heated, and cooled.
12. Possessed of adequate, accessible space between floors to allow for future installations of machines and equipment.
13. Possessed of an innovative, imaginative form which reflects and allows for flexibility without being "tricky."[9]

When confronted with the design of a new learning resources building, it's easy to be limited by perceptions of what it "should" be like. In many cases there is a propensity to design and build a learning resources building for existing functions whether they be housed in an existing library facility or spread among separate facilities throughout the school. In the first instance, the result will be a learning resources building that will represent an improvement in services to students and faculty. In the last instance, the services to students and faculty will remain essentially the same, but the convenience of administering the learning resources center will be improved.[10]

Four major areas that should be included among the facilities of any learning resources center are the library department, the audiovisual department, the learning systems and automation department, and the data processing department. Each of these four areas would be divided further to provide for internal school use and external use by other schools and other users. These four areas can then be described in more detail as follows:

Library Areas:
  Study
  Circulation
  Card Catalog
  Processing (acquisitions and cataloging)
  Automated learning
  Collections (assigned)
    Books
    Periodicals and Serials
    Pamphlets
    Newspapers
    Reference
    Reserve
    Transparencies
    8 mm Films
    16 mm Films
    Microfilm-Microfiche

Slides
Audio and Automated Programs
Maps
Audiovisual Areas:
  Circulation
  Preview
  Production (Slides, Transparencies, etc.)
  Processing (May be combined with Library)
  Collections (Distributed)
    16 mm Motion Pictures
    8 mm Super, Motion Pictures
    8 mm Super, Single Concept Films
    Audio Tapes
    Slides
    Filmstrips
    Curriculum Materials
    Learning Kits
  Transparency Editing (16 mm, 8 mm, Slides)
  Graphics
  Closed Circuit Television Collections
  Maintenance Workshop
  Photographic Production
  Media Index Collection
  Equipment Storage
  Television Production
Learning Systems and Automation Areas:
  Program Development
  Software Processing
    Tape Duplication
    Filmstrip Conversion
    Phono-Record Conversion
    Kit Development
  Woodwork and Machine Shop
Computer Areas:
  Programming
  Systems Analysis
  Central Computer System
  Program Collection
  Production Preparation
Student Areas:
  Carrels
  Seminar-Workroom (30 persons)
  Small Group Workrooms (10 persons)
  Exhibit
  Planetarium

Observatory
Smoking Lounge
Faculty Area:
  Reading Room-Lounge
    Professional Journals
    Professional Books
    Newspapers
    Audio Tape Listening
    Lockers

The building of a new learning resources center will probably enhance learning and teaching methodology as much or more than the building of any other kind of facility. One thing is certain: all other facilities will be affected by learning resources services, and this makes the center's design of utmost concern to assure that the developing practices, offering so much hope to improve learning and teaching, will not inadvertently be left out.[11]

The spatial relationships and operation of the various functions of the learning resources center are very important to the overall success of the center. Ralph Ellsworth has noted that there are five basic relationships common to college libraries:

1. There should be one central exit control point at which all who leave the building can be checked to make certain the library materials they are taking out have been properly checked out.

2. As soon as the reader has passed the vestibule, he goes into a lobby, a place the architect uses for various purposes: an area for displays, an area to quiet down readers as they come into the building, an area to lead the reader to the key library books and operations, a place to house new book exhibits, and even as a place for receptions.

3. Immediately beyond the lobby one should see the tools and services that serve as keys: catalog, reference services, bibliographies.

4. Traffic patterns should be planned so that as one enters a building they can use the cloak room, locker check room, and toilets before they pass the control exit point.

5. Provisions for books and readers will be dependent on two factors: (a) the type of building (fixed function vs. modular), and (b) the type of organization to be used.[12]

A spatial relationship diagram of the library functions of the learning resources center includes the following areas: lobby, offices, circulation, card catalog, periodicals area, technical services, reference area, reading

FIGURE 66
Spatial relationships-library

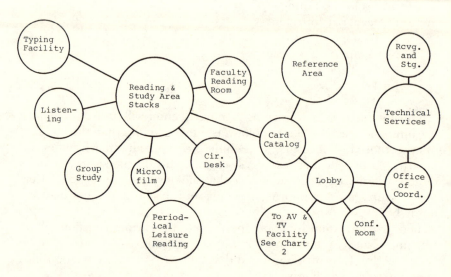

Ellsworth, Ralph, *Planning Colleges and What Does a Modern Learning University Library Building Do?* (Boulder, Colorado, Pruett Press, Inc., 1968) (1, pp. 41–49)

and study area, stacks, faculty reading area, typing facility, microfilm reading area, group study facilities, and receiving and storage. A visual diagram of these relationships is presented in Figure 66. This diagram will change from institution to institution as reflected in their differing philosophies.[13]

The consideration of spatial relationships of the audiovisual facility for the learning resource center is also very important. Some colleges may separate audiovisual facilities within the learning resource center complex; others may integrate all media in one facility. A visual arrangement of a separate audiovisual facility is represented by Figure 67. Within the center there are areas for lobby, reception and scheduling, storage and repair, graphics and production, television, basic skills laboratory, preview rooms, recording studio, and a darkroom.

The relationships illustrated in Figures 66 and 67 are not the only emerging patterns of development, and each institution should develop its own patterns as reflected by the needs of the particular institution and community.[14]

What are recommended space requirements for a learning resource center? In the library the reading and stack storage areas have as their

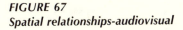

FIGURE 67
Spatial relationships-audiovisual

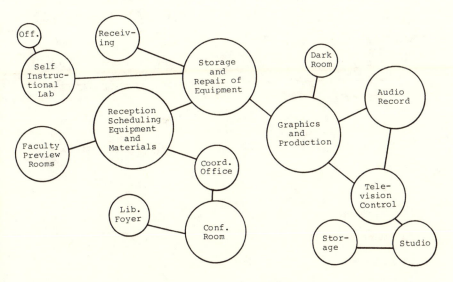

Ellsworth, Ralph F., *Planning Colleges and University Library Buildings*, (Boulder, Colorado, Pruett Press, Inc., 1968), (1, pp. 41, 49).

major purposes the storage of printed materials, and accommodations for the reading public. A unified effort of library planning in concise form has been organized in *Manual Four, Academic Support Facilities*, published by the Western Interstate Commission for Higher Education (WICHE). A generally acceptable standard indicates that approximately 25 percent of the student body (full-time equivalent) should have seating accommodations and that twenty-five square feet per reader is an acceptable standard.

Few standards have been established with respect to the space required for housing the audiovisual facility. Perhaps the best unified effort has been WICHE's condensation of the findings of the Office of the Vice Chancellor, State University of New York. Table 13 gives one of the best condensed findings for the space needed by an audiovisual facility.[15]

The guidelines used previously are only points for preliminary planning in a learning resources center. The real space allocations will be determined by the philosophy of the institution and the budget on which it is to operate.[16] An example of total space requirements is found in Table 14.

TABLE 13
Space needs for audiovisual facility

SPACE NEEDS FOR AUDIOVISUAL FACILITY			
Facility Function or Category	1 to 3,000 FTE	3,001 to 5,000 FTE	5,001 to 7,000 FTE
Core Service			
Graphics	800	800	800
Photography	600	800	1,020
Equipment and Materials			
Circulation	1,000	1,400	1,640
Equipment			
Maintenance	400	400	400
Studios	1,200	1,500	1,500
T.V. Audio			
Distribution	1,200	1,200	1,200
Audio Services			
and Radio	480	600	800
Shops and			
Storage	1,400	1,600	1,800
Administration	480	600	840
Instructional			
Development	540	860	1,000
Total Assignable Square Feet	8,100	9,760	11,000

Higher Education Facilities Planning and Management Manuals. Manual Four, Academic Support Facilities, (Boulder, Colorado, Western Interstate Commission for Higher Education, 1971) (6 p. 68).

TABLE 14
Space needs for LRC with 5,000 FTE students

SPACE NEEDS FOR LRC WITH 5,000 FTE STUDENTS

A. Library (excluding lobby)

   1. Student stations (1,250 (25% of

      5,00 FTE) X 25 sq. ft. = 3.250   31,250

   2. Area needed for printed materials

      storage:

      Book storage   6,000

      Special collection   1,500

   3. Staff requirements (10 positions)   1,800

   4. Processing and technical services   1,700

   5. Typing   350

   6. Microfilm reading and storage   350

   7. Staff reading room and lounge   300

   8. Group study rooms (6 at 150 sq. ft.)   900

                                   44,150

B. Audiovisual and Television   11,000

C. Listening and Audio-Video retrival   1.200

D. Self Instructional Laboratory   1,200

    GRAND TOTAL   Square Feet   57,550

Higher Education Facilities Planning and Management Manuals. Manual Four, Academic Support Facilities, (Boulder, Colorado, Western Interstate Commission for Higher Education, 1971) 6 p. 68.

ORGANIZATION OF LEARNING RESOURCE CENTERS

The administrative organization of the learning resource center depends on many factors. There is the impact of history, or, differently expressed, the persistence of an established pattern even after the basis for its continued existence has disappeared. There is the general administrative college pattern into which the learning resource center must fit. There is the size of the institution; generally, the larger the institution the more administrative levels are necessary. There is the preferred administrative style of the persons or groups in policy-setting positions. There is the inclination to adopt "qualitative recommendations and professional expertise based on successful practices" used in other leading institutions.[17]

Guidelines exist for developing the organization of learning resource centers. The American Library Association and the Association of College and Research Libraries jointly developed the "Guidelines for Two-Year College Learning Resources Programs", cited above, in December 1972. Several states have approved this document for application to their community and junior college libraries.

The responsibilities and functions of learning resources programs within the institutional structure and the status of the chief administrator and heads of learning resources units must be clearly defined. The effectiveness of services provided depends on the understanding by faculty, college administrators, students, and learning resources staff of their responsibilities and functions as they relate to the institution. A written statement, endorsed by the institution's trustees or other policy-setting group, should be readily available.[18]

To function adequately, the chief administrator of a learning resources program (whose title may vary in different institutions) usually reports to the administrative officer of the college responsible for the instructional program and has the same administrative rank and status as others with similar institution-wide responsibilities. These responsibilities are delineated as part of a written statement so that the learning resources dean or director has adequate authority to manage the internal operations and to provide the services needed. The relationship of a learning resources program to the total learning program necessitates involvement of the professional staff in all areas and levels of academic planning.[19]

Provision of learning materials is central to the academic program. As a result, the professional staff has broad interests which go beyond the scope of its day-to-day operations. Professional staff members are involved in all areas and levels of academic planning. The chief administrator and heads of learning resources units should work closely with other chief administrators of the college, and all professional staff members participate in faculty affairs to the same extent as regular faculty.[20]

The learning resource center requires a staff broadly educated and well-qualified in the area of communication. Familiarity with both print and nonprint media and their implications and effectiveness in the process of communication is a necessity. Furthermore, media personnel need an understanding of student and faculty characteristics at the local institution, for those following baccalaureate and occupational as well as adult education curricula. The roles of professional and semiprofessional staff members must be understood in order to effectively serve the students and faculty. The success of the operation in meeting the objective and goals of the institution requires a well-qualified and numerically adequate staff.[21] Following are guidelines for learning resources staff:

1. The chief administrator of the learning resources program is selected on the basis of acquired competencies which relate to the purposes of the program, educational achievement, administrative ability, community and scholarly interests, professional activities, and services orientation.

2. The administrative (or supervisory) heads of the separate learning resources units are selected on the basis of their expertise in and knowledge of the function and role of the particular unit which they will manage and to which they will give leadership.

3. A well-qualified, experienced staff is available in sufficient numbers and area of specialization to carry out adequately the purposes and objectives of the LRC.

4. Professional staff members should have degrees and/or experience appropriate to the position requirements.

5. Every professional staff member has faculty status, faculty benefits, and obligations.

6. Professional development is the responsibility of both the institution and the professional staff member.

7. Teaching assignments by learning resources staff members are considered dual appointments in calculating staff work loads.

8. Supportive staff members are responsible for assisting the professional staff in providing effective services.

9. Student assistants are employed to supplement the work of the supportive staff.[22]

Sarah K. Thomson found from visits to twenty-seven community college library/learning resource centers, in California, Florida, Illinois, Texas, Virginia, and Maryland, that personnel expenditures accounted for about two-thirds of the learning resources budgets. Of the campuses visited, the personnel expenditures in the 1972–1973 fiscal year ranged from $106,000 to $484,135, the mean was $286,232 and the medium $301,000. Staffs ranged in size from thirteen to sixty; the median size was twenty-nine. Twenty-two of the colleges were organized with the library and the audiovisual or media program as separate units within the college; although separate units, they might be within the same department, have a common administrative head, and share the same building. In addition to these two units, there were sometimes separate units for production services, and perhaps separate (central) technical

FIGURE 68
Richland College organization chart

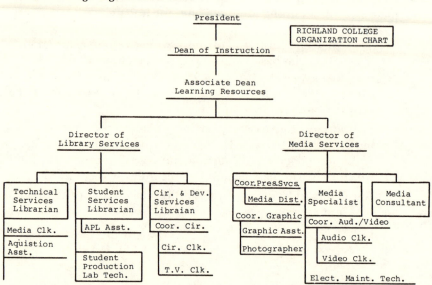

Richland College, *Rights, Sites and Rituals,* Revised, 1976, 1977. (Dallas, Texas, Richland College Print Shop, 1976 (9, P, 105).

processing services. Fourteen of these units were headed by a common administrator of learning resources. Eight had no chief administrator for learning resources as such, although the librarian and the head of audiovisual services might have reported to a common general administrator, such as a dean or vice president of instruction.[23]

At Richland Community College in Dallas, Texas, the learning resource center is headed by an associate dean. As may be seen from Figure 68, the associate dean of the learning resource center reports to the dean of instruction. Reporting to the associate dean of the LRC are the director of library services and the director of media services.[24]

SERVICES OF LEARNING RESOURCE CENTERS

Two very important decisions must be determined relative to the services provided by the learning resource center: (1) to whom should the services be given and (2) what will be the nature of the services?

The nature of the services will vary from institution to institution. How the learning resource center will sell its services to faculty and students is an important question. Knowledge of the utilization requirements of faculty and students must be obtained before the center can efficiently administer an effective program. One method of determining utilization requirements is through student and faculty surveys. An analysis of such surveys indicates that students tend to use materials because they are required to use them and that the majority of students utilize their own materials and not the center's when studying in the learning resource center.

The technical services area is responsible for the ordering of magazines, books, and other print and nonprint materials; checking invoices against purchase orders; accounting of funds allocated to the department; cataloging and classifying materials; filing catalog cards; and other processing techniques that may be required to make materials available for student and faculty use. The department should be organized in a manner to allow a work flow beginning with the ordering process to the finished product for patron usage. Utilization may be increased through interfiling print and nonprint materials in the card catalog.[25]

Some of the services offered in the library section of the learning resource center are as follows: high-speed tape duplicator, photocopy machines, maintenance of reserve collection, hold for reserve service, circulation art production service, center for independent study, short answer directional information, reference questions, reader advisory service, machine instruction, interlibrary loan preparing of bibliographies, bibliographic information supplies, orientation tours, student use of typewriters, reel-to-reel, and cassette recorders, tapes and monitors, slide projectors, instructional television viewing and microcomputers with program selection.

Classroom media services found in a learning resource center, or LRC, are responsible for the distribution of media equipment and materials to the classroom. The physical delivery of equipment is usually done by LRC personnel. Specific types of media available in an LRC usually include the following: 16 mm projectors, 16 mm film, super 8 mm projectors, slides, filmstrips, slide carousels, filmstrip projectors, overhead projectors, opaque projectors, super 8 mm camera, reel-to-reel (audio) recorders, cassette recorders, videotape recorders, public address system, phonographs, and miscellaneous equipment such as metal easels, roller chalkboards, screens, and extension cords.

Thomson found that of the twenty-three learning resource departments that relied primarily on a central pool of equipment, twenty-two provided pick up and delivery service to and from the classroom and one required the faculty members to arrange their own pick up and delivery. This pick up and delivery service required a major commitment of time, seldom less than seventy man-hours per week and often considerably more. Estimates of numbers of staff that would be delivering equipment simultaneously during a normal busy change of class time ranged from one regular staff and three students to ten people. One campus did not use student aides for pick up and delivery, but had four full-time staff with this assignment. Most directors thought that this service was essential if they wanted faculty to use the materials. One campus, threatened with a budget cut, discontinued pick up and delivery. All the faculty petitioned. The protect was so strong that funding was restored in forty-eight hours. In addition to pick up and delivery, four campuses supplied operators and most campuses set up the software so that all the faculty member had to do was to start the machine.[26]

Thomson also found that, in addition to the central equipment pool, seventeen campuses supplemented their pick up and delivery by permanent room assignments of heavily used equipment, semester or extended loan to faculty or to departments, and standing orders. Some pools to which faculty had keys were kept in each building. Lecture halls often had projection booths where equipment was locked in or bolted down. Remote control from the lectern by the instructor saved having to schedule operators. Many campuses had overheads and screens in every teaching space; one campus provided permanent placement of an overhead, a 16 mm projector, a tape recorder, and a slide projector in 70 percent of its classrooms. Some campuses where theft rate was very low were moving more and more toward permanent installation, which was considered a small risk in proportion to the greatly increased convenience and high savings. Some campuses were able to run their pick up and delivery systems on as few staff as they did because they delivered equipment as much as a half-hour ahead and left it standing outside the door in the hall unattended. This was considered a calculated tradeoff, of utility vs. convenience vs. theft risk. On four campuses most of the software was retained permanently in the departments.[27]

Instructional services of an LRC include both consultant and production services. LRC consultants work directly with faculty in preparing material for classroom use. The LRC consultants should be able to provide the following basic services to the faculty: (1) Instructional design and development, (2) Units or modules of instruction, (3) Implementation research (identifying appropriate learning-teaching processes), (4) Course management, (5) Materials reproduction, and (6) Investigation of commercial products.

Production services provided by an LRC usually consist of four areas: graphics, photography, audio, and video. Generally the faculty member makes a written request to production services for what he or she wants produced. This service is only for faculty and college staff use. On many campuses a special student production lab is available for use by the students. This lab is for the production of mediated projects such as films, posters, maps, slides, tapes, transparencies, and many more. An LRC consultant is on duty to assist in the selection of appropriate media as well as with technical aspects of the production. This unit may be of even more importance than other aspects of the LRC since it provides services directly to students.

Eleven campuses in Thomson's survey has special facilities and provided advisory and other assistance to students doing their own independent production of audiovisual materials. Sometimes these materials were related to courses the students were taking and would be presented by them in class; sometimes they were not related to their course program. In several schools the English department would accept such a production in place of term papers. Production facilities for students often included a student operated darkroom and, in four cases, a black-and-white television studio. Some campus bookstores stocked supplies for this use. One school had an independent production room for students and faculty, including audio, photography, and graphics capability. Staff were available to tell students how to make their projects and sometimes to give them help all the way down the line. One school had a regular media workshop for students and a full-time person to help them. Another school had a slide collection especially for students to incorporate into their productions. It started as an accident, was too useful to discard, and was then regularly augmented.[28]

SELECTION OF LEARNING MATERIALS

The need for selection tools became evident several decades ago, and comprehensive aids for book selection specifically tailored to the needs of higher education in the first two years were published as early as 1930. Since that time a number of lists have been issued. Several have been produced within the past few years.[29]

Many selection aids can be effectively used by learning resource center personnel and faculty. Some of the guides are as follows: *Choice, Books for College Libraries, Books for Junior Colleges, The Junior College Library Collection, A Basic Book Collection for The Community College, The Julian Street List, Publisher's Weekly, Library Journal, New York Times Book Review, Books in Print, Reader's Advisor,* the NICEM directories, *National Audio Tape Catalog,* and *Audiovisual Equipment Directory.* A well-balanced collection is not acquired by chance, and adequacy should be measured according to the goals and objectives of the institution.[30]

In selection of print material the following evaluation criteria will be helpful. Think in terms of, Who is the author? Does he have qualifications that fit him for dealing with the subject? Is he by education, occupation, or experience in a position to write anything of value? If he has written other books on the subject, check to see how they were received by the knowledgeable.

After the authority of the author has been established, the scope of the book should be ascertained. Does it concern itself with the history of the

TABLE 15
Criteria for selection of non-book materials

CRITERIA FOR SELECTION OF NON-BOOK MATERIALS

1. AUTHENTICITY
   Accurate facts
   Facts impartially presented
   Up-to-date information
   Other acceptable works of
     producer

2. APPROPRIATENESS
   Vocabulary at user's level
   Concepts at user's level
   Useful data
   Media-subject correlation
   Titles, captions, etc,
     related to subject
   Narration, dialogue, sound
     effects related to subject

3. SCOPE
   Full coverage as indicated
   Superior concept development
     by this means
   Content to satisfy demands
     for current subjects

4. INTEREST
   Intellectual challenge
   Curiosity satisfaction
   Credibility

5. ORGANIZATION
   Logical development
   Pertinence of all sequences
   Balance in use of narration
     and dialogue; background
     elements

   Imagination appeal
   Human appeal
   Sensory appeal

6. TECHNICAL ASPECTS
   Tone fidelity
   Clarity
   Intelligibility
   In-focus pictures
   Complete synchronization of
     sound and image

7. SPECIAL FEATURES
   Descriptive notes, teachers
     and/or users guide
   Pertinent accompanying material

8. PHYSICAL CHARACTERISTICS
   Ease in handling, for user, for
     storage
   Attractive packaging, Durability
   Ease of repair

Hicks, Warren B. and Tillan, Alma M., *Developing Multi-Media Libraries*, New York, RR topic or some present aspect of it? Is its treatment, either of the whole subject or part of it, exhaustive or brief? Once its scope has been determined, it should be compared with titles already in the library to decide if it really makes a contribution to the collection in terms of material covered.

Analyze the manner in which the material is treated. Is there anything in the writing itself that recommends the book? Is the style clear and readable, or muddied and tortured? Does the author organize the material so that the reader can follow his thought easily, or is he disjointed and confusing? Does the text have vitality and interest, or is it characterized by tedium and monotony? If the text popularizes a technical subject, is it done with accuracy and care, or is it so oversimplified that it is misleading. Does the author attempt to summarize the facts only, or does he present the material in such a way as to support some thesis? Look for evidence of bias in the collection of the materials and try to decide whether the author is fair-minded or a strong partisan.

Discriminating choice of audiovisual materials cannot be based on the traditional idea that they are nothing more than handmaidens to the book. They must be clearly and objectively viewed in their own right. Their merits must be evaluated, not in comparison to books and magazines, but in an assessment of their own specific contribution to satisfying the often unexpressed needs of the library public. When the customary evaluation criteria of authenticity, appropriateness, scope, interest, organization, special features, and physical characteristics are seen in the light of such factors as the goals of the institution, the type of students, and availability of materials, their relative importance will vary. A more detailed look at these selection criteria is contained in Table 15.

SENIOR COLLEGE OR UNIVERSITY LEARNING RESOURCE CENTERS

Even though many senior colleges and universities are older than community colleges the basic concepts for learning resource centers should be the same. The authors of this book have made the assumption that learning resource administrators are well prepared through basic curricula in the LRC areas of audiovisual and library materials, but may have had in their college studies little emphasis on management theories and techniques. Another assumption has been made that too many academic administrators know very little about learning resource centers, which are usually under their jurisdiction.

As stated previously, the LRC administrator usually reports to the academic vice president. This position is a line position when dealing with his or her own staff, but is usually a staff relationship when dealing with other administrators and faculty members on campus. In this latter position the title and position of the administrator is valuable only insofar as the individual is able to influence people not under his or her direct supervision. In a college the administrator and his staff should remember the basic principle that the entire LRC operation is a *service* component for faculty and students, designed to aid and assist in the improvement of the educational program.

In directing the activities of the LRC it is necessary that top management in the college be sold on the benefits of the learning resource center. To be effective and efficient, planning, leading, organizing, implementing, and evaluating must occur in coordination with superordinates in the organization as well as with subordinates.

The LRC administration must constantly be aware of three basic functions, all of which maintain quality control factors: maintenance, problem solving, and innovative procedures. The excellent programs of the present and past need to be maintained, decisions made and problems solved. Also remember that an organization cannot maintain the status quo, but moves forward with new ideas and creations. Several items which the LRC administrator should keep in mind are as follows:

1. The task of an LRC is the facilitation of learning, which includes learning spaces, learning resources, instructional design, and competent staff.

2. The student is the center of the learning process. All other aspects of this process should be evaluated on the basis of how they facilitate the education process.

3. The instructor is the "content specialist" and the learning manager. This is the person who should be consulted in connection with educational specifications or the learning environment.

4. The facilities, the LRC specialist, the student, and the faculty member all will determine the type of media or print material to be utilized in the classroom.

Higher education today is unique in that its instruction depends greatly upon different approaches and technological elements. Comprehensive education depends heavily upon the materials, services, and technologies of a properly administered learning resource centers.

In many instances, the instructor asking for instructional materials is thinking in terms of format rather than the results expected from the learner and the means or strategy used to obtain those results. The learning resource center as a change agent is systematically involved in the instructional process. It is involved to the extent that measuring the students performance based on the learning objectives also includes measuring the impact and relevance of the media used and the strategies or techniques employed to facilitate the observable, measurable, or perceptible results of the process in respect to the learner.

As a change agent, the learning resource center does not necessarily restructure the administrative organization of the institution. Change may occur elsewhere in the institution as a result of feedback provided to the appropriate agencies through the learner evaluation process. The change that the learning resource center is concerned with is the perceptible change in the behavior of the learner as a result of utilization, application, or evaluation of the learning resources provided by the center.

The center is not the physical area; it is the configuration administered systematically as a subsystem within the learning process. Support in terms of materials provided may occur. The services and items required of a support unit are necessary to facilitate the functions of the learning resource center.

The learning resource center as a support center may be, in some instances, a workable although limited concept. Limited, insofar as support may be considered as an aggregate of services, entities, or activities. The cry for involvement in the instructional process which may be heard informally from some may be due to the lack of recognition that support is a supply function; a necessary component. Without it the operation might be slowed or halted. In education, the support function provides the logistics or supplies that are not the primary concern of the learning activity. The problem becomes a refinement of design, strategy, and performance evaluation to indicate whether or not learning objectives are being reached.

Quality control of the learning process is the concern of the LRC. Influencing or persuading the participants in the instructional process is one of the major challenges confronting the LRC. One way to meet this challenge is in systematic planning and implementation of plans with appropriate evaluation and feedback. For the LRC the feedback is more than a count of the number of services rendered, it is an appraisal of the effectiveness of the services.

The change facilitated by the LRC is the change that occurs when somebody learns. Learning resource centers should write their objectives from the vantage point of the change expected in the learner rather than the activity inherent in the support function.

NOTES

1. Gary T. Peterson, *The Learning Center: A Sphere for Non-Traditional Education* (Hamden, Conn.: Shoe String Press, 1975), pp. 8, 5.

2. Stephen J. Knesevich, *Program Budgeting (PPBS)* (Berkeley, Calif.: McCutchan Publishing Corp., 1973), p. 330.

3. Commission on Instructional Technology to Improve Learning, *A Report to the President and the Congress of the United States* (Washington, D.C.: Government Printing Office, 1970).

4. Ibid.

5. Kenneth Allen and Loren Allen, *Organization and Administration of Learning Resources Center in the Community College* (Hamden, Conn.: Shoe String Press, 1971), p. 140.

6. Richard H. Perrine, *Library Space Survey of Texas Colleges and Universities*, CB Study Paper No. 10 (Austin, Tex.: Coordinating Board, Texas College and University System, June 1970), p. 4.

7. Harry F. Anderson, "The Architect Views the Building and Planning Process," in *Junior College Libraries: Development, Needs and Perspectives*, ed. Everett L. Moore (Chicago: American Library Association, 1969), p. 96.

8. Ibid.

9. Ibid.

10. Herbert E. Humbert, "What Does a Modern Learning Resources Building Look Like?" *Community and Junior College Journal* 43 (June/July 1973), pp. 16–17.

11. Ibid.

12. Ralph E. Ellsworth, *Planning College and University Library Building* (Boulder, Colo.: Pruett Press, 1968), pp. 41–49.

13. Ibid., p. 107.

14. Anderson, "Architect Views the Building and Planning Process," p.

15. Higher Education Facilities Planning and Management, *Manual Four: Academic Support Facilities* (Boulder, Colo.: Western Interstate Commission for Higher Education, 1971), p. 68.

16. Allen and Allen, *Organization and Administration of Learning Resources Center,* p. 119.

17. *College & Research Libraries News,* 11 (December 1972). ACRL *News Issue* (B) of College and Research Libraries 33, no. 7, pp. 305–15. "Guidelines for two-year college learning resources programs," approved by ACRL Board of Directors on June 29, 1972, American Library Association (Association of College and Research Libraries); American Association of Community and Junior Colleges; Association for Educational Communications and Technology.

18. Ibid., p. 308.

19. Ibid., pp. 308–9.

20. Ibid., pp. 308–9.

21. Allen and Allen, *Organization and Administration of Learning Resources Center,* p. 26.

22. "Guidelines for Two-Year College Learning Resources Program," pp. 57–58, 311–12.

23. Sarah K. Thomson, *Learning Resource Centers in Community Colleges: A Survey of Budgets and Services* (Chicago: American Library Association, 1975), p. 67.

24. Richland College, *Rights, Rites and Rituals, Revised, 1976–1977* (Dallas, Tex.: Richland College Print Shop), 1976, p. 105.

25. Allen and Allen, *Organization and Administration of Learning Resources Center in the Community College,* p. 147.

26. Thomson, *Learning Resource Centers in Community Colleges*, p. 113.

27. Ibid., p. 114.

28. Ibid., pp. 128–29.

29. Fritz Veit, *The Community College Library* (Westport, Conn.: Greenwood Press, 1975), p. 80.

30. Anderson, "Architect Views the Building and Planning Process," p. 146.

National Organizations and Higher Education Administration

JACK D. TERRY, JR.

There is no doubt that the American public is composed of "joiners," seemingly willing to join any association as long as that association seems to have something to do with a profession, skill, hobby, art form, or fraternal affairs, religion, athletics, or social welfare. The 1983 *Encyclopedia of Associations* lists 16,519 known active participating associations and another 1020 which are termed missing because of the lack of a location, address, or executive director, 2876 defunct or inactive associations, bringing the total to 20,418.*

All of these associations were formed to bring like qualities together into associations which could through strength of membership bring to bear pressures, politics, lobbying prominence, recognition, or what have you to a group of like-minded individuals.

This does not diminish the importance of associations. If they were not important, there would not be such an impressive list. On the contrary, associations are very important and necessary to the continuation and propagation of some form of activity. Therefore, in higher education associations are important to the continuance and promotion of the various facets important to the propagation of the field of higher education.

This chapter will introduce the reader to the national associations that intersect and impact higher education administration and operation. The nutshell capsulated data bits are gleaned from the *Encyclopedia of Associations*, 1983. Selection of the material from each of the encyclopedia entries is used to simply introduce the associations and give a brief overview of their intent, purpose, philosophy, and publications. These capsulated data bits are by no means exhaustive. The author

*ENCYCLOPEDIA OF ASSOCIATIONS, 17th edition, edited by Denise S. Akey (copyright © 1959, 1961, 1964, 1968, 1970, 1972, 1973, 1975, 1976, 1977, 1978, 1979, 1980, 1981, 1982 by Gale Research Company), Gale, Detroit, Mich., 1983.

would encourage the reader to secure the entire encyclopedia for a complete data base of information.

The associations included in this overview are those most closely associated with higher education administration and operations. Those excluded are not excluded by choice but simply for lack of space to include them all here.

ACCREDITATION

COUNCIL ON POST SECONDARY ACCREDITATION (COPA)

One Dupont Circle, N.W., Suite 760   Phone: (202) 452-1433
Washington, DC 20036   Richard M. Millard, Pres.
Founded: 1975. Nongovernmental organization intended to support, coordinate and improve all voluntary accrediting activities conducted at the postsecondary educational level in the U.S. Supported by nearly 4000 accredited institutions of postsecondary education. Recognizes, monitors and coordinates more than 52 regional and national accrediting bodies that accredit both institutions and programs. **Publications:** Accreditation (newsletter), quarterly; also publishes occasional special papers and general information brochure. **Formed by Merger of:** The Federation of Regional Accrediting Commissions of Higher Education and the National Commission on Accrediting. **Convention/Meeting:** semiannual board meetings.

NATIONAL COUNCIL FOR ACCREDITATION OF TEACHER EDUCATION (NCATE)

1919 Pennsylvania Ave., N.W., Suite 202   Phone: (202) 466-7496
Washington, DC 20006   Lyn Gubser, Dir.
Founded: 1954. **Members:** 34. **Staff:** 8. Representatives from constituent groups (24), colleges and universities, state departments of education, school boards, teachers and other professional groups (10). Extra-legal, voluntary accrediting body devoted exclusively to evaluation and accreditation of institutions for preparation of elementary and secondary school teachers; and for preparation of school service personnel, including school principals, supervisors, superintendents, guidance counselors, school psychologists, and other specialists for school oriented positions. Has accredited 545 colleges and universities. **Committees:** Appeals Board; Audit. **Publications:** Annual List of Accredited Institutions; also publishes Standards for Accreditation of Teacher Education, and Update. **Convention/Meeting:** 2–3/year.

MIDDLE STATES ASSOCIATION OF COLLEGES AND SCHOOLS (MSA)

3624 Market St.   Phone: (215) 662-5605
Philadelphia, PA 19104   Calvin L. Crawford, Exec. Dir.
Founded: 1887. **Members:** 2600. **Staff:** 25. Colleges and universities (500); secondary schools (1700) and elementary schools (400) in Panama, Delaware, District of Columbia, Maryland, New Jersey, New York, Pennsylvania, Puerto

Rico and the Virgin Islands, which have been accredited by either the Commission on Higher Education, the Commission on Secondary Schools or the Assembly of Elementary Schools. One of six similar regional organizations in the U.S. **Committees:** School/College Relations. **Publications:** (1) Elementary Assembly Newsletter, quarterly; (2) Higher Commission Newsletter, quarterly;

NEW ENGLAND ASSOCIATION OF SCHOOLS AND COLLEGES (NEASC)

131 Middlesex Tpke.   Phone: (617) 272-6450
Burlington, MA 01803   Richard J. Bradley, Exec. Dir.
Founded: 1885. **Members:** 1254. **Staff:** 19. Institutions of higher education, public and independent schools and vocational-technical schools (1142) in Connecticut, Maine, Massachusetts, New Hampshire, Rhode Island and Vermont, accredited on recommendation of the Commission on Institutions of Higher Education, the Commission on Independent Schools, the Commission on Public Schools (includes junior high or middle schools), or the Commission on Vocational, Technical, Career Institutions. Other members of the NEASC are: educational associations (12); individuals (100). One of six similar regional organizations in the U.S. **Committees:** Overseas Schools. **Publications:** (1) Newsletter, 3/year; (2) Membership Directory, annual. **Formerly:** (1972) New England Association of Colleges and Secondary Schools. **Convention/Meeting:** annual—always December, Boston, MA.

NORTH CENTRAL ASSOCIATION OF COLLEGES AND SCHOOLS (NCA)

P.O. Box 18   Phone: (303) 449-7110
Boulder, CO 80306   John W. Vaughn, Sec.
Founded: 1895. **Members:** 5900. **Staff:** 30. Colleges and universities and schools in Arizona, Arkansas, Colorado, Illinois, Indiana, Iowa, Kansas, Michigan, Minnesota, Missouri, Nebraska, New Mexico, North Dakota, Ohio, Oklahoma, South Dakota, West Virginia, Wisconsin, Wyoming and Overseas Dependents' Schools of Department of Defense, accredited by appropriate commissions. One of six similar regional accrediting organizations in the U.S. **Publications:** (1) NCA Quarterly; (2) NCA Today, 3–4/year; also publishes Optional and Special Function Schools, Policies and Standards for Secondary Schools, Junior High/Middle Schools, Elementary Schools, Independent College-Preparatory Schools, Vocational/Adult Schools; and handbooks on accreditation. **Formerly:** (1976) North Central Association of Colleges and Secondary Schools. **Convention/Meeting:** annual—always March or April. Chicago, ILL.

NORTHWEST ASSOCIATION OF SCHOOLS AND COLLEGES (NASC)

3700-B University Way, N.E.   Phone: (206) 543-0195
Seattle, WA 98105   Dr. James F. Bemis, Exec. Sec.-Treas.
Founded: 1917. **Members:** 997. **Staff:** 2. Colleges, universities and community colleges (141) and schools (856) in Alaska, Idaho, Montana, Nevada,

Oregon, Utah and Washington, accredited by appropriate commissions. One of six similar regional organizations in the U.S. **Committees:** Research and Service. **Publications:** (1) Newsletter, semiannual; (2) Directory of Accredited and Affiliated Institutions, annual; (3) Proceedings, annual; has also published a history of the association. **Formerly:** (1975) Northwest Association of Secondary and Higher Schools. **Convention/Meeting:** annual.

SOUTHERN ASSOCIATION OF COLLEGES AND SCHOOLS (SACS)

795 Peachtree St., N.E.   Phone: (404) 875-8011
Atlanta, GA 30308   Dr. Felix C. Robb, Exec.Dir.
Founded: 1895. **Members:** 10,433. **State Groups:** 22. Colleges, universities, occupational schools, secondary schools and elementary schools in Alabama, Florida, Georgia, Kentucky, Louisiana, Mississippi, North Carolina, South Carolina, Tennessee,Texas, Virginia, and Latin America, accredited by an appropriate commission. Conducts educational research and development through education improvement program. Projects: Vocational-Technical Education Consortium of States; Motor Vehicle Mechanics Training Project. One of six similar regional organizations in the U.S. **Commissions:** Colleges; Elementary Schools; Occupational Education Institutions; Secondary Schools. **Committees:** Investments; Personnel Policies; Research, Projects and Studies. **Publications:** (1) Newsletter, 7/year; (2) Proceedings of Annual Meeting; also publishes membership lists, special project and research reports, and standards, policies and procedures for accreditation. **Convention/Meeting:** annual - always December.

WESTERN ASSOCIATION OF SCHOOLS AND COLLEGES (WASC)

1614 Rollins Rd.   Phone: (415) 697-7711
Burlingame, CA 94010   Lyle E. Siverson, Sec.-Treas.
Founded: 1962. **Staff:** 12. Accredited educational institutions in California, Hawaii, Guam, and other areas of the Pacific. **Commissions:** Accrediting Commission for Community and Junior Colleges; Accrediting Commission for Schools; Accrediting Commission for Senior Colleges and Universities. **Publications:** Directory, annual.

ADMINISTRATION

AMERICAN ASSOCIATION OF SCHOOL ADMINISTRATORS (AASA)

1801 N. Moore St.   Phone: (703) 528-0700
Arlington, VA 22209   Paul B. Salmon, Exec.Dir.
Founded: 1865. **Members:** 19,000. **Staff:** 55. **State Groups:** 74. Professional association of administrative officers of boards of education; school district superintendents; central building and service unit administrators; presidents of colleges, deans, and professors of educational administration; placement officers; executive secretaries and administrators of education associations;

heads of private schools. Sponsors numerous seminars annually including in-service seminars for administrators through the AASA National Academy for School Executives, and "dedicated to the continuing professional and personal development of school administrators." Distributes Project Teams workshop training materials to assist educators in developing full service programs for handicapped students. Presents awards; founder of Educational Research Service. Maintains 12 committees including: American Association of Educational Service Agencies; National Center for Improvement of Learning; and Network for Outcome Based Schools. **Publications:** (1) the School Administrator, 11/year; (2) Report, annual; also publishes books, special reports, pamphlets and filmstrips. **Absorbed:** (1968) County Intermediate Unit Superintendents (of NEA). **Formerly:** (1870) National Association of School Superintendents; (1907) Department of School Superintendence of the National Education Association; (1937) Department of Superintendence of the National Education Association. **Convention/Meeting:** annual - always February.

AMERICAN ASSOCIATION OF UNIVERSITY ADMINISTRATORS (AAUA)

1000 Vermont Ave., N.W.   Phone: (202) 628-4634
Washington, DC 20005   John H. Ganoe, Exec.Sec.
Founded: 1970. **Members:** 1100. **Chapters:** 7. To promote excellence in the administration of higher education and to assist career administrators to continue their professional growth through organizational affiliation. Operates placement service; bestows awards. **Committees:** Chapter Development; Future Directions; Issues of the Professions; National Assemblies; Policies of the Profession; Professional Development; Professional Services; Standards and Review. **Publications:** (1) Administrators Update, quarterly; (2) Communique, quarterly. **Convention/Meeting:** annual national assembly - always June.

AMERICAN FEDERATION OF SCHOOL ADMINISTRATORS (AFSA)

110 E. 42nd St., Rm. 1510   Phone: (212) 697-5111
New York, NY 10017   Peter S. O'Brien, Pres.
Founded: 1971. **Members:** 10,000. **Staff:** 6. **Regional Groups:** 2. **State Groups:** 4. **Local Groups:** 57. National Offices: 4. Regional Offices: 1. Principals, vice-principals, directors, supervisors, administrators involved in pedagogical education. Purposes are: to achieve the highest goals in education; to maintain and improve standards, benefits and conditions for personnel without regard to color, race, sex, background or national origin; to obtain job security; to protect seniority and merit; to cooperate with all responsible organizations in education; to promote understanding, participation and support of the public, communities and agencies; to be alert to resist attacks and campaigns which would create or entrench a spoils system; and to promote our democratic society by supporting every effort to enhance full educational opportunities to every child and student in our nation. **Publications:** News, 7/year. **Affiliated with:** AFL-CIO. **Formerly:** (1976) School Administrators and Supervisors Organizing Committee. **Convention/Meeting:** triennial.

ASSOCIATION OF GOVERNING BOARDS OF UNIVERSITIES AND COLLEGES (AGB)

One Dupont Circle, N.W., Suite 400   Phone: (202) 296-8400
Washington, DC 20036   Robert L. Gale, Pres.
Founded: 1921. **Members:** 24,000. **Staff:** 20. Governing boards of publicly and privately supported colleges and universities. Individual members include regents, trustees, presidents, supervisors, visitors and other board members of colleges and universities. Addresses the problems and responsibilities of trusteeship in all sectors of higher education and the relationships of trustees and regents to the president, the faculty and the student body. Operates Trustee Information Center; conducts special projects and programs. **Publications:** (1) News Notes, monthly; (2) Reports, bimonthly. **Formerly:** (1963) Association of Governing Boards of State Universities and Allied Institutions. **Convention/Meeting:** semiannual—always April and October.

COLLEGES AND UNIVERSITY SYSTEMS EXCHANGE (CAUSE)

737 29th St.   Phone: (303) 449-4430
Boulder, CO 80303   Charles R. Thomas, Exec. Dir.
Founded: 1971. **Members:** 1300. **Staff:** 4. Individuals engaged in the development, use and management of information systems in higher education. Purpose is to enhance the effectiveness of college and university administration through the use of computer-based information systems and related management techniques; to serve as an information interchange. Participates in cooperative workshops and seminars with member institutions and other associations. Presents awards. Maintains exchange library. Provides information request service and consulting services. **Committees:** Editorial; National Conference; National Issues; Recognition. **Publications:** (1) CAUSE-EFFECT (magazine), bimonthly; (2) CAUSE Information (newsletter), bimonthly; (3) Proceedings of National Conference, annual; (4) Directory, biennial; also publishes monograph series. **Formerly:** College and University Systems Exchange. **Convention/Meeting:** annual.

COLLOQUIA FOR PRESIDENTS AND ACADEMIC ADMINISTRATORS (**Administration**) (CPAA)

Office of Leadership Development in Higher Education
American Council on Education
One Dupont Circle   Phone: (202) 833-4780
Washington, DC 20036   Jerry Miller, Co-Dir.
Founded: 1955. **Staff:** 4. Organized to provide professional development seminars on administrative decision making and academic leadership for recently-appointed top-level officials in higher education. Programs are conducted for presidents; vice presidents; academic deans; financial, advancement and student personnel officers; other senior administrators. Sessions offer a balanced program of prominent speakers, seminars, case study analyses simulations and small group discussions covering concerns, problems, issues and opportunities in academic administration. Enrollment for each program is limited. The ICUA also cooperates with other higher education

national and regional associations in developing and conducting programs for their clientele, both prospective and practicing administrators. Sponsored by the American Council on Education.

NATIONAL COUNCIL OF ADMINISTRATIVE WOMEN IN EDUCATION (NCAWE)

%Mary Walsh
17 Forsythe Rd.
Pittsburgh, PA 15220   Mary Walsh, Exec. Officer
Founded: 1915. **Members:** 3500. Women educators in administrative or supervisory positions in a public or private school system, college or university, foundation, agency, government or non-government education programs; also offers auxiliary and associate memberships. To encourage women to prepare for careers in educational administration and to urge educational institutions, systems and agencies to employ and advance women in this field. Monitors national and local legislation pertaining to women's education. Works to eliminate discrimination against women in educational administration. Maintains placement service and speakers bureau; conducts research; presents awards. **Committees:** Action Program; Board of Inquiry; Editorial; Intergroup and Public Relations; Status of Women. **Publications:** News, 5/year; also publishes Wanted More Women, a book series. **Convention/Meeting:** annual.

ADMISSIONS

AMERICAN ASSOCIATION OF COLLEGIATE REGISTRARS AND ADMISSIONS OFFICERS

One Dupont Circle, N.W., Suite 330   Phone: (202) 293-9161
Washington, DC 20036   Dr. J. Douglas Conner, Exec. Dir.
Founded: 1910. **State Groups:** 29. Member institutions (2000) and member representatives (7200), including college and university registrars, admission financial aid and institutional research officials. **Publications:** (1) College and University, quarterly; (2) Newsletter, quarterly; (3) Transfer Credit Practices by Educational Institutions, annual; also publishes world education series, guides to academic placement of students from foreign countries in educational institutions of the U.S. **Formerly:** American Association of Collegiate Registrars. **Convention/Meeting:** annual—always April.

NATIONAL ASSOCIATION OF COLLEGE ADMISSION COUNSELORS (NACAC)

9933 Lawler, Suite 500   Phone: (312) 676-0500
Skokie, IL 60077   Charles A. Marshall, Exec. Dir.
Founded: 1937. **Members:** 3000. **Staff:** 20. **Regional Groups:** 7. **State Groups:** 13. Public, parochial and independent secondary schools; school systems; public and private two-year colleges; public and private four-year colleges and universities; educational organizations concerned with high school guidance, college admission and financial aid. Seeks to establish and

maintain high professional standards in college admission guidance; to develop useful and efficient college guidance programs and materials; to develop and expand the relationships between and among secondary schools and colleges. Conducts state and regional conferences; seminars and workshops; research projects; National College Fairs for colleges and other post-secondary institutions, students and parents in several cities each year. Provides a computerized college search hot-line service. Maintains library of publications pertinent to guidance, admissions, and financial aid. **Publications:** (1) Newsletter, 6/year; (2) Journal, quarterly; (3) Membership Directory, annual; also publishes The Researcher, National College Fair Directory, Bibliography for Counselors and Admissions Officers, studies and surveys. **Formerly:** (1969) Association of College Admissions Counselors. **Convention/Meeting:** annual—always October.

BUSINESS ADMINISTRATORS

NATIONAL ASSOCIATION OF COLLEGE AND UNIVERSITY BUSINESS OFFICERS (NACUBO)

One Dupont Circle   Phone: (202) 861-2500
Washington, DC 20036   D. F. Finn, Exec. V. Pres.
Founded: 1950. **Members:** 2000. Non-profit institutions of higher education which are members of a regional association. To develop and maintain interest on a nationwide basis in continuous improvement of principles and practices of business and financial administration in higher education. Sponsors workshops in fields such as cash management, risk management, accounting, investment, student loan administration and energy conservation. Maintains library of 1500 volumes. Sponsors program of information exchange between college and university personnel. Maintains a placement service. Bestows annual "Cost Reduction Incentive Awards." **Committees:** Accounting Principles; Facilities Planning and Management; Federal Paperwork; Financial Management; Governmental Relations; Insurance and Risk Management; Investments; Minority Institutions; Personnel; Postal Regulations; Professional Development; Programs for Small Colleges; Publications; Student-Related Programs; Taxation; Two-Year Colleges. **Publications:** (1) Business Officer, monthly; (2) Special Reports, monthly; (3) Administrative Service, 6/year; (4) Annual Report; also publishes College and University Business Administration Service with monthly supplementation and revision and numerous books and guides for college and university administrators. **Formerly:** (1962) National Federation of College and University Business Officers Associations. **Convention/Meeting:** annual.

COMMUNITY COLLEGES

ASSOCIATION OF COMMUNITY COLLEGE TRUSTEES (ACCT)

6928 Little River Tpke., Suite A
Annandale, VA 22003   William H. Meardy, Exec. Dir.
Founded: 1969. **Members:** 680. Community college or technical institute districts, or other accredited post-secondary educational institutions whose

courses lead to degrees or objectives less than a baccalaureate degree, and educational institutions of other nations which are considered as being post-secondary, but not baccalaureate, by that nation; any group of individuals or any single individual; individual lifetime members who have been so designated by the association. Objectives are: to unify trustees in order to give direction to the community college movement through the development of resolutions and policies; to promote the philosophical concept of the community college and technical institute and the elimination of all existing and potential barriers with regard to race, creed or sex which may hinder development of the community college and technical institute philosophy. Develops liaisons with other national and international organizations concerned with the community college and technical institute movement. **Committees:** Awards; Federal Relations; Future Directions; Liaison with AACJC; Past Presidents. **Publications:** (1) ACCT-O-Line (and supplement), weekly; (2) Advisor (newsletter), monthly; (3) Quarterly; also publishes books, reports, guidebooks, glossaries and other materials. **Formerly:** (1972) Council of Community College Boards. **Convention/Meeting:** annual—always October.

CURRICULUM

ASSOCIATION FOR INNOVATION IN HIGHER EDUCATION (AIHE)

%Dr. Frederick Geib
P.O. Box 48   Phone: (207) 873-1131
Waterville, ME 04901   Dr. Frederick Geib, Exec. Dir.
Founded: 1970. **Members:** 50. Degree-granting institutions of higher education. Purposes are: to encourage innovation in education with special emphasis on the "4-1-4" curriculum; to provide channels for communication and to disseminate information relative to such concerns; to establish and strengthen a common bond among institutions committed to innovative reforms; to help establish guidelines for successful organization, operation and evaluation of innovative academic programs; to arrange for and conduct annual meetings, workshops, consulting services and other assistance on matters relevant to innovative calendars and curriculum. **Publications:** (1) Newsletter, quarterly; (2) Cooperative Listing of Interim Term Courses, annual; (3) Exchange Directory, annual. **Formerly:** 4-1-4 Conference. **Convention/Meeting:** annual.

NATIONAL ASSOCIATION FOR CORE CURRICULUM (NACC)

407-D White Hall
Kent State University   Phone: (216) 672-7977
Kent, OH 44242   Gordon F. Vars, Exec. Sec.-Treas.
Founded: 1953. **Members:** 300. Teachers, administrators, guidance specialists, professors of curriculum, curriculum directors, supervisors. "To promote the development of secondary general education programs variously known as core, common learnings, unified studies, block-time, etc." Provides for exchange of information on problems and resources as a means of im-

proving and extending core programs and teacher education for the core curriculum by circulating videotapes, films, filmstrips and slides. Presents Nelson L. Bossing Research Scholarship. **Publications:** The Core Teacher, quarterly; also publishes position paper, Core Today: Rationale and Implications; history of NACC; and audiotapes of major convention addresses. **Formerly:** (1966) National Conference of Core Teachers. **Convention/Meeting:** annual—always fall.

DEANS AND ACADEMIC OFFICERS

AMERICAN CONFERENCE FOR ACADEMIC DEANS (ACAD)

1818 R St., N.W.   Phone: (202) 387-3760
Washington, DC 20009   Robert O. Tilman, Chm.
Founded: 1944. **Members:** 600. Academic deans of four-year colleges of liberal arts and sciences. **Publications:** Proceedings, annual. **Affiliated with:** Association of American Colleges. **Convention/Meeting:** annual—always January.

NATIONAL ASSOCIATION OF COLLEGE DEANS, REGISTRARS AND ADMISSION OFFICERS

917 Dorsett St.   Phone: (912) 435-4945
Albany, GA 31701   Helen Mayes, Exec. Sec.
Founded: 1925. **Members:** 325. Deans, registrars and admissions officers of collegiate institutions with predominantly black student bodies. **Committees:** Findings; Research; Time and Place. **Publications:** (1) Directory, annual; (2) Proceedings, annual. **Formerly:** (1949) National Association of Collegiate Deans and Registrars in Negro Schools; (1970) National Association of College Deans and Registrars. **Convention/Meeting:** annual - always second Sunday of March.

NATIONAL ASSOCIATION FOR WOMEN DEANS, ADMINISTRATORS AND COUNSELORS (NAWADAC)

1625 I St., N.W., Suite 624-A   Phone: (202) 659-9330
Washington, DC 20006   Dr. Patricia A. Rueckel, Exec.Dir.
Founded: 1916. **Members:** 1900. **Staff:** 3. **State Groups:** 21. Individuals holding positions in academic administration, student personnel, and counseling. Includes: deans, principals, student and academic deans, vice principals, social directors, advisers of girls, college presidents, professors of education, directors of residence halls. Promotes study of new trends in problems of women's education and counseling of women students, and in student personnel, curriculum and guidance. Maintains career placement service and job referral service. Bestows Ruth Strang Research Award. **Committees:** Intercultural Education; Minority Concerns; Professional Employment Practices. **Sections:** College; Community and Junior College; Continuing Education; Elementary, Middle and Junior High School; High School; University. **Publications:** (1) Journal, quarterly; (2) Newsletter, quarterly; also publishes an-

nual directory and monographs. **Formerly:** (1956) National Association of Deans of Women; (1973) National Association of Women Deans and Counselors. **Convention/Meeting:** annual.

EDUCATION (GENERAL)

AMERICAN COUNCIL ON EDUCATION (ACE)

One Dupont Circle   Phone: (202) 833-4700
Washington, DC 20036   J. W. Peltason, Pres.
Founded: 1918. **Members:** 1632. A council of colleges and universities (1392), educational organizations (174) and affiliates (66). Advances education and educational methods through comprehensive voluntary action on the part of American educational associations, organizations and institutions. Bestows annual award to an individual who has made an outstanding contribution to higher education. Maintains library of 5000 volumes on higher education and administration. **Divisions:** External Relations; Governmental Relations; Institutional Relations; International Educational Relations (see separate entry); Policy Analysis and Research. **Publications:** (1) Higher Education and National Affairs, weekly; (2) Educational Record, quarterly; also publishes A Fact Book on Higher Education, publishes or distributes yearbooks and directories of institutions of higher education in the U.S. **Convention/Meeting:** annual - usually October.

AMERICAN EDUCATION ASSOCIATION

663 Fifth Ave.   Phone: (212) 687-6865
New York, NY 10022   Evelyn Peavey, Pres.
Founded: 1938. "Teachers, parents, and others interested in preserving sound American education, the Constitution and Declaration of Independence and traditional tenets of social and economic freedom." Opposes sex education and the prohibition of prayer in the schools. Conducts research on curriculum, textbooks, methods, and evaluation; engages in tutoring; grants several awards. Publishes Educational Signpost. **Committees:** Captive Nations; Classroom Sex Education; Equal Rights Amendment; Parent Education; To Restore Prayer to Schools. **Absorbed:** Guardians of American Education. **Convention/Meeting:** seminannual - usually fall, New York City.

HIGHER EDUCATION PANEL (HEP)

One Dupont Circle   Phone: (202) 833-4757
Washington, DC 20036   Frank Atelsek, Dir.
Founded: 1971. **Members:** 760. **Staff:** 5. Established by the American Council on Education (see separate entry) as a service to educational and governmental policy makers. Members have agreed to supply the council quickly, on request, with a limited amount of information concerning higher education. Surveys conducted deal with such subjects as enrollment, finances, salaries, degrees, and policies of various institutions. Surveys are conducted by telephone or mail, depending on the urgency of the issue. Publishes Panel Reports.

NATIONAL EDUCATION ASSOCIATION (NEA)

1201 16th St., N.W.   Phone: (202) 833-4000
Washington, DC 20036   Terry E. Herndon, Exec. Dir.
Founded: 1857. **Members:** 1,600,800. **Staff:** 600. **State Groups:** 53. **Local Groups:** 10,000. Professional organization and union of elementary and secondary school teachers, college and university professors, administrators, principals, counselors and others concerned with education. **Committees:** Affiliate Relationships; Higher Education; Human Relations; Instruction and Professional Development; Legislative and Financial Support; Teacher Benefits; Teacher Rights. **Divisions:** Affiliate Services; Communications; Government Relations; Instruction and Professional Development; Political Affairs; Research; Teacher Rights. **Publicatons:** (1) Reporter, 8/year; (2) Today's Education, quarterly; (3) Handbook, annual. **Absorbed:** (1966) American Teachers Association; (1981) NEA Higher Education Council (founded 1974 and superseded the combined activities of: National Association of College and University Administrators, founded 1969; National Society of Professors, founded 1967; National Faculty Association of Community and Junior Colleges, founded 1967). **Formerly:** (1870) National Teachers Association. **Convention/Meeting:** annual.

FINANCIAL OFFICERS

FINANCIAL MANAGEMENT ASSOCIATION (FMA)

School of Business
Univ. of South Florida
Tampa, FL 33620   Phone: (813) 974-2084
                                          Jack S. Rader, Admin.
Founded: 1970. **Members:** 4000. Professors of financial management; corporate financial officers. Facilitates exchange of ideas among persons involved in financial management in "both the academic and practical world of affairs." Sponsors workshops for comparison of current research projects and development of cooperative ventures in writing and research. Maintains placement service for academic and professional positions. Has special study groups in various fields of financial management. Sponsors honorary society for superior students at 95 colleges and universities. **Publications:** (1) Financial Management, quarterly; (2) Membership/Professional Directory, irregular. **Convention/Meeting:** annual conference—always October.

NATIONAL ASSOCIATION OF STUDENT FINANCIAL AID ADMINISTRATION (NASFAA)

1776 Massachusetts Ave., Suite 100   Phone: (202) 785-0453
Washington, DC 20036   Dr. A. Dallas Martin, Jr., Exec. Dir.
Founded: 1968. **Members:** 2300. **Regional Groups:** 6. Institutions of postsecondary education; agencies, financial aid administrators, students and other interested individuals. Seeks to "promote the professionalism of student financial aid administrators; serve as the national forum for matters related to student aid; represent the interests and needs of students, faculties and other persons involved in student financial aid." National council serves as the association's executive body. **Publications:** (1) Newsletter, monthly;

(2) Journal of Student Financial Aid, 3/year. **Convention/Meeting:** annual—always July.

NATIONAL COUNCIL OF HIGHER EDUCATION LOAN PROGRAMS (NCHELP)

% Nancy M. Berve
Education Commission of the States
1860 Lincoln St., No. 300 Phone: (303) 830-3792
Denver, CO 80295 Paul P. Borden, Pres.
Founded: 1961. Directors of state and private nonprofit corporations that guarantee student loans under the Higher Education Act of 1965 as amended. Seeks to coordinate federal, state and private functions in the student loan program. **Committees:** Bankruptcy Legislation and Procedures; Collections and Default Prevention; Data Processing; Lender Relations; Reauthorization; Research. **Publications:** Directory, annual. **Formerly:** (1969) National Conference of Executives of Higher Education Loan Plans. **Convention/Meeting:** semiannual.

HIGHER EDUCATION

AMERICAN ASSOCIATION FOR HIGHER EDUCATION (AAHE)

One Dupont Circle, Suite 600 Phone: (202) 293-6440
Washington, DC 20036 Russell Edgerton, Pres.
Founded: 1870. **Members:** 7000. **Staff:** 14. Administrators, students, trustees, faculty, public officials and interested individuals from all segments of postsecondary education; public and private, nonprofit and proprietary, large and small, two-year, four-year, graduate and professional. Seeks to clarify and help resolve critical issues in postsecondary education through conferences, publications and special projects. **Publications:** (1) Bulletin, 10/year; (2) Research Reports, 10/year; (3) Journal of Higher Education, 6/year; (4) Current Issues in Higher Education, annual; also publishes books and reports developed from special projects. **Formerly:** Association for Higher Education (of NEA); Department of Higher Education (of NEA). **Convention/Meeting:** annual - always March.

ASSOCIATION FOR THE STUDY OF HIGHER EDUCATION (ASHE)

One Dupont Circle, Suite 630 Phone: (202) 296-2597
Washington, DC 20036 Jonathan D. Fife, Exec.Sec.-Treas.
Founded: 1972. **Members:** 900. Professors, researchers, administrators, policy analysts, graduate students, and other persons concerned with the study of higher education. To facilitate the evolution of an emerging profession; to promote communication among groups concerned with higher education; to provide a forum for discussion of priority issues for research in the study of higher education. Presents annual Distinguished Dissertation Award in high-

er education. **Committees:** Council of Higher Education Journal Editors; Curriculum, Instruction, and Learning; Dissertation Award; Research Classification and Publication. **Publications:** (1) Review of Higher Education, 3/year; (2) Directory of Higher Education Programs and Faculty, biennial; (3) Membership Roster, biennial. **Formerly:** Association of Professors of Higher Education. **Convention/Meeting:** annual - in conjunction with the American Association for Higher Education annual conference.

NATIONAL ASSOCIATION OF STATE UNIVERSITIES AND LAND GRANT COLLEGES (NASULGC)

One Dupont Circle, N.W., Suite 710   Phone: (202) 293-7120
Washington, DC 20036   Robert L. Clodius, Pres.
Founded: 1962. **Members:** 140. **Staff:** 22. Education association representing the principal public universities of the 50 states, including the nation's 72 land grant colleges and universities. Seeks to focus public attention on problems of this special segment of higher education and on contributions these institutions have made to the nation. Special areas of interest include legislation at both the federal and state level affecting public higher education, curriculum revision, academic structure, urban involvement, extension activities, university research, education of the disadvantaged, enrollment, cost trends and degree production. **Publications:** (1) For Your Information, monthly; (2) Facts, annual. **Formed by Merger of:** Association of Land-Grant Colleges and State Universities (founded 1887 and formerly the Association of Land Grant Colleges and Universities); National Association of State Universities (founded 1895); State Universities Association (founded 1917 and formerly Association of Separated State Universities). **Formerly:** (1963) Association of State Universities and Land-Grant Colleges. **Convention/Meeting:** annual - always November.

WESTERN INTERSTATE COMMISSION FOR HIGHER EDUCATION (WICHE)

P.O. Drawer P   Phone: (303) 497-0200
Boulder, CO 80302   Dr. Phillip Sirotkin, Exec.Dir.
Founded: 1953. **Members:** 13. **Staff:** 55. Member states are Alaska, Arizona, California, Colorado, Hawaii, Idaho, Montana, Nevada, New Mexico, Oregon, Utah, Washington, and Wyoming. Administers of the Western Regional Education Compact, which was created to help the states develop professional and technical manpower to meet the needs of the region; to improve access to higher education for western residents; and to improve the efficiency and effectiveness of postsecondary education in the west. Serves as a fact-finding agency and a clearinghouse for information; studies educational needs. Conducts programs in mental health and human services, nursing education, internships, health resources, economic development, and minority education. Maintains library of 15,000 volumes on higher education, health and human services, nursing, adult education and management information systems. Offers various student exchange programs. **Publications:** (1) Reports (newsletter), quarterly; (2) Annual Report; (3) Graduate Education News, irregular; also publishes other reports. **Convention/Meeting:** semiannual.

JUNIOR AND COMMUNITY COLLEGES

AMERICAN ASSOCIATION OF COMMUNITY AND JUNIOR COLLEGES (AACJC)

One Dupont Circle, No. 410   Phone: (202) 293-7050
Washington, DC 20036   Dale Bonnell, Pres.

Founded: 1920. **Members:** 1250. Community, junior and technical colleges (900); individuals interested in community college development (250); associate members (100). Programs include: Center for Women's Opportunities; Energy Communication; Humanities and Occupational Education; International Education; Older Persons in Small Business; Public Broadcasting; Service to Aging; Small Business Administration. Office of governmental affairs monitors federal educational programming and legislation. Maintains library of junior college catalogs, reference books, textbooks, journals. Compiles statistics. **Publications:** (1) Community and Junior College Journal, 8/year; (2) Community, Junior and Technical College Directory, annual; also publishes many booklets and pamphlets for two-year college faculty and students. **Formerly:** (1972) American Association of Junior Colleges. **Convention/Meeting:** annual.

NATIONAL COUNCIL OF STATE DIRECTORS OF COMMUNITY JUNIOR COLLEGES

% Dr. Max J. Lerner
Ohio Board of Regents
30 E. Broad St.   Phone: (614) 466-5810
Columbus, OH 43215   Dr. Max J. Lerner, Chm.

Members: 39. Officials with state-level responsibility for community/junior colleges. The Council is an informal group that works closely with the American Association of Community and Junior Colleges. **Convention/Meeting:** 3/year.

PERSONNEL ADMINISTRATORS

AMERICAN ASSOCIATION OF SCHOOL PERSONNEL ADMINISTRATORS (AASPA)

6483 Tanglewood Ln.   Phone: (516) 524-3030
Seven Hills, OH 44131   Arch S. Brown, Exec. Dir.

Founded: 1940. **Members:** 1000. **Regional Groups:** 28. Persons employed in school personnel administration. To establish acceptable school personnel standards, techniques and practices. Conducts research. Presents annual award for exemplary personnel practices. **Committees:** Research and Projects. **Publications:** (1) Report, bimonthly; (2) Bulletin, quarterly; (3) Membership Roster, annual; also publishes Standards for School Personnel Administration. **Formerly:** (1959) American Association of Examiners and Administrators of Educational Personnel. **Convention/Meeting:** annual—always October.

COLLEGE AND UNIVERSITY PERSONNEL
ASSOCIATION (CUPA)

11 Dupont Circle, Suite 120   Phone: (202) 462-1038
Washington, DC 20036   Stephen S. Miller, Exec. Dir.
Founded: 1947. **Members:** 3500. **Regional Groups:** 5. **State Groups:** 17. Professional organization made up of colleges and universities interested in the improvement of campus personnel administration. Carries out special research projects and surveys, including annual administrative compensation survey for higher education. Operates Consultants' Academy providing professional consulting referral services in all areas of human resource management. Sponsors training seminars in personnel management. Disseminates information to members regarding federal rules and regulations affecting higher education institutions. Cosponsors placement service; compiles statistics; bestows awards. **Councils:** Affirmative Action/EEO; Benefits; Employment; Faculty/Staff Relations; Management Information Systems; Training and Development; Union Relations; Wage and Salary. **Publications:** (1) Personnelite (newsletter), weekly; (2) Journal, quarterly; (3) Directory, biennial; also publishes research reports and monograph series. **Convention/Meeting:** annual.

NATIONAL ASSOCIATION OF STUDENT
PERSONNEL ADMINISTRATORS (NASPA)

160 Rightmire Hall
1060 Carmack Rd.   Phone: (614) 422-4445
Columbus, OH 43210   Richard F. Stevens, Exec. Dir.
Founded: 1919. **Members:** 4600. **Regional Groups:** 7. Representatives of degree granting institutions of higher education (1200) which have been fully accredited. "To discuss and study the most effective methods of aiding students in their intellectual, social, moral and personal development; to cooperate with agencies and associations representing higher education, government, community resources and specialized interests in student personnel work." Maintains placement service and conducts seminars. Bestows Dissertation of the Year and Ruth Strang Research awards. **Divisions:** Career Development and Placement; Communications Services; Professional Development and Standards; Research and Program Development. **Publications:** (1) Placement Bulletin, semimonthly; (2) National Newsletter-Forum, 8/year; (3) Journal, quarterly; also publishes monographs, regional newsletters and special papers. **Formerly:** (1951) National Association of Deans and Advisers of Men. **Convention/Meeting:** annual—always March/April.

PROFESSIONAL ORGANIZATIONS FOR PROFESSORS

AMERICAN ASSOCIATION OF UNIVERSITY
PROFESSORS (AAUP)

One Dupont Circle   Phone: (202) 466-8050
Washington, DC 20036   Irving J. Spitzberg, Gen. Sec.
Founded: 1915. **Members:** 70,000. **Staff:** 40. **Local Groups:** 1371. State and Regional Conferences: 45. College and university teachers, research scholars, and academic librarians. Purpose is to "facilitate a more effective cooperation among teachers and research scholars in universities and colleges, and in

professional schools of similar grade, for the promotion of the interests of higher education and research, and in general to increase the usefulness and advance the standards, ideals, and welfare of the profession. Maintains toll-free phone number: 800-424-2973. Bestows awards and compiles statistics. **Committees:** Academic Freedom and Tenure; Accrediting of Colleges and Universities; College and University Government; College and University Teaching, Research and Publication; Economic Status of the Profession; Historically Black Institutions; Junior and Community Colleges; Professional Ethics; Relationships of Higher Education to Federal and State Governments; Representation of Economic and Professional Interests; Status of Minorities in the Profession; Status of Women in the Academic Profession. **Publications:** (1) Academe, 6/year; (2) Chapter/Conference Newsletter, 6/year; (3) Collective Bargaining Newsletter, 6/year; also publishes documents, reports, monographs, and the AAUP Redbook. **Convention/Meeting:** annual.

UNIVERSITY PROFESSORS FOR ACADEMIC ORDER (UPAO)

635 S.W. Fourth St.   Phone: (503) 753-7446
Corvalis, OR 97330   Dr. Karl F. Drlica, Pres.

Founded: 1970. **Members:** 600. **Staff:** 2. **Regional Groups:** 8. **Local Groups:** 20. Professors, academic research personnel, and administrators connected with institutions of higher learning; associates are alumni, trustees and supporters of higher education. Purposes: to foster and maintain the integrity of the academic teaching and research professions; to study and improve the administration of universities and professional schools; to advance and promote the study of legitimate ideals of higher and professional education; to preserve and advance the ideals of the freedom to teach and the freedom to learn; to promote academic standards for universities and professional schools and their teaching and research staffs; to advance the professional and economic interests of teaching and research staffs; to promote cooperation among members of teaching and research staffs. Upholds the function of the university to "impart knowledge, wisdom and culture rather than serve as a center for political activity and social activism;" believes that persons working for or attending a university should not engage in pursuits against university regulations and/or the laws of the community. Opposes collective bargaining and compulsory unionism for higher education faculties. Supports administrative rejection of a Marxist to chair a university department. Sponsors lectures; maintains speakers bureau and placement service; conducts research. **Publications:** Universitas, (newsletter), 10/year; also publishes Continuity in Crisis, U.S. China Policy Today and other books. **Convention/Meeting:** annual - always December or January.

WOMEN IN HIGHER EDUCATION

AMERICAN ASSOCIATION OF UNIVERSITY WOMEN (AAUW)

2401 Virginia Ave., N.W.   Phone: (202) 785-7700
Washington, DC 20037   Dr. Quincalee Brown, Exec.Dir.

Founded: 1881. **Members:** 190,000. **Staff:** 80. **State Groups:** 50. **Local Groups:** 1950. Women graduates of regionally accredited colleges; colleges and universities. Works for advancement of women, education and lifelong learning; engages in advocacy, action and research. Conducts a study-action program on topics selected each program cycle (1981–83 topics will focus on money as power and on technology's impact and how it can be harnessed for a better quality life) and other programs of continuing interest in the areas of international relations, education, the community, women and culture. Through Action for Equity: Advancement for Women, advocates the ratification of the ERA and the advancement of women in education, family and employment; educates the public in "gender-based discriminatory practices," including encouraging colleges to abolish discriminatory practices (result of study showing little progress for women in higher education after Title IX and affirmative action). Adopts biennial legislative program and resolutions supporting AAUW interests and actively lobbies on behalf of these programs. Supports Fellowships Program and Research and Projects Grants of AAUW Educational Foundation (see separate entry). Maintains comprehensive library and archival collection on women. **Committees:** Corporate Member Relationships; Educational Foundation Programs; Legislative Program; Women; also has implementation committees for each study topic. **Publications:** (1) Action Alert, biweekly (while Congress is in session); (2) Graduate Woman, bimonthly; (3) Leader in Action, quarterly; also publishes brochures, research studies, study guides and booklets. **Affiliated with:** International Federation of University Women. **Formerly:** Association of Collegiate Alumnae. **Convention/Meeting:** biennial.

AMERICAN ASSOCIATION OF UNIVERSITY WOMEN EDUCATIONAL FOUNDATION (AAUWEF)

2401 Virginia Ave., N.W.   Phone: (202) 785-7700
Washington, DC 20037   Dr. Quincalee Brown, Exec.Dir.
Founded: 1958. An arm of the American Association of University Women (see separate entry). Established to: expand AAUW's primary emphasis on educational work; facilitate the building of endowments for fellowships, research, and public service projects; supplement and further specified areas of AAUW concern; and assume administrative and managerial responsibilities in the AAUW Educational Center. Sponsors conferences; encourages development of the Educational Center in Washington, DC, as a center for women scholars from throughout the world; seeks support from other foundations for research and educational projects; also receives contributions from AAUW members. Is especially concerned with women's participation in the community and in higher education. Administers Educational Foundation Library, AAUW Fellowships Program, and Research and Projects endowment funds. Brings 50 women from other countries to the U.S. for study each year. Presents 100 fellowship awards annually to American women for advanced study. Awards public service grants to member divisions and branches; presents individual members with special research project grants. Library includes 4000 volumes on higher education, women and subjects related to AAUW programs. Issues various publications on education. **Convention/Meeting:** annual - always October or November, Washington, DC.

CLEARINGHOUSE ON WOMEN'S STUDIES (CWS)

P.O. Box 334   Phone: (516) 997-7660
Old Westbury, NY 11568   Florence Howe, Editor
Founded: 1970. **Staff:** 20. An educational project of the Feminist Press. The

principal repository of curricular information about women's studies courses throughout the U.S. Seeks to eliminate sexism in education at all levels. Offers in-service training for teachers. Provides consultant services. Maintains 300 vertical file drawers of materials on publications, conferences, awards and statistics connected with women's education. **Publications:** Women's Studies Newsletter, quarterly; also publishes Who's Who and Where in Women's Studies.

HIGHER EDUCATION RESOURCE SERVICES (HERS)

Cheever House
Wellesley College   Phone: (617) 235-7173
Wellesley, MA 02181   Lilli S. Hornig, Exec. Dir.
Founded: 1972. Women administrators who are members of Committeee for the Concerns of Women in New England Colleges and Universities (Concerns Committee). As action arm of Concerns Committee, purposes are: to improve status of women faculty and administrators; to expand career opportunities for professional women; to aid institutions of higher education in achieving equal opportunity. Programs and activities include: search, referral and placement service for academic positions for women; women's resource file and talent service for academic positions for women; women's resource file and talent bank; Career Cooperatives (career counseling services, workshops, and seminars for women graduate students and junior faculty); early and mid-career re-orientation programs; speakers on academic women's issues; women administrators conferences. Holds seminars in higher education administration for junior to mid-level women academic administrators and faculty preparing to be administrators. Conducts research on equal educational and employment opportunity for women.

The crucial question about associations may be, Which one do I join? Perhaps a better question is, To which of these is my college or university already obligated? Often group memberships are available at reduced rates if your institution has a membership. However, don't let the lack of an institutional rate deter you from joining an association. Your decision to join should be determined by the answers to three basic questions: Does the association have a proven track record which demonstrates substantial benefits to the membership and not a self-perpetuating philosophy of growing larger and more powerful? Does the association impart and interest the pertinent questions which need to be answered for the personal and professional growth of the membership? Is the end product of the association more than meetings, committees, and publications; that is, does it honestly speak to the issues and situations that would assist professional growth and expertise?

When you can answer these three questions a choice of association membership can also be determined. Choose your association carefully. The continued growth of professionalism and personal direction is the important consideration.

Glossary

PREPARED BY JACK D. TERRY, JR. FROM CHAPTER MATERIALS

Academic freedom: a community of teaching and learning in which freedom of the mind and spirit are accepted as fundamental privileges which cannot be directed through administrative or coercive channels.

Accountability: to be responsible for goals and objectives either developed individually or superimposed from above.

Accrediting agencies: regional accrediting bodies which develop a set of standards for the purpose of accrediting the institution as a whole. The regional accrediting agency assures that the total program of a complex institution is coordinated, administered, and held in proper balance.

Achievement management: how well a student achieves and masters content at a given level.

Administration: the managing of a business, office, school, etc. The group of persons in charge of the management of affairs.

Administrative evaluation: area persons with hard data concerning individual faculty members who evidence improvement of instruction, professionalisms, publications, classroom skills, classroom management, etc. The area from which professionalism in teaching can be evaluated.

Adversary hearing: the process of allowing a person of divergent views (political, social, sectarian, religious) the freedom and privilege of speech in opposition to a popular view.

Affirmative action: a series of positive measures to make opportunities available to individuals belonging to groups which have been discriminated against in the past.

Affirmative action program: the use of selection procedures which have been validated to assure equal employment opportunity for all in order that discrimination may be avoided.

Alumni public: the most vocal and dependable external group dating back to the beginning of the education endeavor.

American Association of University Professors (AAUP): organized in 1915. Has been involved in protecting academic freedom, tenure, due process, advancing faculty salaries, and gaining faculty involvement in the governance of the college or university.

American Federation of Teachers (AFT): organized in 1916 and a member of the American Federation of Labor. The more aggressive organization for teachers' rights.

Antinepotism: restrictions against more than one member of a family being employed by a college or university within the same work team, division, or department. If this law discriminates against a woman by denying her employment it can be termed unfair.

Appropriate practice: (a) equivalent appropriate practice occurs when the practice situation is essentially the same as that called for in the performance or behavioral objectives. (b) analoguous appropriate practice provides practice activities that are comparable but not identical to the performance or behavioral objectives.

Arbitration: a process of negotiation between a professional negotiator and an employment group. All decisions from this process are binding on the collective group.

Assessed needs: a statistical data-based investigation via survey and other evaluative instruments to determine specific needs for a projected program.

Audiovisual department: develops and maintains all audiovisual equipment for classroom support and for LRC usage.

Authoritarian leadership: associated with bureaucratic organizational structure. Authority comes downward.

Automation department: develops the material which can be automated for learning system use.

Budget: a statement of the estimated income and authorized expenditures for a fixed period, usually one year.

Bureaucracy: academic governance in which the faculty has little to say about the implementation of the school enterprise but are handed down decisions and determination from above.

Bureaucratic paradigm: budgeting, facilities, design, and intraadministrative relations.

Campus autonomy: each campus has the privilege of interpretations of the broad state guidelines under the direction of its president and board of trustees. Each campus is a separate entity and must be dealt with individually.

Centralization: all institutional or consortial involvement is vested in one central office or administrative cluster.

Chief administrative officer: directly responsible to the local governing body for insuring that the institution is in compliance with the rules, laws, and various regulations impacted from the various internal and external agencies.

Clear and present danger: clear and convincing proof that the speech and speaker would cause danger to the orderly functions of the institution.

Clear and present danger doctrine: a person cannot be restrained from speaking or the audience prevented from listening merely because the presence may constitute a danger.

Colleague evaluation: the use of peers to determine colleagues' comprehensiveness, up-to-dateness of course content, textbooks, assignments, grapevine feedback, and grading procedures.

Collective bargaining: a process of joining persons in a collection of common needs and bargaining with an employing agency for specific physical or spatial needs. Commonly used by unions to achieve desired ends.

Collegial: academic governance in which the faculty has a strong voice in the implementation of the school enterprise.

Commonalities: a system of rewards which are available to all staff personnel without regard to rank, tenure, race, sex, or national origin. Faculty have objectives in common.

Community public: the most important yet delicate external group for the program of public relations because of the desired image with residents of a community.

Comprehensive community colleges: institutions in a community setting which offer a wide variety of services seemingly appropriate to the needs of a nontraditional education. These programs involve occupational, university parallel and continuing education.

Conceptual areas: considers ways these can effect teaching either positively or negatively—lesson plans, course outlines, goals, objectives, individual differences, etc.

Conflict model: a model in which organization is conceived as a basis of group differences not individual differences. Conflict acts as a stimulus to proffer competition in an effort to reduce conflict among groups.

Conflict resolvement strategies: field-tested strategies that resolve specific conflict situations.

Conflict theory: a theory that views organization as the hierarchy of subordinate-superordinate relationships within the social system which allocates, integrates, and facilitates in order to achieve goals of the social system.

Consortium: formal arrangements for cooperation in one or more areas of activity among two or more institutions.

Contingency management: a process stressing the effectiveness of a leader according to the type of industry he/she is in as well as his/her personal style of leadership.

Continuing education units (CEUs):   credit given in unit measures for nontraditional educational services. Domains: (a) cognitive domain involves intellectual process (b) affective domain involves the feelings or emotions (c) psychomotor domain involves the manipulative skills.

Coordinating boards: elected institutional bodies set up by the state legislature to coordinate all the work of the various institutions within the learning cluster.

Cost analysis: a process which may be employed through three kinds of costs: research and development, investment, and operating costs (placed on physical qualities such as time, space, equipment, supplies).

Counseling paradigm: humanizing one-to-one relationships; administrative credibility based on personal credibility.

Current operating fund: the income that is needed to finance the instructional programs, maintain the educational plant, and meet instructional costs.

Curriculum flowchart: an administrative flowchart for curriculum revisions. These suggestions gathered from throughout the campus from students, department chairpersons, division chairpersons, deans, academic and administrative vice presidents form a planning cycle which imparts the system design to improve and assure proper operation and procedure. Keeps the process on target.

Curriculum paradigm: curriculum development with the student in mind.

Data processing department: the department that catalogues materials on a computer. The data is immediately retrievable for update, future acquisition, present acquisition, and inventory.

Decision-making theory: a theory that may be equated with the problem-solving process which assists an organization to pass judgment on a problem and thereby terminate a controversy.

Democratic leadership: associated with a participative structure of organization. Authority stems from the group.

Designs approach: the basic elements of the management process, including long- and short-range planning, organizing, staffing, directing and controlling.

Discriminatory conditions: conditions resulting from unintentional biases which have been reflected in certain personnel policies or the reflections of personal biases on the part of individual administrators, faculty members, or the college or university as a whole.

Due process and tenure: the process of arbitration given a faculty member in danger of losing a job. Sets forth the conditions under which that arbitration may take place.

Due process protection: giving individuals fair notice of proceedings as required by civil statutes.

EEOC: the Equal Employment Opportunity Commission is a federal agency created to monitor instances of discrimination in all processes involving a minority constituency.

Endowment capital: gifts and donations received that form an institutions' endowment principle.

Enrichment management: provision for in-depth study to allow a student to apply what has been learned.

Enroute behaviors: any skills preliminary to the accomplishment of the stated objectives.

Environmental paradigm: helping students to interface with their universe.

Equal educational opportunity: the development of measures and procedures providing equal educational opportunity for all Americans no matter their race, creed, color, or national origin.

Equal Pay Act: prohibits discrimination in pay on the basis of sex.

Evaluation of teaching: a process of determining the efficiency, professionalism, classroom skills, goals, and outcomes of a faculty member through the use of professionally prepared or personally developed objective evaluation instruments. The main purpose of evaluation of teaching to improve the holistic concept of the student and faculty member.

Ex parte restraining order: a restraining order that allows for a partisan presentation only.

External degree: a degree achieved away from a college setting with little or no time spent in residence at the college.

External groups: groups of individuals not closely associated with the institution by virtue of salary or governance responsibilities. (Sometimes termed external publics.)

External publics: groups outside of the academic environment.

Faculty development: a program for continuing professionalism for faculty members. Either developed individually by the professor with support from the institution or an individually funded program at a regional development center. Faculty development provisions are often an enticement in faculty recruitment.

Federal control: multiple laws enacted by the federal government which assure the high quality of various forms of educational programs and provide funds to assist these programs.

Fee: a one time or recurring request such as admissions filing fee, graduation fee, late examination fee, etc.

Feudal patronage: discrimination in job placement preferring those persons who graduated from particular colleges or universities or were closely associated with college or university alumni.

Final authorization: an adjudicatory board to pass final judgment on the establishment of a particular program.

Financial aid: the distribution of allocated funds, both federal and institutional, based upon a predetermined dissemination formula or policy.

Formulas: a process of securing funds based on an equivalent student attendance on a full-time basis.

Free choice model: a planning model to develop projections predicated on the number of students expected to exit from a particular discipline and the number of faculty expected to teach in that discipline.

General purpose tax: tax for any authorized expenditure; used mainly for general operations.

Goals forecasting: includes an element of flexibility in predicting the educational and institutional needs of the organization on a long-range basis.

Goals setting: three dimensions in the planning process—priority, time, structure.

Grievance citation: a petition which may be presented to an institution by the representatives of a collective union representing the needs and interests of all under the umbrella of that particular collective union.

Guidance and counseling: provisions ranging from information via printed materials to individual confrontations or group activities that determine decision making.

Health program: the provision of medical services and outpatient care on a limited or extended basis.

Hygiene theory: identifies motivational factors in terms of satisfiers and dissatisfiers. These likewise are developed from lower needs to higher related needs producing genuine personal satisfaction.

Implementation: a step-by-step process to achieve stated objectives in program development design to bring the program into full operation.

Individualized instruction: an individualized system designed on goals and objectives. Developed in sequential steps to a particular predetermined outcome.

Institutional image: the concept of an institution held by a number of publics that are not totally associated with the institution or its institutional life.

Institutional public image: the process of communicating to the public an institution's view of itself and the view to be held by the public and private secto

Instructional package: an organization of devices and other materials which pre ents a complete body of information and is largely self-supporting rathe than supplementary to the teaching-learning process.

Internal publics: communication within the institution's boundaries for the pur pose of persuasion or motivation toward institutional goals and objective

Laissez-faire leadership: a participatory approach to leadership where almost n decisions are made by the administrator.

Leadership Models: differing types of leadership styles (that is, Theory X, Theo ry Y, Theory Z, Contingency Theory, are examples).

Learning resource center (LRC):   this center houses all the materials, print o nonprint, used for instructional and research purposes. Includes both the mediated center as well as the library.

Learning systems: software that is used in the learning process and playable on the equipment maintained by the audiovisual department.

Life-style cycle theory leadership: associated with an understanding of the relation ship between an effective style of leadership and the level of maturity o the members of the organization.

Line management: administrators in the direct line who report to the presiden or chancellor through whom all communications materials, both beneficia and detrimental, should flow in due process.

Local governing boards: the legislative and policy-making body of an institution of higher education charged with the supervision and control of the institution's activities.

Maintenance management: opportunity and review in the system to maintain skills and values learned.

Management: the controlling, handling, and directing of a business, office, school, etc. The group of persons who skillfully administer the guidance of those affairs.

Management by Objectives (MBO):   a system of management that requires the formulation of goals and the construction of objectives to meet those goals.

Manpower planning model: projects manpower needs then develops projections of the number of individuals needed to fill those requirements.

Maslow's Hierachy of Needs: a pyramid of elevated levels that describe a progression from base needs (physiological) to achievement needs (self-actualization), with descriptive indicators as achievement success.

Mass media: the combination of all reporting devices (newspaper, radio, television, magazines, etc.) by private corporations to provide newsworthy items to the public for the purpose of information for the masses.

Measurability model: a model that establishes specific performance objectives the educator expects the learner to accomplish.

Media public: the "new kid on the block" in terms of external groups, and potentially the most visible public. This group has the power to make or break the institution through the printed or mediated word.

Merit: an increment, either monetary or advancement in rank or tenure, for the demonstration of professionalism through local, state, or national recognition; expertise in the classroom; or publications and services.

Merit ratings: a criterion system for recognizing faculty achievers. Based on a nonbiased set of standards available to all faculty and staff.

Minorities: specifically defined by the Department of Labor as Negros, persons with Spanish surnames, American Indians, and Orientals.

Mirror image: a person hired in a division or department who has feelings, beliefs, and life-styles similar to the department or division head.

Modeling: a teaching tactic which allows the student to see those behaviors he is expected to adopt.

Morale and esprit de corps: a feeling of togetherness and companionship usually generated by a common cause.

Motivation: a conscious and unconscious effort to stimulate efficient productivity by means of meeting a taxonomy of human needs—biological, sociological, and sociocultural.

Motivational Theory: a theory that considers organization as a cooperative system which is conscious, deliberate, and purposeful.

Motivation Management: rewards built into the system to motivate the student to stay involved.

National Education Association (NEA):   a professional organization effective at state levels; is strong in community colleges and public school districts.

Needs assessment: an evaluation of students' needs in order to develop objectives to reach new levels of learning.

Negotiation: a due process carried on with a school employer by delegated representatives of the teachers union for the purpose of reconciling a grievance or personnel problem.

New students: members of minority groups, and those with previous military service; physical handicaps and women.

Nondiscrimination requirements: apply to all persons including citizens of the United States and those who enjoy the benefits of citizenship through legal or temporary residence. No discrimination shall be directed toward these persons though not members of a legal minority.

Nonprint material: any material for use in LRCs that is not traditionally considered print material.

Nonresolvement: a collective bargaining request that cannot be resolved is turned over to a professional negotiator. In most union organizations all decision-making processes are forfeited to the negotiator and all decisions are binding on the members of the collective union.

Nontraditional student: a student who attends college for some purpose other than strictly academic. (For example, vocational-technical, noncredit, continuing education, etc.)

Objectives: statements written in terms of personal performance, observable by one or more of the five senses, specific enough to be meaningful, and measurable in terms of level of behavior and conditions, sequential in relation to prior subsequent objectives, relevant in relation to prior and

subsequent objectives, attainable within the time period allowed, and cha
lenging to each individual person.

Ombudsman paradigm: student and faculty problems and solutions facilitated.

Performance appraisal: scientific instruments for the purpose of evaluating an
appraising a workman's performance.

Placement: the process of identifying potential job opportunities in the publi
and private sector and the assessment of students for placement or recom
mendation to these job opportunities.

Planning, Programming, Budgeting System (PPBS): developed by the Departmer
of Defense in 1961. Designed to provide a systematic process to identif
communalities in programs with similar objectives.

Planning system: functional organization of the planning sequences into
super- and subsystem design to effectuate the planning process.

Positive action: the process employed to overcome the systematic exclusion o
members of various minority groups from access to career opportunitie
and advancement tracks available to other citizens.

Prescriptive management: a plan developed from tests and assessments for
student to master content learning.

Press relationship: a working relationship formed with the media-producing
agencies of a community for the purpose of presenting a positive image t
the public.

Print materials: books, magazines, abstracts—any material whose primary deliv
ery system is print.

Private donors: include philanthropic foundations, nonalumni individuals
alumni, business corporations, religious groups. Their gifts may be gener
al, or restricted to specific programs of particular interest to the donor

Proactive: a stance that anticipates problems or difficulties rather than reacting
to them.

Proactive student development: a developmental plan that anticipates problems
and difficulties in student life and provides objectives to meet those
difficulties.

Problem-solving and decision-making techniques: models for solving specific problems or making specific decisions.

Professional development: a process of evaluating all levels of educational administrative and teaching functions and prescribing additional studies or
workshops to improve performance.

Program development: a systematic process involving analysis of the key elements
of need, desirability, and ability to carry out the program.

Program evaluation: an on-going systematic process to determine the index of
program success and to determine the continuing feasibility of a program
or its deletion.

Program idea: an idea for an educational program which may emanate from
manpower surveys, publications, advisory committees, students, faculty,
conferences, or business and industry.

Political: academic governance in which faculty and administration have little
to say about the implementation of the school enterprise, which is determined by the political system governing the institution. The assumption is
that the political force is the state government.

Promotion: a criterion-based process for the purpose of progressing professionally through the academic ranks of an institution on a clearly stated schedule.

Public information: the method or process of transmitting the image of the institution to the minds and consciousness of the various publics.

Public relations: the methods and activities employed by an individual, organization, corporation, or institution to promote a favorable relationship with the public.

Quality control: the process of assuring the best possible environment in which learners may grow, make positive changes, and be active in student and public life.

Quality control programs: programs of checks and balances in a system design to monitor the quality of the present administrative flow and project the quality of the future process. Brings the program together for flow analysis.

Rational model: a model in which organization is conceived as a means for the realization of announced group goals.

Reactive student development: a developmental plan that does not anticipate problems and difficulties in student life. Provides management by crisis rather than Management by Objectives.

Recycling: a function in systems design that returns the process to a given point in the system to pick up an inadequate procedure and cycle that procedure back through the flow of the system.

Resident life: the concern of housing is to be responsive to the total needs of students, which include comfort, safety, and a wholesome environment.

Revenue bonds: bonds issued to repay investors from receipts derived from an operation.

Reward system: an incentive program available to all personnel; constructed on a criterion basis and is not biased in its administration. May include increased pay, release time from teaching responsibilities, sabbatic leave, national recognition, etc.

Scientific decision-making process: the logical ordered exploration of any problem in a systematic approach to management.

Scientific management: the traditional or classical approach concerned more with the measurement of work than with the workman or the description of the organization.

Strike: a process whereby members of a union cease to work in a collective fashion, none performing their assigned task until grievance issues can be settled or clarified.

Structuralistic management: a bureaucratic organization equated with rules and expectations flowing from superordinates downward.

Student development: an integrated process that includes all functions of the student services and academic domain involving students, faculty, and student personnel professionals.

Student evaluation: national testing instruments or personally prepared instruments that allow the student to judge a multiplicity of classroom skills firsthand. Data demonstrates that the most accurate evaluation of teaching probably comes from the student.

Student fees: may include tuition, student activity fees, and building usage fees.

Student public: the most significant external group in the public relations program of the institution.

Superordinate: a supervisor who is immediately above a person in line supervision and supervises all activities of that person, including all academic privileges.

System: an analysis of past and present strengths and weaknesses designed into an administrative flow developed on goals and objectives for the future success of the administrative procedure.

Systematic exclusion: a process of systematically excluding particular persons from professional or occupational advancement or training because of race, creed, color, or national origin.

Systems approach to administration: a planning approach to administrative procedure which analyzes problems, organizes past and present processes, analyzes present priorities, writes general statements of goals and objectives in long-range terms, and states short-range objectives in order that long-range goals can be reached.

Systems theory: a theory of administration organized in such a manner as to accomplish objectives and goals.

Task force feasibility study: a group of persons representative of all areas involved in new program development, including internal and external representatives, to assess program feasibility.

Teaching-learning process: includes the total educating environment of teaching values, social conflicts, goal and objective setting, synthesis process, teaching methods, and teaching strategies.

Teaching machines: manipulative machines which have a body of materials available through a systems-designed form for an individualized study approach.

Team management concept: a concept of management that considers the total strength of the entire management team and uses each member's strength rather than one person's weakness.

Technical skill: the functioning area capabilities of an individual.

Tenure: a provision offered teachers in institutions that provides for job continuance, academic freedom, protection of constitutional rights, and the right to be employed.

Terminal behavior: that exit behavior designed for the final performance of the behavioral objective.

Theory X: authoritative style of management with a work centered approach to structure and productivity and an external force as authority figure.

Theory X management: views the work group from the classical or scientific approach and directs and controls through authority exercised. Hard management techniques are embraced.

Theory Y: participative style of leadership with all members of the group integral contributing partners in the enterprise.

Theory Y management: views the work group from the human element standpoint. The process is the integration of the worker into the organization to achieve his own goals and within those to achieve the organization's goals.

Theory Z: systems management designed to allow prediction of effects of organizational change with some degree of correctional action as a result of external or internal change. A type of situational motivation and leadership.

Theory Z management: a recirculating type of process capable of some degree of corrective action either as a result of internal changes within the system or in answer to environmental changes.

Tripartite: the three parts of the educational process—administrator, professor, student.

Union: a collection of persons employed in a common enterprise joined together for the purpose of exerting collective pressure on the employer to improve working conditions.

Universal principles of management: an authoritarian approach to management that considers workmen as mere machines.

Zero Based Budgeting (ZBB):   a budget control system with "decision packages" which relate goals and objectives to budgeting priorities and needs.

Selected Bibliography

Abbott, Joan. *Student Life in a Class Society*. Oxford, England: Pergamon Press, 1971.

Abilene Christian University Catalogue, 1977–78. Abilene, Tex.

Ackoff, R. L. *Scientific Method: Optimizing Applied Research Decision*. New York: John Wiley and Sons, 1962.

Allen, James E., Jr. *Emerging Patterns in American Higher Education*. Edited by Logan Wilson. Washington, D.C.: American Council on Education, 1965.

Allen, Kenneth. *Use of Community College Libraries*. Hamden, Conn.: Shoe String Press, 1971.

_____, and Allen, Loren. *Organization and Administration of Learning Resources Center in the Community College*. Hamden, Conn.: Shoe String Press, 1973.

American Association of Colleges for Teacher Education and Association of Teacher Educators. *Perspectives on Organization*. Washington, D.C.: American Association of Colleges for Teacher Education, 1976.

American Library Association, American Association of Community and Junior Colleges, and the Association for Educational Communications and Technology. "Guidelines for Two-Year College Learning Resources Programs." *Audiovisual Instruction* 18 (January 1973), pp. 50–61.

Anderson, G. Lester. *Readings in Organizations*. Edited by James L. Gibson, John M. Ivancevich, and James H. Donnelly, Jr. Dallas, Texas: Business Publications, Inc., 1973.

Anderson, Harry F. "The Architect Views the Building and Planning Process." In *Junior College Libraries: Development, Needs, and Perspectives*, edited by Everett L. More. Chicago: American Library Association, 1969.

Anderson, Scarvia B.; Ball, Samuel; and Murphy, Richard T. *Encyclopedia of Educational Evaluation: Concepts and Techniques for Evaluating Education and Training Programs*. San Francisco: Jossey-Bass, 1974.

Andrew, W. W. *Cooperation within American Higher Education*. Washington, D.C.: Association of American Colleges, 1964.

Anthony, R. N. *Planning and Control Systems*. Boston: Harvard University Press, 1965.

Anzalone, J. S. *An Interinstitutional Admissions Program for the State University of Florida*. Tallahassee, Fl.: State University System of Florida, 1967.

Argyris, Chris. *Executive Leadership: An Appraisal of a Manager in Action.* New York: Harper and Brothers, 1953.

Arner, T. D. "Student Personnel Education: A Process Outcome Model." *Journal of College Student Personnel* 17, (1977), pp. 334–41.

Associated Colleges of the Midwest. *Associated Colleges of the Midwest Faculty Handbook, 1970–71.* Chicago, 1971.

Astin, Alexander W. "The Impact of Dormitory Living on Students." *Educational Record,* 54 (Summer 1973), pp. 347–52.

Aussiecker, Bill. "Student Involvement with Collective Bargaining." *Journal of Higher Education* 5 (September/October 1976), pp. 533–43.

Averill, Lloyd J. "Autonomy: Myth and Reality." *Trends and Issues in Cooperation.* Washington, D.C.: American Association for Higher Education. Fall 1973, pp. 10–16.

Baker, E. L., and Popham, W. J. *Expanding Dimension of Instructional Objectives.* Englewood Cliffs, N.J.: Prentice-Hall, 1973.

Baker, James H. *American University Progress.* New York: Longmans, Green and Company, 1916.

Baker, Robert L., and Schutz, Richard E. *Instructional Product Development.* New York: Van Nostrand Reinhold Co., 1971.

Barger, Ben, and Lynch, Ann Q. "University Housing: A Healthy Learning Laboratory." *New Directions for Higher Education* 1 (Autumn 1973), pp. 5–17.

Bargon, Paul E. "Human Resources, the Changing Labor Market and Undergraduate Education." *Liberal Education* 61 (May 1975), pp. 275–84.

Barnard, Chester I. *The Functions of the Executive.* Cambridge, Mass.: Harvard University Press, 1938.

Barnhart, Clarence L. *Thorndike Barnhart Dictionary.* New York: Doubleday, 1967.

Barzun, Jacques. *The American University.* New York: Harper and Row, 1968.

Bender, Marylin. "When the Boss Is a Woman." *Esquire,* 28 March 1978, pp. 35–41.

Bendig, A. W. "The Use of Student-Rating Scales in the Evaluation of Instructors in Introductory Psychology." *Journal of Educational Psychology* 43 (1952), pp. 167–75.

Benewitz, Maurice C. "Grievance and Arbitration Procedures." In *Faculty Bargaining in the Seventies,* edited by Terrance N. Tice. Ann Arbor, Mich.: The Institute of Legal Education, 1973.

Benezet, Louis T. "The Office of the President." In *Administrators in Higher Education,* edited by Gerald P. Burns. New York: Harper & Brothers Publishers, 1962.

Benjamin, Harold, ed. *Dictionary of Education.* 2d ed. New York: McGraw-Hill, Series in Education, 1959.

Bennis, Warren G. *Changing Organizations: Essays on the Development and Evolutions of Human Organizations.* New York: McGraw-Hill, 1966.

————. "Leadership Theory and Administrative Behavior: The Problem of Authority." *Administrative Science Quarterly* 4 (December 1959), pp. 273–85.

————. "Revisionist Theory of Leadership." *Harvard Business Review,* January–February 1961, pp. 26–36; 148–50.

_____; Benne, Kenneth D.; and Chin, Robert. *The Planning of Change*. New York: Holt, Rinehart, and Winston, 1962.

Bergevin, Paul. *A Philosophy for Adult Education*. New York: Seabury Press, 1967.

Bernays, Edward L. *Public Relations*. Norman, Okla.: University of Oklahoma Press, 1963.

Berqquist, W. H., and Phillips, Steven R. "Components of an Effective Faculty Development Program." *Journal of Higher Education* 46 (March 1975), pp. 177–211.

Bess, James L. "The Motivation to Teach." *Journal of Higher Education* 48 (May/June 1977), pp. 243–56.

Birney, Robert C. *Employment by Hampshire College Progress Report*. No. 1. Amherst, Mass.: Hampshire College, 1975.

Blackburn, R. T., and Clark, M. J. "An Assessment of Faculty Performance: Some Correlates Between Administrator, Colleague, Student, and Self-Ratings." *Sociology of Education* 48 (1975), pp. 242–56.

Blocker, Clyde; Bender, Louis; and Martorana, S. V. *The Political Terrain of American Postsecondary Education*. Fort Lauderdale, Fl.: Nova University Press, 1975.

Bloland, P. A., and Siegman, A. B. "An Instructional Approach to Student Development." *Journal of College Student Personnel* 18 (1977), pp. 174–76.

Bloom, Benjamin S. *Taxonomy of Educational Objectives: Cognitive Domain*. New York: David McKay, 1974.

Board of Trustees Policies and Administrative Procedures Manual. Dallas: Dallas County Community College District, 1977.

Boe, Edmund S., and Damp, Harry S. "The Elements of Program Budgeting." *Journal of Accountancy*, April 1971, pp. 84–86.

Bolin, John G., and Muir, John W. *Merit Rating for Salary Increases and Promotions*. Athens, Ga.: University of Georgia, Institute of Higher Education, 1966.

Boone, Jerry N.; Hampton, Clarence O.; and Jones, John D. "Student Affairs and Academics: A Team Approach." *National Association of Student Personnel Administration Journal* 13 (Fall 1975), pp. 43–45.

Borich, G. D., ed., *Evaluating Educational Programs and Products*. Englewood Cliffs, N.J.: Educational Technology Publications, 1974.

Borland, D. T., and Thomas, R. E. "Student Development Implementation Through Expanded Professional Skills." *Journal of College Student Personnel* 17, (1976), pp. 145–49.

Borland, David. Unpublished lecture notes, EDHE 673. Denton, Texas: North Texas State University, Spring 1977.

Bowman, Garda, and Klopf, Gordon J. *New Careers and Roles in American Schools*. Washington, D.C.: Bank Street College of Education for the Office of Economic Opportunity, 1968.

Bradley, A. P. "Academic Consortium Effectiveness: An Investigation of Criteria." Ph.D. dissertation, University of Michigan, 1971.

Brandes, F. M. "Point of View." *Chronicle of Higher Education*, 16 April, 1973, p. 12.

Breneman, D. W. "Selected Aspects of the Economics of the Five College Cooperation." Mimeographed. Amherst, Mass: Amherst College, 1971.

Brooks v. *Auburn University*. 412 F. 2nd. 1171.

Brown, Robert D. *Student Development in Tomorrow's Higher Education*. Washington, D.C.: American Personnel and Guidance Association, 1972.

Brown, William F. *Student-to-Student Counseling*. Austin, Tex.: University of Texas Press, 1972.

Brown, William H., III. "Can Collective Bargaining Survive without Protecting the Rights of Minorities and Women?" In *Collective Survival in the 70's*, edited by Richard Rowan. Philadelphia: University of Pennsylvania Press, 1972.

Brubacker, John S. *Higher Education in Transition*. New York: Harper and Brothers, 1958.

Burnett, H. J., ed. *Institutional Cooperation in Higher Education*. Corning, N.Y.: College Center of the Finger Tahres, 1970.

Buxton, C. E. *College Teaching: A Psychologist's View*. New York: Harcourt Brace, 1956.

Campbell, P. B., and Beers, J. S. *Evaluation: The State of the Art*. Princeton, N.J.: Educational Testing Service, 1972.

Carman, Harry J. "Boards of Trustees and Regents." In *Administrators in Higher Education*, edited by Gerald P. Burns. New York: Harper and Brothers, 1962.

Carnegie Commission on Higher Education. *The More Effective Use of Resources: An Imperative for Higher Education*. New York: McGraw-Hill, 1972.

Carnegie Foundation for the Advancement of Teaching. *Missions of the Curriculum: A Contemporary Review with Suggestions*. San Francisco: Jossey-Bass, 1977.

Caro, F. G. *Readings in Evaluation Research*. New York: Russell Sage Foundation, 1971.

Centra, J. A. *The College Environment Revisited: Current Descriptions and a Comparison of Three Methods of Assessment*. Research Bulletin RB-70-44. Princeton, N.J.: Educational Testing Service, 1970.

_____, and Linn, R. L. *Student Points of View in Ratings of College Instruction*. Research Bulletin RB-73-60. Princeton, N.J.: Educational Testing Service, 1973.

_____, and Sobol, M. G. "Faculty and Student Views of the Interim Term." *Research in Higher Education* 2 (1974), pp. 231–38.

Central Steering Committee of the CCFL Self Study and Long-Range Plan. *Patterns for Voluntary Cooperation: Self-Study Report of the College Center of the Finger Lakes*. New York: College Center of the Finger Lakes, 1971.

Chambers, M. M. *Financing Higher Education*. Washington, D.C.: The Center for Applied Research in Education, 1963.

Chandler, E. M. "Student Affairs Administration in Transition." *Journal of College Student Personnel* 14, (1973), pp. 392–98.

Chickering, Arthur W. "College Advising for the 1970's." *New Directions for Higher Education* 1 (Autumn 1973), pp. 69–80.

Churchman, C. W.; Askoff, R. L.; and Arnoff, E. L. *Introduction to Operations Research*. New York: John Wiley, 1957.

Clark, Michael C. *Systematic Curriculum and Program Development (C & PD) at Saint John's University: An Evaluation Report*. Collegeville, Minn.: Saint John's University, 1976.

Coffman, W. E. "Determining Students' Concepts of Effective Teaching from Their Ratings of Instructors." *Journal of Educational Psychology* 45 (1954), pp. 277–86.

Cohen, Arthur M. *Community College Review* 2 (1974), pp. 121–21.

_____. *Objectives for College Courses.* Beverly Hills: Glencoe Press, 1970.

_____. *Measuring Faculty Performance.* Washington, D.C.: ERIC Clearinghouse for Junior College Information, American Association of Junior Colleges, 1969.

_____. "Political Influences on Curriculum and Instruction." *New Directions for Community Colleges* 2 (Autumn 1974), pp. 29–53.

_____, and Brewer, Florence B. *Community Colleges*, 1972, pp. 33a–33s.

Cohen, J., and Humphreys, L. G. "Memorandum to Faculty." Mimeographed. Illinois: University of Illinois, Department of Psychology, 1960.

Cohen, S. A., and Berger, W. G. "Dimensions of Students' Ratings of College Instructors Underlying Subsequent Achievement on Course Examinations." *Proceedings of the 178th Annual Convention of the American Psychological Association*, vol. 5 (1970), pp. 605–6.

Coladarci, Arthur P., and Getzels, Jacob W. *The Use of Theory in Educational Administration.* Stanford: Stanford University Press, 1955.

Cole, Richard R., and Bowers, Thomas A. "An Exploration of Factors Related to Journalism Faculty Productivity." *Journalism Quarterly* 52 (Winter 1975), pp. 638–44.

Coleman, James C. *Abnormal Psychology and Modern Life.* 4th ed. Glenview, Ill.: Scott, Foresman and Company, 1972.

Colleagues as Raters of Classroom Instruction. Research Bulletin RB-74-18. Princeton, N.J.: Educational Testing Service, 1974.

Commission on Instructional Technology to Improve Learning. *A Report to the President and the Congress of the United States.* Washington, D.C.: Government Printing Office, 1970.

Cook, J. M., and Neville, R. F. *The Faculty as Teachers: A Perspective on Evaluation.* Washington, D.C.: ERIC Clearinghouse on Higher Education, George Washington University, 1971.

Coolie, Verner, and Booth, Alan. *Adult Education.* Washington, D.C.: The Center for Applied Research in Education, 1964.

Cordes, David C. "Project PRIME: A Test Implementation of the CAMPUS Simulation Model." In *Managing the University: A Systems Approach*, edited by Paul W. Hamelman. New York: Praeger, 1972.

Corson, John J. *Governance of Colleges and Universities.* New York: McGraw-Hill, 1960.

Costin, F. "Intercorrelations Between Students and Course Chairmen's Ratings of Instructors." Mimeographed. Carbondale, University of Illinois, Division of General Studies, 1966.

_____; Greenough, W. T.; and Menges, R. J. "Student Ratings of College Teaching: Reliability, Validity, and Usefulness." *Review of Educational Research* 41 (1971), pp. 511–35.

Council of the Clairmont Colleges. *The Constitution of the Clairmont Colleges.* Clairmont, Calif.: 1970.

Cramer, Jerome. "How Would Your Faucets Work if Plumbers Were Shielded by Tenure Laws?" *American School Board Journal* 163 (October, 1976), pp 22–24.

Crannell, C. W. "An Experiment in the Rating of Instructors by their Students." *College and University* 24 (1948), pp. 5–11.

Crase, Dixie, R., and Crase, Darrell, "New Tenure and Promotion Guidelines Produce Growth Pains." *Peabody Journal of Education* 54 (October 1976), pp. 56–59.

Crawford, P. L., and Bradshaw, H. L. "Perception of Characteristics of Effective University Teachers: A Scaling Analysis." *Educational and Psychological Measurement* 28 (1968), pp. 1079–85.

Cronback, L. J., and Gleser, G. C. *Psychological Tests and Personnel Decisions.* 2d ed. Urbana, Ill.: University of Illinois Press, 1965.

Cross, K. P. "Student Personnel Work as a Profession." *Journal of College Student Personnel* 14, 1973, pp. 77–81.

Crow, Mary Lynn, ed. *Faculty Development Centers in Southern Universities.* Atlanta: Southern Regional Education Board, 1976.

Cutlip, Scott M. *A Public Relations Bibliography.* Madison, Wis.: University of Wisconsin Press, 1965.

———, and Center, Allen H. *Effective Public Relations.* Englewood Cliffs, N.J.: Prentice-Hall, Inc., 1964.

Davis, Allison. "The Motivation of the Underprivileged Worker." In William Footewhyte, *Industry and Society.* New York: McGraw-Hill, 1946.

DeCoster, David A., and Mable, Phyllis, eds. *Student Development and Education in College Resident Halls.* Washington, D.C.: American College Personnel Association, 1974.

Deegan, William L. "Should Students Evaluate Faculty?" *Community and Junior College Journal* 43 (1972), pp. 25–26.

Deighton, Lee C., ed. *Encyclopedia of Education.* Vol. 5. Macmillan Co., Free Press, 1971.

Desatnick, Robert L. *A Concise Guide to Management Development.* Washington, D.C.: American Management Association, 1970.

Developing Programs for Faculty Evaluation: A Sourcebook for Higher Education. San Francisco: Jossey-Bass, 1974.

Dickson v. *Sitterson.* 250 F. Supp. 486.

District Policy and Procedure Manual. Dallas: Dallas County Community College District, 1977–78.

"Do Alumni and Students Differ in Their Attitudes toward Instructors?" *Journal of Educational Psychology* 42 (1951), pp. 129–43.

Dolan, W. Patrick. *The Ranking Game: The Power of the Academic Elite.* Lincoln, Neb.: Study Commission of Undergraduate Education and the Education of Teachers, 1976.

Donnelly, James H. *Fundamentals of Management.* Dallas, Texas: Business Publications, 1975.

Donoar, G. T., ed. *College and University Interinstitutional Cooperation.* Washington, D.C.: Catholic University of America Press, 1965.

Doty, Charles R., and Gepner, Ronald, eds. *Post-Secondary Personnel Development,* vol. 1. Trenton, N.J.: Mercer County Community College, 1976.

Downie, N. W. "Student Evaluation of Faculty." *Journal of Higher Education* 23 (1952), pp. 495–96, 503.

Dressel, Paul L. *Handbook of Academic Evaluation*. San Francisco: Dressel-Jossey-Bass, 1976.

_____. "Evaluation of the Environment, the Process, and the Results of Higher Education." In *Handbook of College and University Administration*, vol. 2., edited by A. S. Knowles. New York: McGraw-Hill, 1970.

_____, and Mayhew, Lewis B. *Higher Education as a Field of Study*. San Francisco: Jossey-Bass, 1974.

Drucker, A. J., and Remmers, H. H. "Do Alumni and Students Differ in Their Attitudes Toward Instructors?" *Purdue University Studies in Higher Education* 70 (1950), pp. 62–64.

Drucker, Peter F. *Management: Tasks, Responsibilities, Practices*. New York: Harper and Row, 1973.

Duane, James E. "Humanizing Instructional Packages." *Educational Technology* 14 (November 1974), pp. 32–33.

Duke v. *State of Texas*. 327 F. Supp. 1218.

Eble, K. E. *The Recognition and Evaluation of Teaching*. Salt Lake City: Project to Improve College Teaching, 1970.

Eden, Colin, and Harris, John. *Management Decision and Decision Analysis*. New York: John Wiley and Sons, 1975.

Earnest, Ernest. *American Procession*. New York: Bobbs-Merrill Co., 1953.

Edwards, Harry T. "Legal Aspects of the Duty to Bargain." In *Faculty Bargaining in the Seventies*, edited by Terrence N. Tice. Ann Arbor, Mich.: The Institute of Legal Education, 1973.

Eisner, E. W. "Emerging Models for Educational Evaluation." *School Review* 80 (1972), pp. 573–90.

Eko, E. V. "Voluntary Academic Consortia: The Impact of Multiple Memberships on Private Colleges and Universities." Doctoral Dissertation, Union of Experimenting Colleges and Universities, 1972.

Ellsworth, Ralph E. *Planning College and University Library Building*. Boulder, Colo.: Pruett Press, 1968.

Enarson, Harold. "The Academic Vice-President or Dean." In *Administrators in Higher Education*, edited by Gerald P. Burns. New York: Harper and Brothers, 1962.

Erickson, Carlton W. H. *Administering Instructional Media Programs*. New York: Macmillan Company, 1968.

Erickson, S. C., and Kulik, J. A. "Evaluation of Teaching." *Memo to the Faculty* 53 (February 1974), pp. 1–6.

Evans, N. Dean, and Neagley, Russ L. *Planning and Developing Innovative Community Colleges*. Englewood Cliffs, N.J.: Prentice-Hall, 1973.

Ewing, David W. *The Human Side of Planning: Tool or Tyrant?* London: The Macmillan Company, 1969.

Farley, Alan, and Moore, David M. "Utilizing Self-Instruction of Learning Packages." *Educational Technology* 15 (August 1975), pp. 9–13.

Farrar, W. E. "Dimensions of Faculty Performance as Perceived by Faculty." *Dissertation Abstracts* 29 (1969), p. 3458.

Fayol, H. *General and Industrial Management*. Translated by C. Storrs. London: Si Isaac Pitman and Sons, 1949.

Ferguson, John H., and McHenry, Dean E. *The American System of Government* New York: McGraw-Hill, 1969.

Five College Long-Range Planning Committee. *Five College Cooperation: Directions for the Future*. Amherst, Mass.: University of Massachusetts Press, 1969.

Flippo, Edwin B. *Management: A Behavioral Approach*. Boston: Allyn and Bacon, 1966.

Fox, Lawrence E. "Putting Cooperation into Purchasing Yields Increased Savings for Consortium Savings." *College and University Business* 53, no. 2 (Aug. 1972), p. 17.

Franks, B. D., and Deutsch, H. *Evaluating Performance in Physical Education*. New York: Academic Press, 1973.

Frederick, E., and O'ostdan, B. L. *Directory: The Marine Science, Inc*. Millersville, Penn.: Millersville State College, 1972.

Freeman, Robert E. *Crisis in College Finance*. Washington, D.C.: Institute for Social Science Research, 1965.

French, G. M. "College Students' Concept of Effective Teaching Determined by Analysis of Teacher Ratings." *Dissertation Abstracts* 17 (1957), pp. 1380–81.

Gadzella, B. M. "College Student Views and Ratings of an Ideal Professor." *College and University* 44 (1968), pp. 89–96.

Garbarino, Joseph W., and Aussiecker, Bill. *Faculty Bargaining: Change and Conflict*. New York: McGraw-Hill, 1975.

Genova, William J., and others. *Mutual Benefit Evaluation of Faculty and Administrators in Higher Education*. Cambridge, Mass.: Ballinger Publishing Company, 1976.

Getzels, Jacob W. "Administration as a Social Process." In *Administrative Theory in Education*, edited by Andrew W. Halpin. New York: Macmillan Company, 1958.

Gibb, G. A. "Classroom Behavior of the College Teacher." *Educational and Psychological Measurement* 15 (1955), pp. 254–63.

Gibson, James L. *Readings in Organizations*. Dallas: Business Publications, 1976.

Gillespie, Marcus. "The New Rules for Interviewing Job Applicants: Schools Ignore Them at Their Peril." *American School Board Journal* 164 (March 1977), pp. 27–30.

Good, Carter V., ed. *Dictionary of Education*. 3d ed. New York: McGraw-Hill, 1973.

Good, Harry G., and Teller, James D. *A History of Western Education*. New York: Macmillan Company, 1969.

Gose, Frank J. *Yavapai County Community College District—Verda Valley Community Needs Assessment Project*. Prescott, Ariz.: Office of Institutional Research, 1979.

"A Graduate Course in the Teaching of Psychology: Description and Evaluation." *Journal of Teacher Education* 19 (1968), pp. 425–32.

Gray, C. E. "The Teaching Model and Evaluation of Teaching Performance." *Journal of Higher Education* 40 (1969), pp. 636–42.

Greenwood, Gordon E.; Bridges, Charles M.; Ware, William B.; and McLean, James E. "Student Evaluation of College Teaching Behaviors." *Journal of Higher Education*, November 1973.

Griffiths, Daniel E. "The Nature and Meaning of Theory." In *Theory Development and Educational Administration*, edited by Eddy J. Van Meter. New York: MSS Information Corporation, 1973.

Gronlund, N. E. *Measurement and Evaluation in Teaching*. New York: Macmillan, 1965.

Grupe, Fritz H. "Consortia and Institutional Change." *Trends and Issues in Cooperation* Spring 1974, pp. 12–21.

Gustad, J. W. "Policies and Practices in Faculty Evaluation." *Educational Record* 42 (1961), pp. 194–211.

Guthrie, E. R. "The Evaluation of Teaching." *Educational Record* 30 (1949), pp. 109–15.

Haas, Frederick C. *Executive Obsolescense: Research Study No. 90*. New York: American Management Association, 1968.

Halerston, W. "Early Attempts at Cooperation Among Member Colleges of Colleges of Mid-America, Incorporated." Mimeographed. Sioux City, Iowa: Colleges of Mid-America, 1972.

Haller, Emil J. "Cost Analysis for Educational Program Evaluation." In *Evaluation in Education: Current Applications*, edited by W. James Popham. Berkeley: McCutchan, 1974.

Halpin, Andrew W. "Administrative Theory: The Fumbled Torch." In *Issues in American Education*, edited by Arthur M. Kroll. New York: Oxford University Press, 1970.

———, ed. "The Development of Theory in Educational Administration." In *Administrative Theory in Education*. New York: Macmillan Company, 1958.

Halstead, D. Kent. *Statewide Planning in Higher Education*. Washington, D.C.: Government Printing Office, 1974.

Hammons, James D. "Suggestions Concerning Institutional Training of New Faculty." *Community College Review* 1, pp. 49–60.

Hankin, Joseph N. "What's Past Is Prologue." In *Adjusting to Collective Bargaining*, edited by Richard J. Ernst. San Francisco: Jossey-Bass, 1975.

Harpel, Richard L. "Accountability: Current Demands on Student Personnel Programs." *National Association of Student Personnel Administration Journal* 13 (Winter 1975), pp. 144–57.

Harrington, Thomas F. *Student Personnel Work in Urban Colleges*. New York: In Text Educational Publishers, 1974.

Harrison, Frank R., III. "Constructing Theories of Education." In *Theory Development and Educational Administration*, edited by Eddy J. Van Meter. New York: MSS Information Corporation, 1973.

Harvey, J. "Administration by Objectives in Student Personnel Programs." *Journal of College Student Personnel*, July 1972, pp. 293–96.

———, and Barker, D. G. "Student Evaluation of Teaching Effectiveness." *Improving College and University Teaching* 18 (1970), pp. 275–78.

Harvey, T. R. "Some Future Directions for Student Personnel Administration." *Journal of College Student Personnel*, July 1974, pp. 243–47.

Hawkridge, D. G.; Campeau, P. L.; and Trickett, P. K. *Preparing Evaluation Reports: A Guide for Authors.* AIR Monograph 6. Pittsburgh: American Institutes for Research, 1970.

Hayes, John R. "Research, Teaching, and Faculty Fate." *Science* 172 (April 1971), pp. 227–30.

Heath, Raymond P. "The Reality of Student Development Programs in the Private Liberal Arts College." *National Association of Student Personnel Administration Journal* 12 (Summer 1975), pp. 16–21.

Heiner, H., and Nelson, J. M., eds. *A Manual for Student Services.* Olympia, Wash.: Washington State Board for Community College Education, 1977.

Helper, John E. "Timetable for a Takeover." In Everett Carl Ladd, Jr. and Seymour Martin Lipset, *Professors, Unions, and American Higher Education.* Washington, D.C.: American Enterprise Institute for Public Policy Research, 1973.

Henderson, Algo D., and Henderson, Jean Glidden. *Higher Education in America.* San Francisco: Jossey-Bass, 1974.

Herron, Orley R., ed. *New Dimensions in Student Personnel Administration.* Scranton, Pa.: International Textbook Co., 1970.

Hersey, Paul, and Blanchard, Kenneth H. "Life Cycle Theory of Leadership." In *Readings in Management,* 4th ed. Edited by Max D. Richards and William A. Nielander. Dallas: South-Western Publishing Co., 1974.

Herzberg, Frederick; Mausner, Bernard; and Snyderman, Barbara Bloch. *The Motivation to Work.* 2d ed. New York: John Wiley and Sons, 1959.

Heyel, Carl. "Management Movement: Leaders in Thought." In *Encyclopedia of Management,* 2d ed. Edited by Carl Heyel. New York: Nostrand Reinhold Company, 1973.

Hicks, Warren, B., and Tillin, Alma M. *Developing Multi-Media Libraries.* New York: R. R. Bowker Co., 1970.

Higginson, M. Valliant. *Management Policies.* New York: American Management Association Research Study, 1966.

Higher Education Facilities Planning and Management Manuals. *Manual Four: Academic Support Facilities.* Boulder, Colo.: Western Interstate Commission for Higher Education, 1971.

Hildebrand, M.; Wilson, R. C. ; and Dienst, E. R. *Evaluating University Teaching.* Berkeley: Center for Research and Development in Higher Education, University of California, 1971.

Hill, R., Jr. "Human Management Concepts for Student Development Administrators." *Journal of College Student Personnel,* 1974, pp. 168–70.

Hind, Robert R., et. al., "A Theory of Evaluation Applied to a University Faculty." *Sociology of Education* 47, pp. 114–28.

Hodghmanson, H. T. *Import of Consortia on Institutional Vitality.* Mimeographed. Berkeley: Center for Research and Development in Higher Education, University of California, 1972.

Hodgkinson, H. L.; Hurst, J.; and Levine, H. *Improving and Assessing Performance: Evaluation in Higher Education.* Berkeley: Center for Research and Development in Higher Education, University of California, 1975.

Hopkins, Bruce R., and Roha, Thomas A. "Legal Liabilities of Administrators and Trustees." *Legal Issues for Post-Secondary Education.* Washington, D.C.: American Association of Community and Junior Colleges, 1975.

Horn, Francis H. "The Organization of Colleges and Universities." In *Administrators in Higher Education,* edited by Gerald P. Burns. New York: Harper and Brothers, 1962.

Hostrop, Richard W. *Education Inside the Library—Media Center.* Hamden, Conn.: Shoe String Press, Linnet Books, 1973.

Hotes, Robert W. "Communication: A Critical Function in Learning Resource Center Management." In *The Administration of Learning Resources Centers,* edited by Robert W. Hotes and Jack D. Terry. Washington, D.C.: University of America Press, 1977.

"How the Effective Supervisor Does His Job." *Supervisory Management,* October 1965, n.p.

Hughes, Graham. "Rules, Policy and Decision Making." *Yale Law Journal* 77 (January 1968), pp. 411–38.

Humbert, Herbert E. "What Does a Modern Learning Resources Building Look Like?" *Community and Junior College Journal* (June/July, 1973), pp. 16–17.

Hungate, Thad L. *Finance in Educational Management of College and Universities.* New York: Columbia University Press, 1954.

Hunter, John O. "Faculty Evaluation as a Liberal Persuasion." *Improving College and University Teaching* 17 (1969), pp. 90–92.

Huse, Edgar R., and Bowditch, James L. *Behavior in Organizations: A Systems Approach to Managing.* Reading, Mass.: Addison-Wesley, 1973.

Iacobelli, John L., and Musczyk, Jan P. "Overlooked Talent Sources and Corporate Strategies for Affirmative Action, Part II." *Personnel Journal* 54 (November 1975), pp. 575–77, 587.

Johnson, Michael T. "Constitutional Rights of College Students." *Texas Law Review* 41 (February 1964), pp. 344–63.

Johnson, Rita B., and Johnson, Stuart R. *Developing Individualized Material.* New York: Westinghouse Learning Press, 1971.

Jones, J. A. C. "The Costs and Benefits of Management Training." *Personnel Management* 5 (September 1973), pp. 31–33.

Jones, Wayne; Sommers, Paul A.; and Joiner, Lee M. "Three Structures for a Teacher Evaluation." *Educational Technology* 16 (February 1976), p. 48.

Kahn, Kenneth F. "Faculty Bargaining Units." In *Collective Bargaining in Higher Education—The Developing Law,* edited by Judith P. Vladeck and Stephen C. Vladeck. New York: Practicing Law Institute, 1975.

Kaludis, George. *Strategies for Budgeting New Directions for Higher Education.* San Francisco: Jossey-Bass, 1963.

Kaplowitz, Richard A. *Selecting Academic Administrators: The Search Committee.* Washington, D.C.: American Council on Education, 1973.

Katz, Ellis. "Faculty Stakes in Collective Bargaining: Expectations and Realities." In Jack H. Schuster, *Encountering the Unionized University.* San Francisco: Jossey-Bass, 1974.

Katz, Joseph, ed. *Services for Students.* San Francisco: Jossey-Bass, 1973.

Katzell, Raymond A. "Contrasting Systems of Work Organization." *American Psychologist.* Washington, D.C.: American Psychological Association (February 1962).

Keezer, Dexter M. *Financing Higher Education.* New York: McGraw-Hill, 1959.

Keller, J. E. *Higher Education Objectives: Measures of Performance and Effectiveness.* Berkeley: Office of the Vice President, Planning and Analysis, University of California, 1970.

Kells, H. R. "Institutional Accreditation: New Forms of Self-Study." *Educational Record* 53 (1972), pp. 143–48.

Kemerer, Frank R., and Baldridge, Victor J. *Unions on the Campus.* San Francisco: Jossey-Bass, 1975.

Kiernan, Irene R. "Student Evaluations Re-Evaluated." *Community and Junior College Journal* 45 (April 1975), pp. 25–27.

Kilgour, Frederick G. "Library Networks: What to Expect." *Institutional Interface: Making the Right Connection* (Spring 1974), pp. 22–28.

Klein, G. D., and Denham, C. H. "A Model for Determining the Validity of Faculty Ratings of University Administrator Effectiveness." *Educational and Psychological Measurement* 34 (1974), pp. 899–902.

Knezevich, Stephen J. *Program Budgeting (PPBS).* Berkeley: McCutchan, 1973.

Knoell, Dorothy, and McIntyre, Charles. *Planning Colleges for the Community.* San Francisco: Jossey-Bass, 1974.

Kobre, Sidney. *Successful Public Relations for Colleges and Universities.* New York: Hastings House, 1974.

Kopan, A., and Wlaberg, H., eds. *Rethinking Educational Quality.* Berkeley: McCutchan, 1974.

Korn, Harold A. "From Selective to Adaptive Education Through Human Services." *New Directions for Higher Education,* Fall 1973, pp. 19–36.

Kreplin, H. *Credit by Examination: A Review and Analysis of the Literature.* Berkeley: Office of the Vice President, Planning and Analysis, University of California, 1971.

Laabs, Theodore R. "Integrating the Educational Resources Concept." Masters thesis, University of Wisconsin, 1973.

Lahti, R. E. *Innovative College Management.* San Francisco: Jossey-Bass, 1973.

Landrith, Harold F. *Introduction to the Community Junior College.* Danville, Ill.: Interstate Printers and Publishers, 1971.

Lane, Willard R.; Corwin, Ronald G.; and Monahan, William G. *Foundations of Educational Administration: A Behavioral Analysis.* New York: Macmillan, 1967.

Lansner, Lawrence A. "Evening College Placement." In *Student Personnel Services for Adults in Higher Education,* edited by Martha L. Farmer. Metuchen, N.J.: Scarecrow Press, 1967.

Lathrop, R. G. "Unit Factorial Ratings by College Students of Courses and Instructors." Mimeograph. Chico, Calif.: California State University, 1968.

———, and Richmond, C. "College Students' Evaluation of Course and Instructors." Mimeograph. Chico, Calif.: California State University, 1967.

Lavin, D. E. *The Prediction of Academic Performance.* New York: Russell Sage Foundation, 1965.

Lawrence, Ben. "The WICHE Planning and Management Systems Program: Its Nature, Scope, and Limitations." In *Managing the University: A Systems Approach,* edited by Paul W. Hamelman. New York: Praeger, 1972.

Lee, C. B. T., ed. "Evaluation of Teaching Performance: Issues and Possibilities." *Improving College Teaching.* Washington, D.C.: American Council on Education, 1967.

Lelftwich, W. H., and Remmers, H. H. "A Comparison of Graphic and Forced-Choice Ratings of Teaching Performance at the College and University Level, Purdue University." *Studies in Higher Education* 92 (1962), pp. 3–35.

Leslie, David W. *Conflict and Collective Bargaining.* Washington, D.C.: American Association for Higher Education, 1975.

Lewis, James, Jr. *Administering the Individualized Instruction Package.* New York: Parker Publishing Company, 1971.

Likert, Rensis. "Motivation: The Core of Management." In *Management: A Book of Readings,* edited by Harold Koontz and Cyril O'Donnell. New York: McGraw-Hill, 1972.

———. *New Patterns of Management.* New York: McGraw-Hill, 1961.

———. *The Human Organization.* New York: McGraw-Hill, 1967.

Lippitt, Gordon L. "Managing Change: Six Ways to Turn Resistance into Acceptance." *Supervisory Management,* June 1968, n.p.

Lopez, F. M., Jr. *Evaluating Executive Decision Making: The In-Basket Technique.* AMA Research Study 75. New York: American Management Association, 1966.

Lovell, G. D., and Haner, C. F. "Forced-Choice Applied to College Faculty Rating." *Educational and Psychological Measurement* 15 (1955), pp. 291–304.

Lumsdaine, A. A. "Instruments and Media of Instruction." *Handbook of Research and Teaching.* Chicago: Rand McNally, 1963.

Lynem, S. F. "An Old Dimension with New Emphasis." *NASSP Bulletin* 60 (November 1976), pp. 103–6.

McAllister, Jeanne Ployhart. *The Transition of a Library into an Instructional Media Center.* Michigan: University Microfilms, 1974.

McCarter, W. Ronald, and Grigsby, Charles E. *Staff Development: A Community College Plan.* Whiteville, N.C.: Southeastern Community College, n.d.

McConnell, T. R. *The Redistribution of Power in Higher Education: Changing Patterns of Internal Governance.* Berkeley: Center for Research and Development in Higher Education, University of California, 1971.

McDaniel, J. W., and Lombardi, Robert. "Organization and Administration of Student Personnel Work in the Community Junior College." In *Student Development Programs in the Community Junior College,* edited by Terry O'Banion and Alice Thurston. Englewood Cliffs, N.J.: Prentice-Hall, 1972.

McDill, E. L.; McKill, M. S.; and Sprehe, J. T. *Strategies for Success in Compensatory Education: An Appraisal of Evaluation Research.* Baltimore: Johns Hopkins University Press, 1969.

McGregor, Douglas. *The Human Side of Enterprise.* New York: McGraw-Hill, 1960.

McKeachie, W. J.; Line, Y.; and Mann, W. "Student Ratings of Teacher Effectiveness: Validity Studies." *American Educational Research Journal* 8 (1971), pp. 435–45.

McNeil, J. D., and Popham, W. J. "The Assessment of Teacher Competence." In *Second Handbook of Research on Teaching,* edited by R. M. W. Travers. Chicago: Rand McNally, 1973.

McVey, Frank I., and Hughes, Raymond M. *Problems of College and University Administration.* Ames, Iowa: Iowa State College Press, 1952.

Mager, Robert F. *Developing Attitudes Toward Learning,* Belmont, Calif: Fearon Publishers, 1968.

———. *Preparing Instructional Objectives.* Belmont, Calif.: Fearon Publishers, 1962.

———, and Beach, Kenneth M., Jr. *Developing Vocational Instruction.* Belmont, Calif.: Fearon Publishers, 1967.

Mahler, Walter R. *How Effective Executives Interview.* Homewood, Ill.: Dow Jones-Irwin, 1976.

Mann, Dale. *Policy Decisionmaking in Education.* New York: Teachers College Press, 1975.

Manning, C. W., and Romney, L. C. *Faculty Activity Analysis: Procedures Manual.* Boulder, Colo.: Western Interstate Commission for Higher Education, 1973.

Manual of Instructions for the Purdue Rating Scale for Instructors. Rev. ed. West Lafayette, Ind.: University Book Store, 1960.

March, J. C., and Simon, H. A. *Organizations.* New York: John Wiley and Sons, 1958.

Martin, Thomas W., and Berry, K. J. "The Teaching-Research Dilemma: Its Sources in the University Setting." *Journal of Higher Education,* 40 (December 1969), pp. 691–703.

Martorana, S. V. *College Boards of Trustees.* Washington, D.C.: The Center for Applied Research in Education, 1963.

Marvin, Philip. *Product Planning Simplified: Sharpening Up Decision Making.* New York: American Management Association, 1972.

Maslow, A. H. *Motivation and Personality.* New York: Harper and Row, 1954.

———, and Zimmerman, W. "College Teaching Ability, Scholarly Activity and Personality," *Journal of Educational Psychology* 47 (1956), pp. 185–89.

Masterson, Thomas R., and Mara, Thomas G. *Motivating the Underperformer.* New York: American Management Association, 1969.

Mayhew, Lewis B. *The Carnegie Commission of Higher Education.* San Francisco: Jossey-Bass, 1973.

———, and Ford, Patrick J. *Changing the Curriculum.* San Francisco: Jossey-Bass, 1971.

Meckley, Shirley M., and William, P. Anthony. "Experience with Affirmative Action." *Journal of the College and University Personnel Association* 28 (Winter 1977), pp. 11–17.

Mee, John F. "Management Movement." In *Encyclopedia of Management,* 2d ed., edited by Carl Heyel. New York: Van Nostrand Reinhold, 1973.

Meyer, D. Eugene, and Smith, Charles W. "A Nationwide Survey of Teacher Education Faculty Evaluation Practices." *College Student Journal Monograph* 11 (Spring 1977), pp. 1–11.

Miller, Bob W. *Higher Education and the Community College.* Washington, D.C.: University of America Press, 1977.

Miller, David, and Webster, Murray, Jr. "Theoretical Constructs and Observables." In *Theory, Development, and Educational Administration,* edited by Eddy Van Meter. New York: MSS Information Corporation, 1973.

Miller, R. I. *Evaluating Faculty Performance.* San Francisco: Jossey-Bass, 1972.

Miller, Theodore D., and Prince, Judith S. *The Future of Student Affairs*. San Francisco: Jossey-Bass, 1977.

Miller, William A. *Developing Effectiveness and Competence Within the Administrative Team*. Denton, Tex.: North Texas State University Printing Office, 1975.

_____. *Faculty Personnel Administration in Higher Education: A Systems Approach*. Denton, Tex.: North Texas State University Printing Office, n.d.

_____, and Carter, John L. *Financing Public Institutions in the State of Texas*, 1974.

Millett, John D. *Financing Higher Education in the United States*. New York: Columbia University Press, 1952.

Moesteller, Frederick, and Moynahan, Daniel P. *On Equality of Educational Opportunity*. New York: Vintage Books, 1972.

Molpus v. Fortune. 311 F. Supp. 240.

Monagen, Henry P. "First Amendment 'Due Process'," *Harvard Law Review* 83 (January 1970), pp. 518–51.

Monroe, Charles R. *Profile of the Community College*. San Francisco: Jossey-Bass, 1973.

Moore, Leila V. "Some Problems in the Study of Students' Perception of Personnel Services." In *College Student Personnel*, edited by New York: Houghton-Mifflin, 1970.

Morphet, Edgar L.; Johns, R. L.; and Reller, Theodore L. *Educational Administration: Concepts, Practices, and Issues*. Englewood Cliffs, N.J.: Prentice-Hall, 1959.

Morris, William, ed. *Effective College Teaching*, 1970.

Mortimer, Kenneth P., and Lozier, Gregory G. *Collective Bargaining: Implications for Governance*. University Park, Pa.: Center for the Study of Higher Education, Pennsylvania State University, 1972.

Murray, Thomas, J. "Zero Budgeting." *Dun's Review*, October 1974, p. 71.

Musella, D., and Rusch, R. "Student Opinion on College Teaching." *Improving College and University Teaching* 16 (1968), pp. 137–40.

Naples, Caesar, Jr. "Collective Bargaining: Opportunities for Management." In Jack H. Schuster, *Encountering the Unionized University*. San Francisco: Jossey-Bass, 1974.

National Committee on Standard Reports for Institutions of Higher Education. *Financial Reports for Colleges and Universities*. Chicago: University of Chicago Press, 1935.

Newsweek, 3 April 1978, pp. 33.

Nolting, Earl. "A Center for Student Development: Concept and Implementation." *National Association of Student Personnel Administration Journal* 13 (Fall 1975), pp. 46–49.

Norris, Donald M. "Speculating on Enrollments." In *Individualizing the System*, edited by Dyckman W. Vermilye. San Francisco: Jossey-Bass, 1976.

North Texas State University. *Faculty Tenure and Promotion Policy*, 1978.

O'Banion, T. "A Program Proposal for Preparing College Student Personnel Workers." *Journal of College Student Personnel* 9, 1969, pp. 249–53.

_____, and Thurston, Alice. *Student Development Programs in the Community Junior College*. Englewood Cliffs, N.J.: Prentice-Hall, 1972.

_____, and Gulden, J. "Student Personnel Work: An Emerging Model." *Junior College Journal*, November 1970, pp. 6–14.

_____. *Teachers for Tomorrow*. Tucson: University of Arizona Press, 1973.

O'Neill, June A. *Sources of Funds to Colleges and Universities.* Washington, D.C.: Carnegie Commission on Higher Education, 1973.

Onushkin, Victor G. *Planning the Development of Universities—II.* Paris: International Institute for Educational Planning, 1973.

Oral Roberts University Catalogue, 1977–1978. Tulsa, Okla.

Pace, C. R., ed. *Evaluating, Learning, and Teaching New Directions for Higher Education.* San Francisco: Jossey-Bass, 1973.

Padgett, Jack F. "How Beneficial is a College Education Today?" *Liberal Education* 61 (December 1975), pp. 473–77.

Paltridge, J. G. "Urban Higher Education Consortia." Berkeley: Center for Research and Development in Higher Education, University of California, 1971.

Parlminson, R. D. "Selected Voluntary Consortia in Higher Education: Financial Aspects." Ph.D. dissertation, Indiana University, 1972.

Patterson, Lewis D. "A Descriptive Study of the Governing of Selected Voluntary Academic Cooperative Arrangements in Higher Education." Ph.D. dissertation, University of Missouri, 1971.

————. "Evolving Patterns of Cooperation." *ERIC Higher Education Research Current,* June 1975.

————, ed. *Comprehensive Bibliography on Interinstitutional Cooperation with Special Emphasis on Voluntary Academic Consortia in Higher Education.* 5th ed. Kansas City, Mo.: Kansas City Regional Council for Higher Education, 1971.

————. *Consortium Directory: Voluntary Academic Cooperative Arrangements in Higher Education.* 5th ed. Kansas City, Mo.: Kansas City Regional Council for Higher Education, 1971.

Pelfrey, R. H. "What a Manager Can Learn from Pro Football." *Supervisory Management,* December 1966, n.p.

Penn, J. Roger; Manspeaker, Jewell; and Millette, Brain J. "The Model Merry-Go-Round." *National Association of Student Personnel Administration Journal* 12 (1975), pp. 222–24.

Penney, James F. *Perspective and Challenge in College Personnel Work.* Springfield, Ill.: Charles C. Thomas, 1972.

Perrine, Richard H. *Library Space Survey of Texas Colleges and Universities.* CB Study Paper No. 10. Austin, Tex.: Coordinating Board, Texas College and University System, 1970.

Perry, R. R. "Evaluation and Teaching Behavior Seeks to Measure Effectiveness." *College and University Business* 47 (1969), pp. 18–22.

Peters, Herman J. *Interpreting Guidance Programs to the Public.* Boston: Houghton-Mifflin, 1968.

Peters, Thomas J., and Watterman, Thomas J., Jr. *In Pursuit of Excellence.* New York: Harper & Row, 1983.

Peterson, Gary T. *The Learning Center: A Sphere for Non-Traditional Education.* Hamden, Conn.: Shoe String Press, 1975.

Phi Delta Kappa National Study Committee on Evaluation. *Educational Evaluation and Decision Making.* Itasca, Ill.: F. E. Peacock, 1971.

Pickings v. *Bruce.* 430 F. 2nd, 595.

Popham, W. James, ed. *Evaluation in Education: Current Applications.* Berkeley: McCutchan, 1974.

_____. "A Preliminary Attempt to Identify the Factors in Student-Instructor Evaluation." *Journal of Psychology* 36 (1953), pp. 417–22.

_____, and Baker, Eva L. "Humanizing Education Objective." *Teacher Competency Development System.* Englewood Cliffs, N.J.: Prentice-Hall, 1973.

_____, and Bahn, E. L. *Systematic Instruction.* Englewood Cliffs, Prentice-Hall, 1970.

_____, and Baker, Eva L. "Humanizing Education Objective." *Teacher Competency Development System.* Englewood Cliffs, N.J.: Prentice-Hall, 1973.

Prior, J. J. "The Reorganization of Student Personnel Services: Facing Reality." *Journal of College Student Personnel,* vol. 13 1973, pp. 202–5.

_____. *Professors as Teachers.* San Francisco: Jossey-Bass, 1972.

Provo, J. L. "A Change Process Model for Bilateral Interinstitutional Cooperation in Higher Education." Ph.D. dissertation, Kansas State University, 1971.

Pyhr, Peter. *Zero-Based Budgeting.* New York: John Wiley and Sons, 1973.

Raines, Max R., and Gunder, Myraw. "Community Services: Goals for 1980." *Junior College Journal* 42 (April 1972), pp. 12–16.

Reck, W. Emerson. *Public Relations: A Program for Colleges and Universities.* New York: Harper and Row, 1946.

The Recognition and Evaluation of Teaching. Washington, D.C.: American Association of University Professors, 1971.

Bendig, A. W. "Relation of Level of Course Achievement of Students, Instructor, and Course Ratings in Introductory Psychology. *Educational and Psychological Measurement* 13 (1953), pp. 437–58.

Report of Phase One of a Study to Determine the Quality of Teacher Education Programs in the State of Alabama. Montgomery, Ala.: Alabama State Department of Education, 1976.

Remmers, H. H. "Reliability and Halo-effect of High School and College Students' Judgements of their Teachers." *Journal of Applied Psychology* 12 (1928), pp. 602–10.

Richards, Tudor. *Problem Solving Through Creative Analysis.* New York: John Wiley and Sons, 1974.

Richardson, Richard C., Jr.; Blocker, Clyde E.; and Bender, Louis W. *Governance for the Two-Year College.* Englewood Cliffs, N.J.: Prentice-Hall, 1972.

Richland College. *Rights, Rites, and Rituals, Revised, 1976–77.* Dallas: Richland College Print Shop, 1976.

Richman, B. M., and Farmer, R. N. *Leadership, Goals, and Power in Higher Education: A Contingency and Open-Systems Approach to Effective Management.* San Francisco: Jossey-Bass, 1974.

Riker, Harold C. *College Students Live Here.* New York: Educational Facilities Laboratories, 1966.

Ritchie, M. A. F. *The College Presidency: Initiation into the Order of the Turtle.* New York: Philosophical Library, 1970.

Rivlin, Alice M. *The Role of the Federal Government in Financing.* Washington, D.C.: The Brookings Institute, 1961.

Roach, Anne C. "State-Aid Programs." *Chronical of Higher Education* 14 (October 1977), pp. 13–14.

Roach, James H. L. "The Academic Department Chairperson: Functions and Responsibilities." *Educational Record,* Vol. 57 (1976), pp. 13–23.

Roberson, E. W., ed. *Educational Accountability Through Evaluation.* Englewood Cliffs, N.J.: Educational Technology Publications, 1971.

Rogers, Carl R. "The Interpersonal Relationship: The Core of Guidance." In *Guidance: An Examination,* edited by Ralph L. Mosher, Richard F. Carle, and Chris D. Kehas. New York: Harcourt, Brace and World, 1972.

———. "Toward a Theory of Creativity." *ETC: A Review of General Semantics,* Summer 1954, pp. 248–50.

Rogers, Jean L., and Fourtson, Walter L. *Fair Employment Interviewing.* Reading, Mass.: Addison-Wesley, 1976.

Rosenthal, Jane, and Gessner, Arlys. "Guidelines for Contemporary Employment Interviewing." *Journal of the College and University Personnel Association* 27 (October–November 1976), pp. 50–61.

Rouche, John E. "Accountability for Student Learning in the Community College." *Educational Technology* 11 (January 1971), pp. 46–47.

———, and Herrscher, B. R. *Toward Instructional Accountability: A Practical Guide to Educational Change.* Sunnyvale, Calif.: Westinghouse Learning Press, 1973.

Rowland, Virgil K. *Managerial Performance Standards.* New York: American Management Association, 1960.

Royce, J. D. "Popularity and Teacher." *Education* 56, pp. 233–37.

Rubenstein, Albert H. "Organization Theory." In *Encyclopedia of Management.* 2d ed., edited by Carl Heyel. New York: Van Nostrand Reinhold, 1973.

———. *Participative Problem Solving: How to Increase Organization Effectiveness.* New York: John Wiley and Sons, 1977.

Rubin, Louis J., ed. *Improving In-Service Education.* Boston: Allyn and Bacon, 1971.

Russell, John D. *The Finance of Higher Education.* Chicago: University of Chicago Press, 1944.

Sagen, E. L. "A Network Model of Steps for the Implementation of the Planning and Establishing of Higher Education Consortiums," Ph.D. dissertation, Ohio State University, 1969.

Said, K. E. "A Goal Oriented Budgetary Process." *Management Accounting,* January 1975, pp. 31–36.

Sanford, Nevitt; Borgstrom, Karl; and Lozoff, Marjorie. "The Role of Athletics in Student Development." *New Directions for Higher Education* 1 (1973), pp. 51–58.

Sartain, A. Q., and Waring, E. G. "Interest in and Value of College Courses." *Journal of Applied Psychology* 28 (1944), pp. 520–26.

Satryb, Ronald P. "A Budget Model for Student Personnel." *National Association of Student Personnel Administrators Journal* 13 (1974), pp. 51–56.

Schein, Edgar H. *Process Consultation: The Role of Organization Development.* Boston: Addison-Wesley, 1969.

Scheps, Clarence, and Davidson, E. E. *Accounting for Colleges and Universities.* Baton Rouge: Louisiana State University Press, 1970.

Schimmel, David, and Fisher, Louis. *The Civil Rights of Students.* New York: Harper and Row, 1975.

Schulman, Benson, R., and Trudell, James W. "California's Guidelines for Teacher Evaluation." *Community and Junior College Journal* 43, (October 1972), pp. 32–34.

Schultz, Raymond E. "Judging an Academic Dean—The Dean's Role: No Assignment for the Faint Hearted." In *Perspectives on the Community-Junior College,* edited by William K. Ogilvie and Max R. Raines. New York: Appleton-Centory-Crofts, 1971.

Schumann, Paul F. "Questions an Administrator Should Ask." *NASSP Bulletin* 61 (January 1977), pp. 62–65.

Semas, Phillip W. "Hutchins' View of the University." *Chronicle of Higher Education* 14 (1977), pp. 5–6.

Sergiovanni, Thomas J., and Carver, Fred D. *The New School Executive.* New York: Dodd, Mead, 1975.

Shaffer, R. L. H. "An Emerging Role of Student Personnel—Contributing to Organizational Effectiveness." *Journal of College Student Personnel* 13 (1973), pp. 386–91.

Shark, Alan. "A Student's Collective Thoughts on Bargaining." *Journal of Higher Education* 43 (1972), pp. 552–58.

Siegel, Max, ed. *Counseling of College Students.* New York: Free Press, 1968.

Silver, Gerald A., and Silver, Joan G. *Introduction to Systems Analysis.* Englewood Cliffs, N.J.: Prentice-Hall, 1976.

Silverman, R. J. "Toward an Inter-Organizational Theory in Higher Education." Ph.D. dissertation, Cornell University, 1969.

Simerly, Robert G. "Improving Institutional Accountability Through Faculty Development: Reacting to Conflicting Pressures in Post-Secondary Education." Paper presented at the Annual Conference of the Association for Institutional Research, May 1976.

Simon, Herbert A. *The New Science of Management Decision.* New York: Macmillan, 1947.

Sisk, Henry L. *Principles of Management: A Systems Approach to the Management Process.* Cincinnati: South-Western Publishing Co., 1969.

Smith, R., and Fielder, F. E. "The Measurement of Scholarly Work: A Critical Review of the Literature." *Educational Record* 52 (1971), pp. 225–32.

Smock, H. R., and Crooks, T. J. "A Plan for the Comprehensive Evaluation of College Teaching." *Journal of Higher Education* 44 (1973), pp. 577–86.

Snyder v. Board of Trustees of the University of Illinois. 268 F. Supp. 927.

Southern Methodist University Catalogue, 1977–1978. Dallas, Texas.

Southern Regional Education Board, *Proceedings: A Symposium on Financing Higher Education,* 1969.

Spaeth, J. L., and Greeley, A. M. *Recent Alumni and Higher Education: A Survey of College Graduates.* New York: McGraw-Hill, 1970.

Stacy v. Williams. 306 F. Supp. 963.

Standards of the College Delegate Assembly. Atlanta: Southern Association of Colleges and Schools, 1977.

Stark, Matthew. "Human Relations Programs: Social Reconstruction Through Collegiate Extracurricular Activities." In *College Student Personnel,* edited by Laurine E. Fitzgerald, Walter F. Johnson, and Willa Norris. Boston: Houghton-Mifflin, 1970.

Stickgold, Arthur. "Policy Implications of Changing Student Values in the Collegiate Culture." *Liberal Education* 61 (1975), pp. 173–86.

Stogdill, Ralph M. *Handbook of Leadership: A Survey of Theory and Research.* New York: Free Press, 1974.

The Student as Godfather? The Impact of Student Ratings on Academia. Research Memorandum RM-73-8. Princeton, N.J.: Educational Testing Service, 1973.

Stufflebeam, D. L., and others, *Educational Evaluation and Decision Making.* Itasca, Ill.: F. E. Peacock, 1971.

"Survey of Opinions About Lecturers." Mimeographed. Illinois: University of Illinois, Department of Psychology, 1968.

Swerdlow, K. G. "Selected Voluntary Academic Consortia in Higher Education: Academic Program." Ph.D. dissertation, University of Indiana, 1972.

Tannenbaum, Robert, and Schmidt, Warren H. "How to Choose a Leadership Pattern." In *Readings in Management,* edited by Max D. Richards and William A. Nielander. 4th ed. Dallas: South-Western Publishing, 1974.

Tarrant County Junior College, "Faculty Evaluation Instrument." Fort Worth: 1974.

Taylor, F. W. *Scientific Management.* New York: Harper and Row, 1911.

Taylor, J. G. "College Revenue Bonds to Finance Self-Supporting Projects." *Journal of Finance,* December 1949, p. 238.

Teaching Tips: A Guidebook for the Beginning College Teacher. 6th ed. Lexington, Mass.: D. C. Heath, 1969.

Terry, Jack D., Jr., and Hotes, Robert W., eds. *The Administration of Learning Resources Centers.* Washington, D.C.: University Press of America, 1978.

Thackrey, R. I. "If You're Confused About Higher Education Statistics, Remember: So Are the People Who Produce Them." *Phi Delta Kappan* 56 (1975), pp. 415–19.

Thompson, James D. "Modern Approaches to Theory in Administration." In *Administrative Theory in Education,* edited by Andrew W. Halpin. New York: Macmillan, 1958.

Thomson, Sarah K. *Learning Resource Centers in Community Colleges: A Survey of Budgets and Services.* Chicago: American Library Association, 1975.

Thornton, James W., Jr. *The Community Junior College.* New York: John Wiley and Sons, 1960.

Thurston, A. J., ed., *The Chief Student Personnel Administrator in the Public Two-Year College.* Washington, D.C.: American Association of Junior Colleges, 1972.

Tiller, Darrel Long, and Maidment, Robert. "Effective Women Managers: Fact and Fantasy" *Forum* 5 (1978), pp. 6–7.

Todes, Jay L.; McKinney, John; and Ferguson, Wendell, Jr. *Management and Motivation: An Introduction to Supervision.* New York: Harper and Row, 1977.

Trendler, C. A. "Institutional Cooperation for Academic Development Among Small Church-Related Liberal Arts Colleges." Ph.D. dissertation, Indiana University, 1967.

Tront, W. E. "The Kentuckian Metrouniversity: Case Study of a Consortium." Master's thesis, University of Tonisville, 1972.

Ulich, Mary Ewen. *Patterns of Adult Education.* New York: Pageant Press, 1965.

Undergraduate Cross Registration. A report of the Associated Colleges of the Saint Lawrence Valley and the Office of Higher Education Management Services of the New York State Education Department, Albany, N.Y., 1975.

"Unionized Professors." *Time* 6 November 1972, pp. 74–76.

U.S. Department of Health, Education and Welfare. *Higher Education Guidelines: Executive Order 11246.* Washington, D.C.: U.S. Department of Health, Education and Welfare, 1972.

U.S. Equal Employment Opportunity Commission. *Affirmative Action and Equal Employment: A Guidebook for Employers.* Washington, D.C.: U.S. Equal Opportunity Commission, 1974.

University of Texas at Arlington Catalogue, 1977–1978. Arlington, Tex.

Valley, John R., and Cross, K. Patricia. *Planning Non-Traditional Programs.* San Francisco: Jossey-Bass, 1974.

Veit, Fritz. *The Community College Library.* Westport, Conn.: Greenwood Press, 1975.

Vermilye, Dyckman. *Relating Work and Education.* San Francisco: Jossey-Bass, 1977.

Von der Embse, Thomas. "Choosing a Management Development Program: A Decision Model." *Personnel Journal* 52 (1973), pp. 907–12.

Walton, John. "The Theoretical Study of Educational Administration." In *Theory Development and Educational Administration,* edited by Eddy Van Meter. New York: MSS Information Corporation, 1973.

Warner, W. Lloyd, and Abeggien, James C. *Big Business Leaders in America.* New York: Harper and Brothers, 1955.

Weaver, C. H. "Instructor Rating by College Students." *Journal of Educational Psychology* 51 (1960), pp. 21–25.

Weber, M. *The Theory of Social and Economic Organization,* edited by T. Parsons. Translated by A. M. Henderson and T. Parson. New York: Oxford University Press, 1947.

Weiner, Richard. *Professional's Guide to Public Relations Services.* Englewood Cliffs, N.J.: Prentice-Hall, 1971.

Weisgerber, Robert A., ed. *Instructional Process and Media Innovation.* Chicago: Rand McNally, 1968.

Welliver, Paul W. "Media Through Media! The Design and Implementation of a Mediated Independent Study Course in Instructional Media." *Educational Technology* 15 (1975), pp. 40–46.

Werdell, P. R. *Course and Teacher Evaluation.* 2nd ed. Washington, D.C.: United States National Student Association, 1967.

Wilhelms, Fred J. *Evaluation as Feedback and Guide.* Washington, D.C.: Association for Supervision and Curriculum Development, NEA, 1967.

Willett, Sandra. "Consumer Protection in Higher Education: Why? For Whom? How?" *Liberal Education* 61 (1975), pp. 161–72.

Williams, Richard C. "Administrative Theory and Higher Education Administration." In *Handbook of College and University Administration, Academic Administration,* edited by Asa Knowles. New York: McGraw-Hill, 1970.

Wilson, Richard E. "Staff Development: An Urgent Priority." *Community and Junior College Journal* 43 (1973), pp. 68–69.

Wilson, Robin Scott. "Toward a National Counseling System." In *Lifelong Learners—A New Clientele for Higher Education*, edited by Dyckman Vermilye. San Francisco: Jossey-Bass, 1974.

Wilson, S. R., and Tosti, D. T. *Learning is Getting Easier*. New York: Individual Learning Systems, 1972.

Wood, K.; Linsky, A. S.; and Straus, M. A. "Class Size and Student Evaluations of Faculty." *Journal of Higher Education* 45 (1974), pp. 524–34.

Worthen, B. R., and Sanders, J. R., eds. *Educational Evaluation: Theory and Practice*. Worthington, Ohio: Jones, 1973.

Wren, Daniel A. *The Evolution of Management Thought*. New York: Ronald Press, 1972.

Wygal, Benjamin R. "Will the Economy Crunch the Community-Based Movement?" *Junior College Journal* 46 (November 1975), pp. 12–13.

Zanella, Richard E. "The Art of Interviewing." *NASSP Bulletin* 61 (January 1977), pp. 56–83.

Zimmerman, W. D. "A Foundation Executive's Assessment of the College Consortia Movement." In *Papers of the Academic Consortia Seminar on Assessing the Consortium Movement*, edited by L. D. Patterson. Mimeographed. Kansas City, Mo.: Kansas City Regional Council for Higher Education, 1968.

Zwerling, L. Steven. "Second-Class Education at the Community College." *New Directions for Community Colleges* 7 (Fall 1974), pp. 23–27.

Index

ABOUT THE EDITORS

DR. BOB MILLER is a Professor and Director of Community College Programs at North Texas State University, Denton. His latest book is *Higher Education and the Community College.*

ROBERT W. HOTES is Manager of Training for a division of Denny's Inc., Fort Worth, Texas. He is co-editor with Jack D. Terry of *The Administration of Learning Resource Centers.* Dr. Hotes has experience in both college administration and industrial management.

DR. JACK D. TERRY, JR., is Dean of the School of Religious Education and Professor of Foundations of Education at the Southwestern Baptist Theological Seminary in Fort Worth. He is the co-editor of *The Administration of Learning Resource Centers* and the author of *Getting Ready to Work as a General Officer.*

DATE DUE